KT-569-458

PENGUIN REFERENCE

The Penguin Dictionary of Sociology

Nicholas Abercrombie has worked at the University of Lancaster for many years and is currently professor of sociology. His academic interests include the mass media, the sociology of culture and the sociology of money. He has also published extensively in introductory sociology, most recently in *Contemporary British Society* (2000) and *Readings in Contemporary British Society* (2000).

Stephen Hill is professor of sociology at the London School of Economics. His academic interests cover the sociology of economic life, social stratification and social theory, and he has published extensively in books and academic journals. He is the editor of the *British Journal of Sociology* and was for many years the chair of examiners in sociology at a major school examination board.

Bryan S. Turner is professor of sociology at the University of Cambridge. His academic interests include the sociology of citizenship, medical sociology and social theory. He is the editor of the journal *Citizenship Studies* and co-editor (with Mike Featherstone) of *Body & Society*. He edited *Max Weber: Critical Responses* (1999), in three volumes.

The three authors have collaborated extensively, particularly in writing *The Dominant Ideology Thesis* (1980), *Sovereign Individuals of Capitalism* (1986) and *Dominant Ideologies* (1990).

The Penguin Dictionary of

Sociology

Nicholas Abercrombie
Stephen Hill
Bryan S. Turner

FOURTH EDITION

PENGUIN BOOKS

PENGUIN BOOKS

Published by the Penguin Group
Penguin Books Ltd, 80 Strand, London WC2R 0RL, England
Penguin Putnam Inc., 375 Hudson Street, New York, New York 10014, USA
Penguin Books Australia Ltd, 250 Camberwell Road, Camberwell, Victoria 3124, Australia
Penguin Books Canada Ltd, 10 Alcorn Avenue, Toronto, Ontario, Canada M4V 3B2
Penguin Books India (P) Ltd, 11 Community Centre, Panchsheel Park, New Delhi – 110 017, India
Penguin Books (NZ) Ltd, Cnr Rosedale and Airborne Roads, Albany, Auckland, New Zealand
Penguin Books (South Africa) (Pty) Ltd, 24 Sturdee Avenue, Rosebank 2196, South Africa

Penguin Books Ltd, Registered Offices: 80 Strand, London WC2R 0RL, England

www.penguin.com

First published 1984
Published simultaneously by Allen Lane
Second edition 1988
Third edition 1994
Fourth edition 2000
8
Copyright © Nicholas Abercrombie, Stephen Hill and Bryan S. Turner, 1984, 1988, 1994, 2000
All rights reserved

The moral right of the authors has been asserted
Typeset in 7.5/9.75 pt ITC Stone
Typeset by Rowland Phototypesetting Ltd, Bury St Edmunds, Suffolk
Printed in England by Clays Ltd, St Ives plc
Except in the United States of America, this book is sold subject
to the condition that it shall not, by way of trade or otherwise, be lent,
re-sold, hired out, or otherwise circulated without the publisher's
prior consent in any form of binding or cover other than that in
which it is published and without a similar condition including this
condition being imposed on the subsequent purchaser

Contents

Acknowledgements

The authors wish to thank the following for their help in preparing the fourth edition of this dictionary: Peter Abell, Christopher Badcock, Will Breare-Hall, Rosemary Deem, Jane Falkingham, Bob Jessop, Judith Henderson, Tetsuo Maruyama and John Urry.

Preface to the Fourth Edition

A dictionary of sociology must strike a balance between the changing intellectual debates of an evolving discipline, which requires entries on contemporary issues where these are perceived to be important and durable, and recognizing the importance of the classical sociological tradition. *The Penguin Dictionary of Sociology* has attempted to present the classical legacy in its diversity and complexity, while also keeping abreast of the emerging intellectual needs of different student generations. We have in particular been conscious of the intellectual requirements of students of sociology for systematic entries on key concepts, ample discussion of major theorists, and informed commentary on important social developments in industrial society. The dictionary aims to be informative, discursive and prescriptive. It seeks to be 'user friendly' in providing extensive bibliographies of contemporary and classical sociology, entries that systematically cover topics, concepts and authors, and up-to-date information on such matters as criminal statistics. The system of cross-referencing permits readers to explore issues within a cluster of concepts.

Sociology continues to develop and expand as an academic discipline, and the fourth edition reflects new trends and developments in theory and research. The principal difficulty is what to exclude rather than what to include. Our selection attempts to express what we feel are genuine contributions to the vocabulary of sociology. We also want to provide students with concepts and theories that directly respond to the academic needs of programmes in sociology and related areas. Finally, we have attempted to be contemporary without being merely fashionable. Some new entries such as 'actor-network theory' are included, because they both question conventional sociological categories in provocative and innovative ways, and contribute to a classical legacy of theories of social action. Other new entries such as 'embodiment' are included, because they are relevant to an understanding of the nature of social phenomena and they support other entries on social action and interaction. We have also expanded and enhanced our entries on contemporary sociologists.

Because we have sought to develop a dictionary that evolves with each new generation of students, the character of the dictionary has changed significantly over time. The first edition of *The Penguin Dictionary of Sociology* was published in 1984. It necessarily and appropriately reflected many of the dominant intellectual concerns of British sociology in the 1970s and 1980s, which differed in some respects from the American sociology of that era. For example, whereas the issues of race and migration shaped American sociology, class and class relations dominated the analysis of social stratification in British sociology. This intellectual preoccupation also required full coverage of the debate between Marxist and Weberian sociology.

The dictionary has not abandoned these early preoccupations, and concepts such as 'alienation', 'anomie' and 'critical theory' remain. In the 1988 and 1994 editions, we systematically revised and updated entries to take account of new developments and the increasing convergence, at least at the level of theory and concepts, between sociology as practised in Europe and America. In preparing the fourth edition, we have added a number of important new emphases. We can identify eight substantial and important developments in recent sociology that have shaped this edition.

(1) We have greatly expanded our treatment of feminist theory, women and work, women's studies, gender and sexuality. This emphasis on feminist issues is a response to the increasing importance of gender and identity politics in contemporary society. There are new entries on feminist thinkers such as Julia Kristeva and on substantive contributions such as feminist criminology. Alongside these changes, the dictionary has enlarged its discussion of the work of major intellectuals in this expanding field, such as Michel Foucault. The importance of the politics of sexual identity is also illustrated by new entries on the sociology of the body and embodiment.

(2) A major expansion of sociology over recent years has been concerned with the analysis of popular culture, the media and information technology. The social impact of information technology, computerization and the entertainment industry is reflected in cultural studies, the sociology of the media, and research on virtual reality. These changes in intellectual interests have been associated with the work of Jean Baudrillard and the notion that 'the social' has been replaced by 'the cultural', and the writings of Manuel Castells on the 'information society'. In the university curriculum, the popularity of sociology has been challenged by cultural studies, film studies and media studies. The fourth edition has in response to these developments incorporated many new entries in the fields of postmodernism, cultural analysis, informationalism, popular culture and the media.

(3) The growth of new technologies of communication has been connected with the globalization of human societies. Although the sociological debate about global society was influential from the 1960s, concern for the consequences of globalism became particularly acute in the 1990s. The new edition reflects the growing complexity and importance of the theme of globalization, and associated issues such as migration and the development of risk society. New entries also explore such issues as hybridization and Orientalism. A substantial entry on world religions will help readers understand the sociological importance in the modern world of organized religions.

(4) With the fall of the Berlin Wall and the final demise of the Soviet system towards the end of the 1980s, the contrast between communism and capitalism became less relevant to sociological analysis. Traditional areas of study, such as development, underdevelopment and dependency that had been influential in earlier editions, have been re-evaluated. In addition, the post-communist societies have experienced new tensions and conflicts around questions of ethnicity and national identity. In contemporary capitalism, ethnic division has also become more salient in a period where class conflict has declined. The dictionary has sought to include these social and political changes through a sharper focus on ethnicity, racial categories and religious divisions. The problems of social exclusion in modern societies have been associated with a revival of interest in such notions as civil society, social citizenship and human rights. We have expanded the dictionary's coverage through a more elaborate treatment of social rights and associative democ-

racy. We have also updated and expanded the entries on politics. Finally, the new interest within the discipline in issues of economic sociology is reflected in new or substantially revised entries on markets, labour markets, networks, management, managerial strategies of control, work attitudes, organization theory and culture, bureaucracy and, of course, economic sociology itself.

(5) The dictionary also attempts to reflect important changes in the intellectual currents of modern society. For example, while Charles Darwin had an important impact on early sociology (through Marx and Spencer), few sociologists in the 1980s would have anticipated the revival of neo-Darwinist theories of competition and selection. The return of the debate on Darwinism is connected with revolutionary changes in the scientific understanding of genetics and with the application of scientific discoveries to medicine. Social anxiety about the implications of new reproductive technologies, the human genome programme and cloning are associated with a new interest in the relationship between biology and sociology. The dictionary has expanded its coverage of sociobiology to reflect this debate. In contemporary society, these scientific developments are transforming the relationship between the environment and society. Sociologists have, as a consequence, become increasingly concerned to understand ecology, environmental politics and risk society.

(6) It is conventional for sociology dictionaries to include entries on social change, but the idea that there is a special or separate topic on social change in the sociology curriculum is becoming obsolete. Social change in contemporary societies is ubiquitous, continuous, and cannot be effectively treated as a separate issue. The dictionary contains entries on many changing aspects of contemporary society: the greying of the population, ageism, the globalization of disease, the dominance of the service sector, the postmodernization of culture, the political importance of religious fundamentalism, single-parent families, the changing nature of work and the labour market, the nature of crime, and the decline of the welfare state. These social changes are reflected in sociological discussions of risk, regulation, globalization, McDonaldization, postmodernity, virtual reality, youth culture and consumer society.

(7) Given the speed of social change in contemporary societies, it is perhaps not surprising that sociologists should be increasingly preoccupied by questions of time and space. Modern sociology as a result shares much in common with the spatial interests of social and human geography. For example, the sociology of spatial relationships has transformed the traditional study of the city and urban culture. With globalization, the city has taken on new cultural and political functions. These social changes are expressed in innovative sociological studies of space, culture, city life and information technology.

(8) The substantial revival of interest in the individual subject among contemporary sociologists has informed many of our revisions. Social theories which foreground individuals rather than collectivities in the explanation of social phenomena have become increasingly important. We include expanded or new entries on sociological approaches to agency and structure, collective action, game theory and rational choice theory. Identity, subjectivity, emotions and emotional labour, individualism, intimacy and reflexivity are issues that have attracted considerable attention over the last few years and are fully covered in this edition.

While there are changes in topics and contents, we can perhaps also detect a change in the intellectual mood of the dictionary as it has evolved over the last fifteen years. Sociology was often described as fashionable, immature and pretentious. It was sometimes dismissed as an upstart discipline that disguised its lack of intellectual substance behind a wall of jargon. The convoluted language of the theory of social systems of Talcott Parsons was taken as a key illustration of the vacuity of sociological 'Grand Theory'. The tone of the first edition in 1984 was characteristically defensive. In the first Preface, we sought to defend sociology against the charge that it was immature, riddled with jargon and politically biased. A defence of sociology along these lines now appears to be inappropriate. Sociology has expanded considerably as a component of the secondary-school curriculum, is popular in the higher-education system and there is strong demand for sociology as a perspective that is important in medicine and the health sciences.

From the perspective of critical sociology, the incorporation of sociology in the higher-education system may blind sociological theory to new perspectives and ideas. In North America, the classical sociological canon has been challenged by a variety of social movements that have been articulated through feminist theory, queer theory, Islamic science and Native American consciousness. In this respect, the challenge to sociological orthodoxy might be seen to parallel the criticism of the literary canon by the oppositional literature of post-colonialism. These diverse social movements and their intellectual expression have been somewhat muted in Europe. We can argue that the vitality of sociology as a discipline can only be sustained if it can successfully respond to diverse social and political forces. The classical sociological tradition remained robust, because it responded vigorously to the social dislocations brought about by urbanization and industrialization, and engaged with the ideologies of Marxism, socialism and Darwinism. Contemporary sociology, if it is to avoid being merely a decorative social perspective, must also respond vigorously to the new challenges from biology and technology, from globalism and postmodernism. The growing size, diversity and complexity of *The Penguin Dictionary of Sociology* can be taken as a measure of its response to these challenges.

January 2000

Nicholas Abercrombie
Stephen Hill
Bryan S. Turner

How to Use This Dictionary

In this dictionary we have tried to represent concepts, debates and schools that are both important and current. Our entries include not only technical definitions (like 'standard deviation') but also running debates ('agency and structure', for example), types of argument (like 'organic analogy'), major writers (such as Durkheim), and whole schools ('labour process approach', for instance). We therefore recommend readers to use the book freely to provide guidance on any sociological topic and not only to give a simple definition of a troublesome word.

As with any dictionary, we have provided a cross-referencing system. Throughout the text of an entry, any terms or names that refer to relevant or explanatory entries have been made into cross-references – indicated by small capitals – wherever they first appear in the entry. At the end of an entry there is usually a list of other relevant entries (in italics) not specifically referred to, or not referred to in the preceding text in the exact form of the relevant entry word. For example, under 'leadership' you will find cross-references in the text of the entry to the related concepts of 'power', 'authority' and 'legitimacy'. If you then take a look at the list at the end of this entry, you will find 'human relations' (a relevant entry not specifically referred to), as well as 'charisma' and 'group' (of which related forms, 'charismatic' and 'groups', occur in the text of the entry). Some terms or names are used so frequently throughout the dictionary that, in many instances, we have not made them into cross-references. This is particularly true of Durkheim, Marx and Weber.

At the end of many entries we have suggested some further reading, the full details of which are given in the bibliography at the back of the book. In general we have given further reading for entries which cover a large subject or are technically difficult. When an author's name is followed by a date in brackets in the text of an entry, this indicates that a corresponding publication will be found in the bibliography.

A

abstracted empiricism See: GRAND THEORY.

accommodation In the sociological analysis of race relations this describes the process whereby individuals adapt to situations of racial conflict, without resolving the basic conflict or changing the system of inequality. The term derives from experimental psychology, where it denotes how individuals modify their activity to fit the requirements of the external social world.

SEE ALSO: *acculturation; assimilation; racism.*

accounts The language by which people justify their behaviour when challenged by another social actor or group is an 'account'. Following the philosopher J. L. Austin (1962), who was particularly interested in 'excuses', and C. W. Mills (1940), who referred to the 'vocabulary of motives', the idea of accounts has been widely used in the sociology of deviance to study the ways in which criminals or deviants attempt to deny or to reduce their responsibility for behaviour which is regarded as untoward or socially unacceptable. The use of accounts is a method of avoiding the stigma of an accusation of criminality or deviance. For example, G. Sykes and D. Matza (1957) developed the concept of 'the techniques of neutralization' to describe the methods by which deviants justify their behaviour. Stealing from large companies may be justified by claiming that nobody really suffers or that an insurance company will cover the cost. Murder may be justified by arguing that the victim deserved it. This theory of DEVIANT BEHAVIOUR was further developed by D. Matza (1964) in his analysis of DELINQUENT DRIFT. Because sociologists have concentrated on denials of responsibility in accounts, they have to some extent neglected the analysis of alternative responses to social accusation, such as confession.

SEE ALSO: *criminology; delinquency; differential association; labelling theory; neutralization.*

acculturation This term is used to describe both the process of contacts between different cultures and also the outcome of such contacts. As the process of contact between cultures, acculturation may involve either direct social interaction or exposure to other cultures by means of the mass media of communication. As the outcome of such contact, acculturation refers to the ASSIMILATION by one group of the culture of another which modifies the existing culture and so changes group identity. There may be a tension between old and new cultures which leads to the adaptation of the new as well as the old.

SEE ALSO: *accommodation.*

achievement motivation The need to perform well, or achievement motivation, significantly determines a person's effort and persistence in reaching some given standard of excellence, or in comparison with competitors, and the level of aspiration that is involved in that standard or competition. This motivation is seen by psychologist D. C. McClelland (1961; 1971) as a major determinant of entrepreneurial activity and as a cause of rapid economic growth when widely dispersed in a society. Many managerial positions are also said to require individuals with a high need for achievement if they are to be performed well. McClelland believes that such needs are learned in childhood, when individuals are socialized into the culture of their societies, rather than being innate. Other needs that may be learned are the needs for power, affiliation and autonomy.

SEE ALSO: *asceticism; capitalism; Protestant ethic; work attitudes.*

achievement orientation See: ASCRIPTION; PARSONS.

act Sociologists distinguish between behaviour and action, where the latter involves purpose, consciousness and an objective. PARSONS has argued that the act is the basic unit of sociological analysis, involving: (1) an agent or actor; (2) an end or future state of affairs to which action is directed; (3) a situation that comprises the conditions and means for action; (4) a set of norms by which actions are guided and means selected. George H. MEAD has defined the act in terms of its impulse, definition of the situation and consummation.

The basic distinction between action and behaviour was made originally by WEBER, when he defined sociology as a science which seeks to interpret the meaning of action. It has been argued by writers like SCHUTZ that the concept of the act is far more complex than Weber's approach would suggest. For example, it is not entirely clear what is meant by ascribing meaning to actions and situations. For sociologists, the principal significance of an act is that it is intentional and directed towards the future realization of a goal.

SEE ALSO: *action theory; agency and structure; behaviourism; methodological individualism; symbolic interactionism.*

action frame of reference See: ACTION THEORY.

action research Conventional social scientific research is concerned to describe, analyse and explain phenomena. The role of the researcher is detached, in order to minimize disturbance of the phenomena under investigation. In action research, however, the research role is involved and interventionist, because research is joined with action in order to plan, implement and monitor change. Researchers become participants in planned policy initiatives and use their knowledge and research expertise to serve a client organization.

SEE ALSO: *evaluation research.*

action theory Subjective action is to be distinguished from behaviour in that it involves meaning or intention. Action theory is the analysis of action starting with the individual actor. Analysis proceeds in terms of typical actors in typical situations by identifying actors' goals, expectations and values, the means of achieving those goals, the nature of the situation and the actors' knowledge of the situation, among other elements. PARSONS refers to these elements as the 'action frame of reference'.

There are two main forms of action theory, the 'hermeneutic' and the 'positivist', and both are also closely related to the doctrine of SYMBOLIC INTERACTIONISM. Both have their origins in the work of WEBER. Weber distinguished four types of action: traditional, affectual, *Zweckrational* and *Wertrational*. Traditional actions are those performed simply because they have been performed in the past. Affectual actions are those performed simply to express an emotion. However, Weber was relatively little interested in these two forms of action, being more concerned with rational action. *Zweckrational* (instrumental action) is action in which the actor not only compares different means to a goal, but also assesses the utility of the goal itself. In *Wertrational* (value rationality), the actor takes the goal as an end in itself and may not even compare different means to that goal. Weber makes it clear that the four types of action are ideal types and it is empirically possible for actions to be a mixture of one or more of the types.

For Weber, it is important that action is defined in terms of 'meaningfulness' and sociological analysis must proceed by identifying the meaning that actions have for actors. Hermeneutic action theories are those which make this meaningfulness an absolute theoretical priority; acting and meaning are inextricably linked. SCHUTZ is one writer who adopts this perspective. He argues that Weber does not provide a satisfactory account of meaningful action in that meaning is too much divorced from the actor; it becomes an objective category imposed by the sociologist.

Schutz holds that the key to the interpretation of action lies in the notion of a stream of experiences in time. Our experiences form a continuous flow. Each experience has no meaning in itself but can be given meaning by reflection on it as it recedes into the past. Actions may, however, be reflected on in what Schutz called the future perfect tense; that is, one may reflect on future actions as if they had been in the past. For Schutz, this form of reflection is crucial, for action is the product of intention and reflection. It is that which is determined by a project or plan. Schutz further distinguishes 'in-order-to motives' from 'because motives'. The former refer to the future and are roughly equivalent to the goals for which actions are the means. The latter refer to the past and are the immediate reasons for undertaking actions. *Social* actions are those whose in-order-to motives contain a reference to someone else's stream of experience, and if social actions defined in this way take place on both sides, there is *social interaction*.

Generally, the more seriously hermeneutic action theorists take the meaningfulness of action, the less easy is it for them to include conceptions of social structure in the theory. Schutz is ambivalent on the question of the relationship of the individual actor to a determining social structure. On the other hand, positivist action theories, the most distinguished example of which is that of T. Parsons, tend to be more interested in social structure and how it sets the goals and means available to actors. There is a tendency in the positivist theory, therefore, to make action and interaction residual concepts less important than the analysis of the social system as a whole; the notion of social structure as simply the outcome of the projects and actions of social actors is largely abandoned in favour of seeing the human actor as socialized into a common culture.

For Parsons, action is behaviour directed by the meanings attached by actors to things and people. Actors have goals and select appropriate means. Courses of action are constrained by the situation and guided by symbols and values. The most important category is interaction; that is, action oriented towards other actors. When interaction between two parties is frequent, mutual expectations will emerge. Both parties will have to adjust both their expectations and behaviour to match up with the other's behaviour and expectations. As expectations are established as reliable predictors of behaviour, they become the norms governing the interaction and following the norms not only makes action more effective, it also gives actors intrinsic satisfaction since, for Parsons, actors 'need' the approval of others. These norms are the basis of social order institutionalized in society and internalized in the individual. Giddens has tried to transcend the limitations of conventional distinctions between actions and structures. His notion of 'duality of structure' emphasizes the knowledgeability of the actor and the existing resources of knowledge.

SEE ALSO: *actor/social actor; agency and structure; behaviourism; hermeneutics; ideal type; methodological individualism; phenomenological sociology; rationality; Verstehen.*

READING: Cohen, I. J. (1996)

actor/social actor Any individual who takes part in social action. There are some similarities with the theatrical sense of the term in that social action can be conceived of as a performance. However, the main implication of the use of the term is a focus on the qualities, feelings, intentions and understandings of the individual as well as on the social constraints acting on that individual.

SEE ALSO: *action theory.*

actor-network theory (ANT) This was initially a French term (*acteur réseau*) which was used to describe networks. The theory has been developed by B. Latour and J. Law in order to explore relationships or networks. ANT grew out of science studies, but it has been applied to a wide range of issues in the social sciences. It is an application of SEMIOTICS to social relationships, based on the premise that entities (people and objects) gain their attributes as a consequence of their relation to other entities. It has been described as 'relational materiality', because it explores the material nature of entities as products or effects of relationships. For example, a museum is a method of organizing the heterogeneity of a collection of objects from a particular archaeological point of view, such that the meaning of the objects is dependent on a series of relationships (to other objects and museums). ANT is a semiotic device that is used to criticize the notion of essential differences. It attempts to overcome the dualisms of social theory (agency and structure, materiality and sociality) by demonstrating that entities have no properties that are not produced by the networks or relations of which they are a part. The approach also attempts to overcome, for example, the division between human bodies and machines – both are seen as entities that are the effects of networks. As a theory of materiality, it treats phenomena in terms of their performativity, because entities arise in, by and through the performance of relations.

ANT is also a contribution to the sociological understanding of space, because it has developed the notion of network as a topological system, where positions are created or held precariously by a set of links or relations. These topological metaphors are designed to overcome the macro/micro distinction, because ANT research is concerned to understand the ordering and durability of networks on whatever scale. The methods of ANT have been compared with ETHNOMETHODOLOGY, in the sense that ANT research involves studying how and why networks are produced and sustained as practical activities.

ANT has been criticized on a number of grounds. A major criticism is that it does not give an adequate account of the actor. Instead ANT is concerned to understand human bodies alongside a range of physical objects that may occur as entities in the flows and circuits that make up networks. The principal characteristic of human beings for ANT is the fact that they are indeterminate; we can predict nothing about them prior to their appearance in networks. As a form of radical semiotics, human beings have no attributes outside or prior to their production in networks. ANT theory can therefore be contrasted with phenomenological theories of human EMBODIMENT. A second criticism is that the concept is expressed in obscure language which conceals the fact that the basic proposition, that things and people are defined in their relation to other things and people, is really quite simple.

SEE ALSO: *actor/social actor; network/social network.*

READING: Law and Hassard (1999)

adaptation See: EVOLUTIONARY THEORY.

addiction This is the devotion to or enslavement by a substance, typically a drug, which is regarded as physically or socially harmful. In one approach, research has concentrated on: (1) the analysis of addictions related to criminal behaviour (such as driving offences); (2) the social distribution of addictions according to age, class and sex; (3) the social and psychological origins of addictions (such as parental influences). Such research emphasizes learning and opportunity in addictive behaviour. By contrast, positivistic approaches that accept BEHAVIOURISM have been more concerned with the physiological and psychological determinants of long-term addiction and with questions related to possible recovery.

A third approach to addiction has been based on SYMBOLIC INTERACTIONISM, and is interested in: (1) the social processes and social context by which individuals become, for example, drug-users within a deviant subculture; (2) the maintenance of a commitment to drug use; (3) social reactions to or labelling of the addict as a social deviant. Becoming an addict is conceptualized in terms of a CAREER with definite stages, in which the addict comes to accept a stigmatizing label and responds to that new identity. The sociology of deviance therefore treats 'addiction' as a label by which law enforcement agencies and public opinion exert social control over individuals regarded as harmful or anti-social. Furthermore, there is evidence of a MEDICALIZATION of behaviour so that the notion of 'addiction' is extended to include a variety of other activities, such as gambling. GIDDENS (1992) sees these extensions as part of the REFLEXIVE project of the self. Treatment of addiction either involves some form of 'aversion therapy' in which the use of drugs comes to be associated with unpleasant experiences, or a programme of learning to reduce and remove addiction through membership of a voluntary association such as Alcoholics Anonymous. However, recovery rates under both methods are low, addiction tending to be a recurrent problem.

SEE ALSO: *body; deviance amplification; deviant behaviour; social pathology; social problems.*

adolescence In general, the sociology of adolescence has been dominated by a 'social problems' approach – that is, basic research has centred around those phenomena which appear to characterize adolescence as a period of individual crisis. Many psychiatric and behavioural problems have their onset or greatest incidence in adolescence. Sociologists and psychologists have focused on the effect of transitions from home to school and to work on emotional stress in young people.

Sociologists have argued that the notion of a separate and specialized age group called 'adolescence' is the product of the late nineteenth century. However, historians claim that specialized youth groups can be traced back to at least the sixteenth century in France.

SEE ALSO: *delinquency; gang; generation; life-cycle; peer group; social problems.*

Adorno, Theodor W. (1903–69)   Associated with the FRANKFURT SCHOOL, Adorno spent much of his life in his native Germany, but between 1934 and 1960 he lived mainly in the United States, where he had fled as a refugee from Nazi Germany. He had wide interests in philosophy and in social and cultural studies generally, especially music. Very much influenced by Marxism, Adorno argued that social theory had to maintain a critical edge. On this basis he attacked many of the approaches used in social studies, particularly those claiming to be scientific and quantitative, on the grounds that they did not provide a basis for the transformation of society. He is probably best known to sociologists for his critique of mass culture in the modern world. This he saw as being purveyed by CULTURE INDUSTRIES and as manipulative of the masses. Adorno's work is diffuse, but the books of most sociological interest are *Prisms* (1967), *Dialectic of Enlightenment* (1973), with M. Horkheimer, and *Minima Moralia* (1974). He also contributed to *The Authoritarian Personality* (1950).

SEE ALSO: *authoritarian personality; Marcuse; Marxist sociology; mass society.*

READING: Jay (1984)

advertising   The means by which goods are promoted and marketed in industrial societies. In sociological work on advertising, two lines of argument have been taken, the second more recent than the first. In the first, the underlying proposition is that advertising persuades people to buy goods that they do not need and generally contributes to the formation and maintenance of CONSUMER SOCIETY. Marxist theorists have been prominent in formulating this view. Members of the FRANK-FURT SCHOOL, for instance, especially ADORNO and MARCUSE, have argued that advertising is instrumental in the preservation of capitalist society by creating false needs in people who are seduced by the flow of goods. Many non-Marxist writers also adopted positions critical of advertising by arguing, for example, that advertising creates and perpetuates materialist values in society or promotes harmful goods (e.g. alcohol or cigarettes) to vulnerable people (e.g. teenagers in Western society). Against arguments of this kind it has been suggested that advertising does not work directly to persuade people that they must have the goods in question, even if they do not need them; at the most it may persuade consumers to switch brands.

It is difficult, however, to believe that advertising does not have a more general cultural role. The second line of argument pursues this point in suggesting that advertising is a form of communication that helps to create a particular societal culture. In most contemporary societies, advertising is omnipresent, being transmitted in a wide variety of media. Thus advertising may indeed contribute to the formation of a consumer culture in which individual consumers look for POSITIONAL GOODS that help them establish an identity. It may also contribute more widely to a postmodern culture which celebrates consumption but also promotes the importance of images. So, for example, recent studies of contemporary advertising have shown how much more dependent on images and how much less on text, it is compared with advertising of fifty years ago.

SEE ALSO: *aestheticization of everyday life; postmodernism.*

READING: Dyer (1982); Schudson (1984)

aestheticization of everyday life The claim that the division between art and everyday life is being eroded. There are two senses: (1) artists are taking the objects of everyday life and making them into art objects; (2) people are making their everyday lives into aesthetic projects by aiming at a coherent style in their clothes, appearance and household furnishings. This may reach the point where people see themselves and their surroundings as art objects. BENJAMIN claimed that mass consumer commodities had liberated artistic creativity, which had migrated into everyday reality. Consumers had broken down the hierarchy of high and low culture.

SEE ALSO: *postmodernity.*

READING: Featherstone (1991)

affect/affective neutrality Typically contrasted with RATIONALITY in the sociology of action, affect refers to emotions as determinants of the choices people make in social interaction. Affective neutrality is action that is not swayed by emotions. In his analysis of the pattern variables in *The Social System* (1951), PARSONS contrasted affective neutrality with expressivity in the selection of means to achieve the ends of action. For example, in the definition of PROFESSION, Parsons emphasized the importance of the professional code of practice that requires professionals to act with affective neutrality in relations with clients.

SEE ALSO: *emotions.*

affective individualism Historical sociologists have argued that changes in the relationship between the family and the economy have placed a greater emphasis on emotional compatibility between marriage partners, because the basis of marriage is no longer simply an economic contract. Marriage is now guided by the romantic norms of affective individualism, namely intimacy, trust and sexual satisfaction. For example, A. Giddens in *The Transformation of Intimacy* (1992) argues that romantic love and FEMINISM have changed the expectations of women about romantic attachments, sexuality and marriage, resulting in a 'democratising of personal life'.

SEE ALSO: *emotions; intimacy; marriage; nuclear family; patriarchy.*

affectivity See: PARSONS.

affinal This refers to a relationship by marriage rather than by the real or mythical ties of descent. For example, mother-in-law is an affinal relationship in contrast to the mother–child relationship, which is one of descent.

SEE ALSO: *descent groups; kinship.*

affluent society A term coined by J. K. Galbraith to indicate the way in which many modern societies have become wealthy enough to eradicate the problems of scarcity. In his view, however, such societies leave affluence in private hands while producing public squalor.

affluent worker It was widely believed during the 1960s that post-war affluence in Britain had led to the EMBOURGEOISEMENT of the manual working class. J. H.

Goldthorpe, D. Lockwood, F. Bechhofer and J. Platt investigated this issue among workers in Luton and published their findings as *The Affluent Worker* (1968a; 1968b; 1969). They distinguished traditional-proletarian and affluent workers. Traditional proletarians lived in closed and isolated working-class communities in single-industry areas, formed gregarious social communities of workmates, kin and neighbours, and had a conflictual, power-based CLASS IMAGERY. Work formed a CENTRAL LIFE INTEREST and was more than just a means to earn money. Traditional proletarians were found in older industries and long-established industrial areas. Affluent workers had migrated to the newer industrial centres of the Midlands, drawn by the attraction of the very high wages. They were privatized workers, in the sense of being home- and family-centred and not participating in community life. They did not see work as a central life interest or as anything more than a means of satisfying their instrumental needs for money and security, displaying none of the 'social needs' assumed by HUMAN RELATIONS. They had a non-conflictual, money image of class. These differences between traditional and affluent workers did not indicate that the Luton workers were becoming more middle-class, however, because the money class image was not similar to the middle-class prestige model, and Luton workers continued to support trade unionism and vote Labour like other workers.

In its time, *The Affluent Worker* represented a major contribution to the sociology of work and social class in Britain. However, given the changes that have occurred in British society, it is now mainly of historical interest.

SEE ALSO: *class consciousness; lifestyle; privatization; work attitudes; working class.*

age cohort See: COHORT.

age differentiation A process by which individuals are located into different status positions and play roles on the basis of social attitudes towards their age; it produces AGE GROUPS.

SEE ALSO: *differentiation; stratification.*

age groups Every society categorizes individuals in terms of their age and therefore by their position in the LIFE-CYCLE, but the STRATIFICATION of society by age has been neglected by comparison with class, ethnicity and gender. S. N. Eisenstadt (1956) defines 'age group' or 'age grade' in terms of the STATUS and role expectations of individuals at specific stages of the life-cycle. The transition of individuals between age grades is typically marked by RITES OF PASSAGE. The term also has a technical meaning in DEMOGRAPHY, where age groups refer typically to five-year periods. Age-group frequencies are used to display demographic data.

SEE ALSO: *age differentiation; aging; generation; gerontology.*

age sets See AGE GROUPS.

ageism A term first employed by Dr R. N. Butler, director of the American Institute of Aging in 1968, it refers to the negative stereotype of elderly individuals, which prejudicially describes them as senile, rigid in their attitudes and psychologically and socially dependent. Ageism has become important as a political issue with the greying of populations in Western societies. 'New ageism' refers to intergenerational conflicts where the elderly are condemned for being 'takers' and not 'givers'.

SEE ALSO: *aging; gerontology; stereotypes.*

READING: Harris (1990)

agency and structure An important debate in sociological theory concerns the relationship between individuals and social structure. The debate revolves round the problem of how structures determine what individuals do, how structures are created, and what are the limits, if any, on individuals' capacities to act independently of structural constraints; what are the limits, in other words, on human agency. There are three main positions in this debate.

(1) Some sociologists argue that structures cannot be seen as determining and the emphasis should be placed on the way that individuals create the world around them. Writers subscribing to the doctrines of METHODOLOGICAL INDIVIDUALISM, ETHNOMETHODOLOGY, or PHENOMENOLOGICAL SOCIOLOGY, mainly take this view; indeed, some might even argue that there is no such thing as social structure.

(2) The contrary position is that sociology should be concerned only with social structures that determine the characteristics and actions of individuals, whose agency or special characteristics therefore become unimportant. E. Durkheim was an early exponent of this position. Functionalists often adopt this view, being concerned simply with the functional relationships between social structures. Many Marxists similarly argue that social relations, not individuals, are the proper objects of analysis. Individuals are only the 'bearers' of social relations.

(3) The third view tries to compromise between (1) and (2), avoiding both the idea of a structure determining individuals and also that of individuals independently creating their world. One of the best-known theories of this kind is that of P. Berger and T. Luckmann (1967). They argue that there is a dialectical process in which the meanings given by individuals to their world become institutionalized or turned into social structures, and the structures then become part of the meaning-systems employed by individuals and limit their actions. For example, if a man and a woman meet for the first time on a desert island, they create their relationship and give it meaning. However, their children are born into the society made by their parents; for them it is a given which constrains their actions to a great extent. GIDDENS has attempted to overcome the division between agency and structure by means of the notion of 'duality of structure'. He argues that 'structure' is both the medium and the outcome of the actions which are recursively organized by structures. He emphasizes the 'knowledgeability' of actors, who depend on existing knowledge and strategy to achieve their ends. Many Marxists have also sought a similar compromise so as to give some meaning to the concept of CLASS STRUGGLE, conceived as actions taken by individuals or groups of individuals against the determining power of social structures. A more recent approach is RATIONAL CHOICE THEORY.

SEE ALSO: *action theory; Althusser; hermeneutics; Marxist sociology; Parsons; social structure; structuration; subject/subjectivity; Verstehen.*

agenda setting This is a concept employed in the sociology of the MASS MEDIA. The suggestion is that television, radio and the press do not simply report events but rather set agendas; that is, they *select* particular issues for discussion in particular ways by particular people. From this it follows that there is a framework of presentation which excludes certain issues or points of view. For example, it has been claimed that the television news coverage of industry neglects industrial accidents but reports strikes in detail.

READING: Glasgow University Media Group (1993)

aggregate data Some data analyses focus on statistics that relate to broad categories or groups rather than to individual cases; for example, social classes, households, or types of person. Aggregate data subsume individual respondents into these broader units so that they cease to be identifiable.

AGIL See PARSONS; SYSTEMS THEORY.

aging While the political role of age groups and generations has been of considerable interest to sociologists, the general area of social aging was neglected by the mainstream of sociology until the late 1960s. Current interest in aging and GERONTOLOGY has been stimulated by the growing proportion of the aged in the population of industrialized societies and by public concern with the aged as a social problem. Societies such as the USA, Canada, Britain, Germany, Italy and Japan are classified by the United Nations as 'old' because more than 7 per cent of their population is over 65 years of age. 'Mature' countries, with 4–7 per cent over 65 years, include Brazil, South Africa and Turkey. 'Young' countries, with less than 4 per cent, include Egypt, India and Mexico. In Britain, people past retiring age (women over 60 and men over 65) increased as a percentage of the population from 6.8 in 1911 to 18.2 in 1998. Social policy towards retirement has had a dramatic effect on the labour force participation rates for the elderly. At the beginning of the century, 67 per cent of men over 65 years were still employed; by the late 1990s, about 7 per cent were employed. With the growth of pensions and early-retirement schemes, it has been argued that the elderly constitute an economic burden on the community. The 'burden of dependency' as a ratio is calculated as those not eligible for employment (young people below working age and those past the age of retirement) over the working population. As this dependency ratio increases, it is thought that as the century progresses the elderly will constitute a considerable brake on economic growth for many advanced industrial societies.

While S. N. Eisenstadt (1956) provided a general perspective on age groups, sociology lacks a theoretical synthesis of existing research into demographic changes, generational politics, age stratification and aging in relation to labour markets.

While gerontology as a branch of biology treats aging as a genetically programmed process of living organisms, social gerontology is concerned with aging (1) as a contingent process relating to the social and demographic structure of human groups; (2) as an aspect of personal status in the life-cycle; (3) as the dynamic component of stratification in terms of generational membership; (4) as a contemporary social problem raising questions about exploitation, victimization and stigmatization. What is of central interest to sociology is not an individual's chronological age but the criteria, in terms of social expectations and cultural values, by which an individual is labelled as 'young', 'middle-aged' or 'elderly'. For example, the problem of old age in modern societies is the product of a dramatic increase in life-expectancy combined with cultural and social changes in values relating to age. In pre-literate societies, the elderly were venerated because they were social repositories of wisdom, custom and property rights. In industrial society, emphasis on achievement rather than ASCRIPTION, early retirement and the significance of youthfulness as a major criterion of personal and aesthetic values have changed the social status of the aged. These changes have given rise to a debate about old age as a disengagement from work, normative commitment and sociability. Functionalist theories of aging as disengagement from social roles have been criticized for assuming that aging is a natural or passive process, whereas it typically involves social exclusion.

Two important issues have come to the forefront of social research into aging. First, there is the historical debate about the changing social status of the elderly with the processes of modernization and industrialization. This issue relates to the problem of whether the decline of the EXTENDED FAMILY has left the aged without kinship support in industrial society. Historical evidence now suggests that households with more than two generations were uncommon in pre-industrial society and, furthermore, the social isolation of the elderly varies with residential, social class and cultural factors. Secondly, the commercialization of personal appearance in societies where youthfulness is prestigious has given rise to research into 'the mid-life crisis', sexual activity in old age, the social implications of the menopause and the general movement for health and fitness.

SEE ALSO: *demographic transition; demography; generation; life-cycle; nuclear family; social problems; welfare state.*

READING: Katz (1996); Phillipson (1998)

agnatic An anthropological term used to describe a system of kinship in which people will establish their pattern of relationships through the father's or the male line only. The term has the same meaning as PATRILINEAL.

SEE ALSO: *cognate/cognatic; descent groups.*

AIDS See: EPIDEMIOLOGY.

alienation This denotes the estrangement of individuals from themselves and others. It was originally a term with philosophical and religious meanings, but K. Marx transformed it into a sociological concept in the *Economic and Philosophical Manuscripts of 1844*. Marx saw human estrangement as rooted in social structures which denied people their essential human nature. He believed that this human essence was realized in labour, a creative activity carried out in cooperation with others by which people transformed the world outside themselves. The process of production is one of 'objectification', whereby men make material objects which embody human creativity yet stand as entities separate from their creators. Alienation occurs when, once objectified, man no longer recognizes himself in his product which has become alien to him, 'is no longer his own' and 'stands opposed to him as an autonomous power'. Objectification, however, only becomes alienation in the specific historical circumstances of capitalism. In capitalist society, one group of people, capitalists, appropriates the products created by others. This is the origin of alienation. Marx saw alienation both as a subjective state – as people's feelings of alienation – and as a structural category which described the social and economic arrangements of capitalism.

Marx identified four particular manifestations of alienation. (1) The worker is alienated from the product of his labour, since what he produces is appropriated by others and he has no control over its fate. (2) The worker is alienated from the act of production. Working becomes an alien activity that offers no intrinsic satisfaction, that is forced on the worker by external constraints and ceases to be an end in itself, and that involves working at someone else's bidding as forced labour. Work in fact becomes a commodity that is sold and its only value to the worker is its saleability. (3) The worker is alienated from his human nature or his 'species being', because the first two aspects of alienation deprive his productive activity of those specifically *human* qualities which distinguish it from the activity of animals and thus define human nature. (4) The worker is alienated from other people, since capitalism transforms social relations into market relations, and people are judged by their position in the market rather than by their human qualities. People come to regard each other as reifications – as worker or as capitalist – rather than as individuals.

Capital itself is the source of further alienation within a developed capitalist economy. This is because capital accumulation generates its own 'needs' which reduce people to the level of commodities. Workers become factors in the operation of capital and their activities are dominated by the requirements of profitability rather than by their own human needs. Within a market economy, the rules which govern accumulation are those of the market place. These rules constitute a set of impersonal mechanisms which dominate all economic actors, capitalists as well as workers, and the market has a coercive force. Marx noted that, although the needs of profit and capital accumulation seem to take on a life of their own, these impersonal mechanisms in fact disguise the human origins of capital and the exploitation that allows one class to appropriate what another has produced.

Since Marx, alienation has lost much of its original sociological meaning and has been used to describe a wide variety of phenomena. These include: any feeling of separation from, and discontent with, society; feelings that there is a moral breakdown in society; feelings of powerlessness in face of the solidity of social institutions; the impersonal, dehumanized nature of large-scale and bureaucratic social organizations. The first pair of usages in fact bear a considerable resemblance to the different, Durkheimian concept of ANOMIE rather than to Marx's conception of alienation. The last usage echoes M. Weber's sentiments about the bureaucratic tendency of modern society.

In the 1950s and 1960s, American social scientists emphasized the subjective or psychological facet of alienation at the cost of the social structural aspect, and when they did consider structural conditions they ignored Marx's sociology of capitalism. M. Seeman (1959) separated a variety of different psychological states, which he measured by ATTITUDE SCALES. The 'powerlessness' dimension of alienation refers to people's feelings that they cannot influence their social surroundings. 'Meaninglessness' is the feeling that illegitimate means are required to achieve valued goals. 'Isolation' occurs when people feel estranged from society's norms and values. 'Self-estrangement' refers to an inability to find activities that are psychologically rewarding. R. Blauner (1964) linked these dimensions of subjective alienation to the different types of work found in modern industry and claimed that production technology was the major determinant of alienation. He claimed that alienation was low in old-fashioned craft work, because craft workers were in control of their work, had 'whole' tasks that were meaningful, opportunities to socialize with colleagues on the job, and found work psychologically rewarding. Alienation was at its peak in the mass production, assembly-line work associated with FORDISM. The pace of work was out of the control of employees, tasks were subdivided into small fragments and social community was absent. He thought that AUTOMATION would make jobs more satisfying and so abolish alienation. Automation meant work would be routine much of the time, but during emergencies would require individual skills, collective team working and an understanding of the process as a whole. The American perspective in effect has equated alienation with people's feelings of dissatisfaction with life, or with work, which is a long way from Marx's original formulation.

The term has been used less often in recent sociology. Many modern Marxists believe that Marx abandoned alienation in his mature work in favour of exploitation and they see little point in preserving the concept. Most non-Marxist sociologists find that it has become too indeterminate to be useful.

SEE ALSO: *cash nexus; division of labour; reification; Marx; Weber; work attitudes.*

READING: Ollman (1971)

alternative medicine Also referred to as *complementary medicine*, these are diagnostic and therapeutic beliefs and practices that attempt to provide alternatives to scientific (allopathic) medicine, which is based on the MEDICAL MODEL. Alternative medicine has the following characteristics: (1) it is typically homoeopathic (rather than allopathic) in treating the patient as unique with idiosyncratic problems and symptoms; (2) it follows the system laid down by S. Hahnemann (1755–1843), who argued (through his teaching on the minimum dose) that less medicine is better than more medicine; (3) it uses natural remedies and traditional (folk) cures rather than manufactured pharmaceutical products; (4) its practitioners are typically not regulated by a professional body recognized by the state; (5) the theories and treatment regimes are characteristically eclectic, drawing upon Western, Eastern and folk systems. Alternative medicine has developed in the twentieth century as a response to consumer dissatisfaction with scientific medicine which is intrusive, interventionist and technologically sophisticated. The practical and philosophical roots of alternative medicine are, however, ancient. Alternative medicine includes acupuncture, chiropractice, Chinese holistic medicines, herbalism, naturopathy, iridology and psychic healing.

SEE ALSO: *health-care systems.*

READING: Cant and Sharma (1996)

Althusser, Louis (1918–90) A French Marxist philosopher, Althusser (1966; 1968, with E. Balibar; 1971) had an influence on contemporary sociology in four main directions.

(1) He attempted to reformulate the BASE AND SUPERSTRUCTURE model, because he objected to the economic DETERMINISM which he believed is implicit in most accounts of that model. Instead of seeing superstructural elements, such as ideology and politics, simply as reflections of the economic base, he proposed a scheme in which ideology and politics are conditions of existence of the economy. Althusser has been partly responsible for the interest shown in the concept of the MODE OF PRODUCTION, which he considered as a complex relationship of economy, ideology and politics.

(2) Althusser attempted to redefine the nature of ideology. He argued that ideology should be seen as a real social relation, or as a practice, not as an illusion as it is in conventional analyses.

(3) The most influential of Althusser's specific proposals is his concept of the IDEOLOGICAL STATE APPARATUS, itself a notion deriving from GRAMSCI. For capitalist societies to continue over time, the RELATIONS OF PRODUCTION must

be reproduced, a requirement that is met by the ideological state apparatuses; for example, institutions of the media and education.

(4) Althusser advanced a number of arguments which touch on the old sociological debate about the relation of AGENCY AND STRUCTURE. Essentially, Althusser objected to theories which reduce explanation to the characteristics of individuals or collections of individuals; for example, classes. Instead, individuals have to be seen as bearers or agents of the *structures* of social relations.

There has been a great deal of criticism of Althusserianism from within conventional sociology, concentrating on the school's theoreticism, its neglect of relevant evidence, its dogmatism and its departure from Marxist principles, particularly that of the primacy of the economy.

SEE ALSO: *Marx; Marxist sociology; structuralism.*

READING: Benton (1984)

altruism Normally contrasted with egoism and individualism, altruism is the principle of unselfish regard for the needs and interests of others. For DURKHEIM, altruistic suicide, that is suicide to serve group interests, was the result of strong collective pressure and social approval. More recently, the question of altruism over egoism has been raised by theories of exchange and RECIPROCITY and by RATIONAL CHOICE THEORY.

SEE ALSO: *exchange theory.*

animism As one of the basic concepts of the nineteenth-century evolutionary theory of RELIGION, animism was held to be part of a primitive philosophy which explained such phenomena as dreams, hallucinations and death by reference to the spiritual existence of animals and plants, and the existence of the human soul. Within an evolutionary scheme of cultural development, positivist science would replace both theology and animistic philosophy. Subsequent theories saw religion more in terms of its social functions rather than as emphasizing its individual and cognitive characteristics.

Annales School An influential group of French social historians associated with the journal *Annales: économies, sociétés, civilisations*, which was founded by L. Febvre and M. Bloch in 1929. The school has made major contributions to the empirical study of European civilization as a whole and to theoretical and methodological debates about historical analysis. Members of the school have, in particular, opposed the conventional approach to history as the chronology of political events by giving greater emphasis to social history, social structure and long-term historical trends. There is an important marriage of interests between some of the classical debates in sociology (over the transition from feudalism to capitalism, for example) and the emphasis on structure and historical process in the *Annales* School. The work of E. Le Roy Ladurie (1975) and F. Braudel (1966; 1979) has become especially important for sociologists. The influence of Braudel on contemporary social science has developed through the Braudel Center in America, under the leadership of I. Wallerstein (1974).

SEE ALSO: *world-system theory.*

READING: Burke (1980)

Année sociologique, L' Edited by E. Durkheim between 1896 and 1913, *L'Année sociologique* has been described as a sociological laboratory rather than a journal, since it provided the principal publishing outlet of the research of the early Durkheimian school. It was certainly a major institutional factor in the dominance of Durkheimian sociology over competitive groups in France.

READING: Nandan (1977)

anomie This is a social condition characterized by the breakdown of norms governing social interaction. Anomie, like ALIENATION, is a concept that bridges the gap between explanations of social action at the individual level with those at the level of the social structure. The classical treatment is that of DURKHEIM in his work on SUICIDE. In *Suicide* (1897), Durkheim argues that people can be happy only when their wants are proportionate to their means. Left to themselves, human desires are boundless and this fact of human nature, together with necessarily limited resources, creates great unhappiness or ultimately suicide. The manner in which societies cope with this problem of unattainable goals is to restrict human desires and goals by imposing a framework of norms which 'permits' only certain goals that have some chance of attainment. Anomie describes the situation when this framework breaks down, goals again outrun means and the suicide rate rises.

Durkheim's concept of anomie has been enlarged by R. K. Merton (1957) into a general theory of deviant behaviour. Merton distinguishes culturally defined goals and institutional means of achieving those goals. Societies vary in the degree to which they stress one or the other. Those societies that lay great emphasis on goals but little on means push individuals into adopting the technically most efficient means to the goal, even if these are illegitimate. An example of such an anomic society is the United States. Here there is an emphasis on wealth and personal success, but the economy limits the real opportunities for SOCIAL MOBILITY. Crime may be normal in certain groups because, while there is a widespread emphasis on the importance of worldly success, particularly in terms of wealth, the available means to these goals are restricted by the class structure and the means of achieving them will also include illegitimate ones.

SEE ALSO: *relative deprivation*.

READING: Parkin (1992)

anticipatory socialization A term describing the behaviour of those who anticipate a future STATUS by taking on the customs, culture or behaviour of a social group that they wish to, or are about to, join. It is most commonly used for changes in the LIFE-CYCLE, as when, for example, children adopt adult ways of behaving, but it can also describe those who are upwardly socially mobile.

SEE ALSO: *socialization*.

anti-psychiatry An intellectual movement of the late 1950s and the 1960s which was critical of the theories and therapeutic treatments of conventional psychiatry. It made various criticisms. (1) The involuntary incarceration of persons regarded as insane is an infringement of basic human rights. (2) Psychiatry is a form of SOCIAL CONTROL by which social deviance is labelled as a form of mental illness. (3) It is not insanity which creates the need for asylums, but rather asylums that create the need for mad people. (4) Diagnostic categories express, not a neutral science, but a set of dominant values, and the use of such diagnostic labels stigmatizes the mentally ill. (5) The therapeutic treatment available to psychiatry, such as electro-convulsive therapy, is degrading and of uncertain value.

The anti-psychiatry movement proposed a range of alternative forms of approach and treatment; the basic proposal was the closure of existing asylums and psychiatric units in favour of COMMUNITY MEDICINE. This movement was associated with T. Szasz (1971) in the USA, FOUCAULT (1961) in France, and R. D. Laing (1959) in Britain. E. Goffman's (1961b) criticism of asylums as total institutions had an influence in sociology. Criticism of psychiatry is now less prominent, because there has been an exodus of patients from mental hospitals since the 1960s and there is a greater use of out-patient treatment. This process of de-institutionalization or decarceration has, in part, been made possible by the improvement in antipsychotic drugs. However, critics of psychiatry would maintain that this change in policy has been produced more by the escalating costs of hospital care.

SEE ALSO: *alternative medicine*; *Freud*; *Goffman*; *labelling theory*; *medicalization*; *mental health*; *sociology of health and illness*; *stereotypes*; *stigma*.

READING: Boyers and Orrill (1972)

applied sociology See: POLICY RESEARCH.

Aron, Raymond (1905–83) French sociologist, philosopher and political actor, he was a professor at the Collège de France from 1970, having held a variety of other university positions from before the Second World War. He was influential in French sociology, but he was also isolated because of his criticisms and opposition to Marxism which was an important theoretical perspective in French sociology, especially before 1968. Aron (1978) divided his own contribution to sociology into four main areas. (1) There was the analysis of contemporary ideologies, as in *The Opium of the Intellectuals* (1955). (2) He wrote extensively on the notion of INDUSTRIAL SOCIETY in *Eighteen Lectures on Industrial Society* (1963b) and *The Industrial Society* (1966). (3) He contributed to the analysis of international relations and warfare in *The Century of Total War* (1951), *Peace and War* (1961), *The Great Debate* (1963a), *De Gaulle, Israel and the Jews* (1968a), *The Imperial Republic* (1973b) and *Clausewitz* (1976). (4) He studied modern political systems and movements in *Democracy and Totalitarianism* (1965a), *An Essay on Freedom* (1965b), *The Elusive Revolution* (1968b) and *Progress and Disillusion* (1969).

In addition, he played an important role in maintaining an awareness of the complexity and richness of the sociological tradition in *German Sociology* (1935) and *Main Currents in Sociological Thought* (1965c). He also wrote on the philosophy of history in *Introduction to the Philosophy of History* (1938) and *History and the Dialectic of Violence* (1973a).

His analysis of industrial society, in which he drew attention to PLURALISM and the complexity of values, was in many respects parallel to the concept of POST-INDUSTRIAL SOCIETY, which has been influential in American sociology. However, he rejected the CONVERGENCE THESIS, arguing that the different political systems of the USSR and the USA were distinctive; in general terms, he attempted to show that political institutions and processes were independent of social and economic relations.

asceticism This is a doctrine or practice in which sensuous pleasures are denied for the enhancement of the spiritual self. The notion is associated with branches of most important religions. For WEBER, Protestant asceticism was of crucial importance for the origins of capitalism, the discipline of labour and capitalist organization.

SEE ALSO: *Protestant ethic; world religions.*

ascribed status See: STATUS.

ascription Ascription means that certain qualities of individuals – status, occupation or income, for example – are given by the position into which those individuals are born or over which they have no control, rather than by their own achievements.

Asiatic mode of production A Marxist concept that explains the alleged stagnation of Oriental societies, it was used by K. Marx and F. Engels in 1853 in a collection of articles published in the *New York Daily Tribune* as a description of 'Asiatic societies' from Egypt to China. Marx and Engels offered various theories to explain the origins of the Asiatic mode of production: (1) the arid conditions of these societies gave rise to the need for state-regulated irrigation systems; and (2) the self-sufficiency of village production in Asia explained the immutability of its social structure. Although there is disagreement as to the origins of the Asiatic mode of production, it has the following characteristics: absence of private property, dominance of the state over public works (such as irrigation), a self-sufficient village economy, the absence of autonomous cities, the unity of handicrafts and agriculture, and the simplicity of production methods. Marx argued that, because of the absence of private property, there was no CLASS STRUGGLE based on a landowning class and peasantry. Because there was no dynamic of class conflict, there was no sociological basis for revolutionary SOCIAL CHANGE. The transformation of these societies was brought about by colonialism, because capitalist exploitation introduced private property in land and hence introduced class relationships.

This concept has given rise to considerable dispute, both within and outside Marxism. Some critics have claimed that it was neither important nor consistently used by Marx and Engels. The concept is politically sensitive for two reasons. (1) It appears to justify colonialism and IMPERIALISM, because their unintended consequences were to create the conditions for progressive social change. (2) It was associated with a controversy over whether pre-revolutionary Russia was a 'semi-Asiatic' society. It has been suggested, following K. Wittfogel's *Oriental Despotism* (1957), that Russian communism reproduced the social stationariness and despotism associated with the Asiatic mode of production.

On more technical grounds, the concept has been criticized by B. Hindess and P. Q. Hirst (1975) for being theoretically incoherent. It has also been rejected because it cannot account for the major social and political differences which existed between imperial China, Iran and Egypt. On empirical grounds, it has been criticized because private property did exist in, for example, Islamic societies. As an alternative framework, some Marxists have proposed a variety of modes of production to analyse the societies of Asia, such as the 'tributary mode of production' which explains the appropriation of a surplus (or tribute) from these societies. However, the concept of the Asiatic mode is no longer in general use.

SEE ALSO: *Oriental despotism.*

READING: Bailey and Llobera (1981)

assimilation This concept was first used in American race relations research to describe the processes by which immigrant groups were integrated into the dominant white culture. Thus, in R. Park's (1950) 'race relations cycle', the social interaction between the host society and new immigrants was conceptualized in terms of four stages – contacts, competition, accommodation and assimilation. In its original usage, assimilation was seen as a unidimensional, one-way process by which outsiders relinquished their own culture in favour of that of the dominant society. Recent research regards assimilation as reciprocal, involving mutual adjustments between host and migrant communities. Furthermore, the particular character of the ethnic group in question may enhance, retard or preclude intermarriage, participation in citizenship and social acceptance. Assimilation is often used interchangeably with ACCULTURATION.

SEE ALSO: *accommodation; migration; racism.*

association, statistical See: CORRELATION.

associative democracy In *Professional Ethics and Civic Morals* (1950), E. Durkheim argued that 'intermediary groups' were a necessary aspect of SOCIALIST SOCIETIES and functioned to connect the individual to the STATE. In a market economy, there was a danger that INDIVIDUALISM in an unregulated environment would result in ANOMIE. Durkheim believed that intermediary groups or VOLUNTARY ASSOCIATIONS provided moral regulation in societies where SECULARIZATION had eroded traditional patterns of morality. In the contemporary debate about the relationship between CIVIL SOCIETY and DEMOCRACY, sociologists have returned to the study of intermediary groups.

Modern theories of associationalism argue that voluntary associations (1) provide local opportunities for representation, (2) offer opportunities for active CITIZENSHIP by encouraging participation, and thus contribute to civic culture, (3) contain the spread of BUREAUCRACY in political organizations, and (4) foster PLURALISM and diversity. Associationalism thus requires devolution or subsidiarity (where decision-making and responsibility are devolved to the lowest level of an organization). It is often associated with the reform of socialism, because it replaces bureaucracy with democracy.

There are a number of criticisms of associative democracy. For example, it is difficult to achieve universalistic standards of service and delivery, where particular needs and perspectives are developed by local associations responding to specific circumstances. As a result, an associative democracy would not remove the state, because associationalism requires a strong legal framework to prevent destructive competition between associations.

SEE ALSO: *communitarianism; community power; justice; political culture; rights.*
READING: Hirst (1990); Cohen and Rogers (1995)

atomism This is the notion that societies can best be seen as entities made up of individual units ('atoms') which interact. Extreme atomistic theories argue that sociology can *only* proceed by examination of these individuals and the meanings that they place on their actions and not by analysis of whole social structures. Atomism is the opposite of HOLISM in sociology.

SEE ALSO: *action theory; agency and structure; exchange theory; methodological individualism; utilitarianism.*

attitude A relatively stable system of beliefs concerning some object and resulting in an evaluation of that object, the concept of attitude is used extensively and technically in psychology but more loosely in sociology. In surveys of attitudes, it is often assumed that relatively superficial attitudes are a good guide to more deeply held values or to actual behaviour. Neither of these assumptions is necessarily true. Expressed attitudes may not relate to deeper feelings, because, for example, people may respond to questions about attitudes in ways that they feel are acceptable to the questioner. Similarly, expressed attitudes have often been shown to be inconsistent with subsequent behaviour. More reliable data on these matters may be elicited by more prolonged contact with respondents, as in ETHNOGRAPHY or PARTICIPANT OBSERVATION.

SEE ALSO: *attitude scales; interview; reliability; work attitudes.*

attitude scales These consist of sets of standardized statements with which people are asked to agree or disagree. Scaling assumes that an attitude will have various aspects that in their totality constitute the attitude being measured. For example, the attitude 'approval of social inequality' might embrace aspects such as class, ethnic and gender inequalities. It also assumes that people can be ranked along a continuum representing the varying degrees of 'strength' or 'intensity' with which an attitude is held. The sets of standardized statements are frequently selected from some larger pool of items that between them cover the relevant aspects of the attitude, selection being based initially on exploratory research in which people respond to all statements, or on the judgement of a panel of evaluators. With certain scales, FACTOR ANALYSIS or CLUSTER ANALYSIS may be applied to the results of the exploratory survey to test whether the selected statements in fact measure a unidimensional attitude or whether they are multidimensional. It is usual to test scales for RELIABILITY and validity before using them in the final questionnaire. The intensity or strength with which people hold the various aspects of the attitude is measured by rating scales for each item, by asking respondents how much they agree with a statement (often on a five-point scale ranging from 'strongly disagree' to 'strongly agree') or by asking them to choose between a number of different statements on each item. Attitude scales produce a single score for each individual that is constructed out of this multiplicity of items, so that each respondent can be placed somewhere along the attitude continuum. The most commonly encountered attitude scales are Guttman, Likert and Thurstone scales.

SEE ALSO: *attitude; measurement levels; questionnaire; reliability; social distance.*

attribution When explaining their own and others' behaviour, people typically follow certain patterns, and attribution theory is concerned with the rules governing these explanations of behaviour. Many attributions involve STEREOTYPES – for example, that all men tend to behave in a certain way and, because the person concerned is male, his behaviour can be explained by reference to men in general. People usually choose to attribute the behaviour of others to personality factors (which are often stereotypes) and their own to external circumstances.

audience Within the sociology of the mass media over the last two decades, there has been much interest in the study of audiences for media events. While most of this interest has centred on audiences for television, there have also been studies of popular music, newspapers and magazines, cinema, radio and theatre. Until the early 1980s, analyses of the media concentrated on interpretations of media texts or on the organizations and practices of media production. In these older analyses, the audience tended to be treated as a residual category, whose responses to the media message could be taken for granted. In contemporary work, the emphasis has been on the active audience which actively interprets, talks about, manipulates, rejects and plays with the material provided by the media.

A variety of approaches to the analysis of audiences have been taken. The *effects approach* concentrates on the ways in which audiences are influenced or affected by the media. In much public debate, as in, for example, argument about television and children, a fairly extreme version of the effects approach is adopted, in which audiences are seen to be directly influenced by the media. More sophisticated effects approaches examine the alteration or stabilization of attitudes, knowledge or behaviour following media exposure in the short or long term. One version of the effects approach, the cultivation approach, focuses on the long-term effects of heavy use of the media. Although much effects research is singularly inconclusive, cultivation analysts suggest that those who, for example, watch a lot of television have different views of the world than those who are otherwise similar but who do not watch as much.

The *uses and gratifications approach* looks not at the effects that media exposure have on the audience, but rather at the uses made by the audience of media messages. This approach considers the way in which the needs of the audience for personal identity or companionship, for example, generate expectations of the mass media which lead to differential patterns of media exposure, which in turn result in gratification of the needs. A third approach to the study of audiences is provided by the *encoding/decoding model*, which derives from debates concerning the concept of IDEOLOGY. The argument is that the media form part of a 'circle of ideology' in which they reinforce a dominant framework of values simply because they assume it. In practice, the output of the media is capable of a number of different interpretations and the question is, therefore, whether audiences will decode media output in terms of the dominant framework or by reference to an alternative set of values which oppose that framework, or by some compromise stance. A very recent approach to audiences concerns the way in which people integrate media use into their everyday lives; the way, for example, in which magazines provide images for their female readers or the way in which television is used to regulate family life.

Although contemporary studies have stressed the way that audiences are active and creative, it is important not to forget that the media can constrain or influence people's knowledge of the world.

SEE ALSO: *dominant ideology thesis; sociology of everyday life; semiotics; sociology of the mass media.*

READING: Moores (1993); Abercrombie and Longhurst (1998)

authoritarian personality This concept indicates the way in which the structure of the personality predisposes it to the acceptance of anti-democratic political beliefs. Early research by E. Fromm and W. Reich argued that the family structure of capitalist societies might typically produce rigid and authoritarian personalities ready to accept fascist ideology. The classical study is by ADORNO *et al., The Authoritarian Personality* (1950). These authors concluded that there is a prejudiced personality characterized by hierarchical and authoritarian parent–child relationships, a dichotomous view of social relationships leading to the formation of STEREOTYPES, conventionality, exploitative dependency, rigidity and repressive denial, all of which may culminate in a social philosophy that worships strength and disdains the weak. They further argue that the authoritarian personality characterized by these traits is produced by a rigid and repressive upbringing. The authors emphasize that their study is, on the one hand, only a psychological one and, on the other, is not any necessary guide to prejudiced or discriminatory *action*.

SEE ALSO: *fascism; Frankfurt School; prejudice.*

authority If power is the exercise of constraint and compulsion against the will of an individual or group, authority is a sub-type of POWER in which people willingly obey commands because they see the exercise of power as legitimate. WEBER distinguished between legal–rational, traditional and charismatic authority. LEGAL–RATIONAL AUTHORITY involves obedience to formal rules which have been established by regular, public procedures. The following of quasi-legal norms in formal bureaucracies is the principal example of this type of authority. By contrast, following a traditional authority involves the acceptance of a rule which embodies custom and ancient practice. In the case of charismatic authority, commands are obeyed because followers or disciples believe in the extraordinary character of their leader, whose authority transcends existing or customary practices. Any regime which has minimal public acceptance as a *de facto* government has, in Weber's terms, some basis of legitimacy even if that regime depends largely on force. In contemporary sociology, the term is often used imprecisely to refer to the influence exercised by LEADERSHIP.

SEE ALSO: *bureaucracy; charisma; legitimacy.*

automation The direction of technological change in modern industry has been towards the replacement of human power and control by mechanical devices. Simple forms of mechanization provide mechanical assistance to what is primarily a manual labour process; for example, when manual workers perform their tasks with the assistance of tools or machines and office workers use typewriters or calculators. More advanced forms are those in which production is primarily performed by machinery and the residual human tasks involve only the control, adjustment and regulation of machines. Automation marks the stage of technical evolution when the remaining human elements are finally removed. Truly automatic processes are 'closed-loop' systems which require no outside human intervention from the moment raw materials are inserted in a machine until the product is completed. The development of information-processing technology during the last quarter of the twentieth century – known universally as information technology (or IT) – which provides computer control of production, has had a dramatic effect. Mechanization was long ago capable of replacing the manual aspect of human intervention in many production systems, but only with computerization have the intellectual and control aspects been capable of automation. The widespread adoption of IT in offices has also transformed non-manual work. Many routine functions previously performed by people have been automated via computerization, and the typical office employee now uses computers in his or her daily work as a matter of course.

There has been considerable sociological interest in the consequences of automation. Sociologists have debated the effects on the content of work. R. Blauner

(1964) believed that automation would benefit employees by removing the unpleasant aspects of work and leaving the more interesting and skilled parts which required employees to use their judgement and discretion. However, the subsequent development of automation has tended to remove even these aspects of work-content among lower-level manual and office workers. It has been fashionable recently to talk of the automation of human control skills as leading to DE-SKILLING. Against this view, others assert that a high-technology society will need a new range of skills. The evidence from manufacturing industry is of a polarization into highly skilled tasks necessary for the design and maintenance of automated processes, at one end, and de-skilled jobs at the other. Among other employees, IT has had different effects for different groups. For example, the use of electronic scanners and cash registers in shops has reduced and simplified the tasks performed by the person on the check-out, but in offices computers require staff with new capabilities and training. Many office staff believe that they are more skilled as a result.

The effect of automation on employment also concerns sociologists. Automation obviously reduces the number of employees needed to produce any given volume of output. This suggests an increase in unemployment. In expanding firms and economies, however, automation may not be associated with job losses if expansion counteracts the effect of labour reduction. It remains difficult to disentangle automation from economic and population factors that also determine employment levels.

SEE ALSO: *alienation; industrialization; labour process approach; scientific management; socio-technical systems; technology.*

READING: Coombs (1985); Gallie *et al.* (1998)

autopoiesis See LUHMANN.

axiom A principle or fundamental assumption in a theoretical system, from which other more specific propositions are derived.

Barthes, Roland (1915–80) Often associated with French STRUCTURALISM, his idiosyncratic approach to literature and society is complex, combining sociology, semiology, literary criticism, structural anthropology and Marxism. He has made important contributions to the analysis of culture, texts and ideology. His works include *Writing Degree Zero* (1953), *Mythologies* (1957), *S/Z* (1970), *Sade, Fourier, Loyola* (1971) and *The Pleasure of the Text* (1975).

SEE ALSO: *myth; semiotics; Tel Quel group.*

READING: Culler (1983)

base and superstructure These terms have been used by Marxist sociologists in the analysis of the relationship between the economy (base) and other social forms (superstructure). The economy is defined in terms of three elements: (1) the labourer; (2) the means of production (which comprises both the materials worked on and the means by which this work is done); and (3) the non-worker who appropriates the product. All economies are characterized by these three elements, but what differentiates one economy from another is the manner in which the elements are combined. There are two kinds of relation that can hold between elements, a relation of possession and a relation of property. Possession indicates the relationship between the labourer and the means of production; either he can be in possession of them, controlling and directing them, or not. In the relation of property, the non-labourer owns either the means of production or labour or both, and can therefore take the product. The superstructure is usually a residual category comprising such institutions as the state, the family structure, or the kinds of IDEOLOGY prevalent in society. As to the relationship between base and superstructure, the strength of the Marxist position comes from saying that the character of the superstructure is determined by the character of the base. As the nature of the base varies, so also will the nature of the superstructure. Therefore, for example, one would expect the feudal political structure to differ from the capitalist one because the economies of these two forms are clearly different.

The model of base and superstructure has inspired a variety of studies ranging from interpretation of the eighteenth-century novel to analysis of family structure in contemporary society. The prevailing form that such studies have taken is class theoretical. That is, the RELATIONS OF PRODUCTION in the base are taken to be relations between social classes, between workers and capitalists, for instance, and to say that base determines superstructure means that the character of the superstructure – its literature, art, politics or family structure – is largely determined by the economic interests of the dominant social class.

The base and superstructure metaphor can be a fruitful analytical device but it has also excited a great deal of debate both from within and without Marxism. One point at issue is the definition of the relations of production. In that these are partly relations of ownership, they appear to involve legal definitions which the model defines as superstructural. It therefore seems difficult to separate base and superstructure analytically. In recent years, attention has been concentrated on formulating a concept of relations of production which is not defined in legal terms. However, the most important bone of contention has been the notion that the base *determines* the superstructure.

A number of critics argue that the model entails an economic DETERMINISM. In fact very few proponents of the notion of base and superstructure adopt such a determinist perspective. MARX and ENGELS never held that doctrine. First, they suggested that superstructural elements could be relatively autonomous of the base and have their own laws of development. Secondly, they argued that the superstructure will interact with, or influence, the base. More recent Marxists have departed still further from economic determinism in claiming that superstructural elements must be seen as conditions of existence of the base, a notion that has been seen as robbing the economy of any primacy and giving all institutions in society equal causal efficacy. Still others have argued that the relationship between base and superstructure is a functional one.

SEE ALSO: *Althusser; capital functions; labour theory of value; Marxist sociology; mode of production.*

READING: Cohen, G. A. (1978)

Bataille, Georges (1897–1962) A French philosopher and sociologist, he criticized the dominant assumptions of economics, notably the concentration on production and saving, and the premise that, in a context of scarcity, human beings attempted rationally but selfishly to satisfy their needs. Bataille, by contrast, attempted to develop a sociology of abundance in *The Accursed Share* (1976) and, in the tradition of DURKHEIM, he proposed an alternative view in which humans joyously destroyed wealth in an orgy of consumption. As a result, social solidarity is brought about by collective rituals which prohibit the emergence of class society. In order to support his views, Bataille turned to such examples as Aztec sacrifice and the potlatch ceremonies of the indigenous peoples of the American north-west coast.

A major focus of his work was the relationship between death and eroticism, which he examined in *Eroticism* (1962). His interest in eroticism followed from his study of prehistoric art (1955). According to Bataille, both death and eroticism create discontinuity, which is the basis of human anguish. In his studies of the SACRED in *Theory of Religion* (1988), he followed WEBER in treating Christianity as a legitimation of an individualized ethic of work and possession of private property. His work has been criticized by anthropologists as factually inaccurate in terms of recent ethnography, especially within the framework of 1960s cultural materialism, but he is credited with providing inspiration for post-structuralism and he directly influenced FOUCAULT, BAUDRILLARD and KRISTEVA. Bataille's approach was complex and holistic: he attempted to develop a theory that embraced the disciplines of literature, economics, sociology, and philosophy. He was also the founder of *Critique*, the French radical journal, and the Collège de Sociologie, which was influential as a platform for the theories of avant-garde intellectuals and social scientists.

SEE ALSO: *Lévi-Strauss; rational choice theory*.

READING: Richardson (1994)

Baudrillard, Jean (b. 1929) A French sociologist, originally critical of the neglect of consumption in Marxist economic theory, Baudrillard has turned increasingly to the analysis of the production, exchange and consumption of signs and symbols in a CONSUMER SOCIETY. He argues that the electronic media of communication falsify social relations which become merely simulations of social reality. He has been concerned to understand the nature of mass society and mass communications. Because social reality is a simulation, he claims that society becomes hyperreal. His major works are: *For a Critique of the Political Economy of the Sign* (1972); *The Mirror of Production* (1973); *L'Echange symbolique et la mort* (1976); *In the Shadow of the Silent Majorities* (1978); *Seduction* (1979); *Simulations* (1981); *Fatal Strategies* (1983); *America* (1986). Critics disagree sharply as to the importance of Baudrillard's work.

SEE ALSO: *postmodernism; sign*.

READING: Rojek and Turner (1993)

Bauman, Zygmunt (b. 1926) Expelled from Poland in 1968, he occupied the chair of sociology at the University of Leeds (1971–90). His early work was concerned with the analysis of such topics as class, elites, socialism and philosophy of the social sciences, in *Culture as Praxis* (1973), *Socialism: The active utopia* (1976), *Hermeneutics and Social Science* (1978) and *Memories of Class* (1982). His work is important because of his serious examination of the role of intellectuals in their contributions to revolutions, the reconstruction of civil society and culture in *Legislators and Interpreters* (1987). Secondly, he has provided a major analysis of GENOCIDE and the Holocaust, which he argues, controversially, in *Modernity and the Holocaust* (1989), is an example of RATIONALIZATION and bureaucracy rather than the irrational beliefs of anti-Semitism. Finally, he has made a major contribution to the study of morality in relation to POSTMODERNISM in *Modernity and Ambivalence* (1991), *Intimations of Postmodernity* (1992), *Postmodern Ethics* (1993) and *Life in Fragments* (1995).

READING: Kilminster and Varcoe (1996)

Beauvoir, Simone de (1908–86) French feminist and existentialist philosopher, she pioneered the study of women's oppression in *The Second Sex* (1949) and contributed to the study of AGING in *Old Age* (1970). She was awarded the Austrian State Prize for her contributions to European literature.

SEE ALSO: *feminism; feminist social theory*.

Becker, Howard S. (b. 1928) As a contemporary representative of the tradition of the CHICAGO SCHOOL, his principal contributions to contemporary sociology have been in occupational socialization in *Boys in White* (1961), to the investigation of deviant subcultures and careers in *Outsiders* (1963), and to the study of youth culture and higher education in *Making the Grade* (1968) and *Campus Power Struggle* (1970a). He also wrote *Sociological Work, Method and Substance* (1970b).

SEE ALSO: *career; deviant behaviour; labelling theory*.

behaviourism This is a school of psychology that deals with observable behaviour and disregards the subjective aspects of human activity such as consciousness, intention or the meaning of behaviour to the people involved. The idea that behaviour divorced from its subjective and social meanings is a legitimate area of study is rejected by sociologists, who use the term 'action' to distinguish meaningful activity from mere behaviour.

SEE ALSO: *action theory*.

Bell, Daniel (b. 1919) An American sociologist who in *The End of Ideology* (1960) claimed that apocalyptic class ideologies had declined in industrialized capitalist societies. In *The Coming of Post-Industrial Society* (1974) he suggested that POST-INDUSTRIAL SOCIETY had superseded industrialism. His other major work is *The Cultural Contradictions of Capitalism* (1976), which postulates that the hedonistic culture typical of advanced capitalist societies is incompatible with the dominance of rationality required by the economic system.

SEE ALSO: *end of ideology theory*.

Bendix, Reinhard (b. 1916) An American sociologist whose comparative study of business ideology and authority in the industrializing societies of Europe and America, *Work and Authority in Industry* (1956), remains a classic work of economic sociology. *Max Weber: An intellectual portrait* (1960) provides a comprehensive analysis of Weber's work. In *Nation-Building and Citizenship* (1964), he elaborated the view of MARSHALL that access to political rights or CITIZENSHIP is important in incorporating the working class into modern society. He also co-authored *Social Mobility in Industrial Society* (1959) with LIPSET.

SEE ALSO: *incorporation; social mobility*.

benefit theory of rights See: RIGHTS.

Benjamin, Walter (1892–1940) A social theorist and philosopher born in Germany, Benjamin is usually associated with the FRANKFURT SCHOOL and particularly with ADORNO. Although his work is diverse (and largely published in essay form), much of it is concerned with the analysis of culture. It is heavily influenced by Marxism in that Benjamin saw art and literature as inseparable from, and conditioned by, technology and social class. However, there is some debate as to how Marxist Benjamin was, and his later work does appear to be moving away from that position. His important works include: *Illuminations* (1973a); *Understanding Brecht* (1973b); *One Way Street* (1979).

READING: Roberts (1982)

Berger, Peter L. (b. 1929) An American sociologist, whose principal interests are social theory and the sociology of religion, but who has also written on Third World issues, the sociology of the family and political sociology. (He is also a novelist.) His works are informed by classical sociology, especially that of Marx, Weber and Durkheim, and PHENOMENOLOGICAL SOCIOLOGY. His work is underpinned by a wish to reconcile human autonomy with the coercive powers of social structure in a sociology of interpretation, which examines how over time the knowledge of social actors becomes legitimate and taken for granted. His most influential books are: *Invitation to Sociology* (1963); *The Social Construction of Reality* (1966); *The Sacred Canopy* (1967); *The Homeless Mind* (1973); *Facing up to Modernity* (1977); *The War*

Over the Family (1983); *The Capitalist Revolution* (1986); *Redeeming Laughter* (1997).

SEE ALSO: *agency and structure.*

Bernstein, Basil (b. 1924) Formerly a professor in the sociology of education at London University's Institute of Education, Bernstein is best known for his pioneering work on the relationship between social class and children's acquisition and use of language in both family and school contexts. In recent years his work has broadened out to provide a general theory of the relationships between class relations, the distribution of power, principles of control, and communication codes. He has published widely, mostly in articles, some of which are collected into the volumes of *Class, Codes and Control* (1971; 1973; 1975).

SEE ALSO: *pedagogical practices; restricted code.*

Beveridge, William Henry (1879–1963) He is best known for his role in the extension of social services and the creation of the WELFARE STATE in post-war Britain. In 1941, Beveridge was appointed chairman of a civil service inquiry into the management of the social services. The report of this inquiry, *Social Insurance and Allied Services* (1942), popularly known as the Beveridge Report, set out the principles which after the war guided the establishment of the welfare state. Idleness, ignorance, disease, squalor and want were identified as the major hazards facing individuals in industrial society, which should be remedied by government. The report recommended a national health service, social insurance and assistance, family allowances, and full-employment policies.

His career was varied, including a fellowship in law at Oxford University (1902–9), a subwardenship at Toynbee Hall in London's East End (1903–5), an early career in the civil service (1908–19), Director of the London School of Economics (1919–37), Liberal MP for a year (1944) and then a Liberal peer.

bias Systematic error or bias is the difference between the true value of a characteristic and the average value obtained by repeated investigations. Any discrepancy between the true value and research value in a *single* investigation is the sum of two factors: bias and SAMPLING ERROR. The idea of bias assumes that there is a 'true' value. This assumption has been disputed on the grounds that such values do not exist independently of the measuring process used. This latter view has much to commend it in the social science field. For example, interviews have social characteristics, thus any data collected via interview may be 'biased' by the interviewer (who may be prejudiced against a respondent, for example), by the respondent (who may lie on socially sensitive topics or react to the personality of the interviewer), or by the interaction between the two. The second and third characteristics apply even when using a structured questionnaire. The method of measurement here determines the data.

SEE ALSO: *interview; non-response.*

biologism/biological reductionism This is the claim that social phenomena or social behaviour can be reduced to, or largely explained by, biological states. The idea arises commonly in debates about INTELLIGENCE, in which it is claimed that any person's intelligence is largely determined by genetic factors, but it is also found in debates in other areas, such as poverty and crime.

SEE ALSO: *eugenics; nature/nurture debate; organic analogy; social Darwinism; sociobiology.*

Birmingham Centre for Contemporary Cultural Studies The CCCS at Birmingham was founded by HOGGART in 1964 and later directed by HALL as a centre for research at the University of Birmingham. Although it developed a distinctive approach to CULTURAL STUDIES, the centre went through various stages in its attempt to come to terms with Marxism, feminism and postmodernism. Frequently criticized for its 'Britishness', it made a lasting contribution to the study of YOUTH CULTURE, race relations and DELINQUENT SUBCULTURE.

SEE ALSO: *culture*; *Williams*.

READING: Centre for Contemporary Cultural Studies (1982)

birth rate See: FERTILITY.

black economy A popular rather than a sociological term, which refers to paid work that is not reported to the tax authorities and, therefore, remains unrecorded in economic statistics.

Black Report Against a background of public anxiety over Britain's falling standards of health (as measured, for example, by infant mortality rates which were higher in Britain than in Singapore and Hong Kong in the 1970s), the Labour government established a Research Working Group in 1977 under the chairmanship of Sir Douglas Black, which reported in 1980. The Report (1980) was received with little enthusiasm by the Conservative administration, which published 260 duplicated copies. In fact, the Report has been influential in identifying the social causes of illness.

Black showed that in the twenty years prior to the Report the mortality rates for men and women in occupational classes I and II aged 35 years and over had declined substantially, while those in IV and V had not changed or had deteriorated. The evidence suggested that the class gradient was becoming more rather than less pronounced. The Report's thirty-seven recommendations argued that redressing the problems of the British health-care system would require more emphasis on primary care, preventive medicine and community health. The conditions for better health lay outside the scope of the National Health Service and any significant improvement in the nation's health would require a radical improvement in the material conditions of the lower social classes.

The Report has been criticized on the following grounds. (1) The relationship between social classes IV and V may be a function of the ways in which 'class' and 'health' are measured. 'The artefact explanation' suggests, for example, that sickness in the lower classes may be a function of the greater average age of these classes. (2) The Report may actually underestimate class differences in health because it depends on the Registrar General's occupational classifications of social class. (3) The poor health of the lower classes may be a consequence of the downward social mobility of the sick. (4) Class differences in health may in fact be a consequence of differences in lifestyle and behaviour (such as smoking, dietary practices and leisure) rather than simply differences in social class. (5) There is some doubt as to what a materialist explanation of health may entail: is it poor housing, hazardous work conditions, low income, urban pollution, work-related stress or inadequate education? Furthermore, how do these 'materialist' factors interact? This debate about the social causes of illness should be seen in the context of a longer and more established dispute about the relative contributions of social, individual and environmental contributions to health.

SEE ALSO: *demography; epidemiology; health-care systems.*

READING: Blane (1985)

Blau, Peter M. (b. 1918) An American sociologist who has contributed to EXCHANGE THEORY and conducted major empirical investigations of the United States occupational structure and the structure of business organizations. His major works are: *The Dynamics of Bureaucracy* (1955); *Formal Organizations: A comparative approach* (1962), with W. R. Scott; *Exchange and Power in Social Life* (1964); *The American Occupational Structure* (1967), with O. D. Duncan; *The Structure of Organizations* (1971), with R. A. Schoenherr.

SEE ALSO: *social mobility.*

blue-collar This is an American term used to describe manual workers.

body The social importance of the body has been a significant topic in both physical and social anthropology, for example in the analysis of RITES OF PASSAGE, but the sociology of the body has been, until recently, neglected. The development of a sociological interest in the body is a consequence of FEMINISM, the AGING of the populations of advanced societies, the emergence of postmodern social theory, changes in the nature of contemporary consumerism which emphasizes the body, developments in medical technology and practice (such as organ transplants) which have made various aspects of the human body politically problematic, the growth of mass sport and leisure which have identified personal worth with the beauty of the body, and the possibility of a radical enhancement of human functions by technology.

The rise of the sociology of the body has been associated with a critique of POSITIVISM and especially with a rejection of the legacy of R. Descartes (1596–1650), whose separation of the body and the mind resulted in a scientific approach (often referred to as Cartesian dualism) in which all mental, spiritual or emotional events were treated as separate from, or simply manifestations of, biochemical changes in the body. This perspective had an important impact on the development of theories of knowledge, but in the twentieth century philosophers have rejected dualism, emphasizing instead the interaction of mental, physical and cultural phenomena. Human beings are not made up of two separate components (mind and body), rather they are embodied.

Sociologists and anthropologists have studied various aspects of the body in relation to fundamental aspects of culture and society: (1) the body has been important in the development of social metaphors of society in such notions as the head of the church; (2) these metaphors are typically normative in that, for example, in many societies the left hand and left side are regarded as evil; (3) notions about body pollution are crucial in defining social normality – for example, dietary regulations form a significant part of religious beliefs and practices about the SACRED, and deviations from these rules are regarded as dangerous for both individuals and the society as a whole.

A number of debates are important in the sociological analysis of the body. (1) There is the view that the human body is not simply a biologically given fact but a social construction; that is, the body is produced by discourses and social practices.

For example, in traditional Japanese society, the menopause was not recognized, therefore women did not report the discomforts associated with this feature of female aging. (2) It is claimed, following the work of FOUCAULT, that the body has become in modern societies the target of endless, minute and detailed forms of surveillance, discipline and control. (3) Other theories, which have been influenced by ELIAS, have examined long-term changes in body practices, which have been brought about by the civilizing process. (4) Feminist theories have been concerned to understand how PATRIARCHY determines social attitudes towards women as frail, irrational and unpredictable; feminists deny that women are determined by their anatomy. (5) In general terms, sociologists are interested in how historically the regulation of the body (through diet, sport, dance, medical intervention, clothing and so forth) has been regarded as necessary for the regulation of society.

The body is an important feature of all social interaction, because body-image is an important aspect of the presentation of the self. For example, obesity is often taken to be an indication of lack of personal control. Sociologists like GOFFMAN have studied the interactional implications of embarrassment and loss of face for personal STIGMA.

SEE ALSO: *addiction; Douglas; embodiment; emotions; gender; habitus; nature/nurture debate.*

READING: Turner, B. S. (1996a)

Bogardus scale See: SOCIAL DISTANCE.

Booth, Charles James (1840–1916) He was a British businessman, social reformer and early social statistician, concerned to improve the economic and social conditions of the mass of the population in urban England. Booth investigated empirically the conditions of the poor and other social groups and pioneered the scientific research of social problems. His mammoth surveys of poverty, industry and religion, published in 17 volumes as *Life and Labour of the People in London* (1889–91), are unrivalled accounts of social conditions at the end of the last century. He was partly responsible for the Old Age Pensions Act of 1908.

READING: Simey and Simey (1960)

Bottomore, Tom B. (1920–92) Until recently a professor of sociology at Sussex University and a past president of the International Sociological Association, Bottomore has written extensively on a variety of subjects. He has played a major role in presenting the ideas of Marxist sociologists, in *Karl Marx: Selected writings in sociology and social philosophy* (1961), edited with M. Rubel; *Marxist Sociology* (1975); *Austro-Marxism* (1978), edited with P. Goode. His other works on classes and politics include: *Classes in Modern Society* (1965); *Elites and Society* (1966); *Political Sociology* (1979). He was the general editor of *A Dictionary of Marxist Thought* (1983) and, with R. Nisbet, *A History of Sociological Analysis* (1978b). His more recent work continues to explore the relationship between sociology, socialism and Marxism, for instance in *Sociology and Socialism* (1984). He has made a major contribution to the sociology of capitalism in *Theories of Modern Capitalism* (1985). With M. Mulkay, he is the editor of the influential series *Controversies in Sociology*.

boundary maintenance This is a term typically used in functionalism, especially by PARSONS (1951), who defines a social system as boundary-maintaining if, in relation to its environment, it preserves certain regularities or patterns. There are social processes which maintain both the boundaries *and* the equilibrium of a system relative to other systems which constitute its environment. For the continued existence of systems, there must also be an exchange of resources across their boundaries with other systems.

SEE ALSO: *functionalism; social systems; systems theory.*

bounded rationality This concept emphasizes the constraints upon rational or optimizing/maximizing decisions. The first constraint is that only limited information is available to decision-makers regarding the range of alternatives and their consequences. The second is the limited ability that people have to process and evaluate all the information which is in fact available. Therefore, when people choose between alternatives, they do not optimize by evaluating every alternative and choosing the best. Instead they *satisfice*; that is, they choose the first satisfactory alternative to emerge. Bounded rationality was originally developed in the analysis of organizational decisions and has been confirmed by psychologists investigating decision-making processes in general. It is now a central element of RATIONAL CHOICE THEORY.

READING: March and Simon (1958)

Bourdieu, Pierre (b. 1930) A professor of sociology at the Collège de France, Paris, Bourdieu's early anthropological work (1956–60) in Algeria among the Kabyle peasantry of the Mahgreb was an attempt to criticize the dominant paradigm of STRUCTURALISM in French social sciences. From this field work, Bourdieu came to elaborate a sophisticated battery of concepts, including practice and strategy, which attempt to avoid the deterministic assumptions of structuralism. These concepts about practical actions were, however, also located in a context where Bourdieu recognized that each 'field' of action has its own specific logic or principles. These logics of action structure the choices and preferences of individuals in these contexts. As a result of these logics, individuals acquire dispositions, or a 'habitus', which regulate the range and types of actions that are possible. Bourdieu's attempts to resolve the analytical relationship between action and structure on the basis of his Algerian ethnography were initially presented in *Outline of a Theory of Practice* (1972) and later elaborated in *The Logic of Practice* (1980).

Bourdieu first became influential in the English-speaking world as a result of his contributions to the sociology of education where, in *Reproduction in Education, Society and Culture* (1970), with J.-C. Passeron, he showed how educational values had the consequence of reproducing social inequality. These studies constructed important theoretical distinctions between economic and CULTURAL CAPITAL. Bourdieu subsequently studied how the taste for cultural goods is organized in terms of economic and cultural divisions in French society in *Distinction: A social critique of the judgement of taste* (1979). This research attempted to demonstrate that appreciation of art, for example, is not governed by an objective set of aesthetic laws, but is grounded in class relationships and status hierarchies. In this study, Bourdieu's contribution to the sociological study of EMBODIMENT became obvious. The dispositions of workers, within a working-class habitus, for particular types of food or sport become inscribed in a particular form of embodiment, which in turn separates or distinguishes them from the middle class who have different and specific tastes for consumer goods, art and sport. Habitus, which has become a crucial aspect of Bourdieu's sociological theory, refers to the ensemble of dispositions by which actions and attitudes in the everyday world are habituated and as a result the everyday world is taken for granted. It becomes thoughtless, because it is embodied.

Despite his growing international reputation, Bourdieu regards himself, and is partly perceived, as an outsider in the academic community. He treats this outsider position as an important aspect of his methodology, because an ethnographic observer perceives modern societies as anthropologically strange. Bourdieu's views on objective and subjective positions are part of a broader philosophical stance, which he has described as 'reflexive sociology' in *In Other Words* (1987) and in *An Invitation to Reflexive Sociology* (1992), with L. J. D. Wacquant. Bourdieu's study of the hierarchies of the field of higher education in *Homo Academicus* (1984a) caused considerable criticism within the academic world. He showed that changes in intellectual fashions, for example during the student revolts of May 1968, were caused by competition between separate generations over educational resources. He claimed that taste in intellectual matters within the educational field is no different from sporting fashions in the recreational field. In *The Political Ontology of Martin Heidegger* (1988), he drew further criticism when he argued that the philosophy of Martin Heidegger was in part a function of Heidegger's outsider position in the 1920s with respect to the elite universities of southern Germany.

In his recent works, he has turned increasingly to the analysis of modern culture in CONSUMER SOCIETY. This is of 'the field of cultural production' (1993) or the production of 'symbolic goods'. In his work on cultural sociology, he has written on sport (1984b), photography (1990), with others, and art appreciation (1992). His critics claim that: (1) his analysis of culture is characterized by economic REDUCTIONISM, in that symbolic power is dependent upon economic wealth; (2) his theory of cultural distinction is specific to France, where Paris has a monopoly over symbolic goods; (3) his view of intellectual fashion is self-defeating, because his own work is fashionable; (4) his social theory is contradictory, because, while he vigorously rejects DETERMINISM, his explanations of cultural differences are deterministic. Despite these criticisms, he has made a significant contribution to sociological theory through his empirical research on culture.

SEE ALSO: *agency and structure; cultural reproduction; generation; praxis; structuration.*
READING: Fowler (1997)

bourgeoisie This term is used loosely to describe either the middle or ruling classes in capitalist society. Both classes are assumed to have an interest in preserving capitalism in a struggle with the working class over the distribution of SURPLUS VALUE. It has become somewhat outdated with changes in the class structure, particularly the rise of joint stock companies, the separation of the ownership and control of industrial and commercial capital, and the fragmentation of the middle class. The term is perhaps more properly applied to the urban social class made up of entrepreneurs, merchants and industrialists active in the earlier stages of capitalist development.

SEE ALSO: *capitalism; class; middle class; periodization.*

bracketing See: PHENOMENOLOGICAL SOCIOLOGY.

bricolage Many social groups adopt a particular style as a component of their CULTURE which distinguishes them from other groups. In some cases, the style may consist of a medley of items, a bricolage, taken from different sources and with different original meanings which, when put together, do convey a unitary meaning. For example, punk style took dustbin liners and safety pins, among other items of style, from different everyday contexts but made them into a coherent ensemble.

Buddhism See: WORLD RELIGIONS.

burden of dependency With the rapid rise in the expectation of life, combined with a gradually falling birth rate, the proportion of people aged 65 or over, and especially 80 or over, in the population of most Western societies has been rising. This allegedly creates additional burdens on the working population since the elderly are typically not only not in paid work but they are also relatively more demanding of certain services, particularly in health. The counter-argument is that the elderly contribute in hidden ways to the support of paid workers, such as those in child care, as well as increasingly making provision for their old age while they are younger and in work.

SEE ALSO: *aging*.

bureaucracy A particular system of administration. Historically it was associated with the rule of government and governmental officials, but sociologists regard it as a form of administration that is found in organizations pursuing a wide variety of goals.

As a technical term in sociology, bureaucracy is associated with WEBER. He gave it a precise definition and suggested that it was the best administrative form for the rational or efficient pursuit of organizational goals. Weber's IDEAL TYPE of bureaucracy comprised various elements: a high degree of specialization and a clearly defined division of labour, with tasks distributed as official duties; a hierarchical structure of authority with clearly circumscribed areas of command and responsibility; the establishment of a formal body of rules to govern the operation of the organization; administration based on written documents; impersonal relationships between organizational members and with clients; recruitment of personnel on the basis of ability and technical knowledge; long-term employment, promotion on the basis of seniority or merit; a fixed salary; the separation of private and official income. In Weber's mind these discrete elements were tied together into a coherent totality by one overarching phenomenon: rationality. Scholarly analysis of Weber's position now suggests that his idea about the rationality of bureaucracy embraced two slightly different things. In one sense the rationality of bureaucracy was that it maximized technical efficiency. The rules defined the most appropriate means to realize organizational ends, were based on up-to-date technical knowledge and directed the behaviour of members along the most efficient lines. In the other sense, bureaucracy was a system of social control or authority that was accepted by members because they saw the rules as rational, fair and impartial – a 'legal–rational' value system. For Weber, however, bureaucracy's major quality was simply its predictability. His main preoccupation was with broad historical and comparative issues and with political administration and its impact on society, and he developed the bureaucratic ideal type for this sort of macro-analysis.

Subsequent sociologists applied the model to the micro-sociology of business organization. Research has shown that many bureaucratic organizations work inefficiently and in ways that Weber's model did not anticipate. R. K. Merton (1957) demonstrated that bureaucracy is likely to become inflexible because of various unanticipated consequences that derive from its structure. Members may adhere to the rules in a ritualistic manner and elevate these above the goals they are designed to realize. This is inefficient if for any reason the rules do not establish the most efficient means; for example, if changing circumstances have made the rules out of date. Subordinates tend to follow orders even if these are misguided. Specialization often fosters a narrow outlook which cannot solve new problems. Colleagues within departments develop feelings of loyalty to each other and their departments, and promote these group interests when they can. M. Crozier (1964) extended these arguments to show that bureaucracies embody vicious circles of decreasing efficiency and effectiveness. Groups of colleagues attempt to maximize their freedom of action by paying lip-service to the rules but ignoring the spirit behind these and bending them when they can. They are able to withhold or distort information so that senior managers do not know exactly what is going on. Senior managers realize that something is amiss, but they are not allowed to take arbitrary or personal action against those they suspect of failing to promote organizational goals, so they create more rules to regulate what goes on below them. These rules make the organization more and more rigid but may still fail to control subordinates. Bureaucracy becomes less efficient and provides only a limited social control. Moreover, Crozier's analysis shows that some tasks within organizations involve unpredictable events for which standardized rules are inappropriate, sometimes where craft or professional knowledge may be a requirement for dealing with unpredictability. He gives the example of the engineering function responsible for dealing with machinery failures in a factory. Senior managers find it difficult to manage such areas of uncertainty, because they do not have the knowledge that would allow them to judge whether subordinates are acting correctly or to regulate behaviour, and social control is particularly weak. There is now a widespread view that bureaucracy is particularly ineffective wherever there is even a moderate degree of unpredictability.

Social theorists who are concerned with the transition from MODERNITY to POSTMODERNITY see Weber as a theorist of modernism. They see bureaucracy as the quintessentially modernist form of organization, which embodies and promotes the dominance of INSTRUMENTAL RATIONALITY in all areas of social life. For BAUMAN (1989), instrumental rationality means that action becomes dissociated from moral criteria. Bureaucracies contribute to this moral vacuum. First, the extreme internal division of labour within bureaucracies leads people to become cogs in a machine without knowledge of, or interest in, the final outcome of what they do. Secondly, bureaucracies also elevate technical responsibility over moral responsibility, consequently moral standards have little relevance to bureaucrats. Finally, bureaucrats are trained to treat people impersonally and as objects, which leads to dehumanization. Bauman believes that an outcome of the pervasiveness of bureaucracies in modern societies is to remove any sense of individual moral responsibility. This helps to create the conditions under which crimes against humanity, including GENOCIDE, may occur.

The Weberian view of bureaucracy as an efficient means to gather information and control individuals has been developed by FOUCAULT and GIDDENS, in the discussion of SURVEILLANCE as a form of social control in modern societies. Modernity is marked by the amount of information on individuals that is held by agencies of the state, such as welfare organizations, tax authorities, schools, local government and the police. Businesses such as banks and credit agencies hold further personal information. Thus individuals depend on bureaucratic organizations that gather information about them and potentially are in a position to exercise some control over their lives. The administrative logic of modernity is said to be the expansion of these supervisory and information processing capabilities of the state and business, which will enhance surveillance and the potential to control individuals.

SEE ALSO: *bounded rationality; legal–rational authority; management; metaphysical pathos; organization theory; postmodernism; rationalization.*

READING: Weber (1946); Perrow (1986); Reed (1992)

bureaucratic control See: MANAGERIAL STRATEGIES OF CONTROL.

C

Canguilhem, G. (1904–96) French philosopher of the life sciences and director of the Institute for the History of Science and Technology in Paris, he has influenced developments in EPISTEMOLOGY, especially SOCIAL CONSTRUCTIONISM. In his research on medical history, he argued that the distinction between normal and pathological was not a fact about organisms but about the structure of medical thought. His ideas influenced FOUCAULT.

SEE ALSO: *mental health; poststructuralism*.

READING: Canguilhem (1966)

capital See: CAPITAL FRACTIONS; CAPITAL FUNCTIONS; CAPITALISM; ENGELS; MARX.

capital fractions In Marxism, capital is seen as being internally divided along several axes. One division can be drawn between large- and small-scale capital; a second occurs between industrial, financial and landed capital. These fractions are believed to have a certain commonality of interest by virtue of their all being forms of capital. This common interest, however, may be offset by sectional conflicts of interest. Such sectionalism is partly overcome by the activities of the state.

SEE ALSO: *capitalism; relative autonomy*.

capital functions The complexity of advanced societies means that the simple division of the population into capitalists and proletarians once favoured within Marxism is no longer viable. The rise of the 'middle classes' of managers, professionals and technicians has followed the growing need to administer and coordinate increasingly complex production processes. At the same time, the dispersal of ownership via shareholdings, often into the hands of institutions such as pension funds, makes it more difficult to identify a capitalist class than was the case in earlier periods. One solution to the problem of how to divide society into capital and labour is to distinguish between the legal ownership of capital and the performance of the functions of capital, which may be carried out by agents who do not legally own the means of production. These functions include the control and supervision of labour, the allocation of resources within the enterprise, and the design of products and of the labour processes to produce them. For capitalism to survive, all these functions must be performed, but the manner in which they are undertaken will vary from society to society.

SEE ALSO: *base and superstructure; capitalism; class; management; managerial revolution; middle class; profession*.

capitalism This type of economic organization in its 'pure' form may briefly be defined by: (1) private ownership and control of the economic instruments of production, that is, capital; (2) the gearing of economic activity to making profits; (3) a market framework that regulates this activity; (4) the appropriation of profits by the owners of capital (subject to taxation by the STATE); (5) the provision of labour by workers who are free agents. Capitalism is a dynamic form of economic activity that is continually evolving. Historically, it has mainly developed and expanded to dominate economic life along with the growth of industrialization. Some of its features, however, were to be found in the commercial sector of the pre-industrial European economy, perhaps as long ago as the medieval period, while in England, a well-developed system of capitalist agriculture predated industrialization by at least a century and a half.

Capitalism has assumed various forms in industrialized societies, which qualify the above definition. It can be misleading to talk of capitalism without some further specification of the form that is being discussed. Early industrial capitalism in Great Britain and the United States in the nineteenth century is regarded as the classical model that approximates the pure form most closely. Economic activity was carried out by a large number of small capitalist firms, owned by individuals or families, with the owners also directly managing their firms. The regulation of economic activity was provided by markets, in which competition between the suppliers of goods and services and demand from consumers were dominant. The market for labour determined wages and allocated workers between employers according to the same forces of supply and demand. The economy embodied LAISSEZ-FAIRE principles, in the sense that the state did not intervene but allowed the market to determine economic activity. The role of government was supportive rather than interventionist, providing the conditions which were necessary for the economy to flourish. This early form of industrial capitalism produced a fragmented, unstable and anarchical economic system which oscillated between booms and slumps.

Elsewhere in Europe and in Japan, however, governments of the nineteenth and early twentieth century intervened more, regulating and directing the emerging capitalist economy. The state was involved in the following activities: directly subsidizing private entrepreneurs; directing credit and investment capital; establishing state-owned firms (notably in Japan, Germany and Italy); regulating labour and product markets by political means; establishing protective tariffs; granting monopoly rights to produce certain goods or to sell in certain markets; granting government contracts. Fairly detailed control of economic life was regarded as essential, in order to enhance national power, maintain healthy state revenues and preserve social order. In the second half of the twentieth century, the newly industrializing societies of South-east Asia repeated this pattern of state regulation and promotion as their governments supervised the transition to industrial capitalism.

Even Great Britain and the United States moved away from the early classical model in the twentieth century. The later forms of 'monopoly' capitalism typical of the second and third quarters of the century were marked by economic concentration, the domination of markets by a small number of large firms rather than there being competition among numerous small firms. Under such conditions (strictly, of oligopoly rather than monopoly), it was not uncommon for firms to agree among themselves to limit competition and manipulate markets, so as to increase profitability and stability. The ownership of capital also became more concentrated. Initially, the spread of joint-stock ownership early in the century led to the diffusion of ownership among a large number of shareholders and the decline of family-owned firms. Diffused ownership weakened the old connection between ownership and the managerial function, and professional managers assumed control of the day-to-day administration of firms. When individual or family shareholders had insufficient holdings on their own or in alliance with several others to control management, then professional managers also determined company policy. However, the last forty years have seen the rise of institutional ownership and the relative decline of privately owned shareholdings in commerce and industry, as financial intermediary institutions (banks, insurance companies, pension funds) have invested in company equity on a large-scale, leading to a new concentration of ownership. 'Finance' capitalism was how some Marxists conceptualized the developmental tendency of monopoly capitalism: the separation of financial from productive capital, its monopolization by a relatively small number of financial institutions, and the domination of the rest of the economy by these.

The economic role of the state also became more influential, even where *laissez-faire* had previously applied. For much of the twentieth century, national governments sought to create economic stability and protect the interests of indigenous capital and labour. The state has done this by using its power as a purchaser of goods and services, by means of state investment, subsidization and, in much of continental Europe, by the public ownership of parts of industry, by directing private investment, by regulating company formation (for example, by controlling mergers and take-overs) and at times by controlling wages, salaries and prices. There is disagreement whether the state's economic role departs so far from the pure capitalist system as to constitute a post-capitalist economy.

In the last two decades of the century, however, monopoly capitalism appears to have changed in various respects. Industrial capitalism has spread further across the globe, as many previously less-developed economies in Asia and Latin America have industrialized. The former socialist societies of the old Soviet Union and central and southern Europe have converted to market economies since 1989 and have also adopted many or all of the other features of capitalism listed at the start of this entry. With this GLOBALIZATION of capitalism, competition in product markets has increased and collusion has declined. State intervention in the economy has been reduced by governments committed to free market philosophies in the USA, Great Britain and some other countries, although these societies continue to regulate economic life to a degree and have not returned to pure *laissez-faire*. International bodies such as the World Trade Organization, the World Bank and the International Monetary Fund have managed to reduce, but not eliminate, governmental protectionism in their efforts to promote a freer international trade. At the same time, recurring economic dislocations since the late 1970s have made the capitalist system less stable. S. Lash and J. Urry (1987) foresaw the end of the 'organized' form of monopoly capitalism, which was at its peak in the third quarter of the twentieth century, and the rise of 'disorganized capitalism'. While this imagery is evocative, the modern world capitalist economy has become less organized than before only in relative terms. Large firms still organize considerable proportions of global production and distribution, thus the world economy remains concentrated. Nation states do continue their attempts to regulate economic life within their borders, even though these may now be less effective in the smaller national economies because large firms operate transnationally across many nations. Within

Europe, however, the member states of the European Union some time ago decided to regulate collectively the economic activity which takes place within the borders of the EU. They created a transnational regime that does regulate transnational firms effectively in one of the most important geographical areas of modern capitalism.

Early sociologists were centrally concerned with the rise and social impact of capitalism. As part of his wider interest in the 'rationalizing' tendency in modern life, WEBER saw capitalism as a concrete manifestation of this tendency: it embodied the qualities of impersonality, calculation and the purposive–rational pursuit of interests, which together constituted efficiency. For Weber, the essential developments that gave industrial capitalism its rational character were both institutional and spiritual. The crucial institutional change was the rise of a free-market economy, particularly the free market in labour. Other important changes included the growth of a money economy and the subsequent development of banks, the rise of universal laws of contract, bureaucratic control of business enterprises, and double-entry bookkeeping. The central spiritual change was the rise of ascetic Protestantism in Europe: the PROTESTANT ETHIC emphasized values of hard work and deferred gratification which favoured the creation of capital and its productive reinvestment rather than consumption. The importance of such values was reaffirmed by W. Sombart (1930), who believed that the 'spirit' of capitalism was the way in which adventurous risk-taking and calculating rationality were fused, and in recent times by the continuing interest in entrepreneurial ACHIEVEMENT MOTIVATION which combines hard work with a competitive attitude.

MARX and Weber shared a concern with the social relations involved in capitalist production. They agreed that employees were denied any part of the ownership and control of the instruments of economic production and that employees were subordinated to those who did own and control. Marx regarded such subordination as an essential feature and defining characteristic of all forms of capitalism, because this was how capital managed to extract SURPLUS VALUE from labour. Weber believed that subordination was necessary for productive efficiency in any type of industrial economy and was not confined to capitalism. For Marx, the exploitative quality of the social RELATIONS OF PRODUCTION in capitalist economies meant that capitalism was based on coercion and a perpetual antagonism between the interests of capital and labour.

In the 1950s and 1960s, sociological interest centred on industrialism, which included both capitalist and non-capitalist economies. The revival of Marxist sociology in the 1970s led to a concern with the distinctive features of capitalism, notably the LABOUR PROCESS and social relations of production in modern capitalist economies, the analysis of MODES OF PRODUCTION, and the discussion of the modes of regulation required to stabilize capitalist relations by the REGULATION SCHOOL. In the 1980s and 1990s, sociologists attempted to describe and explain the changes that monopoly capitalism appeared to be undergoing, focusing on its expansion into a global system and the transformation of FORDISM into the varieties of POST-FORDISM. Most have viewed capitalism as an economic system which, in its different manifestations, has particular political and social correlates.

Capitalism can also be regarded as an ideology which contains doctrines of social justice and individual rights. This ideology suggests that existing inequalities of income and wealth represent the socially just returns for the different contributions that people make to economic activity. It also contains the idea that certain freedoms and rights are necessary for the continued well-being of capitalist society, notably that individuals must be protected from the arbitrary power of the state while the state protects their economic interests by safeguarding property rights and guaranteeing the enforcement of commercial contracts. Political democracy provides safeguards against arbitrary state power and, historically, capitalism has mainly been associated with democratic political forms.

SEE ALSO: *capital fractions; capital functions; convergence thesis; democracy; dependency; dual economy; flexible specialization; globalization; globalization of production; individualism; industrial society; information society; labour market; labour market segmentation; labour process approach; management; managerial revolution; Marxist sociology; mode of production; new international division of labour; post-industrial society; relative autonomy; world-system theory.*

READING: Lash and Urry (1987)

carceral society A number of writers, for example FOUCAULT and GOFFMAN, have argued that institutions such as prisons, hospitals, army camps and asylums have a great deal in common with one another: they all involve separation from the outside world, the collapse of the usual distinctions between work, sleep and leisure, and a powerful discipline. Foucault, in particular, argues that carceral institutions like prison use a disciplinary technology that focuses not on physical punishment but on administration, SURVEILLANCE and registration. In turn, Foucault suggests that contemporary societies as a whole are carceral, because all depend on these disciplinary technologies.

SEE ALSO: *total institution.*

career Careers may be viewed as the sequences of jobs performed by individuals in the course of their working lives. Careers may be structured into ordered sequences that relate to each other or unstructured; if structured, job sequences are frequently arranged as a hierarchy of increasing income and prestige.

The concept of career is most often applied in the study of occupations. Manual workers, particularly if unskilled, typically have unstructured careers marked by job movement of an apparently haphazard nature, though older workers have greater job stability. Skilled workers exhibit more structured patterns. In both cases, peak earnings are usually reached by the early thirties and thereafter may decline, and careers provide little advancement through an income/social prestige hierarchy. Large firms in Japan have developed seniority-based pay and promotion ladders, though these rarely lead into higher-level occupations such as management. In general, non-manual employees, especially men, are more likely to have structured careers. Women non-manual employees who are not in professional or managerial jobs tend to have relatively unstructured careers. Occupationally based careers are found among professionals and semi-professionals, where individuals may shift between employers but their career progression is stable and predictable. Professions are to a large extent self-regulating and their associations protect as far as possible the earnings, status and careers of members. Organizationally based careers have in the past provided managers with structured career routes within the enterprise, but these appear to be much less guaranteed now than they were before, and managers often have to move between firms if they are to gain promotion. There is also more job insecurity for managers now. Non-manual employees above the level of routine white-collar work typically enjoy rising wages throughout most of their working lives and upwards intragenerational social mobility.

H. S. Becker (1963) claimed that the concept was valuable 'in developing sequential models of various kinds of deviant behavior'. For example, he studied the stages by which a person becomes a regular marijuana user. These stages in the career included learning the technique, perceiving the effects and learning to enjoy the sensations. E. Goffman (1961b) used the notion of 'moral career' to describe the experience of mental patients in asylums. He suggested that a moral career had an objective dimension (the official institutional processing of the patient) and a subjective dimension (the personal experience of the patient). The concept has been extensively used in SYMBOLIC INTERACTIONISM.

SEE ALSO: *deviant behaviour; labour market segmentation; middle class; profession; social mobility; stratification; women and work.*

cargo cult See: MILLENARIANISM.

case study The detailed examination of a single example of a class of phenomena, a case study cannot provide reliable information about the broader class. But it is often useful in the preliminary stages of an investigation since it provides hypotheses which may be tested systematically with a larger number of cases.

Case studies are frequently used in sociological research, sometimes as the preliminary to more extensive investigation but often as the primary research method. In the latter case, shortage of resources or difficulties in gaining access to research subjects are often reasons for this choice. Many case-study investigations in fact use more than a single case, for a number of different reasons. Some researchers wish to ascertain the range of variability in the population under consideration. Cases are then selected to represent what, on the basis of theory or prior knowledge, are thought to be contrasting examples. Others try to test hypotheses by the comparison of contrasting cases; for example, the hypothesis of R. Blauner, that ALIENATION varies with the type of production technology used in factories, could be tested by comparing and contrasting a number of factories with different technologies. Sociologists who use techniques of qualitative research such as ETHNOGRAPHY or PARTICIPANT OBSERVATION, which are time-consuming and cannot easily be delegated to research assistants, almost invariably choose the case-study method. But data collection techniques can also include surveys. For example, the investigation of alienation in a factory case study might well include an attitude survey of employees. Case studies may provide data of a richness and detail that are difficult to obtain from more representative research designs, but at the cost of a lack of generalizability.

READING: Yin (1989)

cash nexus This term was used by K. Marx and F. Engels in the *Communist Manifesto* of 1848 and now has a wide currency in industrial sociology. It refers to the character of employment in many modern industries, when the only tie binding employers and employees is the payment of wages for work done and when each side tries to maximize its own interests regardless of the interests of the other. The cash nexus depersonalizes employment relations by turning them into simple economic transactions subject to market forces. Some modern firms, however, try to create loyalty among their employees by creating ties of a non-economic nature.

SEE ALSO: *alienation; class; human relations; labour market segmentation.*

caste A caste system is a form of social STRATIFICATION in which castes are hierarchically organized and separated from each other by rules of ritual purity. The lowest strata of the caste system are referred to as 'untouchables', because they are excluded from the performance of rituals which confer religious purity. In this hierarchical system, each caste is ritually purer than the one below it. The caste system is an illustration of SOCIAL CLOSURE in which access to wealth and prestige is closed to social groups which are excluded from the performance of purifying rituals. This ritual segregation is further reinforced by rules of ENDOGAMY. In M. Weber's study of India (1958a), caste represented an important illustration of social ranking by prestige and formed part of a wider interest in pariah groups. If castes are maintained by social closure, they originated in either the segregation of ethnic groups or in occupational specialization; in both cases, caste regulated access to the market and to social prestige in a competitive struggle between social groups.

There is considerable debate as to whether the caste system is specific to Hindu culture, or whether its principal features are more widely found in other societies where hierarchically organized, endogamous strata are present. In the first position, caste cannot be defined independently of 'caste system', which is specific to classical Hindu society. In the second argument, the term caste is extended to embrace the stratification of ethnic groups, for example in the southern states of the USA.

While the Hindu caste system is organized in terms of four major castes (Brahmin, Kshatriya, Vaisya and Sudra), there is much diversity at the local, village level, where the major castes are further divided into smaller groupings of subcastes which are called *jati*. In principle, one is born into a caste and social mobility between castes is impossible. In practice, however, it is possible for a sub-caste as a whole to bring about an improvement in its standing within the hierarchy of prestige. Those special groups which can successfully acquire or imitate the ritual practices of privileged castes can experience upward mobility by a process known as 'sanskritization'.

The caste system is of interest because (1) it represents an alternative to class as a principle of social stratification, and (2) it has been regarded as a barrier to economic, specifically capitalist, development, in that caste inhibits labour mobility. Against this latter view, it has to be noted that caste does not inevitably or invariably prohibit people of different castes working together. As Weber noted, caste regulations typically end at the workplace. Given this latter possibility and the fact of mobility, the degree to which caste stands in the way of industrialization and mobility of labour is much disputed in the social sciences.

SEE ALSO: *ethnic group.*
READING: Dumont (1970)

causal explanation This is a form of explanation in which one state of affairs is said to bring about another. For example, the shift to an industrial society is said to have caused the replacement of the extended by the nuclear family. Some writers argue that causal explanations in sociology are problematic for three reasons. (1) Most social phenomena are extremely complex and it is difficult to devise procedures which will clearly identify which elements are causally important. (2) One cannot generally set up an experimental procedure with proper CONTROL GROUPS.

(3) Causal explanations cannot succeed because they assume that human beings are like natural objects when they are not, since their actions are partly determined by the meanings that they give to the world.

SEE ALSO: *causal modelling; correlation; Geisteswissenschaften; hermeneutics; positivism; realism; Verstehen.*

READING: Keat and Urry (1975)

causal modelling Sociologists often wish to understand the causal connections among a number of different variables acting simultaneously, yet it is usually impossible t⌐ collect sociological data by means of the EXPERIMENTAL METHOD, which woulᵈ permit a precise specification of the effects of variables on each other and their interactions. Sociological data tend to provide relationships of CORRELATION and not causation. Causal modelling is the generic title for a group of statistical techniques that facilitate the specification of causal linkages among correlations. They are also known as *structural equation models*. These include multiple REGRESSION, PATH ANALYSIS and LOG LINEAR ANALYSIS. The starting point is to construct a MODEL of the assumed causal process. The model is theoretically derived by the investigator. The statistical techniques manipulate the data to see whether they fit the model. Causal models do not prove causal connections, however. Various assumptions are made when building models and these may be invalid in any particular case. One benefit of causal modelling is that, in representing causal mechanisms formally, investigators have to make their assumptions explicit. Such modelling has been used mainly on large-scale survey data, though increasingly it is applied to other data sets including historical statistical series.

SEE ALSO: *measurement levels; multivariate analysis.*

READING: Duncan (1975)

census A census of population is the collection of demographic, economic and social data about all the people within the boundaries of a country or any other geographical unit. Censuses may be designed to provide information about topics other than population, for example industrial production, housing and agriculture, but sociologists normally have population censuses in mind when they use the term census. National governments regularly count their people and the two oldest, continuous, periodic censuses are those of the United States (every ten years since 1790) and Great Britain (every ten years since 1801, except in 1941). Some commentators believe that the development of the census in the nineteenth century provided information necessary for political control of the population.

SEE ALSO: *socio-economic groups.*

central business district See CONCENTRIC ZONE THEORY.

central life interest Older studies of industrial workers distinguished between people who were work-centred – for whom work was a central life interest – and those who were not. Work for the first group provided intrinsic satisfaction, self-realization and valued social relationships, and was an emotionally significant experience. For the non-work-centred, work was unimportant and they fulfilled their needs via their non-work life. The term was coined by R. Dubin and the ideas it expressed had an influence on the AFFLUENT WORKER study. The term itself is rarely used today, but the notion that work is of different degrees of centrality to different people remains influential.

SEE ALSO: *work attitudes*.

central tendency When analysing data, it is always useful to provide a single summary statistic of the central or most characteristic value. Two measures of central tendency are used in sociological data analysis. The most common is the *mean*, which is the arithmetic average obtained by adding up all the data and then dividing by the total number of data. The mean is the most useful because it is used in the most important statistical tests. The other common measure is the *median*, which is literally the middle point in a distribution of data (half the data lie above and half below this point). The median is less affected by skewed data distributions, for example where there are a few very large values at one extreme end of a range, which may render the average less meaningful to an analyst. The median can also be applied to ordinal scale measurements. There is a third measure of central tendency, the *mode* or most frequently occurring value, which sociologists rarely use.

SEE ALSO: *measurement levels*.

centre/periphery Spatial metaphors and imagery are common conceptual devices in sociological theory. There are two important uses of the centre/periphery dichotomy in sociology.

(1) E. Shils (1975) argues that the core of society is the central value system which has a sacred character and is the ultimate source of authority, legitimating the distribution of wealth, rewards and roles in the social system. While the various social elites are fundamentally involved in the centre, other social groups are located at the periphery. As the means of communication are improved with industrialization, the centre becomes more extensive within society and previously peripheral groups become increasingly involved in the central value system and subject to its authority. The emergence of the modern state was thus a condition for the extension of the centre, the creation of national identity and CITIZENSHIP rights. However, the increasing complexity of modern society and the differentiation of roles means that consensus over central values is always partial and problematic. While Shils' theory is developed within functionalist sociology, his notion of centre/periphery has similarities with the Marxist concept of ideology.

(2) In the development theory of Marxist sociologists like A. G. Frank (1969), the centre refers, not to a core of values, but to the loci of economic power in the global organization of production and distribution. In this perspective, the global economy is conceived in terms of a hierarchy of economic centres which, through military, political and trade arrangements, extract an economic surplus from subordinate peripheral economies and regions. The distinction between the industrialized core and the underdeveloped periphery is thus part of a more general theory of imperialism. The backwardness of peripheral economies is held to be a consequence of their dependence on various core economies and not the effect of their poor resources, illiteracy, traditionalism or political instability. The industrial development of the centre is at the cost of the underdevelopment of the periphery. The centre/periphery scheme may also be used to describe regional differences within one country. The economic power of the centre, for example the south-east of the UK, controls

peripheral regions. The analysis of GLOBALIZATION and WORLD-SYSTEM THEORY has now superseded centre/periphery.

SEE ALSO: *dependency theory; dual economy; internal colonialism; sociology of development; underdevelopment.*

charisma A theological term ('gift of grace'), charismatic authority first came to prominence in M. Weber's analysis of domination. Contrasted with LEGAL–RATIONAL AUTHORITY, charisma means the AUTHORITY vested in a leader by disciples and followers in the belief that the leader's claim to power flows from extraordinary personal gifts. With the death of the leader, the disciples either disband or convert charismatic beliefs and practices into traditional ('charisma of office') or legal arrangements. Because charismatic authority is unstable and temporary, it is transformed into permanent institutions through the 'routinization' of charisma.

SEE ALSO: *rationalization.*

READING: Weber (1946); Lindholm (1993)

chi-squared test The test (χ^2) is a statistical technique that sociologists commonly use in the interpretation of data measured at the nominal level (data that are discontinuous and consist of mutually exclusive categories). The test allows one to assess the probability that a particular distribution might simply be the product of chance. It is also used as a simple measure of association when one variable is cross tabulated against another.

SEE ALSO: *cross tabulation; measurement levels.*

Chicago School Between the two world wars, American sociology was dominated by the University of Chicago, which produced an immense amount of sociological work and trained many students who subsequently became teachers in other American universities. Although covering a wide range of topics, both in theory and in empirical research, the Chicago School is best known for its urban sociology and, secondarily, for the development of the symbolic interactionist approach. Impressed by the rapid expansion of Chicago, by the intake of migrants of all nationalities, races and religions, and often influenced by humanitarian considerations, a number of sociologists, notably E. Burgess, R. Mackenzie, R. Park and L. Wirth, developed a distinctive urban theory and their students carried out detailed studies of various areas of the city. The theory was dominated by the assumption that cities manifested a particular way of life radically different from that found in the countryside. Explanation of this urban way of life was founded on the principles of URBAN ECOLOGY, chiefly that the forces of competition in a bounded environment produced a set of natural areas, each inhabited by different social groupings. These areas and groupings became the subject of detailed investigation which produced studies of the hobo, skid row, the Negro family, and the Jewish ghetto, amongst others. These studies were mostly based on ETHNOGRAPHY, a method also used in studies of various occupations in the city: musicians, doctors and waitresses, for instance. QUALITATIVE RESEARCH was the main approach, using the CASE STUDY method and, above all, PARTICIPANT OBSERVATION. The ethnographic tradition in Chicago became closely associated with SYMBOLIC INTERACTIONISM, in that studies of urban areas, social groups and occupations were concerned with the construction of identities by the interaction of individuals' perceptions of themselves and of others' views of them. This concern was supported by the more theoretical work, firstly by W. Thomas, and, more importantly, by George H. MEAD. At the same time, there was an emphasis, notably in the work of W. F. Ogburn, on the collection of detailed statistical information on local communities.

SEE ALSO: *concentric zone theory; natural area; rural–urban continuum.*

READING: Downes and Rock (1995)

childhood Following the historical research of P. Aries (1960), sociologists argue that the child as a social ROLE and childhood as a social category separate from adults began to develop in the eighteenth century among the nobility. The differentiation and specialization of age groups was associated with the emergence of the school as a place of moral training separate from the home. In England, this cultural development was closely connected with the emergence of the public school as a special institution for the cultivation of an elite. Before this period, children were more thoroughly integrated into the world of adults. The growth of childhood as a distinctive category was also connected with new educational theories which argued that children were innocent and required protection from adult society in order to be prepared for maturity at a later stage. By the end of the nineteenth century, this emphasis on the moral development of children required a new set of attitudes towards parental responsibilities and the importance of privacy and domesticity for the nurturing of the child. In the twentieth century, these concerns for an appropriate moral environment for children from birth were expressed by J. Bowlby (1953) in the theory of MATERNAL DEPRIVATION.

The growing importance of social rights for children can be seen as an extension of CITIZENSHIP, starting with the Factory Acts of the 1840s which protected children from unrestricted exploitation at work. In the twentieth century, these rights have been expanded to include rights to education and welfare. The implication of these rights for children is that the state can interfere in the household to protect the child from parental abuse. In the last decade there has, for example, been growing concern over reports of extensive sexual abuse of children in the home (primarily by fathers of their daughters). Some authors, for example J. Donzelot (1977), have suggested that developments in medicine, psychiatry and law have brought about a government of society through the family, in which the state rather than the father functions as the basis of PATRIARCHY.

Children have become increasingly important in social policy issues, because their position in society has become precarious as a consequence of high divorce rates, the more widespread domestic violence and sexual abuse of children, the prevalence of single-parent households and the failure of divorced men to provide adequate financial support for children of previous marriages. Some conservative critics of society argue that this set of circumstances is a recipe for social crisis (such as mounting rates of juvenile delinquency).

SEE ALSO: *adolescence; delinquency; divorce; generation; marriage.*

READING: Jenks (1996)

Chinese religions See: WORLD RELIGIONS.

choice theory of rights See: RIGHTS.

Christianity See: WORLD RELIGIONS.

church E. Troeltsch (1912) identified a central paradox: Christianity could either attempt to influence the whole society as a universal RELIGION open to all people, that is as a church, or it could aim to influence society as an elite of devout followers, that is as a SECT. The cost of being a church was some degree of accommodation to secular institutions, especially the state. The cost of being a sect was isolation, withdrawal and loss of general influence. Troeltsch argued that growing SECULARIZ-ATION spelt the end of the universal church. Contemporary sociologists, however, continue to use the term to describe large religious organizations which accept the importance of the state and other secular institutions in maintaining the social order, which have a hierarchical organization based on a priesthood and which recruit their membership through birth rather than conversion.

SEE ALSO: *world religions*.

circulation of elites See: ELITE.

citizenship The concept of citizenship as a status that provides access to rights and powers is associated with MARSHALL (1963). Civic rights comprise freedom of speech and equality before the law. Political rights include the right to vote and to organize politically. Socio-economic rights include economic welfare and social security. In pre-industrial society these rights were confined to a narrow elite. As long as the mass was denied full civic and political rights, then revolutionary class ideologies flourished. The extension of civic and political citizenship to the bourgeoisie and working class integrated these classes into society, thus leading to decline in revolutionary CLASS CONSCIOUSNESS. The extension of socio-economic rights, including trade unionism, COLLECTIVE BARGAINING in the economic sphere and the growth of the WELFARE STATE, may also be viewed as significant for integration of the modern working class. Critics of Marshall's theory of citizenship argue that the social conditions which sustained citizenship have been eroded. These were full employment, an expanding economy, the nuclear family, the absence of general female employment and an ideology of welfare consensus.

While the Marshallian tradition conceptualized citizenship in terms of resource allocation in welfare capitalism, contemporary approaches have been more concerned with issues relating to identity, cultural difference and national communities. Questions of citizenship identity are important because the sovereignty of the nation state has been partly eroded by GLOBALIZATION.

SEE ALSO: *capitalism; corporatism; democracy; incorporation; institutionalization of conflict; rights; trade unions*.

READING: Turner, B. S. (1993)

civic culture See POLITICAL CULTURE.

civil religion A term first employed by J.-J. Rousseau in *The Social Contract* (1762) and developed by E. Durkheim in *The Elementary Forms of the Religious Life* (1912), it refers to the beliefs, symbols, rituals and institutions which legitimate the social system, create social solidarity and mobilize a community to achieve common political objectives. For example, it has been argued that, in industrial societies where there has been some SECULARIZATION of traditional religions, national symbols and rituals serve the same function as religion in generating social solidarity.

In more recent sociology, the term has been closely associated with the analysis of American society by R. N. Bellah (1967; 1970; 1974; 1975). The American civil religion is composed of: (1) elements of the Judaeo-Christian tradition which emphasize ACHIEVEMENT MOTIVATION and INDIVIDUALISM; (2) events from the national drama (the death of Lincoln and the Civil War); (3) secular values from the Constitution; (4) secular rituals and symbols (the flag, Memorial-Day rites and the Fourth of July). In contemporary America, where ethnic diversity and cultural pluralism create problems of social integration, Bellah has argued that the civil religion generates powerful sentiments of national solidarity and purpose.

This theory of religion in American national life develops perspectives from de TOCQUEVILLE (1835 and 1840), W. Herberg (1955), and T. Parsons' (1951; 1967) analysis of religion and social integration. Bellah's version of the concept of civil religion can be criticized on a number of grounds: (1) it is highly specific to contemporary American society; (2) many societies which are ethnically and culturally diverse do not develop a civil religion; (3) it suffers from the analytical problems associated with FUNCTIONALISM; (4) it represents a version of the DOMINANT IDEOLOGY THESIS.

SEE ALSO: *invisible religion; nationalism; sacred.*

READING: Bellah and Hammond (1980)

civil rights See: RIGHTS.

civil society In the social sciences, there is no consensus as to the theoretical and empirical separation of political, economic and social relations. The shifting meaning of the concept of 'civil society' indicates changing theoretical attitudes towards the relationship between economy, society and state. As sociology emerged out of POLITICAL ECONOMY, social philosophy and 'moral statistics', its province became the phenomena of social, symbolic and normative interactions which constitute 'society', while political relations (state, power, government, political parties, etc.) were left to political science, and economics became the science of the production and distribution of economic resources. Against this trend of intellectual differentiation, sociology can also be treated as, following COMTE, a synthetic science which attempts to integrate political, economic and social phenomena. In Marxism, also, there was a similar theoretical ambivalence. In the BASE AND SUPERSTRUCTURE metaphor, the economic base was contrasted with the superstructure of law, politics and social relations. Alternatively, it was argued that, for example, the relations of production were simultaneously social, economic and legal.

In the eighteenth century, A. Ferguson (1767) treated 'civil society' as a state of civility and as the consequence of civilization. He also, however, treated 'civil society' as a political term, contrasting Western governments with ORIENTAL DESPOTISM. The term also had an economic connotation in that civilization was contrasted with societies (the barbaric state) in which private property did not exist. The term 'civil society' eventually came into sociology via the analyses of G. Hegel and K. Marx. In Hegel (1837), 'civil society' became an intermediate institution between the family and the political relations of the state. In K. Marx and F. Engels, we rarely, if ever, encounter the term 'society' in isolation. Rather there is a more basic dichotomy between 'civil society' (the ensemble of socio-economic relations and forces of production), and the state (the superstructural manifestation of class relations inside civil society). In *The German Ideology* (1845b), they argued that 'civil society is the true source and theatre of all history'; that is, the explanation of political events, legal changes and cultural development was to be sought in the development of the structure of civil society. This Marxist conception was substantially adapted by GRAMSCI (1971), who argued that between the coercive relations of the state and the economic sphere of production lies civil society, namely that area of social life which *appears* as the realm of the private citizen and individual consent. Gramsci's formulation of the relationship between economy, society and state in terms of two contrasts between private and public life, consent and coercion has played a fundamental role in the contemporary Marxist analysis of ideology and power. This influence was especially marked in the contrast between IDEOLOGICAL STATE APPARATUS and 'repressive state apparatus' in the work of L. Althusser. This modern employment of the term 'civil society' does not, however, entirely resolve the traditional problem of the relationship between base and superstructure. With the collapse of communism in Europe after 1989, attempts to introduce democracy looked to CITIZENSHIP and civil society as key concepts.

SEE ALSO: *associative democracy*; *communitarianism*; *rights*; *Scottish Enlightenment*; *society*.

READING: Cohen and Arato (1995)

civilization For ENLIGHTENMENT thinkers, the notion of civilization was inextricably connected with the idea of social progress, namely the triumph of rationality over religion, the decline of local, particular customs and the rise of natural science. It was associated with the growth of the absolutist state and therefore with the reduction of local systems of taxation, local political autonomy and with greater cultural uniformity within states. In the nineteenth century there was growing disillusionment with progress as urban, industrial, capitalist society was seen as producing ALIENATION and ANOMIE.

SEE ALSO: *Elias*; *progress*; *rationalization*; *Scottish Enlightenment*; *secularization*.

READING: Elias (1939a; 1939b)

civilizing process See: ELIAS.

clan See: DESCENT GROUPS.

class Sociologists identify class as one of the fundamental types of social STRATIFICATION, along with CASTE and ESTATES. The major theoretical tradition within class analysis derives from the work of MARX and WEBER on the newly emerging class structure of industrial capitalism in the nineteenth century. In this, classes are defined in economic terms, though views differ as to what are the crucial economic determinants. An alternative tradition found in some American accounts of social stratification is that class is *not* mainly economic.

Marx analysed class in relation to the ownership of capital and the means of production. He divided the population into those who owned property and those who were propertyless, the capitalist class and the proletariat. He recognized the existence of groups which did not fit this framework such as peasants and small proprietors, but suggested that these were hangovers of the pre-capitalist economy which would vanish with the maturation of the capitalist system. Class was more than just a way of describing the economic position of different groups, because Marx saw classes as tangible collectivities and as real social forces with the capacity to change society. The incessant drive of capitalists to create profit led to the exploitation of the proletariat in work and, so Marx believed, to its increasing pauperization. In these circumstances, workers would develop CLASS CONSCIOUSNESS and the proletariat would grow from being a class 'in itself', that is an economically defined category with no self-awareness, to become a class 'for itself', made up of workers with a class-conscious view of the world and ready to pursue class conflict against the capitalists.

Weber divided the population into classes according to economic differences of market capacity that gave rise to different LIFE-CHANCES. Capital was one source of market capacity, but skill and education formed another. While property-owners were a class, as Marx had emphasized, those whose skills were scarce on the market and commanded high salaries also constituted a separate class. Thus Weber distinguished four classes: the propertied class; the intellectual, administrative and managerial class; the traditional petit bourgeois class of small businessmen and shopkeepers; and the working class. Class conflict was common and was most likely to occur between groups with immediately opposed interests, for example between workers and managers rather than workers and capitalists. Weber also noted the significance of another principle of stratification that differed from class, namely social honour or STATUS.

Modern accounts of class have often rejected the Marxist definition. The separation of capital ownership from the management and control of industry makes propertylessness such a broad category that it fails to distinguish between groups with different economic positions, for example managers and shopfloor workers. Nor has the pauperization prediction been realized. British and American class theories have developed in different directions. Post-war American sociologists saw their society as classless. This was partly because they thought there were no sharp breaks in the distribution of material rewards, which they saw as being ranked simply along an unbroken continuum, and partly because they believed that individuals in modern society might just as plausibly be ranked on a whole variety of factors unrelated to economically defined class, such as occupation, religion, education, ethnicity. They took up Weber's notion of status and developed a multidimensional approach which treated social status and PRESTIGE as independent factors which diluted or even replaced economically determined class. Most occupational ranking schemes used in the study of inequality assumed simply that occupations could be ranked as 'better' or 'worse' than others according to the income and prestige their incumbents received.

British sociologists in this period initially took the DIVISION OF LABOUR as the crucial determinant of class, and identified the major class divide as that running between manual and non-manual occupations. This appeared to correspond to major differences in economic and social conditions. The division formed the basis of the old Registrar General's classification of SOCIO-ECONOMIC GROUPS (SEGs) and classes. It was largely an *ad hoc* distinction but ultimately seems to have derived from the Weberian notion of life-chances. The division is no longer useful, however, because there is considerable variation among the economic and social conditions of many low-level, non-manual employees, and there are significant differences between those at the bottom and top of the non-manual ladder. SEGs have been replaced by a new official SOCIO-ECONOMIC CLASSIFICATION (SEC). This derives from the class schema developed by GOLDTHORPE and colleagues, and is a more useful classification for sociologists.

Class is now defined by employment relations and conditions in contemporary society. This is an explicitly Weberian approach to class, which employs the criteria of market and work situations. The initial distinction is between employers, who purchase and control the labour of others, employees, who sell their labour to an employer or employing organization and place themselves under the control of others, and the self-employed, who do neither. A second distinction is between various types of employee position. These comprise different work and market situations. J. Goldthorpe (1987) has distinguished employment conditions which reflect a *labour contract* of employment from those which reflect a *service relationship* (also known as a service contract). The former involves a narrowly focused exchange of wages for effort, along the lines of the CASH NEXUS. This is typically the contract experienced by the working class. The latter is a longer-term and more diffuse relationship, in which employees serve their organization in return for much greater financial rewards and the prospects of future promotion. A service relationship also gives employees more autonomy at work and less supervision and control than labour contracts. Top managers and other senior employees have service relationships. *Market situation* refers to material rewards and life-chances such as pay, security and opportunity for promotion. *Work situation* refers to work tasks and production technology, and the structure of social relations and control systems in firms. There is assumed to be a congruence between the factors, in that market rewards and working conditions become progressively better as one ascends the class hierarchy from manual workers at the bottom to the senior managers, etc., at the top. The process by which classes may be transformed from economic categories into socially meaningful groups, commonly referred to as STRUCTURATION, has received considerable attention. Factors determining structuration include residence in single-class communities, low rates of social mobility which keep people in one class over time, and common lifestyles, all of which tend to turn classes into identifiable social groups. Class variations in social values and political identification may add to the distinctiveness of classes.

The division of the population into three classes – working, intermediate and upper – is now a conventional sociological model of the British class structure. Manual workers are placed in the working class: low-level, non-manual workers such as clerks and lower technicians in the intermediate class; and managers, administrators and professionals in the upper. The most commonly used classification is that developed by J. Goldthorpe and the Social Mobility Group at Oxford University. Goldthorpe has identified eleven social class categories, which may be compressed into three major social classes for many purposes. These are reproduced in the diagram overleaf. The upper class is described as the service class in this scheme, although some sociologists prefer the label 'salariat'.

A criticism of the way class analysis developed in the past is that it concentrated on men and wrongly ignored women. Women constituted 45 per cent of the United Kingdom labour force in the late 1990s. Working women are heavily concentrated in a handful of occupations: mainly in certain professions; in clerical and sales work among the non-manual occupations; and in unskilled factory work and services (e.g. cleaning) among the manual occupations. Their jobs have tended to be segregated from men's – certain jobs being largely reserved for women – although segregation is declining within managerial and professional occupations. They also have lower market rewards than men. Because women are not evenly distributed across the

Service	I	Higher-grade professionals, administrators, and officials; managers in large establishments; large proprietors
	II	Lower-grade professionals, administrators, and officials; higher-grade technicians; managers in small business and industrial establishments; supervisors of non-manual employees
Intermediate	IIIa	Routine non-manual employees in administration and commerce
	IIIb	Personal service workers
	IVa	Small proprietors, artisans, etc., with employees
	IVb	Small proprietors, artisans, etc., without employees
	IVc	Farmers and smallholders: self-employed fishermen
	V	Lower-grade technicians, supervisors of manual workers
Working	VI	Skilled manual workers
	VIIa	Semi-skilled and unskilled manual workers (not in agriculture)
	VIIb	Agricultural workers

Source: Adapted from Marshall *et al.* (1988), *Social Class in Modern Britain*, London, Unwin Hyman

range of occupations, ignoring them would create a distorted image of the shape of the class structure, which would omit whole occupational areas.

The theoretical and practical effects of treating men as central to class analysis were widely debated in the 1980s and 1990s. One problem area is the convention of making the family the unit of analysis in empirical studies of the transmission of material and cultural inequalities through generations, for example research into SOCIAL MOBILITY. In order to assign a class position to families, the class position of *all* family members was conventionally determined on the basis of the occupation of the husband/father, who was regarded as the head of household and main breadwinner. When most women work, this convention is problematic. If husband and wife can be assigned different class positions on the basis of their individual occupations, the class position of the family unit is not clear-cut. Similarly, the lifestyle of families with two wage-earners may differ significantly from others in the same class where there is only one wage. Moreover, some feminists suggest that women who work unpaid in the home are unjustly ignored in class theory, because their work at home supports the labour power of family members in paid employment, while they also reproduce the next generation of employees.

The study of social class in modern Britain by G. Marshall *et al.* (1988) has shown that taking the individual as the unit of class analysis and including women on an equal basis does improve understanding. For example, employed women at every level in the class hierarchy have inferior market and work situations compared with those of men in similar locations, inferior returns on their formal qualifications, and noticeably worse chances of upwards career progression and thus of social mobility. The last point suggests that the chances of men being upwardly mobile would be considerably diminished if women were treated equally; thus the existence of employed women shapes this important social-class process. Cross-class households are common, but the class locations and class trajectories of married women in such households are influenced more by their own attributes (e.g. their formal qualifications) than by the class of the male 'head' of family. The only area where knowledge about the male 'head' predicts married women's behaviour is political allegiance: women in cross-class families are more likely to vote in the way predicted by their husband's class position than by their own.

Marxist class theory revived in America and Britain in the 1970s and 1980s. Modern Marxists tackled the problem of where to place those occupations, such as management and the professions, which do not belong in the capitalist class or the proletariat as traditionally conceived. A distinction was made between those who performed CAPITAL FUNCTIONS and exercised the powers of ownership, in this way defining the capitalist class regardless of whether the people in it actually owned capital or not, and those who performed only the function of labour and were thus in the working class. E. O. Wright (1976), for example, divided ownership power into three aspects: control over resource allocation and investment; control over the physical apparatus of production; and control over labour power. The capitalist class controlled the overall investment process, the physical apparatus of production and labour power. The proletariat was excluded. The two classes stood in an antagonistic relationship, where the former dominated the latter. In this scheme, the capitalist class comprised the top corporate executive of firms (the board of directors), but most managers occupied intermediate and ambiguous ('contradictory') class locations, since they performed some but not all of the functions of capital. The proletariat included all low-level employees, both manual and non-manual. Wright (1985) later substantially revised his earlier analysis. The basis of class division became the unequal distribution of various assets and the associated patterns of exploitation. In capitalism, the principal asset is ownership of the means of production (capital), but there are other and subsidiary assets, which include organizational control and scarce skills and talent. Most managers are excluded from ownership of capital, like labour, but they also have interests opposed to those of labour because they control organizational assets and skill assets. The class typology that results from the intersection of the three principles of stratification is complex. G. Marshall *et al.* (1988) found that the Wright typology was less useful than the conventional classification for understanding social class structure and processes in Britain, and modern Marxist accounts are generally thought to be inadequate.

Class analysis has been criticized by several sociologists on the grounds that social class is no longer relevant to an understanding of modern societies: they even celebrate the 'death of class'. They claim that high rates of social mobility mean that class is a weak determinant of life-chances; that other principles of stratification, such as race and gender, appear to be very influential; that people no longer act or think in class-differentiated ways, hence the old link between class and beliefs (e.g. political allegiance) has largely disappeared and people no longer believe that class and class differences are salient. These claims are linked to sociological theories about economic and cultural change in the contemporary world. POST-FORDISM in the economy is thought to have disrupted in particular the working class, which can no longer be regarded as an organized, fully employed and coherent social group. The decline of the old mass production industries, which employed huge numbers of men in giant factories with full-time and long-term jobs, has been matched by the growth of FLEXIBLE SPECIALIZATION in production. At the same time, new patterns of employment have developed, which include more flexible and insecure jobs, more part-time jobs and more women employees. The sociological theory of POST-MODERNISM suggests that social structures are much more complex and fragmented than before. The new significance of race and gender divisions is evidence of these changes, but for post-modernism the really crucial areas of social division are CONSUMPTION CLEAVAGES and culture. It suggests too that individuals now have the freedom to choose and create their own sense of identity, rather than identity being determined by structural factors such as a person's class location. This perspective on the declining influence of class on personal choices is echoed in recent analyses of VOTING.

The view that class is unimportant is disputed, however. Studies of social mobility show that absolute rates of mobility may have increased but the same is not true of relative rates. Class is still an influential factor in life-chances in industrial societies while, in Britain, attitude surveys show that people still perceive class to be important in terms of social differences and social justice.

SEE ALSO: *affluent worker; class imagery; deferential worker; identity; labour aristocracy; lifestyle; Marxist sociology; middle class; new working class; postmodernity; profession; proletarianization; relations of production; service class; social closure; status inconsistency; underclass; upper class; Veblen; women and work; working class*.

READING: Crompton (1993); Pakulski and Waters (1996)

class attitudes See: CLASS IMAGERY.

class awareness See: CLASS CONSCIOUSNESS; CLASS IMAGERY.

class consciousness Used originally by Marxists to describe a situation when the PROLETARIAT becomes aware of its objective class position *vis-à-vis* the BOURGEOISIE and its historic role in the transformation of capitalism into socialism, this term refers to the 'subjective' dimension of class. The proletariat would develop from a class 'in itself', simply a collection of workers sharing a common class position but with no collective awareness, to become a class 'for itself'. K. Marx believed that consciousness would develop out of the working class's concrete experience of the contradiction between capitalist relations of production based on individual private property and the emerging collective forces of production which created a proletariat whose power was collectively based and experienced. *False* consciousness is a term Marxists use to describe the situation where the proletariat fails to perceive what they believe to be the 'true' nature of its interests and does not develop a revolutionary class consciousness. V. I. Lenin (1902) suggested that workers left to themselves would create only a trade-union consciousness which sought limited social and economic reforms, and that a true revolutionary awareness could only be developed by a communist party with a socialist ideology. Marxist accounts of false class consciousness have raised the problem of how one is to judge CLASS INTEREST.

The term was subsequently used loosely by sociologists outside the Marxist tradition to include any feelings of self-awareness or common identity among members of a social class. M. Mann (1973) gave class consciousness greater precision and captured some of the original spirit of the Marxist usage. He identified four elements: (1) class *identity* – the definition of oneself as working class; (2) class *opposition* – the perception that capitalists and their managers constitute an enduring opponent; (3) class *totality* – the realization that the two previous elements define one's own social situation and the whole of the society in which one lives; (4) an *alternative* society – a conception of the desired alternative which will be realized when class conflict is successfully resolved. These elements, in practice, represent the stages through which a developing class consciousness moves.

SEE ALSO: *class; class imagery; commonsense knowledge; dual consciousness; Gramsci; hegemony; Leninism; new working class; pragmatic acceptance; stratification; working class.*

class dealignment See: CONSUMPTION CLEAVAGES; VOTING.

class imagery Different people perceive class structure in different ways and, whatever the objective reality of class inequality, people may have different images or models of this reality. These images, as well as the actual structure of class inequality, are often assumed to influence people's political and social attitudes and behaviour. Imagery was important in British sociology in the third quarter of the twentieth century. E. Bott (1957) distinguished between power and prestige images. The power image divided society into the working and upper classes whose interests conflicted, the upper having the power to coerce the other. The PRESTIGE image portrayed class structure as a finely graded ladder of positions that differed in terms of their social status, with people moving up or down according to their ability. J. H. Goldthorpe *et al.* (1969) identified in addition a money model. This imagined society as being divided by differences in income and spending, creating a multiplicity of different levels, with most people being somewhere in the middle. The money model indicated low class consciousness. A major influence on class imagery was held to be the character of the primary social groups to which individuals belonged. Power models were thought to be associated with closed working-class communities where there was little geographical or social mobility and where community and work relations were superimposed. Prestige images were thought to be associated with the more open networks of social relationships typical of the middle class.

Class imagery, both as a concept and in the way it has been operationalized, has been heavily criticized. (1) It assumes that people have fairly clearly articulated and internally consistent images, when in fact these are often incoherent. (2) The classification of respondents' images depends heavily on the interpretation of the researcher, thus variations may reflect differences between researchers rather than real differences in the population. (3) The significance of class imagery has not been demonstrated – even if images are coherent, consistent and unambiguously identifiable, it remains unclear what effect, if any, they have on political or social behaviour.

More recent studies of class-based beliefs in Britain, notably the major national surveys of attitudes reported in A. Heath and R. Topf (1987), A. Heath and G. Evans (1988) and G. Marshall *et al.* (1988), no longer refer to class imagery and find no evidence of a *single* set of beliefs that has internal consistency. But they do show the continued salience of perceptions of class and persistent class-based divisions in beliefs about society. They report two major clusters of attitudes: (1) regarding class and issues of economic, social and political inequalities; (2) regarding issues of morality and law and order. On the subject of class, most people have a sense of their own class identity and believe also that class is an important social division; thus class awareness remains strong in contemporary Britain. However, working-class respondents have a more strongly radical-egalitarian and oppositional set of attitudes: they are more likely to see class divisions, economic inequality and a lack of social and political justice than people in the higher social classes. Nevertheless, a substantial minority of the service class of managerial, professional and administrative employees is also radical on these issues. The other cluster covers personal and familial morality, respect for law and order, dutifulness and discipline. Here it is the working class that tends to be conservative and authoritarian, while the highest social class is more liberal.

SEE ALSO: *affluent worker; class consciousness; dual consciousness.*

class interest In the debate between Marxist and non-Marxist sociologies, the notion of class interest, as the aims and aspirations of a class, is of some importance. It may be argued, for example, that the capitalist class adopts a particular IDEOLOGY because of its class interest. Difficulties with the notion arise when the sociologist wants to ascribe an objective interest to a class when members of that class appear to be unaware of this or even to deny it. It is then not clear what evidence would confirm or deny the ascription.

SEE ALSO: *class consciousness.*

class struggle A diversely used term, class struggle is always assumed to belong to the Marxist canon. For K. Marx himself, the class struggle was the motive force of history, as classes tried to realize their class interests. For example, the transition from feudalism to capitalism was produced by a struggle between a landed aristocracy and a rising capitalist bourgeoisie. In contemporary societies, class struggle is used to refer to conflict between social classes which occurs primarily at the economic level, manifest, for example, in wage bargaining, strikes or absenteeism and, secondarily, at the political level, manifest in such issues as the reform of trade union law, the maintenance of the welfare state and economic policy. The most important struggles in capitalist societies are those between capitalists and workers, although other classes, for example the peasantry or the middle classes, may also be involved in alliances with one or other party.

There are difficulties in deciding what is to count as evidence of class struggle, for there is a tendency for all industrial or political conflict to be interpreted as instances of struggles between classes. Within Marxism, these struggles are always seen as manifestations of, and explained by, a deeper CONTRADICTION between capital and labour.

SEE ALSO: *agency and structure; Althusser; class consciousness; Marxist sociology; mode of production.*

classroom interaction The traditional concern of educational sociologists with pupil attainment, in which the pupil's social background or individual psychology were the main explanatory variables, gave way in the 1970s to the investigation of educational institutions themselves and the way they shape educational outcomes. Using the techniques of ETHNOGRAPHY and often working within the perspective of SYMBOLIC INTERACTIONISM, investigators analysed the social interactions and values (often implicit rather than formally acknowledged) that made up the social system of the classroom or school. Since these case-study investigations are limited (often to single schools) and mainly descriptive, the generalizations that can be made about their findings are limited: (1) the HIDDEN CURRICULUM, with its LATENT FUNCTION of controlling pupils, is an integral part of the social system of the school; (2) there are distinct pupil subcultures of commitment to and dissent from school values; (3) these divisions within the body of pupils are influenced by the social organization of the school – for example, segregation into 'able' and 'less able' streams – and by the stereotyping and labelling of individuals by teachers and pupils alike; (4) the social interaction between teachers and pupils is highly complex, based on an asymmetrical distribution of power that sometimes promotes pupil resistance, and influenced by the way pupils accept school values, especially those of the hidden curriculum. Pupil attainment, therefore, appears to be the product not only of the intelligence or innate ability of pupils, but also of complex social processes in the school.

SEE ALSO: *classroom knowledge; educational attainment; labelling theory; pedagogical practices; stereotypes.*

classroom knowledge N. Keddie (1971) has linked the assessment of pupils' abilities that forms the basis of streaming in schools to the criteria that teachers use to evaluate classroom knowledge. She suggests that it is knowledge defined as appropriate by the school – knowledge that is abstract and can be presented in general forms – that is relevant; teachers see this as superior to pupils' own knowledge comprising items of concrete information derived from experience. High-ability candidates are more willing to accept what is defined as appropriate knowledge and to suspend their disbelief when this fails to match their own experience. Once streamed, the more able are allowed access to more highly evaluated knowledge than those assessed as less able.

SEE ALSO: *classroom interaction; cultural capital; pedagogical practices.*

clinical sociology The phrase was first used by L. Wirth (1931), who observed the employment of sociologists in clinics which included psychiatrists, psychologists and social workers. These clinics were primarily concerned with behavioural problems in children, but Wirth anticipated the growth of sociological clinics which would deal with a range of social problems. The sociologist would become part of a therapeutic team providing research, teaching and practical involvement in the problems of its clients. Wirth also argued that sociology was important in providing doctors and psychiatrists with a perspective on the social dimensions of mental and physical illness.

SEE ALSO: *applied sociology; sociology of medicine; social problems.*

closed-ended question See: QUESTIONNAIRE.

closure See: SOCIAL CLOSURE.

cluster analysis A group of statistical techniques used in the analysis of multivariate data to identify internal structure. The purpose is to find groups of objects (individuals and other entities) that share the maximum number of common features and, conversely, share the minimum number of features with other groups. For example, if one has a sample of individuals with measures of the variables of education, salary and occupational status, one could put all those people with university education, high salary and senior professional or managerial jobs into one cluster and the remainder into a second cluster. Because they define similarity and difference, clustering techniques are extremely useful for identifying underlying patterns in sets of data. Thus they are frequently used in exploratory analysis of data and to impose order on complexity, prior to developing hypotheses for CAUSAL MODELLING, and also to create descriptive classifications and typologies. While most of the statistical techniques are designed to produce exclusive clusters and an individual can be assigned to only one, some allow for overlaps. This is sometimes referred to as 'clumping'.

SEE ALSO: *factor analysis*.

code See: RESTRICTED CODE; SEMIOTICS.

co-determination See: INDUSTRIAL DEMOCRACY.

coding This is the process of translating raw research data into a form which can be used in calculation by classifying data into categories and assigning each category a numerical value. For example, in a questionnaire about political beliefs, the answers Labour, Conservative, Lib Dem, Don't Know, to a question asking people how they would vote at the next election, would be assigned the numbers 1, 2, 3, 4, respectively, so that voting intentions can be quantified. Many survey questions are pre-coded and the interviewer (or the respondent if it is a self-completed questionnaire) simply rings the appropriate number. When the range of answers cannot be determined in advance, for example if people are asked to comment on a particularly complex political issue, then a *coding frame* is drawn up after all the replies have been collected and a selection has been analysed in the office. The frame assigns numbers to different answers and these are then coded for quantitative analysis. Coding is often regarded as part of survey research, but in reality it takes place whenever any kind of data are categorized and assigned a numerical value.

coding frame See: CODING.

coercion There are two main senses of coercion: active and situational. (1) The actions of subordinate individuals or social groups are determined or compelled by the use or the threat of physical force. While sociologists recognize that there is an element of coercion in all societies, it is held that the use of force by the state must be supported by some form of legitimation. People accept the exercise of coercion if they believe it is administered by appropriate office-holders. (2) People are compelled to behave in certain ways by situational circumstances, that is by the structure of society and not by individuals. In K. Marx's view, the economic organization of society is coercive in that the propertyless labourer is forced to sell his labour in order to live.

SEE ALSO: *authority; conflict theory; consensus; legitimacy; power; social control; social order*.

cognate/cognatic An anthropological term used to describe a system of kinship in which people will establish their pattern of relationships through either the male or the female line.

SEE ALSO: *agnatic; descent groups*.

cognitive dissonance L. Festinger's theory of cognitive dissonance is that people find dissonance or lack of fit between attitudes or between attitudes and behaviour unacceptable, because they have a need for consistency and harmony, and they will try to reduce it, by modifying their cognitions or adding new ones. For example, if the members of a cult expecting the arrival of aliens by flying saucers find that the saucers do not arrive on the appointed day, the inconsistency will force them either to revise their beliefs or to reinterpret the failure of the prediction.

READING: Festinger (1957)

cohabitation See: HOUSEHOLD; MARRIAGE.

cohesion See: SOCIAL ORDER.

cohort This is a demographic term describing a group of people who share a significant experience at a certain period of time. For example, all the children born in one year form the birth cohort of that year. Cohort analysis, following the history of a cohort over time, has been used to collect data relevant to the study of fertility, health care, education and employment. It can also be a particularly good method of studying social change.

Coleman, James Samuel (1926–96) A professor of sociology at the University of Chicago from 1973 and president of the American Sociological Association (1990–93), he made significant contributions to public policy in respect of education and equality in two reports: *Equality of Educational Opportunity* (1966) and *Public and Private Schools* (1982), with T. Hoffer, S. Kilgore and S. S. Peng. His academic contributions were to the sociological study of education, parenting and youth culture in *Adolescent Society* (1961), *Equality and Achievement in Education* (1990a) and *Parents, their Children and the School* (1993), with B. L. Schneider; and to the study of POWER in *Union Democracy* (1956), with S. M. Lipset and M. A. Trow, *Community Conflict* (1957) and *Power and the Structure of Society* (1973). In his later career he was known primarily for his contributions to RATIONAL CHOICE THEORY in *Individual Interests and Collective Action* (1986), *Foundations of Social Theory* (1990b) and *Rational Choice Theory* (1992b), with T. J. Fararo. He also contributed to mathematical sociology in his *Introduction to Mathematical Sociology* (1964).

READING: Sorensen and Spilerman (1993)

collective action N. M. Olson, in *The Logic of Collective Action* (1965), asked why people who would benefit from acting collectively to advance their common interests, either directly or via an organization such as a pressure group, often fail to do so. Olson argued that, far from people being irrational when they choose not to work together to advance their own interests, they are making a rational choice. If a group is successful in advancing its cause, very often the rewards are also available to non-members who benefit without any expenditure of effort. For example, when a trade union negotiates a pay rise, this is normally paid to all relevant employees in a company whether or not they are union members. Therefore the decision to be a 'free rider', as economists describe this action, on the efforts of others is highly rational. Olson argued that the poorer people are, the relatively more costly they find participation and the more likely they are to free ride. A solution is for collective movements to provide other incentives to join, for example psychological gratification or social approval. Olson's thesis has influenced the development of RATIONAL CHOICE THEORY and GAME THEORY.

collective bargaining This is a method of establishing wages, working conditions and other aspects of employment by means of negotiation between employers and the representatives of employees organized collectively. Employee organizations are typically TRADE UNIONS. As a means of accommodating competing interests in industry, it has played an important part in the regulation and INSTITUTIONALIZATION OF CONFLICT. As an institution that provides employees with some influence over their working lives it has extended the rights of CITIZENSHIP into the economic sphere.

SEE ALSO: *industrial democracy; labour movement.*

collective behaviour The early theory of crowd behaviour is associated with G. Le Bon (1895), who argued that, in periods of social decline and disintegration, society is threatened by the rule of crowds. In the crowd, the individual psychology is subordinated to a 'collective mentality' which radically transforms individual behaviour. In contemporary sociology, there is less interest in crowd behaviour. By 'collective behaviour', sociologists now mean the mobilization of a mass of people to change the general structure of society. Such movements to change society as a whole include both secular movements of social protest and religious attempts to change society, for example MILLENARIANISM. The most influential general theory of collective behaviour is that of N. Smelser (1962), which draws particular attention to the importance of 'generalized beliefs' and values in directing social movements in periods of rapid social change and political disruption. He developed a sequential model, which explained collective behaviour in terms of structural conduciveness; structural strain (such as economic hardship); the spread of generalized beliefs; precipitating factors; mobilization of participants; and the effectiveness, or otherwise, of social control.

SEE ALSO: *social movements.*

collective conscience See: CONSCIENCE COLLECTIVE.

collective consumption This term was introduced into urban sociology by M. Castells (1977; 1978). He argued that LABOUR POWER must be reproduced. That is, there must be means whereby workers are able to offer their labour for sale day after day. Food, housing and transport, for example, have to be provided, as well as an educational system which trains labour power. All these items of consumption are increasingly provided in an urban setting as the population becomes more concentrated. Furthermore, their provision is more and more a matter for the state as private capital finds it unprofitable; it is a collective provision as education, transport, housing and health become state activities and hence matters for political debate and action. However, the state is persistently unable to meet the costs of collective consumption and there is therefore a tendency towards crisis in its provision which generates urban SOCIAL MOVEMENTS. As an explanation of the provision of urban facilities and consequent political action, the concept has been much criticized. There is some ambiguity as to whether it is a matter of collective use or collective provision. If it is the former, it is clear that many facilities, if not all, are consumed individually. If it is the latter, many items that are required for the reproduction of labour power are not provided by the state: for example, housing. Nonetheless, the concept continues to have utility, particularly as it focuses attention on the relationship of the state and private capital in the allocation of urban resources.

SEE ALSO: *reproduction of labour power; state.*

READING: Saunders (1981)

collective labourer K. Marx argued that, at a certain stage in the development of capitalism, when individual workers no longer produced an entire commodity by themselves, it would be proper to speak of the collective labourer. The term refers to the cooperation of workers in a complex LABOUR PROCESS characterized by a high division of labour.

collective representations In *The Elementary Forms of the Religious Life*, DURKHEIM (1912) argued, on the basis of field work undertaken by B. Spencer and F. J. Gillen in the late nineteenth century in *The Northern Tribes of Central Australia* (1904), that religious beliefs about sacred phenomena are in fact collective representations of the society or social group as a whole. These representations are periodically revived by the performance of collective rituals, giving rise to strong emotional attachments to society, which Durkheim called 'collective effervescence'. His SOCIOLOGY OF KNOWLEDGE can also be read as a critique of Kantian idealism, because Durkheim treated the fundamental categories of mind (such as time and space) as being socially produced in collective representations. Even in contemporary society, where there has been a process of SECULARIZATION, collective representations and collective sentiments still play an important role.

SEE ALSO: *religion*; *sacred*; *society of the spectacle*.

collective rights See: COMMUNITARIANISM.

colonialism See: IMPERIALISM; INTERNAL COLONIALISM.

command economy See: SOCIALIST SOCIETIES.

commodification A process whereby more and more human activities come to have a monetary value and effectively become goods to be bought and sold in a market. The theoretical underpinning of the idea comes from the work of MARX, who argued that CAPITALISM is a self-expanding economic system that requires increasing commodification. Capitalism, therefore, brings in its wake a replacement of spiritual or human values by monetary ones.

SEE ALSO: *commodity fetishism*.

commodity fetishism A doctrine originally formulated by MARX, commodity fetishism is a process by which people conceive of their social relations as if they were natural things. The doctrine depends on the prior distinction that Marx made between producing something for one's own use and producing a commodity which is an object created solely to be exchanged (for money or another commodity). Since the producers do not come into contact with each other until they exchange their products, they have no social relationships except in the act of exchange of objects. These objects come to stand for the social relationships. People's thinking about the social relations involved in their work is then characterized by a fetishism, whereby beliefs about the physical products of labour and their exchange substitute for, and mask, the social relations themselves.

The theory of commodity fetishism has been much used, together with the associated concept of REIFICATION, as a basis for theories of ideology and law, in that many forms of thought in capitalist societies are said to be fetishistic. That is, they present as natural and object-like phenomena that are actually socially constructed.

SEE ALSO: *appearance and reality*; *ideology*; *Marxist sociology*.

READING: Abercrombie (1980)

commonsense knowledge (1) A term used technically within PHENOMENO-
LOGICAL SOCIOLOGY to mean that knowledge which is routinely used in the
conduct of everyday life: for example, knowledge of how to post a letter. The
everyday world is the fundamental reality within which most people live. Consciousness of that world is characterized by the 'natural attitude' which takes the world as
natural, constant and pregiven.

(2) GRAMSCI was interested in the way that the concept contrasted with systematic
thought. Commonsense is practical, experimental and critical, but also fragmentary
and incoherent. As a result, it cannot go beyond practical activity into theoretical
construction. Gramsci identified commonsense thought with the mass and theoretical thought with an elite. This relates to the development of revolutionary consciousness: either a dominant class can impose a theoretical consciousness on to the
masses which, although it will be at variance with commonsense, does suppress
revolutionary possibilities; or an intellectual stratum (the party) can develop commonsense categories into a theoretical revolutionary consciousness.

SEE ALSO: *class consciousness*; *dominant ideology thesis*; *hegemony*; *life-world*; *Schutz*.

commune In political sociology, the commune is typically a secular institution in
which members, through their collective labour and common ownership of property, live together in accordance with a common ideology such as anarchism or
communism. In the sociology of religion and sociology of youth cultures, the
analysis of communes in industrial societies became important with the development of the commune movement, in North America particularly, in the 1960s. The
maintenance of the commune as a way of life, however, proves problematic since
communes have to solve basic problems of institutionalized social life, namely
power, stratification and economic subsistence.

SEE ALSO: *cooperative*.

communication The transfer of messages from one party to another. Those who
study communication (communications science) are interested in such questions as
'Who communicates to whom, by what means, with what content and with what
effect?' Communication processes can take place at a number of different levels –
between individuals, between social groups, within a society, or between societies.
Different academic disciplines study different aspects of communication at different
levels. Typically, sociologists' interests are at the higher levels where the complexity
of the communication process is greater. Two kinds of issue arise. First, sociologists
typically see communication as involving the circulation of *meaning*. One way of
understanding this is by SEMIOTICS: the study of the way that signs take on meaning
and are constructed into codes, encoded by the sender and decoded by the receiver.
Second, much important communication in modern societies is organized into
institutions – television companies, for instance – which address a *mass* audience;
communication is from the few to the many. Interest here focuses on the nature
and context of what is transmitted, the ownership, internal structure and values
of the producing organizations, and the way that the audience responds to the
transmission.

The term has a special meaning within the work of HABERMAS.

SEE ALSO: *audience; sociology of the mass media.*

READING: Fiske (1990)

communication management (public relations) Corporations and governments have to pay increasing attention to the successful management of communication with their clients and critics, because consumer pressure groups and organizations such as Green Peace have forced them to take greater responsibility for the consequences of their actions, especially with regard to the physical environment. A variety of major political, medical and environmental crises and disasters (thalidomide victims, the Three Mile Island nuclear power station accident, the Bhopal chemical accident, the Chernobyl nuclear accident and BSE or 'mad cow' disease') and routine consumer difficulties with food poisoning, contaminated products or poor workmanship in commodities have forced commercial companies to take the questions of reputation, corporate image and consumer confidence more seriously. The management of the information environment of the company by means of professional public relations has become a central component of corporate strategy in response to external risk. Communication management is now seen to be as significant as product management or personnel management. The rise of public relations as an academic discipline and as a corporate strategy are both a function of the increasing importance of electronic communication, consumer lobby groups and quality-control systems.

Communication management can also be treated as a component of corporate citizenship, which argues that corporations have duties and responsibilities (with respect to the environment and the societies within which they operate) rather like individuals. Critics argue that 'PR' is designed not to offer clients correct information but to orchestrate PUBLIC OPINION in the interests of corporate profit.

SEE ALSO: *corporate crime; risk/risk society.*

READING: Grunig and Hunt (1984); L'Etang and Pieczka (1996)

communism As a doctrine rather than a practice, communism refers to societies that have no private property, social classes or DIVISION OF LABOUR. K. Marx held that these societies would be formed gradually after the revolutionary overthrow of capitalist societies. He also noted that these three features are possessed by certain tribal societies, a condition he referred to as primitive communism.

There is considerable doubt as to whether these ideals can be realized in practice in more modern societies. Most communist countries have had some private property, an extensive division of labour and what amounts to a class system based on bureaucratic privilege. The actual development of twentieth-century communist societies produced a debate amongst theoreticians of communism, some of whom held that some private property and division of labour were inevitable. The dramatic collapse of the communist governments of Eastern Europe and the Soviet Union at the end of the 1980s was a consequence of economic debt, lack of popular support, the failure of both political and economic reform, nationalist tensions in many communist societies and the withdrawal of the Soviet army.

SEE ALSO: *socialist societies.*

communitarianism Critics of RIGHTS theory often claim that liberal INDIVIDU-ALISM cannot provide an adequate theory of rights as universal entitlements.

Communitarianism proposes to develop a new theory of rights which gives appropriate attention to COMMUNITY and SOCIAL STRUCTURE. Communitarians argue that there are important collective rights which apply to social groups such as, for example, ethnic communities, religious groups or trade unions. Although there is no inevitable connection between communitarianism and welfare rights, there is a relationship between communitarianism and the benefit theory of rights.

A. MacIntyre (1981) and M. Sandel (1982) argue that in liberal CAPITALISM there are disagreements about values, and that the values which underpin individualistic traditions of rights are incommensurable and hence the legitimation of rights doctrines is uncertain. There is no common morality which could provide a general endorsement of rights. Communitarianism involves a quest to reconstitute the values and moral codes which individualism has disrupted.

Although there are many versions of communitarianism, they share the notion that communities as well as individuals can be rights-bearers. Thus in *The Spirit of Community* (1993), A. Etzioni argues that a communitarian moral system is required to rebuild American society, which has been undermined by individualism. He claims that, for example, individualistic interpretations of rights have encouraged the erosion of the family, which is an essential basis of social order.

SEE ALSO: *associative democracy*; *citizenship*.

READING: Macedo (1990)

community The term community is one of the most elusive and vague in sociology and is by now largely without specific meaning. At the minimum it refers to a collection of people in a geographical area. Three other elements may also be present in any usage. (1) Communities may be thought of as collections of people with a particular social structure; there are, therefore, collections which are not communities. Such a notion often equates community with rural or pre-industrial society and may, in addition, treat urban or industrial society as positively destructive. (2) A sense of belonging or community spirit. (3) All the daily activities of a community, work and non-work, take place within the geographical area; it is self-contained. Different accounts of community will contain any or all of these additional elements.

Many nineteenth-century sociologists used a concept of community, explicitly or implicitly, in that they operated with dichotomies between pre-industrial and industrial, or rural and urban societies. F. Toennies, for example, in his distinction between GEMEINSCHAFT and *Gesellschaft*, treats communities as particular kinds of society which are predominantly rural, united by kinship and a sense of belonging, and self-contained. For many nineteenth-century sociologists, the term was part of their critique of urban, industrial society. Communities were associated with all the good characteristics that were thought to be possessed by rural societies. Urban societies, on the other hand, represented a destruction of community values. Some of these attitudes persist today. However, it became clear that societies could not be sharply divided into rural or urban, communities or non-communities, and sociologists proposed a RURAL–URBAN CONTINUUM instead, along which settlements could be ranged according to various features of their social structure. Unfortunately there was little agreement about what features differentiated settlements along the continuum, beyond an insistence on the significance of kinship, friendship and self-containment. This lack of agreement has made it difficult to compare the large number of studies of individual settlements carried out particularly between

1920 and 1950. In the United States there was interest in urban locations, particularly by the CHICAGO SCHOOL and W. F. Whyte (1961), but in Britain rural societies commanded more attention. All these studies were based on the assumption that the communities were largely self-contained and therefore had some community spirit, but the term community no longer referred to only one kind of social structure. This community study tradition was also important in its development of techniques of PARTICIPANT OBSERVATION but has lost favour recently, partly because communities are not so self-contained as national considerations become important and partly because urban sociologists have become interested in other problems.

More recently, the term has been used to indicate a sense of identity or belonging that may or may not be tied into geographical location. In this sense, a community is formed when people have a reasonably clear idea of who has something in common with them and who has not. Communities are, therefore, essentially mental constructs, formed by imagined boundaries between groups.

The term community continues to have some normative force. For example, the rural community ideal continues to have some grip on the English imagination and town planners often aim at creating a community spirit in their designs.

SEE ALSO: *neighbourhood*.

READING: Crowe and Allan (1994)

community care This refers to the social policy of managing individuals with chronic illness, handicap or major social problems outside an institution. It became an important aspect of welfare programmes in response to fiscal crises and economic cut-backs in the United States and Great Britain. In the 1970s, as a result of governmental fiscal controls, it came to be equated, paradoxically, with private provision. The term is imprecise and refers to a wide range of policies from sheltered housing to DECARCERATION.

SEE ALSO: *community medicine*.

community medicine Since the mid 1950s, in both Britain and the United States, there has been a growing emphasis on the use of community facilities (sheltered housing, community nursing, community mental-health centres and the patient's home with appropriate professional support) for treatment, rather than the general hospital. The concept is in fact general, since it embraces the care of the sick outside such institutions as hospitals and hospices; it also includes primary medical care, family medicine and general practice. The growth of interest in community care is associated with: (1) the view that hospitalization is often not the most appropriate response to the patient's needs, especially in the case of mental illness; (2) disillusionment with the effectiveness of conventional, hospital-based, scientific medicine; (3) the cost of hospital services.

SEE ALSO: *alternative medicine; health-care systems*.

community power A theory of POWER that promotes the view that the ELITE no longer enjoys a monopoly over decision-making, it claims that DEMOCRACY has dispersed the control of resources to the COMMUNITY. Decision-making occurs in a variety of VOLUNTARY ASSOCIATIONS and opinion formation is shaped by local interest groups. It claims that power is not exercised exclusively through centralized processes associated with the STATE and BUREAUCRACY.

SEE ALSO: *associative democracy; communitarianism*.

comparative method All sociological research involves the comparison of cases or variables which are similar in some respects and dissimilar in others. The term comparative method denotes a particular interest in institutional and macro-social factors analysed comparatively across different societies, or in the distribution of other specific phenomena in different societies. A major methodological issue is whether the units of comparison (whole societies, major institutions, religions, groups, and so on) and the indicators chosen to compare differences or similarities are genuinely comparable and can legitimately be used outside their specific cultural settings. Comparative research across societies faces a second dilemma: whether to focus on similarity or difference. Studies that set out to prove some general theory tend to emphasize similarity in support of their hypotheses. For example, the CON- VERGENCE THESIS, that industrial societies were becoming similar, failed to appreci- ate national differences that qualified this model. Conversely, comparative method may become comparative description, which illuminates differences between soci- eties but fails to explain these, other than saying that societies differ in their histories. Comparative method is neither a distinct methodology nor a particular theory, but rather a perspective.

SEE ALSO: *understanding alien belief systems.*

READING: Ragin (1987)

competition A competitive situation is one where individuals with different and opposed interests seek to maximize their own advantages or rewards. In economic theory, the competition between buyers and sellers of commodities in the market is held to reduce prices, equalize profits in different enterprises and promote efficiency of production. The beneficial effects of competition were also emphasized in some early social theories. UTILITARIANISM claimed that competition had benign social consequences because it was the most reliable mechanism for producing general wealth. SOCIAL DARWINISM made a parallel between the struggle for survival in nature and competition between people in society: in each case, the processes of natural selection ensured the survival of the fittest and improved the quality of the species. Institutional attempts to protect the weak, the unintelligent and people regarded as socially inferior – for example, state intervention to alleviate the con- dition of the urban poor – were regarded as interfering with natural selection. This particular movement in sociological theory was closely associated with SPENCER. Popular versions of Spencer's evolutionism overlooked his argument that cooperation was the guiding principle of complex society, while competition was a central characteristic of primitive society. SIMMEL categorized competition as 'indirect' conflict, because competitors try to surpass rather than destroy each other. Because people expend more effort and creativity when they are in competition, there are often significant collective benefits to society as a whole. For example, business people who compete for customers become far more sensitive to consumer needs and so benefit the public at large.

In Marxism, competitiveness is not regarded as a universal, constitutive feature of human nature, but as a specific structural aspect of CAPITALISM. In K. Marx's theory of capitalism, three types of competition can be distinguished: (1) there is competition between capitalists to control the market; (2) there is competition between workers to secure employment; (3) there is competition between capital and labour. It was in this competitive struggle with capitalists that the working class would acquire a revolutionary class consciousness. The final outcome of competitive class struggle would be the destruction of capitalist society.

For M. Weber (1922), competition was defined as peaceful conflict, consisting of attempts to gain control over scarce resources. Regulated competition was associated with social selection (e.g. the competition between academics for limited posts is regulated formally by professional standards of conduct). Unregulated or violent competition was associated with natural selection (such as the struggle for survival between species). For Weber, competitive struggles were an inevitable feature of all social relationships and not specific to capitalism.

For T. Parsons (1951; 1954), competition in capitalism is restrained by a variety of conditions: common values, codes of conduct in professional associations, reciprocity between roles and legal regulations.

A number of modern sociobiologists suggest that aggression is a biological fact that underpins certain aspects of human social life. They adopt a neo-Darwinian perspective, that all organisms seek to reproduce themselves and to pass on their genes. They propose that, in any species, the males who have survived genetically are the ones who have succeeded in competing for females and for food and territory. While violent conflicts over sexual mates, food and territory are no longer the norm in modern societies, natural male aggression can find its outlet in political, social and economic competition. GAME THEORY also assumes that much social interaction is inherently competitive, because the interests of individuals often do not coincide and rational individuals selfishly seek to maximize their own advantages. Game theory attempts to explain, however, under what conditions cooperation may be a rational choice for rational individuals who seek to maximize their advantages, even in competitive situations.

Debates in sociology as to the nature of competition have thus concentrated on: (1) its extent and permanence; (2) whether it is a defining characteristic of capitalism; (3) the presence of regulation which controls competition between individuals.

SEE ALSO: *class struggle; conflict theory; industrial conflict; market; sociobiology; urban ecology.*

complementary medicine See: ALTERNATIVE MEDICINE.

complex society This is a society which has undergone structural DIFFERENTIATION. The term was once popular but is now little used.

SEE ALSO: *Comte; division of labour; Durkheim; evolutionary theory; functionalism; Gemeinschaft; industrialization; industrial society; social change.*

Comte, Auguste (1798–1857) Inventor of the term 'sociology', first publicly used in the fourth volume of his *Positive Philosophy* (1838), Comte was secretary to SAINT-SIMON, and there has long been a debate over the relative importance of these two writers for socialism and sociology.

Comte thought that sociology was a science employing observation, experimentation and comparison, which was specifically relevant to the new social order of industrial Europe. Comte's scientific POSITIVISM was conjoined with an evolutionary view of society and thought which he saw progressing through three stages: theological, metaphysical and positive. Human societies evolve through three major stages of development (primitive, intermediary and scientific). Human thought progressed by a process of decreasing generality and increasing complexity.

Employing an ORGANIC ANALOGY, Comte argued that society, through the division of labour, also became more complex, differentiated and specialized. The DIVISION OF LABOUR, along with language and religion, created social solidarity, but also generated new social divisions between classes and between the private and public domains.

Sociology, standing at the pinnacle of the sciences, was to proceed in terms of an analysis of social dynamics and social statics. The first would consider the general laws of social development, while the second concentrated on the 'anatomy' of society and the mutual interaction between its constituents. Comte studied the functional contribution of social institutions (such as the family, property and the state) to the continuity of social order. While his view of the interconnectedness of elements of the social system anticipated FUNCTIONALISM, Comte's view of sociology is now generally regarded as arcane.

SEE ALSO: *Durkheim; evolutionary theory; sociology.*

READING: Coser (1971)

concentric zone theory E. Burgess, a member of the CHICAGO SCHOOL, argued that cities in industrialized societies take the form of five concentric rings. The innermost ring is the central business district, containing most of the better shops, offices, banks, amusement and service facilities. The second, the ZONE OF TRANSITION, is essentially an area in development as the central business district expands outwards. As a result, it is a run-down area of relatively cheap housing. The third zone contains the homes of manual workers, while the fourth comprises middle-class suburbs. On the fringes of the city is the commuters' zone.

Burgess proposed his theory as an IDEAL TYPE. Real cities would not conform exactly to the five zones, which would be deformed by the existence of communication routes, for example. The theory followed the principles of URBAN ECOLOGY. The zones comprise natural areas created by impersonal forces independent of the intentions of the population. Competition for land determines the arrangement, with those activities able to afford high rents taking the best central sites. Successive waves of migration follow one another with a racial or ethnic group starting in the zone of transition and moving outwards as it prospers.

The theory has been extensively criticized. It has been argued, for instance, that cities are really in the form of sectors, not rings, and that land values may not only be dictated by competition but by cultural values. Many of these criticisms were anticipated by Burgess and the theory remains useful, especially in its depiction of the zone of transition.

SEE ALSO: *natural area.*

READING: Savage and Warde (1993)

conflict theory Social conflict assumes various forms. Competition describes a conflict over the control of resources or advantages desired by others where actual physical violence is not employed. Regulated competition is the sort of peaceful conflict which is resolved within a framework of agreed rules. Markets involve competition, both regulated and unregulated. Other conflicts may be more violent and not bound by rules, in which case they are settled by the parties mobilizing their power resources.

Social theorists in the nineteenth and early twentieth centuries were concerned with conflict in society. Mid-twentieth-century functionalists, however, neglected conflict in favour of a unitary conception of society and culture which emphasized social integration and the harmonious effect of common values. When functionalists did consider the phenomenon, they saw conflict as pathological rather than the normal state of a healthy social organism.

Some sociologists in the 1950s and 1960s attempted to revive what they called 'conflict theory' against the dominant functionalism of the time, drawing on MARX and SIMMEL to this end. Marx had presented a dichotomous model of social conflict, in which the whole of society was divided into the two basic classes representing the interests of capital and labour. Conflict would ultimately transform society. Simmel, while emphasizing the salience of conflict, adopted neither the dichotomous model nor the assumption that conflict would in the end destroy existing social arrangements. He believed that conflict had positive functions for social stability and helped preserve groups and collectivities. L. Coser (1956; 1968) developed the Simmelian perspective to show that conflict was usually functional in pluralistic complex societies. He argued that cross-cutting conflicts, in which someone who was an ally in one dispute was an opponent in another, prevented conflicts falling along one axis and dividing society along dichotomous lines. Complex societies contained a plurality of interests and conflicts which provided a balancing mechanism that prevented instability. R. Dahrendorf (1959) similarly concluded that conflicts were cross-cutting and did not overlap, and, unlike Marx, claimed that the central conflict in all social institutions concerned the distribution of power and authority rather than capital, that it was the relationship of domination and subordination which produced antagonistic interests. He thought that the successful containment of INDUSTRIAL CONFLICT within the economy, so that it no longer spilled over into other institutions, was especially important in this context.

D. Lockwood (1964) developed a distinction, implicit in Marxism, between 'system' and 'social' conflict and integration. System conflict occurs when institutions are not in harmony: for example, when the political sub-system pursues policies which conflict with the needs of the economic sub-system. Social conflict is interpersonal and occurs only within social interactions.

With the decline of functionalism and the revival of Marxist and Weberian approaches to sociology since the 1970s, the older debate about conflict and CON-SENSUS has largely disappeared from social theory. Conflict and cooperation among individuals remains a central concern of GAME THEORY and RATIONAL CHOICE THEORY.

SEE ALSO: *competition; contradiction; institutionalization of conflict; market; social and system integration; social order; systems theory.*

conjugal This term refers to relationships between marriage partners, or between a man and woman living together.

SEE ALSO: *conjugal role; domestic labour; nuclear family.*

conjugal role The tasks typically taken up by husband and wife in the household are referred to as conjugal roles. E. Bott (1957) distinguishes *segregated* conjugal roles, in which husband and wife have quite different tasks within the home, from *joint* conjugal roles in which they have tasks which are more or less interchangeable. Segregated conjugal roles are associated with tight-knit networks of friends and kin which support husband and wife in their separate activities at home, leisure and work. Joint roles, on the other hand, are typically associated with the lack of any such network, perhaps following a period of geographical mobility. A number of studies (e.g. M. Young and P. Willmott, 1973), have apparently shown that there is a trend towards more 'egalitarian' marriages with joint conjugal roles, following the decline of traditional occupations and stable communities and with the increase in the number of employed wives and unemployed husbands, increasing social and geographical mobility, and separation from kin. Other writers, such as A. Oakley (1974), have argued, however, that there has been no serious movement towards joint roles, because women still carry the burden of child care and domestic work of all kinds. J. Gershuny (1992) provides comparative evidence from a number of countries, which supports the argument that there is indeed a trend away from segregated roles, although there still remains a substantial amount of inequality between men and women.

SEE ALSO: *domestic labour; nuclear family; sex roles; symmetrical family.*

conjuncture The actual balance of unevenly developed social and political forces in a society at a particular moment is referred to as the conjuncture. Analysis of specific conjunctures is distinguished from the analysis of the forces acting generally within the MODE OF PRODUCTION, which, it is argued, may be seen only at the abstract theoretical level. For ALTHUSSER, the study of the conjuncture is the basis of Marxist politics because it reveals where political pressure will be most effective.

SEE ALSO: *contradiction.*

connotation/connotative meaning See: DENOTATION.

conscience collective This term played an important part in the sociology of DURKHEIM. While the notion of 'conscience' typically refers to the moral attitudes of the *individual*, for Durkheim *conscience collective* was essentially social and exterior to the individual. It referred to an external normative order or SOCIAL FACT which coerced members of the group to behave and think in certain ways. As the division of labour increased, individualism also developed and the *conscience collective* declined. Societies based on organic solidarity are held together by restitutive law and by reciprocal relationships within the division of labour.

READING: Lukes (1972)

consciousness, class See: CLASS CONSCIOUSNESS.

consciousness, false See: CLASS CONSCIOUSNESS.

consensus The question of how SOCIAL ORDER is established and preserved in any society or social group has been a central issue of social philosophy and sociology. In sociology, following T. Parsons' (1937) treatment, this is technically referred to as 'the Hobbesian problem of order'. Broadly speaking, sociologists can be divided into those who emphasize COERCION as the basis of social order and those who argue that some degree of general consensus over values and norms provides the crucial basis of any society. In practice, of course, most sociological theories of social order conceptualize the bases of order in terms of both normative consensus and physical coercion. However, in Parsonian sociology the central explanation of order is in terms of 'ultimate values' which are internalized and shared by the population as a result of common experiences of socialization within the family. The nature and extent of consensus over social values in human society has given rise to a long-standing debate in modern sociological theory. For example, there is much empirical research into the beliefs of the urban WORKING CLASS which suggests that dominant social values are not completely or consistently accepted by large sections of the population. Furthermore, even where common values are accepted, this acceptance may be merely pragmatic and partial. Some MARXIST SOCIOLOGY has adopted notions similar to that of value consensus, which stress dominant ideology and hegemony. Other forms of Marxism, however, have criticized the idea and have stressed the importance not of unity but of class and class conflict.

SEE ALSO: *conflict theory; dominant ideology thesis; Gramsci; hegemony; Parsons; pragmatic acceptance; value.*

READING: Giddens (1997)

conspicuous consumption See: LEISURE CLASS.

consumer culture See: CONSUMER SOCIETY.

consumer society This term embodies the claim that modern societies are distinctive in that they are increasingly organized around consumption. There is a rapidly growing and somewhat incoherent debate about the characteristics of consumer societies but the following have been discussed. (1) Rising affluence. The inhabitants of Western countries have, in general, had more money to spend on consumer goods, holidays and LEISURE. (2) Working hours have been falling since the beginning of the century. There is now more time available for leisure pursuits. (3) People take their IDENTITY as much, if not more, from their activities as consumers and from their leisure time as from their work. Societies have developed a consumer culture. (4) Because of the AESTHETICIZATION OF EVERYDAY LIFE, there is more interest in the presentation of an image and the construction of a LIFESTYLE, both of which involve the purchase of commodities of various kinds. Consumption of these commodities is organized not around need, but around daydreams. (5) Acts of consumption, the development of a lifestyle, the acquisition of certain goods, are increasingly used as markers of social position. People use POSITIONAL GOODS to demonstrate their membership of particular social groups and to distinguish themselves from others. (6) While earlier in the nineteenth and twentieth centuries social class or race or gender were the major sources of social division, these have been replaced in the late twentieth century by patterns of consumption or CONSUMPTION CLEAVAGES. (7) In consumer societies, consumers gain power and authority at the expense of producers, whether these are producers of goods or professionals offering a service, such as doctors, teachers or lawyers. In some respects, the economic position of the consumer is replacing political rights and duties; the consumer replaces the citizen. (8) Increasing numbers of goods and services, but also human experiences and aspects of everyday life, are being commodified, or offered for sale. The market is extending into all areas of life. Shopping becomes a leisure activity. Many of the contributors to the debate about consumer society are, in effect, arguing that sociological analysis has concentrated too much on production – the experience and effects of paid work – and not enough on consumption.

Although modern societies do indeed have some of these characteristics, it is by no means clear that they have all of them, nor what their significance might be or whether they are to be welcomed. For example, it has been argued that class, race and gender continue to be amongst the most important sources of social differentiation, and that it is only a minority that are involved in the aestheticization of everyday life. Many writers doubt that the consumer society results in the empowering of consumers and argue that it simply represents the extension of capitalist values and further divides the rich from the poor.

SEE ALSO: *affluent society; Adorno; advertising; Bourdieu; capitalism; commodification; Frankfurt School; Marcuse; postmodernity; postmodernism.*

READING: Lury (1996)

consumption See: CONSUMER SOCIETY; CONSUMPTION CLEAVAGES.

consumption cleavages In much sociological work, social class has been taken to be the source of important social divisions or cleavages. Recently, however, a number of sociologists have argued that, for a variety of reasons, class divisions are not nearly as important as they were. Social cleavages are increasingly based on differing patterns of consumption and may cut across social divisions, producing class dealignment. For example, it has been argued that voting patterns are better explained by home ownership than by class membership. Saunders (1990a) has taken this argument further in suggesting that a major division in contemporary societies is between those that are dependent on the state and those who provide for themselves through personal ownership whether this be in housing, pensions, education or health.

Another version of the argument may be found in those writers who suggest that IDENTITY in modern societies is increasingly founded on differences in consumption. People therefore do not derive their identity from their class position or from their work lives but rather from the tastes, habits and consumption patterns that they share with others.

SEE ALSO: *class; consumer society; voting.*

content analysis This is the analysis of the content of communication, which involves classifying contents in such a way as to bring out their basic structure. The term is normally applied to the analysis of documentary or visual material rather than interview data, but the same technique may in fact apply to the analysis of answers to open-ended questions in survey research. Researchers create a set of categories which illuminate the issues under study and then classify content according to these predetermined categories. It is essential that the categories are precisely defined to minimize bias resulting from the judgements of different investigators. This technique produces quantitative data which can be processed by computer and analysed statistically. However, content analysis is sometimes criticized as involving subjective judgements which may create data that are quantifiable but not valid.

SEE ALSO: *coding.*

contest mobility See: SPONSORED MOBILITY.

contingency table See: CROSS TABULATION; LOG LINEAR ANALYSIS.

contingency theory See: ORGANIZATION THEORY.

contradiction Two social activities are said to be in contradiction when, because of their very nature, they are incompatible. The term is used most frequently in MARXIST SOCIOLOGY. For example, there is a contradiction between labour and capital because of the way that capital exploits labour by the extraction of SURPLUS VALUE.

Contradictions, although they are systematic in the structure of society, do not necessarily issue in actual conflict. In the case of capital and labour, the presence of actual conflict will depend on the organization of class forces and the activities of the state. The more fundamental the contradictions involved and the more different contradictions fused together, the more serious will be any resultant conflict.

SEE ALSO: *conflict theory; Marx; systems theory.*

READING: Althusser (1966)

contradictory class location See: CLASS.

control group In social science experiments a control group is a group of people matched as closely as possible on relevant variables with an experimental group. The experimental group is exposed to the independent variable whose effects are being investigated while the control group is not exposed. Any differences which are found between the two groups after the experiment are attributed to the independent variable. For example, in studying the effect of television on children, besides exposing the experimental group to television one has to create a similar group matched by important characteristics (e.g. age, sex, education, class) which is not exposed to television. Without such a control, the investigator cannot tell whether any observed effect is due to television or to some other feature of the environment.

Control groups may also be used when experiments are impracticable. A comparison of two groups is made, matching the members as closely as possible, but where only one group has in the past been exposed to the independent variable. The hypothesis that this variable has an influence is tested by comparing the two groups. This method works from the past to the present and is known as a *cause-to-effect* design. Alternatively, two groups selected because they are known to differ in some significant aspect are matched as closely as possible and their past is investigated to find an explanation of the difference. This is an *effect-to-cause* method.

SEE ALSO: *experimental method; statistical control.*

control of labour See: LABOUR PROCESS APPROACH; MANAGERIAL STRATEGIES OF CONTROL.

convergence thesis This argument claims that the process of INDUSTRIALIZATION produces common and uniform political, social and cultural characteristics in societies which, prior to industrialization, may have had very different historical backgrounds and social structures. All societies converge to a common point because industrialization requires certain characteristics in order to function effectively. These are: (1) an extended social and technical division of labour; (2) the separation of the family from the enterprise and the workplace; (3) a mobile, urbanized and disciplined workforce; (4) some form of rational organization of economic calculation, planning and investment. Theories of industrial convergence suggest in addition that, given the 'logic of industrialism', all industrial societies will tend to be secular, urban, mobile and democratic. The convergence thesis is thus linked, on the one hand, with the END OF IDEOLOGY THEORY in suggesting that industrial

society will be based on a new form of consensus and, on the other, with development theory which regards Western society as the only appropriate model for rapid
economic progress.

There are a number of theoretical problems associated with the convergence
thesis. (1) It is not clear whether all societies must assume a common form with
industrialization or whether considerable institutional variation is compatible with
a common industrial base. (2) There is an ambiguity in whether it is the presence of
the large industrial enterprise, industrialization as a process, or certain technological
conditions of production which is held to be the cause of social convergence. In the
latter case, the argument assumes a crude form of technological determinism which
treats the social context of industrialization as directly dependent on changes in
industrial technique. (3) Not all industrial societies are empirically converging
towards a common pattern. (4) Some people argue that the characteristics of industrial society are those of CAPITALISM. Insofar as social convergence takes place, this
may be explained by the dominance of capitalism rather than by the process of
industrialized production itself. (5) The convergence thesis was typical of the optimistic analysis of industrial society which was common in the early 1960s. The
subsequent experience of industrial decline, inflation and unemployment in certain
industrialized economies has shown that regional imbalance, de-industrialization
and economic decline may create important variations between and within industrial societies.

SEE ALSO: *industrial society; post-industrial society; social mobility.*
READING: Scott (1997)

conversational analysis A relatively recent field of study in sociology, conversational analysis has grown out of ETHNOMETHODOLOGY, especially the work of
H. Sacks. This form of analysis attempts to record patterns of conversation, in order
to uncover the rules that permit communication to proceed in a meaningful and
orderly fashion. The use of natural language in conversations provides order and
management of the social settings in which the conversations take place. Conversational analysis provides *descriptions* of the way in which conversations achieve this
order. It is not concerned with the actual subject matter and content of natural
conversations, but with the rules which organize conversation. Empirical studies
include the way in which the first five seconds of telephone conversation are structured and the manner in which courtroom conversational interaction is ordered.
Conversational analysis represents a move away from the earlier ethnographic
studies conducted by ethnomethodologists, towards more rigorous scientific and
quantitative methods of data collection.

READING: Heritage (1987)

cooperative Voluntary organizations characterized by the absence of a distinct
ownership and capital-providing class, cooperatives are jointly owned and wholly or
in part financed by their members, who also determine policy. The origins of the
cooperative movement are associated with the ideas of C. Fourier in France and
R. Owen in Great Britain in the early nineteenth century. Owen's aim was to create a
self-supporting cooperative community where producers and consumers were the
same people. In practice, cooperatives have usually divided into separate consumer
and producer forms. Owen's community ideal has rarely been realized, though Owen-

ism was the inspiration for the modern Mondragon cooperative community in Spain.

Consumer cooperatives are widespread and have a long and successful history, notably in Great Britain and Sweden. Producer organizations include farming cooperatives which purchase, process and market. These are widespread in Europe and America. Producer cooperatives in manufacturing industry have in the past usually proved unsuccessful. The difficulty of raising sufficient capital and the inadequate management of member-controlled organizations reduced the commercial viability of cooperatives. However, the number of producer cooperatives in Western Europe and the USA has grown. The Mondragon group of cooperatives shows that the financial and managerial problems can be overcome, in which case producer cooperation is highly efficient. The commitment and application of cooperative members to organizational goals exceeds that of employees in conventional firms, and industrial relations are transformed when all employees are co-owners. Cooperatives incorporate socialized ownership as an alternative to conventional capitalism yet retain the market economy, which is why K. Marx and modern Marxists have disparaged them as 'worker capitalism'.

SEE ALSO: *commune*.

READING: Cornforth *et al.* (1988); Whyte and Whyte (1988)

corporate crime This is often associated with WHITE-COLLAR CRIME, such as embezzlement, fraud and 'insider-trading'. Such crimes are rarely notified to the police and the perpetrators rarely appear in the courts. The concept is also employed to identify the damage done to society and the economy by corporations, who may not be acting in a way that is technically illegal, such as engaging in price-fixing or causing industrial pollution.

SEE ALSO: *crimes without victims; criminology*.

corporatism A form of social organization in which the key economic, political and social decisions are made by corporate groups, or these groups and the state jointly. Individuals have influence only through their membership of corporate bodies. These include TRADE UNIONS, professions, business corporations, political pressure groups and lobbies, and voluntary associations. Corporatism may be contrasted with decision-making via the market, in which individuals who make their own private market choices collectively and cumulatively shape society. At the political level, corporatism may also be contrasted with the traditional form of liberal DEMOCRACY in which political decisions were taken only by governments representing the electorate directly.

The theory of the corporate STATE – that the political community includes a number of corporate groups and that individuals are to be represented politically via their membership of these groups rather than as individual electors – was adopted in Italian FASCISM.

Many Western European democracies moved towards a tripartite form of corporatism in the 1970s, and governments made social and economic policy in consultatism and negotiation with the powerful vested interests of trade-union movements and employers' associations. Sociologists have suggested that politicians allowed corporate bodies to influence state decisions in return for these bodies controlling their members: corporations delivered the support of their members in return for an influence over political decision-making. Trade unions restrained their members' strike activity and pay demands, employers aligned the pursuit of their private interests with those of the state, while governments in return protected labour and pursued economic expansion. Corporatism was particularly strong in the Scandinavian nations, the Low Countries, West Germany and Austria. During the 1980s, the effect of economic downturns and increased economic competition was to weaken the trade-union movement and, outside Scandinavia, business and government eroded, but did not totally destroy, tripartite corporatism as they found less need to cooperate with unions to curb worker militancy.

Sociologists disagree whether corporatism represents an attempt by the state to incorporate and pacify militant trade unionism at the cost of employees' interests, or whether it marks the successful use of workers' power to constrain business and the state. Where corporatism survived through the 1980s, employees' interests were in fact better protected than where market forces were allowed to dominate economic life, with lower rates of both unemployment and inflation.

READING: Goldthorpe (1984); Crouch (1992)

correlation It is normal to record a variety of data simultaneously in sociological research: for example, to measure respondents' educational attainments and occupational levels in surveys. If one datum provides information about another, they are associated or correlated. In the example of educational attainments and occupational levels, it is generally found that the higher the occupational level the higher the educational attainment – that is, the correlation is normally *positive*, which means that the values of the two variables tend to increase or decrease together. A *negative* correlation describes the case when the value of one variable increases while the other decreases. There are various types of correlation coefficient that are used with different sorts of data, but all measure the strength of the association between two or more variables. The fact that two variables are correlated does not establish which one is antecedent or causes the other, or indeed that they are causally related at all, since they may both be caused by a third factor and the correlation may be spurious.

counter-culture A term made popular in the 1960s, when student radicals and others formulated new and unconventional theories and policies about politics, work and family life that ran counter to conventionally accepted values and patterns of behaviour. Common themes of the counter-culture included the repressive qualities of conventional family life, the desirability of letting people 'do their own thing', experimentation with drugs of various kinds, and the virtues of sexual freedom.

counterfactual A proposition which states what would have happened had something not been the case. It is often claimed that to make any sociological proposition meaningful and testable, there must be a corresponding counterfactual proposition. For example, to argue that the Industrial Revolution caused the decline of the extended family means that one must have some idea of what would have happened to the family had there not been an industrial revolution. Again, to claim, as in some studies of power, that a particular action is against the interests of an individual or group, one must know what actions *would* be in the interests of that group.

SEE ALSO: *falsificationism*.

credentialism This term refers to a modern tendency in society to allocate positions, particularly occupational positions, on the basis of educational qualifications or credentials. The pursuit of such credentials then becomes an end in itself, a process sometimes known as the 'Diploma Disease'. As a result, not only is the educational process distorted but the qualifications demanded and gained may have very little to do with the skills actually used in a job. Qualifications in the much expanded higher-education system, for example, may merely serve as a method of restricting entry to certain occupations and not as a training for them.

READING: Dore (1976)

crimes without victims In most crimes there is a clearly defined victim. However, there is a limited number of crimes which have no victims, sometimes referred to as 'service' crimes. These include drug abuse, gambling and prostitution. Typically these are not reported to the police, because both parties to the crime derive a 'benefit' from it.

criminal statistics (1) *General principles.* In England and Wales, the official statistics used to estimate the crime rate are based on the recording by the police of notifiable offences. Notifiable offences are in effect those crimes for which a suspect has the right to trial by jury, which marks the difference between more and less serious crimes. In fact, the majority of convictions in British courts are for motoring offences, which do not enter the estimation of the crime rate because, with the exception of reckless driving and the theft or unauthorized taking of a vehicle, they are not notifiable. Notifiable offences that are unknown to the police or that the police choose not to record do not appear in the criminal statistics. The annual rate of increase in recorded crime averaged about 5 per cent between 1970 and 1992 and the number of crimes per 100 people in the population rose from 4 to just over 10. Recorded crime doubled between 1981 and 1991, which probably reflects in part the underlying growth in actual crimes and in part an increase in the amount of reporting. There was, however, a fall in recorded crime at the end of the 1990s.

It is generally agreed that all criminal statistics, including notifiable and unnotifiable crimes, prosecutions and convictions, are unreliable as guides to the actual extent of crime, for several reasons. (i) Crimes known to the police are a small fraction, possibly as low as one quarter, of the total – the crimes unknown to the police constitute the so-called 'dark figure'; many trivial offences are not fully reported, while certain types of serious crime such as fraud, blackmail, incest and rape are also under-reported. (ii) Criminal statistics may also reflect police bias (notably leniency towards women, white people and middle-class offenders) and changes in public opinion about specific crimes such as mugging. (iii) The size and composition of criminal statistics are also shaped by the efficiency, deployment and size of the police force. (iv) Changes in law clearly determine the incidence of crime; for example, attempted suicide and homosexuality between consenting adults ceased to be crimes in the post-war period. (v) There is also judicial bias in the variability of treatment of alleged offenders by the courts. As a result, sociologists tend to treat criminal statistics as evidence, not of actual criminality, but of changes in police practice, public opinion and judicial process; that is, they attempt to go behind the statistics to understand the social processes that determine how these statistics are collected and categorized.

In order to get a better idea of actual rather than recorded crime, many nations initiated crime surveys in the 1960s and 1970s. These large-scale surveys of national populations ask people whether they have been victims of crime. The British government carried out its first crime survey in 1982. British surveys have shown that about 1 in 4 incidents of vandalism, 1 in 3 assaults and 9 out of 10 burglaries involving loss are reported to the police. Many offences that are reported by victims do not get recorded by the police, or are not recorded in the proper category. Incomplete reporting and recording mean that only 30 per cent of all crimes mentioned by victims end up in police records. Surveys do not necessarily provide the 'true' record of crime: they do not cover corporate victims; respondents are likely to understate offences involving drugs, alcohol abuse and sex between consenting partners; and there are obvious problems of fabrication and recall among victims.

SEE ALSO: *crimes without victims; official statistics*.

READING: Box (1971); Bottomley and Pease (1986)

(2) *Recent trends*. The long-term trend indicates that the gradual rise in recorded crime in the 1980s and the steeper rise in the early 1990s was reversed in the late 1990s. There was a fall in nearly all offences between 1995 and 1997. In this period, the police recorded a 12 per cent fall in crimes that compared with a fall of 15 per cent in the British Crime Survey (BCS). For example, burglary fell by 7 per cent, violence by 17 per cent, and thefts of vehicles by 25 per cent. Despite this recent improvement, the number of crimes in England and Wales recorded by the BCS has increased by 49 per cent since 1981.

The most common offences involve some form of theft (around 62 per cent of the total number of offences). In 1997, 62 per cent of BCS offences involving theft amounted to 10,134,000 crimes in England and Wales. A minority of crimes are defined as violent offences (21 per cent), of which the majority are common assaults involving minimal injury (14 per cent). Only 4 per cent involve significant injury such as wounding and 2 per cent are muggings. Thefts from vehicles are the most commonly experienced crime. In 1997, 10.2 per cent of vehicle-owning households experienced such a theft. In 1997, 5.6 per cent of households had a burglary or attempted burglary.

Violent incidents are disproportionately experienced, most noticeably by young men between the ages of 16 to 24 years. Whereas these young men were 5 per cent of the BCS sample, they experienced 25 per cent of all violent crime. By contrast, young women in this age group were 7 per cent of the BCS sample and experienced 7 per cent of all violent crime.

Burglary also shows a pattern of unequal risk. Whereas 8.5 per cent of victims of burglary came from the inner city, only 3.4 per cent were in rural areas. Burglary is more common in council estate areas, in areas of high physical disorder (in terms of perceived levels of vandalism, graffiti, litter and rubbish), and in the north-east; it is less prevalent in rural regions, non-council estate areas, cities of low physical disorder and in the eastern regions. For example, 8.3 per cent of the victims of burglary came from the Yorkshire and Humberside region, the figure for Wales was 4.8 per cent.

In conclusion, although there was a significant change in the trends of crime between 1995 and 1997, the general pattern of post-war crime in England and Wales was upwards. The risks of crime are unequally distributed in the community in terms of class, gender, age and region. People who live in areas with the least material advantages are also more likely to become victims of crime.

READING: Walker (1995); Watson (1996); Mirrlees-Black *et al.* (1998)

criminology This branch of social science is the study of criminal behaviour; that is, infractions of the law, especially criminal law. It involves: (1) the study of the causes, nature and distribution of crime in society; (2) the study of the physical, psychological and social characteristics of criminals; (3) the study of the victims of crime and their interaction with criminals; (4) the study of criminal careers, cultures and values. Criminology, in addition to the study of crime, examines the effectiveness of methods of controlling crime. Criminology also embraces the related discipline of PENOLOGY. There are a number of conventional criticisms of traditional forms of criminology: (1) the legal definition of criminal behaviour is inappropriate from a sociological perspective; (2) if the notion of 'crime' is replaced by 'deviance', it becomes clear that no single theory of DEVIANT BEHAVIOUR can explain the complexity of such heterogeneous phenomena; (3) the overlap between the theoretical objectives of criminology and the policy objectives of law enforcement agencies calls into question the objectivity and autonomy of criminological research. In the 1960s and 1970s, new theoretical and empirical research traditions emerged in response to criticisms of criminology by MARXISM, FEMINIST SOCIAL THEORY and SYMBOLIC INTERACTIONISM.

SEE ALSO: *addiction; crimes without victims; corporate crime; criminal statistics; critical criminology; delinquency; delinquent drift; deviance amplification; differential association; feminist criminology; gang; realist criminology; social pathology; victimology; white-collar crime; women and crime.*

READING: Downes and Rock (1995)

critical criminology A perspective on crime which drew on MARXISM and CONFLICT THEORY, it emerged in the 1970s as a critical response to both traditional CRIMINOLOGY and to LABELLING THEORY. Also called 'radical criminology', it studied crime as a social and historical product of CAPITALISM, in which criminals are also victims of class inequality and state oppression. In research terms, it concentrated on the problems of police accountability, the repressive character of prisons, and the class bias of the criminal justice system. Critical criminology was in turn criticized for a propensity to romanticize crime and to neglect features of criminal behaviour, such as race, gender and age, that are not related to class. Critics also claimed that it produced no practical alternative policies, because it was merely reacting to dominant assumptions.

SEE ALSO: *class; feminist criminology; realist criminology.*

READING: Taylor, Walton and Young (1973)

critical theory This form of social analysis is often equated with the FRANKFURT SCHOOL of critical sociology in the twentieth century, but the notion of criticism is clearly older and more comprehensive than this simple equation would suggest. Criticism means the exercise of negative judegment, especially concerning manners, literature or cultural products in general. Textual criticism developed as a weapon of religious conflict during the Reformation, when biblical criticism was held to be a negative but objective judgement on conventional ecclesiastical practice and dogma. Criticism then came to mean uncovering hidden assumptions and debunking their claims to authority, as well as simple fault-finding. G. Hegel saw human history as a progression of human self-awareness which constantly transformed and went beyond existing social constraints. In Hegelian philosophy, therefore, criticism was more than a negative judgement and was given the positive role of detecting and unmasking existing forms of belief in order to enhance the emancipation of human beings in society.

This Hegelian critique of ideological forms of consciousness was enthusiastically espoused by the so-called Left Hegelians who proposed to apply 'critical criticism' to all spheres of human activity, especially in relation to religion and politics. It was in this context that MARX and F. Engels framed their project (1845b) of criticizing society so as to unmask religion and all other forms of bourgeois thought.

For Marx, the idea of critique was not simply a negative *intellectual* judgement on ideological systems of thought, but a practical and revolutionary activity. Under the slogan 'The philosophers have only interpreted the world in various ways; the point is, to change it', Marx (1845) began to develop the idea that, in order to be effective, philosophical criticism had to become an instrument of the working class in its revolutionary struggle against the BOURGEOISIE. For Marx, critique was now conjoined with PRAXIS. While this idea of praxis, or practice, is particularly complicated in Marxism, in one respect it signifies that intellectual criticism can only be actualized fully in the activity of men in society. This conception of the relationship between valid knowledge of the world and revolutionary practice was taken one step further by G. Lukács (1923), for whom true consciousness was the exclusive property of the proletariat as a class acting in its real interests, even when these interests were clouded by 'false' consciousness.

The development of critical theory by the Frankfurt School arose out of their dissatisfaction with the use of 'criticism' by institutionalized Marxism to legitimate political decisions of the Communist Party. Critical theorists also had a deeper perception of the value and importance of 'critique' in its Hegelian form. By its very nature, criticism has to be *self*-critical. Consequently, the Frankfurt School developed an open attitude to any philosophical tradition which held out the promise of human emancipation through social critique. Critical theorists recognized that, since CAPITALISM had changed fundamentally, it was impossible to remain entirely within the framework of Marx's criticism of nineteenth-century capitalism. The principal target of critical theory, therefore, became the claims of INSTRUMENTAL REASON (in particular, natural science) to be the only valid form of any genuine knowledge. The critique of the rational foundations of science and capitalism led critical theory not only to reappraise classical German philosophy, but to debate M. Weber's analysis of capitalism as a rationally organized 'iron cage'. The result was an account of society which tried to fuse Weber's view of RATIONALIZATION with Marx's theory of capitalism, accepting some of the pessimism of the former but with some of the liberating potential of the latter.

The dominant figure of contemporary critical theory is HABERMAS. In common with other critical theorists, he is interested in self-emancipation from domination. However, he stresses rather more the ways in which capitalism has changed, noting the emergence of large-scale corporations, the growing association of the state and capitalism and the decline of the public sphere.

SEE ALSO: *hermeneutics; Marxist sociology; neo-Kantianism; positivism; Verstehen.*
READING: Bronner and Kellner (1989)

cross-sectional design data When data are collected at only one point in time, rather than at several points over time, they are described as cross-sectional.

Cross-sectional research designs cannot provide evidence of change or how processes work over time, for which a longitudinal or PANEL STUDY design is required.

cross tabulation A common way of presenting data is in two-way tables which relate the values of one variable to those of another. The example below is of a cross tabulation of voting intention by social class among 200 people.

	Conservative	Labour	Total
Middle Class	80	20	100
Working Class	30	70	100
Total	110	90	200

The purpose of cross tabulating variables is to see what association they have with each other. It is possible to elaborate the analysis by bringing in further variables. For example, one might introduce male and female categories into the illustration above, to see if the relationship between class and voting is the same for both men and women. The tables that present cross tabulations of variables are normally referred to as *contingency* tables.

SEE ALSO: *log linear analysis*.

cult In its anthropological usage, a cult is the beliefs and practices of a particular group in relation to a god or gods. In sociology, it is often associated with the discussion of church–sect typologies. The cult is regarded as a small, flexible group whose religion is characterized by its individualism, syncretism and frequently esoteric belief. While it has been suggested that religious sects emphasize fellowship and cults enhance private, individual experience, in practice it is often theoretically difficult to distinguish religious groups in these terms. The modern proliferation of cults, often with specifically Oriental religious ideas, has brought into question the nature and extent of secularization in Western industrial societies.

SEE ALSO: *church*; *new religious movements*; *sect*; *secularization*.
READING: Heelas (1996)

cultural capital The phrase was initially used by BOURDIEU in his critique of official sociology of education, *Reproduction in Education, Society and Culture* (1970), with J.-C. Passeron. His claim was that children of middle-class parents acquire from them cultural capital, endowments such as cultural and linguistic competence, and it is these competences which ensure their success in schools. Because such cultural capital is not transferred to working-class children, school assessment systems, which appear neutral and objective, in fact legitimate economic inequality between social classes by reference to the ideological term of natural abilities. In his later studies of universities and academics (1984a), Bourdieu developed a more complex differentiation of *social* capital (power secured through family members, or other networks), *symbolic* capital (such as reputation or honour), *economic* capital (the ownership of economic assets such as property, shares and investments) and finally *cultural* capital (educational qualifications, and distinction in the world of art and science). Cultural capital is thus used by Bourdieu in *Distinction* (1979) to distinguish between different fractions of the dominant class. The fraction of the dominant class that derives its power from culture (primarily educational achievement) will always be finally subservient to the dominant economic class, and therefore Bourdieu describes their class position as 'ambiguous'. Their educational achievements and cultural dispositions separate them from the working class, but they do not belong fully to the dominant economic class. The notion of cultural capital is an important component of Bourdieu's analysis of the hierarchical structure of taste.

SEE ALSO: *classroom interaction; classroom knowledge; cultural reproduction.*

cultural deprivation The failure of children from the working class and some ethnic minorities to reach the same average levels of educational achievement as middle-class children was often explained in terms of cultural deprivation, the failure of the home and neighbourhood to provide these children with the motivational and linguistic attributes necessary for success within the educational system. It is rarely used now, because it implies personal inadequacy when the issue may simply be one of cultural *difference*: the school embodies social values and conceptions of appropriate knowledge which may differ from those of large sections of the population. The emphasis now is on the CULTURAL CAPITAL of the middle classes rather than the deprivation of others.

SEE ALSO: *Bernstein; classroom knowledge; educational attainment; restricted code.*
READING: Keddie (1971)

cultural lag The idea of a cultural lag was developed by W. F. Ogburn (1950) in response to crude economic DETERMINISM in which cultural, political and social phenomena change in direct and immediate response to changes in the economic basis of society. Ogburn noted that changes in culture were not always or necessarily congruent with economic changes. For example, he argued that economic changes influencing the division of labour in the family had not been accompanied by a change in the ideology that 'a woman's place is in the home'. A cultural lag exists when two or more social variables, which were once in some form of agreement or mutual adjustment, become dissociated and maladjusted by their differential rates of change. Although Ogburn's formulation of the problem of social change is no longer central to contemporary sociology, his hypothesis of cultural lag did anticipate debates in sociology about the relationship between the economic base and cultural superstructure of society.

SEE ALSO: *base and superstructure; social change.*

cultural relativism (1) This is a method whereby different societies or cultures are analysed objectively without using the values of one culture to judge the worth of another. A favoured way of achieving this aim is to describe the practices of a society from the point of view of its members. The method is one of the hallmarks of 'modern' anthropology in contrast to the ETHNOCENTRISM of nineteenth-century anthropology. (2) A more commonsense meaning is that beliefs are relative to a particular society and are not comparable between societies.

SEE ALSO: *comparative method; rationality; understanding alien belief systems.*

cultural reproduction This term was introduced into British sociology by P. Bourdieu (1973), who sees the function of the education system as being to reproduce the culture of the dominant classes, thus helping to ensure their continued dominance.

SEE ALSO: *cultural capital; dominant ideology thesis; hegemony; social reproduction.*

cultural studies An area of academic work on the boundary between the humanities and the social sciences. It lacks any kind of unity, being eclectic both in its theoretical perspectives and in its subject matter. It stretches from economic studies of the CULTURE INDUSTRIES to literary–critical analyses of television programmes.

SEE ALSO: *culture; popular culture.*

culture Over the last two decades there has been a burgeoning interest in the concept of culture. There has not unfortunately been much precision in its use. As a result, the concept has been used in a number of different ways which tend to overlap one another.

(1) Culture is contrasted with the biological. Anthropologists, particularly, use 'culture' as a collective noun for the symbolic and learned, non-biological aspects of human society, which include language, custom and convention, by which human behaviour can be distinguished from that of other primates. Human behaviour is seen as culturally and not genetically or biologically determined.

(2) Culture is contrasted with nature. In the Anglo-French intellectual tradition, the concept of culture was often used synonymously with civilization and was opposed to barbarism or a state of nature. In German social thought, by contrast, culture (*Kultur*) was held to be the repository of human excellence, artistic achievement and perfection, while civilization was regarded as a process of material development which threatened individual culture by creating an urban MASS SOCIETY.

(3) Culture is contrasted with structure. For some sociologists, societies consist of a framework of social institutions – the social structure – and culture, which provides a kind of social cement keeping the structure intact. PARSONS, for example, distinguished social structure from culture, which is responsible for integration and goal attainment.

(4) The cultural is contrasted with the material. For many Marxist sociologists, culture is the realm of beliefs, ideas and practices whose form is determined, or heavily influenced, by the economic structure. In this sense, culture has the same meaning as IDEOLOGY.

(5) Culture as way of life. Social groups may be differentiated from each other by their differing attitudes, beliefs, language, dress, manners, tastes in food, music or interior decoration, and a host of other features which comprise a way of life. Such differentiations may occur at different levels. For example, youth cultures may be separated from each other by their different ways of life, as may generations or social classes. At the other end of the scale, it is clear that whole societies have different cultures or ways of life. It is often claimed that modern societies are becoming increasingly culturally fragmented. In these circumstances, it becomes less clear whether or not such societies can be said to have a common culture.

(6) High culture and popular culture. In this last usage, the sociological sense of culture is more like everyday usage in referring to social practices that are artistic in the broadest sense, whether that describes musical or literary tastes or interests in fashion or television. Sociological work in culture in this sense explores the differences between high culture and POPULAR CULTURE or investigates the way in which culture is created, transmitted and received.

SEE ALSO: *audience; civilization; consensus; cultural relativism; custom; dominant ideology thesis; Frankfurt School; Gramsci; hegemony; Marx; Marxist sociology; nature/*

nurture debate; norm; organizational culture; postmodernism; sociobiology; subculture; value; youth culture.

READING: Jenks (1993)

culture, organizational See: ORGANIZATIONAL CULTURE.

culture, popular See: POPULAR CULTURE.

culture industries A term of uncertain reference usually used to designate those organizations that produce popular culture; that is, television, radio, books, magazines and newspapers, popular music. It is also used more widely to include all cultural organizations; for instance, museums, advertising agencies and sporting organizations. The importance of these industries is two-fold. First, they have a considerable and growing economic importance in most Western societies. Second, contemporary everyday life is infused with images of very many kinds, most of which are produced by the culture industries. There is an AESTHETICIZATION OF EVERYDAY LIFE, in which cultural artefacts, whether they be the visual images of television or magazines, or the musical images of popular music, have become inseparable from people's lives.

According to the FRANKFURT SCHOOL, and particularly ADORNO, the culture industries ensure capitalist HEGEMONY by providing a bland and undemanding popular culture. More recent analyses suggest that culture industries actually produce contradictory messages, some of which are hegemonic and some more resistant.

SEE ALSO: *dominant ideology thesis; popular culture; postmodernism.*

culture of poverty It is sometimes argued that the poor create distinctive patterns of behaviour and belief, notably a fatalistic acceptance of being poor and an inability to do anything that might help them to lift themselves out of POVERTY. This condition is disabling and ensures that the poor remain in poverty. It is also reproduced over the generations in a related *cycle of deprivation*, whereby children from poor or deprived families are socialized by their parents into the culture and grow up to be poor too. Originated by O. Lewis (1961) to describe slum dwellers of the Third World, both terms have been used to describe the poor in contemporary developed societies. The pejorative implications of the concept, that the poor are to blame for their own plight and that parents raise children to be socially deprived in turn, have been contested. Critics point to the following: the failure of society, and particularly of governments, to provide the poor with the resources to move out of poverty; the active strategies of mutual aid and self-help that many poor people develop in order to cope with poverty; the existence of a POVERTY TRAP that makes it more difficult for the poor to lift themselves out of poverty.

custom This term is used mainly in anthropology, to denote established patterns of behaviour and belief. It refers both to the routines of daily life and to the distinctive features which mark off one culture from another.

SEE ALSO: *culture.*

cyberspace Sometimes confused with VIRTUAL REALITY, it refers to electronically mediated and simulated space.

SEE ALSO: *globalization; information superhighway; McLuhan; time–space distantiation.*

cycle of deprivation See: CULTURE OF POVERTY.

Dahrendorf, Ralph (b. 1929) A German sociologist who has contributed to class theory and role theory, Dahrendorf was formerly a professor of sociology in Germany, then a European Economic Community Commissioner, then director of the London School of Economics, and finally head of St Anthony's College, Oxford. His major works are: *Class and Class Conflict in an Industrial Society* (1959); 'Conflict after Class' (1967a); *Society and Democracy in Germany* (1967b); *The New Liberty* (1975); *Life Chances* (1979).

SEE ALSO: *conflict theory; imperatively coordinated association; institutionalization of conflict; service class.*

Darwinism See: SOCIAL DARWINISM.

Davis–Moore debate See: FUNCTIONAL THEORY OF STRATIFICATION.

death rate The crude death rate is the number of deaths per 1,000 living members of a population per year. The standardized death rate is the number of deaths for any given COHORT or age group per year. The standardized rate is a common measure in demography since, in this particular instance, the death rate among people of 65 years of age is obviously much higher than that among teenagers. Comparisons of crude death rates and crude birth rates provide the sociologist with basic measures of FERTILITY and population increase. For example, the 'net rate of natural increase' is the excess of the crude birth rate over the death rate.

SEE ALSO: *birth rate; demography.*

decarceration From the 1960s to the 1980s, in both the United States and Europe, a new social policy emerged to reduce the number of residential mental-health patients in more or less permanent institutional care. Radical critics claimed that institutionalized care produced what R. Barton called 'institutional neurosis' (1959), namely that incarceration produced dependency and depression. In Italy in the 1970s, Franco Basaglia and the Psichiatria Democratica movement advocated voluntary psychiatric evaluation and promoted out-patient services. In the United States, the Community Mental Health Centers Act of 1963 presented community medicine as an effective alternative to institutionalization. Economic critics of incarceration suggested that it was expensive and inefficient. As a result of both these left-wing and right-wing criticisms, there was an extensive programme of decarceration, as a result of which asylum populations were significantly reduced. In *Decarceration* (1977), A. Scull has claimed that the process of de-institutionalization was a cynical exercise of cost-cutting, which did not result in the full development of community-based care as an alternative. As a result, the mentally ill experienced a 'revolving door syndrome' in which decarceration from institutions was followed by regular re-admissions.

SEE ALSO: *anti-psychiatry; community care; Goffman; medicalization; total institution.*

deconstruction Originally a critical method for the analysis of the meaning of philosophical and literary works by breaking down and reassembling their constitutive parts ('sentences'). It claims that conventional interpretations of texts concentrate on the author and the overt meaning of the work. Deconstructionism attempts (1) to undermine the importance of the author by concentrating on the structure of texts and on their membership of a literary *genre*, which is seen to exist independently of the author, and (2) to grasp the implicit meanings of texts by exposing their underlying and hidden assumptions. The method is associated with the idea of 'decentring'; that is, attacking the assumption that the structure of a text has a unifying centre providing an overarching significance. Decentring aims to disperse, not to integrate meaning. These implicit meanings are often exposed by (1) discovering the gaps or absences ('aporias') and (2) concentrating on the minor details or peripheral aspects of texts ('margins') such as the footnotes and digressions, where it is argued that significant meanings are often obscured or hidden.

Deconstruction brings about a reversal of the overt and official meanings of a text in favour of a subversive reading. This reversal is achieved by identifying and then reorganizing the explicit contrasts or differences of a text (such as good/bad, male/female, rational/irrational) which are the key elements of a narrative. Deconstructionists such as P. de Man (1983) and J. Derrida (1982) often claim that deconstructionism cannot be reduced to a simple recipe or method for reading texts. However, deconstructive literary methods have in fact begun to influence sociologists who claim that 'society' is a text that can be deconstructed in order to expose its implicit meanings. Critics claim that deconstructive methods are arbitrary, random and subjective, and that society has an objective character which is non-textual and non-discursive.

SEE ALSO: *Heidegger; postmodernism; poststructuralism; structuralism.*

READING: Norris (1988)

deductive See: HYPOTHETICO-DEDUCTIVE METHOD; INDUCTION.

deferential worker This is a working-class conservative who defers to the old-established ruling class as the natural leaders of society. D. Lockwood (1966) suggested that deferential workers were to be found in farming and small firms, where regular contact with and dependence upon superiors created deference and led to the assimilation of these superiors' attitudes and values. This was disputed by H. Newby (1977).

SEE ALSO: *working-class conservatism.*

deferred gratification A concept used to refer to behaviour in which sacrifices are made in the present in the hope of greater future reward. It is often said that this is a feature of middle-class upbringing, accounting for the relatively greater educational success of middle-class children. It is also claimed that deferred gratification is a precondition of both the accumulation of capital and the striving for success that were important in the earlier stages of CAPITALISM.

SEE ALSO: *achievement motivation.*

definition of the situation The importance of the subjective perspectives of social actors for the objective consequences of social interaction is often summarized in sociology by the notion of 'defining the situation'. It was first specified by W. I. Thomas (1928) in a well-known aphorism – 'if men define situations as real, they are real in their consequences'. One implication of this sociological viewpoint is that, for sociology, the truth or falsity of beliefs ('definitions of the situation') are not important issues; what matters is the outcome of social interaction. Thus, if a particular minority group is regarded as 'a threat to society', then there will be major objective consequences – exclusion, intimidation, expulsion – even where the minority group is not a real threat to social order. This approach to what Thomas (1927) called 'situational analysis' has had an important influence on subsequent studies of the conditions for stable interaction and role-taking in SYMBOLIC INTER-ACTIONISM and ETHNOMETHODOLOGY.

degradation-of-work thesis See: DE-SKILLING.

de-industrialization The importance of manufacturing industry has declined in a number of industrial societies, when measured by the share of manufacturing in total output or the proportion of the population employed in manufacturing. In part, this relative decline simply reflects the growth of output and employment in the service sector of the economy which changes the relative shares of manufacturing and services. Employment changes further reflect the implementation of labour-saving technologies which reduce the volume of employment in manufacturing for any given level of output. De-industrialization, defined as a decline in manufacturing, is a feature of such structural shifts within capitalist economies. In the UK and USA, however, de-industrialization has also followed the declining international competitiveness of manufacturing industries in these countries. Britain, for example, became a net importer of manufactured goods in the mid 1980s for the first time since the Industrial Revolution and has experienced an absolute decline in manufacturing capacity.

SEE ALSO: *industrialization*.

delinquency This term covers a wide variety of infringements of legal and social norms, from behaviour that is merely a nuisance to criminal acts such as theft. In criminology, it is typically specified as juvenile delinquency to indicate the high level of indictable offences committed by young males between the ages of 12 and 20 years. The typical crimes of younger males are larceny and breaking and entering, while violent crimes are more common in the age groups over 17 years. Most sociological theories of juvenile delinquency attempt to explain these crimes in terms of the organization of urban gangs, delinquent subcultures, and the limitations on opportunity for working-class males and deprived social groups. For example, the CHICAGO SCHOOL analysed juvenile delinquency in terms of the social structure of local neighbourhoods and the role of the PEER GROUP in the SOCIALIZATION of adolescent generations. Alternatively, delinquency has been explained as the product of anomie or as the result of DELINQUENT DRIFT. Critical criminologists have occasionally regarded delinquency as an expression of opposition to dominant values and social inequality.

SEE ALSO: *adolescence; criminal statistics; criminology; deviance amplification; deviant behaviour; differential association; gang; labelling theory; Merton; social problems; subculture.*

delinquent drift An explanation of delinquent conduct developed by D. Matza (1964; 1969), it claims that delinquents often 'neutralize' legal and moral norms by subjectively defining such norms as inapplicable, irrelevant or unimportant. Once a person feels indifferent towards the law, he or she may commit unlawful acts without a strong sense of guilt or shame. A delinquent who thus neutralizes legal norms may be said to drift into a SUBCULTURE of DELINQUENCY, which makes him or her available for delinquent acts.

SEE ALSO: *criminology; deviant behaviour; neutralization.*

delinquent subculture A concept used in the explanation of DEVIANT BEHAVIOUR, it describes the formation of deviant cultures as a social response to disadvantage and DEPRIVATION, especially by youth groups and minorities. A subculture is typically a variation on the dominant culture rather than a rejection of it. Delinquent youth cultures often accept the material goals of society, but do not have legitimate means to achieve them.

SEE ALSO: *anomie; Merton; youth culture.*

democracy In ancient Greek society, democracy meant rule by the citizens as opposed to rule by a tyrant or aristocracy. In modern democracies, citizens do not rule directly, but typically elect representatives to a parliament by means of a competitive political party system. Democracy in this sense is often associated with the protection of individual freedoms from interference by the state. Sociological discussion of democracy has gone through several phases. Many nineteenth-century accounts, like that of A. de Tocqueville, concentrated on the social consequences of allowing greater political participation to traditionally subordinate groups, and this theme has been developed in the work of the MASS SOCIETY theorists. More recent work has explored the connections between social development and parliamentary democracy. Various attempts have been made to correlate democracy with degree of industrialization, level of educational attainment, and national wealth. It has been argued that democracy is naturally encouraged by higher levels of industrial development which create pressures for wider participation in politics. Other approaches have investigated the way in which democracy may lead to bureaucracy in TRADE UNIONS and the relationship between democracy and CITIZENSHIP.

There is debate as to whether modern democracies represent their citizens or protect individual liberties. Some theorists of the STATE argue that democrats only serve the interests of an elite or a capitalist class.

SEE ALSO: *associative democracy; capitalism; citizenship; elite; industrial democracy; Michels; political participation; political parties; voluntary associations; voting.*

READING: Dahl (1989); Pierson (1996)

democracy, industrial See: INDUSTRIAL DEMOCRACY.

demographic transition The theory of demographic transition attempts to specify general laws by which human populations change in size and structure during INDUSTRIALIZATION. The theory holds that pre-industrial societies were characterized by stable populations which had both a high DEATH RATE and BIRTH

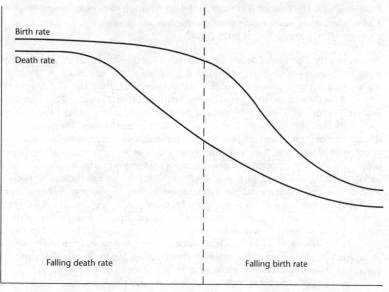

Time

RATE. In the first stage of the transition, death rates begin to fall with improvements in nutrition, food supply, food distribution and improved sanitation and health standards. Since the birth rate continues to remain high relative to the declining death rate, there is a rapid increase in the size of the population. In the second stage, changes in social attitudes, the introduction of cheap forms of contraception and increases in life-expectancy create social pressures for smaller families and for a reduction of FERTILITY. The populations of advanced, urban industrial societies are now stable, with low birth and death rates. The growth pattern of human populations is thus held to be S-shaped, involving a transition from one type of demographic stability with high death and birth rates to another type of plateau with low death and birth rates. This demographic transition can be illustrated by the above diagram.

Demographic transition theory can be criticized under three broad headings. (1) It may provide a *description* of the general features of demographic change in certain Western societies, but it does not provide a sophisticated causal explanation because the theoretical connections between the key variables, and their nature, are often not precisely stated. (2) As a *general* theory, the notion of a common process of population change is difficult to reconcile with specific population changes in modern Africa, Asia and Latin America. (3) Recent research in historical demography also presents a far more complex picture of European population history. The stability of pre-industrial populations in north-eastern Europe was caused by low fertility as a consequence of late marriage and celibacy, while the population stability of societies which lay east of a line connecting Trieste and St Petersburg was the result of early marriage with strictly enforced low fertility. These revisions of traditional transition theory now place greater importance on marriage practices and family structure than on simple technological change in the explanation of population growth.

SEE ALSO: *aging; demography; social change; urbanization.*

READING: Wrong (1966); Andorka (1978)

demography This can be defined as the analysis of the size, structure and develop-ment of human populations, although it is occasionally employed to cover the study of animal populations. The crude statistics of population size and change are provided by the relationship between the birth and death rates and by migration and emigration. Two central features of population structure are the sex and age composition of human groups. Demographic analysis also includes the geographical distribution of populations, population and natural resources, genetic composition, population projections, family planning, and demographic features of the labour supply. Because the demography of human populations is crucial for economic and social planning, the development of demographic analysis has become important for national and international government forecasting. Population change in both size and structure has a direct bearing on, for example, the availability of housing, education, health and employment. In Britain, for example, the proportion of those past retiring age (women over 60 and men over 65) rose from 6.8 per cent in 1911 to 18.2 per cent in 1998. This has clear implications over a wide area from the provision of health, welfare and housing services to the nature of family relationships and the perceived obligation on family members to care for the elderly.

Partly in response to government requirements and partly because of the nature of demographic data, demographers have developed sophisticated mathematical models of population change and structure which permit statistical forecasting, population projections and the creation of actuarial life-tables. It is now common-place, therefore, to distinguish between formal or mathematical demography, which is concerned with the mathematical structure and functions of human populations, and social or historical demography, which studies the historical conditions of population change such as the nature of DEMOGRAPHIC TRANSITION.

The demographic characteristics of human populations are clearly of major impor-tance for any sociological understanding of human society. Despite these obvious connections between demography and sociology, it is perhaps surprising that the two disciplines have tended to develop as separate and distinct approaches to human society. Although the question of population density played an important part in early sociological theories of social contract and division of labour, subsequent sociological theory and research did not take the demographic features of society to be of central *analytical* significance in sociological explanation. While demographers were inclined to ignore the cultural and social factors which mediate between population and environment, sociologists have neglected population variables between society and environment.

This mirror-image ignorance between demography and sociology has now changed fundamentally with recent developments in the social history of human populations, which is centrally concerned with such questions as marriage practices, bastardy, family structure and generally with the impact of social conditions on FERTILITY, MORTALITY and MIGRATION. Historical demography employs the method of *family reconstitution* in which parish records are used to study the major demographic events – births, deaths and marriages – of each family. The use of this method by, for example, the ANNALES SCHOOL transformed sociologists' understanding of the family. In particular, it helped to destroy the myth of the EXTENDED FAMILY in pre-industrial Europe. Historical demography, especially under the impact of the Cambridge Centre for the Study of Population and History, has made a major contribution to the re-evaluation of conventional sociological perspectives on the family, fertility and social class, and the social aspects of population change. This expansion in historical demography has consequently made important contributions to the sociological analysis of SOCIAL CHANGE by improving our understanding of the relationship between population change, social structure and technological improvement.

SEE ALSO: *aging; birth rate; census; cohort; death rate; Malthus; nuclear family; sex ratio.*

READING: Wrigley and Schofield (1982); Coleman and Salt (1992)

denotation This refers to the specific meaning that a word, image, message or sign has. For example, the denotative meaning of the word 'pig' is of a farm animal which is the source of meat of various kinds. This meaning is contrasted with CONNOTATION. Connotative meaning refers to the much wider range of associations that the sign may have. For example, 'pig' not only has a narrow denotative meaning, it also always evokes a range of associations, particularly centred round being a dirty animal living in unclean surroundings. These connotations enable the word to be used no longer to refer to the animal but to a person of unclean or uncouth habits. The range of connotations of a sign will depend on the context in which it is used. For example, the connotations of 'pig' in Muslim religious discourse will clearly differ from those in a farming magazine.

SEE ALSO: *semiotics.*

dependency theory The theory of dependency can be understood as a critical response to the *laissez-faire* model of international trade and economic development which can be traced back to A. Smith's (1776) explanation of the economic benefits of the DIVISION OF LABOUR. Smithian theories of international trade suggest that economic growth is maximized by regional specialization and the reduction of trade tariffs. Since natural resources, climate and labour supplies are unequally distributed between societies, each society should specialize its production around these 'natural gifts', so that international trade exchanges will maximize productivity in certain raw materials, goods and services.

Dependency theory was advanced by P. Baran (1957), who argued that the economic development of industrial societies in the West rested on the expropriation of an economic surplus from overseas societies. Third World countries were underdeveloped as a consequence of their precarious reliance on export-oriented primary production (agricultural and mineral produce). The theory was further elaborated by A. G. Frank (1969), who analysed UNDERDEVELOPMENT in terms of a global network of exploitation between metropolis and satellite societies. Dependency theory argues that the global economy cannot be conceived in the Smithian manner as a system of *equal* trading partners precisely because the superior military, economic and political power of the centre (the industrial societies) imposes conditions of unequal exchange on the periphery (underdeveloped societies). Historically, colonialism undermined industrial production in the Third World by imposing the import of manufactured goods from the colonial power and insisting on the export of cheap agricultural and mineral commodities. In modern times, the industrial societies have maintained this system of unequal exchange in other ways. They distort and retard industrial development in Third World societies: partly by competing with Third World manufactured products in the latter's home and export markets; partly by locating their own factories in Third World countries, in order to take advantage of cheap labour, but transferring only labour-intensive and low-technology industrial processes which preserve technological backwardness. Dependent societies are therefore obliged to give undue weight to the production of raw materials (cotton, rubber, tea, minerals and so forth), but the world markets for such commodities are highly volatile and unpredictable. Thus it is argued that the system of dependency between centre and periphery, while no longer organized under direct colonialism, is still maintained through the power of multinational corporations. Dependency theory has a close affinity with the WORLD-SYSTEM THEORY later developed by I. Wallerstein (1974).

There are several criticisms of the concept. (1) Third World societies differ among themselves and are therefore not homogeneous. (2) Apart from Japan, all the dynamic and modern industrial economies of the Pacific Rim (e.g. Hong Kong, Malaysia, Mexico, Singapore, South Korea, Taiwan) were only a few decades ago members of the Third World periphery and now challenge the economic supremacy of the older industrial societies, which flatly contradicts the dependency thesis. (3) It ignores the contribution of internal factors within various Third World societies to the explanation of their relative lack of development.

SEE ALSO: *centre/periphery; globalization; imperialism; internal colonialism; new international division of labour*.

READING: Mouzelis (1988)

dependent/independent variables In sociological accounts of the relationships between variables, a phenomenon that is explained or caused by something else is called a *dependent* variable, while the causal or explanatory variable is referred to as *independent*. For example, in social mobility studies the dependent variable is usually the level of occupational attainment of individuals while the independent variables include other phenomena that may explain this level, such as the occupations of parents and the educational achievements of the individuals concerned.

deprivation Sociological analysis defines deprivation broadly as inequality of access to social goods. It includes POVERTY and wider forms of disadvantage. M. Brown and N. Madge (1982), surveying the huge volume of research sponsored jointly by the Social Science Research Council and the Department of Health and Social Services in Britain in the 1970s, concluded that the concept was in fact slippery and fraught with problems. Researchers have adopted a wide range of operational definitions, measurement has proved extremely difficult, while the fact that deprivation may occur in several areas of social life diffuses the concept further. *Multiple deprivation* refers to the tendency noted in some studies for inequalities of access in different areas to overlap. Thus low income or UNEMPLOYMENT may go together with poor housing, poor health and access to inferior education. The multiplication of deprivation seems particularly prevalent in inner-city areas in Britain. *Transmitted deprivation* refers to a view that deprivation is transmitted across generations.

SEE ALSO: *distribution of income and wealth; poverty trap; relative deprivation; social mobility; welfare state*.

derivations See: PARETO.

descent groups A descent group is any social group in which membership depends on common descent from a real or mythical ancestor. Thus a lineage is a unilineal descent group in which membership may rest either on *patrilineal* descent (patrilineage) or on *matrilineal* descent (matrilineage). In patrilineal descent, kinship is traced through the father, in matrilineal through the mother. In *cognatic* descent, all descendants of an ancestor/ancestress enjoy membership of a common descent group by virtue of any combination of male or female linkages. However, cognatic descent is sometimes used synonymously with either *bilateral* or *consanguineal* descent. A clan is a *unilineal* descent group, the members of which may claim either patrilineal descent (patriclan) or matrilineal descent (matriclan) from a founder, but do not know the genealogical ties with the ancestor/ancestress. A phratry is a grouping of clans which are related by traditions of common descent. Mythical ancestors are thus common in clans and phratries. Totemic clans, in which membership is periodically reinforced by common rituals such as sacred meals, have been of special interest to social anthropologists and sociologists of religion. Where the descent groups of a society are organized into two main divisions, these are known as moieties (halves).

The analysis of descent groups is crucial for any anthropological study of pre-industrial society, but in most Western industrial societies the principle of descent is not prominent and descent groups are uncommon. In modern Britain, for example, we recognize our cognates as kin and surnames are patrilineally acquired, but there are no descent groups as such.

SEE ALSO: *agnatic*; *cognate/cognatic*; *endogamy*; *exogamy*.
READING: Keesing (1975)

de-schooling This is the proposition that the formal educational system not only excludes certain social groups but also, in emphasizing formal, abstract knowledge, underrates the importance of life-experiences. Originally developed to apply to Third World societies, the idea has been extended to developed societies in order to promote the organization of informal educational systems which build on the learners' previous knowledge and experience.

de-skilling There has been a long-running debate over the effects of technological change on employees' skills. Writers in the 1960s and 1970s, for example D. Bell (1974), believed that the average skill requirements of industrial work were being upgraded, with a consequential transformation of the occupational structure and an expansion of the middle class. H. Braverman (1974) rejected this view, suggesting that manual and lower-level non-manual jobs were being de-skilled. He believed that the strategy of employers was to reduce the skills required in their production processes, often by means of new technologies which simplified tasks. He saw the possession of skills as providing workers with power to resist managerial domination at work, because skilled workers were in short supply on the labour market and because production systems could not function without their expertise. Braverman saw employees becoming proletarian rather than middle class. More recently, the theory of FLEXIBLE SPECIALIZATION has suggested that de-skilling was a managerial strategy associated with FORDISM and is no longer dominant, because the technologies used in modern production systems require a wider range and higher levels of skill among the workforce.

Evaluation of these competing accounts involves several difficulties. (1) The direction of occupational change in all advanced societies is for lower-skill occupations to decline and higher-level, knowledge-based occupations to expand, leading to the growth of the middle class. Therefore, the *average* skill levels of populations are increasing. However, within this overall increase, it remains a possibility that certain categories of jobs (e.g. manual work in industry) might also be losing their skill requirements. (2) Skill is a social construct as well as a reference to real attributes of knowledge and/or manual dexterity, and is thus an ambiguous concept. Official occupational classifications show the skill levels of jobs to be increasing, yet among lower-level occupations at least, some of this apparent increase may be the result of an upwards reclassification of jobs whose 'real' skill level has not increased. (3) Organized resistance among employees may affect definitions of skill; for example, some craft unions in Britain for a long time successfully retained the skilled label for their members, who were paid accordingly by managers and kept their traditional craft control over certain aspects of the production process, even though the work had less 'real' skill than before. (4) There is a distinction between *jobs* and *workers*. Jobs may be de-skilled but for various reasons workers may not. When de-skilling takes place during periods of economic growth, the actual number of jobs available to skilled workers may increase even though they decline as a proportion of all jobs. De-skilling in the past often resulted from new industries with lower skill requirements growing alongside older ones: the loss of skills which might show through in statistics would not reflect any de-skilling of existing workers and jobs in existing industries and firms, but the changes in the industrial structure. (5) The evidence cited by those who believe a particular category of jobs (notably manual work in manufacturing industry) has been de-skilled or re-skilled is of poor quality. Typically, small numbers of case studies of individual workplaces are cited, without any evidence that these are representative of workplaces in general. There have been no adequate, large-scale, representative investigations of the effects of new technology on jobs and work skills. However, surveys of employees' *perceptions* of their jobs indicate that most people, in most types of jobs, believe that new technology has raised the skill levels of their work.

SEE ALSO: *automation; labour process approach; proletarianization.*

READING: Gallie *et al.* (1998)

determinism Usually a term of abuse in sociology, determinism is used in several senses. (1) Theories are said to be deterministic to the extent that they emphasize the causal primacy of social structure to the exclusion of the autonomy or 'free-will' of the human subject. Explanations have to be sought in the nature of social structure, not in the characteristics of individuals. (2) Marxist sociology is often accused of using an economic determinism in which all social phenomena are explained in terms of the economic structure or RELATIONS OF PRODUCTION. (3) Technological determinist theories are those that suggest that social change is dependent on technological change. (4) Occasionally social scientists argue that social phenomena are to be explained by reference to biological or genetic characteristics. These would manifest a biological determinism.

SEE ALSO: *agency and structure; base and superstructure; methodological individualism; reductionism; sociobiology; technological determinism.*

development, sociology of See: SOCIOLOGY OF DEVELOPMENT.

deviance amplification This term was originally coined by L. T. Wilkins (1964) who used the expression 'deviation amplification'. It suggests that much of the alleged deviance in society is the unintended consequence of police control, mass-media coverage and popular reaction to deviant stereotypes. The theory suggests that distorted information and ignorance about minorities in a MASS SOCIETY produce inappropriate responses to perceived deviance. In turn, this distorting knowledge results in a further amplification of deviance. Thus, societal reaction and deviant response create a 'spiral of deviance' by which relatively minor patterns of deviance may be amplified. The concept of deviance amplification has been particularly useful in studies of police reaction to drug abuse and sexual offences. It has been argued, for example, that the identification of drug-users as evil or immoral leads to legislation and police action which places the users into a category of deviants or offenders, which in turn leads to calls for further action and another round of police intervention. The theory of the spiral of deviance was criticized by J. Ditton (1979) for failing to show how these spirals are eventually terminated, diminished or abandoned. The theory of amplification was associated with LABEL-LING THEORY and the concept of STIGMA as an explanation of crime and deviance. While the theory may be particularly relevant to certain crimes (e.g. sexual offences), it may be inapplicable in others (e.g. murder). Public reaction to crime is in fact far more variable and ambiguous than deviancy theory would suggest.

SEE ALSO: *deviant behaviour; folk devils; stereotypes.*

READING: Downes and Rock (1995)

deviance disavowal An addition to the theory of DIFFERENTIAL ASSOCIATION as an explanation of DEVIANT BEHAVIOUR, it describes the processes of disavowal by which individuals who have been labelled 'criminal' or 'deviant' frequently deny responsibility for their actions. The principal way of denying individual responsibility is generally to blame 'society'.

SEE ALSO: *labelling theory; Lemert.*

deviant behaviour The study of deviant behaviour or the sociology of deviance is most adequately understood as a reaction against traditional CRIMINOLOGY. There are three important areas where criminology and the sociology of deviance have diverged.

Criminology was historically largely concerned with the infraction of legal norms, whereas deviancy research has taken a much broader definition of deviance as any socially proscribed departure from 'normality'. Thus, many different forms of behaviour may be socially condemned or challenged even though the behaviour is not specifically illegal – foul language, keeping 'bad company', habitual failure to keep appointments, and heavy drinking would be obvious examples. The sociology of deviance thus takes a far broader, more heterogeneous category of behaviour as its object of study than is the case for traditional criminology. It also tends to include any behaviour which is socially defined as 'deviant' as an operational definition. Deviancy studies have embraced a great diversity of behaviour from drug abuse to football hooliganism to witchcraft as behaviour which is labelled as deviant.

The second area of difference is that traditional criminology concentrated on the causes of crime which were seen to reside, as it were, within the individual criminal, whereas the sociology of deviance maintains that at least some categories of criminal behaviour are the result of the imposition of social control on subordinate or marginal social groups. Paradoxically the enforcement of law may have the unintended consequence of amplifying deviance in society. Deviancy theory has been particularly concerned with the role of criminal STEREOTYPES and STIGMA in the creation of deviant careers.

Thirdly, there was little analytical distinction in criminology between the existence of crime in society, the criminal personality or character and the criminal act. It seemed that to explain why criminals existed was also to explain the presence of crime in society. The sociology of deviance suggests that the question of deviance in society and the making of a deviant should be kept analytically separate.

The criminological definition of crime as simple infractions of legal norms raises a variety of problems. Legal definitions are subject to change (with judges' decisions and with changes in legislation) so that 'crime' is an unstable, shifting phenomenon. On the other hand, the notion that deviance is simply any deviation from accepted, common normative standards implies that societies are, or must be, characterized by some normative consensus. An alternative view is that modern industrial society does not have any cultural uniformity or value consensus, but on the contrary is typified by a wide pluralism in values and norms. In this case, the distinction between 'normality' and 'deviance' becomes blurred and imprecise. The claim that 'deviance' is simply behaviour so labelled runs into similar difficulties. It presupposes that the social reaction to deviance is unambiguous and normally sufficient to confer a deviant stigma on the offender – in other words, it assumes some form of value consensus.

The assumption of a deviant identity is normally assumed to involve a successful process of stigmatization, social isolation, membership of a deviant subculture and acceptance of a deviant role. In this perspective, the deviant is the product of definite social processes which ostracize individuals from 'normal' roles and groups, forcing them to adopt deviant self-conceptions and restricting the availability of conventional roles and activities. Primary deviance, the initial infraction of social norms, leads through social isolation to secondary deviance. For example, if a person is sentenced for some sexual offence, such as homosexual abuse of children, this may severely limit the range of 'normal' sexual contacts such an individual might subsequently make. The isolation from normal sexual interaction may further increase the likelihood of additional deviance. In order to cope with social isolation and stigmatization, the deviant may find support in membership of a deviant SUBCULTURE and thereby adopt the role of permanent deviancy. E. Lemert (1951; 1967) made the distinction between primary and secondary deviation in order to draw attention to the importance of social reactions to deviance. Individuals who commit deviant acts find that they need to cope with negative social reactions. The process of coping may involve individuals in redefining themselves in ways that promote further deviance.

Underlying this model is the idea of a CAREER. The deviant career may be seen as a process of development over time, leading through identifiable stages towards the end state of permanent deviancy. The end may be in doubt to participants until it is reached, but each stage of the unfolding career progression is recognized by the deviant and other people. As just described, career has a strong meaning: there is a conventional and structured pattern of rule-breaking which over time socializes an individual into deviance. A weaker use is simply that any deviance can be described after the event as having a pattern. While the strong version may help us to understand deviant careers in sexual and drug offenders, it is less relevant to other forms of crime such as murder. It also assumes that deviants uniformly accept and adopt external social labels as personal self-conceptions. There has been very little exploration of the possible conflicts and contradictions between such social labels and personal identities in the social formation of the deviant. The limitations of the symbolic interactionist paradigm, however, have brought into prominence the need for a theory of deviance which incorporates the notion of 'social control' as a central feature.

SEE ALSO: *addiction; Becker; deviance amplification; delinquency; delinquent drift; differential association; gang; Goffman; labelling theory; moral panics; norm; social problems; symbolic interactionism.*

READING: Downes and Rock (1995)

deviant subculture See: SUBCULTURE.

diachronic Although originally used specifically in linguistics, diachronic is now more widely used to refer to the analysis of change, while *synchronic* refers to the analysis of static states.

dialectical materialism MATERIALISM rejects idealist explanations of social and other phenomena and suggests that *all* phenomena are material. The notion of *dialectic* expresses the view that development depends on the clash of contradictions and the creation of a new, more advanced synthesis out of these clashes. The dialectical process involves the three moments: thesis, antithesis and synthesis. K. Marx used the notion to account for social and historical events, but ENGELS extended the scope of dialectical analysis so far as to establish it as a general law of development that applied equally in social, natural and intellectual spheres. He believed both that the real world, whether of society or nature, developed according to dialectical sequences of contradiction and synthesis, and that dialectical logic was the means by which one could comprehend this development.

SEE ALSO: *historical materialism.*

READING: Kolakowski (1978a)

dialogic A term coined by M. Bakhtin to describe cultural texts such as novels, films or plays which are made up of several discourses or systems of meaning that interact or conflict. The contrast is with monologic texts that have a single meaning or DISCOURSE. Bakhtin cites Dostoevsky's novels as dialogical texts and Tolstoy's as monological.

READING: Bakhtin (1981)

differential association A general theory of criminal behaviour developed by E. H. Sutherland (1934) on the basis of an earlier theory by G. Tarde. It attempts to explain crime in terms of cultural transmission; crime is learned within primary groups whose members are criminally inclined. Individuals become delinquent because of an excess of definitions favourable to law violation over definitions which are not favourable. The theory is in fact more concerned with differential definitions than differential association. It was subsequently developed and expanded by D. R.

Cressey (1955), D. Glaser (1956), and Sutherland and Cressey (1955). The theory was important as a critique of explanations which treated criminals as abnormal persons, because it located the cause of crime in general social processes. While the theory may be useful in the study of professional criminals who have a deviant career, it is less relevant where crimes are isolated acts. It is not much used in modern CRIMINOLOGY.

SEE ALSO: *deviant behaviour.*

READING: Lemert (1967); Downes and Rock (1995)

differentiation A notion with a long history in sociology, differentiation is mainly used in theories of social change. Social or structural differentiation refers to a process whereby sets of social activities performed by one social institution become split up between different institutions. Differentiation represents an increasing specialization of the parts of a society, giving greater heterogeneity within the society. For example, whereas the family once had reproductive, economic and educational functions, in modern societies specialized institutions of work and education have developed outside the family.

For classical nineteenth-century sociology, differentiation was an important concept in the analysis of social change and in the comparison of industrial and pre-industrial societies. There was often an explicit analogy between the social and the biological. For SPENCER, for example, differentiation was a necessary accompaniment of the growth in size of both biological and social aggregates. As units grow, there must be differentiation of structures if the unit is to survive. With increased specialization of parts, there is a corresponding requirement for a greater interdependence and integration of parts.

In the 1950s, sociologists developed classical themes by tying differentiation to functionalist or evolutionary theories of social change. PARSONS, for example, argued that social evolution had proceeded by variation and differentiation from simple to progressively more complex forms. He showed that SOCIAL SYSTEMS differentiate into sub-systems, each of which has distinct functions with respect to various environments which include other sub-systems. This process continues over time, producing a greater range of sub-systems, each with its own peculiar structure and function, all tending to the general enhancement of adaptive capacity.

A good example of the empirical use of the concept of differentiation was provided by N. Smelser (1959). He tried to analyse nineteenth-century industrialization in terms of the differentiation of family structure in relation to the changing economy. There is a sequence of change where an existing structure generates discontent, which eventually leads to a more differentiated structure.

There are some similarities between the concepts of differentiation and DIVISION OF LABOUR, except that the latter mainly concentrates on the specialization of tasks within the economic sphere. Occasionally differentiation is used, not as a concept in theories of social change, but to indicate the way in which various groups in a society are separated from one another and ranked along a hierarchy of status or wealth. In this sense it is equivalent to social STRATIFICATION. The concept of structural differentiation has little support in contemporary sociology, because of its association with EVOLUTIONARY THEORY and FUNCTIONALISM.

SEE ALSO: *Comte; Durkheim; international division of labour; organic analogy.*

READING: Parsons (1966)

diploma disease See: CREDENTIALISM.

discourse This is a body of language-use that is unified by common assumptions. For example, FOUCAULT describes the existence of discourses of madness – ways of talking and thinking about madness and associated practices – which have changed over the centuries. In the early medieval period, the mad were not seen as threatening but almost as possessing an inner wisdom. In the twentieth century the discourse of madness emphasizes the condition as an illness in need of treatment. In the intervening centuries there have been other discourses of madness, treating madness and the mad in quite different ways. For Foucault there may also be similarities (or articulations) between discourses of different topics at any one time. He suggests that the discourse of political economy in the eighteenth and nineteenth centuries, for instance, takes the same *form* as the discourse of natural history. However, it is also important to stress that, although discourses may overlap or reinforce each other, they may also conflict. For example, at certain moments in the history of Western societies, different and often contradictory discourses of the individual have coexisted, some of which stress a freedom to act, others of which emphasize the individual's duty to society.

Radical views of the concept of discourse, largely inspired by Foucault, argue that the world is constituted by discourse. In particular, our knowledge of the world is discursively determined. For example, to identify someone as mad is a discursive product, because it only makes sense within a set of classifications that is established by a particular discourse of madness. Other discourses might see quite different behaviour as mad. This is not to say that there is no such thing as madness caused, perhaps, by the presence of particular chemicals in the brain, it is only to say that the designation 'mad' only has meaning within a specific discourse. All this implies that discourses make certain things sayable, thinkable and doable but others not. Sociological attention concentrates on the social effects of this characteristic of closing off possibilities. Take, for example, IDENTITY and POWER. Discourse will define identity, describe what characteristics are possible for a person. For example, contemporary Western societies have particular discourses of gender which dictate what it is – and what it is not – to be a man or a woman. This determination of identity is a closing-off of possibilities and, hence, is an exercise of power.

In many ways, the concept of discourse resembles that of IDEOLOGY, but without the latter's involvement in class relations and its insistence that there is a separate realm of truth. The definition of discourse as an ordered and structured framework within which people see their world has proved to be useful. It has, however, been criticized for its apparent relativism and for a failure to distinguish what is inside a discourse and what outside.

SEE ALSO: *interpellation; mental health.*
READING: Barratt (1991)

discrimination See: PREJUDICE.

disembedding When social relationships are removed from the purely local environment that gives them meaning, they are said to be disembedded.

SEE ALSO: *reflexive modernization.*

disorganized capitalism See: CAPITALISM; POST-FORDISM.

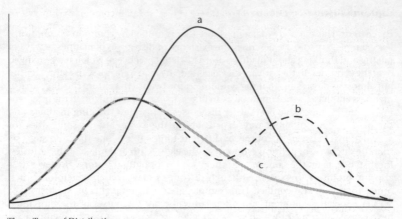

Three Types of Distribution
(a) Unimodal Symmetrical
(b) Bimodal
(c) Skewed

distribution In statistics this refers to the set of values, together with their relative frequencies, of any variable, often expressed graphically. Sociologists need to ascertain and then explain the particular shape of any distribution. The diagram above shows three common types of distribution.

A commonly encountered unimodal symmetrical distribution is the *normal* distribution with mean 0 and variance 1. This forms the basis of probability theory and many important statistical measures derive from its mathematical characteristics, including the measure of variability known as the STANDARD DEVIATION. Empirically, distributions in many different situations often do closely approximate this normal distribution.

distribution of income and wealth The spread of material resources among the population is an important indicator of social inequality, while changes in this distribution over time indicate whether society is becoming more or less equal. The investigation of the spread of personal income and wealth, however, is fraught with difficulty because of inaccuracies in the data, the problem of deciding the relevant unit of analysis (whether to use individuals, families or households), how to assess the non-monetary benefits derived from government expenditure, and the way individuals' positions may change over the life-cycle.

One simple way to present data about the distribution of income is to compare original income (that received by households from employment, occupational pensions and investments) with post-tax income (which equals original income plus state benefits minus income taxes, VAT and national insurance). The tax-benefit system clearly has an effect on the distribution of income. In 1992 in the UK, for example, the top decile (the one-tenth of the population at the top of the income distribution) had an original income thirty times that of the poorest decile. After making allowances for taxes and benefits, however, the top decile had an income eleven times greater than the bottom decile.

From the 1940s to the 1970s, the trend was for post-tax income to become more equal. From the late 1970s, however, the distribution of income has become more unequal. In the period 1977–88 the richest quintile's proportion of total post-tax income rose from 37 per cent to 44 per cent, while the proportion taken by the rest of the population fell. Households in the top quintile (one-fifth) in effect took income from all four of the other quintiles, most particularly from the poorest two. The total income of the poorest tenth of the population actually fell in the period 1979–92.

There are a variety of factors responsible for this reversal. For those in work, the disparity in hourly wage rates rose rapidly over the period: wages for the lowest paid hardly changed at all in real terms while high wages grew by 50 per cent. At the same time, during the 1980s more people were dependent on state benefits, partly because of rising unemployment. The value of these benefits, compared with the wages of those in work, fell because benefits are pinned to prices. Lastly, the tax system has done nothing to correct these rising pre-tax inequalities and the discretionary elements of the tax system have actually shifted the burden of taxation away from the better off. While in the period from the late 1970s there has been a move to greater inequality in many countries, it has been greater still in the UK than in any other country, with the exception of New Zealand.

Wealth distribution is more difficult to investigate because of the greater unreliability of the data, which depend largely on estate tax returns that are inaccurate and so require extensive adjustment, the difficulty of establishing a consistent set of data over time, and the problem of whether to define wealth simply as marketable assets or to include non-marketable assets (e.g. the capital value of state and occupational pension schemes). Taking marketable assets as the measure, the wealthiest 10 per cent in the UK owned more than one-half of the marketable property in 1989. A good deal of the nation's wealth is in the ownership of houses. If these are taken out of wealth measures, inequality is sharper still. In 1989 the proportion of marketable wealth, less the value of houses, taken by the wealthiest 1 per cent of the population was 28 per cent. Historically, over a long period, there has been some equalization of wealth. Since 1923, the share of the top 1 per cent has declined significantly from about 61 per cent to about 32 per cent. However, this has essentially been a redistribution within the richer half of the population and the poorer half has not increased its share. Moreover, there is evidence that the narrowing of wealth differences slowed down, or even stopped, in the period 1976–92. For example, in 1976 the richest 1 per cent owned 50 per cent of all wealth, while in 1992 they still owned 49 per cent. This period, therefore, showed a reversal of the older trend to greater equality in both income and wealth.

SEE ALSO: *class; poverty; stratification; welfare state.*

READING: Hills (1995)

division of labour This concept has been used in three ways: (1) in the sense of the *technical* division of labour it describes the production process; (2) as the *social* division of labour, it refers to differentiation in society as a whole; (3) as the *sexual* division of labour, it describes social divisions between men and women.

(1) The eighteenth-century economist A. Smith (1776) used this term to refer to the extreme specialization in the process of production that results from minutely subdividing work into limited operations performed by separate workers. He recom-

mended this technique to raise the productivity of labour, by increasing people's dexterity as they endlessly repeated one simple task, reducing time lost in shifting between tasks, and simplifying operations in a way that facilitated the introduction of machinery. C. Babbage (1832) noted another advantage: the separation of work into components, some of which were simpler than others and all of which were simpler than the whole. This enabled the employer to purchase cheaper (less skilled) labour to do the simpler jobs instead of using expensive, skilled workers to do the whole process as before. The division of labour thus forms the basis of modern industrial production.

While classical political economy had focused on the positive consequences of the division of labour in enhancing profitability, MARX, in his early writings, associated the division of labour with social conflict. It was a primary cause of social class inequality, private property and ALIENATION. In capitalist society, it was associated with the dehumanization of labour, because it destroyed all the interesting and creative aspects of work, leaving only boring and repetitive operations. In his later works, he suggested that the technical division of labour was required in any industrial society, and would continue even under socialism and the abolition of private property and inequality, indicating that class and the division of labour were separate phenomena. Some Marxist sociologists assert that the extreme division of labour found in many firms is not technically required for efficiency and that managers use it to increase their power in the workplace by weakening the control over production of skilled operatives. Unlike specialization which allows those with the greatest aptitude to do various expert activities, the division of labour tries to reduce all specialisms to simple components which anyone can do.

(2) While COMTE recognized that the division of labour tended to increase social solidarity by creating mutual relations of dependence between individuals, he also emphasized negative aspects of the process which were divisive of society. Following this view, DURKHEIM thought that the division of labour in modern societies created a new basis for social integration which he called 'organic solidarity'. The growing complexity and differentiation of society created a new basis of reciprocity arising from socio-economic specialization rather than from commonly held beliefs.

(3) While in classical political economy the concept referred to the specialization of technical and economic processes, some modern sociologists have extended and elaborated the concept to include, for example, the sexual division of labour, the division of activities and roles between men and women. While this sexual division is often explained biologically by reference to the reproductive functions of women, feminists see these divisions as an effect of PATRIARCHY and as a feature of the separation of the domestic domain and the public sphere in capitalist society.

SEE ALSO: *de-skilling; differentiation; domestic labour; labour market segmentation; evolutionary theory; new international division of labour; labour process approach; scientific management roles; women and work.*

divorce The legal dissolution of a valid MARRIAGE while both partners are still alive, leaving them free to remarry. Divorce rates have increased markedly in most industrial societies in recent times, from 2.1 people per thousand of the married population in Britain in 1961 to 13.4 people per thousand in 1995. Divorce rates expressed in this way are a little crude since they ignore the age structure of society. A more meaningful method of measurement is to express the divorce rates as the number of divorces per thousand people who were married in a particular year. On this basis, it is estimated that two in five marriages contracted in the 1990s will end in divorce.

Rates vary: divorce rises with early childbearing, pre-marital pregnancy and childlessness; people who marry in their teens or early twenties are more likely to divorce than those who marry later; the longer the marriage lasts the lower the propensity to divorce; people in lower socio-economic groups have higher divorce rates. The increased propensity to divorce does not necessarily reflect any growth in family disorganization, because it appears that many marriages used effectively to break down though they did not end in divorce. Legal changes have made divorce easier, in particular the 1971 Divorce Reform Act which added 'irretrievable marriage breakdown' as a reason for divorce to the older notion of matrimonial offence, when one or both parties had to be 'guilty' of cruelty or adultery. Social values have also changed and now sanction divorce as an appropriate response to marital disorganization. Lastly, the position of women has altered and they are more likely to petition for divorce. Marriage, however, remains a popular institution and two-thirds of divorcees will eventually remarry; 14 per cent of all marriages in 1961 were remarriages involving at least one divorced partner, but by 1994 the proportion had risen to 36 per cent.

The rise in divorce rates has been the major cause of the rise in the number of SINGLE-PARENT FAMILIES, even if the parents remarry eventually. The rate of remarriage among divorcees has also increased the number of reconstituted families; that is, those families with children in which one or both parents have been divorced.

READING: Coleman and Salt (1992)

domestic division of labour See: DOMESTIC LABOUR.

domestic labour This term refers to those tasks in the household that are needed to keep it going from day to day, including cooking, cleaning, child care and looking after the sick and elderly. The domestic division of labour, or the allocation of domestic tasks between men and women, is notably unequal, with women taking on very much the greater burden. The introduction of machines of various kinds has not helped greatly, for this has often meant the transfer of a task from men to women as it has become mechanized, and women have set higher standards which their families come to expect. The growth of women's paid employment outside the home has not altered the division: women continue to perform the same domestic chores as well as working outside. Even when men are unemployed, women still take on the bulk of domestic labour. There is some evidence, however, that the balance between men and women is altering. One study (Gershuny, 1992) showed that over the period from 1974/5 to 1987, husbands of full-time employed wives doubled the amount of time they spent in cooking and cleaning, although women still carried the major burden.

The division of labour between men and women in the home is reproduced in employment, for women also tend to have routine and badly paid jobs. Furthermore, women's domestic work is largely unpaid, although it is obviously necessary for a successful economy and society for people to be fed, cared for and reproduced. Two interpretations have been offered of this apparent paradox. First, it has been argued that women are exploited by men who have services performed for them free of charge. Secondly, a number of writers have suggested that women's work, and the institutions of the family generally, serve a function for capitalism in feeding, clothing and caring for workers (and future workers) without any cost: it is capital that exploits women. In a sense, both interpretations are correct. Women's domestic labour reproduces the inequality between men and women and it also subsidizes the economy.

SEE ALSO: *conjugal roles; nuclear family; patriarchy; sex roles; symmetrical family; women and work.*

READING: Morris (1990)

dominant ideology thesis Many Marxists have explained the political passivity of subordinate classes as the consequence of ideological INCORPORATION. They interpret K. Marx as claiming that the ruling class everywhere establishes its own ideology as dominant in society, and that this indoctrinates subordinates who uncritically accept it as true. The thesis has been criticized both on theoretical grounds, that it is not a correct interpretation of what Marx actually believed, and empirically, that throughout history subordinate groups have developed their own beliefs and frequently rejected those of dominant classes. A less crude version of the doctrine was provided by GRAMSCI in his notion of HEGEMONY.

SEE ALSO: *discourse; ideology; social order.*

READING: Abercrombie *et al.* (1980)

domination A term often used in a general sense to indicate the POWER that one social group has over another, such as the domination of the old over the young, or men over women. WEBER used it in a more specific sense to mean 'the likelihood that a command within a given organization or society will be obeyed'.

SEE ALSO: *authority.*

Dore, Ronald P. (b. 1925) Formerly director of the Centre for Japanese and Comparative Industrial Research, and visiting professor at Imperial College, London, he has made a major contribution to the understanding of modern Japan in *City Life in Japan* (1958), *Land Reform in Japan* (1959), *Education in Tokugawa Japan* (1965), *British Factory, Japanese Factory* (1973), *Shinohata* (1978) and *Flexible Rigidities* (1986). He has also written on economic development and, in *The Diploma Disease* (1976), on the role of education in developing societies.

SEE ALSO: *credentialism.*

Douglas, M. (b. 1921) A British social anthropologist whose field work was completed in the Belgian Congo (Zaïre) in 1949–50 and 1953, Douglas has made major contributions to such diverse topics as magic and witchcraft (1970a), pollution (1966), risk (1982), with A. Wildavsky, institutional forms (1986), social meanings (1973, 1975), and consumer behaviour (1978), with B. Isherwood. Her work is integrated by an interest in how groups respond to risk and uncertainty, and her intellectual development was significantly influenced by E. Evans-Pritchard's work (1937) on WITCHCRAFT among the Azande (Douglas, 1980). For example, in *Purity and Danger* (1966) she showed how notions about pollution help to establish social order against uncertainty and danger, and how the human body functions as a metaphor of social stability. She has also developed a theory of social relations which is referred to as the grid/group dichotomy (1970b). The group variable refers to the strength of collective attachment to social units; the grid refers to social constraints on individuals which result from ascribed STATUS. She has also been critical of utilitarian theories of consumption (1978), with B. Isherwood. Her other works include: *The Lele of the Kasai* (1963); *Cultural Bias* (1978); *In the Active Voice* (1982a); *Essays in the Sociology of Perception* (1982b); *Risk and Blame* (1992).

SEE ALSO: *body*; *profane*; *risk/risk society*; *trust*.

dramaturgical This approach within SYMBOLIC INTERACTIONISM is particularly associated with GOFFMAN. The basic idea is that in interaction people put on a 'show' for each other, stage-managing the impressions that others receive. Social roles are thus analogous to those in a theatre. Thus people project images of themselves, usually in ways that best serve their own ends, because such information helps to define the situation and create appropriate expectations.

SEE ALSO: *sociodrama*.

dual-career families This is a term introduced by R. N. Rappoport and R. Rappoport (1971; 1976) to designate families in which both husband and wife have careers. These families should be distinguished from those in which both husband and wife are in paid work, but not necessarily in careers with relative job security and promotional prospects.

SEE ALSO: *career*.

dual consciousness In sociological debates in the 1970s about the CLASS CONSCIOUSNESS of industrial workers, people were said to manifest a dual consciousness when they held two apparently inconsistent sets of beliefs at the same time. The term was commonly applied to members of the WORKING CLASS in European societies, who had sets of beliefs formed by the dominant culture through the educational system as well as different sets of beliefs generated by the experience of work and working-class life. It was suggested that the former type of belief would be typically revealed in questionnaire research which asks abstract questions, while the latter shows most clearly in practical activities. For example, many people would say in response to social surveys that they disapproved of strikes, while participating in such strikes at their own workplace.

SEE ALSO: *dominant ideology thesis*; *Gramsci*; *hegemony*; *pragmatic acceptance*.
READING: Parkin (1971)

dual economy This term was originally associated with J. H. Boeke's analysis in the early twentieth century of economic growth in underdeveloped nations. European-owned plantations in Java, run along rational and efficient capitalist lines, coexisted with an indigenous agrarian economy where peasants made no effort to emulate the European model. This was a dual economy of advanced and backward sectors which remained distinct. Europeans were dominated by economic needs whereas Javanese peasants had social needs. His ideas about needs are no longer accepted, but his description of economies segmented into advanced and backward sectors continues to inform the study of developing societies.

The idea of dualism has been applied *within* advanced capitalist economies, notably Japan and the United States. Both economies include a 'core' sector of large corporations that have sufficient economic power to manipulate their environments and reduce the disruptive effects of competition. There are also 'peripheries' of smaller, less prosperous and less stable firms. Where the two sectors relate, the relationship is asymmetrical because some firms on the periphery may depend on large corporations for business, whereas the latter rarely depend on the former.

SEE ALSO: *centre/periphery*; *dependency theory*; *internal colonialism*; *labour market segmentation*.

dual labour markets See: LABOUR MARKET SEGMENTATION.

Durkheim, Emile (1858–1917) He is widely acknowledged as a 'founding father' of modern sociology who helped to define the subject matter and establish the autonomy of sociology as a discipline. He taught first at the University of Bordeaux and then at the Sorbonne in Paris.

He was greatly influenced by the French intellectual tradition of J.-J. Rousseau, SAINT-SIMON and COMTE. His work is marked by an opposition to the utilitarian tradition in British social thought, which explained social phenomena by reference to the actions and motives of individuals. He adopted a collectivist perspective throughout his sociological analysis. He denied that the utilitarian version of individualism could provide the basis on which to build a stable society. He also asserted that the sociological method was to deal with SOCIAL FACT.

In his first major work, *The Division of Labour in Society* (1893), he argued against the British writer H. Spencer that SOCIAL ORDER in industrial societies could not adequately be explained as an outcome of contractual agreements between individuals motivated by self-interest, because the pursuit of self-interest would lead to social instability, as manifest in various forms of social deviance such as suicide. He distinguished the forms of social order found in primitive and modern societies. Mechanical solidarity in primitive societies was based on the common beliefs and consensus found in the CONSCIENCE COLLECTIVE. As societies industrialized and urbanized and became more complex, the increasing DIVISION OF LABOUR destroyed mechanical solidarity and moral integration, thus rendering social order problematic. He was well aware at the time he was writing that industrial societies exhibited many conflicts and that force was an important factor in preventing social disruption. He believed, however, that a new form of order would arise in advanced societies on the basis of organic solidarity. This would comprise the interdependence of economic ties arising out of differentiation and specialization within the modern economy, a new network of occupational associations such as guilds that would link individuals to the state, and the emergence within these associations of collectively created moral restraints on egoism. T. Parsons (1937; 1968a) interpreted organic solidarity as the continuation of the *conscience collective* in a modified form, suggesting that Durkheim's analysis of social order in modern society demanded a prior consensus and moral order, and this view has proved influential. Evidence for this interpretation can be drawn from a variety of Durkheim's publications. For example, in two pamphlets written during the First World War Durkheim noted that the communal experience of warfare had created a moral consensus in France and involvement in public ceremonies which resembled religious festivals. In his sociology of religion, Durkheim also argued that modern society would require some form of *conscience collective* relevant to contemporary circumstances – an argument clearly dependent on Saint-Simon's conception of the New Christianity. However, it is difficult to reconcile this view of the continuing importance of religious values in modern societies, which Durkheim appears to have accepted towards the end of his life, with the argument of *The Division of Labour in Society* which recognized the importance of economic RECIPROCITY in creating social consensus. There has been considerable controversy over the continuity of the theme of moral consensus in Durkheim's sociology. Parsons (1937) argued that the early emphasis on social facts in a positivistic framework collapsed as Durkheim adopted a voluntaristic action framework. An alternative view suggests that the central theme of Durkheim's sociology was the idea of moral compulsion and normative constraint. The changes in Durkheim's epistemology did not produce significant discontinuities in his sociology of moral life.

He saw the domain of sociology as the study of social facts and not individuals. He believed both that societies had their own realities which could not simply be reduced to the actions and motives of individuals, and that individuals were moulded and constrained by their social environments. In 1895 he wrote *The Rules of Sociological Method*, in which he demonstrated that law was a social fact, embodied in formal, codified rules and not dependent on individuals or on any particular act of law enforcement for its existence.

In *Suicide* (1897), he explained how even apparently individual decisions to commit suicide could be understood as being affected by the different forms of social solidarity in different social settings. He identified four types of SUICIDE on the basis of his analysis of the suicide statistics of different societies and different groups within them. 'Egotistic' and 'anomic' forms of suicide were most commonly found in modern societies where, as *The Division of Labour in Society* had previously shown, traditional forms of social regulation and integration like the *conscience collective* of mechanical solidarity had declined. The higher incidence of 'egotistic' suicides among modern Protestants than Catholics reflected an individualistic ethos in which individuals were responsible for their own salvation. 'Anomic' suicides occurred when the individual experienced a state of normlessness or when norms conflicted. Both forms were to be found when the social checks on individual behaviour typical of traditional societies had lost their force. In primitive societies and in armies in modern societies, where mechanical solidarity was stronger, 'altruistic' suicides for the good of the group were more common. Fatalistic suicides, for example among slaves, were the result of excessive social regulation. Although there have been major criticisms of his approach (J. M. Atkinson, 1978), Durkheim's *Suicide* represents the most influential sociological contribution to this issue.

He came to see social norms as regulating people's behaviour by means of institutionalized values which the individual internalized, rather than society simply acting as an external constraint. In 1912, in *The Elementary Forms of the Religious Life*, he suggested that primitive religions embodied the idea of society and that sacred objects were so because they symbolized the community. Religious culture consisted of the collective values which comprised a society's unity and personality. Religious ceremonies served to reinforce collective values and reaffirm community among individuals. This process was clearly identifiable in primitive societies, though Durkheim recognized how difficult it was to find similar SACRED objects and collective rituals in modern organic societies. His approach to the sacred/profane dichotomy represents a major alternative to arguments about SECULARIZATION. Durkheim was concerned to understand the universal functions of religious systems for the continuity of society as such. In *Primitive Classification* (1903), written with M. Mauss, he argued that the fundamental categories of human thought, such as number, time and space, were modelled upon features of social organization.

In his political writings he expressed concern at the dangers to society of individuals who do not feel that social norms are meaningful to them, who are in a state of ANOMIE. He saw the attraction of socialism to the working class as a protest against the disintegration of traditional social bonds and values, rather than as a desire for the abolition of private property *per se*. He advocated guild socialism as a means of rebuilding cohesive and solidary social communities. He also placed great importance on intermediary associations between the individual and the state in maintaining the moral integration of modern societies.

SEE ALSO: *differentiation; guild; norm; official statistics; religion; social pathology.*

READING: Parkin (1992)

dysfunction A social activity or institution has dysfunctions when some of its consequences impede the workings of another social activity or institution. Any particular activity may have dysfunctions for one other activity and *eufunctions* (helpful functions) for another or, indeed, a mixture of dysfunctions and eufunctions for the same activity.

SEE ALSO: *functionalism.*

ecological fallacy This is the fallacy of drawing conclusions about individual people from data that refer only to aggregates. For example, sociologists often conduct their studies by comparing the social characteristics of collectivities. The relationship between voting and social class might be studied by comparing a geographical area with a high proportion of, say, manual workers with one containing a high proportion of professional managerial workers, and seeing how many votes each political party receives in each area. This is a permissible technique, because some evidence of a connection between the social class composition of an area and voting behaviour can be established. However, such a study would commit the ecological fallacy if it led to imputations about *individual* voting behaviour on the basis of data that derived from collections of individuals.

ecology See: SUICIDE; URBAN ECOLOGY.

economic determinism or **economic reductionism** See: DETERMINISM; ECONOMISM; REDUCTIONISM.

economic sociology or **sociology of economic life** The development of a sociological analysis of economic phenomena was a central concern of classical sociologists such as MARX, WEBER and, in his early work, DURKHEIM. However, sociological attention to economic phenomena declined during the twentieth century, until the revival of Marxist and Weberian sociology in the 1970s and the development from the 1980s onwards of what is sometimes known as the new economic sociology (NES). Economic sociology is a broad field that covers many substantive economic phenomena. These include: all aspects of the economic activities of individuals and groups; the sociology of organizations, markets and other economic institutions; consumption and leisure; macro-issues such as the development of CAPITALISM, the comparative analysis of economic systems and the economic effects of different cultures and religions. It is also a field within which many of the different theoretical traditions in sociology operate, thus there is no single 'school' of economic sociology.

However, a common feature of all forms of economic sociology is the relationship to economics. Starting with UTILITARIANISM in the nineteenth century, most economists have subscribed to individualistic models of action, in which individuals maximize their own material interests in a rational manner and where society may largely be seen as an aggregation of 'atomized' individuals who are brought together by self-interest. Marx, Weber and Durkheim reacted against this perspective and asserted the social nature of economic life, and the notion that the economy is a social system continues to be central to all forms of economic sociology. Historically, economic sociologists tended to leave areas which were apparently more purely economic to the economists. They focused first on the aspects of economic life where the social dimension was particularly self-evident; for example, how the behaviour of social groups within a BUREAUCRACY may affect its efficient operation. Secondly, they considered the links between the economy and the rest of society, two examples being the analysis of CLASS and the relationship of the PROTESTANT ETHIC to modern capitalism. However, contemporary economic sociologists advocate a sociological analysis of all economic issues, including those previously seen as the preserve of economists. A comparison of economic sociology with economics helps define the sociological approach.

In the first place, sociology assumes that economic actors are social entities. The relevant economic actors for many sociologists are groups and institutions. But the social aspect remains dominant even when economic actors are defined as individuals, as did Weber. This is because individual actors inhabit networks of social relationships with other people who influence them, and also because SOCIALIZATION affects how actors define themselves. The sociological position contrasts with the primacy given to individuals as economic actors in economics and the assumption that, when they act as economic agents, individuals are largely unaffected by social ties.

Second, sociologists differ about the nature of economic action. (1) Neo-classical micro-economics assumes that individuals act in a rational manner to maximize their own self-interests. One consequence of people acting in this way is that scarce resources are used efficiently. Sociologists, however, see this type of rational decision-making in pursuit of one's own self-interest as only one form of economic action. Drawing on Weber's distinctions among types of action, ACTION THEORY indicates that many economic decisions may be based simply on tradition and that there is also more than one type of rationality. The view that both motives and rationality are variable is supported by RATIONAL CHOICE THEORY. Although this branch of social theory is particularly sympathetic to economics, it shows that assumptions about the universality of egoistic, self-interested motives and a particular form of rationality cannot be sustained. (2) Economic action is meaningful action but its meaning is socially constructed rather than arising out of the individual. The process of social construction is typically a combination of prior socialization and ongoing social interaction. (3) Sociologists see economic action as embodying POWER, and assume as a consequence that exchange relationships are normally unequal. While markets may appear to be formally free, in reality market exchanges favour those with power as Marx and Weber recognized long ago. In economics, however, exchange is in principle assumed to be uncoerced and fair (provided that markets are operating in conditions of perfect competition).

Third, it follows that economic action occurs within a social context. Thus economic phenomena cannot be explained in terms of the motives of individuals and the scarcity of resources, divorced from social structure and culture, as is the tendency in economics. The socially situated and shaped nature of economic activity has been emphasized recently. Adapting insights from the anthropologist Karl Polyani, advocates of NES point to the importance of social networks and embeddedness. In M. Granovetter's formulation, social structure is conceptualized as a series of networks of social relationships; that is, as sets of regular contacts or interactions, among individuals or social groups. All economic actions are embedded within networks and are expressed in concrete social relationships. Network links may be among individuals, groups, firms and economies. Economic action is also embedded in culture as well as social structure. Modern economic sociologists attempt in these ways to give more precision to the conventional sociological wisdom, that the economy is part of society and governed by social as well as economic rules.

Social networks that are regularly repeated and remain stable over time become institutionalized – that is, they develop a fixed pattern – and these economic institutions then influence the shape of networks in the future. Economic institutions are socially constructed by previous interactions and in turn influence future interactions. NES is particularly concerned with economic institutions, because 'pure' economic forces are filtered through institutions which determine how these forces will operate. For example, prices in pre-industrial societies do not simply follow the 'law' of supply and demand, because market relations among buyers and sellers are embedded in institutions and culture that are based on principles of social reciprocity which reduce the force of this 'law'. Another example is the introduction after 1989 of a capitalist economy into Russia, formerly a socialist society. This was refracted by pre-existing social networks and shared cultures to produce a distinct form of capitalism, which differs from those found among older capitalist economies. Many members of the political elite of the socialist era, which was based on the Communist Party, used their control of state assets to install themselves as the owners or controllers of the capitalist firms that were created when the assets were privatized. The prosperity of businesses often still depends on access to the state's influence and resources, notably subsidies, contracts and collusion in the non-payment of taxes. Networks of personal relationships within the new capitalist class are also important and most were formed in the days of the socialist ruling elite. Within economics, the New Institutional Economics school is also concerned with institutional variations and the ways in which these modify neo-classical economic principles in practice. Despite these signs of convergence, however, the new institutionalism in economics shows little concern for the social construction and modification of economic institutions.

While more precise concepts have been developed, there is still no dominant theory and the field remains broad and encompasses a considerable range of phenomena. *The Handbook of Economic Sociology*, edited by N. Smelser and R. Swedberg (1994b), contains a full overview of the empirical and conceptual research in this field.

SEE ALSO: *atomism; institutional theory; labour market; labour market segmentation; market; network/social network.*

READING: Swedberg and Granovetter (1992); Smelser and Swedberg (1994a)

economism This term has two distinct meanings in Marxist sociology, both pejorative. (1) Economism in the sense of economic REDUCTIONISM explains all social, political and cultural activity in terms of the economic base, which denies the 'superstructure' any independent significance. A related meaning is that the key to the subordination of one class by another is found in the organization of production. (2) A variant meaning widely used in industrial sociology describes the CLASS CONSCIOUSNESS and aspirations of the working class as economistic, when workers' activities are geared to improving their material conditions within capitalism rather than to its overthrow. This variant is similar to the use of 'trade-union consciousness' by V. I. Lenin (1902).

SEE ALSO: *base and superstructure; determinism; Leninism; Marxist sociology; trade unions.*

education, sociology of See: SOCIOLOGY OF EDUCATION.

educational attainment Despite formal equality of opportunity and access to education, levels of educational attainment vary systematically within Western societies. Children from lower social class families do less well than those from higher, and girls used to do less well than boys. Because of the linkage between educational qualifications and occupations, sociologists concerned with SOCIAL MOBILITY and CLASS have been especially interested to explain class variations in attainment.

British educational sociologists in the 1950s and 1960s identified a number of factors affecting social class differences in attainment. (1) The organization of schooling, with selection on the basis of a competitive examination (the 11+) for different types of public secondary school and the streaming of children within schools, was one factor. The spread of comprehensive schools since the late 1960s has largely ended selection in public education, while the point at which streaming takes place has been raised in many schools. But the continuation of private selective schools and streaming may perpetuate class differences. The experience of countries with longer comprehensive traditions, with less emphasis on streaming and with relatively smaller private sectors, such as the USA, suggests that systematic differences in attainment may survive changes in the overall organization of the school system. Research in Britain by M. Rutter *et al.* (1979) indicated that even within one type of school (comprehensive), differences in the internal organization of individual schools would lead to different levels of achievement in public examinations. (2) Teachers' expectations were thought to be influential, since teachers appeared to expect higher levels of achievement from middle-class pupils than working-class ones, and pupils responded to these different expectations. Moreover, middle-class children shared the same culture as middle-class teachers. (3) Working-class culture was thought to be one of CULTURAL DEPRIVATION, marked by low aspirations for educational attainment in family and community, and embodying a RESTRICTED CODE. The second and third factors emphasized cultural phenomena as important sources of difference, and this emphasis has been continued in more recent treatments of CLASSROOM INTERACTION, CLASSROOM KNOWLEDGE and CULTURAL REPRODUCTION.

Gender differences have recently attracted the attention of sociologists. Until the mid-1980s girls did better at school until adolescence, gaining more passes at GCE Ordinary level and GCSE, but they did less well at Advanced level and were less likely to attend university. They were also less likely than boys to study mathematics, the sciences or engineering. These attainment differences were explained by the sexual division of labour which gave priority to men's education and work. It was further argued that schools were reinforcing these expectations via the HIDDEN CURRICULUM. Since the mid-1980s, however, the position has changed dramatically. By 1996, girls were awarded significantly more higher-grade GCSEs than boys and were also more successful at A level (16 per cent of 17-year-old girls gained three or more A levels compared with 14 per cent of boys). Similarly, in 1975, 35 per cent of undergraduates were female, a proportion that had increased to about 50 per cent by 1997. Gender segregation in the subjects studied at universities has also declined.

SEE ALSO: *Bernstein; equality; intelligence; nature/nurture debate; peer group; sponsored mobility; stereotypes; women and work.*

READING: Stanworth (1983)

egoism See: SUICIDE.

elaborated code See: RESTRICTED CODE.

elective affinity When two systems of thought overlap with one another or contain ideas that are similar or which resonate together, they are said to have an elective affinity. The best-known use is in M. Weber's *Protestant Ethic and the Spirit of Capitalism* (1930). WEBER argued that the PROTESTANT ETHIC emphasized ASCETI-CISM, hard work and INDIVIDUALISM, qualities also implicitly valued in capitalist practice. The systems of thought behind Protestantism and capitalism had an elective affinity which contributed to the establishment of capitalism in Protestant countries.

Elias, Norbert (1897–1990) After fleeing from Germany in 1933, Elias held academic posts in sociology at the universities of Leicester (1954–62) and Ghana (1962–4). He was also professor emeritus at the University of Frankfurt and visiting professor at the Institute of Interdisciplinary Research at the University of Bielefeld. His major work (*Über den Prozess der Zivilisation*) was neglected at the time of publication in 1939, but has subsequently come to be regarded as a classic of historical sociology since its publication as *The Civilizing Process* (1939a and 1939b). His major interest has been the pacification of medieval society through the development of individual, moral forms of restraint in codes such as table-manners and etiquette. The develop-ment of the state as a system of social regulation has been accompanied by the emergence of civilized systems of self-control. In *The Court Society* (1969), he studied the evolution of ceremony in the French court before the Revolution, the economic decline of aristocratic society as a result of its internal competition for influence, and the emergence of bourgeois society. The impact of individual norms of restraint on the process of dying in a secular society has been outlined in *The Loneliness of the Dying* (1982). He has also made important contributions to theoretical problems in sociology. For example, in *What is Sociology?* (1970) he developed the idea of figura-tional analysis; the reciprocity between people creates the figurations of social interaction which develop in ways which are unplanned. Concepts like group or community refer to figurations of interdependent individuals. His figurational or processual sociology was critical of both FUNCTIONALISM and structuralism, on the grounds that they tended to reify social processes. Thus he argued that sociology should analyse not civilization but civilizing processes. His contribution to the sociology of knowledge has been published in *Involvement and Detachment* (1986).

elite This refers to a minority group which has power or influence over others and is recognized as being in some way superior. The sociology of elites has traditionally dealt with the ruling elites within societies, as in the work of PARETO and MOSCA, or within organizations as in the study of political parties conducted by MICHELS. The assumption has been that there will always be a divide between the rulers and the ruled or those with power and those without, even in nominally democratic societies and institutions. Ruling elites vary in the extent to which they are open to outside influences: in some societies elites recruit new members from the non-elite and/or are open to pressures from below, whereas elsewhere elites may be less open to outside recruits and influence. Elites also vary in the extent to which they are integrated into socially cohesive or solidary groups. The traditional sociological model of the United States was of a plurality of elites in different spheres which remained unintegrated and acted as checks and balances on each other. MILLS, however, has claimed to have found a well-integrated and partly self-perpetuating power elite. He has noted that the top groups in political, economic and military organizations are linked by ties of family and friendship and share common social backgrounds.

Ruling elites are sometimes distinguished from ruling classes in terms of the fluidity of their membership and the way outside pressures influence them. This is a poor criterion, since some elites are not fluid or open and the concept of CLASS does not entail that dominant classes do not recruit from lower classes or remain uninfluenced by outside pressures. The difference between class and elite rests largely on the fact that classes are defined in terms of economic position and power, whereas elites may have a non-economic basis. Indeed, a ruling elite is sometimes simply that section of the dominant class with political power.

SEE ALSO: *oligarchy*; *political parties*; *ruling class*.

READING: Scott, J. (1990)

embedding/embeddedness See: DISEMBEDDING; ECONOMIC SOCIOLOGY.

embodiment The concept is derived from the phenomenology of M. Merleau-Ponty, especially his *Phenomenology of Perception* (1962). His basic question was about how we experience reality. He argued that, to experience the world, we have to perceive it and to perceive it we have to possess language. The embodiment of the human being is fundamental to these processes of the apprehension and perception of immediate reality. He argued that the conventional psychology of perception had ignored the fact that the way in which individuals perceive external reality involves their bodily experiences of the physical world and a capacity to manipulate the everyday world through the motor activities of the body. This perceptual world is not distinct from what he referred to as the motor-practical world. Our experience of the world is made possible by language; Merleau-Ponty argued that language, as a system of signs, is based in the speech capacities that form the operational gestures of the body and can be manifest verbally, auditorily or visually. Language is necessarily embodied in these material forms. As a result, he rejected the Cartesian mind/body dualism and argued that thinking, doing and feeling are practical activities that require our embodied presence. Understanding and other mental predicates refer to embodied and reflexive forms of behaviour.

His philosophy followed a distinction in the German language between the body as an object (*Körper*) and the body as lived experience (*Leib*). The body is simultaneously an object that can be observed and a mode of being that makes that observation possible. The relationship of an individual to their own bodies is never an external, objective or neutral relationship, because identity is inextricably bound up with subjective being in the material or objective world.

We can define embodiment as the mode by which human beings practically engage with and apprehend the world. In this respect, the concept of embodiment also has a close affinity with the sociology of BOURDIEU, which attempts to overcome dichotomies between action and structure in the notions of practice and 'habitus'.

SEE ALSO: *actor-network theory; body; Foucault; phenomenological sociology.*

READING: Turner, B. S. (1996a)

embourgeoisement An explanation of declining working-class support for radical political movements, as the result of increased affluence causing workers to adopt middle-class (bourgeois) values and lifestyles, embourgeoisement was a popular concept in Britain in the 1950s and 1960s. It was criticized in the AFFLUENT WORKER research, which showed that the working class still had distinctive values, styles of life and political beliefs, and was less affluent than much of the middle class. The notion of PROLETARIANIZATION held, conversely, that some of the middle class were becoming like the working class.

SEE ALSO: *class imagery; end of ideology theory; lifestyle.*

READING: Goldthorpe *et al.* (1969)

emergent properties This concept was formulated by PARSONS (1937) in his analysis of social systems. There are three related notions. (1) Social systems have a structure which emerges from the process of social interaction. (2) These emergent properties cannot be reduced to the biological or psychological characteristics of social actors; for example, culture cannot be explained by reference to biology. (3) The meaning of a social act cannot be understood in isolation from the total context of the social system within which it occurs. The concept is thus an element of Parsons' argument against REDUCTIONISM.

In SYMBOLIC INTERACTIONISM, emergence arises out of the combination of the divergent elements of the body, mind, self and society, which are synthesized into a new form. Thus all social objects have emergent properties which cannot be reduced to a single factor.

SEE ALSO: *agency and structure; social system; systems theory.*

emotional labour For organizations which provide services to customers on a face-to-face basis, the quality of the relationship between customers and employees with whom they deal is very important. Emotional labour may be defined as the work of presenting organizationally prescribed emotions in face-to-face transactions with customers. In her pioneering analysis of airline flight attendants, A. R. Hochschild (1983) analysed how organizations try to manage the ways in which employees present themselves and interact with customers. For women attendants, this requires their manufacturing EMOTIONS such as warmth, concern, friendliness and pleasure, particularly towards male passengers, for the benefit of the company. Conversely, they should never express boredom or irritation. Managing one's emotions requires both planning and effort, thus it really is labour. Moreover, what were once regarded as private emotions have become commodities with a commercial value.

Subsequent literature has suggested that organizations are concerned to manage the expression of emotion and not to control the actual feelings of their employees. There are social norms of appropriate emotional expression in different contexts, often referred to as *display rules*, which managers follow when directing the emotional performance of their employees. For example, smiling is appropriate among flight attendants and check-out staff in supermarkets, but not among pall bearers at a funeral. Emotional labour research is also concerned with emotional dissonance, where the organizationally required display contrasts with an employee's actual feelings.

READING: Morris and Feldman (1996)

emotions In the nineteenth century, research on the emotions focused on their physical and psychological characteristics. C. Darwin (1872) developed a comprehensive and influential classification of emotions. W. James (1884) produced a peripheral theory of emotions in which the perception of arousing stimuli brought about changes in the peripheral organs such as the viscera and the voluntary muscles. From this perspective, an emotion is the perception of these physical changes. In James' theory, we run not because we are afraid; rather we are afraid because we run. James' theory was criticized by W. B. Cannon, who argued that the bodily changes that allegedly produce an emotion are too general to permit one to distinguish between specific emotions. Researchers subsequently became interested in the individual's cognitive interpretation of emotional states. These cognitive and motivational components have been described by K. R. Scherer (1984) as the functions of emotion. Opinion in psychological research is still divided between those who believe that there are distinctive, innate physiological changes of neural, facial and motor activity, awareness of which produces a subjective experience of emotions, and those who believe that, in the absence of specific physiological states, cognitive awareness of an emotion is crucial. There is also no agreement concerning the classification of separate emotions, nor about the distinction between emotions and other affective states such as feelings or sentiments.

These psychological theories are not interested in cultural variations in emotions, nor in their historical development or collective nature. For example, anthropologists have been concerned to differentiate between SHAME and guilt cultures. Shame involves a public, external means of control; guilt is individualized and private. Sociologists such as ELIAS have been concerned to understand emotions within a historical context by arguing that emotions have changed as a consequence of the civilizational process. It is no longer thought to be civilized to give expression in public to violent emotions of rage or passion; the exception might be in modern sport where such violent emotions are thought permissible or appropriate. Modern societies require a high level of control over the emotions. Thus, sociological theories suggest that emotions are not simply an awareness of arousal, because they are shaped by culture and social situations. For example, in her influential study of EMOTIONAL LABOUR, A. R. Hochschild (1983) has shown that women in service industries, such as air hostesses, are required by their employers to manufacture emotions, in order to make their customers feel pleased about the services they are receiving. She regards this artificial production of affect as a feature of ALIENATION at work.

It is also argued that these changes in the social context of emotions are closely associated with the changing nature of family life, courtship and intimacy. Partly as a consequence of romanticism and the women's movement, according to A. Giddens (1992) there has been a transformation of intimacy. A democratization of the private sphere has followed the democratization of the public realm, and this has put a greater emphasis on trust, mutual respect, reciprocity and affection. The stability of affectual ties in both heterosexual and homosexual relationships is now dependent on the mutual satisfaction of intimacy. Thus family life is no longer merely dependent on property relations, legal enforcement or sexual reproduction. Without a continuous satisfaction of intimacy, such familial relations are likely to be short-lived. This argument suggests that, while violent emotions related to violent encounters are rejected in modern society, men are forced to accept the expectations of women for sensitive, intimate and affectual partnerships. Whereas feminists might argue that the household is still dominated by the values of the patriarchal family, the continuity of domestic violence could be seen as evidence of the inability of men to adapt to these changes in the emotional relationships between men and women.

SEE ALSO: *affective individualism; feminist social theory; marriage; nuclear family; patriarchy.*

READING: Kemper (1990); Barbalet (1998)

empathy In sociology the concept of empathy – the ability to assume or take on the social roles and attitudes of other social actors – appears in a variety of different contexts. (1) In the social psychology of George H. MEAD the ability to empathize with social roles and positions is a basic social skill, acquired in the process of socialization. In order to anticipate the response of others to our social gestures it is important for us to be able to put ourselves in the social position of other actors. (2) In the sociology of development, empathy has been treated by D. Lerner (1958) as a basic psychological concomitant of modernization which requires social actors to identify with new political leaders and programmes, new economic commodities and modern social institutions. In an open, democratic society, each citizen has to be able to imagine alternative social arrangements and different political policies. (3) In methodological terms, the ability of the sociologist to empathize with the individuals who are being studied is often mistakenly confused with M. Weber's concept of 'interpretative sociology'. Weber's methodology is less concerned with sympathetic interpretation and more with the attribution of meaning to actions and motives by the use of theoretical constructs.

SEE ALSO: *actor/social actor; hermeneutics; Verstehen.*

empirical An empirical statement or theory is one which can be tested by some kind of evidence drawn from experience.

empiricism This is a doctrine based on the supposition that the only source of knowledge is experience. In sociology, it is used positively to describe that style of sociology that tries to avoid untested theoretical speculation and to aim always at the provision of quantitative, empirical evidence. Negatively, it is suggested that empiricism tends to reduce the importance of theory on the one hand and, on the other, underestimates the technical and theoretical difficulties of gathering reliable data.

SEE ALSO: *attitude; interview; official statistics; positivism; theory-laden.*

end of ideology theory In the 1950s, American sociologists, especially BELL and LIPSET, put forward the theory that, because of important changes in the nature of capitalism, democratic participation of the working class in politics and the growth of welfare, the old ideologies of the right and the left had lost their relevance and force. Western societies, having solved their earlier social problems, were thus characterized by a CONSENSUS and by a pragmatic approach to the remaining problems of the distribution of resources.

Although the theory, to some extent, adequately reflected the existence of consensus and welfare politics in the 1950s and early 1960s, it was thought during the 1970s that the prevalence of racial conflict in America, student riots in Europe, the polarization of attitudes during the Vietnam war and an upsurge of industrial conflict were empirical disconfirmation of the notion of the 'end of ideology'. Other writers suggested that the 'end of ideology' was itself an ideology of welfare consensus.

SEE ALSO: *citizenship*; *ideology*; *institutionalization of conflict*; *social order*.

endogamy All human societies possess social rules which specify certain categories of persons who are regarded as eligible marriage partners. The rules for marrying within and without certain defined kinship groups are fundamental to any study of kinship. The rule of endogamy permits or prescribes marriage *within* a specific group, based on kinship, tribal, class or religious affiliation.

SEE ALSO: *descent groups*; *exogamy*.

Engels, Friedrich (1820–95) A German-born industrialist whose family partly owned a textile business in Manchester, Engels spent most of his adult life working in England. He was the close collaborator and friend of MARX, introducing him to economics in the 1840s, later supporting him financially, then spending years preparing the manuscripts of *Capital*, vols 2 and 3, for publication after Marx's death.

In 1844 Engels published a newspaper article, 'Outlines of a Critique of Political Economy', which analysed capitalism as an economic system based on private property and class conflict and criticized the contradictions of liberal economics. This led to the association with Marx, and jointly they wrote *The Holy Family* (1845a), *The German Ideology* (1845b) and the *Manifesto of the Communist Party* (1848). Engels' own contributions to the development of Marxism were varied. (1) After Marx's death, he suggested that superstructural elements such as law and ideology had some independence of the economic base and might on occasion determine it, separating the economic from other factors in a way that Marx rarely did. (2) He laid the foundations of what came to be known as DIALECTICAL MATERIALISM in *Anti-Dühring* (1877–8) and the posthumously published *Dialectics of Nature* (1952). (3) Influenced by C. Darwin, he believed that social development followed evolutionary principles and he emphasized the notion of unilinear development more strongly than Marx. (4) He attempted to develop Marxism on a natural scientific basis, natural science being conceived as both materialistic and following dialectical laws.

His work also covered history, anthropology and military commentary. *The Condition of the Working Class in England* (1845), based mainly on direct observation of Manchester and Salford, remains the classic description of working-class life in industrializing England, though modern historians debate whether the wretched living standards Engels describes were in fact an improvement on what went before or, as Engels claims, a deterioration. *The Origin of the Family, Private Property and the State* (1884) is notable for its condemnation of women's subjugation and its association of PATRIARCHY with private property, though its anthropological base is discredited.

SEE ALSO: *base and superstructure*; *ideology*; *matriarchy*.
READING: McLellan (1977)

Enlightenment A European philosophical and social movement of the eighteenth century, often referred to as 'the Age of Reason'. Enlightenment philosophers developed a variety of progressive ideas: freedom of thought and expression, the criticism of religion, the value of reason and science, a commitment to social progress and the significance of INDIVIDUALISM. These critical, secular ideas played a crucial role in the emergence of modern societies. The principal adherents of the Enlightenment included M. Condorcet (1734–94), D. Diderot (1713–84), D. Hume (1711–76), I. Kant (1724–1804), J.-J. Rousseau (1712–78) and Voltaire (1694–1778). The Enlightenment has also been subject to criticism. In the nineteenth century, the Romantics argued that Enlightenment reason was soulless, and conservatives regarded it as too radical. In the twentieth century, the Enlightenment has been criticized as a movement which was in fact intolerant of individual differences and cultural variation. FEMINISM has criticized Enlightenment ideas as presenting a view of reality which is biased by one-sided male values. A self-confident, robust commitment to Reason is uncommon in late-twentieth-century thought.

SEE ALSO: *Habermas; postmodernism; rationalism.*

READING: Gay (1966–9)

enterprise culture A particular societal culture that emphasizes qualities of individual initiative, energy and self-reliance. Societies that have such cultures, and contain enterprising individuals, are said to perform better economically, as well as offering more freedom to individuals, than societies with a substantial degree of state regulation, public ownership and extensive welfare states, all of which are claimed to suppress individual initiative. Conservative governments in Britain in the 1980s and 1990s attempted to promote enterprise culture chiefly by the introduction of market principles into all areas of economic and social life. For example, financial markets were deregulated, publicly owned utilities like gas and water were sold to private interests (PRIVATIZATION), and commercial principles were introduced into the public sector including the health and education services. Besides providing incentives for individuals to innovate, these changes were supposed to empower consumers, diminish producer power (partly by encouraging competition) and encourage or force individuals to take responsibility for their own welfare. Particularly in the delivery of public services, this has meant an attack on professional expertise and authority. It is too early to tell if these changes have produced more enterprising individuals and organizations. They have, however, resulted in a substantial dismantling of the welfare state and of public ownership.

SEE ALSO: *capitalism; entrepreneurship; New Right; postmodernity.*

READING: Keat and Abercrombie (1991)

entrepreneurship The economist J. A. Schumpeter (1934) saw innovation as the criterion of entrepreneurship. Entrepreneurial activity formed the engine of economic development because profits were created by doing new things or finding new ways of doing existing things. Managers in business organizations were entrepreneurs when they made creative and innovative decisions. This view of the determinants of economic growth has been influential in sociological analyses of developing societies, and it has been suggested at times that the extent to which social values favour the emergence of the entrepreneurial personality influences the likelihood of economic development. This interest in entrepreneurship links with

M. Weber's famous discussion of the PROTESTANT ETHIC and the socio-religious values and personality type conducive to the emergence of modern CAPITALISM. A distinction is sometimes made now between *entrepreneurs*, defined as owner-managers of small businesses, and *intrapreneurs*, who are innovative managers within larger organizations.

SEE ALSO: *achievement motivation.*

epidemiology The study of the causes of the incidence and distribution of diseases and illness in human populations. In medical sociology, it involves the study of how culture influences the presence of illness. While orthodox epidemiology examines social factors in the distribution of disease, it has been criticized by some sociologists because it treats disease as a problem for the individual in relation to the social environment and ascribes responsibility for illness to the individual, rather than treating illness as an effect of social structure. Because epidemiology has been developed in the framework of the MEDICAL MODEL, it does not give sociological variables a central place in the causal explanation of disease and its social distribution. However, some medical sociologists describe themselves as social epidemiologists.

From the early 1980s, there has been considerable scientific interest in AIDS (Acquired Immune Deficiency Syndrome), ARC (Aids Related Complex) and HIV (Human Immunodeficiency Virus). Unfortunately sociologists were latecomers to the study of AIDS, but the sociologists' AIDS Network is now providing an important forum for debate and research. Sociologists have contributed to the study of the aetiology of AIDS, its distribution and reception, how PWAs (people with AIDS) cope with its effects, and the health education programmes on sexual behaviour modification. Early conceptualization associated AIDS exclusively with gay men and with epidemiologically defined 'risk groups' such as Haitians and IVDUs (intravenous drug users). This view of AIDS as an epidemic in the homosexual community disguised the growth of AIDS among white, heterosexual males and the spread of HIV among women and among drug-users who use unclean needles. In the USA, 90 per cent of PWAs are male, and ethnic minorities constitute 40 per cent of AIDS cases. There have been major changes in the behaviour of the gay community which have reduced 'risky' sexual practices (such as having multiple partners). Research shows that race, class and gender are the major determinants of the spread of AIDS.

SEE ALSO: *sociology of health and illness.*

epistemology In philosophy this concept is used technically to mean the theory of knowledge, or the theory of how it is that people come to have knowledge of the external world. The term is more loosely used in sociology to refer to the methods of scientific procedure which lead to the acquisition of sociological knowledge. For example, a sociology founded on REALISM would have a different epistemology from one founded on POSITIVISM.

READING: Keat and Urry (1975)

equality It is conventional to identify four types of equality: (1) the doctrine of equality of persons, or ontological equality; (2) equality of opportunity to achieve desirable goals; (3) equality of condition, in which the conditions of life are made equal by legislation; (4) equality of outcome or result.

Type 1, ontological equality, is normally associated with a religious belief. For example, in Christianity there is the doctrine that all people are equal, because God is the Father of humanity. The spread of SECULARIZATION has made such beliefs problematic.

The idea of equality of opportunity (type 2) is the legacy of the French Revolution, the idea being that all positions in society should be open to a competitive system of entry by means of educational attainment, on the basis of personal talent. This form of equality requires universalistic criteria in the selection of people to positions in society and also places a value on ACHIEVEMENT MOTIVATION. By employing the analogy of society as a competitive contest, equality of opportunity suggests that all persons, regardless of race, gender or age, have the right to compete. Critics of this standard of equality argue that, as a result of CULTURAL CAPITAL, many people entering the competition already enjoy many advantages. This argument was frequently used in Britain in the 1960s against the principle of competitive selection for grammar-school education, on the grounds that it reinforced existing inequalities; children from middle-class homes already possessed many cultural advantages over working-class children. To ensure a more fundamental equality, it is sometimes argued that, by means of legislation on welfare and education, there should be an equality of condition (type 3) to compensate for social disadvantage. Positive discrimination in favour of minority groups to promote SOCIAL MOBILITY would be a further illustration of changes designed to bring about equality of condition.

Radical critics of society argue that equality of opportunity is a position supported by liberalism and equality of condition is a form of change which aims to reform rather than abolish the prevailing system of inequality. Radical objections against these two forms of equality also argue that the analogy between society and a competition itself reflects the dominant ideology. For example, in the nineteenth century, SOCIAL DARWINISM conceptualized society in terms of a struggle for survival. Against these metaphors, socialists argued for equality of outcome (type 4) through a programme of political and economic revolution which would remove the social causes of inequality. The aim of socialism is to destroy inequalities (the ultimate cause of which is private ownership of the means of production) and to satisfy human needs equally regardless of the accidents of birth (such as sex).

These types of equality have been criticized as either not feasible or not desirable. For example, it is argued that the achievement of radical equality is unrealistic, because it would require the SOCIALIZATION of children away from the family in order to minimize the inheritance of cultural benefits, the abolition of all forms of inheritance of property, the prohibition of competition and achievement, and a universal training programme in cooperative values and ALTRUISM. Critics argue that empirical research shows that radical attempts to secure equality over a long period (the Israeli kibbutz, religious communities, secular communes, peasant revolutions and communist revolutions) have not been successful, because inequalities of class, status, power and authority can never be wholly eradicated. It is further argued that equality of condition and outcome are not necessarily desirable, because they conflict with other values such as personal freedom and INDIVIDUALISM. For example, in Britain it is often claimed that parents have a right to choose private education for their children and that governments should not, in the name of equality of opportunity or condition, prevent freedom of choice with respect to the type of education parents desire for their children. Against this, it has been suggested that privileged social groups use an IDEOLOGY such as 'freedom of choice', not to defend freedom, but to maintain the privileges they enjoy as a consequence of continuing inequality.

While sociologists have devoted considerable energy to the study of inequality, the conditions for equality and the development of egalitarian social movements have been neglected in mainstream sociology. The contemporary value placed on equality is the product of egalitarian ideologies (such as socialism), the expansion of social rights as a consequence of CITIZENSHIP, the erosion of status hierarchies as a result of URBANIZATION and the development of mass consumption as an aspect of the rise of a MASS SOCIETY. In Britain, the WELFARE STATE played an important part in bringing about greater equality of opportunity and condition. These social changes were largely based on the implementation by governments of the economic ideas and policies of J. M. Keynes (1883–1946). Since the economic recession of the mid-1970s, government has moved away from Keynesianism towards a policy which cuts state expenditure on welfare in order to encourage private investment and profitability. The result has been an increase in inequality and a greater tolerance, at least on the part of governments, of inequality.

SEE ALSO: *capitalism; caste; class; class imagery; classroom knowledge; commune; competition; cultural deprivation; democracy; distribution of income and wealth; dual consciousness; educational attainment; estates; industrial democracy; industrial society; justice; life-chances; Marshall; progress; stratification.*

READING: Tawney (1931); Turner (1986b)

equilibrium Societies or social systems are said to be in equilibrium when the forces acting within them are balanced and the society is consequently stable. PARSONS holds that societies are systems which always tend to equilibrium, even if they do not reach it. He conceives of social change as the movement from one equilibrium position to another (or one tendency to another) as the internal forces are changed and rebalance themselves. This is referred to as *dynamic* equilibrium.

SEE ALSO: *Pareto; systems theory.*

error See: BIAS; SAMPLING ERROR.

essentialism Arguments which reduce the complexity of social phenomena to a single dimension (an essence) are often criticized as essentialist. FEMINIST SOCIAL THEORY has attacked unidimensional explanations of gender and sex differences in terms of biology as being flawed by essentialism.

SEE ALSO: *sexualities.*

estates A system of STRATIFICATION found historically in Europe and Russia which, like caste, contained sharp differences and rigid barriers between a small number of strata. Unlike castes, estates were created politically by man-made laws rather than religious rules. These laws served both to define the system and control mobility between strata, and also to create an orderly framework of rights and duties which applied to all. Each estate had its own code of appropriate behaviour (e.g. etiquette). Estates were commonly found in FEUDALISM and the post-feudal, early modern period. The normal divisions were threefold: clergy, nobility and the commons, though sometimes fourfold when the commons were separated into city dwellers and peasants.

estimation This refers to the method of estimating characteristics of a population from sample data. SAMPLING on a random basis allows statistical distribution theory to be used to make estimates of a known degree of accuracy.

ethnic group There has been much conceptual confusion in sociology with respect to the distinctiveness of such terms as 'ethnic group', 'racial group', 'caste' and 'social stratum'. In general, sociologists have rejected the notion that human groups can be unambiguously defined in terms of their genetic constitution. Social groups in sociological theory are more commonly defined by reference to shared culture such as language, customs and institutions. There is a difference between a group which claims ethnic distinctiveness and one which has distinctiveness imposed upon it by some politically superior group in a context of political struggle. Ethnicity may, therefore, become the basis either for national separatism or for political subordination. The ambiguity of the definition of 'ethnic group' thus reflects the political struggles in society around exclusive and inclusive group membership.

SEE ALSO: *caste; group; internal colonialism; nationalism; racism; social closure; stratification.*

ethnocentrism This term, first coined by W. G. Sumner (1906), is used to describe prejudicial attitudes between in-groups and out-groups by which *our* attitudes, customs and behaviour are unquestionably and uncritically treated as superior to *their* social arrangements. The term is also used to criticize sociologists and anthropologists who, often unwittingly, import narrow, parochial assumptions drawn from their own society into their research.

SEE ALSO: *cultural relativism; prejudice; understanding alien belief systems.*

ethnography The direct observation of the activity of members of a particular social group, and the description and evaluation of such activity, constitute ethnography. The term has mainly been used to describe the research technique of anthropologists, but the method is commonly used by sociologists as well.

SEE ALSO: *participant observation.*

ethnomethodology This is a term, literally meaning 'people's methods', invented by GARFINKEL to describe a branch of sociology which he initiated. In its origins the subject was based on a critique of mainstream sociology, which Garfinkel saw as imposing a set of sociological categories on the ordinary person. Conventional sociology re-describes what ordinary people do, treating their own accounts as somehow deficient. For example, the concept of social structure is an invention to the extent that it departs from people's own sense of structure. At the same time, sociology is really a commonsense practice, not a technical one, for the sociologist uses his or her commonsense categories for organizing data. The subject as conventionally practised, therefore, claims to be something it is not, and treats people as 'cultural dopes'.

Instead, ethnomethodology proposes to investigate how people ('members') construct their world. The assumption is that everyday life is fairly orderly and that orderliness is produced – reflexively – by people in everyday life. Members have to work continuously at making their own activities make sense to others, yet despite this, the way in which the social world is constructed is entirely taken for granted. One important feature of everyday life is the indexical character of 'conversation'.

The understanding of conversation depends on the participants being able to fill in a set of background assumptions unique to every interaction. Members, therefore, have to 'repair' INDEXICALITY, perhaps by GLOSSING.

Ethnomethodology aims to study members' methods as they are persistently used in the construction of the social world. There are two main varieties of investigation. The first is illustrated by Garfinkel's experiments in the disruption of everyday life. Garfinkel asked his students to go home and behave as if they were lodgers. The reactions of parents and relatives were dramatic, at first puzzled and then hostile. For Garfinkel this illustrates how carefully constructed, yet delicate, is the social order of everyday life and, in other studies (of jurors, for example), he investigated how people constructed this order in different settings while taking it entirely for granted. The second type of ethnomethodological investigation is CONVERSATIONAL ANALYSIS, the study of the social organization of talk.

Ethnomethodology was a topic of considerable debate in sociology in the early 1970s but is less prominent now. It has been criticized on a number of grounds: (1) it deals with trivial subjects; (2) it presents an over-ordered notion of everyday life, which is, in fact, riven by conflict and misunderstanding; (3) it has no notion of social structure and consequently neglects the way in which the activities of people are constrained by social factors; (4) it uses the methods of inquiry which it criticizes in others.

SEE ALSO: *phenomenological sociology; reflexive/reflexivity; Schutz; symbolic interactionism.*

READING: Sharrock and Anderson (1986)

ethology This is the comparative study of animal behaviour, particularly its non-learned aspects. There have been unsuccessful attempts to apply the lessons learned with animals, particularly primates, to human behaviour. However, as a method of study that emphasizes the limitations imposed on behaviour by genetic structure, it complements social scientists' concern for what is learned and socially created.

SEE ALSO: *sociobiology.*

READING: Hinde (1982)

eufunction See: DYSFUNCTION; FUNCTIONALISM.

eugenics A term coined by F. Galton in 1883 to refer to the improvement of the human race by the use of a 'genetic policy' based on the principles of HEREDITY. As a social movement, it was influential in the United States between 1890 and 1920, where it was associated with SOCIAL DARWINISM. The American Genetic Association was founded in 1913. The aim of eugenics was to maintain and improve human populations by positive means (the encouragement by financial support of parents who were thought to be intelligent or in some sense superior) and negative means (the prohibition on reproduction by parents who were allegedly inferior). These ideas began to have a practical application in the United States when the state of Indiana adopted a sterilization law in 1907. During a period of massive migration to the United States, eugenics was used to give expression to anxieties about the consequences for American culture of a sustained policy of immigration. Sociologists have been critical of the use of biological models in the explanation of social action and interaction; they have also criticized the ORGANIC ANALOGY. Although eugenics as such is no longer fashionable, the basic issues are still important in the NATURE/NURTURE DEBATE.

SEE ALSO: *intelligence*; *sociobiology*.

evaluation research Social scientists are increasingly called upon to use their research expertise to evaluate the success of policies in reaching goals. Evaluation research is often linked to ACTION RESEARCH. It has been employed most widely in the United States.

everyday life, sociology of See: SOCIOLOGY OF EVERYDAY LIFE.

evolutionary theory This doctrine embraces a variety of principles in different usages and there is no real agreement as to its essence. There are two types of evolutionary theory: (1) that which postulates the unilinear, ordered or progressive nature of social change; (2) that which is based on an analogy with evolution in plant and animal populations, following Darwinian theory.

(1) Evolutionary perspectives were central to the nineteenth-century approach to the study of society. Some commentators saw *any* change as evolutionary, but the major sociological contributions emphasized the ordered and directional nature of change. SAINT-SIMON started from the idea, conventional in late eighteenth- and early nineteenth-century conservatism, of society as an organic equilibrium, stabilized by the fact that individuals and social classes depended on the success of the whole for their survival. To this he added an evolutionary idea of social development, a sequential progression of organic societies representing increasing levels of advancement. Each society was appropriate in its own time but was later superseded by higher forms. He saw the growth of knowledge as defining and determining evolution, and his three stages were later elaborated by COMTE in the latter's evolutionary scheme. Comte linked developments in human knowledge, culture and society. Societies passed through three stages, the primitive, intermediary and scientific, which corresponded to the forms of human knowledge arranged along a similar continuum of theological, metaphysical and positive reasoning. All mankind inevitably passed through these stages as it developed, suggesting both unilinear direction and PROGRESS. Moreover, Comte saw society in organismic terms, as an entity made up of interdependent parts which are in balance with each other and create an integrated whole. He saw evolution as the growth of functional specialization of structures and the better adaptation of parts.

SPENCER also displayed a linear conception of evolutionary stages. The degree of complexity in society was the scale on which he measured progress. The trend of human societies was from simple, undifferentiated wholes to complex and hetero-geneous ones, where the parts of the whole became more specialized but remained integrated. He worked with an ORGANIC ANALOGY but did not describe society as an organism. The concern with change and stages of development can also be found in non-organismic thought in the second half of the century, among anthropologists interested in the comparative study of cultures, in the succession of modes of production outlined by MARX and F. Engels, and in E. Durkheim's view of the progressive DIVISION OF LABOUR in society.

(2) Twentieth-century anthropologists and sociologists have tended to pay less attention to social evolution, except for a revival of interest among American func-tionalists in the 1950s and 1960s. This revival, sometimes referred to as *neo-*

evolutionism, borrowed, in a modified form, the principles of natural selection and adaptation drawn from evolutionary theory in the biological sciences. FUNC-TIONALISM used an organismic model of society and found in Darwinian evolutionary theory an explanation of how organisms changed and survived that appeared compatible with its own assumptions. The starting point was the adaptation of societies to their environments. Environments included both the natural world and other social systems. Changes in society, deriving from whatever source, provided the basic material of evolution. Those changes which increased a society's adaptive capacity, measured by its long-run survival, were selected and became institutionalized, following the principle of the survival of the fittest. Sociological functionalism located the main source of adaptation and selection in DIFFERENTIATION, the process whereby the main social functions were dissociated and came to be performed by specialized collectivities in autonomous institutional spheres. Functional differentiation and the parallel structural differentiation would enable each function to be performed more effectively. Anthropological accounts have often referred to specific evolution (the adaptation of an individual society to its particular environment), whereas sociologists have concentrated on general evolution, which is the evolution of superior forms within the total development of human society. This general perspective suggested a unilinear direction of change and that some societies were higher than others on a scale of progress, assumptions that specific evolution did not make.

SEE ALSO: *biologism/biological reductionism; Durkheim; mode of production; Parsons; social Darwinism; sociobiology; urban ecology.*

READING: Eisenstadt (1968a); Peel (1969a)

exchange theory The conceptualization of social interaction, social structure and social order in terms of exchange relations has a long history in anthropology and more recently has been adopted by some sociologists. Two approaches can be identified: individualistic and collectivist exchange theories.

The American individualistic approach, as found in the work of G. C. Homans (1961) and P. M. Blau (1964), follows the hedonistic, utilitarian perspective that individuals seek to maximize their own private gratifications. It assumes that these rewards can only be found in social interaction and thus that people seek rewards in their interactions with each other. Exchange theorists see a similarity between social interactions and economic or market transactions, namely the expectation that benefits rendered will produce a return. The basic paradigm is a two-person interaction model. There is an emphasis on mutual reciprocity, though the basis of exchange remains calculative and involves little trust or shared morality. This approach is one of the precursors of RATIONAL CHOICE THEORY. It faces several criticisms. (1) Its psychological assumptions are naive and exaggerate the self-seeking, calculative elements of personality. (2) The theory is stunted because it cannot go beyond the two-person reciprocity level to social behaviour on a larger scale. (3) It does not explain social processes such as domination or generalized values that cannot be derived from the paradigm of two-person exchange. (4) It is an elegant conceptualization of the sociologically trivial.

The traditional emphasis on collective exchange in French anthropology, associated with M. Mauss and LÉVI-STRAUSS, is not subject to these criticisms. The emphasis is on generalized exchange involving at least three actors, in which any individual participant may not receive from the person to whom he gave, rather than on mutually reciprocal exchange. Exchange involves shared values and trust, the expectation that others will fulfil their obligations to the group or society rather than pursue self-interests. In Lévi-Strauss' work, exchange theory explains the development of these integrative cultural ties through the social networks which generalized exchanges create. Although directed at non-industrial societies, Lévi-Strauss deals with issues of social structure and culture that are more relevant sociologically than the concerns of individual exchange theories.

SEE ALSO: *utilitarianism*.

READING: Bredemeier (1979); Cook (1987)

exchange value See: LABOUR THEORY OF VALUE.

exogamy The concept of exogamy refers to those formal rules or social preferences compelling marriage *outside* the immediate group.

SEE ALSO: *endogamy*.

experimental method In the physical sciences, experimentation is a method of research whereby changes are deliberately made in a process and their effects are observed and measured. The experiment allows the investigator to control all the factors that might affect the phenomenon under study. In sociology it is seldom, if ever, possible to achieve complete control and many investigations are better described as uncontrolled observational studies. In order to provide some estimation of cause and effect within such studies, various techniques may be used. One method is that of the CONTROL GROUP, which reduces, but does not eliminate, the uncontrolled factors. When the investigation is of social processes where control groups cannot be used – the majority of research situations – CAUSAL MODELLING of the data may be attempted.

explanans/explanandum In any explanation, the thing that is to be explained is called the explanandum. The explanans refers to the set of statements which together constitute the explanation of the explanandum.

explanation See: AGENCY AND STRUCTURE; CAUSAL EXPLANATION; CAUSAL MODELLING; DEPENDENT/INDEPENDENT VARIABLES; EXPLANANS/EXPLANANDUM; FALSIFICATIONISM; FUNCTIONALISM; HERMENEUTICS; HYPOTHETICO-DEDUCTIVE METHOD; NATURALISM; PHENOMENOLOGICAL SOCIOLOGY; POSITIVISM; REALISM; RULE; SOCIOLOGY AS SCIENCE; STRUCTURALISM; VERSTEHEN.

extended family This is conventionally defined as a social unit comprising parents and children and other more distant relatives, perhaps including grandparents or uncles and aunts, living under one roof. It is now more widely used to describe a looser set of relationships in which the NUCLEAR FAMILY keeps in contact with wider kin by a variety of means, but does not form a single HOUSEHOLD. The typical family form in modern industrial societies is not, therefore, the isolated nuclear family but is a modified extended family.

Links between members of modified extended families in modern Britain are maintained in a number of ways. For example, recent studies presented in *Social Trends* (1997) have established that most people live within one hour's journey of parents, siblings and other relatives and say that they see them at least monthly. More remotely, contact is maintained by telephone or other means. As J. Finch and J. Mason (1993) show, the extended families are united by a network of obligations and exchange of services from the loan or gift of money to babysitting. Lastly, it is clear from attitude surveys that people continue to hold positive views of the role that wider family members play in their lives. For instance, when asked (*Social Trends*, 1997), only 7 per cent of people say that their friends are more important than their family.

SEE ALSO: *conjugal role; group; kinship*.

READING: Finch (1989)

F

facticity This term, drawn from PHENOMENOLOGICAL SOCIOLOGY, and sometimes confused with ALIENATION, refers to the way in which the external social and natural world appears to individuals as solid, taken-for-granted, and 'thing-like'.

SEE ALSO: *Schutz.*

READING: Berger and Luckmann (1967)

factor analysis This collection of statistical techniques is often used to explore the underlying structure of a set of variables. By identifying underlying dimensions within a data set, factor analysis can simplify complex data. Principal-component factor analysis is often employed in the analysis of survey data to identify any common components or factors underlying a set of items. Frequently, attitude scales that deal with a variety of different items – for example, politics, industrial relations, inequality, capital and corporal punishment, the family, sexual morality – may be shown to contain a single general factor (perhaps authoritarianism in this hypothetical case) that contributes to all items.

false consciousness See: CLASS CONSCIOUSNESS.

falsificationism This doctrine, originally associated with POPPER, claims that scientific advance can only come about through the testing and falsifying of hypotheses, which are then replaced by new hypotheses, also subject to test and falsification. One cannot ultimately verify, only falsify. It is further argued that hypotheses are only meaningful to the extent that a test can be conceived that would falsify them.

It has been argued against this position, originally by T. Kuhn (1970), that scientific change does not come about through the systematic testing and falsification of hypotheses, but through the replacement of one PARADIGM by another. It is also argued that science depends critically on propositions that cannot be falsified, like 'every event has a cause'.

SEE ALSO: *counterfactual; positivism.*

family See: DIVORCE; EXTENDED FAMILY; HOUSEHOLD; NUCLEAR FAMILY; SOCIOLOGY OF THE FAMILY; SYMMETRICAL FAMILY.

fascism Mussolini's corporatist political system, fascism, existed in Italy between 1922 and 1945. The term fascism is often applied, however, to cover somewhat similar political movements elsewhere, for example German Nazism and the Spanish Falange. Fascism was an authoritarian, nationalistic and illiberal political movement arising out of the social and economic crises following the First World War, which were perceived as proving the inadequacy of liberalism and the democratic process.

It had no developed or coherent political philosophy but embraced NATIONALISM, a hatred of communism, a distrust of democratic politics, commitment to the single-party state and faith in charismatic leaders. It glorified violence and supported totalitarianism. In Germany, Nazism was also racialist and anti-Semitic. The social support of fascist movements came from the military, middle-class groups who felt threatened by the social disorder and economic depressions of the inter-war period and by the rise of socialist movements, and some parts of the working class.

The fascist state was corporatist in the sense that many of the autonomous institutions of democratic PLURALISM were suppressed, in order that the state should be the sole representation of the social collectivity. Independent trade unions and political parties were the notable casualties. Italian fascists at one time suggested that professions and industries should act as representative groups which would link the people to the state, but in practice this idea was ignored.

There are a number of theories which seek to explain fascism. (1) W. Reich (1933) argued that fascism resulted from sexual repression in an authoritarian and inhibited society; he concentrated on the sexual symbolism of fascist collective rituals. (2) B. Moore (1967) argued that whether capitalism developed along the lines of democracy or dictatorship depended on the forms of alliance between the landed classes, the peasantry and the urban bourgeoisie; where capitalist agriculture is slow to develop (as in Prussian Germany) and repressive forms of agricultural production predominate, a repressive, fascist state apparatus is necessary for the continued subordination of agricultural labourers. (3) N. Poulantzas (1974) argued that fascism is the result of a deep economic and ideological crisis of the dominant class. When no fraction of the dominant class can impose its leadership on the 'power bloc', the fascist state replaces democratic, parliamentary politics as a solution to the crisis of capitalist society which is threatened by the organized working class. The petty bourgeoisie, which is squeezed by the concentration of large capitalist enterprises, comes to play an important part in government because it is being forced into the working class by capitalist development. The collapse of traditional parliamentary politics results in a reorganization of the political system through the formation of the fascist party and the use of 'extra-parliamentary means' with the support of monopoly capitalism. The conclusion to these class struggles is the dominance of finance capitalism over other CAPITAL FRACTIONS within the political system.

SEE ALSO: *authoritarian personality*; *class struggle*; *corporatism*.

READING: Kitchen (1976)

fatalism A habit of mind or way of perceiving the world in which everything is seen as ordained by fate or beyond human intervention. Individuals with a fatalistic viewpoint believe that there is little that they can do to change their circumstances. The viewpoint has been explored in two main ways in sociology – in E. Durkheim's theory of SUICIDE and in accounts of the images of society held by different social classes. Some sections of the British working class have marked fatalistic attitudes (Marshall *et al.*, 1988).

fatalistic suicide See: DURKHEIM; SUICIDE.

fecundity It is conventional in demography to distinguish between the biological capacity for reproduction (fecundity) and actual reproduction (fertility). FERTILITY is less than fecundity in all societies, and varies considerably among societies without any apparent relation to differences in fecundity. Such differences are largely determined by biology. There is some evidence, for example, that fecundity in Western societies is declining because of a general reduction in levels of female sex hormones.

femininity Many societies have ascribed different and distinctive qualities to men and women. In modern Western societies, it is considered 'feminine' to be caring, warm and sexually attractive, as well as passive, weak and dependent. There is considerable debate as to whether such qualities really are actual characteristics of the genders and, if so, whether they are biologically or socially determined, and in what ways they maintain male power.

SEE ALSO: *gender; masculinity; patriarchy; sex roles; sociology of gender.*

feminism This doctrine, originating in the late eighteenth century, suggests that women are systematically disadvantaged in modern society and advocates equal opportunities for men and women. It is also a social movement which has gradually improved the position of women in twentieth-century Western societies in respect of voting rights, position in the workplace and in marriage. Feminism in the early part of the century was oriented mainly to winning political and legal equality. 'Second wave' feminism, from the 1960s onwards, showed, however, that women still have a way to go in securing equal rights and opportunities.

Feminist ideas have had a great and deserved influence in sociology in recent years. Feminist sociologists have argued that sociologists, who are mostly men, have neglected the sociological significance of women in all areas of the subject. For example, many studies of social stratification have until recently concentrated on the paid work of men as a determinant of the class position of women family members. Sociology is now far more sensitive to issues of gender, and feminism has had a substantial influence on social theory.

SEE ALSO: *class; domestic labour; feminist social theory; patriarchy; sex roles; women and work.*

feminist criminology A critical perspective in CRIMINOLOGY, which emerged in the 1970s alongside CRITICAL CRIMINOLOGY in response to the neglect and misunderstanding of the relationship between GENDER and crime. It used FEMINIST SOCIAL THEORY to develop a new agenda in research and theory. Feminist criminology initially recognized that a significant proportion of victims of crime are women, especially in cases of domestic violence, rape and sexual offences. But it also criticized the sexist assumptions of traditional criminology and fostered a research agenda which examined women offenders, differential court responses according to gender, and the impact of women's prisons. Feminists have argued that women are traditionally governed by the informal controls of domestic life and that female crime is typically a product of the erosion of informal social regulation, for example when young girls are placed in institutional care. When women offend, they are more likely to be regarded as mad rather than bad; that is, female offenders are more likely to experience MEDICALIZATION than their male counterparts. More recently, it is argued that the principal topic of feminist criminology should be the relationship between gender, PATRIARCHY and crime, and not the empirical details of the lives of female offenders.

SEE ALSO: *sexism; sociology of gender; women and crime.*
READING: Smart (1977)

feminist methodology See: FEMINIST SOCIAL THEORY.

feminist social theory Twentieth-century feminist social theory cannot be isolated or understood separately from FEMINISM as a social movement. As the feminist movement has changed from being a campaign for equal voting rights in the 1920s to being a radical movement for fundamental gender equality at work and in domestic activities, legal relations and cultural practices, so feminist social theory has evolved through a variety of forms: liberalism, Marxism and POSTMODERNISM. In general terms, feminist social theory is concerned to understand and explain the subordinate position of women in society by reference to gender differences and specifically in terms of a theory of PATRIARCHY.

Feminist versions of equal-rights doctrines, which had their philosophical origins in M. Wollstonecraft's *A Vindication of the Rights of Woman* (1792), were eventually expressed through the suffragette movement, which attempted to remove various political and social barriers to women's full participation in society. These reformist struggles can be interpreted as political attempts to achieve CITIZENSHIP for women. The 'first wave' of feminism was primarily concerned with the problem of formal equality between men and women.

In the 1960s, feminism assumed a more radical focus, seeking a revolutionary transformation of society as a whole. In theoretical terms, this radical turn involved the adoption of ideas from a variety of radical traditions, including Marxism, psychoanalysis and anarchism. In America, this 'second-wave' feminism was associated with the struggle for civil rights for black people. This political struggle produced the view that the subordination of women was comparable to the colonization of blacks under conditions of IMPERIALISM. Black and female liberation has to take place not only in economic and political terms but also at the level of psychology and culture. This struggle against patriarchy was also associated with anti-militarism and with ecological concerns about the environmental destruction of the planet. Social hierarchy, RACISM, warfare, violence and environmental destruction were seen to be the effects of men's psychological need for dominance and the social organization of patriarchy. In Britain, the occupation of Greenham Common (a US air base where ninety-six cruise missiles were sited) in March 1982 by 250 women is one illustration of feminist opposition to male militarism (Young, 1990). Violent sports, domestic violence, pornography and rape were also treated as general manifestations of male violence towards women. In social and political terms, lesbianism and separatism were responses to male violence and patriarchy. At the level of social theory, there were many experiments to combine feminism with various branches of socialist and CRITICAL THEORY. The key publications in second-wave feminism were: S. de Beauvoir, *The Second Sex* (1949); K. Millet, *Sexual Politics* (1969); S. Firestone, *The Dialectics of Sex* (1970); G. Greer, *The Female Eunuch* (1970); J. Mitchell, *Women: The longest revolution* (1974).

In the 1980s and 1990s, feminist social theory was influenced by poststructuralist and postmodernist analysis. Following postmodernist emphasis on difference and plurality, feminist theorists have argued that traditional feminist analysis 'tended to reflect the viewpoints of white, middle-class women of North America and Western Europe. The irony was that one of the powerful arguments feminist scholars were making was the limitations of scholarship which falsely universalized on the basis of limited perspectives' (Nicholson, 1990, p. 1). It is claimed that 'third-wave' feminism is more sensitive to local, diverse voices of feminism and rejects a universalistic perspective on a single feminist standpoint. Some of the critical publications of contemporary feminism include: C. Gilligan, *In a Different Voice* (1982); B. Hooks, *Feminist Theory* (1984); C. Weedon, *Feminist Practice and Post-Structuralist Theory* (1987); N. Chodorow, *Feminism and Psychoanalytic Theory* (1989). Feminist theorists such as D. Riley (1988) are anxious that postmodernism will dilute feminist criticism of patriarchy and undermine their ability to act as a unified political movement, because postmodern RELATIVISM will challenge the universalistic thrust of feminist opposition to male dominance. Some postmodern feminists claim that traditional forms of female oppression still exist in modern society and that feminist politics cannot be abandoned prematurely.

Feminist social theory has been very important in France, where it has been combined with poststructuralist theories of language, radical literary criticism and post-Freudian psychoanalysis. French writers have been especially interested in the ways in which the human (female) body is represented or suppressed in male-dominated writing. French feminist literary production and theory is often referred to collectively as *écriture féminine*. The key publications include: M. Wittig (1973); H. Cixous (1975; 1976); L. Irigaray (1977).

Feminist social theory has had a general impact on sociology in terms of the conceptualization of sex and GENDER, the analysis of patriarchal POWER and social CLASS. Gender along with AGE, ethnicity and class is regarded as one of the major dimensions of social inequality in human societies. Feminist social theory has also had a significant impact in recent years on methodology. In *Feminist Methods in Social Research* (1992), S. Reinharz argues that there is no single feminist methodology, but feminist methods include research which is qualitative, reflexive, client-focused and interactive. Although feminist theory has been influential in sociology, feminist critics claim that a feminist perspective has yet to be fully incorporated into mainstream sociology, where the 'founding fathers' remain dominant.

SEE ALSO: *body; emotions; Freud; marriage; Mead, Margaret; sexism; sex roles; body; social movements; sociology of the family; sociology of gender; women and work.*

feminization Occupations are said to be feminized when women enter them in significant numbers. For example, clerical work at the beginning of the twentieth century was predominantly a male occupation. Now it is overwhelmingly female.

SEE ALSO: *women and work.*

fertility The crude fertility rate is defined as the actual number of live births per thousand of the population in one year. A slightly more precise measure is the actual number of live births per thousand women of reproductive age. However, neither of these measures is particularly useful, because women of different ages have different intentions about family size. Cohort fertility is a more meaningful measure of changes in fertility over time. This expresses the number of live births per thousand women in a given year during their reproductive span. But even this measure does not yield precise predictions of population size, since later cohorts of women will not have finished their childbearing. Defined in this way, fertility in the United Kingdom has declined from 3.4 births per thousand women born in the early 1870s to a low of 1.8 for those born in the early years of the twentieth century, and stands at just over 2.0 for those born in the early 1950s. 'Fertility' – actual live births – is thus contrasted in DEMOGRAPHY with 'fecundity', which is the *potential* capacity for biological reproduction. The principal factors influencing fertility in a population are the age of marriage, the availability of contraception and attitudes towards family size. A decline in fertility is characteristic of urban, industrial societies and has significant social and economic consequences for the size of the workforce.

SEE ALSO: *birth rate*; *demographic transition*; *fecundity*.

feudalism The social, economic and political structure known as feudalism was found in its most developed form in northern France in the twelfth and thirteenth centuries. Feudalism is conventionally a label applied also to Japan and to other parts of Europe where feudal characteristics have been found, and the system is thought to have lasted in Europe for the five hundred years known as the Middle Ages. Feudalism cannot be defined exactly because of the diversity of cases and the fact that no individual case remained unchanged over the half millennium of the feudal period in Europe.

J. Prawer and S. N. Eisenstadt (1968) list five characteristics common to most developed feudal societies: (1) lord–vassal relationships; (2) personalized government that is mainly effective at local rather than national level and where there is relatively little separation of functions; (3) a pattern of landholding based on granting fiefs in return for services, primarily military; (4) the existence of private armies; (5) rights of lords over the peasants who are serfs. These characterize a political system that was decentralized and depended on a hierarchical network of personal ties within the ranks of the nobility, despite the formal principle of a single line of authority stretching upwards to a king. This provided for collective defence and the maintenance of order. The economic base was the manorial organization of production and a dependent peasantry who provided the surplus that lords needed to perform their political functions.

Sociological interest in feudalism has taken the following directions. M. Weber (1922) was concerned with its political and military arrangements, especially with the socio-economic structure which was required to maintain a feudal cavalry. Weber contrasted the *feu* (a heritable, traditional title to land) and the *benefice* (a title which could not be inherited) to mark the essential difference between feudalism and prebendalism. Weber distinguished several types of feudalism. In Japan, the *daimyo* were patrimonial governors who did not possess a fief but were officials of the emperor. In Islamic feudalism, landlords had territorial rights but there was no feudal ideology; landlords existed on the basis of tax farming. The essence of these various models of feudalism was the nature of rulership: decentralized domination by local lords, who were inculcated with a sense of obligation and loyalty to a sovereign.

K. Marx and F. Engels dealt only briefly with pre-capitalist modes of production, but in the 1970s some Marxist sociologists became interested in the feudal MODE OF PRODUCTION. Unlike capitalism, where workers were dispossessed of all control over the means of production, feudalism did permit peasants effective possession of some of these means (though not legal title). Class struggle between lords and peasants centred on the size of the productive units allocated to tenants, the conditions of tenancy, and control of essential means of production like pasture, drainage and mills. In later Marxist approaches, therefore, it was argued that, because the peasant-tenant has some degree of control over production through, for example, possession of customary rights, 'extra-economic conditions' are required to secure control over the peasantry by landlords. These conditions are basically forms of political and ideological control. The feudal mode of production is thus one which secures the appropriation of surplus labour in the form of rent. Feudal rent may assume a number of forms – rent in kind, money or labour. Variant forms of the mode can be defined in terms of these variations in rent. For example, rent-in-labour requires a particular type of labour process, which is the combination of independent production by tenants with demesne production under the supervision of the lord or an agent. The transition of feudalism to capitalism is, in this perspective, the outcome of continuous struggle over the nature and extent of appropriation by rent. However, there are competing theories of transition; causal primacy may be given to exchange relations, markets, relations and forces of production, and to cultural factors.

SEE ALSO: *patrimonialism; relations of production.*

READING: Holton (1985)

field work This term is used loosely to describe the activity of collecting data in empirical sociological research.

SEE ALSO: *participant observation.*

figurational sociology A perspective associated with ELIAS (1970), figurational or process sociology has three interrelated aspects. (1) It attempts to overcome the false dichotomy of AGENCY AND STRUCTURE, by arguing that individuals are located and understood in terms of enduring social configurations of relationships. (2) It rejects the artificial distinction between the individual and society, by demonstrating that the rise of the individual is itself a social process. (3) All social phenomena have to be understood as social processes. Thus sociology should not study the economy, for example, but economizing processes. Figurational sociology is an argument against METHODOLOGICAL INDIVIDUALISM and REIFICATION.

READING: Mennell (1989)

flexible firm As part of the debate about the decline of FORDISM and the rise of POST-FORDISM, the idea that firms have become internally more flexible has become commonplace. Three types of flexibility have been identified: (1) functional flexibility, which refers to more flexible work tasks and organization in association with a more multi-skilled workforce; (2) numerical flexibility, when firms use non-standard forms of employment (e.g. part-time work, temporary work, consultancy and subcontracting) in order to allow them to expand or contract the size of the firm as product markets change; (3) flexible payment systems which relate pay more than before to employees' performance. While there is evidence that many firms have become more flexible on some of these dimensions, there is little sign of a general shift on all three dimensions and among all firms.

SEE ALSO: *flexible specialization.*

flexible specialization First formulated by M. Piore and C. Sabel (1984), the theory of flexible specialization (FS) attempted to describe and explain a new form of manufacturing organization which emerged with the decline of FORDISM.

FS theory distinguishes between two basic technological paradigms or models: mass production, as found in Fordism, and flexible specialization. Mass production is the manufacture of standardized products in large volumes for mass consumer markets, using special-purpose machinery and semi-skilled labour that specializes in one simple task. Flexible specialization is the production of a wide and changing variety of products in small volumes (including single items) for specialized markets, using general-purpose machinery and skilled and adaptable labour; it can be viewed as a modern form of craft production. *Flexibility* refers to the nature of production systems: new technology, particularly computerization, now permits general-purpose machines to be programmed to produce many different products, while multi-skilled workers, often with an understanding of computer applications, are needed to get the best out of flexible machinery. *Specialization* refers to the nature of product markets: mass markets have fragmented into a multiplicity of specialized markets, as customers now want more variety, individuality and innovation.

Against the LABOUR PROCESS APPROACH, FS theory implies the following changes in work: (1) employees will be re-skilled rather than de-skilled; (2) jobs will become more satisfying, with more freedom and discretion; (3) wages will rise, because employees produce more added value and companies also have to pay more to attract skilled people; (4) industrial relations are likely to become more harmonious, and organizational cultures with a greater feeling of teamwork will develop – partly because jobs and wages improve and partly because managers need to trust employees more, as rapidly changing tasks and employee discretion make tight control inappropriate.

FS maintains that each technological paradigm has particular regulatory require-ments, which are met by institutional arrangements at the micro and macro levels. For flexible specialization, the requirement is to encourage innovation by estab-lishing the optimal balance of competition and cooperation between productive units. Micro-level regulation is provided by the organizational contexts within which productive units are embedded, which take two institutional forms: *industrial districts* and *decentralized large companies*. A particular form of macro-level regulation by the state of the national economy and social welfare system is thought to be required by Fordism, whereas FS has less requirement of any specific form of macro-level state regulation.

In industrial districts – that is, local geographical areas specializing in particular products or processes – independent small or medium-sized firms undertake related activities and create dense networks of interlinkages as the result of subcontracting among themselves. Subcontracting allows firms to specialize in certain things. Thus they can buy expensive equipment and benefit from economies of scale, like larger firms. Firms in industrial districts may share common services (e.g. training, techni-cal and market research, credit and quality control), which no single firm is large enough to provide for itself. Districts develop means of controlling competition which encourage firms to compete on the basis of innovative products and manufac-turing processes, rather than by means of low pay and poor conditions. A range of institutions may have a regulatory role in providing common services and control-ling competition: for example, trade unions and employers' associations, local government, local banks and credit unions, churches. Classic examples of industrial districts are what is sometimes known as Third Italy, a collection of industrial districts specializing in engineering, furniture, shoes and clothing, and Silicon Valley, in California, which is devoted to electronics. In decentralized large companies, pro-ductive units have considerable autonomy and almost resemble small firms or workshops. They have links with other relatively autonomous units in the company and access to common services, while the company regulates the degree of competition and cooperation among the units. Some writers indicate that shared organizational cultures also assist cooperation and coordination among units. Large companies increasingly contract out operations to other companies and develop networks similar to those in industrial districts, and relations between a company and its suppliers are regulated by trust as well as by contract.

The theory is notable for its attempt to link a number of different levels: the manufacturing system at the factory or productive unit level; the intermediate, micro-regulatory level of companies and local economies; the macro-regulatory level of governmental regulation of the national economy. It rightly draws attention to the importance of changing product markets and technologies, and to the fact that networks in local economies and the structure of large companies are also changing. However, FS has been criticized on various grounds. (1) By creating two opposed technological paradigms, it oversimplifies present-day reality and history. Both models have coexisted in many national economies, while, even within a single firm, mixes of mass and craft production may occur. (2) More flexible manufacturing methods have been adopted by mass producers to make the more varied and innovative products required by modern market conditions. Computerized technologies provide special-purpose machines with more flexibility than before, so mass producers can switch between different products within a limited range while still manufacturing in high volumes. Moreover, products made for specialized markets may simply be special combinations of mass-produced parts: for instance, many motor-car manufacturers produce some special models in low volumes, but these use standard engines, drive trains, chassis components, etc. Most exponents accept these two criticisms and recognize that the two paradigms are not opposed and various elements of each can be combined in hybrid forms. (3) The theory is impossible to test, because the various elements are not precisely specified and cannot be measured, while their interrelationships are vague. (4) New technology need not cause upskilling, autonomy and job satisfaction, since managers may not choose to use it in ways which improve low-level jobs. (5) Many small firms are old-fashioned 'sweat-shops', with poor pay and conditions and with little record of innovation. Thus the progressive character of industrial districts may be overemphasized in FS theory. (6) So far, large firms do not seem to have decentralized to the extent suggested by the theory; nevertheless they are still dominant in the world economy and are the main source of innovative products and processes.

SEE ALSO: *flexible firm*; *management*; *organization theory*; *organizational culture*; *post-Fordism*; *postmodernity*; *regulation school*.

READING: Pollert (1991)

focus group A technique used in qualitative research, in which a small group of people is asked to focus on an issue and discuss it in depth with an interviewer, often on a number of separate occasions over time. It is used extensively in market research and political opinion polling as an alternative or supplement to traditional questionnaire surveys.

folk culture A term used to refer to the CULTURE of pre-industrial societies. It is often contrasted with, on the one hand, the culture of industrial societies and, on the other, the culture of simple or tribal societies.

SEE ALSO: *anthropology*; *industrial society*; *mass society*.

folk devils Many societies scapegoat certain minority groups as being immoral or evil – that is, as folk devils – and deserving control and punishment. In recent times, groups such as black youths, drug-users, hippies, football fans and homosexuals have been demonized in this way. In modern societies, this process is often promoted by the mass media, which may portray these groups in such simplistic terms that the police and the courts feel obliged to act against them; this is sometimes known as a 'societal reaction'. Such campaigns can become MORAL PANICS.

The classical study by S. Cohen (1991) describes how young people visiting British seaside towns in the 1960s on motorscooters and motorbikes in large numbers became involved in fights. The fighting was relatively minor, but its importance was exaggerated by newspapers and other agencies, who characterized the perpetrators as folk devils. The police were obliged to intervene forcefully, producing a process of DEVIANCE AMPLIFICATION.

SEE ALSO: *deviant behaviour; labelling theory; stereotypes.*

folk society A concept used by R. Redfield to designate one pole of a continuum between folk and secular or urban societies, his version of F. Toennies' distinction between GEMEINSCHAFT and *Gesellschaft*. Folk societies are relatively more isolated, homogeneous, and traditionally organized, and less secular and individualistic.

SEE ALSO: *rural–urban continuum.*

folkways This concept, introduced by W. G. Sumner (1906), describes the everyday activities within a small-scale society which have become established and are socially sanctioned. Folkways differ from MORES in that they are less severely sanctioned and are not abstract principles.

forces of production A concept used within Marxist sociology, the forces of production refer to both the materials worked on and the tools and techniques employed in production of economic goods. They have to be distinguished from RELATIONS OF PRODUCTION.

SEE ALSO: *Marx; mode of production.*

Fordism Initially, this referred to the mechanized, mass-production manufacturing methods developed in the USA by Henry Ford between 1908 and 1914. He divided previously complex work tasks into a number of simple operations, applying the principles of SCIENTIFIC MANAGEMENT, and also standardized the design of the product to eliminate all variation. These changes enabled Ford to mechanize the production of motor cars by means of special-purpose machinery (dedicated to one product and one operation) and moving assembly lines. Labour costs were lowered, because work simplification increased output and also substituted cheaper, unskilled labour for expensive, skilled workers, while production volumes were higher as the result of mechanization, thus creating economies of scale. Ford in fact paid his unskilled labour higher wages than were available to unskilled workers elsewhere, in order to persuade them to work in his factory. Nevertheless, the net effect was to lower the cost of each unit of production. Machine pacing of work and tight supervision also ensured labour discipline. In addition, Ford integrated all the operations involved in manufacturing on one site.

As a manufacturing system, Fordism can be defined as the mass production of standardized goods, using dedicated machines and moving assembly lines, employing unskilled or semi-skilled labour in fragmented jobs, with tight labour discipline, often in large, integrated factories, resulting in scale economies and lower unit costs. This system spread from motor cars to other consumer products and from the USA to other societies: by the 1970s it was the normal method of manufacturing standardized products in high volumes in many industries around the world. In industries that produced in lower volumes and where more worker skill was required, Fordist manufacturing was less likely to be found.

Fordism has been extended by some to include a particular set of economic and social welfare arrangements that are thought to be associated with this manufacturing system. The argument is that the system requires regulation or governance by the state to maintain its profitability. Huge investments in dedicated machinery and purpose-built factories mean that Fordism needs large and stable markets for consumer goods in order to recover these costs; therefore the role of the state is to regulate the economy in ways that maintain full employment and avoid severe fluctuations in consumers' purchasing power, and to use social-welfare payments to maintain high levels of consumption. Keynesian economic management and the welfare state are seen as a natural corollary of Fordism.

However, a number of developments in the final quarter of the twentieth century threatened Fordism: global economic fluctuations that reduced the stability of product markets and could not be regulated by individual nation states; intensified competition for established producers in the traditional industrial economies from lower-cost manufacturers in newly industrializing societies; shifts in consumer demand that reduced the markets for mass-produced, standardized goods, as these markets reached saturation and as preferences changed to favour greater variety and less standardization; the development of new forms of more flexible automation that reduced investment in dedicated equipment; political change that meant some governments changed their mode of regulation, withdrawing from state intervention in the economy and social welfare in favour of free markets. Commentators speak now of POST-FORDISM.

SEE ALSO: *automation; flexible firm; flexible specialization; globalization; globalization of production; labour process approach; postmodernity; regulation school.*

formal organization All social collectivities involve some form of organization, but the term formal organization is reserved for collectivities that have developed formal procedures for regulating relations between members and their activities. The sociological investigation of such collectivities is the domain of ORGANIZATION THEORY, which focuses primarily though not exclusively on economic and political or governmental formal organizations. *Informal organization* describes social relationships and actions that do not coincide with formal procedures and roles.

SEE ALSO: *bureaucracy; role.*

formal sociology This approach, associated particularly with SIMMEL and early-twentieth-century German sociology, took the *form* of social relationships as the object of analysis and studied relationships which differed in substance but displayed the same formal properties. For example, competition may be viewed as a relationship with distinct formal characteristics, no matter what the setting – whether it occurs in the market place, on the sports field, or in the political arena. WEBER was also associated with formal sociology, and part of his endeavour was to outline the basic forms of human interaction which occur in any society, such as power, competition and organization.

Foucault, Michel (1926–84) Elected to the Collège de France in 1969 and the chair of the History of Systems of Thought, Foucault had spent much of his early career outside France as an assistant at the University of Uppsala (1955–8), director of the French Centre at the University of Warsaw, Poland (1958), and director of the French Institute in Hamburg, Germany (1959). He returned to France in 1962 as professor of philosophy at the University of Clermont-Ferrand. His thesis *L'Histoire de la folie* (1961) established his reputation outside France when it was translated as *Madness and Civilization* in 1971.

Foucault did his undergraduate studies in philosophy and psychology, when he was influenced by ALTHUSSER and by philosophers of science like CANGUILHEM. He shared with these authors the view that the history of ideas cannot be written as a lineage of individual thinkers. Rather one has to study systems of thought and their revolutionary changes and ruptures. Knowledge and power are intimately connected and the growth of power is accompanied by new forms of knowledge. At the same time, he rejected the existentialist philosophy of writers like J.-P. Sartre and implicitly embraced the so-called anti-humanism of POSTSTRUCTURALISM. His views on EPISTEMOLOGY and methodology were outlined in *The Archaeology of Knowledge* (1969) and *The Order of Things* (1966).

His research interests were broadly in three areas of history. (1) He was concerned to understand the rise of discipline and the regulation of the individual in his study of psychiatry in *Madness and Civilization*, PENOLOGY in *Discipline and Punish* (1975) and medicine in *The Birth of the Clinic* (1963). Foucault attacked the official view of the history of psychiatry that interprets the professional growth of psychiatry as a triumph of reason over madness. Foucault emphasized instead the regulation of the individual that was made possible by psychiatric practice. (2) He studied the regulation of sexuality in Christianity, which attempted to control sexual desire by its denunciation, and in the classical world, which managed sexuality through a series of techniques or arts of the self. The results of these historical studies were published as *The History of Sexuality* (1976), *The Care of the Self* (1984a) and *The Use of Pleasure* (1984b). Foucault's main but controversial claim was that Victorian society, far from suppressing sexual discussion and inquiry, was obsessed by sex. In the case of the Christian legacy, he attempted to show how the Western notion of truth emerged from the confessional tradition, where sexual secrets could be brought into the open. (3) An integrating theme that ran through all his work was a concern with the socio-political practices or technologies by which the self is constructed. From these inquiries, commentators have argued that the central and overarching concept of Foucault's sociology was governance or *governmentality*, namely the administrative structures of the state, the patterns of self-government of individuals and the regulatory principles of social structure. Foucault argued that governmentality has become the common foundation of all forms of modern political rationality; that is, the administrative systems of the state have been extended in ways that maximize its control over the population. This extension of administrative rationality was first concerned with demographic processes of birth, morbidity and death, and later with the psychological health of the population. These processes have been described by N. Rose (1989) as 'governing the soul'.

Foucault's research gave rise to a distinctive notion of POWER, in which he emphasized the importance of the local or 'micro' manifestations of power, the role of professional knowledge in the legitimation of such power relationships and the productive rather than negative characteristics of the effects of power. His approach can be contrasted usefully with the concept of power in MARXIST SOCIOLOGY, where power is visible in terms of the police and army, concentrated in the state and ultimately explained by the ownership of the economic means of production. Foucault's view of power is more subtle, with an emphasis on the importance of knowledge and information in modern means of SURVEILLANCE. 'Governmentality' is the generic term for these power relations. Foucault has defined this as 'the ensemble formed by the institutions, procedures, analyses and reflections, the calculations and tactics, that allow the exercise of this very specific, albeit complex, form of power, which has as its target populations' (1991, p. 102). The importance of this definition is that, historically, the power of the state is less concerned with sovereignty over things (land and wealth) and more concerned with maximizing the productive power of administration over population and reproduction. Furthermore, Foucault interpreted the exercise of administrative power in productive terms; that is, enhancing population potential through, for example, state support for reproductive technology.

Foucault's political theory suggests that there is not one but many forms of rationality, just as there are many forms of political practice. His critical theory attempted to provide a criticism of the forms of knowledge (rationality) that are contained in political practices. As a result, he examined the treatment of marginal groups in society (criminals, hermaphrodites, the mentally ill and so forth). His approach to social theory continues to be a source of inspiration for social criticism. FEMINIST SOCIAL THEORY has drawn on Foucault's interest in how governmental rationality controls the human body and how institutions regulate the lives of women.

Foucault has been criticized for his neglect of the formal power of the state, on the grounds that the sovereign powers of the state cannot be ignored. His anarchistic political orientation treats every aspect of government as an instance of regulatory, albeit productive, power. Foucault has been attacked by HABERMAS, on the grounds that his criticism of rationality is ultimately self-defeating: it cannot justify or legitimate any alternative forms of politics, apart from offering a specific defence of some local resistance to authority. Similarly, every oppositional social movement – for example, the Islamic struggle against the Shah of Iran – was automatically interpreted by Foucault as a struggle for liberation. Other critics have argued that Foucault's social analysis cannot be converted into a social policy or a political programme. His emphasis on DISCOURSE has been criticized, because it effectively precludes the subjective interpretation of action and does not offer solutions to issues raised, for example, by PHENOMENOLOGICAL SOCIOLOGY. Finally, Foucault failed to recognize that his ideas had been anticipated by earlier sociologists. For example, there is a close intellectual relationship between Foucault's study of sexual regulation in early Christianity and the study of the Protestant sects by WEBER. Despite these critical responses, Foucault's thought has been influential in the study of MENTAL HEALTH, the sociology of the BODY, the SOCIOLOGY OF MEDICINE and GENDER. Because he was a staunch critic of MODERNITY, he is often mistakenly associated with POSTMODERNISM.

SEE ALSO: *carceral society; ideology; panopticism.*

READING: Hoy (1986); Simons (1995); Dumm (1996)

Frankfurt School An influential movement in contemporary Marxism, the Frankfurt School was a group of social scientists who worked in the Institute of Social Research (1923–50), which was connected to the University of Frankfurt. Members of the Frankfurt School were predominantly Jewish and as a group went into exile during the Nazi ascendancy. The Institute moved to Columbia University, New York, at this time, returning to Frankfurt in 1949. Although principally important for their theoretical writing on epistemology, Marxism and culture, the school undertook important empirical research in America on racism and prejudice, resulting in the publication of *The Authoritarian Personality* (1950). Leading figures in the school included ADORNO, BENJAMIN, E. Fromm, M. Horkheimer and MARCUSE.

Members of the Frankfurt School had a very wide range of interests and influences. They depended primarily upon the work of MARX, but also owed intellectual debts to FREUD and WEBER, among others. They engaged in empirical work on music, literature and radio audiences, on the one hand, and in theoretical studies in epistemology and social theory on the other. Their principal lines of argument were as follow.

(1) The critique of advanced capitalism. Members of the Frankfurt School combined Marx's analysis of CAPITALISM with Weber's of RATIONALIZATION. Although rationalization had its origins in pre-capitalist society, they argued that the two social forms have become intertwined, with rationalization providing the means by which the aims of capitalism are achieved. The Frankfurt School provided an essentially pessimistic view of contemporary society: rationalization provides an iron discipline and capitalism a set of exploitative social relations. Despite the many sources of oppression, members of the school saw little possibility of revolutionary social change.

(2) The critique of economism. The Frankfurt School adopted a particular view of Marxism in proposing a synthesis of Marx and Weber. In criticizing ECONOMISM, they took issue with some versions of Marxist theory, particularly those that saw the economy as the only or overriding force in social change. The result was a greater emphasis on the role of CULTURE than would be adopted by many Marxists.

(3) The critique of POSITIVISM. Members of the Frankfurt School took issue with the epistemology that they saw as dominant in Western society, namely positivism, which regards knowledge as rooted in, and testable by, sense experience. They favoured, rather, a form of RATIONALISM, in which dialectical thought reveals a stream of contradictions which are resolved only to reappear in a new guise.

(4) The relationship to Freud. Another theoretical innovation of the Frankfurt School was the incorporation of psychoanalysis, primarily in its Freudian versions, into their account of society. This represented another variation on Marxism, in that the school saw that a theory of human needs and desires was needed to complement a structural theory of society.

SEE ALSO: *authoritarian personality; critical theory; dialectical materialism; Habermas; instrumental reason.*

READING: Jay (1973); Held (1980)

free rider See: COLLECTIVE ACTION.

frequency distribution See: DISTRIBUTION.

Freud, Sigmund (1856–1939) Born in Moravia of Jewish parents, he was brought up in Vienna where he studied medicine and specialized in neurology. His early work was in the histology of the nervous system, but, influenced by J. Breuer's use of hypnosis, he made an important contribution to the study of hysteria by the use of free association (or 'talking therapy'). Their research on hysterical phenomena and psychotherapy was published as *Studies on Hysteria* (1895). As a consequence of this clinical work, Freud developed the basic concepts of psychoanalysis (the unconscious, repression, abreaction and transference), which were described in, for example, *Five Lectures on Psycho-Analysis* (1910a). Freud became interested in how jokes and dreams might reveal the nature and problems of human sexuality in *The Interpretation of Dreams* (1900) and *Jokes and their Relation to the Unconscious* (1905a). He applied the same approach to the study of lapses of memory and verbal slips in *The Psychopathology of Everyday Life* (1901). Freud also developed a psychoanalysis of art in *Leonardo da Vinci* (1910b), where he argued that paintings like 'Madonna and Child with St Anne' were products of Leonardo's homosexuality, rejection of parental authority and narcissism. The theory of childhood sexuality was outlined in *Three Essays on the Theory of Sexuality* (1905b); his conception of the dynamics of personality was published in *The Ego and the Id* (1923). Freud and his colleagues founded the International Psycho-Analytical Association in 1910 in Nuremberg; they also created journals to disseminate their ideas. These were the *Central Journal for Psycho-Analysis* and *Internal Journal for Medical Psycho-Analysis*. Freud wrote an account of these institutional and theoretical developments in *On the History of the Psycho-Analytical Movement* (1914) and *An Autobiographical Study* (1925).

Although Freud's psychoanalytical research covered a wide variety of issues, it was his perspective on the conflict between the instinctual gratification of the individual and the requirements of social order which was particularly influential in sociology. In his later work – *The Future of an Illusion* (1927), *Civilization and its Discontents* (1930) and *Moses and Monotheism* (1934–8) – Freud emphasized the contradiction between the satisfaction of sexuality and aggression for the individual and the importance of social control for civilization. The social order is a fragile compromise between sexual fulfilment, social discipline and work.

Freud's theories have been influential in both sociology and Marxism. PARSONS adopted Freud's account of personality development to provide the psychological underpinnings of the socialization process, but, in stressing the complementarity between personality and social systems, Parsons neglected the contradictory relationship between sexuality and social order. In Marxism, ALTHUSSER referred to Freud's discovery of the unconscious as parallel to K. Marx's discovery of the laws of modes of production. In the FRANKFURT SCHOOL, psychoanalytical theories were adopted to develop a materialist conception of personality as a companion to Marx's materialist analysis of society. Equally, Freud has been criticized by many feminists, on the grounds that his theory of sexuality was a reflection of male prejudice.

SEE ALSO: *feminism; Foucault; Gellner; gender; myth; patriarchy; taboo.*
READING: Bocock (1983)

friendship Nuclear families are tied to the wider community by a variety of links of which KINSHIP is particularly important and much researched. Friendship is, however, conceivably of greater significance but is very under-researched. Willmott and Young (1960), for example, found that a middle-class suburban neighbourhood community was based on friendship, not kinship.

Friendship patterns differ by class and gender. In general, although the working class have more frequent contact with kin than the middle class do, the reverse is true of friendship. Allan (1979) argues that class differences are due to different ways of organizing friendship. Although middle-class friendships start in particular settings – work or the tennis club, for instance – true friendship only develops when the interaction is continued outside that setting. Working-class friendships, on the other hand, remain confined to the original setting. So middle-class people will tend to plan friendship meetings and entertain in their homes; the working class do not plan meetings and keep their homes to themselves.

In all social classes, women have less contact with friends (and more with relatives) than men do. This must have a good deal to do with the greater tendency for women to be confined to the home: they have a greater degree of PRIVATIZATION.

SEE ALSO: *community; extended family; household; nuclear family; sociology of the family*.

READING: Allan (1989)

functional imperative or **functional prerequisite** These concepts refer to the basic needs of a society which have to be met if it is to continue to survive as a functioning system. For example, a system of social STRATIFICATION is said to be necessary to ensure that the most able people are recruited to the most important positions, a requirement for an efficient society. The concept has been much criticized on the grounds that it is difficult to establish what are the functional imperatives in any society.

SEE ALSO: *evolutionary theory; functionalism; need; Parsons; teleology*.

functional theory of stratification This theory was important in American discussions of inequality in the 1950s and 1960s. K. Davis and W. E. Moore (1945) asserted that in all societies there are positions that objectively have more functional importance than others and need special skills if they are to be performed adequately. These skills, however, are in short supply because talent is scarce and training is costly of people's time and resources. So, there must be adequate rewards to induce the right people to develop their skills. Such rewards are typically a mix of monetary inducements and high social status or PRESTIGE. STRATIFICATION is universal and results from the need to fill positions of functional importance. It should be noted that Davis and Moore recognized that the existence of inherited wealth and property might prevent a tight relationship between material rewards and functional importance and, also, that they made fewer assumptions than other functionalists about a social consensus of occupational importance.

SEE ALSO: *functionalism*.

functionalism Now a controversial perspective within sociology, functionalism has a long history. Nineteenth-century sociologists were greatly impressed by the way in which the various elements of a society were interdependent, and they often explained this interdependence in terms of EVOLUTIONARY THEORY or the

ORGANIC ANALOGY. Just as the heart has the function of circulating the blood, so also do social institutions have functions for society as a whole. Functionalist ideas were also introduced into sociology via social anthropology.

As a minimal definition, functionalism accounts for a social activity by referring to its consequences for the operation of some other social activity, institution, or society as a whole. There are a large number of types of functionalist argument, but three have been especially important. (1) A social activity or institution may have latent functions for some other activity. For example, some contend that whatever the intentions of individual members of families, the change from an extended family form to a nuclear one benefited (had latent functions for) the process of industrialization; mainly, that people were freed of family ties and were able to be geographically mobile. This claim of latent functionality for industrialization is part of an explanation of the change in family structure. (2) A social activity may contribute to the maintenance of the stability of a SOCIAL SYSTEM. For example, E. Durkheim argued that religious practices were best understood as contributing to the integration and stability of a society. Some theorists would go so far as to say that one should look at all social institutions as performing this function. (3) A social activity may contribute to the satisfying of basic social needs or functional prerequisites. PARSONS argued that societies have certain needs that must be met if they are to survive, and institutions have to be seen as meeting those needs.

There has been a great deal of debate about functionalist argument, much of it very repetitive, although the debate has lessened since the 1980s. Four important arguments have been adduced against one or all of the variations of functionalism outlined above. (1) Functionalism cannot account for social conflict or other forms of instability, because it sees all social activities as smoothly interacting to stabilize societies. Functionalists have responded to this claim by suggesting that social conflict may, in fact, have positive functions for social order, or, in the concept of DYSFUNCTION, admitting that not all social activities will have positive functions for all other activities. (2) Functionalism cannot account for change, in that there appears to be no *mechanism* which will disturb existing functional relationships. The functionalist response to this has been to employ concepts such as DIFFEREN-TIATION. (3) Functionalism is a form of TELEOLOGY in that it explains the existence of a social activity by its consequences or effects. (4) Functionalism neglects the meanings that individuals give to their actions by concentrating simply on the consequences of actions. In the 1980s, following T. Parsons' death in 1979, there was a revival of interest in Parsons' functionalism, which attempted to answer many traditional criticisms of functionalism. This movement has been called 'neo-functionalism'.

SEE ALSO: *functional imperative; holism; latent function; Malinowski; Radcliffe-Brown; reciprocity; social structure; stratification; systems theory.*

READING: Cohen, P. S. (1968); Ryan (1970)

G

game theory This component of RATIONAL CHOICE THEORY extends the theory of rational individual action to situations of interdependence or social interaction; that is, where two or more individuals do not act independently but interact and are mutually dependent. In one form of interdependence, an actor needs to take into account the actions of others but can treat these as given and need not calculate how the others will react to what he or she decides to do. Rational choice theorists are more concerned with 'strategic' interdependence: where the individual, in choosing a course of action, does need to consider what actions others will take in response to his or her decision or, indeed, in response to what they anticipate his or her decision will be. In strategic interdependence, the social environment is reactive and not given, thus the outcome of interaction cannot be explained by the actions of one individual. Game theory seeks to explain social action and interaction in such situations: it attempts to clarify the strategic interdependencies in which individuals are enmeshed and to predict their actions. It permits the mathematical modelling of possible and likely choices in situations with common characteristics (including the structure of the game, the number of players and whether there are zero-sum or non-zero-sum outcomes – see below). It assumes that all 'players' (individual actors) in a 'game' (an interaction) will normally act rationally to promote their own preferences/desired outcomes.

The Prisoner's Dilemma, which focuses on the problem of cooperation, is one of the games that has long interested social scientists. Two people are arrested on suspicion of committing a crime. They are questioned by the police in separate rooms, which prevents any communication between the two. The police know that they have no firm evidence, so they present each prisoner with the following set of alternatives. If one confesses and also provides evidence against the other, he will be released immediately while the other will go to prison for ten years. If they both confess, each will be sent to prison but the police will recommend a more lenient sentence of five years. But if neither confesses, the police will find a lesser charge – being in possession of stolen goods, for example – which will guarantee that both are imprisoned for one year. Each prisoner has the choice to confess or not, but neither can control the outcome on his own, because this depends on what they both decide. The best strategy for the two of them jointly is to cooperate and not to confess (then both go to prison for one year). But each is unsure about what the other will choose to do and, should one of them decide to deny his guilt while the other confesses, then one gets ten years and the other goes free. Given this uncertainty about the other, the best strategy for each individually is to confess (and they both go to prison for five years). The game highlights how strategic interactions may deliver outcomes that are less than optimal for all concerned. It is not that people are irrational or fail to understand the situation, rather that, by acting rationally in pursuit of one's own interest and with a correct understanding of the range of choices, poor outcomes still result.

One solution to the problem of cooperation is to be found in repeated games. Faced with the prospect of the game being repeated, people have been found to develop different strategies which generally promote cooperative outcomes that are to both players' long-term advantage. Tit-for-tat strategies are particularly effective. If one player starts with a cooperative move, then the other responds similarly and a cycle of cooperation develops. Game theorists assume that people may promise to cooperate but will break their promises if it is in their interests to do so. For example, the two prisoners might have agreed prior to their arrest that neither would confess, but once in the police station both will choose to break the agreement. In repeated games or social interactions, however, it becomes rational for self-interested individuals to keep promises and to trust others to do the same.

The other solution is to change the costs and benefits of making different choices. One could add a further element to the Prisoner's Dilemma: that if one person confesses and goes free while his partner gets ten years, then the friends of the second criminal will take their revenge on the first. In this new situation, it is more likely that rational players will not confess and both will choose the one-year sentence.

A basic distinction has been made between games with *zero-sum* and *non-zero-sum* properties. In the former, one player can only gain at the cost of the other, because the size of the 'cake' is fixed and if one gets more, others get less, while in the latter all can gain because the size of the cake can be increased. In the Prisoner's Dilemma, the prison sentences vary according to the strategies of the prisoners and only in one case would one party gain at the expense of the other. More recently, the divide has been between games with *complete information* and those with *incomplete information*. This gives priority to ascertaining what each player knows about the objectives of the others and allows the analyst to incorporate the notion of BOUNDED RATIONALITY. The main focus of game theory has been situations where players' interests are, at least in part, in COMPETITION, but social coordination and cooperation in non-competitive situations have now begun to attract attention.

To date, game theory has largely downplayed the possibilities of trust, communication and social norms of reciprocity as bases of social interaction. It has assumed as well that social actors are primarily self-interested and motivated by personal gain, although in principle game theory can handle any set of individual preferences and does not require this limited view of motivation. Consequently, many sociologists have been sceptical of its relevance. *Rationality and Society* and *Journal of Mathematical Sociology* are the main sociological journals that publish in this area. However, economists and political scientists have taken to game theory with enthusiasm. They have used it, for example, to analyse business strategies of companies, pay bargaining between employers and employees, and rivalry between political parties and between nations.

SEE ALSO: *collective action.*

READING: Axelrod (1984); Hargreaves Heap and Varoufakis (1995)

gang This term is typically used to refer to small groups which are bound together by a common sense of loyalty and territory, and which are hierarchically structured around a gang leader. Although the term occurs in a variety of contexts – such as 'work gang' – it is most commonly employed in the sociology of deviance to refer to groups of male adolescents engaged in various deviant activities. In F. M. Thrasher (1927) and W. F. Whyte (1956), the existence of delinquent gangs was seen to be the product of the urban disorganization of working-class communities, providing young men with a sense of identity and excitement. Thrasher demonstrated that gangs were not loosely organized collections of individuals, but integrated groups, bound together by conflict with the wider community, with a strong sense of loyalty and commitment. A. Cohen (1955) treated working-class gangs as subcultures which rejected middle-class values. He argued that the gang values were non-utilitarian, negative and delinquent. R. Cloward and L. Ohlin (1960) argued that delinquent gangs were caught between the opportunity structures of the working and middle classes; this gave rise to three different subcultures, namely criminal (concerned with illegal methods of making money), conflict (concerned with violence) and retreatist (concerned with drugs). Subcultures were seen as defensive reactions to limited social opportunities by young (predominantly male) adolescents. This theory was an application of ANOMIE to JUVENILE DELINQUENCY. Subsequent debates questioned whether gangs were tightly organized, primary groups or merely diffuse, impermanent groups. Interest in gangs is now much less and they are rarely discussed.

SEE ALSO: *adolescence; Chicago School; deviance amplification; deviant behaviour; differential association; group; peer group; primary relationship; subculture; youth culture.*

Garfinkel, Harold (b. 1917) Between 1946 and 1952, Garfinkel trained in the Department of Social Relations at Harvard University under the supervision of PARSONS. Responsible for initiating a school of sociology known as ETHNOMETH-ODOLOGY, Garfinkel is interested in analysing the methods used by people in everyday life to describe and make sense of their own activities. His main publication is a collection of essays, *Studies in Ethnomethodology* (1967).

gatekeeper A person of influence, often informal, who controls access to resources. For example, the term has been used in the sociology of science to describe the way in which influential scientists – as journal editors, referees for grant proposals or job applications, or conference organizers – control what is to count as good science or bad science. In doing so, it is argued, they can regulate careers and reputations.

gay studies See: GENDER.

Geisteswissenschaften A generic term used to cover the human sciences, it is usually associated with a particular view of human sciences as disciplines employing methods radically distinct from those of the natural sciences, particularly as they involve an *understanding* of human beings.

SEE ALSO: *empathy; hermeneutics; Simmel; Verstehen; Weber.*

READING: Outhwaite (1975)

Gellner, Ernest (1925–96) Born in Paris, he became professor of social anthropology at the University of Cambridge. He was highly critical of linguistic philosophy in *Words and Things* (1959) and of the reluctance in modern anthropology to engage in rational criticism of other societies in *Saints of the Atlas* (1969). In *Thought and Change* (1964), he argued that the promotion of wealth through industrialization and government by co-nationals are the principal bases of legitimacy of modern societies. In *Legitimation of Belief* (1974), he criticized modern pluralism and relativism. In *Muslim Society* (1982), he considered the impact of social change on Islamic cultures. His work is noted for its use of social anthropology to explore traditional philosophical issues and vice versa. In *The Psychoanalytic Movement* (1985), he provided an explanation of the social success of Freudian therapy, which questioned the basic assumptions of psychoanalysis as a coherent theory or effective practice. His other works include *Postmodernism, Reason and Religion* (1992) and *Revolutions in the Sacred Grove* (1995).

Gemeinschaft Usually translated as COMMUNITY, this term is contrasted with *Gesellschaft* or 'association'. Societies characterized by *Gemeinschaft* relations are homogeneous, largely based on kinship and organic ties, and have a moral cohesion often founded on common religious sentiment. These relationships are dissolved by the DIVISION OF LABOUR, INDIVIDUALISM and competitiveness; that is, by the growth of *Gesellschaft*-relationships. Whereas TOENNIES (1887) regarded *Gemeinschaft* as the expression of real, organized life, *Gesellschaft* is an artificial social arrangement based on the conflict of egoistic wills.

   SEE ALSO: *civilization; rural–urban continuum; urban way of life.*

gender If the sex of a person is biologically determined, the gender of a person is culturally and socially constructed. There are thus two sexes (male and female) and two genders (masculine and feminine). The principal theoretical and political issue is whether gender as a socially constructed phenomenon is related to or determined by biology. For example, in the nineteenth century various medical theories suggested that the female personality was determined by anatomy and women's reproductive functions. These views have been challenged by FEMINISM. Anthropological research has also shown the cultural specificity of notions about gender, sexuality and sex roles. For example, Margaret MEAD showed in a number of cross-cultural studies that, while gender differentiation is widespread, the social tasks undertaken by men and women are highly variable. There is no general relationship across societies between social roles and biological sex. Social psychologists have treated gender identity as the product of child training rather than as biologically given. ETHNOMETHODOLOGY studies 'gender' as the problem of how individual sexuality is assigned.

More recently, critics have challenged these interpretations, because (1) while sociologists distinguish between sex and gender, they often treat the latter as an expression of the former, thereby giving biology a determining significance, and (2) they fail to provide the connection between the economic subordination of women and its expression through the family and personal life. In the radical critique, it is the place of women in relation to economic production which ultimately determines male/female differences. In this sense, it has been argued that 'gender' is analogous to class relationships. The task of establishing systematic, causal connections between CAPITALISM, CLASS and PATRIARCHY has, however, proved to be highly problematic. Theoretical attempts to develop a sociological perspective on biological sex, gender, SEX ROLES and personality have nevertheless transformed many taken-for-granted assumptions in a number of sociological topics. For example, feminists within the psychoanalytic tradition have challenged the basic ideas of FREUD by showing that the Oedipus complex, penis envy and castration complex should be interpreted as features of the symbolic world of patriarchal power. Modern SOCIOBIOLOGY questions the sociological emphasis on culture over biology.

SEE ALSO: *body; domestic labour; feminism; feminist social theory; nature/nurture debate; sociology of gender.*

READING: Abbott and Wallace (1990); Robinson and Richardson (1997)

gender stereotyping See: EDUCATIONAL ATTAINMENT; LABOUR MARKET SEGMENTATION; SEX ROLES; STEREOTYPES.

generalized order See: MEAD, GEORGE H.

generation There is an important distinction between generation as a term to describe KINSHIP relationships, namely the structural relationships between parents and children, and the use of generation to describe COHORT processes. The idea of generational or cohort structures was originally developed in sociology by MANNHEIM as a critical reflection on the Marxist theory of CLASS. Following Mannheim's essay 'The problem of generations' (1952a), 'generation' is sometimes claimed to be as important as 'social class' or 'gender' in the explanation of individual and group differences in culture, interests and behaviour. 'Generational conflicts' and the stratification of society by 'age groups' are thus held to be parallel or analogous to 'class conflict'. As a concept, it has been used to study significant changes in consciousness, especially under the impact of such traumatic events as warfare, decolonization and revolution. For example, the experience of trench warfare in the First World War shaped the political consciousness of troops who became the backbone of the fascist movement in Germany two decades later. A generation can be defined more sharply, therefore, as a social cohort whose collective experience of history is shaped by a significant event or events, and whose memory is constructed around recurrent rituals and significant places, as in the Sixties Generation.

SEE ALSO: *age-group; aging.*

READING: Pilcher (1995); Eyerman and Turner, B. S. (1998)

genocide The term was coined by the Polish jurist Raphael Lemkin during the implementation of Hitler's Final Solution (mass extermination of the Jewish people). The word is derived from the Greek *genos* (people or race) and the Latin *caedere* (to kill). A legal definition of genocide as acts intended to destroy a national, ethnic, racial or religious group became the basis of the Convention on the Prevention and Punishment of the Crime of Genocide, as a condemnation of the Nazi Holocaust, and the concept was first employed at the United Nations in General Assembly Resolution 96 (1) of 11 December 1946.

The United Nation's definition can be regarded as minimalist. Genocide is the deliberate act, typically of a state, to destroy a specific group, typically defined in ethnic terms. Critics of this legal concept argue for a maximalist definition, because genocide can occur by neglect rather than intent and it may not be exclusively concentrated on an ethnic group. They point out that nuclear deterrence, which involves a threat of mass destruction, is a genocidal policy. By a policy of neglect, a state can genocidally threaten a community by polluting its water, destroying its food supply or appropriating its land. Under this maximalist definition, the destruction of native North American tribes in the nineteenth century by the slaughter of plains bison was a policy of genocide.

Both approaches share a concern for the impact of the sovereignty of the STATE on social, especially ethnic, minorities; the legitimacy of claims to RIGHTS and JUSTICE; and the global responsibility of agencies like the United Nations to police relations between states. From a sociological point of view, genocide appears to be paradoxically bound up with the process of MODERNIZATION in relation to the state apparatus.

SEE ALSO: *Bauman; citizenship; civil society; legitimacy.*

READING: Stoett (1995)

genre A term that refers to a type of text, such as detective story, romance, science fiction, soap opera. Each genre has its own conventions, which are well known by both producers and audiences, and can cross different media. It has been argued that genres produce their own pleasures precisely because audience members know what will happen next and want to see how it will be done.

gerontology The study of AGING, old age and the problems of the elderly, it was in the 1960s dominated by the welfare needs of the elderly within a social-policy framework. Recent social gerontology, however, has been influenced by the cultural movements of the 1970s and by the political organization of the elderly (by such associations as the Gray Panthers in the United States). There is now considerable interest in the social construction of the concept of age, the politics of aging, the experience of aging and in the idea of aging as a normal (as opposed to pathological) process. Despite these changes, gerontologists are still concerned with social rather than sociological questions.

SEE ALSO: *demographic transition; demography; health-care systems; sociology of medicine.*

READING: Jerrome (1983)

Gesellschaft See: GEMEINSCHAFT.

ghetto Although this term is commonly applied to the Jewish quarters of pre-war European cities, in sociology it refers to any urban area, often deprived, which is occupied by a group segregated on the basis of religion, colour or ethnicity. In contemporary debates, it has been suggested that the notion of an 'internal colony' is a more accurate description of the racial segregation of the black community in North America. However, while the colonial analogy implies the possibility of social change (i.e. 'de-colonization'), in historical terms ghetto status was permanent.

READING: Neuwirth (1969)

Giddens, Anthony (b. 1938) Currently director of the London School of Economics and formerly professor of sociology at Cambridge, he has contributed extensively to the interpretation of classical sociological theory in *Capitalism and Modern Social Theory* (1971), *Politics and Sociology in the Thought of Max Weber* (1972), *Emile Durkheim* (1978) and *Sociology* (1982). He attempted a resolution of the traditional problems of class analysis in *The Class Structure of the Advanced Societies* (1973). The central theme of his perspective has been to develop the theory of action, AGENCY AND STRUCTURE and the knowledgeability of the social actor, through a theory of

STRUCTURATION, in *New Rules of Sociological Method* (1976), *Studies in Social and Political Theory* (1977), *Central Problems in Social Theory* (1979), *Profiles and Critiques in Social Theory* (1983) and *The Constitution of Society* (1984). He has begun an extensive critique of the theoretical limitations of HISTORICAL MATERIALISM in *A Contemporary Critique of Historical Materialism* (1981). He has also presented an innovative framework for an integration of sociology and geography in the analysis of time and space (1984). He has criticized sociology for its failure to provide an analysis of the development of the state and the impact of international conflicts on social relations in *The Nation-State and Violence* (1985). Giddens has been critical of POSTMODERN-ISM as a theory of society in *The Consequences of Modernity* (1990), preferring as an alternative the idea of the reflexivity of modernity and 'high modernity' as a definite stage in the development of society. Reflexivity is important in the development of the self, a topic explored in *Modernity and Self-Identity* (1991). He has also explored the sociology of EMOTIONS in *The Transformation of Intimacy* (1992). *Beyond Left and Right* (1994), *The Third Way* (1998) and *The Third Way and its Critics* (2000) reflect on the changing nature of political life in an era when the political philosophies of socialism and the NEW RIGHT are in decline.

In the 1999 Reith Lectures, published as *Runaway World* (1999), he discusses the impact of GLOBALIZATION, focusing on risk, tradition, family and democracy. He argues that the positive effects of global change include wealth generation, more egalitarian personal and familial relationships, and the possibility of more democratic societies. But the emergence of a global cosmopolitan society also ruptures tradition, diminishes nation states and generates high levels of personal anxiety. The new global economy also perpetuates economic inequalities.

SEE ALSO: *reflexive modernization; third way politics*.

READING: Craib (1992)

gift The analysis of gifts has played an important part in the anthropology of kinship systems where, especially in the case of cross-cousin marriages, the exchange of women between families is an instance of a gift relationship. The exchange of gifts is regarded either as a method of creating and reinforcing binding social relationships or as an exhibition of superior wealth. M. Mauss (1925) sees gift giving as an act of social exchange which reinforces social solidarity and is underpinned by a powerful sense of obligation to reciprocate the original gift. R. Titmuss (1970) has applied the idea to contemporary societies in analysing the giving of blood as a gift to strangers, an act accompanied by a feeling of moral obligation.

SEE ALSO: *exchange theory*.

glass ceiling See: MANAGEMENT.

Glass, David V. (1911–78) A British demographer and sociologist, his contributions to the development of historical demography and the empirical study of SOCIAL MOBILITY were of major significance. He held the senior chair in sociology at London University and was on the faculty of the London School of Economics. His major contributions to historical demography were *Population in History* (1965), edited with D. Eversley, and *Population and Social Change* (1972), edited with R. Revelle. He supervised the pioneering investigation into British social mobility, published with other contributors as *Social Mobility in Britain* (1954). He was a founder of *The British Journal of Sociology* and of *Population Studies*, and was elected a Fellow of the Royal Society – a unique distinction for a sociologist.

globalization This refers to the process by which the world is said to be transformed into a single global system. It became an issue of great significance in the 1990s. Aspects of what is now called globalization were first seriously discussed by sociologists during the 1960s and 1970s. In 1960, MCLUHAN introduced into the analysis of culture and the mass media the phrase 'the global village', in order to describe how, in his view, the world was shrinking as a result of new technologies of communication. In the same period, changes in the global economy, notably the growth of multinational companies (MNCs), the expansion of international trade, the international division of labour, prompted the development of WORLD-SYSTEM THEORY as a model of the global economy. In current discussions, globalization has three dimensions or manifestations: economic, cultural and political.

The *economic* dimension is the expansion and transformation of capitalism into an integrated global economy. The most important change has been the expansion of world financial markets. The globalization of financial flows, in which capital is moved around the world in order to finance international trade, for investment purposes (by financial institutions investing in intangible assets as well as by MNCs investing in physical goods), and through foreign-currency exchanges, accelerated rapidly in the last quarter of the twentieth century. Financial globalization has been greatly assisted by the development of information technology, which makes possible global markets that operate in real time and the electronic transmission of funds. The other significant contribution to economic globalization has been the continued development of MNCs, which account for the greater part of the substantial increase in world trade in the last quarter of the twentieth century. The largest MNCs earn more income than many small nations and their worldwide activities are largely beyond the control of any national government. In their internal operations and their dealings with other MNCs, they help to integrate economic activity on a global scale. One aspect of this economic role that has received particular attention is the GLOBALIZATION OF PRODUCTION.

Globalization of *culture* is said to be the result of the rise of mass tourism, increased MIGRATION of people between societies, the commercialization of cultural products and the global spread of an ideology of consumerism, which have the effect of replacing or supplementing more localized cultures. The marketing activities of MNCs and the development of the mass media of communication (which are mainly owned by MNCs) contribute to cultural globalization; MCDONALDIZATION is a frequently cited example.

In the *political* sphere, globalization has seen the rise of international agencies, including the World Bank, the International Monetary Fund and the World Trade Organization, which regulate the global economy and, therefore, set limits on the freedom of nation states. Global financial markets and MNCs also reduce the capacity of national governments to control activities within the borders of the state, because companies can move business elsewhere should they dislike the policies of a government. The European Union further limits national sovereignty in economic, social and political affairs for member states. Some sociologists have identified the emergence of an international managerial bourgeoisie or transnational capitalist class, although this remains empirically contentious. Political sociologists are concerned with a number of issues arising out of globalization in its various manifestations. These include: the erosion of the authority of the NATION STATE; environmental problems, aboriginal rights and CITIZENSHIP; migration and interracial and -ethnic conflict; and the tension between human and civil RIGHTS. Globalization appears to have threatened the continuity and authenticity of local cultures, which has given rise to social movements protesting against this perceived homogenization of cultures. These tensions between the local and global have led to a new terminology which expresses reactions against incorporation into the global system; for example, GLOCALIZATION. Globalization has also been analysed with reference to the possibilities of new forms of governance and democracy in the global order (Held, 1995).

The principal analytical problems of the theory of globalization cover six broad topics. (1) Globalization was initially interpreted through the sociology of PARSONS as an extension of the process of MODERNIZATION. But many sociologists now regard globalization as a feature of POSTMODERNITY, because, for example, it implies the end of the modern nation state. (2) There is disagreement as to whether globalization produces a standardization of culture or increased cultural diversity (and an associated fragmentation of identity), in a process of accommodation and diffusion which is labelled HYBRIDIZATION. (3) Globalization offers the possibility of a new global political system, because the communication problems of political organization are reduced. But globalization and cultural hybridization also create greater ethnic and religious tensions, which would need to be handled by any globalized political system. (4) There is considerable disagreement as to the causes and extent of globalization. Some treat the global order as simply a product of economic growth and integration, others as essentially a cultural consequence of new electronic media of communication. (5) Historians have noted that, in the late nineteenth century, there was already a liberalized and international trading economy. Thus economic globalization at the end of the twentieth century may have been, at least in part, a return to an older economic model. (6) Evaluations of globalization range from optimistic views of an emerging world order based on universal values to a pessimistic view, which concentrates on ecological disaster, cultural standardization and ethnic wars.

SEE ALSO: *capitalism; dependency theory; identity; information society; modernity; new international division of labour; post-Fordism; post-industrial society*.

READING: Albrow (1996); Giddens (1999)

globalization of production Large multinational companies operating in many different countries have existed throughout the twentieth century, but it was only in the 1970s that they began to integrate the production of their goods and services on a global scale. Until then, operations were mainly nationally based and products were made in one country, even though they might be sold around the world. Globalization of production means that companies integrate their production facilities in different countries into a single system, with the result that products contain components made worldwide. Companies also buy more components from outside suppliers in preference to making these themselves, and these suppliers too may be dispersed around the globe (e.g. many electronic components used in Europe and the USA originate in the Far East). Moreover, the same range of products may also be assembled in several different countries. Companies globalize production to lower costs; for example, by moving operations to countries with cheaper or more productive labour, weaker trade unions, less state regulation of employment conditions, where the state offers subsidies, or where transport is cheaper. They may also reduce costs by making their operations in each country compete with each other for future investment.

Globalization of production has been helped by the globalization of *products*, as companies via their marketing efforts have educated consumers to purchase a global product rather than one designed for a particular national market. A familiar example of this is the design, manufacture and marketing of cars. As recently as the 1970s, the major US-based multinationals operating in Europe produced different model ranges for different European countries, while by the 1990s they each had a single European range. At the start of the twenty-first century, these, in turn, share major components with, and are visually similar to, models on sale in the USA and elsewhere, as companies develop 'world' cars which are manufactured and sold around the world. Globalization strategies are part of the neo-Fordist variety of POST-FORDISM rather than FLEXIBLE SPECIALIZATION.

SEE ALSO: *globalization; new international division of labour.*

glocalization A term adopted by sociologists from the marketing strategies of global companies which introduce minor modifications into global products for different local markets, to comply with local tastes. In sociology, it expresses the tension between local and global cultures. As a process, it refers to the GLOBALIZATION of the local, and the localization of the global.

SEE ALSO: *hybridization.*

glossing For ethnomethodologists, all utterances and actions are indexical; that is, their meaning is uniquely given by their context. Actors have to make sense of such utterances and actions by referring to their context; they have to 'repair' INDEXICALITY. Since specification of the context can be an unending task, actors produce a shorthand description, or gloss, of what is going on, of what makes sense to them.

SEE ALSO: *ethnomethodology.*

READING: Cuff and Payne (1979)

Goffman, Erving (1922–82) In contemporary sociology, Goffman made a major contribution to the study of social interaction, encounters, gatherings and small groups in *Behavior in Public Places* (1963), *Interaction Ritual* (1967) and *Relations in Public* (1971). He also made important contributions to role analysis in *Encounters* (1961a). His principal concern was with the constituents of fleeting, chance or momentary encounters; that is, with the SOCIOLOGY OF EVERYDAY LIFE. To grasp the orderliness of such meetings, Goffman employed drama as an analogy for the staging of social meetings in *The Presentation of Self in Everyday Life* (1959). For Goffman, the social order is always precarious because it is disrupted by embarrassment, withdrawal and the breakdown of communication; these issues are explored in *Stigma* (1964). He also contributed to the analysis of inmates in mental institutions in *Asylums* (1961b). His other publications include *Frame Analysis* (1974) and *Gender Advertisements* (1979).

SEE ALSO: *dramaturgical; ethnomethodology; role; stigma; symbolic interactionism; total institution.*

READING: Burns (1992)

Goldthorpe, John H. (b. 1935) Currently a fellow of Nuffield College, Oxford, he was co-director with LOCKWOOD of the AFFLUENT WORKER investigation and co-authored the three volumes (1968a; 1968b; 1969) resulting from this research. He subsequently directed a part of the Social Mobility Group's investigation at Nuffield College, leading to the publication of *The Social Grading of Occupations* (1974), with K. Hope, and *Social Mobility and Class Structure in Modern Britain* (2nd edn, 1987). The classification of social classes that he developed with colleagues is widely used in empirical research on CLASS and SOCIAL MOBILITY, and forms the basis of the SOCIO-ECONOMIC CLASSIFICATION to be used in the 2001 census. He also reintroduced the concept of the SERVICE CLASS into class analysis. In collaboration with researchers in other countries, he has studied comparative social mobility in order to analyse the social structures of advanced industrial societies; this research is summarized in *The Constant Flux* (1992), with R. Erikson. He has published papers on class, industrial relations and inflation, and edited *The Political Economy of Inflation* (1978), with F. Hirsch, and *Order and Conflict in Contemporary Capitalism* (1984).

SEE ALSO: *class imagery; management; privatization.*

goodness of fit See: SIGNIFICANCE TEST.

Gouldner, Alvin Ward (1920–80) Born in New York, he was professor of sociology at Washington University (1959–67), president of the Society for the Study of Social Problems (1962), professor of sociology at Amsterdam (1972–6) and Max Weber Professor of Sociology at Washington University (from 1967). His early works such as *Patterns of Industrial Bureaucracy* (1954) and *Wildcat Strike* (1955) explored aspects of WEBER's theory of bureaucracy in relation to strikes, management and control. He emphasized the capacity for working-class action and industrial disruption despite the constraints of bureaucracy. Features of Weber's sociology of religion were explored in *Notes on Technology and the Moral Order* (1962), with R. A. Peterson: he argued that certain moral orders (the Apollonian) that emphasized order, reason and activism were causally important in the development of technology.

An important change of direction occurred in the 1960s when he turned to theoretical debates with Marxism and scientific sociology. He worked on a project which would provide a historical and critical study of social theory from Plato (in *Enter Plato*, 1965) to Marxism (in *The Two Marxisms*, 1980), to contemporary sociology (in *Against Fragmentation*, 1985). In these publications, Gouldner rejected the fashionable distinction between neutral science, moral discourse and political commitment. These criticisms were first formulated in *The Coming Crisis of Western Sociology* (1970), a major and controversial study of FUNCTIONALISM and Marxism as it had developed as a scientific theory within the Soviet bloc. In 1974, he founded the influential journal *Theory and Society*, which has done much to develop and elaborate his views on critical theory.

Gouldner was always concerned with the possibilities for progressive social change, and specifically with the role of intellectuals in directing and contributing to change in *The Future of Intellectuals and the Rise of the New Class* (1979). He called upon sociologists to be more reflexive about their theories and role in society in *The Dialectic of Ideology and Technology* (1976).

Following his death, there has been much debate as to the dominant intellectual forces which shaped his vision of critical theory. His views on rationality and criticism were influenced by the FRANKFURT SCHOOL, but his radical style and outlook were also shaped by MILLS. However, his concern for bureaucracy, power and knowledge reflected his debt to the Weberian tradition.

governmentality See: FOUCAULT.

Gramsci, Antonio (1891–1937) Initially a journalist, then a militant in the Italian Communist Party and imprisoned for ten years by Mussolini, Gramsci was one of the most important Marxist thinkers of the twentieth century. His work, a deliberate attempt to unify social theory and political practice, was dominated by a rejection of economic DETERMINISM and the attempt to find an alternative way of interpreting Marx. This rejection was achieved in two ways: (1) by insisting on the independence of politics and ideology from economic determination; (2) by emphasizing the way that men and women can change their circumstances by struggle.

Gramsci argued that the domination of the capitalist class could not be secured by economic factors alone but required political force and, much more importantly, an ideological apparatus which secured the consent of the dominated classes. In capitalist societies, these apparatuses were effectively the institutions of CIVIL SOCIETY, the churches, the family and even trade unions. Political coercion was essentially the province of the state. The stability of capitalist societies was mostly dependent on the ideological domination of the working class. Gramsci suggested that this domination could not be complete, however, for the working class has a DUAL CONSCIOUSNESS, one part of which is imposed by the capitalist class while the other part is a COMMONSENSE KNOWLEDGE derived from the workers' everyday experience of the world.

This commonsense knowledge is potentially revolutionary but requires development by party intellectuals to make it an effective force. For Gramsci, radical social change can only come about when a revolutionary consciousness is fully developed, and hence the role of the party is crucial in articulating and promoting this consciousness. The CLASS STRUGGLE is very largely a struggle between intellectual groups, one beholden to the capitalist class and the other to the workers.

SEE ALSO: *class consciousness; dominant ideology thesis; hegemony; Leninism; Marxist sociology.*

READING: Mouffe (1979)

grand narrative See: POSTMODERNISM.

Grand Theory A term coined by MILLS to refer, pejoratively, to sociological theories couched at a very abstract conceptual level, like those of PARSONS. He similarly criticized abstracted empiricism, the practice of accumulating quantitative data for its own sake. Instead he advocated sociology as the study of the relationship of the individual's experience to society and history.

green movement See: ECOLOGISM; NEW SOCIAL MOVEMENTS.

grounded theory In contrast to formal, abstract theory obtained by logico-deductive methods, grounded theory is grounded in data which have been systematically obtained by social research. The development of grounded theory was an attempt to avoid highly abstract sociology. Grounded theory was part of an important growth in QUALITATIVE RESEARCH in the 1970s which sought to bridge the gap between theoretically uninformed empirical research and empirically uninformed theory by grounding theory in data. It was a reaction against GRAND THEORY and extreme empiricism. The concept is a truism, because one cannot collect data without theory or develop theory without an empirical reference.

READING: Glaser and Strauss (1968a)

group Social groups are collectivities of individuals who interact and form social relationships. C. H. Cooley (1909) classified groups as *primary* and *secondary*. The former are small, being defined by face-to-face interaction. They have their own norms of conduct and are solidaristic. Within this category may be included the family, groups of friends and many work groups. The latter are larger and each member does not directly interact with every other. Some secondary groups, for example trade unions, can be described as associations when at least some members interact, when there is an identifiable normative system and some shared sense of corporate existence.

There was a remarkable growth of interest in small groups in the 1930s based on three distinct approaches that have subsequently fused. E. Mayo and colleagues in the business school at Harvard University investigated industrial work groups as part of their sociological approach to the study of HUMAN RELATIONS in industry; experimental psychologists associated with K. Lewin became interested in groups as the result of investigations of LEADERSHIP; and J. L. Moreno pioneered SOCI-OMETRY, the empirical investigation of the structure of social interaction and communication within small groups. The resulting social psychology of groups has been concerned with issues of group structure and cohesion, morale, group leadership and the effects on the individual. The relevance of this small-group sociology to an understanding of larger social collectives has still to be shown, although the work of R. F. Bales greatly influenced T. Parsons' analysis of social systems.

SEE ALSO: *Homans*; *Parsons*; *primary relationship*; *self*.

READING: Homans (1950; 1961)

guild Guilds were occupational associations of pre- and early industrial society which communicated the lore and skills of a trade by means of formal apprenticeships, control of members' occupational activities and the exclusion of outsiders from practising the trade. They were normally fraternal and corporate bodies.

In *Professional Ethics and Civil Morals* (1950), DURKHEIM suggested that guilds were significant 'intermediary associations', which in traditional society had exercised moral restraint over economic behaviour. He believed that they could continue to provide moral control of market relationships in industrial societies, and he anticipated the future growth of guild socialism in Europe.

SEE ALSO: *associative democracy*; *pluralism*.

H

Habermas, Jürgen (b. 1929) Habermas is one of the principal exponents of CRITICAL THEORY and is also closely associated with the FRANKFURT SCHOOL. The main theme of Habermas' theory (1970a; 1970b) is that valid knowledge can emerge only from a situation of open, free and uninterrupted dialogue. The ideal society permits unconstrained communication and encourages free public debate. In *The Structural Transformation of the Public Sphere* (1962), he described the evolution of the public sphere in eighteenth-century Europe, in which public debate was possible, and charted its decline during the following centuries. In *Towards a Rational Society* (1970c) and *Theory and Practice* (1963), he argued that the idea of a neutral, apolitical science, based on a rigid separation of facts and values, is untenable since questions of truth are inextricably bound up with the political problems of freedom to communicate and to exchange ideas. He has been a prominent critic of POSITIV-ISM and economic DETERMINISM in *Knowledge and Human Interests* (1968). Habermas has also been highly critical of SYSTEMS THEORY, engaging in a prolonged debate with LUHMANN in *Theorie der Gesellschaft oder Sozialtechnologie?* (1971). He has been influential in recent studies of the state and the decline of normative legitimacy in *Legitimation Crisis* (1973). *Communication and the Evolution of Society* (1979) was concerned with the problems of power and legitimacy. In *The Theory of Communicative Action* (1981), he criticized Western social theory for its failure to avoid reductionism and to develop a valid theory of COMMUNICATION and rationality. In *The Philosophical Discourse of Modernity* (1988), he has criticized POSTMODERNISM for its relativism. Most recently, he has developed his ideas about communication, norms, law and political legitimacy in *Between Facts and Norms: Contributions to a discourse theory of law and democracy* (1997).

SEE ALSO: *hermeneutics*.

READING: Rasmussen (1990)

habitus See: BOURDIEU.

Halévy thesis E. Halévy (1961) explained the social and political stability of England in the nineteenth century in terms of the importance of Protestantism. He said that Wesleyan Methodism acted as a social ladder between artisan, nonconformist dissent and the Anglican establishment, thereby contributing to the process of social EMBOURGEOISEMENT and reducing social conflicts.

READING: Hill (1973)

Hall, Stuart McPhail (b. 1932) Formerly director (1972–9) of the BIRMINGHAM CENTRE FOR CONTEMPORARY CULTURAL STUDIES, editor of the *New Left Review*

(1957–61) and professor of sociology at the Open University, he made contributions to the study of YOUTH CULTURE in *Resistance through Rituals* (1976), edited with T. Jefferson, and *Policing the State* (1978). He was a determined critic of the government of Mrs Thatcher in *The Politics of Thatcherism* (1983, with M. Jacques) and *The Hard Road to Renewal* (1988). However, his principal contribution was to the development of CULTURAL STUDIES, which was driven by a critical theory of society in *The Popular Arts* (1964, with P. Whannel), and *Questions of Cultural Identity* (1996, with P. du Gay).

SEE ALSO: *Hoggart; Williams.*

READING: Morley and Chen (1996)

Halsey, A. H. (b. 1923) Formerly professor of social and administrative studies at Oxford University, he has written extensively on education, social mobility and other topics. As director of the Oxford Social Mobility Project, he published *Origins and Destinations* (1980), with A. F. Heath and J. M. Ridge, which analysed the inter-relationships of family, education and class in twentieth-century Britain. He has written on the academic profession in *The British Academics* (1971) and *Decline of Donnish Dominion* (1992). He gave the Reith Lectures for 1977, published as *Change in British Society* (4th edn, 1995). His other major publications include: *Social Class and Educational Opportunity* (1957); *Education, Economy and Society* (1961); *Power in Co-operatives* (1965); *Social Survey of the Civil Service* (1968); *Trends in British Society since 1900* (1988); *Power and Ideology in Education* (1977), with J. Karabel; *Heredity and Environment* (1977).

Hawthorne Studies See: HUMAN RELATIONS.

health and illness, sociology of See: SOCIOLOGY OF HEALTH AND ILLNESS.

health-care systems This term encompasses the various institutions by which the health needs of a society are satisfied. In medieval Europe, the church provided some charitable relief through the hospice (for sick pilgrims) and the lazar-houses (for the victims of venereal disease and leprosy). The period of religious foundations (1335–1550) was followed by the age of the charity hospital (1719–1913). Health-care delivery in industrial societies is highly complex. The modern hospital, offering both a general and specialized service, has dominated modern health-care systems following improvements in care (associated with the professionalization of medicine and nursing) and in hygiene for the management of infections. In the majority of industrial societies, there was a significant programme of construction and modernization of hospitals in the 1960s. With the escalation of the cost of hospitalization, there has been, since the late 1970s, a new emphasis on containment. In the period of hospital expansion, there was, in America, the growth of an alliance between private industry, the state and the medical profession, which sociologists called 'the medical–industrial complex' (B. and J. Ehrenreich, 1970). However, since then there has been a greater emphasis on preventive medicine (e.g. anti-smoking campaigns), COMMUNITY MEDICINE and other local services (such as health centres).

Health-care systems can be considered in terms of the level of health delivery and the means of funding. In terms of level, it is conventional to distinguish between primary, secondary and tertiary care. *Primary* care refers to all forms of out-patient care, typically provided by a general practitioner. *Secondary* care refers to more specialized forms of service, such as the services of a cardiologist. *Tertiary* care incorporates complex procedures provided within a specialized hospital or hospital unit such as open-heart surgery. Furthermore, health-care systems can be considered along a continuum of private and public health care. At one extreme, health care in the USA is decentralized and depends extensively on private health insurance and private sources of funding; at the other extreme, the former USSR had until recently a highly centralized, unitary system funded by the state. Societies like Britain and Sweden fall in the middle of the continuum, combining both public provision and private insurance schemes. There has been much controversy as to the desirability of different types of health-care delivery. The basic issue is that a public system of health (such as the National Health Service in Britain) provides a minimum standard of health which is more or less egalitarian, but the economic cost of such a service is very high. In contrast, private health schemes are not an economic burden on the state, but they are highly inegalitarian since privileged social groups enjoy far higher standards of health. The dispute is, therefore, about EQUALITY versus efficiency. In the 1980s, governments in Great Britain, Australia and New Zealand attempted to improve efficiency by deregulation and privatization. Critics argue that these NEW RIGHT policies merely push responsibility out of the public domain on to the family and women.

It is difficult to resolve this debate by the use of comparative health statistics. Societies have different procedures for measuring morbidity rates and for evaluating effectiveness, and the statistics are complicated by the fact that populations may have different age structures. There are also important cultural variations in attitudes towards sickness and hospital care. For example, in Japan a period of treatment in a hospital is regarded as an important form of rest. Therefore, statistics that show that patients are hospitalized for longer periods in Japan than in many other countries reflect differences of culture rather than morbidity. However, the principal difficulty in evaluating different systems is the disagreement over objectives – whether these are to achieve a more egalitarian distribution of health or an efficient system which is economically sensitive to consumer demand. The health-care systems of industrial societies are, as a result, a topic of intense political debate.

SEE ALSO: *Black Report; sociology of health and illness; sociology of medicine.*

READING: Ham (1997); North and Bradshaw (1997)

hegemony This was a term used by GRAMSCI to describe how the domination of one class over others is achieved by a combination of political and ideological means. Although political force – coercion – is always important, the role of IDEOLOGY in winning the consent of dominated classes may be even more significant. The balance between coercion and consent will vary from society to society, the latter being more important in capitalist societies. For Gramsci, the state was the chief instrument of coercive force, the winning of consent by ideological domination being achieved by the institutions of CIVIL SOCIETY, the family, the church and trade unions, for instance. Hence the more prominent civil society is, the more likely it is that hegemony will be achieved by ideological means.

Hegemony is unlikely ever to be complete. In contemporary capitalist societies, for example, the working class has a DUAL CONSCIOUSNESS, partly determined by the ideology of the capitalist class and partly revolutionary, determined by their experiences of capitalist society. In Gramsci's view, for capitalist society to be overthrown, workers must first establish their own ideological supremacy derived from their revolutionary consciousness.

SEE ALSO: *class consciousness; dominant ideology thesis; ideological state apparatus; Marxist sociology.*

READING: Anderson, P. (1976a)

Heidegger, Martin (1889–1976) A German philosopher, critical in *Being and Time* (1927) of abstract theories of human existence because they neglected the concrete, actual, everyday world. He developed a view of this mundane social world which subsequently influenced the sociology of the life-world or everyday life. Heidegger formulated a philosophical methodology for the analysis of texts which contributed to the modern technique of DECONSTRUCTION. His analysis of technological society (1954) was an important conservative criticism of capitalism, but his association with FASCISM has damaged his reputation.

SEE ALSO: *Foucault; ontology; phenomenological sociology; poststructuralism; sociology of everyday life; structuration.*

READING: Dreyfus (1991)

heredity The basic principles of the science of heredity – the study of the transmission by breeding of discrete units of inheritance (genes) from parents to children – were discovered by G. J. Mendel (1822–84) through a study of peas in 1865. These experiments laid the foundations for genetics (the science of heredity), a term coined by W. Bateson in 1905. These laws of genetic inheritance in the natural world were adopted by F. Galton (1822–1911), who developed the idea of EUGENICS as a science for the improvement of humanity through the adoption of 'genetic politics'.

Mendelian principles of heredity or genetic transmission may be expressed crudely in the idea that 'like begets like'. Although this theory proved to be useful and important in biology, its application to anthropology and sociology has been much contested. In nineteenth-century sociology, assumptions about genetic inheritance were used to suggest that 'criminals beget criminals'. As a consequence of SOCIAL DARWINISM, it was argued that people with poor genetic attributes should be discouraged or prevented from breeding, because it would have disastrous consequences for society. Sociologists have challenged these assertions on the grounds that: (1) it is very difficult to prove the truth of Mendelian laws in the case of human populations; (2) CULTURE is more important than biological inheritance in social groups, and the SYMBOL not the gene is the basic unit of transmission; (3) eugenics is morally objectionable.

SEE ALSO: *intelligence; nature/nurture debate; racism; sociobiology.*

hermeneutics This is the theory and method of interpreting meaningful human action. It has a long history, being rooted in the problems of biblical interpretation. Before printing, when bibles were produced by hand-copying, numerous errors were introduced. Hermeneutics referred to the problem of recovering the 'authentic' version. In the early part of the nineteenth century, hermeneuticians became interested in how to interpret any text, not just by concentrating on the text itself, as in the case of biblical interpretation, but also by reference to the experiences of the author.

The subject became more developed in the work of W. Dilthey, who argued that there is a marked difference between the study of nature and the study of human action, which, being an expression of 'lived experience', requires a special method of analysis. Dilthey effectively provided two such methods. In the first, the focus was on the relationship of the creator of an act, a book or a picture to the interpreter. The latter understands by putting himself in the position of the former. Understanding is possible because both share a common humanity or, in another formulation, because they are both expressions of the Spirit. In the second, the characteristics of individuals are disregarded. Instead, hermeneutics understands human action in relation to some wider whole which gives it meaning. For example, a painting is understood by reference to the outlook or WORLD VIEW of the society in which it is produced. Similarly, the analyst can construct such a world view out of its individual manifestations. This circular relationship between a whole and its parts is known as a hermeneutic circle.

MANNHEIM advanced similar arguments. He suggested that individual cultural manifestations can be understood by seeing them as part of a larger world view. The analyst attaches 'documentary meaning' to human action. This has nothing to do with intentions, but makes sense in the context of a world view. For example, the documentary meaning of a painting can be understood by locating it within the world view of the society or group which produced it.

Hermeneutics has formed part of a general critique of positivism in sociology, in which human action is seen as caused by social structures of various kinds. However, the difficulty of hermeneutic analysis has always been how to validate interpretations. On the face of it, one interpretation of the meaning of an action or a text is as good as another. The solution offered to this problem is the 'hermeneutic circle' mentioned above. The most distinguished recent writer to advocate this solution is H. G. Gadamer, who insists that hermeneutics has to understand the part in terms of the whole, and the whole in terms of the part. The interpreter, in judging a book, for example, has to recapture the perspective within which the author formulated his or her views. For Gadamer, the spatial and temporal gap between author and interpreter is bridged by tradition and by what he calls a 'fusion of horizons'. However, the gap can never be completely bridged; there can never be a completely correct interpretation. Interpretations are therefore always tentative and subject to revision in the hermeneutic circle.

SEE ALSO: *Geisteswissenschaften; phenomenology; positivism; Verstehen.*

READING: Connerton (1976); Bauman (1978)

hidden curriculum Most educational institutions have a formal curriculum comprising those areas of academic knowledge which pupils are expected to acquire, such as mathematics. Besides this academic and explicitly taught curriculum, however, there is also a set of values, attitudes or principles – a hidden curriculum – that is implicitly conveyed to pupils by teachers. The hidden curriculum is believed to promote social control at school and in society at large by training people to conform and to obey authority, teaching them to regard social inequalities as natural, and ensuring CULTURAL REPRODUCTION.

S. Bowles and H. Gintis (1976) argued that schools have an important role in teaching punctuality, discipline, obedience and diligence, which are the qualities they believe are needed by the workforce in a capitalist society. In this account, the success of the school in teaching technical skills and knowledge is less important than its success in imparting a hidden curriculum that corresponds to the disciplinary requirements of employment. This principle of correspondence has been criticized, on the grounds that many pupils are not socialized to become disciplined workers by schools, as has been shown by the prevalence of industrial conflict and employee resistance to managerial control at various times. Resistance may be found even within the school itself, since pupil subcultures that reject authority and school values have been identified, mainly among the academically less successful.

SEE ALSO: *classroom interaction; classroom knowledge; educational attainment.*

Hinduism See: WORLD RELIGIONS.

histogram Any distribution of variables measured on an interval scale may be presented pictorially as a histogram, where blocks of differing areas represent the number of observations falling within each interval on the scale used to measure the variable. For example, the above table, which gives the age distribution of a sample of respondents in a survey, can also be presented as a histogram.

Age	Number
Under 10 years	5
10 and under 20	10
20 and under 30	20
30 and under 40	30
40 and under 50	20
50 and under 60	25
60 and under 70	10
Total	120

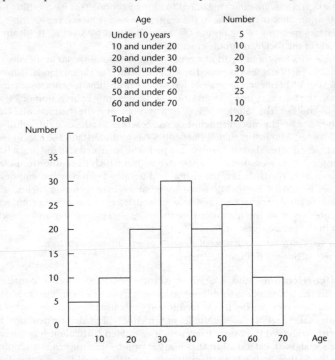

historical materialism K. Marx propounded the materialist interpretation of history that social, cultural and political phenomena were determined by the mode of production of material things. This gave causal priority to the economy rather than to ideas in the explanation of historical processes, summarized in the base–superstructure distinction.

SEE ALSO: *base and superstructure; dialectical materialism; materialism.*

historical sociology In the past thirty years, the two disciplines of history and sociology have converged in terms of empirical interests and methodological approaches. For example, the ANNALES SCHOOL employs quantitative methods for the analysis of historical data, while historians of European witchcraft often depend on anthropological theories of magic for historical analysis. Similarly, sociologists frequently utilize detailed historical studies of the working class in one locality in order to build a picture of the development of a national working class during industrialization. This convergence has occurred despite acrimonious debates which proclaim the necessary divisions between the two disciplines.

The term 'historical sociology' can have two trivial meanings. These are either that historical analysis should be more concerned with the social context or that sociology should be given a deeper historical background. P. Abrams (1982) provides a more compelling definition of historical sociology in terms of three theoretical concerns. (1) Sociology is specifically concerned with the transition to industrialism as an historical process. (2) Sociology is concerned with the pattern of freedom and constraint in the life-histories of individuals in social contexts. (3) Sociology is concerned with the dynamic interaction between human agency and social structure, not as an abstract problem, but as an empirical issue in world history. In this sense, all sociology is historical sociology because it is inevitably concerned with change, process and development.

SEE ALSO: *Comte; evolutionary theory; historicism; periodization; progress; social change.*

historicism (1) As used by POPPER (1957), this refers to interpretations of history that purport to show the existence of fixed laws of historical development.

(2) In a different sense, historicism refers to the doctrine that every age can be understood only in its own terms and that meaningful comparison cannot be made across historical periods. This view is usually associated with a conception of the human sciences contrary to NATURALISM and utilizing such concepts as VERSTEHEN. It has been argued that historicism falls into RELATIVISM in providing no independent means of validating claims about any society or historical period.

SEE ALSO: *Geisteswissenschaften; hermeneutics.*

Hoggart, Richard (b. 1918) Formerly foundation director of the BIRMINGHAM CENTRE FOR CONTEMPORARY CULTURAL STUDIES (1964–73), assistant director-general of UNESCO (1970–5) and warden of Goldsmiths College, University of London (1976–84), his *The Uses of Literacy* (1957) explored the transformation of working-class culture and solidarity in post-war Britain, and criticized the impact of mass culture. He wrote extensively on the problems of teaching English in relation to CULTURAL STUDIES in *An English Temper* (1982a) and *Speaking to Each Other* (1970). He also contributed to the emergence of broadcasting studies in *The Future of Broadcasting* (1982b).

SEE ALSO: *Hall; mass society; McDonaldization; Williams.*

holism This is the doctrine that societies should be seen as wholes, or as systems of interacting parts. Analysis should, therefore, start from large-scale institutions and their relationships, not from the behaviour of individual actors. Societies, in this view, have properties as wholes which cannot be deduced from the characteristics of individuals.

SEE ALSO: *action theory; atomism; functionalism; methodological individualism; social system; systems theory.*

Homans, George C. (1910–89) An American sociologist concerned with the functioning of small groups and face-to-face social interaction, he made notable contributions to EXCHANGE THEORY. His major works were: *The Human Group* (1950); *Social Behavior: Its elementary forms* (1961); *Sentiments and Activities* (1962); *The Nature of Social Science* (1967). In a famous paper (1964), he argued that all social phenomena are to be explained in terms of the characteristics of individuals rather than social structures.

SEE ALSO: *group; methodological individualism.*

homoeostasis See: SOCIAL SYSTEM.

household A single person or group sharing living accommodation. For many purposes of sociological analysis, this is a term preferable to the more widely used FAMILY. The latter implies a uniformity in the structure of households formed around a man and woman legally married and not married previously, with two or three children. Households may consist in families defined in this way, but just as commonly they may not. In Britain, in recent years, households have become much more diverse. Thus, in 1961, 11 per cent of households were made up of single people. By 1991, this had grown to 26 per cent. Part of this increase was caused by a rise in the number of elderly people in the population, but the proportion of single-person households of those under pensionable age also grew rapidly (from 4 per cent to 11 per cent of the total), a change due to a number of factors including a trend towards later marriages. At the same time, the proportion of households consisting of lone parents (almost always women) with dependent children has also risen over the past thirty years from 2 per cent of all households in 1961 to 6 per cent in 1991. The result of these changes is that the stereotypical household consisting of a married couple, with or without children, has become less well represented in the population, falling from 72 per cent of all households in 1961 to 60 per cent in 1991.

It is important to realize, though, that even households consisting of married couples with children are becoming more complex. DIVORCE rates have risen sharply (2.1 divorces per thousand of the married population in 1961, compared with 13.4 in 1995). At the same time, remarriage rates following divorce remain reasonably high (half of women divorced in the 1980s had remarried within eight years). The result is that many households will contain children from at least two marriages. At the same time, changing MARRIAGE patterns have altered the nature of households. An increasing number of households consist of a couple living together without being married, and often with children. In 1966, 4 per cent of women married in that year had lived with their husband before marriage, but by 1993 the proportion had risen to 68 per cent. In 1996, 37 per cent of all births were to unmarried women, compared with 8 per cent in 1971.

SEE ALSO: *extended family; nuclear family; single-parent family.*

READING: Pullinger and Summerfield (1997)

housework See: DOMESTIC LABOUR.

housing class The theory of housing classes was introduced by J. Rex and R. Moore (1967). Their argument is that the population can be grouped into distinct housing classes – the owners of houses or council-house tenants, for example – that are usually geographically segregated. The constitution or numbers of classes will vary from place to place. Housing classes are independent of social classes, although they are also a feature of social inequality since not all housing is equally desirable. Rex and Moore assume that everybody wants suburban housing but not everybody has access to it, and hence there is competition and struggle between housing classes which is responsible for much apparently racial conflict. The regulation of access to housing classes is of great importance, since it tends to confine ethnic minorities to city centres. The theory has been criticized because it is difficult to draw the boundaries of housing classes, a very large number of classes are often introduced, conflicts are as often within housing classes as between them, suburban housing is not universally desired and, most importantly, housing classes are really a function of the social class structure.

SEE ALSO: *zone of transition*.

human capital Individuals who invest time and money (including foregone earnings) in education, training, experience and other qualities that increase their productivity and thus their worth to an employer, are said to have a greater endowment of human capital. The idea of differing human capitals is used by many labour economists to explain inequalities in the labour market: variations in pay are assumed to reflect the different values of the human capital that different employees bring to work. Groups who are apparently disadvantaged in the labour market, including women and ethnic minorities, are held to owe at least part of their inferior rewards to their lower investments in human capital, whether these be education and training or, particularly in the case of women, lack of continuous work experience. A problem with the concept is that productivity is not in fact measured directly but is only inferred from the higher pay received by, for example, the better-educated men. The inference depends on an assumption that employers are rational people who maximize profits by paying only what the productivity of each individual employee justifies. Another problem is that, empirically, human-capital differences explain only part of the observed differences in earnings and there remains a large proportion of variance to be explained by other factors.

SEE ALSO: *labour market segmentation; women and work*.

READING: Rubinson and Browne (1994)

human ecology See: URBAN ECOLOGY.

Human Relations This interdisciplinary movement in the study of social relations in industry, embracing sociology, social anthropology and social psychology, was influential between the late 1930s and early 1960s in academic and managerial circles. It focused on the behaviour of employees in groups, and marked a shift away from the SCIENTIFIC MANAGEMENT view of employees as isolated individuals maximizing income, to regard employees as oriented towards groups and needing socially supportive relationships at work, placing group interests above their own individual financial rewards. Pioneering research carried out in the Western Electric Co. by E. Mayo and colleagues between 1927 and 1932, sometimes known as the Hawthorne Studies after the name of the main plant, suggested that employee productivity was influenced by group factors. In one experiment, output increased when the creation of small work groups raised morale, leading individuals to become more productive. However, in another, the work group developed social norms that restricted output. Subsequent investigation has concentrated on the factors influencing work-group formation, such as the technology and layout of production systems, and the ways of channelling group dynamics to the benefit of the company – for example, by training supervisors to act as group leaders. Criticisms of Human Relations include: (1) that it has ignored the wider social system of the organization, including conflict between workers and management; (2) that it has ignored the influence of trade unions on output and the wider economic environment; (3) that it exaggerates the 'social' needs of employees and downplays their economic motivations; (4) that it focuses on issues of concern to management and does not maintain academic neutrality.

SEE ALSO: *affluent worker; cash nexus; group; industrial conflict; Pareto; socio-technical systems.*

READING: Rose, M. (1988)

human rights See: RIGHTS.

hybridization Originally an anthropological interpretation of the relationship between Westernization and local cultures – that indigenous cultures are not simply destroyed but combined and merged with Western cultures through a process of adaptation – it has been adopted in the sociological analysis of POSTMODERNITY to question the alleged lack of authenticity in hybrid cultural arrangements. If there are no 'pure' cultures, then 'hybridity' is a general component of cultural diffusion. Gianni Vattimo in *The End of Modernity* (1988) has employed the notion of hybridity to identify the conservative nature of those critics who regard Westernization as a threat to cultural authenticity. In the process of GLOBALIZATION, it refers to the articulation of global processes with local and regional customs and traditions.

SEE ALSO: *glocalization.*

hyperreality A term employed by BAUDRILLARD to describe the growth of an advertising culture – especially in the United States, where images and signs begin to replace or stand in for reality – it is employed to criticize MASS SOCIETY. This visual culture, in representing the social world, permits fakes to appear more realistic than reality. Hyperreality involves 'the generation by models of a real without origin or reality' (Baudrillard, 1983, p. 2).

SEE ALSO: *postmodernism; postmodernity; society of the spectacle.*

hypothesis A proposition or set of propositions put forward for empirical testing. The word is often used more loosely to mean suggestion, explanation or theory.

SEE ALSO: *hypothetico-deductive model.*

hypothetico-deductive model A common view of theory construction and explanation in the natural sciences runs as follows. Scientists think up a theory which might explain certain phenomena. They then deduce logically from that theory certain more specific propositions – hypotheses – which take the form of predictions about what will actually be found in nature. These hypotheses are then subjected to empirical tests in the laboratory. The predictions will either be true or false. If false, the theory is said to be *disconfirmed*. If true, it is *confirmed*, though it is always liable to be disproved by further laboratory tests. In practice, such a rigorous method is not often adhered to in the natural sciences and only very rarely in sociology and other social sciences.

The hypothetico-deductive model is often contrasted with the inductive model, in which theory is gradually evolved or built up out of observations or experiments in the natural or social world. It is a process whereby the truth of the theory is made more probable by the accumulation of confirming evidence. It cannot ever be ultimately valid, because there is always the possibility of a disconfirming instance.

SEE ALSO: *falsificationism; hypothesis; Popper; positivism.*

READING: Keat and Urry (1975)

iatrogenesis See: SOCIOLOGY OF HEALTH AND ILLNESS.

idealism In philosophy, this is the position that the external material world is either constructed by or dependent upon the mind. In sociology, subjectivist idealism is occasionally employed to describe such positions as SYMBOLIC INTERACTIONISM, in which the external social reality cannot exist independently from the everyday interactions and subjectivity of social actors. Marxists argue that sociology as a whole is idealist because it neglects or minimizes the causal role of objective economic conditions. For some Marxists, the economic base determines the superstructure of beliefs. However, it should be noted that Marxists in recent years have often appeared to stress the causal importance of the superstructure, while the emphasis on subjectivity in sociology has the merit of drawing attention to the active role of social actors in the construction of social reality.

SEE ALSO: *base and superstructure; determinism; materialism.*
READING: Benton (1977)

ideal type There has been considerable confusion surrounding the exposition of ideal-type constructions in sociology. WEBER first drew attention to ideal types in order to make explicit the procedures by which he believed social scientists formulate general, abstract concepts such as 'the pure competitive market', the 'church-set typology' or 'bureaucracy'. He suggested that social scientists selected as the defining characteristics of an ideal type certain aspects of behaviour or institutions which were observable in the real world, and exaggerated these to form a coherent intellectual construction. Not all the characteristics will always be present in the real world, but any particular situation may be understood by comparing it with the ideal type. For example, individual bureaucratic organizations may not exactly match the elements in the ideal type of BUREAUCRACY, but the type can illuminate these variations. Ideal types are therefore hypothetical constructions, formed from real phenomena, which have an explanatory value. 'Ideal' signifies 'pure' or 'abstract' rather than normatively desirable. However, the precise relationship between ideal types and the reality to which they refer remains obscure. Weber did suggest that major discrepancies between reality and an ideal type would lead to the type being redefined, but he also argued that ideal types were not models to be tested. However, other sociologists treat them as testable models of the real world. Further confusion may arise since Weber himself often implicitly used ideal types as testable models.

SEE ALSO: *model.*
READING: Albrow (1990)

identity This is the sense of self, of personhood, of what kind of person one is. Identities always involve both sameness and difference. Thus, if you are British, you are like other Britons and different from non-Britons. There is a tendency to see identities as being fixed or given. Sociologists, however, argue that identities are fluid and changeable and that we can acquire new ones. The concept has been used by sociologists in a number of different but related contexts.

(1) The acquisition of identity. It is widely agreed that there are primary identities acquired in childhood – gender or ethnicity, for example – that are relatively durable. Even these can be changed, as transsexuals will attest. In later life, there may be important moments of transition in identity, as in the process of moving from childhood to adulthood. There are numerous, less profound transitions, as in changing occupations or even moving house. All these involve alterations in the individual's sense of what kind of person she or he is. They also all involve a process of negotiation (the theory of which owes much to the work of George H. MEAD) between the self and external agencies. Someone who is a Muslim, for instance, has that identity confirmed in a constant negotiation between his or her sense of being a Muslim and others' definition of what that means.

(2) The work of GOFFMAN focuses attention on how identities are managed. In his view, individuals present an image of themselves to others, who are free to accept or reject that image. Goffman describes in detail the mechanisms of this impression management and draws extensively on dramatic metaphors. He has been criticized for presenting identity simply as a series of masks put on for different audiences.

(3) It has sometimes been claimed that identities in contemporary society are becoming fragmented. In the recent past, individuals would have had a number of central elements to the construction of their identity – family, locality, nation, social class, ethnicity, gender. However, modern, or postmodern, societies introduce more sources of identity which cross-cut these, producing a more complex pattern of identity and belonging. So, for example, there is more geographical mobility, with the result that individuals lose their ties to locality and family. GLOBALIZATION undermines the sense of nationhood. Large social CLASS formations break up. Identities based upon a multiplicity of lifestyles come to be important.

(4) At the same time, it is claimed, identities are more fluid in contemporary societies. People can change identities over their lifetime. They can choose who they want to be in a society in which traditional loyalties are breaking down. GIDDENS, for example, argues that one of the key features of modernity is what he calls 'the reflexive project of the self'. Individuals reflect on their own identity and continuously rework it.

(5) A certain amount of sociological work has concentrated on identity as a sense of belonging. This makes identity very much a feature of the imagination. Individuals imagine themselves as belonging to some wider entity, such as a local community. In doing so, they implicitly do not belong to other entities. Public debate often trades on this sense of identity, especially when politicians reflect on the British national character, by contrast with continental Europe, for instance, or contrast British ways with those of immigrants.

SEE ALSO: *interpellation; lifestyle; ontological security; postmodernism; reflexive/reflexivity; symbolic interactionism.*

READING: Jenkins (1996)

ideological state apparatus (ISA) A term popularized by ALTHUSSER. This refers to one of the means by which the domination of the capitalist class is secured. ISAs, examples of which are religious and educational institutions, the media of communication, the family, even trade unions and political parties, function by incorporating all classes in societies within a dominant ideology. The HEGEMONY of dominant classes can also be secured by repressive state apparatuses (RSAs) which operate by force rather than IDEOLOGY. The balance between ISAs and RSAs will vary from society to society. The concept of ISA has been criticized for exaggerating the impact of ideology in making societies coherent.

SEE ALSO: *civil society; dominant ideology thesis; Gramsci; ideology; incorporation.*

READING: Abercrombie (1980)

ideology One of the most debated concepts in sociology, ideology may be provisionally defined as beliefs, attitudes and opinions which form a set, whether tightly or loosely related. The term has been used in three important senses: (1) to refer to very specific kinds of belief; (2) to refer to believes that are in some sense distorted or false; (3) to refer to any set of beliefs, covering everything from scientific knowledge, to religion, to everyday beliefs about proper conduct, irrespective of whether it is true or false.

(1) Ideology in this sense has figured mainly in American political science literature and is defined as a tightly knit body of beliefs organized around a few central values. Examples are communism, fascism and some varieties of nationalism. These types of ideologies are frequently oppositional to dominant institutions and play a role in the organization of devotees into sects or parties. Investigation of these sorts of belief typically takes the form of studies of the ideological personality or of the social functions that ideology performs, as in, for example, the industrialization of a society.

(2) This conception of ideology is associated with Marxist literature. There are many different usages but the fundamental arguments are, firstly, that the character of ideologies is largely determined by the economic arrangements of a society and, secondly, that in class societies such as capitalism, ideologies are distorted by CLASS INTEREST. The first argument is represented in the notions of BASE AND SUPER-STRUCTURE and in the idea that membership of a social class determines ideology. The second is often expressed in the concepts of a dominant class ideology and false consciousness.

Areas of debate revolve around the degree of economic determination and the consequences of holding that ideologies are necessarily distorted in capitalist society. It has been argued that some sorts of ideology – concerning art, for example – are relatively unaffected by the economy or class membership. Again, social groups other than class have been shown to have an influence on the character of ideology. Various arguments have been advanced concerning the mechanism by which distorted beliefs are produced. For instance, class interest is said to narrow and constrain perceptions of the world, and Marx's ideas on COMMODITY FETISHISM have also been invoked. These arguments do, however, raise the difficulty of how one obtains objective knowledge. Thus, if the economic base or class interests distort knowledge in capitalist societies, how is one to obtain a perspective outside capitalism in order to claim that there is distortion?

(3) The notion of ideology as constituting any set of beliefs, true or false, is found

in the SOCIOLOGY OF KNOWLEDGE. The idea here is simply that all beliefs are socially determined in some way or another, although there is no assumption that any one factor, the economy for instance, is most important. For example, it has been argued that bureaucracies generate particular styles of thought. There is, therefore, room for argument about the degree of social determination and about which social groups generate ideologies. Some writers have argued that the principle that beliefs are socially caused creates a difficulty, since this seems to imply that these beliefs are false. Against this, it has been suggested that social causation does not imply falsity, and showing that a proposition is false and that it is socially caused are quite separate activities. Other writers, working within the tradition of HERMEN-EUTICS, have argued that it is incorrect to speak of social factors causing beliefs.

Contemporary European debates about ideology have fused (2) and (3). There are three major points of argument. (1) There has been a general movement against economic determinism and towards the recognition that ideology may be relatively independent of class or the economic structure. (2) Many recent writers have argued against the notion that ideology consists of 'ideas in people's heads'. First, it is suggested that ideology should be seen not only as an intellectual product but also as comprising the ideas of ordinary men and women. Second, some writers have argued that ideologies are not ideas at all, but rather should be viewed as practices engaged in every day by everybody in an entirely unreflecting way. Third, it may be that DISCOURSE, a unified and structured domain of language-use that constrains what can be said or thought, is equivalent to ideology. (3) More abstractly, the role of the subject, the individual human agent, in ideological creation and function has been the subject of extensive debate, particularly where sociology overlaps with other disciplines like linguistics.

SEE ALSO: *Althusser; appearance and reality; class consciousness; culture; determinism; dominant ideology thesis; end of ideology theory; Foucault; Gramsci; hegemony; interpellation; myth; poststructuralism; semiotics; subject; subjectivity; world view.*

READING: Larrain (1979); Barratt (1991)

idiographic A term used to describe methods of study of individual, unique persons, events or things. It contrasts with nomothetic methods in which the object is to find general laws that subsume individual cases.

SEE ALSO: *empathy; hermeneutics; historicism; Verstehen.*

imperatively coordinated association This is a term used by DAHRENDORF (1959), derived from M. Weber, to describe groups which possess an authority structure, such as the state and firms.

imperialism In its broad and conventional meaning, imperialism is the imposition of the power of one state over the territories of another, normally by military means, in order to exploit subjugated populations and extract economic and political advantages. As a form of conquest and domination, empires are an ancient form of political rivalry between human societies. In the social sciences, attitudes towards imperialism are sharply divided. Liberal economists, like J. A. Schumpeter (1951), have argued that the imperialist expansion of European societies in the nineteenth century was not a necessary feature of capitalist growth and competition, but in fact contrary to the political and economic characteristics of CAPITALISM. Imperialism was simply the survival into capitalism of the militaristic nationalism of absolute monarchies. By contrast, radical writers have treated imperialism as an essential feature of capitalist development at a particular stage. V. I. Lenin (1915) associated capitalist imperialism with the dominance of finance capital, the export of capital in response to domestic stagnation of the economy, the growth of international trusts and the capitalist division of the globe. Economic theories of imperialism either claim that capitalism is pushed into imperialism because of a crisis of profitability in home markets or pulled into imperialism by the need for cheap raw materials. Critics of these Marxist theories point out that (1) imperialism pre-dates capitalism and (2) political rather than economic causes explain imperialist rivalry.

The terms 'imperialism' and 'colonialism' are often used interchangeably, but colonialism – the settlement of foreign territories, the separation of foreign and indigenous peoples by legal means, and the growth of racialism – can be regarded as a special or direct form of imperialism. 'Neo-colonialism' refers to a situation where, despite formal political independence, previous colonies are still dependent upon and subordinated to a metropolis.

SEE ALSO: *dependency theory; new international division of labour; underdevelopment; world-system theory.*

READING: Barratt Brown (1974); Mommsen (1980)

income See: DISTRIBUTION OF INCOME AND WEALTH.

incorporation This is the process by which individuals and groups are integrated into a larger social grouping, either by creating rights and obligations for individuals and groups, or by other mechanisms that reduce SOCIAL CLOSURE, such as SOCIAL MOBILITY. In the most common use of the term, incorporation has referred to the channelling of working-class political and economic activity into existing institutions, along with the development of INDUSTRIAL SOCIETY, rather than allowing it to remain on the outside where it poses a threat to the established order. This process is thought to involve both the growth of the rights and obligations of CITIZENSHIP and a change in working-class culture from radical, oppositional values based on CLASS CONSCIOUSNESS to an acceptance of the socially dominant values in society. Whereas MARSHALL and BENDIX believed that the growth of citizenship established effective democratic participation that destroyed privilege, Marxist sociologists argued that inequality remained and incorporation was mainly the result of growing bourgeois ideological HEGEMONY over the working class and the 'betrayal' of the working class by their political and trade-union leaders.

SEE ALSO: *dominant ideology thesis; ideological state apparatus; institutionalization of conflict; oligarchy; trade unions.*

independent variable See: DEPENDENT/INDEPENDENT VARIABLES.

index (1) In survey analysis, a number of variables may be combined into a composite measure or index which is expressed as a single score. For example, an investigator may ask several questions about various aspects of social inequality, such as housing, education, income and health, and then combine the answers into a single measure of reported inequality. Each respondent can then be assigned a single score on this composite scale.

(2) Index can also refer to an indicator of something that is not measured directly.

For example, voting for socialist political parties is sometimes used as an index of politically militant attitudes among manual workers.

indexicality Ethnomethodologists argue that all actions and utterances are indexical; that is, they depend for their meaning on the context in which they occur. This feature means that actors will normally make sense of actions and utterances of others by referring to their context, an activity which requires work, even if unconscious, particularly as each context is unique.

SEE ALSO: *ethnomethodology*; *glossing*.

individualism This term refers to a diverse collection of doctrines that stress the rights, freedom and importance of the individual in relation to other entities such as the state, the church or the king. For example, Protestantism is a form of religious individualism, in that it argues for a direct relationship between individuals and God rather than one mediated by the church.

It is often argued that doctrines of individualism are associated with the rise of CAPITALISM in the West, in that capitalism requires people to be constructed as autonomous and enterprising economic agents, able to relate to one another in a free market. WEBER, for example, argued that the individualism of Protestant religions in early modern Europe was a pre-condition for the rise of capitalism. Abercrombie *et al.* (1986) argued that individualism is not necessary to capitalism but nevertheless has constructed capitalism in a particular individualistic way.

Whatever its origins and whatever its relationship to capitalism, there is widespread agreement that individualism is a dominant feature of the culture of the contemporary West. Indeed, governments have actively attempted to encourage individualism in the belief that enterprising individuals who are as free as possible of state influence and control are the best guarantors of a successful economy and ENTERPRISE CULTURE. It has also been argued that contemporary societies are undergoing a process of individualization, in which individuals are being taken out of their traditional ties of family or locality and are having to make their own individual choices and fashion their own identities and biographies. More technically, individualism is sometimes used to denote an argument (more often known as METHODOLOGICAL INDIVIDUALISM) in the philosophy of the social sciences, in which all sociological explanations are reducible to the characteristics of individuals.

SEE ALSO: *invisible religion*; *New Right*; *Protestant ethic*; *reflexive modernization*; *third way politics*.

induction See: FALSIFICATIONISM; HYPOTHETICO-DEDUCTIVE MODEL; POPPER.

industrial conflict The relationship between the owners and managers of industry on the one hand and working people on the other is frequently one of conflict. The term refers both to the forms which conflict may take and to the sources of conflict. There is general agreement among industrial sociologists that the forms of conflict are various and include absenteeism, sabotage, restriction of output and non-cooperation, all of which may occur on an individual or collective basis, and COLLECTIVE BARGAINING and strikes, which are collective manifestations.

There are competing accounts of the sources of conflict. The HUMAN RELATIONS movement suggested that conflict occurred when industry failed to integrate workers into a socially supportive community at work and that conflict between managers and workers was not inevitable. Other approaches believe that conflict is inevitable. R. Dahrendorf (1959) claimed that there would always be conflict between those with authority and those without. Many Weberian sociologists attribute conflict to the clash of economic interests in employment, because workers and managers have different interests with regard to wages and effort. Marxists also adhere to an economic explanation, namely that employment in capitalism is by nature exploitative and places management and labour in opposed camps. Economic accounts have had primacy in recent years.

Accounts of conflict reflect three alternative models of the firm and the employment system. Human Relations had a *unitary* model of the firm as a homogeneous community with shared interests and values, with the potential of great harmony. The Marxist perspective is *dichotomous* and oppositional, emphasizing the fundamental and all-embracing nature of conflict. Exploitation means that firms are split into two camps which have no identity of interests and workers are compelled to work against their will. Modern Marxists therefore have to explain why industrial conflict, at least in its overt and collective manifestation, is so subdued in the contemporary economy. Modern Weberian economic accounts are usually *pluralist*, since they see firms as containing a plurality of divisions and competing interests, that is within the ranks of management and labour as well as between them. Moreover, pluralism suggests that the various parties within the firm have an interest in cooperating, since by working together they do better than they would on their own, and so conflict occurs within this broader cooperative framework. While WEBER believed that the LABOUR MARKET allowed employers to dominate employees, it is an assumption of some modern accounts that, because people can choose whether or not to work, employment should not be seen as coercive.

SEE ALSO: *imperatively coordinated association; industrial democracy; inflation; institutionalization of conflict; labour market; labour process approach; managerial strategies of control; pluralism; scientific management; strikes; trade unions.*

READING: Hill, S. (1981)

industrial democracy This concept refers to the participation of employees in managerial decisions which affect their working lives. The mechanisms by which democracy may be promoted are various. They include: (1) trade unionism and COLLECTIVE BARGAINING; (2) works councils and consultation between management and employees; (3) co-determination, which provides employee representatives with seats on company boards and a share in company decision-making; (4) workers' control of industry. Workers are primarily interested in having influence in the areas that most directly affect their working lives, such as wages, working conditions and the power of managers over employees. Trade unionism and collective bargaining proved effective at this level in Britain during the middle decades of the twentieth century, although less so after 1980. In continental Europe, works councils have formed the main vehicle of participation on issues other than wages. However, certain crucial issues, such as new investments or plant closures, are beyond the scope of TRADE UNIONS working through collective bargaining or works councils dealing with day-to-day problems, and other mechanisms of industrial democracy are required in addition. In a number of European countries, employees have representation on company boards and participate in high-level decision-making, but, being in the minority, these employees do not determine the outcome of decisions. Industrial democracy in Germany involves both works councils and co-determination via union representatives on the company boards.

SEE ALSO: *citizenship; cooperative.*

READING: Poole (1986)

industrial districts See: FLEXIBLE SPECIALIZATION.

industrial relations This phrase covers the employment relationship and the institutions associated with it. It embraces the relations between workers, work groups, worker organizations and managers, companies and employer organizations. The study of industrial relations is an interdisciplinary enterprise, drawing heavily on industrial sociology, labour economics and trade-union history, and to a lesser extent on psychology and political science.

industrial society The defining characteristics of an industrial society are: (1) the creation of cohesive nation states organized around a common language and culture; (2) the commercialization of production and the disappearance of a subsistence economy; (3) the dominance of machine-production and the organization of production in the factory; (4) the decline of the proportion of the working population engaged in agriculture; (5) the urbanization of society; (6) the growth of mass literacy; (7) the enfranchisement of the population and the institutionalization of politics around mass parties; (8) the application of science to all spheres of life, especially industrial production, and the gradual RATIONALIZATION of social life. Industrial society is frequently associated with MASS SOCIETY. Western Europe and North America went through the process of INDUSTRIALIZATION in the period 1815–1914, although there was considerable variation in the rate of change for individual societies.

The principal area of controversy in the analysis of industrial society centred on whether such societies were cooperative or conflictual, adaptive or self-destructive. In the nineteenth century, sociologists like H. Spencer and E. Durkheim emphasized the cooperative, integrative nature of the DIVISION OF LABOUR in industrial society. Similarly, twentieth-century structural FUNCTIONALISM treated industrial society as a highly differentiated and coherent social system. In contrast, twentieth-century Marxist sociologists regarded industrial society as inherently conflictual by pointing to, for example, the contradictory interests of wage labour and capitalist owners and managers. While non-Marxist sociologists treated both capitalism and socialism as industrial societies, Marxists typically regarded industrial society as specific to capitalism, emphasizing the essentially exploitative nature of capitalist relations. For Marxists, however, the technological basis of machine-production in industrial society was incidental to the defining characteristics of capitalism, namely the separation of the worker from the means of production, production of commodities by wage labour and the realization of an economic surplus in the form of profits. The crises of capitalist production resulted in class struggle and imperialism. Not all conceptions of industrial society were formulated in such sharp contrasts between cooperation or conflict. Both M. Weber and the economist J. M. Keynes recognized the instability of the capitalist market without accepting a Marxist analysis. Weber recognized the instability of competitive capitalism and the discipline of factory production, while denying that socialism could avoid completely the sociological characteristics of industrialism. Keynes (1936) thought that the basic problem of the business cycle was inadequate aggregate consumer demand, which could be solved by state provision of programmes of public works rather than through war and class conflict.

SEE ALSO: *automation; capitalism; convergence thesis; industrial conflict; post-industrial society; socialist societies; technology.*

READING: Aron (1963b); Scott, J. (1997)

industrialization This term refers to sustained economic growth following the application of inanimate sources of power to mechanize production. Industrialization initially took the form of factory production, later spreading to agriculture and services. Compared with pre-industrial organization, it has involved DIVISION OF LABOUR, new social RELATIONS OF PRODUCTION between the owners of capital, managers and workers, URBANIZATION and the geographical concentration of industry and population, and changes in occupational structure. Initially a development within capitalist economies, industrialization now transcends any single economic system. The understanding of the nature and consequences of industrialization and industrial society has always been central to sociology from the nineteenth-century 'founding fathers' through to the present.

SEE ALSO: *de-industrialization; industrial society; post-industrial society.*

READING: Aron (1963b)

inequality See: DEPRIVATION; DISTRIBUTION OF INCOME AND WEALTH; EQUALITY; JUSTICE; STRATIFICATION.

inflation This is a rise in the general level of prices which has the effect of reducing the purchasing power of a given amount of money. The investigation of inflation has mainly been confined to economics, but in the 1970s sociologists became interested in the social processes that lie behind this phenomenon.

Within market economies, the interests of capital and labour compete with regard to the distribution of the product between profits and wages, with both sides trying to maximize their own interests. Historically, when labour was weak – as the result of high unemployment levels, a political and legal system that favoured business interests, and a poorly organized labour movement – pressure to raise wages was resisted. In the post-war era through to the major recession of the later 1970s, all these conditions changed and business was less able to resist pay demands. These demands became inflationary to the extent that higher wages did not reflect more output; by increasing prices, business resisted the reduced profits implied by increased wage costs. Governments played a part by increasing the money supply to permit higher money wages to be accommodated without widespread business bankruptcies.

This analysis suggested a number of important social conditions. (1) There was little natural harmony of interests between employers and workers. (2) There was no effective set of shared social values which would restrain workers' aspirations and demands – a state of ANOMIE. (3) The balance of power within industry and in politics between labour and capital was more evenly balanced. (4) Government played a significant role in reconciling economic conflicts. When inflation reduced after the 1970s, so sociological interest in its social conditions and consequences declined.

SEE ALSO: *corporatism; industrial conflict.*

READING: Gilbert (1986)

information society Working within the intellectual framework of the POST-INDUSTRIAL SOCIETY, that knowledge is now the primary source of value in the economy, a number of sociologists have suggested that information and its use define a new form of society. Their claim is that the INFORMATION SUPERHIGHWAY – that is, the convergence of various technologies into an integrated information technology (IT) – and the growing financial importance of knowledge-intensive services have together created a new technical and economic basis for contemporary capitalism. This in turn has profound effects on the nature of society.

M. Castells (1996) states that the information economy, which he calls *informationalism*, has five characteristics. (1) Information is the raw material of the economy. (2) IT has pervasive effects on society and individuals. (3) IT provides an information-processing capability which enables the logic of networks to be applied to economic organizations and processes. (4) IT and networking logic permit vastly greater flexibility, with the consequence that processes, organizations and institutions can easily be changed and new forms are continually being created. (5) Individual technologies have converged into an integrated system. For Castells and other sociologists, informationalism is also intimately bound up with GLO-BALIZATION.

While the information economy is fairly well specified, the nature of information society is less so. It is said to have social effects, such as the potential to 'empower' people with access to sources of information and learning. While this is the potential, information society writers also believe that, in reality, there will be a major division between those who can access information and others who cannot; in other words, a new form of social STRATIFICATION between the information-rich and the information-poor. But effects such as these, while important, do not change the form of society. In terms of the bigger picture – systemic change – it is claimed that IT assists the globalization of culture and the consequential weakening of national cultures and nation states as units of social organization. If these systemic changes were indeed occurring (the consequences of globalization are disputed), then it would be the broader process of globalization which would be significant rather than information as such.

Critics point out that the information economy coexists with manufacturing and services which do not use information as their raw material; thus the claim of economic dominance is much exaggerated. Information has clearly become more important as a source of economic value, but the claim that there are now information economies and societies which differ fundamentally from previous forms, remains contentious.

information superhighway A new telecommunications infrastructure, based on the merging of the separate technologies of telephone, facsimile, computer, cable and satellite communications, has created the information superhighway. The term is used metaphorically, to describe the development of CYBERSPACE, in which individuals can interact or 'travel' on the Internet.

SEE ALSO: *globalization; McLuhan; virtual reality.*

infrastructure See: BASE AND SUPERSTRUCTURE.

inner city See: ZONE OF TRANSITION.

insanity See: ANTI-PSYCHIATRY; DISCOURSE; MEDICAL MODEL; MEDICALIZ-ATION; MENTAL HEALTH.

instinct A term used in sociology to indicate unlearned, pre-social, or genetically coded characteristics of human beings.

SEE ALSO: *ethology; nature/nurture debate; need; sociobiology.*

institution The term is widely used to describe social practices that are regularly and continuously repeated, are sanctioned and maintained by social norms, and have a major significance in the social structure. Like ROLE, the term refers to established patterns of behaviour, but institution is regarded as a higher-order, more general unit that incorporates a plurality of roles. Thus a school as a social institution embraces pupil roles, teacher roles (which usually include different roles for junior, senior and head teachers) and, depending on the degree of autonomy a school has from outside agencies, parent roles and the managerial/inspectorial roles associated with the relevant educational authority. *The* school as an institution embraces these roles across all the schools that jointly constitute the school system in a given society.

Five major complexes of institutions are conventionally identified. (1) Economic institutions serve to produce and distribute goods and services. (2) Political institutions regulate the use of, and access to, power. (3) Stratification institutions determine the distribution of positions and resources. (4) Kinship institutions deal with marriage, the family and the SOCIALIZATION of the young. (5) Cultural institutions are concerned with religious, scientific and artistic activities.

Institutionalization is the process whereby social practices become sufficiently regular and continuous to be described as institutions. The notion is a useful corrective to the view that institutions are given and unchanging entities, indicating that changes in social practice both modify existing institutions and create novel forms. This is the correlate of the idea in role theory that people have some freedom to 'role make' in their interactions with others and do not simply act out prescribed patterns of behaviour.

The concept of institution is widely used in sociology, though often without precise specification. Different schools of sociology treat it in different ways. For example, functionalists can see institutions as fulfilling the 'needs' of individuals or societies, while phenomenologists may concentrate on the way in which people create or adapt institutions rather than merely respond to them.

SEE ALSO: *comparative method; economic sociology; need; norm; social structure.*
READING: Eisenstadt (1968b; 1968c)

institutional theory This branch of ORGANIZATION THEORY, sometimes referred to as the 'new' institutional theory, developed in the 1970s and 1980s. The basic proposition is that the actions of organizations are not determined solely by the logic of economic and technological factors, but also by the institutions which comprise their social environments. These include, for example, the state, professions, other organizations, together with the values and culture of the broader society in which an organization is embedded. Institutional pressures influence both organizational goals and means.

It follows from the basic proposition that organizations within a particular institutional environment should tend to be similar. For example, it is a legal requirement of the German system of INDUSTRIAL DEMOCRACY in large firms that employees' representatives occupy a certain proportion of seats on the company's top board of directors and that managers also consult regularly with employees about workplace issues via works councils. This legal framework, enacted by the state, reflects, and is reinforced by, a wider culture that values participative management. Thus business organizations in Germany are likely to share similarities in their structure and how they are managed and to differ from organizations in, say, the UK or USA. Institutionalists contend that organizations select institutionalized practices which are appropriate within a particular environment. *Isomorphism* describes the fact that organizations typically copy each other. When new organizational practices are developed, other organizations will follow suit once a certain minimum number has adopted these. There are several reasons for isomorphism: coercive pressures, the need to seek social legitimacy, or the wish to reduce uncertainty.

The *process* of institutionalization is also emphasized. In this process, repetition and familiarity lead over time to organizational structures and activities becoming firmly embedded in, and legitimized by, the culture of organizational members. Therefore, the internal social environment of the organization also influences structure and activity. Innovations that are introduced from outside, or designed internally for a particular purpose, may be modified in the process of institutionalization, as members adapt them to be compatible with existing practices and social norms. The term *path dependency* describes the fact that initial conditions influence the future path of development of an innovation. In this case, the initial conditions are institutional. For example, the same new technology may be used differently in different firms, either to enhance employees' skills or to de-skill. One explanation of these outcomes is cultural variation among firms and societies with regard to appropriate forms of work organization and the determinants of job satisfaction. Institutionalization means, in addition, that practices may persist even when they have ceased to be appropriate for the goals of those who control an organization.

Institutional theory is a useful corrective to the notion that there is a simple link between economic and technological variables and how organizations act. This link is made in the contingency approach to organizational theory and also in the rational profit-maximizing assumption of neo-classical economics. But it should be treated more as a general orientation than as a fully developed theory, because there is a significant lack of agreement among its adherents as to its precise specification.

SEE ALSO: *economic sociology.*

READING: Scott, W. R. (1995)

institutionalization of conflict Early capitalist industrialization was marked by violent social conflict in industry and society, which at times threatened to culminate in revolution. As capitalism has matured, so conflicts have declined and become less threatening. A major sociological explanation is the institutionalization of conflict.

It is assumed that one reason why conflict was severe during early capitalism was the destruction of traditional, pre-industrial social bonds and normative regulation. With the completion of the transition to mature industrialism, new regulatory and integrative institutions and values developed. Institutionalization results from the separation and autonomy of political and INDUSTRIAL CONFLICT, so that one is no longer superimposed upon the other. The growth of *citizenship* rights such as universal suffrage and political representation means that the interests that dominate industry no longer control politics. CITIZENSHIP directly integrates workers into society as well. Another process is subsumed under institutionalization: the development of specialized institutions for regulating conflict in industry once industrial conflict has been separated from political. TRADE UNIONS, together with COLLECTIVE BARGAINING between employers and trade unions, are institutions which negotiate and reconcile the differences between employers and workers.

SEE ALSO: *end of ideology theory; incorporation; strikes.*

instrumental rationality or **instrumental reason** A term derived from the work of WEBER, and much used by members of the FRANKFURT SCHOOL, to signify the use of the technically most efficient and rational means (instrument) to reach a desired end or purpose. The concept is usually used critically to indicate the harmful consequences of the spread of RATIONALIZATION, of which instrumental rationality is a part.

SEE ALSO: *critical theory; rationality.*

instrumentalism This term describes the orientation of workers who seek instrumental satisfactions from work, such as high pay or secure employment. It is sometimes contrasted with the orientation of those who value satisfactions relating to the intrinsic nature of work tasks or the social community aspects of work. In practice, people usually appreciate a combination of all three. PARSONS also uses the term to describe an orientation to action.

SEE ALSO: *affluent worker; cash nexus; work attitudes.*

integration (1) One of the abiding problems of classical sociological theory was how the various elements of society hold together, how they integrate with each other. Various accounts of social integration are proposed, the two most important being integration by commonly held values, following the perspective of FUNCTIONALISM, and integration by interdependence in the DIVISION OF LABOUR. The concept has been criticized as implying an over-integrated view of societies, ignoring the possibilities of conflict. The development of the concept of SOCIAL AND SYSTEM INTEGRATION is an attempt to advance the discussion of how elements of society do or do not hold together. (2) Integration also refers to the process by which different races come to have closer social, economic and political relationships.

SEE ALSO: *dominant ideology thesis; Durkheim; Parsons; social order.*

intelligence Defined as an innate ability, it is measured in terms of an individual's performance in mental tests which provide an intelligence quotient (the IQ), giving the ratio of a person's intelligence to the average, which is set at 100. A. Binet (1857–1911), a French psychologist, was commissioned in 1904 by the French minister of public instruction to inquire into the education of retarded children. He constructed an intelligence test which graded children in terms of their mental age (determined by a variety of cognitive tests) and their chronological age.

Considerable controversy surrounds the concept. (1) Is intelligence a fixed, innate ability that is genetically given, or is it a skill which can be developed by environmental factors? (2) Do intelligence tests measure ability or performance which is determined by other factors such as class, race or gender? (3) Do the tests measure a child's conformity to classroom expectations which are set by the teacher? (4) Some critics suggest that IQ tests are produced by representatives of the middle class in terms of the prevailing culture of such privileged groups, and that IQ tests are biased towards certain dominant norms. For these reasons, many sociologists would not regard current intelligence tests as wholly reliable. The debate about the degree to which intelligence is genetically determined has lasted for over fifty years and shows no sign of resolution.

SEE ALSO: *classroom interaction; classroom knowledge; nature/nurture debate.*

interaction See: ACTION THEORY; DRAMATURGICAL; EXCHANGE THEORY; NEGOTIATED ORDER; PARSONS; RATIONAL CHOICE THEORY; SIMMEL; SYMBOLIC INTERACTIONISM.

interaction of variables This term describes the situation when there are two or more *independent* variables which interact together to influence a *dependent* variable. For example, an investigation of the effect of teaching methods (an independent variable) on educational achievement (the dependent variable) might show that formal methods produce higher levels of achievement among school pupils than informal methods. Introducing the IQ (intelligence quotient) score of pupils as a second independent variable, however, could produce an interaction effect between the independent variables, with the result that formal teaching methods would not produce improvements in educational achievement for all IQ scores: pupils at the extremes, with very high and very low IQ scores, might achieve higher levels with informal methods whereas the great bulk of pupils might do better with formal. The main effect of formal methods in this hypothetical example is to raise achievement levels, but interaction means that the effect of one independent variable is not the same for every category of another independent variable.

SEE ALSO: *dependent/independent variables; multivariate analysis.*

intergenerational mobility See: SOCIAL MOBILITY.

internal colonialism This concept was used by Marxists like V. I. Lenin and A. Gramsci to describe political and economic inequalities between regions within a given society, by political sociology to characterize the uneven effects of state development on a regional basis, and by race relations theory to describe the underprivileged status and exploitation of minority groups within the wider society. These variations in application have a number of common elements: (1) they reject the assumption that industrial development will, in the long run, produce an integrated society, bound together by common culture and by equality of citizenship rights; (2) regional inequalities are not temporary but necessary features of industrial society. In colonialism, the relationship between metropolis and colony is unequal and exploitative; in internal colonialism, the relationship between the core and its geographical periphery is also exploitative. An internal colony produces wealth for the benefit of those areas most closely associated with the state. The members of these colonies may be differentiated by ethnicity, religion, language or some other cultural variable; they are then overtly or covertly excluded from prestigious social and political positions, which are dominated by members of the metropolis. This model has also been used to explore the role of Celtic regions within British national development.

SEE ALSO: *centre/periphery; underdevelopment.*

READING: Hechter (1975)

internalization This concept refers to the process by which an individual learns and accepts as binding the social values and norms of conduct relevant to his or her social group or wider society.

SEE ALSO: *norm; socialization.*

international division of labour See: NEW INTERNATIONAL DIVISION OF LABOUR.

interpellation Within certain branches of social theory, this refers to the process by which individuals acquire their sense of identity. For many writers, this effect is largely achieved by the action of discourses which position and create the individual as a subject. For example, discourses concerning Britishness construct certain people, those to whom these discourses are addressed, as British. Needless to say, that positioning simultaneously excludes other people from being British. Early versions of this concept tied it closely to the notion of IDEOLOGY. ALTHUSSER argued that ideologies interpellate individuals and contribute to identity formation, fixing those individuals into given positions in society as British, as a worker, or as a woman, for instance.

SEE ALSO: *discourse; identity.*

interpretation See: EMPATHY; GEISTESWISSENSCHAFTEN; HERMENEUTICS; PHENOMENOLOGICAL SOCIOLOGY; RULE; VERSTEHEN.

intersubjectivity Many forms of sociological theory have, as their starting point, the experiences of the individual subject. Such theories have to explain how it is that individuals relate to one another; that is, how intersubjectivity is created.

SEE ALSO: *action theory; phenomenological sociology; Schutz; symbolic interactionism.*
READING: Berger and Luckmann (1967)

interval scale See: MEASUREMENT LEVELS.

intervening variable This is a variable that mediates the effect of one variable on another. For example, the positive correlation between the occupational levels of fathers and sons is mediated by several intervening variables, one of the most important being educational attainment.

SEE ALSO: *correlation.*

interview The interview is an important research technique in empirical sociology. Interviews may either be formal, using a structured interview schedule, or informal, the interviewer being able to follow up points made by the interviewee. Interviews may also provide either quantitative or qualitative data. Doubts have been expressed concerning the reliability of the interview, as its social nature can lead to various sorts of unreliability. Interviewers may introduce BIAS, by the sort of questions that they ask or the way that they ask them. Interviewees may choose not to answer truthfully. A third element of bias may occur as the result of the social interaction between the interviewer and interviewee.

SEE ALSO: *ethnography; participant observation; qualitative research; questionnaire; unobtrusive measures.*

interview schedule See: QUESTIONNAIRE.

interviewer bias See: BIAS; INTERVIEW; REPLICATION.

intimacy With the growth of AFFECTIVE INDIVIDUALISM in modern marriages and partnerships, there is an emphasis on the satisfaction of intimacy as a central criterion of permanent relationships. T. Zeldin in *An Intimate History of Humanity* (1994) identified three historical meanings of intimacy. (1) It meant spatial proximity between couples in their domestic environment. (2) The romantic movement and FEMINISM redefined intimacy in terms of erotic relationships. (3) There is the intimacy which comes from a union of minds. The development of the NUCLEAR FAMILY on the basis of intimacy and trust encourages individuals to find erotic love and friendship inside MARRIAGE.

SEE ALSO: *divorce; emotions; sexualities; sociology of the family.*

intragenerational mobility See: SOCIAL MOBILITY.

invisible religion P. L. Berger and T. Luckmann (1963) criticized the traditional SOCIOLOGY OF RELIGION for its narrow focus on Christian institutions; they argued that the sociology of religion and the SOCIOLOGY OF KNOWLEDGE were both alike in explicating the processes by which the everyday world was rendered meaningful. They argued in *The Social Construction of Reality* (1967) that RELIGION was fundamental to the creation and preservation of social reality. These perspectives on religion were further developed in Berger (1967) and Luckmann (1967). Luckmann claimed that INDIVIDUALISM in contemporary, urban, consumer society contained elements of transcendence and sacredness which were components of an invisible religion. The themes of contemporary individualism are the pursuit of individual autonomy through self-expression and self-actualization. He associated this emphasis on individual experience and expression with SOCIAL MOBILITY, ACHIEVE-MENT MOTIVATION, sexuality, and the privatized world of the modern family. His theory of religion is consequently a significant challenge to the conventional view of SECULARIZATION.

SEE ALSO: *civil religion; privatization; profane; religion, sacred.*

Irigaray, L. (b. 1930) Director of research at the Centre National de la Recherche Scientifique, Paris, Irigaray is a philosopher and psychoanalyst, and a major figure in FEMINIST SOCIAL THEORY. Her work is concerned with the social construction of femininity and sexual differences, about which she has published in *Speculum of the Other Woman* (1974) and *This Sex Which Is Not One* (1977).

SEE ALSO: *feminism.*

iron law of oligarchy See: OLIGARCHY.

Islam See: WORLD RELIGIONS.

J

Jainism See: WORLD RELIGIONS.

James, William (1842–1910) An American psychologist and philosopher, James attempted to establish psychology on a scientific basis (that is, as experimental physiology and biology) in his *The Principles of Psychology* (1890). He established a new perspective in philosophy in his *Pragmatism* (1907), in which the truth of a theory is not whether it corresponds to nature, but whether its results are practical; things are 'true' if they work. He also analysed the psychological dimension of religion in *The Varieties of Religious Experience* (1902). His philosophy influenced the sociological study of EMOTIONS, RELIGION and the development of SYMBOLIC INTERACTIONISM.

Japanese religions See: WORLD RELIGIONS.

joint conjugal role See: CONJUGAL ROLE.

Judaism See: WORLD RELIGIONS.

justice As a concept fundamental to ethical theory and political philosophy, justice is associated with the notion of equity (or impartiality) and EQUALITY, especially with the injunction to treat equals equally. From Aristotle (*c*.384–322 BC), it is conventional to distinguish between (1) distributive justice, which is concerned with questions of who should get what, and (2) corrective (or commutative) justice, which is concerned with the treatment of individuals in social transactions (especially punishing an individual for an offence). The notion of distributive justice is important in contemporary social philosophy and policy as social justice. A modern theory of distributive justice has been put forward by the American philosopher J. Rawls in *A Theory of Justice* (1971), in which he defends INDIVIDUALISM while also arguing a case for equality. His general definition is that 'All social values – liberty and opportunity, income and wealth, and the bases of self-respect – are to be distributed equally unless an unequal distribution of any, or all, of these values is to everyone's advantage' (1971, p. 62). We can take two examples. It may be 'to everyone's advantage' to have legislation prohibiting the possession of firearms; instead, society has an unequal distribution of firearms to the police force in order to maintain an equal security of life. Secondly, it may be 'to everyone's advantage' to prohibit young people under a certain age from riding a motorbike. In both illustrations there is a tension between personal liberties and social justice. An alternative view of justice, that emphasizes liberties, has been propounded by R. Nozick in *Anarchy, State and Utopia* (1974) in an argument supporting private property, individual rights and self-determination. For Nozick, the state can be justified provided it is minimal; that is, it does not interfere with the enjoyment of personal freedoms.

The concept has been the topic of perennial dispute in philosophy. In practice, the principles of justice are often ambiguous and therefore difficult to apply. In the case of distributive justice, when we say 'treat equals equally' it is often difficult to determine in what sense people are equal. In the case of corrective justice, there are always problems associated with criminal responsibility, retribution and the justification of punishment. The ancient principle of *lex talionis* ('an eye for an eye') expressed a basic notion of justice, but most contemporary legal systems prefer to support some notion of correction and rehabilitation. While justice may be difficult to define and achieve, few governments have ever entirely abandoned the appeal of justice (especially as fairness), since justice is an essential feature of LEGITIMACY.

SEE ALSO: *citizenship; relative deprivation.*

K

kinship The social relationships deriving from blood ties (real and supposed) and MARRIAGE are collectively referred to as kinship. Anthropologists often distinguish between ties based on descent and ties based on affinity – that is, ties resulting from marriage.

Kinship is universal and in most societies plays a significant role in the socialization of individuals and the maintenance of group solidarity. In simple societies, kinship relations may be so extensive and significant that in effect they constitute the social system. For this reason, the concept is vitally important to anthropologists. In more complex societies, kinship normally forms a fairly small part of the totality of social relations which make up the social system. Sociologists are less concerned with kin relations, therefore, and treat these as important mainly in the SOCIOLOGY OF THE FAMILY.

SEE ALSO: *conjugal role*; *descent groups, extended family*; *network*; *nuclear family*.

knowledge, sociology of See: SOCIOLOGY OF KNOWLEDGE.

Kristeva, Julia (b. 1941) French psychoanalyst and professor of linguistics at the Université de Paris VII, Kristeva was originally a follower of BARTHES. She made significant contributions to SEMIOTICS in *Revolution in Poetic Language* (1974), and has influenced FEMINIST SOCIAL THEORY in her studies of love, desire and the self in *Powers of Horror* (1980) and *Tales of Love* (1983).

SEE ALSO: *intimacy*; *sexualities*.

READING: Moi (1986)

labelling theory In the sociology of deviance, the 'labelling theory of deviant behaviour' is often used interchangeably with the 'societal reaction theory' of deviancy; both phrases point equally well to the fact that sociological explanations of deviance treat it as a product, not of individual psychology or of genetic inheritance, but of social control. Labelling theory was significantly influenced by the CHICAGO SCHOOL and SYMBOLIC INTERACTIONISM. The foundations for this view of deviance were first established by E. Lemert (1951) and were subsequently developed by H. S. Becker (1963). The perspective of the DEFINITION OF THE SITUATION is employed to assert that, if individuals or groups are defined as deviant, there will be important and often unanticipated consequences at the level of behaviour. Labelling theory has subsequently become a dominant paradigm in the explanation of deviance. The theory is constituted essentially by two propositions. The first is that deviant behaviour is to be seen not simply as the violation of a norm, but as any behaviour which is successfully defined or labelled as deviant. The deviance does not inhere in the act itself but in the response of others to that act. The second proposition claims that labelling produces or amplifies deviance. The deviant's response to societal reaction leads to secondary deviation by which the deviant comes to accept a self-image or self-definition as someone who is permanently locked within a deviant role. The distinctiveness of the approach is that it draws attention to deviance as the outcome of social imputations and the exercise of social control.

Labelling theory has spread outside the confines of the sociology of deviance; for example, the imputation of the label 'insane' to a person may represent an important stage in the process of becoming mentally ill. Labelling theory has also been used to explain WITCHCRAFT. The theory has thus proved a fruitful development of sociological understanding of the relationships between deviance, self-conceptions, social reaction and control. It is important to remember, however, that labelling theory is not a causal explanation of primary deviance, but only of secondary deviance as a response to imputed deviance from norms.

Labelling theory has been criticized from various perspectives. Radical criminologists such as I. Taylor, P. Walton and J. Young (1973) have suggested that it neglects the significant effects of power and economic influence on the detection of crime. It is also argued that the theory neglects the victim by concentrating on the deviant and the criminal. Labelling theory has, however, been significant in generating an important body of empirical research evidence on crime and deviance.

SEE ALSO: *criminology; delinquency; delinquent drift; deviance amplification; deviant behaviour; differential association; mental health; stigma.*

READING: Downes and Rock (1995)

labour aristocracy This refers to an upper and privileged stratum of the manual WORKING CLASS, which, by means of scarce skills, strategic position, or organizational and trade-union strength, establishes better conditions for itself. It has been influential among Marxist accounts of the nineteenth-century British working class, where the existence of a labour aristocracy has been used to explain the lack of revolutionary class action in the second half of that century. Their claim is that the labour aristocracy was divided from the rest of the working class by its favourable conditions and was more likely to collaborate with the bourgeoisie than to oppose it. Although correctly highlighting the internal divisions within the nineteenth-century working class – social historians point to many other sources of division as well – the concept remains vaguely defined and its use ambiguous. It appears to have little relevance for understanding modern class structure in Britain, although it may have some relevance to Japan, where workers in the primary labour market do have a privileged position.

SEE ALSO: *labour market segmentation; labour process approach.*

READING: Gray (1981)

labour market The basic requirement of a labour market is that a person's capacity to work – that is, their LABOUR POWER – should exist as a commodity which can be bought and sold. The market is the allocative mechanism which matches the demand for, and supply of, this commodity. Most contemporary uses assume also that both the buyers and sellers of labour are formally free to choose. This distinguishes labour markets from the administrative matching of employers and employees by the state that occurred in many socialist societies, or the coercion that was characteristic of slavery and other forms of unfree labour. Labour markets have been most characteristic of capitalist industrialization and are now the standard way of organizing paid employment in modern CAPITALISM.

C. Tilly and C. Tilly (1994) identify six key components of labour markets: (1) *workers*, who formally are free to work for any employer, or not to work at all; (2) *employers*, who formally are free to hire and fire employees; (3) *jobs*, which are the result of dividing work between firms and, within firms, into distinct roles; (4) *hiring*, which can be viewed as an exchange whereby an employer agrees to pay a certain wage in return for the rights to assign employees to jobs and to control their labour power; (5) *networks*, which describe the lines of communication that link numerous employers with numerous potential employees (and vice versa); (6) *contracts*, the formal agreements and informal norms that regulate work tasks, working conditions, levels of worker effort and payment.

Economists and sociologists by and large have different perspectives on labour markets. Neo-classical economists make a number of theoretical assumptions. Both employers and employees are free to choose. Hiring, therefore, is an exchange that is entered into voluntarily by both parties, because they expect to gain more jointly than they could on their own. In general, markets are efficient mechanisms for allocation of resources and price-setting under conditions of perfect competition and perfect knowledge. In labour markets, competition among many employers for workers, and among many workers for employment, means that wages will reach an equilibrium price that reflects the balance of supply and demand, at least in the long run. When there are imperfections in the competition among potential employees or among employers that affect the equilibrium, as, for example, where strong trade unions and professions restrict competition among employees or where there are only a few employers, in theory these should be ironed out over time. Employers and employees are assumed in theory to be rational decision-makers and knowledgeable about their opportunities in the labour market, therefore they will actively search out the most advantageous deals for themselves. However, many neo-classical economists now accept that, in reality, people may not have complete information and that there is an issue of BOUNDED RATIONALITY, which may introduce some degree of market imperfection.

In an early sociological analysis of labour markets, MARX contended that the freedom of workers to choose employers became purely a formal freedom with the growth of capitalism. The dispossession of workers from the means of production, which is a characteristic feature of capitalism in his account, meant that workers had no opportunity to work for themselves rather than an employer. This led to a relationship of exploitation of workers by employers. In a similar vein, WEBER maintained that theoretical assumptions about the voluntary nature of hiring relationships and an equality of exchange that is mutually beneficial, could conceal a reality of power and inequality in which employers dominated workers in labour markets.

Sociologists have continued to focus on the social relationships involved in the production of goods and services. These include social relations within the labour market and the workplace. Sociologists have largely ignored the market efficiency issues that economists favour. There have been a number of important insights.

(1) The hiring relationship between a potential individual employee and an employer is not equal. One consequence is that employees will often seek to increase their strength *vis-à-vis* employers by means of collective action. TRADE UNIONS bargain collectively with employers, in order to influence wages and the terms and conditions of employment. Historically, some trade unions also succeeded in limiting the competition among potential employees in the labour market by restricting access to certain jobs to their members. PROFESSIONS act similarly in the labour market to limit competition by restricting membership and excluding non-members, in a process known as SOCIAL CLOSURE.

(2) Contracts are always indeterminate and liable to re-negotiation, and, ultimately, reflect social processes more than formal agreements. Indeterminacy stems from the nature of the commodity that employers hire: an employee's *capacity* to work, rather than a precisely defined quantum of effort or output. Given this lack of definition, the terms of contract are capable of interpretation by both parties. For example, effort and output may be affected by prevailing social norms and group interaction, as the HUMAN RELATIONS school demonstrated, and by the distribution of power within companies, following the LABOUR PROCESS APPROACH.

(3) The social relationships involved in production, including those in the labour market, are significantly influenced by law and politics, and ultimately, therefore, by social values. In general, many aspects of capitalist labour markets are determined administratively rather than by competition and free choice in the market, while specific patterns of regulation vary across societies. Labour market regulation may include any of the following examples: national minimum wages; limits on hours worked; restrictions on the ability of employers to dismiss employees; specification of the employment contract; specification of the rights of trade unions (whether these favour employers or employees); the allocation of rights to professions to

monopolize certain jobs; anti-discriminatory hiring and firing laws; requirements for positive discrimination in hiring and promotion ('affirmative action' in the USA).

(4) Sociologists maintain that labour markets are never fully competitive and will always be more or less imperfect, because they are segmented. The notion of LABOUR MARKET SEGMENTATION was pioneered by institutional economists, against neo-classical orthodoxy, and has been adopted by sociologists to describe the reality that labour markets comprise interrelated but non-competing sub-markets. Jobs cluster into segments and, while potential employees may compete with each other for employment within a segment, there is far less competition across these. Segmentation is an outcome of the social relations between employers and employees, when the patterns of interaction between the parties within the workplace have consequences for the labour market (e.g. an understanding that more senior posts within a company will be filled by means of internal promotion favours insiders and excludes outsiders). Segmentation is also shaped by wider social norms about employment (e.g. that certain jobs are more appropriate to men than women and vice versa).

The sociology of labour markets has been developed in recent years with the analysis of networks. These provide the lines of communication that link potential employees with potential employers. A celebrated analysis of how people get jobs, by M. Granovetter (1974), showed that most people find work via acquaintances, rather than via formal methods such as job advertisements or employment agencies. Neither employers nor employees choose to search widely and anonymously, contrary to what neo-classical economics suggests, but prefer to use networks of acquaintances in order to match people and jobs. 'Weak' rather than 'strong' ties are more useful to potential employees. 'Strong ties' (with close friends) give access to the same sources of information and jobs as oneself, whereas 'weak ties' (with more distant acquaintances) bring different information and contacts. Employers prefer to recruit among people known to themselves or their existing employees, because this reduces the cost of recruitment and the risk of hiring an unsatisfactory employee. Research shows that the number of useful contacts people have increases with their educational level and contacts are especially important among managerial and professional employees (although they are not unimportant to manual employees). It also shows that, once a network exists, its members tend to be promoted faster within an organization and, secondly, that they tend to recruit into the organization other people similar to themselves. Exclusion from the networks of male managers is often cited as one reason that women managers fail to be promoted as rapidly or as far as men.

SEE ALSO: *management; market network/social network; women and work.*

labour market segmentation Institutional economists believe that national labour markets comprise interrelated yet non-competing sub-markets. Jobs are clustered into segments that are internally fairly homogeneous in terms of their skills, responsibility, autonomy, job interest, security, promotion prospects and pay. While potential employees may compete with each other for jobs within one segment of the LABOUR MARKET, there is little competition among segments or movement of individuals across. The model departs markedly from the assumptions of neo-classical economics about competitive labour markets and an unbroken distribution of jobs and workers. Sociologists and institutional economists share common ground in this analysis. Segmentation can be viewed as a form of SOCIAL CLOSURE, which limits particular jobs to certain people and excludes others. The classic definition of closure sees this as a process whereby one group excludes others from the advantages that it enjoys, but, in segmentation, closure is promoted by employers as well as the employees who overtly benefit. There have been different views about the underpinnings of segmentation, whether it is due to technological factors or to the nature of social relationships involved in production, but the latter is now the orthodox position. In addition, segmentation draws on prevalent social norms about what forms of exclusion might be permissible (e.g. that some jobs are women's and not men's work).

Early accounts proposed a dualistic model of primary and secondary labour market segments. While more than two segments are recognized today, the primary/secondary division remains an important one and can be found in a number of economies. *Primary* markets are composed of jobs which offer high wages, CAREER structures (albeit with low ceilings for manual employees), the chance to acquire skills on the job, and stable and secure employment. *Internal* labour markets are often held to be characteristic of primary employment. In these, firms recruit from outside (the *external* labour market) for certain fairly low positions and then fill higher-level vacancies by the promotion of existing employees. *Secondary* labour market jobs provide low wages, few possibilities for advancement or the acquisition of skills, and unstable, insecure employment. To some extent, the primary/secondary labour market division corresponds to the divisions within the DUAL ECONOMY: 'core' firms tend to offer primary jobs and peripheral firms to offer secondary ones. The overlap is not complete, because 'core' firms may also offer secondary jobs. In Japan and the United States, where the dual labour market is highly developed and well documented, certain groups of workers have tended to get jobs in one market rather than another: ethnic minorities and women are more likely to be selected for secondary jobs; ethnic majority males for primary ones. It is now common to distinguish between upper and lower segments of the primary market in the USA. The lower comprises manual and lower white-collar employees who lack transferable skills and are therefore dependent on their employers. The upper segment comprises managers, professionals and certain craftsmen with transferable skills, who are not tied to a single employer and move among firms seeking the best deal.

P. B. Doeringer and M. J. Piore (1971) attributed duality mainly to technological factors: advanced technology is believed to require firm-specific skills and stable labour forces, which in turn lead firms to offer training and to commit workers to their jobs by means of high pay, a career structure and good benefits. Because technological demands are not constant for all jobs within a firm, companies frequently work with a mix of primary and secondary markets. Women and minorities are stereotyped as making insufficiently reliable and stable employees, which is why they may be discriminated against and excluded from the better jobs. Job changing and absenteeism have tended on average to be higher among these groups, which reinforces employers' STEREOTYPES. But it may be the case that an apparent lack of job commitment follows from the inferior jobs on offer in the secondary market rather than the characteristics of employees. Equally, the labour-force attachment of women is now changing, since women work for more of their lifetime than in the past and, when they are working, may not change jobs any more often than men. Oligopolistic product markets are needed if firms are to pass on the extra costs of creating a privileged stratum. M. Reich *et al.* (1973) analysed segmentation as a managerial strategy of divide-and-rule. Because 'monopoly' capitalism in the twentieth century created larger enterprises, standardized production methods and de-skilled craftwork, the WORKING CLASS began to grow more homogeneous and potentially more able to organize collectively against capital. Management therefore created artificial divisions and bought off a large segment of labour in order to prevent organized class struggle. Neither account of segmentation gives much weight to employee organization. Yet experience in America and elsewhere is that both unions and professional associations have helped to develop and maintain segmentation, ensuring that companies adopt employment practices that are beneficial to their members and protecting their members against competition from new arrivals on the external labour market.

Sociologists take account of segmentation in the analysis of internal stratification within the working class, the study of the position of women and ethnic minorities in employment, and accounts of work and industrial relations. Market segmentation is universal. Outside the USA and Japan, however, some of the particular features of primary markets as described by US economists – namely internal labour markets, career ladders and skill acquisition – may be less prevalent. Nor, in the case of the USA, is it clear how far these features have survived the ongoing restructuring initiated by large corporations in the late 1980s. Job security in the primary sector was eroded when companies decided to 'downsize'; that is, to reduce significantly the numbers of their employees. There seem now to be fewer opportunities for promotion, because the numbers of layers within organizations have also been reduced (in a process of 'delayering'), but what promotion remains may still be internal. Skill acquisition has been unaffected, however. It should be noted that segmentation models differ from the labour process approach, which claims that labour has been homogenized.

SEE ALSO: *de-skilling; human capital; labour aristocracy; profession; sex roles; underclass; women and work.*

READING: Gordon *et al.* (1982); Tilly and Tilly (1994)

labour movement Worker dissatisfaction and protest are ubiquitous in industrial society. The organizations that develop to give effective voice to these sentiments constitute the labour movement.

American social scientists for long regarded the term 'labour movement' as being interchangeable with trade unionism, and unionism as being concerned with collective bargaining. However, the European experience and that of currently industrializing societies show that there is a wide range of organizational forms. Individual labour movements often comprise both TRADE UNIONS and political parties. The British labour movement, for example, embraces the Trades Union Congress and the Labour Party; indeed, trade unions finance the political party. Nor do trade unions always value COLLECTIVE BARGAINING as the means of promoting workers' interests: French trade unions, for example, acted largely to mobilize worker support for political parties until recently.

SEE ALSO: *institutionalization of conflict; Leninism.*

READING: Regini (1992)

labour power MARX distinguished between the labourer's work (labour) and his capacity to work (labour power). In capitalism, the employer buys labour power and not labour.

SEE ALSO: *labour theory of value; Marxist sociology; surplus value.*

labour process This term refers to the process of production, in which labour power is applied to raw materials and machinery to produce commodities. The substitution of 'labour' for the term 'production' reflects the Marxist view that it is labour which creates all value and that the more conventional term disguises this fact.

SEE ALSO: *labour process approach; labour theory of value.*

labour process approach H. Braverman in *Labour and Monopoly Capitalism* (1974) claimed that the LABOUR PROCESS in advanced capitalist economies should be seen as determined by capitalist social relations, not as the product of technological or organizational factors that have their own requirements irrespective of the form of economic ownership. He contended that the way labour processes are organized reflects the antagonism that is inherent in CAPITALISM, which is based on the exploitation of labour by capital. This antagonism has meant that the managers who represent capital in modern corporations cannot rely on labour voluntarily to work diligently and effectively to produce SURPLUS VALUE. When they employ workers, employers hire a capacity to work – LABOUR POWER – rather than a fixed amount of output or effort, and they then have to convert this capacity into effective work. Managers therefore look for ways of maximizing their control over the labour process and minimizing that of workers. In this account, the evolution of production technology and the organization of work are both determined by the requirement for capital to dominate the labour process and weaken any power that labour has to resist. Historically, management has attempted to do this by introducing SCIEN-TIFIC MANAGEMENT principles of work organization and new technologies that are less dependent on workers' skills, which together de-skill labour. In the future, managers may reduce their dependence on workers altogether by replacing people with automated machinery if possible. At the same time, because the profitability of capital may be increased by reducing labour costs, economic pressures reinforce the trend towards de-skilling and technological replacement, in order to cheapen labour.

Braverman was responsible for a major intellectual shift within industrial sociology that led to a new concern with the nature of the labour process, including the evolution of managerial practices and production technology and the character of the social relations involved in production. Subsequent research has concentrated on two issues, DE-SKILLING and MANAGERIAL STRATEGIES OF CONTROL, and Braverman's arguments have now been greatly qualified.

(1) The long-term trend towards the AUTOMATION of production and routine office tasks reduces employment opportunities but has no necessary effects on skill. New technologies create new skills, for example in design and maintenance, while the evidence for the de-skilling of production and routine office tasks is inconclusive since many examples can be found of re-skilling as well as de-skilling.

(2) The resistance of employees to de-skilling and tight control has often retarded and modified managerial policy, particularly where trade unions have been strongly established.

(3) Managers now see unacceptable costs in tight control of the labour process. Where automation is not sufficiently advanced to dispense altogether with labour, the financial cost of close supervision can be high. If companies can reduce their supervisory personnel and still achieve adequate output from employees, there is a strong incentive to do so. Many have now expanded the range of tasks performed by their employees, to include traditional supervisory tasks such as inspection, quality control and responsibility for organizing work. More responsibility and independence is now thought to improve productivity and quality. FLEXIBLE SPECIALIZATION suggests that companies need to employ people with multiple skills or competences (a concept often referred to as 'polyvalency'), in order to work on new technologies and to cope with the rapid product changes characteristic of many industries, and also to give more discretion to their labour forces. Outside manufacturing and routine office work, tight managerial control may be even more inappropriate. Where employees deal directly with customers, as for example in retailing, customers will respond more favourably when employees have sufficient discretion to provide a personal service. Many technical and professional jobs are difficult to de-skill or replace by technology, and people in such occupations typically expect to be given a reasonable amount of discretion, thus tight control may be counter-productive. It is necessary, in fact, for management to adopt various strategies, not just one.

(4) Thus the conclusion is that Braverman's analysis has no general relevance in the contemporary economy. It may, however, fit the few remaining cases of FORDISM.

SEE ALSO: *division of labour; industrial conflict; labour market; post-Fordism; relations of production.*

READING: Littler (1990); Grint (1993)

labour relations See: INDUSTRIAL RELATIONS.

labour theory of value For MARX, the aim of any economy is the creation of use values; that is, useful objects. However, in many economies, especially capitalist ones, people do not produce things for their own use directly, but for exchange with other commodities. All commodities are produced by labour and, ultimately, it is the labour time expended in their production that determines exchange value. Commodities may not, however, actually exchange at their values, because their prices will be determined by a whole range of factors, including supply and demand.

SEE ALSO: *commodity fetishism; Marxist sociology; surplus value.*

labour unions See: TRADE UNIONS.

Lacan, Jacques (1901–81) A French psychoanalyst who believed that there was a need for psychoanalysis to recognize the role of speech and language. He therefore sought to re-interpret FREUD in the light of structural linguistics. The result was a conceptualization of the self as a dynamic, precarious and divided entity. Lacan has had a considerable influence on film theory and FEMINIST THEORY. His major work in English is *Ecrits: A selection* (1977).

SEE ALSO: *semiotics; structuralism.*

laissez-faire A traditional description of an economy where government intervention is kept to the minimum possible level. During the ascendancy of the NEW

RIGHT in the 1980s, the term regained currency, to describe the withdrawal of government from most of its by then customary activities in the economic sphere, including the PRIVATIZATION of publicly owned industry, de-regulation of the markets for capital, labour and products, and reduced personal and corporate taxation, in order to promote an economy free of restraints.

langue See: SAUSSURE.

latent function This term refers to the unintended and unrecognized consequences of social action upon other social actors or institutions. In an example used by MERTON, the Hopi Native Americans engage in ceremonial dances designed to encourage rain. Whatever the effects on the weather, these dances have the unintended consequence or latent function of uniting the tribe.

SEE ALSO: *functionalism; manifest function.*

READING: Merton (1957)

latifundia A large estate, characteristic of the agrarian structure of Latin America, in which the labourer is subject to the authoritative control of the normally absentee *patron*. The *latifundismo* is a system of such estates.

SEE ALSO: *paternalism.*

law, sociology of See: SOCIOLOGY OF LAW.

Lazarsfeld, Paul F. (1901–76) An Austrian sociologist who emigrated to the USA in 1933, he was the major influence on the growth of modern quantitative sociology. In the early 1940s, he founded the Bureau of Applied Social Research at Columbia University as the first university-based social survey centre. His main contributions to research methodology included the systematic development of CROSS TABULATION as a technique for the analysis of survey data, the construction of indicators and the training of a generation of quantitative sociologists. His substantive work was in the area of mass communications and political, applied and mathematical sociology.

Lazarsfeld taught in the Sociology Department of Columbia University from 1940 to 1969, where he collaborated with MERTON. He published widely in scholarly journals and monographs. Among his best-known works are: *Mathematical Thinking in the Social Sciences* (1954); *Personal Influence* (1955), with E. Katz; *Latent Structure Analysis* (1968), with N. W. Henny; *The People's Choice* (1969), with others; *Qualitative Analysis: Historical and critical essays* (1971).

leadership In social psychology, leadership is frequently treated in the analysis of small groups. In sociology, it is defined as the exercise of influence or POWER in social collectivities. Weberian sociology has identified three types of leadership corresponding to the different forms of AUTHORITY and LEGITIMACY. Charismatic leaders lead by virtue of the extraordinary powers attributed to them by their followers. Traditional leaders lead by virtue of custom and practice, because a certain family or class has always led. Legal leadership based on expertise and implemented according to formal rules is typically found in public administration and modern business enterprises. From this perspective, modern management represents the exercise of leadership on the basis of technical or professional competence.

Recent sociologists have emphasized power rather than leadership, being particularly concerned with the structural conditions that allow some to exercise power over others. They have questioned the Weberian assumption that leadership roles must be legitimated by subordinates.

SEE ALSO: *charisma; group; human relations.*

legal–rational authority For M. Weber (1922), legal–rational authority is the characteristic form of AUTHORITY in modern society. Within BUREAUCRACY, a command is held to be legitimate and authoritative if it has been issued from the correct office, under the appropriate regulations and according to appropriate procedures. The authority of officials depends, not on tradition or CHARISMA, but on a consensus as to the validity of rules of procedure which are perceived as rational, fair and impartial.

SEE ALSO: *legitimacy.*

legitimacy The modern problem of legitimacy is a problem of political representation and consent. The issue of political legitimacy emerges with the disappearance of direct political relationships in small-scale societies; the modern problem thus centres on which individuals are legitimately entitled to act as representatives of political POWER. Legitimacy is consequently bound up with the nature of political LEADERSHIP.

In classical civilization there was no essential difference between 'lawfulness' and 'legitimacy'. Legitimate power was simply lawful power. In modern discussions of political legitimacy, however, law and morality have been partially separated. The positivist definition of law treats law as a command supported by appropriate sanctions, and the moral content of law is secondary. Governments can have legal authority without being morally just governments.

Modern theories of legitimacy are often subjectivist in defining legitimate power as power which is believed to be legitimate. M. Weber's theory of legitimacy is one which stressed the importance of followers' beliefs. There are three ideological bases of legitimacy (traditional, charismatic and legal–rational) which may confer authority on rulers. Since Weber thought that the state could not be legitimated by any absolute standards based on natural law, the modern state has a 'legitimation deficit'; its operations are extended beyond the scope of public consent. Notions of legitimation deficits and crises have become common in political sociology.

SEE ALSO: *charisma; legal–rational authority; natural law.*

READING: Merquior (1980)

legitimation See: HABERMAS; LEADERSHIP; LEGAL–RATIONAL AUTHORITY; LEGITIMACY; LEGITIMATION CRISIS.

legitimation crisis A term introduced in the work of HABERMAS, who argues that all social systems have to have some mechanism that gives them LEGITIMACY. Modern capitalist societies require extensive state planning of the economic system. This state intervention is given legitimacy by parliamentary democracy which, for Habermas, boils down to periodic and occasional voting by citizens who are otherwise politically inert. This inertia, or civil privatism, is necessary for the survival of the system. However, civil privatism is undermined by the very process of state intervention and planning, which systematically interferes in citizens' private lives, thus generating a potential crisis of legitimacy.

READING: Habermas (1973)

leisure Frequently defined as the time left over after paid work. This definition is somewhat misleading for those people who do not have paid work – women at home, the unemployed and the elderly.

The amount of time that people spend at work in the UK has been declining steadily since the beginning of the century, from about 53 hours per week to about 40 hours for industrial manual workers, although there are signs that this began to reverse in the late 1990s. There are many different ways of spending leisure time, but it is usually spent in the home (70 per cent for men, 80 per cent for women), chiefly watching television. There are, however, significant gender, life-cycle, and class differences in leisure patterns. In particular, men are more involved in leisure pursuits outside the home and, generally speaking, women, whether in paid employment or not, have less free time. Professional and managerial classes do more in all leisure fields than other social classes, partly a reflection of financial resources. The young and the elderly have more free time than other age groups and, in a sense, the lives of these two groups are organized around leisure.

With rising incomes in the West, many households have more money available for their leisure pursuits. This is related to the growth of a leisure industry which will provide for a very large variety of tasks. These developments have led some commentators to argue that a leisure society or a CONSUMER SOCIETY has been created in which a person's IDENTITY is given by their leisure pursuits and not by their paid employment.

SEE ALSO: *privatism.*

leisure class A term coined by T. Veblen (1899). The leisure class is wealthy enough not to have to work. Its members live a life of leisure, marked by the conspicuous acquisition and display of consumer goods. They therefore show their STATUS and social position by distancing themselves from the world of work yet are engaged in conspicuous consumption.

SEE ALSO: *positional goods.*

Lemert, Edwin M. (1912–96) Generally recognized as the founder of the LABEL-LING THEORY of social deviance, or 'societal reaction theory', he was president of the Society for the Study of Social Problems in 1972 and of the Pacific Sociological Society in 1973. *Social Pathology* (1951) is a classic sociological study of DEVIANT BEHAVIOUR.

SEE ALSO: *deviance amplification.*

Leninism The Russian revolutionary leader V. I. Lenin produced little systematic theory but certain of his political doctrines have had some influence in sociology. His analysis of labour movements (1902) suggested that workers spontaneously produced only a reformist outlook, which sought piecemeal improvements of the working class's lot within capitalism rather than seeking to overthrow the system. Trade unionism, according to this perspective, is reformism *par excellence*, since its objectives of improving pay and conditions at work and persuading governments to act in the realms of social welfare and labour law can be met and, once achieved, serve to incorporate workers within capitalism. Moreover, trade unionism encourages sectionalism between different trades and occupations within the working class. He believed that the revolutionary socialist party, led by Marxist intellectuals, was necessary to furnish the working class, including the LABOUR ARISTOCRACY with a true revolutionary CLASS CONSCIOUSNESS rather than trade-union consciousness. These ideas, that there are inherent limitations to working-class ideology, that unions are sectional bodies, and that class consciousness has to be taught by a political party, have informed some more recent analyses of class consciousness and the labour movement. Lenin himself also produced analyses of IMPERIALISM and UNEVEN DEVELOPMENT.

SEE ALSO: *economism; Gramsci; incorporation; trade unions.*

READING: Kolakowski (1978b)

Lévi-Strauss, Claude (b. 1908) A French anthropologist, who worked for many years at the New School of Social Research in New York, before returning to France in 1958. While Lévi-Strauss made a major contribution to modern anthropology in *Structural Anthropology* (1958), to the study of mentality in *The Savage Mind* (1962b) and, more generally, to STRUCTURALISM in *Introduction to a Science of Mythology* (1964), he has had only a slight influence on sociology. The point of his anthropology is primarily to provide an understanding of human conceptual activity, and thus to contribute to the study of the human mind. While his structuralist analyses of MYTH, totemism (1962a) and primitive classifications often appear to bear a close affinity with the social anthropology of E. Durkheim and M. Mauss, Lévi-Strauss himself claims to have been influenced by the Anglo-Saxon tradition of empirical anthropology, but his analysis of myth depends on structural linguistics and cybernetics.

Lévi-Strauss' anthropology is essentially cognitive anthropology aimed at an analysis of the relationship between nature and culture in terms of language. His work has been organized around three areas: kinship theory (1949), the analysis of mythology and the nature of primitive classifications. These three areas are connected by social exchange, especially the exchange of women, words and commodities. Structuralist analysis is applied to these social phenomena to isolate the underlying patterns, regularities and types which, for Lévi-Strauss, point to the universal features of the neuro-physiological constitution of the human brain. His autobiographical work, *Tristes Tropiques* (1955), is a major guide to the nature of the anthropological imagination.

SEE ALSO: *exchange theory; Foucault; Lacan; semiotics; taboo.*

READING: Leach (1970)

life-chances The chances an individual has of sharing in the economic and cultural goods of a society are referred to in Weberian sociology as 'life-chances'. The distribution of such goods is usually asymmetrical. Material rewards are clearly distributed unequally in most societies, but so are cultural goods, as is shown, for example, by differential access to education. This inequality reflects the access that different social classes have to the benefits of society.

SEE ALSO: *class; cultural capital; stratification.*

READING: Dahrendorf (1979)

life-course See: LIFE-CYCLE.

life-cycle This term is used primarily to describe the development of a person through childhood, adolescence, mid-life, old age and death. The sociological concept of 'life-cycle' does not refer to the purely biological process of maturation, but to the transitions of an individual through socially constructed categories of age and to the variations in social experience of AGING. For example, men and women have very different social experiences of biological aging, while the length and importance of 'childhood' varies between cultures.

There is a secondary meaning of the concept, which may refer to the history of individual families or households rather than to persons. In this alternative sense, the life-cycle of a family or household is a process that includes courtship, marriage, child-rearing, children leaving home and dissolution of the family unit.

In both senses, therefore, the idea is to represent families or households through time. It is also important to note the diversity of households, families and persons, and the diversity of experiences and trajectories through time. It is for this reason that the term 'life-course' is sometimes preferred, because it does not suggest that the stages through which a person, household or family moves are fixed.

SEE ALSO: *generation*.

READING: Morgan (1985)

life-expectancy See: AGING.

life-world This refers to the everyday world as it is experienced by ordinary men and women. For PHENOMENOLOGICAL SOCIOLOGY, the life-world is the 'paramount reality' and the main object of sociological inquiry. Its chief characteristic is that it is unproblematic and is taken for granted, and is therefore to be contrasted with the world of scientists and sociologists in which natural objects and social interactions are not taken for granted. The term is used by HABERMAS to refer to the everyday world, which is informed by practical considerations.

SEE ALSO: *commonsense knowledge*; *Schutz*.

lifestyle A concept that has been used in several ways. In the British sociology of stratification of the 1960s and 1970s there was an interest in the differences between social groups, in patterns of social relationships, the consumption of material goods, and culture, which together constitute lifestyles. Such differences are visible indicators of class position, and lifestyles form one of the ways in which economic classes have a social presence. The debate about EMBOURGEOISEMENT revolved around the assertion that workers were adopting middle-class lifestyles. The AFFLU-ENT WORKER research disproved this claim.

In American sociology, the notion of style of life has been used to distinguish between rural and urban, urban and suburban forms of social life. In more recent work, the concept has been used more widely still to designate the tastes, attitudes, possessions or ways of behaving of any social group which distinguish it from other social groups. In this sense, any connection between the concept and that of social CLASS has been severed.

SEE ALSO: *consumer society*; *postmodernism*; *postmodernity*; *rural–urban continuum*; *youth culture*.

lineage See: DESCENT GROUPS.

Lipset, Seymour M. (b. 1922) Formerly a professor of government at Stanford University, his intellectual contributions are diverse, covering SOCIAL MOVEMENTS and political radicalism, modernization, democracy in trade-union government and SOCIAL MOBILITY. He is regarded as one of the leading figures of post-war American sociology. His major works are: *Agrarian Socialism* (1950); *Union Democracy* (1956), with M. A. Trow and J. S. Coleman; *Social Mobility in Industrial Society* (1959), with BENDIX; *Political Man* (1960); *The First New Nation* (1963); *Revolution and Counter-Revolution* (1969); *The Politics of Unreason* (1971), with E. Raab.

SEE ALSO: *end of ideology theory*.

Lockwood, David (b. 1929) A British sociologist, formerly professor of sociology at Essex University, who has contributed to the theory of social conflict and social class, and to the empirical investigation of stratification in Britain. His study of clerks, *The Blackcoated Worker* (1958), was significant for its conclusion that the historically privileged position of clerks was threatened (though he disputed that clerks were becoming more proletarian), and as a contribution to modern Weberian class theory. Two papers in 1956 and 1964 contributed to the conflict–consensus debate from the conflict perspective, and introduced the distinction between social and system integration. He was one of the senior members of the research team which conducted the AFFLUENT WORKER investigation; this used his conceptual typology of the British working class (1966). A more recent study is *Solidarity and Schism: 'The Problem of Order' in Durkheimian and Marxist Sociology* (1992).

SEE ALSO: *class imagery; conflict theory; deferential worker; orientation to work; social and system integration*.

log linear analysis The techniques of multivariate data analysis used by sociologists have largely been borrowed from other disciplines and depend on assumptions that may be inappropriate for sociological research findings. In particular, sociologists may wrongly believe that their data fit the assumptions of the general linear model and erroneously use REGRESSION and PATH ANALYSIS techniques deriving from the model. For example, it is not uncommon for sociologists to treat ordinal variables as if they had the properties of interval scales, or to use nominal categories in the 'dummy variable' regression procedure, but they run a risk of spurious results. CROSS TABULATION does not make assumptions about linearity and is often used by sociologists. However, the relationships within cross-tabulation tables (also known as *contingency* tables) become increasingly difficult to interpret as the number of variables increases. A simply analysed, bivariate (two-by-two) cross tabulation of, say, voting intention by the social class of the respondent, becomes much more complicated as extra variables are added. In this case, if one were to add the sex and age of respondents into the contingency table, one would have four variables and their relationships and interaction effects to analyse.

Log linear analysis has been developed to meet the specific needs of sociologists. It transforms non-linear into essentially linear models by the use of logarithms. This transformation both simplifies the statistical analysis and permits the use of linear techniques as required. Its main application is in the elaboration of contingency tables comprising many variables, some or all of which are nominal or ordinal measurements, and in the CAUSAL MODELLING of data. It has been used extensively in the analysis of data on SOCIAL MOBILITY. Like other modelling devices, it requires that the user specify a theoretical model that is then tested against the data. Analysis usually proceeds by testing successive models against the data until the best 'fit' is found. The use of logarithms in regression models is another application.

SEE ALSO: *measurement levels; multivariate analysis*.

READING: Gilbert (1981)

longitudinal study See: PANEL STUDY.

Luhmann, Niklas (1927–98) Formerly professor of sociology at the University of Bielefeld, Germany, Luhmann was enormously productive, writing over fifty books and three hundred articles between 1964 and 1997. He developed an original general theory of social systems, which treated human beings as elements of the environment and rejected ACTION THEORY. Society is defined as a system that covers all forms of communication. Communication requires meaning, and meaning requires the creation of distinctions. A system is a set of distinctions or meanings that are stored in symbolic generalizations, such as language. Luhmann argued, therefore – contrary to PARSONS – that a general theory of social systems was prior to a general theory of action.

According to Luhmann, social systems function to reduce complexity. As social systems become differentiated, their sub-systems become increasingly autonomous; this process is conceptualized as the *autopoietic* reproduction of social systems. Luhmann adopted the concepts of self-reference and autopoiesis from contemporary biology to describe the processes by which social systems reproduce themselves. In order to understand how social systems process information from their environments through codes, structures and systemic processes, Luhmann introduced the concept of autopoiesis, which may be defined broadly as the capacity of organisms to monitor, regulate and adapt to environments. Social systems can be conceptualized as systems of communication that are constituted autopoietically through the management of information, especially information about the meaning of their environments. Social systems reflect on meaningful information from the environment in order to monitor their external relationships, including their relations with other social systems. In this respect, social systems are sophisticated structures, because they can collect, process and act on information about themselves. In the development of social systems, this capacity for self-referential knowledge means that they become increasingly independent and autonomous. They can process information critically and self-reflexively to manage and cope with threats from their environment.

Luhmann's research objective was to analyse the principal functional systems in this process of differentiation, such as law, politics, the economy, religion and so forth. His aim in producing a critical theory of contemporary society was to show how modern social systems are destroying their natural environment. Because it is difficult for complex systems to gain a comprehensive overview of their functions, modern social life is contingent and therefore risky. Luhmann applied this complex theory to a great variety of issues in: *The Differentiation of Society* (1982); *Religious Dogmatics and the Evolution of Society* (1984); *Love as Passion* (1986); *Ecological Communication* (1989); *Risk: A sociological theory* (1993); *Social Systems* (1995).

SEE ALSO: *differentiation*; *Habermas*; *risk/risk society*; *social system*; *systems theory*.

Lukács, Georg (1885–1971) Partly a political organizer but more of a Marxist theoretician, Lukács has contributed a good deal to Marxist theory, especially the critique of epistemology and ONTOLOGY in *The Ontology of Social Being* (1978). As far as sociologists are concerned, his major works are *History and Class Consciousness* (1923) and *The Historical Novel* (1955). In the analysis of consciousness he developed the notion that the working class had a unique insight into historical truth. However, because there were occasionally divergences within the working class and it was prey to false consciousness, he argued that the analyst might have to impute a consciousness to it. He also argued for the importance of the concept of REIFICATION for the analysis of capitalist society. He made a major contribution to the sociology of literature in *Essays on Thomas Mann* (1964), *Goethe and his Age* (1968) and *Studies in European Realism* (1972). He suggests that the novel was realistic in the nineteenth century and reflected man's experience as a whole because the BOURGEOISIE was triumphant. The novel becomes modernist, reflecting only a fragmented experience, in the twentieth century, because of the rise of a potentially revolutionary working class. His work on the novel argues for a connection between social class and literary form. Lukács suggested in *The Destruction of Reason* (1954) that there was a strong current of irrationalism in German intellectual history, which had contributed to the rise of FASCISM.

SEE ALSO: *Marxist sociology.*

M

macro-sociology In sociology there are different levels of analysis. Macro-sociology is the analysis of either large collectivities (the city, the church) or, more abstractly, of social systems and social structures.

SEE ALSO: *micro-sociology*.

madness See FOUCAULT; MENTAL HEALTH.

male chauvinism A term used to describe the masculine attitudes – and practices – which treat masculine concerns and interests as paramount while treating women as inferior or even invisible beings. Such attitudes may lie behind the discrimination against women in many areas of social life.

SEE ALSO: *gender; patriarchy; stereotypes*.

Malinowski, Bronislaw (1884–1942) Malinowski did anthropological field work among the Trobriand Islands, New Guinea, shortly after the First World War, publishing *Argonauts of the Western Pacific* in 1922. His academic life was subsequently spent at the London School of Economics where he became reader in anthropology (1924) and professor of anthropology (1927). Malinowski made major contributions to the study of magic in *Coral Gardens and their Magic* (1935), functionalist theory in *A Scientific Theory of Culture* (1944), and the study of sexual behaviour in *Sex and Repression in Savage Society* (1927).

The principal features of the empiricist tradition in British anthropology following Malinowski's perspective were: (1) a concentration on intensive, detailed empirical study of small-scale societies; (2) an emphasis on direct participation with native informants; (3) an adherence to functionalist theory in which cultural institutions were treated as direct expressions of human needs.

SEE ALSO: *functionalism*.

Malthus, Thomas (1766–1834) His *Essay on Population* (1789) argued that the human capacity for reproduction exceeded the rate at which subsistence from the land can be increased. Living conditions of the working class could not be improved without the population increasing, thereby reducing living standards by decreasing the food supply. Human populations were checked by positive means (famine, disease or war) or negative means (late marriage and chastity). SOCIAL DARWINISM adopted Malthusian DEMOGRAPHY, arguing that working-class poverty resulted from moral irresponsibility.

SEE ALSO: *demographic transition*.

READING: Petersen (1979)

management Sociological interest in management is focused on four issues: (1) a concern with managers as a privileged social grouping; (2) the character of the social relationships internal to managerial hierarchies in enterprises; (3) management as a process with both technical and social control functions; (4) the position of women in management.

(1) The occupational category of managers and administrators has grown considerably in this century, from 3.6 per cent of the employed population in the British census of 1911 to nearly 13 per cent in 1991. Managers are placed at or near the top of the CLASS structure in all accounts of stratification. In modern Weberian accounts, managers have an elite position by virtue of their market and work situations. The market position and LIFE-CHANCES of managers are highly favourable with regard to income, terms and conditions of employment, prospects of career advancement and pensions. Job security and prospects of career advancement declined in the 1980s and 1990s in comparison to earlier periods. But the managerial market position is still relatively favourable. The managerial work situation normally provides more interesting work and autonomy than many other occupations. These market and work advantages increase the higher the level of a manager in the managerial hierarchy. Entry to managerial careers has become more selective over time, especially in terms of required educational qualifications. J. Goldthorpe uses the term SERVICE CLASS. This recognizes the special relationship managers (particularly top managers) have with the owners of capital: they serve owners' interests and are rewarded for their loyalty by their privileged position compared with other employees. Because managerial work is difficult to simplify, codify and control, managers have to be trusted to use their discretion properly on behalf of the interests they serve, hence their privileges. Modern Marxist class analysis has placed top management (particularly the board of directors) in the upper of two classes, because they control various CAPITAL FUNCTIONS. It has more difficulty precisely locating managers below this top level, since they are not fully part of the upper class but are definitely not in the working class.

(2) Along with the growth in numbers, there was initially an elongation of the organizational hierarchy and greater division of labour and specialization within the ranks of management. It became usual to distinguish top management, including the board of directors, concerned with corporate strategy and with the distribution of resources in the enterprise; middle management, with functional responsibilities such as production, research and development, marketing, personnel, accountancy and finance; and first-level operational management, including foremen and supervisors. An increase in the number of vertical levels and greater horizontal division as the result of specialization of functions created a complex structure of relationships within the management hierarchy. The sociological investigation of these has become a specialized area in its own right that is conventionally known as ORGANIZATION THEORY. From the late 1980s and through to the late 1990s, large US and UK companies halted and partially reversed the trend to elongation, by reducing the number of vertical layers ('delayering') and cutting the number of managers ('downsizing'). This was most noticeable among first-level and middle management.

(3) The process of management has two important attributes. Management is in one sense an economic resource that comprises the technical functions connected with administering other resources. These include planning, organizing and integrating a complex division of labour and directing the activities that occur within

an enterprise. Management is secondly a structure of control, which ensures the compliance of subordinates and the direction of their activities along the lines laid down from above.

The social control aspect has become prominent in sociology. Starting from the premise that subordinates do not share the same interests as management, which may variously be explained as a consequence of exploitation as in Marxist accounts, of an inevitable conflict between those with and without authority as in R. Dahrendorf's account (1959), or of the competing claims between wages and profits, attention is focused on how managers persuade or compel others to comply with their commands. From this perspective, a large part of the history and development of management in the twentieth century may be seen as the attempt to impose control over potentially recalcitrant employees. The control issue can also be applied to managers, since subordinate managers do not always share the interests and objectives of their superiors, and there is now a recognition that management is not necessarily homogeneous or united. Conflicts within management are also the subject of organization theory.

(4) Historically, few women entered management. This used to be an important aspect of gender inequality, because managerial occupations have always been among the best-paid and most interesting. However, the proportion of women managers in Britain is growing. As management tends to be full-time and permanent employment, rather than part-time and temporary, a comparison of women's share of managerial jobs (28 per cent) with their share of all full-time and permanent jobs (35 per cent) shows that women remained under-represented even in 1990, but the discrepancy was no longer huge. In particular areas, which include local government, personnel management, and professional and related jobs supporting management, women were well represented.

But women are much less likely than men managers to be promoted to the top jobs. The same is true of women's chances of getting to the top of the professions. *Glass ceiling* describes the subtle and barely visible obstacles in the way of women's promotion. First, young women managers are more likely than men to be allocated to support functions that are less central to the business (these include personnel, sales, administration), which therefore provide a poorer basis to get to the top. Second, selection processes may discriminate against women in promotion. It has been suggested that there are implicit criteria (rather than formal discrimination) which disadvantage women. One is the tendency of male senior managers to stereotype women managers as having certain 'female' characteristics. The positive female stereotype is being adept in the areas of human relationships, caring, dependable and conscientious. The negative one is of women, compared to men, being less innovative, ambitious and analytical, and more influenced by emotions. Women managers are labelled with these characteristics, regardless whether they apply in any particular case (or at all). Women's attributes are deemed to be suitable for certain managerial roles (e.g. personnel, sales, customer relations), but not for most senior jobs. Another implicit process that probably affects women is the tendency for people to select those whom they will feel comfortable working with. Because the great majority of senior managers are male, therefore men may be promoted in preference to women. Third, women are unlikely to be members of male social networks. A network often provides its members with mutual assistance, which may help individuals to perform more effectively in their jobs. This, in turn, will influence the chances of promotion. Networks, moreover, can bring junior managers to the attention of more senior managers outside their own areas.

SEE ALSO: *bureaucracy; industrial conflict; labour process approach; managerial revolution; managerial strategies of control; middle class; network/social network; organizational culture; scientific management; women and work.*

READING: Grint (1995)

managerial revolution J. Burnham, in *The Managerial Revolution* (1941), suggested that the rise of professional managers would create a new CLASS to replace the old ruling class of capitalists. Along with A. A. Berle and G. C. Means (1932), he was responsible for highlighting changes in the way modern firms were run, with the managerial employee replacing the owner as the controller of the corporation. This separation of the ownership of firms from their administration and control resulted from the way share ownership was becoming fragmented and dispersed among numerous small shareholders instead of being concentrated in a few hands.

Some commentators believed that the new influence of salaried employees at the top of corporations would lead to changes in the running of firms. Managers were thought no longer to maximize profits like old-style capitalist owners and to be more socially responsible. In particular, as R. Dahrendorf (1959) suggested, it was thought that the nature of managerial authority would change, creating a new state of shared interests in place of the old conflicts between labour and capital. Managerial legitimacy was thought to depend on managers' claims to technical and professional competence.

More recent research has shown that the managerial revolution thesis was overstated. There are still a few giant corporations where individuals and families retain control by virtue of their large private shareholdings. The recent trend towards the institutional ownership of shares by pension funds, insurance companies and other corporations means that the older tendency of shareholdings to fragment has been reversed and a small number of institutions own the great bulk of shares (though this new trend does not re-establish individual private ownership, of course). This concentration of ownership allows a few shareholders acting together to exert considerable influence over the top managers who run the companies in which they invest, particularly as shareholders have the legal right to appoint and dismiss boards of directors. In practice, directors have usually been given considerable freedom to run companies on behalf of their shareholders; although, since the 1990s, shareholders in Britain and the USA have begun to use their powers more often to ensure that companies are directed as they wish them to be. There is no evidence, moreover, that salaried managers are any less interested in company profitability than capitalist owner-controllers, nor that they run their firms differently. The payment of top managers normally incorporates a performance-related bonus that is based on profitability or the level of the share price, which aligns managerial interests with those of the owners.

The phenomenon of what are known as corporate networks or interlocking directorships has also attracted attention. It is normal both in Britain and the USA for the boards of directors of large companies to include non-executive, outside directors who also sit on the boards of other companies. Many of these directors have links with the financial institutions that own the bulk of company shares. The precise significance of such networks is not clear, but one implication is that, at the highest level, the business world is more integrated than was thought previously. Another implication is that top managers who are executive directors will be closely monitored by non-executives acting as intermediaries for the owners, in order to ensure that a company is run on lines approved by its major shareholders.

SEE ALSO: *capital functions; capitalism; industrial conflict; management; network/ social network.*

READING: Scott, J. (1997)

managerial strategies of control Because the interests of employees and those who manage them are not identical, managers cannot assume that employees will always do what they are supposed to do. There has been considerable interest among sociologists in how managers achieve compliance when interests diverge. The LABOUR PROCESS APPROACH was an important early attempt to understand managerial control, which has been modified in more recent accounts.

Control systems broadly may be categorized as: (1) *market control* of employees; (2) *personal control* of employees by supervisors/managers; (3) *technical control* of the production process (or 'labour process'); (4) *bureaucratic control* of workplace and organizational rules and procedures; (5) *normative control* via organizational culture; (6) *discursive control* of meaning and a person's sense of identity. In any particular case, all modes of control are likely to occur to some extent, while their relative weights may change over time.

(1) *Market control* refers to the hiring and firing of employees and the design of payment systems. Incentive payment systems, for example, which are fairly widespread in American and British companies, are thought to align employees' interests with those of senior managers, because they create financial incentives to achieve specified targets. (2) *Personal control* involves the direct supervision of employees by individuals who have the power to give orders, exercise discipline and, in some cases, determine whether an individual is hired or fired. (3) *Technical control* describes how production systems are organized in ways that structure and prescribe employees' activities. One form is SCIENTIFIC MANAGEMENT. (4) *Bureaucratic control* establishes formal and codified procedures that are binding on employees and managers alike. It creates an impartial and reasonably fair system of managerial authority at the workplace and in hiring, firing and remuneration. Employees comply, adopting the required behaviours, because they understand and accept the rules, feel the company treats them fairly and have little sense of exploitation. (5) *Normative control* occurs when senior managers try to create among employees a positive identification with the norms and values of the organization. Employee compliance goes beyond simply behaving as managers wish and is internalized as the natural and right thing to do. (6) *Discursive control* involves the structuring of meaning. It is closely related to normative control and may be difficult at times to separate in practice. Sociological accounts are influenced by the analysis of DISCOURSE, which focuses on how language structures meaning and shapes personal IDENTITY. While normative control indicates that people come to accept and endorse the organization's values, discursive control works through the moulding of identities. This proposition, that managers may establish such a powerful and dominant discourse within an organization that people come to define their own identity in its terms, is, however, contested by many writers.

Japanese management practices show how the strategies may coexist. LABOUR

MARKET SEGMENTATION in Japan means that large firms in the primary market offer a much better deal than firms in other labour market segments: higher wages, guaranteed rises with each year of service (a seniority-based wage system) and better terms of employment (notably the offer of permanent or lifetime employment). These advantages are a positive source of compliance and also work through fear, because a dismissed employee is unlikely to be hired by another primary-sector firm and will fall into the secondary segment. Personal control is exercised by supervisors, who in Japan have considerable powers to allocate work and supervise employees. There are, in addition, technical controls that follow from prescribed tasks and the organization of the flow of work. However, large Japanese companies have never followed a de-skilling strategy based on scientific management. They have relied more than on worker skills, coupled with fairly tight direction by supervisors. Large Japanese companies are also bureaucratized and employees and their unions appear to feel that the rules and procedures are fair. Normative control is actively promoted by managers. They attempt to instil company values in employees by means of, for example, extensive propaganda which emphasizes how everyone is part of the same community, the provision of social and leisure facilities where employees are subjected to corporate culture even during their non-work lives, and the communal singing of company songs at the start of the working day. It is said that normative control may even have sufficient discursive power to shape employees' identities. Finally, companies can rely on the wider norms and values of Japanese culture, elements of which support obedience and deference.

SEE ALSO: *bureaucracy; capitalism; industrial conflict; organizational culture; paternalism; post-Fordism; relations of production.*

READING: Littler (1990); Deetz (1992); Gallie *et al.* (1998)

manifest function The intended and recognized consequences of social action upon other social actors or institutions.

SEE ALSO: *functionalism; latent function.*

READING: Merton (1957)

Mannheim, Karl (1893–1947) He was born in Hungary, fled to Germany in 1919 where he became a university teacher, left Germany in 1933 after the emergence of Nazism and moved to England, where he continued his academic career at the London School of Economics. His major works, many of which were collected and published in English after his death, are: *Ideology and Utopia* (1936); *Man and Society in an Age of Social Reconstruction* (1940); *Diagnosis of Our Time* (1943); *Freedom, Power and Democratic Planning* (1951); *Essays on the Sociology of Knowledge* (1952b); *Essays on Sociology and Social Psychology* (1953); *Essays on the Sociology of Culture* (1956).

His work can be divided into two phases. The first saw the development of his SOCIOLOGY OF KNOWLEDGE. (1) He insisted that a sociology of knowledge was possible, that there was an association between forms of knowledge and social structure, and that membership of particular social groups conditioned belief. (2) He attempted to deal with what he saw as the relativistic implications of the sociology of knowledge. He assumed that, if all beliefs could be socially located, then there was no place for true beliefs and no socially independent criteria of truth. He experimented with various solutions to this problem, initially by postulating a class of socially independent propositions, and latterly by recognizing that his initial assumption that social origins determined truth was incorrect. (3) He rejected Marxist explanations of knowledge or IDEOLOGY, which he regarded as reducing all knowledge to class membership. In Mannheim's view, a number of social groups or processes (e.g. generation, sect, class and competition) could be correlated with forms of knowledge.

In the second, less appreciated phase of his work, Mannheim argued for the necessity of social reconstruction. Contemporary societies had become mass societies, disordered groups of atomized individuals with no social ties. Such societies were the outcome of liberal capitalism, and their repair was to be effected by social planning.

SEE ALSO: *atomism; mass society; relativism.*

READING: Loader (1985)

manual/non-manual distinction See: CLASS.

Marcuse, Herbert (1898–1979) Trained at the universities of Berlin and Freiburg, Marcuse was influenced by the phenomenology of E. Husserl and M. Heidegger. In 1934, he joined the FRANKFURT SCHOOL in exile at Columbia University. Approaching Marxism via phenomenology and CRITICAL THEORY, his central concern has been the possibility of authentic existence in industrial capitalism; for example, *One-Dimensional Man* (1964) argued that modern societies generate artificial needs, giving the working class a false consciousness in which the pursuit of consumer goods distracts from the realization of class interests. In *Eros and Civilization* (1955), he tried to integrate the work of FREUD and Marx, arguing that civilization has, through a process of continuing labour, obstructed the development of human happiness. His interpretation of Freud was challenged by E. Fromm (1993) on the grounds that Freud was a conservative, not a revolutionary thinker. Marcuse's critical views on American liberal democracy were reflected in *An Essay on Liberation* (1969), but he was equally critical of Soviet society in *Soviet Marxism* (1961). Marcuse is also known for his controversial studies of philosophy in *Reason and Revolution* (1954) and of sociology in *Negations* (1968).

SEE ALSO: *Marxist sociology.*

market The market has always occupied a central place in economic theory but has been less significant in sociological analysis. In its broadest sense, a market is an arena of exchange in which individual buyers and sellers attempt to maximize their own advantages in the exchange of commodities. In the process, the market also serves to coordinate activities. Economists have tended to view markets abstractly, as price-setting mechanisms that determine the allocation of resources within an economy. As arenas of exchange, however, markets are also social institutions: they have a social structure of patterned and recurrent social interactions, which are sanctioned and maintained by social norms. While WEBER began to develop the sociological analysis of markets early in the twentieth century, subsequent sociological theorists mainly ignored markets for the next half century. For Weber (1922), the interactional structure of the market starts with struggle and COMPETITION (which he defines as 'peaceful' conflict), which evolves into exchange. In competitive social relationships, parties seek to control opportunities and advantages which are also desired by others. In exchange, the parties compromise their interests in the course of reciprocal compensation. Nevertheless, for Weber, market-based social action remains the extreme case of rational action and is the most calculative and instrumental social relationship possible in society.

The sociological theory of markets revived in the last quarter of the twentieth century, as part of a new interest in ECONOMIC SOCIOLOGY. The so-called 'structural' approach to markets focuses on social structures, insofar as these are revealed by patterns of social relationships and their clustering into networks. For example, W. Baker (1984) observed patterns of trading between dealers in a US financial market and deduced that the market's social structure comprised two segments. One was a small and dense network of ties, while the other was larger and more differentiated and its members were more loosely linked. This sociological perspective on markets questions the assumptions of the dominant, neo-classical, economic model, that markets are undifferentiated and fully competitive. Baker also demonstrated that the market's social structure had direct economic effects: prices were more volatile in the larger and more differentiated network than in the smaller and denser one. The cultural, legal and political aspects of markets are also relevant to sociologists. A well-known example of how cultural values affect markets is the failure in Britain to develop a market in human blood (donors expect to give their blood without payment), whereas in many other societies the selling and buying of blood is socially legitimated. The existence of markets depends, in turn, on there being laws that enforce property rights and contracts. Marxist sociologists regard such laws as the conditions of existence of the capitalist market economy. There is, however, little interest now in developing a systematic theory of the cultural, political and legal dimensions of markets. Instead, their influence is analysed case by case.

Despite the relative paucity of sociological theorizing about markets, sociologists working within the tradition of POLITICAL ECONOMY have long been concerned with a particular application of the concept, namely the market economy. This is one where the greater part of the economic activities of production, distribution and exchange are carried out by private individuals or corporate bodies following the dictates of demand and supply, in which state intervention is minimized. Markets are becoming more widespread as more human activities become commodities which are bought and sold. Weber regarded the rise of a market economy as a major contribution to the growth of capitalist industrialism, and in his analysis of class assumed that stratification reflected the distribution of different LIFE-CHANCES in the market place for labour. Modern Weberian class analysis has followed this lead, and there is a growing interest in the workings of LABOUR MARKETS. Marxist and Weberian schools join in characterizing labour markets as agencies by which one group or class dominates another, since the parties to the exchange are not of equivalent strength.

SEE ALSO: *capitalism; class; commodification; commodity fetishism; enterprise culture; entrepreneurship; individualism; industrial society; labour market segmentation; marriage; network/social network.*

READING: Swedberg (1994)

market situation See: CLASS.

marriage Mate selection operates rather like a MARKET, and the rules of selection determine the forms of exchange between partners and their households. These rules in human societies are extremely complex but they may be regarded as a continuum from arranged to formally free marriages. In a closed market, selection is made by parents to consolidate property and form family alliances. Parental choice is more important than affection, and marriages are based on prudence and calculation. In an open market, romantic attachment becomes the basis of marriage, parental wishes are minimized and, in principle, partners select from an infinite range of eligibles. Marriage is a cultural phenomenon which sanctions a more or less permanent union between partners, conferring legitimacy on their offspring. As an institution, marriage is either monogamous (i.e. being married to one person at a time), or polygamous (i.e. having more than one marriage partner at a time). Polygamy includes: (1) polygyny (one man and two or more wives); (2) polyandry (one woman and two or more husbands); (3) group marriage (several husbands and wives in a common marital arrangement). The eligibility of partners in any form of marriage is determined either by EXOGAMY or ENDOGAMY. The permanence of the marriage union is also variable. Common law marriages have a stability without legal recognition; they are based on custom and may result in a legal union. Legislation in Britain (under various matrimonial causes acts) has extended the grounds for divorce and made litigation less costly. The increase in DIVORCE results in 'serial monogamy' where most divorcees subsequently remarry. Feminists argue that marriage may reinforce the subordination of women by men. For example, it is clear that in many marriages men can be physically violent towards their wives without much fear of intervention by the police. In addition, there is substantial evidence from attitude surveys that marriage may be less beneficial to women than men. Certainly, three-quarters of divorces are initiated by women.

Marriage patterns in Britain have been changing. The average age at first marriage fell steadily for much of the twentieth century, but throughout the 1970s, 1980s and 1990s it rose again (reaching 28 years for men and 26 years for women in 1993). Cohabitation before marriage has increased: 5 per cent of women had lived with their husband before marriage in the 1960s; by the 1990s the proportion had risen to almost 70 per cent. The number of babies born outside marriage has also increased: from 1901 to 1961 the rate remained constant at 5 per cent; by 1996 it had jumped to 37 per cent.

SEE ALSO: *domestic labour; household; single-parent families; sociology of the family*.

Marshall, Thomas H. (1893–1982) A professor of sociology at the London School of Economics, he is best known for his influential analysis of CITIZENSHIP and social class in the course of industrialization, contained in the essay 'Citizenship and Social Class' (1949), republished in *Sociology at the Crossroads* (1963). In *Social Policy* (1965), he analysed the development of welfare policies between 1890 and 1945 as an illustration of the expansion of social rights. Marshall (1981) saw modern capitalism as a 'hyphenated society' where there are inevitable contradictions between democracy, welfare and class.

Martin, David (b. 1929) Formerly professor of sociology at the London School of Economics and professor of human values at the Southern Methodist University, Dallas, Texas (1986–8), he has made a major contribution to the sociology of religion, in which he has been a leading critic of the contention that industrial societies are characterized by an inevitable process of SECULARIZATION. In *A Sociology of English Religion* (1967), he showed that the evidence on belief and practice did not support the secularization thesis and, in *The Religious and the Secular* (1969a), he challenged the implicit historical and sociological assumptions behind the theory. He has shown, in *A General Theory of Secularization* (1978a), that it is important to combine political sociology and the sociology of religion in order to understand the divergent patterns of state–church relations. He has also contributed to the sociological analysis of pacifism (1965) and to our understanding of the Christian challenge to violence in *The Breaking of the Image* (1980). Professor Martin has written extensively on the problem of the loss of authority and continuity in modern cultures in *Anarchy and Culture* (1969b), *Tracts against the Times* (1973) and *The Dilemmas of Contemporary Religion* (1978b). He has played a major role in defending the traditional 'Book of Common Prayer', about which he has written extensively since 1979. He writes also on the theoretical relation of religion to politics and of religion to sociology.

Marx, Karl (1818–83) A political revolutionary and social theorist, Marx was born and educated in Germany. After finishing his education, he married and became a journalist but, being unable to find permanent employment, he migrated to Paris in 1843. There he mixed with émigré radicals, became a socialist and met ENGELS with whom he formed a life-long friendship and collaboration. Expelled in 1845, he moved to Brussels and, after travelling around Europe, finally settled in London in 1849. There he stayed for the rest of his life in considerable poverty, occupied in writing and political activity, and supported financially largely by Engels and occasional journalism.

Marx's major works of sociological importance are: *The German Ideology* (1845b), with F. Engels; *The Poverty of Philosophy* (1847); *Manifesto of the Communist Party* (1848), with F. Engels; *The Eighteenth Brumaire of Louis Bonaparte* (1852); *Capital* (1867; 1885; 1894); and two manuscripts published after his death, *The Economic and Philosophic Manuscripts of 1844* (1964) and *Grundrisse* (1973).

Marx has been a major influence on the development of sociology, as often a subject of criticism as of inspiration. There are five important sociological areas covered by his writings.

(1) In his early work, Marx was interested in the concept of ALIENATION. One of the senses that he gave to the term was that of alienated labour, in which condition man had work imposed on him by others, a theme that was to run through all his subsequent contributions.

(2) Marx is best known for his views on the relationship between economic life and other social institutions. It is often suggested that he was an economic determinist, believing that the nature of a society was determined by the manner in which its economy was owned and organized. This is certainly not the case. Although he thought that human labour was the basis of social activity, he also held that social institutions, like the state or the family, were relatively independent of the economy in their development and even had an influence on the operation of the economy. Marx's views on this question are best summed up in the theory of BASE AND SUPERSTRUCTURE.

(3) Although Marx was influenced by his anthropological reading and speculated on primitive states of human society, he was primarily interested in the analysis of societies organized into social classes. The basis of social classes lay in the RELATIONS OF PRODUCTION in the economy. Those who own and control the means of production, and are able to take the product, form one class and those depending

on their own labour alone, the other. The form of the relations of production will vary from society to society, producing different class relations. For example, in capitalist societies the relationship between capitalists and workers is based in the control the capitalist has over both the FORCES OF PRODUCTION and the product. He can direct the use to which equipment is put, control the labour process and take the product, whatever it is. In feudal societies, however, the lord does not have direct control over the means of production, which remains in the hands of the peasant, but he can appropriate the product. For Marx, the basic model of such societies is of a two-class structure. He argued, however, that in all real societies the picture will be more complicated, with several classes, particularly those left over from earlier stages of society. Marx's analysis of social class as applied to contemporary capitalist societies has attracted a great deal of criticism, because of the difficulties in fitting the middle class into his scheme and of identifying a class of *persons* who own and control the means of production when ownership of capital passes increasingly to institutions such as pension funds. For Marx, the relations of production necessarily involve conflict because the owners of the means of production, for example capitalists within a capitalist society, effectively exploit workers by appropriating the product of their labour.

(4) This conflict, or CONTRADICTION, at the heart of class societies also suggests a theory of social change. Marx argues that CLASS STRUGGLE is the 'motor of history'; the rising capitalist class overthrew the feudal aristocracy and will be similarly displaced by the working class or PROLETARIAT. In capitalist societies, Marx suggests that, other things being equal, the society will become polarized with the working class becoming poorer and poorer. It should be clear that change does not follow automatically from changes in the economic structure; class struggle as the *active* intervention of human beings is necessary. Historical change takes the form of a succession of societies dominated by different modes of production, FEUDALISM or CAPITALISM, for example, each of which represents greater technological control over nature. Marx's analysis of class struggle and social change has proved controversial. It has been argued that class struggle has little to do with change from one society to another and, specifically for capitalist society, there is no sign of impending disintegration, polarization, or progressive impoverishment of the working class.

(5) Marx was pre-eminently a theorist of capitalist society. *Capital*, his most detailed work, spells out the economic mechanisms of capitalist society, developing the LABOUR THEORY OF VALUE, the theory of capital accumulation, and the possibilities of capitalism's internal collapse. Also in *Capital* is a discussion of other issues which have become important recently; for example, commodity FETISHISM and APPEARANCE AND REALITY.

SEE ALSO: *Althusser; bourgeoisie; capital fractions; capital functions; class; determinism; division of labour; historical materialism; ideology; labour market; labour power; labour process; labour process approach; Marxist sociology; mode of production; periodization; political economy; praxis; ruling class; socialist societies; surplus value.*

READING: Craib (1997)

Marxist sociology Since the death of MARX in 1883, an enormous literature has grown up around his work. A good deal of this has been critical and much early sociology, that of WEBER, for example, was partly formed by a critique of Marx.

There has also been a stream of work that is broadly Marxist, often involving reinterpretations of Marx, although that term is now employed so widely that it has begun to lose all meaning. There are several areas of sociology where Marx's work has been extended, while remaining faithful to at least some of his principles.

(1) In the analysis of CLASS structure, several early Marxists argued that Marx's scheme had to be revised because there was no real sign of the collapse of CAPITALISM or of heightened class struggle. A good deal of effort has been expended in trying to adapt the basic idea of a necessary conflict between capital and labour to the conditions of contemporary capitalism. This has taken the form of new theories of social class to take account of changes in the patterns of property ownership, the growth of the MIDDLE CLASS, and changes in relationships at work. In addition, some Marxists have given attention to the notion of CLASS CONSCIOUSNESS as a prerequisite for CLASS STRUGGLE, especially GRAMSCI, V. I. Lenin and LUKÁCS.

(2) In the analysis of politics, arguments that the state is the instrument of the ruling class have given way to a more complex analysis of the state as relatively autonomous of the ruling class, responsive to pressures from the working class via the institution of parliamentary democracy, but ultimately favouring the interests of capital.

(3) Revisions of Marx's economics have taken the form of distinguishing different CAPITAL FRACTIONS, and of providing an account of the monopoly phase of capitalism, which is distinctively different from the earlier, competitive phase dominant in Marx's day.

(4) A feature of twentieth-century capitalism noted by Lenin was its capacity to seek markets in underdeveloped countries and often to colonize and control those countries. Following Lenin's account of IMPERIALISM many studies have connected the persistence of underdevelopment in the world with capitalism's need for expansion.

(5) A great deal of twentieth-century Marxist sociology has been dominated by an interest in the analysis of IDEOLOGY. In particular, it has been argued that the continued persistence of capitalism has been due in large part to the ideological control exercised by the dominant class. This sort of analysis has often been inspired by the notion of HEGEMONY as propounded by Gramsci or by the writings of the FRANKFURT SCHOOL.

(6) There has been a continuing interest in the study of the philosophy and method of Marxism, particularly in the Frankfurt School and CRITICAL THEORY, and more recently in the work of HABERMAS and followers of ALTHUSSER. Very often the study of methodology has been informed by an attempt to rescue Marxism from POSITIVISM.

(7) Many sociologists have utilized the work of Marxist historians interested in the analysis of social change through class struggle and, more recently, in the utility of the concept of MODE OF PRODUCTION for historical analysis.

SEE ALSO: *capital functions; conjuncture; dominant ideology thesis; economism; Engels; feudalism; historical materialism; ideological state apparatus; labour process; labour process approach; Leninism; Marx; overdetermine; patriarchy; political economy; power; relative autonomy; reproduction of labour power; socialist societies.*

masculinity Many societies have ascribed different and distinctive qualities to men and women. In modern Western societies, it is considered 'masculine' to be aggressive, independent and active. There is considerable debate as to whether these qualities really are actual characteristics of the gender, whether they are biologically or socially determined, and in what ways they maintain male power.

SEE ALSO: *femininity; gender; patriarchy; sex roles; sociology of gender.*

READING: Seidler (1989)

mass observation This was an organization founded in 1936 with the aim of conducting social surveys of the population and reporting the results as widely as possible. The founders believed that social science should not be purely academic. To this end they carried out a large number of studies based on diaries and reports from regular participants as well as questionnaires. Their methods may not always have been technically perfect but they furnished a very full picture of British social change before and during the Second World War.

mass media, sociology of the See: SOCIOLOGY OF THE MASS MEDIA.

mass society The concept of mass society holds that contemporary society has the following characteristics: most individuals are similar, undifferentiated and equal, showing no individuality; work is routine and alienating; religion has lost its influence and there are no deeply held and important moral values, although the masses are prone to ideological fanaticism; the relationships between individuals are weak and secondary and ties of kinship are not important; the masses are politically apathetic and open to manipulation by dictatorships and bureaucracies; culture – art, literature, philosophy and science – has become a mass culture; that is, reduced to the lowest level of taste.

Writers who describe society in these terms use the concept of mass society pejoratively and usually attribute the ills of society to capitalism or industrialization. Some of these themes are present in the work of nineteenth-century social theorists, A. de Tocqueville (1835–40) and TOENNIES, for example, and in the very general dichotomy between pre-industrial and industrial society current at that time. However, the specific theory of mass society was developed between 1920 and 1960 in three main directions. (1) In England, a number of writers, especially literary critics like T. S. Eliot and F. R. Leavis, concentrated on the loss of excellence in literature and culture generally and the disappearance of a cultivated public. Theirs was essentially a conservative reaction to capitalist society and was taken up by a number of sociologists, especially MANNHEIM. (2) Members of the FRANKFURT SCHOOL, especially after their flight from Hitler's Germany to the USA, analysed the political rather than cultural aspects of mass society. Their argument was that capitalism had, by producing a mass society, created the conditions for the political manipulation of the masses by ruling elites. This showed a rather more socialist response to the social and international problems of the inter-war period. (3) In making use of the concept of mass society, some American writers saw it more positively. For E. Shils (1962), for example, the masses were being drawn into political participation, thus making elitist politics more difficult.

Some early research into the mass media was influenced by mass society theory, particularly that of the Frankfurt School, in that the audience was seen as relatively undifferentiated and easily influenced (or manipulated) by programmes. However, the concept of mass society is not now influential in sociology. (1) Contemporary societies are not seen as undifferentiated masses but as made up of numbers of competing groups. (2) Subordinate classes are not manipulated by an elite but are quite capable of active dissent. (3) There has not been a breakdown of family and community ties.

SEE ALSO: *dominant ideology thesis.*

READING: Giner (1976)

materialism In sociology, this term has a specific sense in referring to theories in which economic relations are the basic cause of social phenomena. More generally, materialist explanations in which concrete social relations are determinant are contrasted with idealist explanations in which ideas are seen as the ultimate cause of social relations.

SEE ALSO: *dialectical materialism; Engels; historical materialism; idealism; Marx; Marxist sociology.*

maternal deprivation It has been argued, most notably by J. Bowlby (1953), that young children need a stable, continuous and affectionate relationship with their mothers, and that maternal deprivation, the absence of such a relationship, may result in mental illness or delinquency. The theory has important implications for women in society, suggesting that they ought to stay at home with their children. Feminists have attacked it as an ideology which keeps women out of the labour force. Recent research suggests that stable relationships with a range of adults may be more important for mental health than an intense maternal relationship.

SEE ALSO: *socialization.*

matriarchy A term used in nineteenth-century anthropology to designate a society ruled by women. In contemporary use, it refers more narrowly to a form of the family in which the mother is the head and descent is reckoned through her. The notion of matriarchal systems of domination is controversial. ENGELS, in *The Origin of the Family, Private Property and the State* (1884), argued that pre-modern societies, before the emergence of private property, had been matriarchal. These societies were eventually replaced by patriarchal systems with the transition from nomadic (hunter–gatherer) to agricultural communities. An alternative argument is that PATRIARCHY results from conquest. The archaeological evidence to support or to refute these theories is clearly difficult to obtain. The concept is important, however, because it is now used to add weight to the feminist perspective on the differences between GENDER and biologically determined sex roles. Matriarchy suggests that male domination has not been universal. The term is also used more loosely to designate family forms dominated by the mother.

SEE ALSO: *feminism; nature/nurture debate.*

matrilineal A system of descent in which kinship is traced through the mother. In such systems, the important relatives for men are those other men related to the mother.

SEE ALSO: *agnatic; cognate/cognatic; descent groups; patrilineal.*

McDonaldization This social and economic development can be described as 'the process by which the principles of the fast-food restaurant are coming to dominate more and more sectors of American society as well as the rest of the world' (Ritzer, 1993, p. 1). The creation of McDonald restaurants originally involved the application of SCIENTIFIC MANAGEMENT and FORDISM to the product of a simple range of edible items such as the hamburger. The extension of these principles has given rise to RATIONALIZATION in the service industries such as McDentists, McDoctors and 'junk-food journalism'; that is, the standardization of news for easy consumption.

SEE ALSO: *Weber*.

McLuhan, Marshall (1910–80) A Canadian social critic, he analysed the impact of new technologies of COMMUNICATION on society and culture in *The Gutenberg Galaxy* (1962) and *Understanding Media* (1987), in which he treated technology as an extension of the human body. He argued that each form of communication has its own logic. For example, print has a linear, sequential logic and is associated with INDIVIDUALISM. He summarized this theory in a famous slogan: 'The medium is the message'. He was convinced about the possibility of a universal culture resulting from new technologies and coined the phrase 'the global village' in *Explorations in Communication* (1960), with E. Carpenter. His controversial theories have been described as 'communication determinism', but they have contributed significantly to the SOCIOLOGY OF THE MASS MEDIA.

SEE ALSO: *globalization; hyperreality; virtual reality*.

Mead, George H. (1863–1931) Although publishing little in his lifetime, Mead, through his lectures, came to have a profound effect on the development of SYM-BOLIC INTERACTIONISM in American sociology. His lecture notes were post-humously published in a number of major volumes – *Mind, Self and Society* (1934), *The Philosophy of the Act* (1938) and *The Philosophy of the Present* (1959). In Mead's philosophy, the self emerges through the process of social interaction with others. In his social behaviourism, the conditioned responses of human beings include gesture and role-taking, which are the bases of social life. Gestures and conversation are crucial features of the symbolic interaction, the distinctive feature of which is that the individual can imagine the effect of symbolic communication on other social actors. Human actors carry on an 'internal conversation' with the self and anticipate the response of other actors. We imaginatively assume other social roles and internalize the attitudes of 'the generalized other' – the attitudes of the social group.

SEE ALSO: *act; actor/social actor; action theory; Chicago School; identity; role; significant others*.

READING: Strauss (1964)

Mead, Margaret (1901–78) An American cultural anthropologist whose early field work was on child-rearing in the Pacific, she made a major contribution to the NATURE/NURTURE DEBATE and the study of CULTURE and SOCIALIZATION. While not denying the importance of biology and the natural environment, Mead demonstrated the central role of culture in shaping human behaviour and attitudes through a series of empirical studies of different societies. There is a social division around social activities which are assumed to be relevant to GENDER, but these divisions have no general or systematic relationship to biological sex. In short, her studies of culture in *Coming of Age in Samoa* (1928), *Growing Up in New Guinea* (1930) and *Sex and Temperament in Three Primitive Societies* (1935) emphasized the importance of nurture over nature. Her anthropological ideas provided significant support for

FEMINISM and her contribution to the development of sexual politics was further reinforced by *Male and Female* (1949). Her field work also showed how primitive societies were relatively tolerant towards the sexual behaviour of adolescents, contrasting sharply with the anxiety shown in Western (especially Protestant) cultures towards sexual development. Her interpretations of her own empirical research in *Culture and Commitment* (1970a) contributed to a more sympathetic understanding of the conflict of generations. Her anthropological studies generated controversial debate, but she retained an enduring commitment to the development of aboriginal societies within the modern world in *New Lives for Old* (1956). She contributed to the debate on race in *Science and the Concept of Race* (1970b) and remained optimistic about the future developments of religion, sexuality and culture in *Twentieth Century Faith* (1972).

Her work has been challenged by D. Freeman (1983) on the grounds that her basic field work was unreliable: she did not learn the Samoan language, her period of research in Samoa was too short, and her informants were not reliable. Freeman has argued that her results do not support her theories and that cultural anthropology is not an adequate PARADIGM. Against Freeman, it has been argued that Mead did not deny or neglect HEREDITY and that her subsequent research more than adequately replicated her earlier findings.

mean The arithmetic mean or average of a set of values is obtained by adding the values together and dividing by the number (n) of items in the set.

meaning See: ACTION THEORY; EMPATHY; HERMENEUTICS; PHENOMENOLOGICAL SOCIOLOGY; RULE; VERSTEHEN; WEBER.

meaningful action Action which actors invest with meanings deriving from definite motives and intentions, rather than that which follows from mere habit or INSTINCT, is meaningful action.

SEE ALSO: *actor/social actor; action theory; phenomenological sociology; rule; Verstehen.*

measurement levels Data can be measured at different levels, on scales of measurement of different strengths. The lowest level is the *nominal* scale. In this, a score indicates simply to which group an individual datum belongs. For example, a population replying to an attitude survey might be divided into those replying 'yes' and 'no' to various questions, 'yes' being given the scale point 1 and 'no' point 2. The numbers denote categories and nothing else: those saying 'yes' could just as easily be numbered 2, while 2 carries no sense of being of a greater order of magnitude than 1. Indeed, the two categories could be given any other numbers.

The next level of measurement is the *ordinal* scale. In this, categories are arranged in a hierarchy. For example, ATTITUDE surveys often use a technique of measuring attitudes, which asks respondents to indicate the strength of their agreement with certain statements according to the following ordinal categories: Strongly Disagree; Disagree; Uncertain; Agree; Strongly Agree. Each point is given a number, in this case 1 to 5. Replies are ordered and movement along the scale indicates an increasing or decreasing magnitude of agreement. Ordinal scales, however, do not allow measurement of the differences between categories: it is not possible to say that Strongly Agree indicates a feeling that differs from Agree by a precise amount.

Interval-level scales are also ordered, but have the additional property that the distances between points on the scale are uniform. Thus scores on an interval scale can be compared in terms of the distances between them as well as their order, since they represent equal units of measurement. *Ratio* measurement shares the properties of interval scales and in addition has an absolute zero point. The Celsius scale for measuring temperature is an interval scale, because 0° in fact refers to the amount of heat available at the freezing point of water and not to the absence of heat. The Kelvin scale, however, is based on ratio measurement, because 0° here represents an absolute zero at which no heat is present. Measurement at the interval and ratio levels is metric, while nominal and ordinal levels are non-metric.

Measurement levels are important because they influence the sorts of statistical techniques that can be used in the analysis of research data. At the nominal level, there is a restricted range of techniques based on frequencies or counting, such as the mode, CHI-SQUARED TEST, contingency tables and CROSS TABULATION. Ordinal-level measurement is appropriate for the full range of NON-PARAMETRIC statistics. Interval and ratio levels allow all statistical techniques to be employed. Many sociological data are nominal or ordinal, and LOG LINEAR ANALYSIS has been developed for such data. This allows more elaborate MULTIVARIATE ANALYSIS and CAUSAL MODELLING to be undertaken.

SEE ALSO: *attitude scales; regression.*

mechanical solidarity See: DURKHEIM.

media sociology See: SOCIOLOGY OF THE MASS MEDIA.

median In a distribution of values, the median is the point with half the distribution on either side.

mediascape A term invented by A. Appadurai (1986) to indicate the omnipresence of the media of mass communication in contemporary societies. It is not only that there are so many types of media available but also that they infuse, become a part of, everyday life. The consequence is that the media become a crucial resource for the imaginative life of people in the modern world.

SEE ALSO: *audience; sociology of the mass media.*

medical model As the basic PARADIGM of medicine since the development of the germ theory of disease in the nineteenth century, it is the principal form of explanation in scientific medicine. Its fundamental assumptions are: (1) all disease is caused by a specific aetiological agent (the 'disease entity') such as a virus, parasite or bacterium; (2) the patient is to be regarded as the passive target of medical intervention, since scientific medicine is concerned with the body as a sort of machine rather than the person in a complex social environment; (3) restoring health (a state of EQUILIBRIUM in the body conceptualized as a machine with functional parts) requires the use of medical technology and advanced scientific procedures.

This model has been criticized on the following grounds: (1) it is an IDEOLOGY which justifies the use of medical technology, thereby precluding alternative therapies and procedures; (2) the model was developed as a response to infectious diseases in the nineteenth century, but, partly because of the AGING of populations, modern societies require HEALTH-CARE SYSTEMS which can respond to chronic illness; (3) the model is inappropriate in the treatment of mental illness and DEVIANT

BEHAVIOUR; (4) it is not appropriate to regard the patient as simply an organism, and therapy is more likely to be effective where the patient is regarded as a person with social and psychological needs.

SEE ALSO: *alternative medicine; anti-psychiatry; clinical sociology; medicalization; mental health; sick role; sociology of health and illness; sociology of medicine.*

READING: Veatch (1981)

medical sociology See: SOCIOLOGY OF MEDICINE.

medicalization This refers to the increasing attachment of medical labels to behaviour regarded as socially or morally undesirable. The implication is that modern medicine can cure all problems (including vandalism, alcoholism, homosexuality, dangerous driving or political deviance) once these are recognized as 'diseases'. The term is used by critics of modern medicine who argue that doctors have too much political influence in issues where they are not in fact professionally competent to make judgements.

SEE ALSO: *addiction.*

medicine, sociology of See: SOCIOLOGY OF MEDICINE.

members' methods See: ETHNOMETHODOLOGY.

mental health In psychiatry and abnormal psychology, mental illnesses are divided into neuroses and psychoses. The causes of mental illness are either organic malfunctioning or in personality conflicts which have their origin in childhood.

Psychoses (e.g. schizophrenia) involve a loss of contact with reality; neuroses (e.g. anxiety neurosis or reactive depression) are less severe, involving an over-reaction to reality. Phobias (such as agoraphobia) are regarded as a sub-category of anxiety neurosis. Critics of these categories argue that (1) they are not logically coherent and (2) they reflect, behind the neutral language of science, commonsense views on SOCIAL DEVIANCE.

The sociology of madness, by contrast, treats psychological abnormalities from a critical perspective. 'Madness' is a social label for classifying and controlling deviancy. 'Madness' belongs to a collection of labels – WITCHCRAFT, 'vagrancy' and 'hysteria' – by which deviants may be incarcerated. While there may be organic causes of insanity, insane behaviour contravenes social norms and treatment is a form of social control. T. Szasz (1971) has drawn attention to the loss of individual rights which follows from the attribution of mental illness to deviants. Similarly, FOUCAULT (1961) has examined historical changes in the criteria used to incarcerate people, from leprosy to venereal disease to madness. Scientific psychiatry does not represent an advance in knowledge, but merely a more subtle and sophisticated form of social control. For Foucault, psychiatry is the triumph of 'reason' over 'madness' in the form of social exclusion and confinement.

There is also a feminist critique which makes several claims. (1) Women are more likely than men to be labelled as insane. (2) Psychiatry, by accepting the values of a patriarchal society, treats women as hysterical or neurotic. (3) Psychoanalysis also treats women as deficient. (4) These negative STEREOTYPES of women are reflected in different forms of treatment and rates of admission; for example, in Britain while one man in twelve will be a psychiatric in-patient at some point in his life, one woman in eight will be admitted as a psychiatric in-patient. (5) Marriage seems to protect men, but also exposes women to mental illness.

SEE ALSO: *anti-psychiatry; Freud; labelling theory; medical model; medicalization; sociology of health and illness.*

READING: Scheff (1966); Mangen (1982)

meritocracy In a meritocracy, social positions in the occupational structure would be filled on the basis of merit, defined in terms of universal criteria of achievement, rather than ascribed criteria such as age, sex or inherited wealth. However, the meritocratic ideal is faced with the problem of securing an objective measurement of talent that can be ascertained independently of inherited advantages.

SEE ALSO: *credentialism; stratification.*

Merton, Robert K. (b. 1910) An American sociologist and the author of very wide-ranging work, chiefly in essay form, much of which was collected in *Social Theory and Social Structure* (1957). Most influential have been his theory of ANOMIE, his views on BUREAUCRACY, his account of FUNCTIONALISM, and his sociological account of the growth and direction of science in the seventeenth century.

SEE ALSO: *latent function; middle-range theory.*

metaphysical pathos This phrase describes the underlying mood of pessimism informing some analyses of BUREAUCRACY. MICHELS and WEBER, for example, assumed that all large-scale social activity necessarily results in bureaucracy and the loss of democratic freedom.

SEE ALSO: *oligarchy.*

meta-theory This term refers to the general background of philosophical assumptions that provide rules for the construction of particular sociological theories and justify particular sociological methods. There are several such meta-theories in sociology, an example of which is HERMENEUTICS.

Methodenstreit This term refers to the dispute over methodological principles and procedures which was central to debates within the social sciences in Germany in the 1890s. The key issue was whether the new discipline of sociology could be based on the EPISTEMOLOGY and methodology of the natural sciences or whether it required special methods peculiar to the study of social action and social institutions.

SEE ALSO: *hermeneutics; naturalism; neo-Kantianism; positivism; Verstehen.*

methodological individualism This is the doctrine that all sociological explanations are reducible to the characteristics of individuals. It was originally formed in opposition to the work of such sociologists as E. Durkheim, who argued that the characteristics of individuals could safely be ignored in sociological explanations, because 'social facts' have an existence of their own and can be studied independently of individuals whose actions they determine. Less radically, many functionalists argue that social groups have EMERGENT PROPERTIES – that is, characteristics that are produced when individuals interact but are not reducible to individuals. The response of methodological individualists is a claim that all such functionalist arguments rest ultimately on assumptions about individual behaviour. Nevertheless, it is quite possible that individual characteristics are socially derived in the interaction between individuals.

Debates about methodological individualism are not as popular as they once were. In discussion of the relationship of individual to society, or of psychology to sociology, attention has mainly shifted to issues such as AGENCY AND STRUCTURE. Contemporary rational choice theorists do, however, adopt a position of methodological individualism. They assume that individual action is egoistic and oriented to maximizing self-interest.

SEE ALSO: *rational choice theory; social fact; subject/subjectivity.*

READING: Lessnoff (1974)

methodology This has a number of meanings. In its simplest usage, it refers to the methods and procedures used in an individual piece or a general type of research activity. More broadly, it describes the methods of investigation, the concepts and the underlying analytical structures of a particular academic discipline or sub-discipline. This broader usage may, in turn, introduce more complex issues that relate to the nature of knowledge and reality, and our ability to understand the world. In the context of a social science, therefore, this final meaning raises three issues: (1) the possibility of scientific knowledge based on the principles of POSITIV-ISM as against HERMENEUTICS, VERSTEHEN or REALISM; (2) the relative primacy to be given to AGENCY AND STRUCTURE; (3) the respective roles of quantitative and qualitative methods of investigation.

SEE ALSO: *qualitative research.*

metropolitan fringe On the outskirts of many industrial cities lies a belt of commuter housing, often located in scattered villages. It has been argued that a distinctive style of life prevails in these areas, characterized chiefly by a radical separation between middle-class commuters and old-established working-class residents.

SEE ALSO: *concentric zone theory; suburban way of life.*

Michels, Robert (1876–1936) A German sociologist and economist, he wrote on nationalism, socialism, fascism, the role of intellectuals, social mobility and elites. He is best known for *Political Parties* (1911), in which he spoke of the 'iron law of oligarchy' in democratic organizations.

SEE ALSO: *elite; oligarchy; political parties; trade unions.*

micro-sociology This level of sociological analysis is concerned with face-to-face social encounters in everyday life and with interpersonal behaviour in small groups. In the micro–macro debate, RATIONAL CHOICE THEORY has recognized that one of the principal challenges for social theory is to find an analytical bridge between individual social actions and their structural outcomes.

SEE ALSO: *agency and structure.*

middle class Sociologists have long debated the limits, homogeneity and even existence of the middle class, which is usually defined as comprising those in non-manual occupations. The motive for the debate comes from two directions. (1) There is a continuing argument, now increasingly threadbare, about the allegedly Marxist notion that there are two main classes in society and hence little room for a genuine middle class. (2) The growth in occupations usually referred to as middle class has also inspired debate. In the period 1911–81, for example, the size of the manual-worker group fell from some 80 per cent to just over 48 per cent of the employed population of Britain, while higher professionals increased from 1 per cent to over 3 per cent, lower professionals from 3 per cent to almost 9 per cent, and clerks from almost 5 per cent to 15 per cent. There are three main lines of argument. The first stresses that the middle class is fairly large and enjoys pay and conditions of work more favourable than those of the WORKING CLASS, but less so than the UPPER CLASS. This relatively favourable market capacity of the middle class is often said to be based on the possession of educational and technical qualifications. The second and more popular view is that the middle class is composed of a number of discrete segments, with one segment effectively part of the working class, another smaller one part of the upper class, leaving a third grouping truly in the middle. This second view therefore undermines the significance of the distinction between manual and non-manual occupations. The third account sees the major division within the middle class as being between routine white-collar workers and a SERVICE CLASS which has a much more favourable work and market situation.

There is widespread agreement that there is a considerable gap between manual and non-manual earnings. However, this comparison is misleading since a number of non-manual categories, such as clerks and shop assistants, have earnings very little different from manual workers. In respect of hours of work, fringe benefits, pension schemes, sick-pay schemes and job security, these routine white-collar workers may be a little better placed than many manual workers, though the differences are being eroded. It has recently been argued that clerks have good promotion prospects and that this occupation is, for very many, a route to managerial positions. However, this seems to apply almost entirely to male clerks and, since some three-quarters of those employed in this occupation are women, overall promotion prospects are not particularly good. White-collar conditions of work may be little better, as an increasing DIVISION OF LABOUR and the introduction of computers and other equipment have affected office work, making it much more routine, less demanding, less skilful, more controlled by management and offering reduced scope for independent action. A recent study offers a different view. Marshall *et al.* (1988) argue that one should differentiate clerical workers from personal-service workers, such as shop assistants; only the work situation of the latter approximates that of the working class. What is not so clear is whether these changes in the market and work situation of some white-collar occupations result in changes in beliefs, political action, trade-union membership and militancy among white-collar workers.

In contrast with the position of routine white-collar workers, the upper sections of the middle class, especially higher professionals and higher managers, have high levels of pay with well-defined career expectations, shorter hours of work, and better pension and sick-pay arrangements. Their work situation is also more favourable, allowing much greater independence, a measure of control over others and opportunities to use their skills. The situation of these occupations is in many respects like that of the traditional upper class of employers, and it has been argued that only middle management, smaller businessmen and lower professionals truly constitute a middle class.

Some recent accounts of the middle class have revived an older notion of the service class. For example, M. Savage *et al.* (1992) argue that the service class, whose position should be seen as radically different from that of routine white-collar workers, is founded in three types of asset – organizational, property and cultural.

Organizational assets are given by position in a bureaucratically defined hierarchy. Members of the service class are better placed in organizations in which they work and are able to use these positions to help their careers. However, these organizational assets have become less important as lifetime careers in bureaucracies are now less common. At the same time, members of the service class have, in recent years, accumulated considerable amounts of property, chiefly, though not solely, in the form of houses. Lastly, the service class is founded on cultural assets – education and lifestyle – which give its members an advantageous position. Savage *et al.* note that, although the service class is founded on possession of these three assets, whether or not it is actually formed as a unified CLASS depends on other factors – for example, patterns of spatial and social mobility – which may potentially serve to fragment the class.

SEE ALSO: *career; class imagery; credentialism; management; proletarianization; professions; social mobility; trade unions.*

middle-range theory This term was coined by MERTON, who believes in the necessity for sociological theory constructed between 'minor working hypotheses' and 'master conceptual schemes'. For example, between an abstract conceptual scheme such as FUNCTIONALISM, which sees society as a system of functionally interrelated parts, and a minor working hypothesis like 'the majority of the UK population no longer supports the monarchy', there might be a middle-range theory concerned with modelling the social processes involved in the distribution and exercise of power.

READING: Merton (1957)

migration The migration of people on a huge scale between societies was an important feature of the second half of the twentieth century. There were major migrations from countries within the less developed European periphery and parts of the Third World into northern Europe during the 1960s; from Latin America to the USA throughout the period after 1965; from Asia to America, Australia and New Zealand, and even more within Asia itself, during the 1980s and early 1990s; and from the former socialist societies of Eastern Europe and the old Soviet Union after 1989. This movement of people across the globe is an important component of the GLOBALIZATION of the world economy. Much migration has been created by labour shortages in economically expanding host countries which coincide with shortages of work in exporting societies with less dynamic economies. Political persecution and social dislocation in some population exporting countries have further fuelled international migration.

Historically, certain nations encouraged inwards migration as a way of increasing their populations, notably the USA in the nineteenth and early twentieth centuries, and Australia, New Zealand and South Africa until the later years of the twentieth. Migrants to these societies were normally entering for life and had full CITIZENSHIP rights in their host societies (though if they were not white, full rights might take longer). Early sociological writing on migration had this model in mind when developing the concepts of ACCULTURATION and ASSIMILATION to describe how outsiders became incorporated into a host society. Many migrations of the later twentieth century, however, were expected to be temporary, with the host society intending to receive migrant workers only for a limited period while there was an economic need. In these cases, migrants were denied full rights of citizenship and were not expected to integrate. Illegal migrants were denied all citizenship rights and might be deported if discovered. In either case, migrants faced restrictions on where they could work and so constituted a form of 'unfree labour'. In fact, many temporary and illegal migrants managed to stay in their host societies permanently, but without full rights.

The effects of migration on society and individuals have been immense. Public policy issues such as MULTICULTURALISM, the unity of the NATION STATE, RACISM, who is to count as a citizen, have become salient largely because of immigration. The effects on traditional cultures and family relationships, and individual IDENTITY, are also significant. Sociologists tend to concentrate on individual aspects of the overall phenomenon and as yet there is no comprehensive analytical framework for the sociology of migration.

READING: Portes (1995)

millenarianism In Christianity, the belief that the Messiah would return for a thousand years (millennium) has given rise to numerous SOCIAL MOVEMENTS among the poor. In sociology, a millenarian movement is a collective, this-worldly movement promising total social change by miraculous means. Millenarianism in Europe flourished between the eleventh and sixteenth centuries among the disprivileged, for example the Anabaptist movement. Anthropologists sometimes include Melanesian 'cargo cults' and 'nativistic movements' in this category. Millenarian movements in this wider context (e.g. Native American Ghost Dance or Islamic Mahdi movements) are pre-political responses to social tensions following European colonialism.

READING: Lanternari (1963)

Mills, C. Wright (1916–62) An American professor of sociology, he was highly critical of conventional social science for perpetuating prevailing prejudices regarding political power and social inequality. In *White Collar* (1951), he looked at the social characteristics of the American middle class. In *The Power Elite* (1956), he explained the power structure of the United States as an integrated array of elites in different spheres. These elites were to some extent self-perpetuating. In *The Sociological Imagination* (1959), he provided a historical interpretation of the evolution of the social sciences in America and a vigorous polemic against the dominance of FUNCTIONALISM and EMPIRICISM in sociology.

SEE ALSO: *elite; grand theory.*

mobility, social See: SOCIAL MOBILITY.

mobilization In MODERNIZATION theory, the term refers to the process by which peasants or workers are brought together to achieve collective goals. Political mobilization is the process by which a population is brought into the political arena by the formation of new parties and other political institutions. The 'mobilization system' is the ensemble of values, institutions and groups which are organized to achieve societal goals (such as the creation of a nation state). It is the process by which individuals and groups are led to become involved in various forms of political activity. Thus it is a precondition of major political change in society.

SEE ALSO: *collective behaviour; nationalism.*

mode of production This concept, of great importance in Marxist theory, has also had considerable influence in various areas of sociology, especially in the sociologies of development, ideology and politics. A mode of production is the relationship between the RELATIONS OF PRODUCTION and the FORCES OF PRODUCTION. Modes of production can be distinguished from one another by the different relationships between the forces and relations of production. For example, in the feudal mode of production, the lord does not have direct control over the peasant's forces of production, tools and land, but does have control over the disposition of the peasant's produce. In the capitalist mode of production, on the other hand, the capitalist controls both the forces of production and the disposition of the product. Many theorists argue that different modes of production have, associated with them, different forms of IDEOLOGY and politics. For example, in the feudal mode of production, ideology in the form of religion is prominent. Although attention has largely focused on the feudal and capitalist modes of production, other types have been distinguished, particularly the Asiatic and slave modes of production.

The concept of mode of production is intended as an abstract analytical model. No society is likely to contain only one mode of production. This will be so particularly in periods of social change when more than one mode will coexist in the same society. Recent work has concentrated on three main areas: (1) the concept has been given more precision by defining relations of production more tightly; (2) the relationship of the economy or relations of production to politics and ideology has been redefined, so that the latter are now seen as being crucial to the existence, and form, of the former; (3) forms or stages of modes of production have been differentiated. An example of this last point is the separation of the monopoly form of the capitalist mode of production from the competitive form.

SEE ALSO: *Althusser; asiatic mode of production; base and superstructure; capitalism; feudalism; Marx; Marxist sociology; oriental despotism; patriarchy; regulation school; slavery; underdevelopment.*

READING: Abercrombie, Hill and Turner (1980)

model This is an abstract way of presenting the relations between social phenomena. Models of social processes will not necessarily perfectly represent the actual social world but will provide devices which simplify and aid understanding of the essential mechanisms involved. For example, social networks or family structures may be modelled. More formal models may also be employed in which relations between elements are expressed mathematically.

SEE ALSO: *causal modelling; ideal type.*

modernism A term referring to a movement within the arts in Western societies between about 1880 and 1950, represented by figures such as Picasso in painting, Eliot in poetry, Joyce in literature, Stravinsky in music and the Bauhaus in architecture. Modernist authors challenged the view that character or personality could be regarded as whole and finished. They promoted the notion that life is fragmented. The movement above all emphasized novelty, although by the middle of the twentieth century it had almost become the orthodoxy. Some argue that it has been superseded by POSTMODERNISM.

SEE ALSO: *modernity.*

READING: Kumar (1995)

modernity A term describing the particular attributes of modern societies. A good deal of sociological work is based on the assumption of a sharp divide between pre-modern and modern societies. There is considerable debate as to the qualities of the two kinds of society as well as to when Western societies became modern. Modernity is distinguished on economic, political, social and cultural grounds. For example, modern societies typically have industrial, capitalist economies, democratic political organization and a social structure founded on a division into social classes. There is less agreement on cultural features, which are said to include a tendency to the fragmentation of experience, a COMMODIFICATION and RATIONALIZATION of all aspects of life, and a speeding up of the pace of daily life. Modernity has required new systems of individual surveillance, discipline and control. It has emphasized regularity and measurement in everyday life. The values of modernity include activism, universalism and affective neutrality. There is disagreement about the PERIODIZATION of modernity, some writers associating it with the appearance and spread of CAPITALISM from the fourteenth to the eighteenth centuries, some with the religious changes of the fifteenth century onwards, which provided the basis for rationalization, others with the onset of industrialization in the late eighteenth and nineteenth centuries, and still others with cultural transformations at the end of the nineteenth and the beginning of the twentieth century which coincide with MODERNISM. Recently it has been argued that contemporary societies are no longer modern but postmodern.

SEE ALSO: *affect/affective neutrality; democracy; industrialization; industrial society; postmodernism; postmodernity.*

READING: Kumar (1995)

modernization Modernization theory was a dominant analytical paradigm in American sociology in the middle of the twentieth century, providing an explanation of the global process by which traditional societies achieved modernity. (1) Political modernization involves the development of key institutions – political parties, parliaments, franchise and secret ballots – which support participatory decision-making. (2) Cultural modernization typically produces SECULARIZATION and adherence to nationalist ideologies. (3) Economic modernization, while distinct from industrialization, is associated with profound economic changes – an increasing division of labour, use of management techniques, improved technology and the growth of commercial facilities. (4) Social modernization involves increasing literacy, urbanization and the decline of traditional authority. These changes are seen in terms of increasing social and structural DIFFERENTIATION. Modernization theory has been criticized on two grounds: (1) modernization is based on development in the West and is thus an ethnocentric model of development; (2) modernization does not necessarily lead to industrial growth and equal distribution of social benefits, since it is an essentially uneven process resulting in underdevelopment and dependency.

SEE ALSO: *dependency theory; international division of labour; mobilization; sociology of development; urbanization; world-system theory.*

READING: Lerner (1958)

monogamy The practice whereby people marry only one spouse at a time. This is the form of marriage generally practised in Europe, the Americas and Australasia, but there are societies in which it is the custom for a man to have several wives at the same time (*polygyny*) or a woman several husbands (*polyandry*).

monologic See: DIALOGIC.

Montesquieu, Charles-Louis de Secondat, Baron de (1689–1755) A French aristocrat who travelled widely in Europe and developed a comparative perspective on the political systems of his time, he was elected to the French Academy in 1727 and became an important figure in the Enlightenment. His social theory was dominated by the problem of political despotism. His *Persian Letters* (1721) was a fictional correspondence between two Persian travellers in Europe which allowed him to reflect upon French society. In his sociological analysis of the harem, Montesquieu argued that any society based on total force or despotism was not viable in the long term. This theme was further pursued in *Considerations on the Causes of Roman Greatness* (*Considérations sur les causes de la grandeur des Romains*, 1734), a comparative analysis of the social causes of the rise and fall of empires. His most significant contribution came in *The Spirit of the Laws* (1748), where he argued that, following the English experience of parliamentary government, despotism could be avoided by the institutional separation of the executive, legislative and juridical functions of the state. This involved an important 'separation of powers' which would prevent the absolute power of despotism. In this work, Montesquieu wrote a comparative sociology of institutions that showed the interconnections between religion, education, government and geography. He established a sociological tradition which continued to be influential in the nineteenth-century work of N. Fustel de Coulanges, DURKHEIM and de TOCQUEVILLE.

SEE ALSO: *comparative method; oriental despotism.*

Moore, Barrington, Jr (b. 1913) A lecturer in sociology and senior research fellow in the Russian Research Centre at Harvard University since 1951, he has made a major contribution to comparative and HISTORICAL SOCIOLOGY. His most influential work is *Social Origins of Dictatorship and Democracy* (1967). In this, he examined the relationship between social classes (especially the peasantry and landlords) in England, France, the United States, Imperial China, Japan and India to see how historical class formations have determined the forms of politics in the modern world, giving rise to bourgeois democracy (England and America), fascism (pre-war Japan and Germany), and communism (China). In *Soviet Politics* (1950) and *Terror and Progress USSR* (1954), he adopted a functionalist framework in POLITICAL SOCIOLOGY to analyse the contradictions between totalitarian politics, INDUSTRIALIZATION and ideology in post-revolutionary Russia. He has also contributed to political and sociological theory in *Political Power and Social Theory* (1958). His historical and political studies can be seen as social inquiries into the relationships among freedom, truth and happiness. These issues were reflected in a collection of essays in honour of MARCUSE that he edited with K. H. Wolff (1967). In his later works, he turned to certain major ethical and social issues. In *Reflections on the Causes of Human Misery* (1972), he addressed himself to 'war, cruelty and general human nastiness'; in *Injustice* (1978), he studied the bases of political authority, obedience and revolt by means of an historical inquiry into the German working class. Finally, he has contributed to the sociological analysis of privacy (1984).

SEE ALSO: *comparative method; peasants.*

READING: Smith, D. (1983)

moral crusade See: MORAL PANICS.

moral entrepreneur/moral enterprise See: MORAL PANICS.

moral panics Episodes of widespread anxiety and fear triggered by apparently trivial events. Moral panics have a long and varied history from accusations of witchcraft in the sixteenth century to fears about drug-users or muggers in contemporary society. They usually involve the identification of a folk devil who is held to be responsible for whatever moral or social damage has occurred. There will be calls for punishment or the restoration of proper moral values. These may take the form of a moral crusade (e.g. against drugs or drink) led by moral entrepreneurs who may make the rectification of the perceived evil into their life's work. In contemporary societies, the mass media may play a very large role in moral panics, spreading rumour and contributing to a spiral of anxiety and fear.

Moral panics are social movements that require sociological explanation. Most theories see them as responses to social stress, although others see them as mainly driven by elites which control the mass media.

SEE ALSO: *deviance amplification; folk devils; stereotypes.*

READING: Goode and Ben-Yehuda (1994)

moral statistics An aspect of the nineteenth-century French antecedents of sociology, moral statistics involved the collection of aggregate social data, which were regarded as a feature of SOCIAL PATHOLOGY – SUICIDE, divorce, homicide and illegitimacy.

SEE ALSO: *Durkheim; official statistics.*

mores W. Q. Sumner (1906) defined mores as the patterns of cultural and moral action which contributed to the continuity of the human group. Mores are traditional, prescriptive standards which maintain the social group by regulating individual behaviour.

SEE ALSO: *culture; custom; folkways.*

mortality Mortality data are often expressed in terms of the crude DEATH RATE; that is, number of deaths per thousand individuals. This measure is not usually very useful, because so much depends on the age and gender composition of a population. Other measures do standardize the crude mortality rate for age, gender and class. Mortality rates are important social indicators. The infant mortality rate, especially the neo-natal rate (covering the first four weeks of life), provides a sensitive indicator of general social welfare in different societies and different regions within any one society. Differential mortality rates between social classes indicate inequalities in health care, wealth and working conditions. In Britain, there has been a marked shift in the principal causes of death away from infectious to degenerative diseases.

SEE ALSO: *demography.*

Mosca, Gaetano (1858–1941) An Italian jurist and political theorist, he contributed to the sociology of elites. In *The Ruling Class* (1896), he contended that, whatever the form of government, power would be in the hands of a minority who formed the ruling class. This class, however, always had to justify its rule by appeals to the moral or legal principles that are acceptable to the governed. His ideas influenced MICHELS and form part of a sociological tradition concerned with elites.

SEE ALSO: *elite*; *ruling class*.

multiculturalism Britain, in common with other advanced Western societies, has seen substantial immigration from other countries within the last fifty years. Immigrants bring with them their own cultural traditions, which are often at variance with those of the host country. For example, immigrants to the UK from Pakistan are predominantly Muslim and may have quite different views about the family and the role of women from those held by the indigenous population or other immigrants, such as from the Caribbean. Originally, it was thought that such immigrants, perhaps by the second generation, would assimilate to the host culture and lose their distinctive identity and that the process of integration would be beneficial. That has not happened and, in turn, the integrationist ideal has given way to a celebration of cultural diversity. In turn, strong national identities have been undermined by the demands of indigenous groups for a separate cultural IDENTITY. Whether it is the Scots or Welsh in Britain, the Maoris in New Zealand, or Native Americans in the United States, groups all over the world are calling for legal, political and moral recognition of their linguistic, ethnic, religious and cultural differences. Such multiculturalism has been further enhanced by the process of GLOBALIZATION. The global sale of goods from many countries, the growth of international travel and the influence of a global mass media have combined to bring a diversity of cultural influences to bear in any one society.

SEE ALSO: *ethnic group*; *migration*; *nationalism*; *nation state*.

READING: Friedman (1994)

multidimensional scaling (MDS) When there are two or more dimensions to be considered in the examination of data, researchers may choose to analyse these by means of MDS. This refers to a group of models which portray data as a set of points in space, such that the relationships in the data are reflected spatially in the geometry of the model. Observations that are associated in different degrees in the data set will appear as points separated by distances that correspond to their coefficients of association; that is, distances between the points represent exactly the amounts of similarity and difference within the data set. MDS presents complex data in a visual form that is usually easier to absorb and interpret than in tabular form. The original metric MDS had a restricted use in sociology, because it assumed interval or ratio MEASUREMENT LEVELS. Non-metric MDS, however, represents data that are merely ordered in some way and uses this rank-order in the plotting of the coordinates for each point. Any sets of data that contain measures of similarity or dissimilarity can be used in such scaling. The technique has proved useful for the analysis of subjective perceptions of similarity and difference in attitude research.

READING: Kruskal and Wish (1978)

multinational companies (MNCs) See: GLOBALIZATION.

multiple methods See TRIANGULATION.

multivariate analysis Multivariate techniques are used in the statistical analysis of data comprising more than two variables. The term describes the analysis of relationships between a number of independent and dependent variables, when techniques such as multiple CORRELATION, REGRESSION, CLUSTER ANALYSIS, FACTOR ANALYSIS, LOG LINEAR ANALYSIS and PATH ANALYSIS are employed.

SEE ALSO: *causal modelling; dependent/independent variables; survey.*

myth A myth is a narrative account of the SACRED which embodies collective experiences and represents CONSCIENCE COLLECTIVE. Nineteenth-century anthropology sought to discover the origins of myths, treating them as unscientific explanations of social institutions and practices. For MALINOWSKI, myths provided LEGITIMATION of social arrangements. Contemporary perspectives have been profoundly influenced by LÉVI-STRAUSS, who treats myths as a system of signs from the perspective of structural linguistics. For Lévi-Strauss, myths are not legitimating charters of institutions and they do not attempt to explain social arrangements. The function of myth is essentially cognitive, namely to account for the fundamental conceptual categories of the mind. These categories are constituted by contradictory series of binary oppositions – nature and society, raw and cooked, man and woman, left and right. Myths do not carry a message which the anthropologist seeks to decipher. Any one myth is merely a variation on a theme which presents one particular combination of elements. Thus, the Oedipus myth is simply one variation on the elements of mother/son, wife/husband and father/son that are organized in relations of love, hatred, service and dominance. While this approach has proved theoretically fruitful, Lévi-Strauss' methodological presuppositions have often been criticized as arbitrary and ethnocentric.

While traditional anthropology was concerned with the study of myths in primitive society, the structural analysis of myth has also been applied to modern industrial societies. For example, R. Barthes (1957) treats myths as a system of communication, consisting not only of written discourses, but also the products of cinema, sport, photography, advertising and television. To some extent, these myths are delusions. More importantly, however, they represent images, communicated widely, in which a society tries to make its own culture seem entirely natural. For example, the French have a myth about wine, which is not simply one drink among many, but somehow symbolizes 'Frenchness'.

SEE ALSO: *ideology; semiotics; structuralism.*

READING: Barnard and Spence (1996)

N

narcissism This refers to a type of personality that is allegedly found widely in modern Western societies. Named after the ancient myth of Narcissus, the narcissistic personality has a mixture of self-love and self-hate, believes that he or she is the centre of attention, is plagued by an anxiety produced by unrealizable desires, and tends to disregard the boundary between the self and the external world. There is some disagreement as to whether narcissism is best seen as a pathological disorder or a cultural condition. In either case, an important causal factor is said to be changing patterns of child-rearing.

nation state In most modern societies, the STATE is coterminous with the nation. Most contemporary states have the military and administrative power to unify the disparate elements of their population within well-defined borders and to give a sense of national cultural, linguistic and, perhaps, religious identity. Within recent history, the stability of nation states has been fundamental to world order or disorder. They have been powerful entities, frequently in violent conflict with one another.

There are signs, however, that a world system based on powerful nation states is changing. Economic GLOBALIZATION, in particular, has meant that nation states have much less control over their economies. Thus, global flows of capital, increased intensity of international trade, the capacity of very large international companies to escape regulation by any nation state, and the vulnerability of individual nations to economic forces beyond their control have all contributed to the gradual emergence of a global economy independent of nation states. These tendencies have been reinforced by cultural changes which have contributed to much greater cultural diversity, undermining the unity so important to the nation state. These changes have been external, including immigration, international travel, a global mass media and the availability of goods and services from many countries. There have also been internal pressures, as many countries have linguistic, regional, religious or ethnic minorities pressing for greater recognition of cultural difference.

SEE ALSO: *multiculturalism; nationalism.*

nationalism Nationalism is an IDEOLOGY based on the belief that a people with common characteristics such as language, religion or ethnicity constitutes a separate and distinctive political community. Nationalists attempt to preserve this social distinctiveness to protect the social benefits which follow from national identity and membership. Nationalism locates the political legitimacy of the STATE in self-government by co-nationals. It is often argued that nationalism as a political doctrine did not exist before the eighteenth century and that the rise of nationalist movements coincides with the development of nation states in Europe after the Napoleonic period. By the end of the nineteenth century, however, it was assumed by many social theorists that nationalism would tend to decline and would be replaced by internationalism and cosmopolitanism. These interpretations of industrial society suggested that: (1) the growth of trade would undermine particularistic differences between societies; (2) conflicts would be expressed through class rather than national ideologies; (3) the working class would develop a commitment to international socialism. These assumptions were shattered by the First World War when there was relatively little organized working-class opposition to a war fought on nationalist principles. Nationalism subsequently became closely associated with movements for self-determination against IMPERIALISM in the Third World.

There are three major contemporary interpretations of nationalism: (1) it was a romantic movement related to the unification of Germany and Italy, and was subsequently exported to Africa and Asia on the back of European colonialism; (2) nationalism is a form of reactive politics in societies where traditional modes of social organization have collapsed; for instance, as a result of social changes introduced by external colonialism, or following the collapse of the socialist system in Eastern Europe; (3) the UNEVEN DEVELOPMENT of capitalism creates profound regional imbalance, and peripheral regions embrace nationalist politics to secure a more equal distribution of wealth. An example is Scottish nationalism within the United Kingdom. In this interpretation, nationalism within advanced capitalist societies develops in response to INTERNAL COLONIALISM.

Nationalism is often regarded as an artificial, parasitic ideology, because it is often impossible to identify a single characteristic common to all members of a society who claim to belong to a common nation. In this view, nationalism is a myth created by intellectuals, who are the exponents of romantic notions of national language, folk heritage and national identity. Nationalism is thus also associated with political extremism and xenophobia. However, the liberal equation of nationalism and FASCISM tends to obscure the positive political merits of nationalist movements in the Third World, which have achieved self-government and some measure of social development.

In the classical Marxist approach to nationalism, there were three common arguments: (1) nationalism was a bourgeois ideology, because it served the class interest of the rising bourgeoisie in its opposition to the traditional aristocracy which ruled by, for example, the principle of divine right; (2) the rise of the nation state was closely associated with the economic requirements of early capitalism, but nationalism would decline as late capitalism became more international in character; (3) national struggle was a special form of class struggle, often referred to as 'external class struggle' that is conducted on the international rather than the national level. These three arguments have not been supported by political developments in the twentieth century. Nationalism has often been associated with working-class radicalism, because nationalist politics may imply social equality for all members of the nation. Nationalism may also be part of a revolutionary socialist struggle for national autonomy against foreign domination and internal exploitation – for example, the Mexican Revolution of 1910–17. It is, furthermore, difficult to treat national struggles as a special form of class struggle and some Marxists have argued that nationalism has to be regarded as an 'autonomous force' in political struggles.

Since nationalism can take many different political directions – democracy, fascism or communism – and can be associated with different classes, it has been argued that there can be no general theory of nationalism. There is no theory that can identify a social process (such as industrialization) which will explain the emergence of all forms of nationalism, or which is able to define the essential and universal features of nationalist movements. This negative conclusion is not, however, widely shared. The consensus in social science is that, despite its empirical complexity, nationalism has the following general features: (1) it is based on the demand that governments should share the same cultural identity as the governed; (2) as a result, cultural nationalism, which seeks to preserve or recreate the national heritage through, for example, the revival of a language, prepares the basis for political nationalism, which seeks self-determination and political supremacy; (3) the development of modern systems of mass communication facilitates the dissemination of unifying nationalist ideologies; (4) nationalist ideologies have a strong appeal to subordinate classes by providing them with some economic protection against non-nationals, but the content of the ideology is typically developed by marginal intellectuals – black intellectuals, for instance, excluded from white educational establishments, were drawn to nationalism; (5) nationalism was, for most of the twentieth century, associated with de-colonization and the economic development of Third World societies, and with the struggle for regional equality within existing capitalist societies. In the post-socialist societies of Eastern Europe, however, there was, from the early 1990s, a revival of violent nationalist movements based on ethnic and religious differences.

SEE ALSO: *ethnic group; mobilization; modernization; political sociology.*

READING: Gellner (1983); Smith, A. D. (1991)

natural area Within the theory known as URBAN ECOLOGY, an area of the city inhabited by a population of a particular type (e.g. the suburb or the ghetto) is known as a natural area. Such an area is relatively homogeneous socially and culturally, and the assumption is that it is created by ecological forces which drive similar populations into similar areas.

SEE ALSO: *Chicago School; concentric zone theory; urban way of life.*

natural law Within the natural law tradition, the justice of social laws and institutions was thought to depend on their conformity to certain universal laws of nature. All human beings, by virtue of their membership in humanity and as part of this natural order, enjoyed certain natural rights, such as a right to freedom. Natural law theory concerned itself with the moral content of laws and developed the criterion that true laws could not be unjust laws. However, the secularization of Western culture and intellectual relativism have brought into question the basic assumptions concerning the universality of human nature.

Contemporary legal theory, including the sociology of law, has inclined towards a view of law as command, supported by relevant sanctions and the coercive apparatus of the state. This is known as *positive* law. The legitimacy of law resides not in its moral content but in the procedures by which it is developed and enforced by the appropriate authorities. The positivist view of law does not provide a criterion by which the justice of governments can be assessed.

SEE ALSO: *legal–rational authority; legitimacy.*

READING: Dworkin (1991)

naturalism Sociologists who argue that the methods of sociology are, for all practical purposes, the same as those of the natural sciences, propose a naturalistic account of sociology. It is commonly suggested that naturalism is equivalent to POSITIVISM, particularly by those who oppose positivist methods in sociology. This is a mistaken view, since other doctrines opposed to positivism, for example REALISM, also unite the methods of natural and social sciences.

nature/nurture debate Human beings are simultaneously features of the natural world (by virtue of having bodies) and members of the cultural world (by virtue of language). The precise relationship between biology and culture in the constitution of human society has long been a controversial issue in social philosophy and social sciences. There are two extreme positions in the nature/nurture debate: (1) geneticism argues that the characteristics of individuals, groups and nations can be explained exclusively in terms of genetic inheritance; (2) cultural determinism and anti-naturalism argue that individual differences and national character are entirely explained by SOCIALIZATION. Explanations in terms of genetic inheritance have been common in theories of criminal behaviour, INTELLIGENCE and educational performance. Theories that emphasize genetic factors maintain that intelligence, for example, is not significantly affected by CULTURE and educational training. Feminists have objected to the emphasis on biological sex in many accounts of the differences between men and women, on the grounds that these accounts reflect the values of PATRIARCHY, while differences are often socially produced by GENDER. While sociologists traditionally rejected all forms of geneticism, some, like PARSONS, sought a more fruitful theoretical relationship between biological and social systems. Parsons (1977) considered the parallel between symbols, information and cybernetics in social systems, and the communication of 'information' in biological systems through DNA.

SEE ALSO: *biologism/biological reductionism*; *Mead, Margaret*; *mental health*; *sociobiology*.

need The concept is used in two senses. (1) As a theory of individual motivation, actions are explained by reference to needs. While it is possible to recognize certain physiologically based needs – food, sleep and shelter – which must be satisfied for human survival, other needs are culturally malleable. Even when needs are physiological, such as a need for sexual satisfaction, they may be achieved in various ways, including homosexuality, marriage, celibacy, promiscuity or prostitution, some of which may be socially determined. For MALINOWSKI, social institutions function to satisfy human needs. Sociologists also recognize needs which are not physiological – the need for companionship, recognition or meaning. The concept also has a critical significance among Marxist sociologists; capitalist society is said to create false needs through advertising. Recent social theory, influenced by POST-MODERNISM, has become more concerned with wants and desires, which are thought to be stimulated by consumerism.

(2) In social systems theory, it is part of the concept of functional prerequisites. For example, PARSONS believes that any social system has four needs or 'functional imperatives', which must be met if the system is to survive.

SEE ALSO: *functional imperative*; *functionalism*; *needs hierarchy*; *sociobiology*; *systems theory*.

READING: Heller (1974)

needs hierarchy For American psychologist A. Maslow (1954), human needs are both universal (shared by everyone) and arranged as a hierarchy with five levels. Once needs at each level of the hierarchy are met, individuals then seek to satisfy their needs at the next level. The basic need is for physiological well-being (which includes sustenance, sleep, warmth). When this is satisfied, then the need for security becomes dominant. Then we progress to the third level, a need for love and belonging. The fourth level is the need for self-esteem, which includes the respect of others as well as of oneself. The fifth and highest level, which can be achieved only when the other four levels have been satisfied, is for self-actualization; that is, the need to develop and realize one's potential and to be or do whatever one is capable of being or doing.

The needs hierarchy remains probably the most influential of all psychological theories which relate individual needs to work motivation. It has been used in explanations of why, once a company has corrected one set of employee dissatisfactions (e.g. by meeting their needs for well-being and job security), employees may still be dissatisfied, because now they look to meet their higher needs in the workplace. Despite its great influence, however, psychologists have been unable to establish the validity of the hierarchy in empirical research. It is still not proven that people have only five types of needs, that needs are structured hierarchically, or that satisfaction at one level triggers needs at the next.

SEE ALSO: *work attitudes.*

negotiated order Negotiated order theory regards social organization as emerging from the ongoing process of interaction between people. The interaction process involves constant negotiation and renegotiation of the terms of social action. Negotiated order theory emphasizes the fluidity and uncertainty of social arrangements. This perspective has been used primarily in the analysis of organizations, for example the modern hospital. Critics claim that the theory neglects the structural limitations on social action, since there are many features of society which are simply not negotiable.

SEE ALSO: *symbolic interactionism.*
READING: Strauss (1978)

neighbourhood A term with a commonsense use in sociology to denote residential areas. The nature of the social ties formed in neighbourhoods was for long the subject of active investigation in urban sociology. For example, a number of studies showed that the residents of suburbs formed fairly close, family-like ties with one another, although the prevailing myth was that suburbanites had essentially private lives.

SEE ALSO: *affluent worker; community; organization man; suburban way of life.*

neo-colonialism See: IMPERIALISM.

neo-evolutionism See: EVOLUTIONARY THEORY.

neo-Fordism See: POST-FORDISM.

neo-functionalism See: FUNCTIONALISM.

neo-Kantianism This term is a general label for a variety of intellectual trends in Germany between 1870 and 1920 which returned to I. Kant's philosophy. In sociology, neo-Kantianism has been important in shaping debates concerning EPISTEM-OLOGY. In the work of SIMMEL, for instance, the Kantian principle that mind has an active part to play in the apprehension of the natural world became a guiding feature of his sociology. Knowledge of the social world is always constructive knowledge which involves selection and interpretation and not simply a question of collecting facts. Just as Kant argued that experience of natural phenomena is determined by *a priori* categories, so Simmel attempted to show how social reality could be studied in terms of enduring social forms in which the varied content of social life was distilled. While neo-Kantianism was superseded by, for example, the debates between critical theories and positivists, the basic assumptions of the neo-Kantian position are still influential in the philosophy of the social sciences.

SEE ALSO: *critical theory; hermeneutics; Methodenstreit; positivism; Weber.*

network/social network The term 'network' is used to describe the observable *pattern* of social relationships among individual units of analysis. Sociologists derive these patterns by mapping interactions. The *content* of the social relationships involved in these networks will vary from case to case: for example, sociologists have studied patterns of friendship, kinship, influence, domination, economic exchange and assistance. Depending on the research focus, the units in a network may be individuals, groups or corporate entities (e.g. companies). Researchers show networks as maps containing a series of points, which represent the units, and lines joining the points, which represent the interactions among units. The mathematics associated with graph theory provide the technical basis for analysing networks. Several computer programs are available which simplify the plotting and analysis.

Network analysis illuminates the structure of actually existing social relations, so it is a useful tool to study the relational level of the broader social structure. Some analysts go further and suggest that the patterns of social relations among individuals in fact constitute the social structure. Networks may also be used in explaining the actions of individuals. The arrangement of social relationships and the location of the individual in these are both a constraint and a resource. Individuals face demands and expectations from other members of their networks, which constrain what they can do. But at the same time, other members are also resources who may be used, for example, to get a job, to borrow money, to meet sexual partners and spouses, to influence those in positions of power. Different types of network structure provide different levels of advantage. Immediate networks, which are dense with strong and close ties, but which overlap more distant networks based on weaker ties (e.g. acquaintances rather than friends), and where resources do not duplicate what is available in the immediate network, provide the most benefits. LABOUR MARKET studies often use these aspects of networks to explain how some people get jobs.

Network analysis is also used to illuminate the relations between companies. These include corporate networks based on interlocking directorships, which are the linkages created when company directors hold directorships in several major firms at the same time, and the inter-firm networks that are crucial to the operation of industrial districts in the theory of FLEXIBLE SPECIALIZATIONS.

SEE ALSO: *actor network theory; economic sociology; management; managerial revolution; market; sociogram.*

READING: Burt (1992); Scott, J. (1992)

neutralization People who commit deviant acts frequently attempt to neutralize their guilt by techniques such as denying responsibility, denying that injury has occurred, blaming the victim and criticizing those who condemn the deviant act. Neutralization is a coping response that allows DEVIANT BEHAVIOUR to continue. The phrase 'techniques of neutralization' was coined by G. Sykes and D. Matza (1957).

SEE ALSO: *accounts*.

new economic sociology (NES) See: ECONOMIC SOCIOLOGY.

new international division of labour (NIDL) Multinational companies have always located some manufacturing operations in countries with low labour costs. NIDL was used by F. Frobel *et al*. (1980) to describe the substantial relocation of operations to Third World countries during the 1970s, which was one of the ways multinationals responded to intensification of competition in world markets, reduced rates of economic growth in the world economy and lower profitability. This shift was facilitated by new technologies, such as computerization of management information systems and new forms of telecommunication, and by better transport. It is an aspect of the process known as GLOBALIZATION. NIDL theory attempted to resolve the inadequacy of earlier explanations of economic backwardness in the Third World, notably DEPENDENCY THEORY and WORLD-SYSTEM THEORY, which were unable to account for the economic growth that had taken place in the NEWLY INDUSTRIALIZING COUNTRIES (NICs). It maintains that the operations that multinational companies relocate are basic manufacturing processes involving low levels of skill, while more skilled processes such as research, design and development, and certain high technology manufacturing tasks, are not relocated. Thus the new international division of labour is one where some regions of the world specialize in low-paid, routine manufacturing operations while others specialize in the high value-added parts of the production process.

Relocation has since occurred within the First World, to countries which offered lower labour costs than other industrialized economies (within the European Union, to Spain and Britain, for example). Multinationals may find it more profitable to use an experienced and well-educated labour force and to produce closer to the final marketplace, even at higher labour costs than are available in the Third World. In part, this has been made possible by the continued advance of technology, which so reduces the labour content of manufacturing operations that it is no longer crucial to use the cheapest possible labour, but which requires skills and education not presently available in many Third World societies.

newly industrializing countries (NICs) A term sometimes used to describe a group of previously 'dependent' and economically underdeveloped societies, which achieved sustained economic growth and successful industrialization during the fourth quarter of the twentieth century. They include Brazil and several Pacific Rim societies, notably Hong Kong, South Korea, Singapore, Taiwan, Malaysia and Mexico.

SEE ALSO: *dependency theory*.

new religious movements (NRMs) Groups of people strongly involved in unorthodox religious beliefs and practices sometimes, but not always, of Eastern origin. A great deal of press attention has been given to NRMs or cults in recent years, particularly regarding their alleged brainwashing of recruits. Such cults are not, in fact, all that new. In the nineteenth and twentieth centuries in Europe and America there has been a continuous history of religious innovation. However, religious fervour of all kinds may also come in cycles. It has been argued, for example, that the 1960s' counter-culture was associated with the growth of new religious movements which have declined since. NRMs are given publicity out of all proportion to their relatively small size. Barker (1984) estimated that in 1982 there were, for example, only 700 Moonies and 200 followers of Transcendental Meditation. Heelas (1996) reports that only 5 per cent of the American population have beliefs that are associated with NRMs and a much smaller proportion are actually members of an NRM.

NRMs are diverse in their religious beliefs. While some are derived from Eastern religions like Buddhism or Hinduism, others are evangelically Christian. Still others are mixtures or are infused with the personal and often idiosyncratic beliefs of a founder. Wallis (1984) distinguishes between different types of NRM – world-rejecting, world-affirming and world-accommodating. The first type (e.g. members of the Unification Church, known as the Moonies) tend to be exclusive: converts are expected to renounce their past lives and the outside world is seen as threatening. Recruits tend to be young, middle-class and highly educated but socially marginal. World-affirming NRMs (e.g. Transcendental Meditation) tend to see sources of unhappiness as lying within individuals, not society. They do not reject the world but try to relate to it more effectively. They recruit from socially integrated people of all social classes in middle age. For world-accommodating movements (e.g. the House Church movement), religious experience is personal, not collective, and is enthusiastic and vital.

NRMs, particularly world-rejecting ones, are often accused of brainwashing recruits. There is little evidence of this and actually the recruitment process is very inefficient. Only a tiny proportion of those approached ever become members and most NRMs experience a high drop-out rate. Given the small size of NRMs, the severity of public reaction has elements of moral panic, enhanced by the world-rejecting qualities of some movements which lead to a renunciation by adherents of their previous family life.

SEE ALSO: *cult*; *moral panics*; *new social movements*; *secularization*; *sociology of religion*.

READING: Heelas (1996)

New Right This political philosophy and practice was associated with the governments of Margaret Thatcher in Britain and Ronald Regan in the USA in the 1980s. It was characterized by a commitment to individualism, enterprise culture, *laissez-faire*, populism and the ideology of capitalism. In the eyes of some commentators, it also displayed elements of the authoritarian personality. Its political programme included a reduction in the scope of the welfare state, weakening the role of trade unions in companies and in politics, and breaking the hold of social democratic values on political life. It is generally credited with permanently changing the nature of political discourse in both societies.

new social movements (NSMs) See: SOCIAL MOVEMENTS.

new working class In the 1960s, the French sociologists S. Mallet (1963), A. Gorz

(1964) and A. Touraine (1969) suggested that the evolution of production technology had created a new segment within the WORKING CLASS. The new working class comprised people employed in advanced, high-technology industries. It was asserted that high technology required better-educated workers, organized work along communal, teamwork lines and integrated workers into their firms. These changes promoted greater industrial and social militancy – that is, CLASS CONSCIOUSNESS – because they made various 'contradictions' of capitalism more visible.

One contradiction that this new class was thought to experience acutely was between the communal production of goods and the private appropriation of profits. Their high levels of education meant the new workers understood how production processes worked and they had real control over these processes. Teamwork brought home to them the communal nature of production. They were thus able to penetrate the contradiction that was concealed from traditional workers. A second contradiction was the discrepancy between their skill, responsibility and training and their inability to influence company policy. Mallet and Gorz thought that the new class comprised both skilled manual workers and non-manual technicians and professionals operating the new technologies.

There have been several criticisms of the concept, which is now discredited. (1) Other research shows that high-technology workers may have little control or understanding of the new processes. D. Gallie (1978) found that most manual workers in four oil refineries in France and Britain were little more than semi-skilled labourers. DE-SKILLING may occur in high technology just as it does elsewhere. (2) There is in fact a considerable variation among the levels of skill and responsibility of the groups that make up the new working class, even within an apparently homogeneous category such as technicians. (3) In the 1970s, the French new working class was less radical and militant than the traditional workers, and was reconciled to capitalism. It is worth noting that R. Blauner (1964) argued that workers on automated systems in America were *less* alienated than others, though his views have also been criticized.

SEE ALSO: *alienation; automation; post-industrial society.*

READING: Rose, M. (1979)

Nisbet, Robert A. (b. 1913) Currently Albert Schweitzer Professor of Humanities Emeritus at Columbia University and Scholar at the American Enterprise Institute for Public Policy Research, his approach to sociology has been remarkably consistent and influential. His work falls into two fields: (1) the study of developmentalism in social thought; and (2) order and disorganization in the social sphere, or community and conflict. His argument is that revolutionary social change has undermined community and communal values, with the result that authority no longer has a significant social underpinning. His analysis of social change has been presented in *Tradition and Revolt* (1968), *Social Change and History* (1969) and *History of the Idea of Progress* (1980). The study of the collapse of community was a central theme of *The Quest for Community* (1953), *The Social Bond* (1970), *The Social Philosophers* (1974a) and *Prejudices* (1982). He has also been involved in a number of edited works which have been influential in the development of theoretical and applied sociology; these include *Emile Durkheim* (1965), *Contemporary Social Problems* (1961), with MERTON, and *A History of Sociological Analysis* (1978b), with BOTTOMORE. He has contributed to the study of the ideas of E. Durkheim in *The Sociology of Emile Durkheim* (1974b). Nisbet's most influential book on the history of sociology is *The Sociological Tradition*

(1967), in which he argues that social theory has been profoundly influenced by the French and the industrial revolutions: three systems of thought (liberalism, radicalism and conservatism) emerged as responses to the disruptions following these revolutions. Sociology is primarily dependent on the conservative legacy in terms of its unit-ideas (such as status, the sacred and community). In *Conservatism* (1986), he explores the primary themes of political conservatism and the present crisis of conservative thought.

nominal See: MEASUREMENT LEVELS.

nomothetic See: IDIOGRAPHIC.

non-parametric Non-parametric statistics make no assumptions about the parameters of a DISTRIBUTION of values. Therefore they are distribution-free, whereas many of the statistics commonly used in social science assume certain distributions (usually the 'normal' distribution). They are useful to sociologists for three reasons: (1) they are effective with small sample sizes; (2) they are effective with the ordinal data that sociologists often work with; (3) they do not depend on assumptions that the population distribution is 'normal', which are often difficult to justify in sociological research. Some statisticians argue that non-parametric statistics are likely always to be more appropriate for sociological data. Two common techniques are the Mann-Whitney U and the Wilcoxon T.

non-response BIAS in the selection of a sample can result from the refusal of some sections of the population to cooperate. Bias arises if the people who refuse to cooperate differ from those who do in some important respect, since the final sample of respondents does not represent the total population that is being investigated. The bias is greater in proportion to the numbers who fail to respond, and to the magnitude of the difference between the respondents and non-respondents. The effects of non-response can be reduced in well-designed surveys by keeping the amount of non-response down to reasonable levels and by approximately estimating the bias that it may introduce into the results.

non-zero sum See: GAME THEORY.

norm Norms are expectations about appropriate conduct which serve as common guidelines for social action. Human behaviour exhibits certain regularities, which are the product of adherence to shared norms. In this sense, human action is 'rule governed'. A social norm is not necessarily actual behaviour, and normative behaviour is not simply the most frequently occurring pattern. Since the term refers to social expectations about 'correct' or 'proper' behaviour, norms imply the presence of legitimacy, consent and prescription. While deviation from norms is punished by sanctions, norms are acquired by INTERNALIZATION and SOCIALIZATION. The concept is central to theories of SOCIAL ORDER.

SEE ALSO: *consensus; institution; Parsons; role; value.*

normal distribution See: DISTRIBUTION.

normative control See: MANAGERIAL STRATEGIES OF CONTROL.

nuclear family Social units comprising a man and a woman living together with their children, nuclear families are often contrasted with extended families. One theoretical position assumes a 'functional fit' between the nuclear family and industrialization, in that the nuclear family, free of wider KINSHIP ties, is more geographically and socially mobile, gives greater emotional support via the unconstrained choice of MARRIAGE partners, and permits occupational roles to be filled by achievement criteria – all requirements of industrial society. The family structure of contemporary society is thus said to be composed of relatively isolated nuclear family households, although there will be considerable social variations.

Recent work shows the following. (1) Family structures before the Industrial Revolution were not all of the classical EXTENDED FAMILY form. Indeed, because of high mortality rates the predominant form was nuclear. (2) The *process* of industrialization was accompanied by a greater use of extended kin contacts, partly by exchange of services and financial aid. Such systems of mutual aid were a support for people made insecure by migration from rural to urban areas. (3) There is now considerable evidence that the family structures of industrial societies are not characterized by isolated conjugal households. Contemporary families are more accurately described as modified extended families in which there are extensive contacts between kin not necessarily living together, contacts taking the form of visits, telephone calls and the exchange of services. In this system of mutual support, non-kin will also be important, creating a modified primary group around each family.

To some extent the notion of the family as a unitary phenomenon is misleading. There are a whole variety of HOUSEHOLD structures besides the conventional nuclear one of wife, husband and children. The trend in Britain is towards smaller households, more people living together before or instead of marrying, more divorces, more remarriages, and an increase in the numbers of children born outside marriage.

These changes in household structure cast some doubt on functional theories of the family current some forty or fifty years ago. Writers of this persuasion argued that the family was a universal human institution because it performed certain crucial functions for society such as SOCIALIZATION, caring for the young, and reproduction. However, not only are there fewer families of this type in contemporary societies, it is also probable that the family structure also creates difficulties for society and for family members; families may be functional but they are also DYSFUNCTIONAL. For example, some recent writers have argued that women are oppressed in the family, which also routinely causes psychological damage to the individuals concerned.

SEE ALSO: *conjugal role*; *divorce*; *domestic labour*; *group*; *patriarchy*.

READING: Allan (1985); Morgan (1985)

null hypothesis See: SIGNIFICANCE TEST.

nurture See: NATURE/NURTURE DEBATE.

O

objectivity The goal of scientific investigation, sociological or otherwise, is often said to be objective knowledge, free of bias or prejudice. There is a division of opinion here, some holding that objectivity in sociology is possible, others not. Five different kinds of arguments are advanced for sociology not being objective. (1) Sociological judgements are subjective, being coloured by actors' own experiences. SEE ALSO: *phenomenological sociology*. (2) All propositions are limited in their meaning to particular language contexts. SEE ALSO: *ethnomethodology*; *indexicality*. (3) All sociological theories are produced by, and limited to, particular social groups. Such a doctrine is often taken to be an outcome of the sociology of knowledge which treats all knowledge as a function of social location. SEE ALSO: *Mannheim*; *relativism*. (4) All observations are necessarily THEORY-LADEN. (5) In that all members of society have different values, sociologists will unconsciously, but necessarily, have their arguments influenced by their values. SEE ALSO: *value freedom*; *value neutrality*; *value relevance*.

Some sociologists argue that objectivity in some or all of the above senses is not necessarily desirable; they suggest that the sociologist, for example, should be critical and espouse particular values. Yet others argue that objectivity in sociology is both possible and desirable. Positions here range from the claim that sociology is like natural science and objectivity can be protected by open debate and the use of rigorous methods, to more complex arguments like those of WEBER, who argues for the position of value-relevance.

SEE ALSO: *critical theory*; *Gouldner*; *sociology as science*.

occupational prestige See: PRESTIGE.

occupational segregation See: WOMEN AND WORK

occupational transition See: SOCIAL MOBILITY.

official statistics These are statistics produced by national and local governments, and by international agencies. Sociologists approach such data with caution, for two reasons. (1) Some official statistics are known to lack accuracy because of the way they are collected: for example, strike statistics. Inaccuracies are often systematic and do not cancel each other out, making the use of official statistics perilous: the classic example of these dangers is E. Durkheim's use of SUICIDE statistics, which under-recorded suicides in socially integrated and rural communities. (2) The categorization of data reflects the interests of government and may not be meaningful to sociologists. For example, United Kingdom UNEMPLOYMENT statistics are presented in two different ways. The first records as unemployed people who have registered at the local benefits office and excludes those who are out of work but do not register. The second records people who are available to start work within two weeks and have either been looking for work over the last month or are waiting to start a job already obtained. Many of those excluded from the official categories are people (mainly women) who for one reason or another fail to qualify for benefits and those who have taken early retirement, willingly or otherwise, rather than search for work in adverse labour market conditions. Data collected by government for its own use are in this case not useful to sociologists concerned with, say, the incidence of unemployment among different groups.

The investigation of the social processes that lie behind the collection and categorization of official statistics, however, has proved a fertile area of research, as criminologists have demonstrated with CRIMINAL STATISTICS.

SEE ALSO: *strikes*.

oligarchy In his analysis of the German Social Democratic Party in the early twentieth century, MICHELS (1911) argued that labour organizations with democratic aims, such as POLITICAL PARTIES and TRADE UNIONS, experienced a tension between the need for efficiency and membership control of the making and execution of policy. As they grew in size, labour organizations became more complex and permanent bureaucracies developed to cope efficiently with the problems of administration. The officials, by virtue of their expertise and experience, became indispensable and difficult to change even when subject to periodic re-election. Once they occupied this strong position, the leaders began to emancipate themselves from member control and to displace member goals with their own. These goals were usually less radical than those of the members and the official party or union ideology. As they controlled the channels of communication, they manipulated the flow of information to help buttress their positions. In the final analysis, goal displacement depended on the apathy and lack of involvement of members with issues of party or union government.

The modern study of trade-union government and the internal structure of mass political parties has been deeply influenced by Michels' pessimism, though research shows that the 'iron law' of oligarchy does not always apply in such organizations.

SEE ALSO: *elite; incorporation*.

ontological security This term refers to the security, order and regularity that people feel in their lives, which are likely to be most clearly experienced in a stable sense of personal IDENTITY over time.

ontology This branch of philosophy or metaphysics is concerned with the nature of existence. Ontological assumptions are those assumptions that underpin theories about what kind of entities can exist.

open-ended question In interview research, this sort of question allows respondents to say what they want, rather than require them to choose among answers that the interviewer has fixed in advance. Interviewers write down or tape-record the answers. The replies of all respondents are considered together later and are either coded for statistical analysis or used as they are for the purposes of quotation.

SEE ALSO: *coding; questionnaire*.

operationalization To operationalize a concept is to provide a way of measuring and quantifying it so that it may be tested. In the process, a relatively abstract theory is turned into a set of more concrete propositions. For example, the concept EXTENDED FAMILY may be operationalized by counting the number of times adults see their parents in any one week, or by measuring the financial flows among members of an extended family. Some sociologists, but certainly not all, believe that if a concept cannot be operationalized, it is fruitless or meaningless.

SEE ALSO: *falsificationism; Popper.*

ordinal See: MEASUREMENT LEVELS.

organic analogy This attempts to understand the structure and function of human society by analogy with the nature of living organisms. For example, society, like an organism in nature, becomes more complex and differentiated in terms of its social structure through evolutionary change. The organic analogy is often contrasted with the mechanistic analogy of society. The former treats society as a natural phenomenon which exists independently of human planning; the latter regards society as the project of human construction, just as a machine is an artefact of human design. The organic analogy is often associated with conservative thought because it suggests that society cannot be changed by political intervention. The mechanistic analogy was associated with the notion of 'social engineering' by which deliberate changes in social arrangements could be achieved. The so-called 'organistic school of sociology' was represented in England by SPENCER.

SEE ALSO: *evolutionary theory; functionalism; social Darwinism; urban ecology.*

organic solidarity See: DURKHEIM.

organization man In *The Organization Man* (1956), W. H. Whyte identified a new breed of business executives, working for large corporations, whose lives were dominated by their firms. Firms demanded total commitment and expected executives to move from town to town, even between continents, as they were shifted from post to post. The more successful the executive, the more moves he made as he spiralled upwards within a firm. The total dedication of organization men meant they adapted their personalities to fit the bureaucratic organizational environment, they had no roots in any local community, no real friends and little contact with their extended families.

SEE ALSO: *spiralist.*

organization theory This describes a set of empirical and conceptual observations about (1) the factors affecting organizational structure and (2) the social behaviour of people in enterprises, particularly of technical, professional and managerial staff.

Organization theory grew out of the analysis of the sociology of BUREAUCRACY. This led to the recognition that there are a variety of organizational forms and managerial structures. In *The Management of Innovation* (1961), T. Burns and G. M. Stalker distinguished between bureaucratic systems, which they called 'mechanistic' and described as being suitable for stable conditions such as uncompetitive markets and unchanging technology, and non-bureaucratic or 'organic' forms which maximize personal discretion, decentralize decision-making and minimize rule-bound behaviour where possible. They saw the latter as better for changing conditions. This insight fostered what became known as the *contingency* approach, which establishes relationships among different structures and various contextual factors, notably economic environment, technology and size. Organizational forms differ on several dimensions: complexity; specialization of tasks; and formalization of roles and procedures. The contingency approach assumes that different forms of organization are appropriate for different contexts. The approach is descriptive, demonstrating associations among structural and contextual variables rather than explaining causal connections. Nor are the associations particularly close and they allow for a variety of structures in any given context.

Research into business history has also influenced the study of organizational structure. The traditional firm was an enterprise based on a single unit with all operations under one roof, or at least on one site. The rise of the giant corporation in the twentieth century has created firms that are multi-unit, operating in a variety of different industrial and commercial sectors and across vast geographical distances. Business historians note that there has been a corresponding organizational shift from a unitary organization (known as U-form), with a direct chain of command and tight control of all operations from the top of the company, to a new form of decentralization. Multi-divisionalism (M-form) groups together various subsidiary units into divisions, and each division is run as a semi-autonomous business. Corporate headquarters set financial targets, approve divisional business plans, appoint senior managerial staff, monitor performance and raise funds in the capital market, but they do not intervene in the day-to-day running of the divisions. The M-form was developed in the USA prior to the Second World War and was widely adopted by large companies in the second half of the century. Although the corporate structure is decentralized, there is no single organizational form or managerial structure within divisions.

During the 1980s and 1990s, many large companies decentralized further. One common innovation was the introduction of business units within divisions, whereby responsibility for all or most of the activities associated with a particular product or service was assigned to a single sub-unit, which was turned into a semi-autonomous profit centre with its own budget and control of its own resources. The aim was to create less bureaucratic organizations that would foster initiative and entrepreneurial behaviour among managers. They also developed their networks of outside suppliers, with whom they established close working relationships, and contracted out many operations previously done within the firm. In this way, they might benefit from the expertise of their suppliers and spread business risks outside the firm. Decentralization within the organization and to outsiders was intended to create a system that is more flexible and responds to change more rapidly. These developments in organizational structure have been conceptualized by theorists of organization in a number of ways. The most influential has been the theory of FLEXIBLE SPECIALIZATION.

Other approaches focus more on managerial behaviour, in particular on those aspects that are not determined by the organization's formal role prescriptions. These aspects are sometimes known as 'informal' or 'emergent' behaviour. The importance of interest groups is widely recognized. The hierarchical division of managers into different strata and the horizontal division into different specialist functions create conditions for distinct sub-groups to form. These often develop their own goals which may conflict with those of other groups or top management.

This indicates that managerial role performance can be problematic. The officially prescribed roles which appear as the formal organizational structure do not in fact determine behaviour. Managerial performance has attracted attention recently, as corporations have tried to devise more effective ways of ensuring that managers behave in desired ways. One method, following the structural changes in organizational design noted above, is to decentralize responsibility and authority and to make managers more directly responsible for outcomes. Others include: performance-related pay, where individuals are rewarded for achieving specified objectives; closer monitoring and surveillance of managers, made possible by the development of better information systems following computerization. Indeed, analysis of MANAGERIAL STRATEGIES OF CONTROL has become an important sub-area of study.

The importance of organizational power-holders for the determination of organizational structure and managerial behaviour was emphasized in a seminal paper by J. Child (1972). The adjustment of structure to contingencies is not automatic, but mediated through top corporate managers who make strategic choices. Their choices may include the sort of structure to establish (centralized or decentralized, for example) and the contextual factors that are to surround the enterprise – which markets to enter, such as what technology to use and how large to let the firm grow. The main power centre is the board of directors, which controls the distribution of resources. Such control provides top management with a major source of influence over the behaviour of subordinates, since groups lower down the hierarchy need resources if they are to survive, while individuals depend on top management for access to resources and rewards in the form of career advancement, or indeed to avoid dismissal.

The institutional approach to organizations, known as INSTITUTIONAL THEORY, assumes that organizations are significantly affected by their social environment. Thus contingencies will have different effects in different social milieux. According to their social environment, organizations will also differ in their structures and in the social behaviour of their members.

Bureaucratic theory maintained that there was one best form of organization, whereas the contingency approach has assumed that different forms are appropriate in different circumstances. In the 1980s and 1990s, the belief that there might be one best way reappeared in some quarters, because change was thought to be so pervasive that an 'organic' form would be the only viable one. The structure advocated by writers on management and the theory of flexible specialization is: (1) the maximum decentralization, within and outside the corporation; (2) managerial teams that cut across internal boundaries, such as departments, functions and divisions; (3) roles that are weakly prescribed and remain fluid, which do not constrain individuals but facilitate their initiative; (4) the minimum of rules and regulations. Because such a structure has a potential for chaos and loss of control, some adherents to this approach to organizational theory emphasize the importance of ORGANIZATIONAL CULTURE as the means to ensure that activities are coordinated in an orderly manner and that control is maintained. Sociologists are mainly critical of this approach to organizational culture, which they view as a complex phenomenon that need not produce these results.

SEE ALSO: *bounded rationality; labour process approach; management; managerial revolution; organization man; role; scientific management.*

READING: Reed (1992)

organizational culture CULTURE refers to the customary patterns of behaviour and shared values, beliefs and assumptions found within social groups. The concept has been extended to organizations in recent years by writers on management and organizations and, because they are mainly concerned with business organizations, it is used interchangeably with *corporate culture*. Management writers make three assumptions about organizational culture. (1) It is plastic and manipulable, and can be designed and shaped by the leaders of a business. (2) It is a unifying force. (3) It is linked to organizational effectiveness and business performance via employee motivation.

The management literature advocates that top managers should create 'strong' cultures. These foster the belief among employees that they belong to a firm which is also a social community with shared values and where there are no conflicts of interest; they lead people to identify positively with the goals of the company (i.e. of top management) and thus to work effectively with few formal controls; and they result in the internalization of the sorts of behaviour desired by top management, which in turn allows organizational rules and monitoring to be reduced. Effective cultures should allow organizations to become more 'organic' in the language of ORGANIZATION THEORY. The success of Japanese companies is partly attributed to strong organizational cultures.

Other social scientists are critical of these normative views. E. Schein (1985) analyses organizational culture as a product of the experience of social groups. Groups are likely to develop strong cultures if they have a stable and homogeneous membership and stay together for a long period of time. Cultures embody the solutions that groups have found to two issues: problems of internal integration and problems of adaptation to the outside environment. Culture forms and changes slowly, particularly at the level of taken-for-granted assumptions. New members of a group have to be socialized into its culture. This analysis has significant implications. (1) Organizations may contain various subcultures based on different groups, rather than a single organizational culture. Organization theory shows how emergent behaviour in groups differs from the formal organizational role prescriptions, and group cultures may similarly differ from those propounded by top management and be resistant to manipulation. (2) Group cultures may be forces of organizational disunity; for example, when a labour force unites around a set of assumptions and beliefs that oppose top management. (3) Creating an organizational culture is likely to be a difficult and slow business and, if it contradicts existing group cultures, is unlikely to succeed however long organizational leaders persevere. (4) A further point, additional to Schein's analysis, is that existing cultural patterns deriving from the wider society will affect the cultures within an organization.

Sociologists have in the past focused on group subcultures. However, the claims of management writers and the efforts made by practising managers to manipulate meanings and symbols have led to a new interest in defining the concept more rigorously and investigating organizational cultures empirically.

SEE ALSO: *labour process approach*; *managerial strategies of control*.
READING: Alvesson (1993)

Oriental despotism Contemporary debates concerning despotism originated in eighteenth-century France. For C. Montesquieu (1748), political systems were divided into republics, monarchies and despotisms according to the principles of virtue, honour and fear. The differences between monarchy and Oriental despotism were: (1) monarchies were based on stable hierarchical stratification, but despotism involved general slavery; (2) in monarchy, the prince followed custom, whereas the potentate ruled by arbitrary whim; (3) in despotism, there were no intervening institutions between the subject and government. In the physiocratic tradition, the enlightened despot was expected to remove traditional constraints on progress and economic development, whereas the Oriental despot was enslaved by arbitrary inclinations. For utilitarians, despotisms were the basis of tradition and ignorance, reinforced by priestly control. In Marxism, Oriental despotism was associated with the ASIATIC MODE OF PRODUCTION; the arbitrary character of political life was connected with the fact that, in Oriental societies, the state controlled the land. Oriental despotism was a society in which the state dominated civil society in the absence of individualism, rights of representation or personal freedoms. Oriental despotisms were arbitrary, stagnant and backward.

Recent debates have been organized around K. Wittfogel's (1957) argument that the nationalization of land under Stalin involved the continuity of despotism from Tsarist to socialist Russia. Asiatic conditions were preserved in the transition from Oriental to party bureaucracy. WEBER (1950; 1951; 1958b) also argued that the political systems of the Orient were patrimonial bureaucracies; these states were arbitrary and despotic. The social conditions for patrimonial despotism were the absence of autonomous cities, rational law and private property.

SEE ALSO: *patrimonialism*.

READING: Venturi (1963)

Orientalism Defined by E. Said (1978) as an academic DISCOURSE that creates a rigid East–West dichotomy, in which dynamic and positive values are ascribed to Western civilization. The original conflict between East and West was first expressed in Christian theology, in its criticism of the claims to revelation in Judaism and Islam which were defined as 'false' religions. With the development of IMPERIALISM in the nineteenth century, the term was used more widely to justify colonial settlement, because indigenous peoples were assumed to be incapable of social development. Orientalism came (1) to create the racial myth of the 'lazy native', who was unable to work efficiently for a wage; (2) to argue that Oriental societies were stationary, because they had no dynamic mechanism for social change such as a property-owning bourgeoisie; and (3) to claim that modernization had to be imposed through imperial administrations. Classical Orientalism was a product of power struggles to establish colonial dominance. Although in the twentieth century there has been a significant process of de-colonization in Asia and the Middle East, Orientalism continues to create a sense of strangeness (or 'otherness') towards 'outsiders' – for example, towards followers of Islam. The critique of Orientalism has argued that the distinction between East and West is arbitrary, and that attitudes towards 'outsiders' are typically based on PREJUDICE and STEREOTYPES which ignore historical and regional variations.

SEE ALSO: *Asiatic mode of production; globalization; Oriental despotism; racism; world religions*.

orientation to work See: WORK ATTITUDES.

other-directedness The other-directed person depends exclusively on constant approval and support of others for confirmation of his or her self-image. This conformist personality is seen as the product of mass consumer society.

overdetermine This term expresses the notion within modern Marxism that even the most important element of the social structure not only determines other elements but is also affected by them. It was originally used by ALTHUSSER to indicate that what he and other Marxists saw as the basic CONTRADICTION in society, between capital and labour, could be modified (overdetermined) by other contradictions, for example that between urban and rural. The concept therefore forms part of his objection to economic DETERMINISM in Marxism.

oversocialized conception of man A phrase coined by WRONG (1961) to describe and criticize the functionalist approach to ROLE. He argued that there will always be a tension between human nature and conformance to social expectations, because people are not dominated by their need for social acceptance.

ownership and control See: MANAGERIAL REVOLUTION.

Pacific Rim See: DEPENDENCY THEORY; NEWLY INDUSTRIALIZING COUNTRIES.

panel study This technique, also known as a longitudinal study, involves collecting data from the same sample at intervals over time. Panels are useful for studying trends and the effects of particular changes. Difficulties include the initial selection of the sample, when it may be hard to find people willing to join a long-term investigation; conditioning, which is a real problem as panel members may cease to be representative of the wider population simply as the result of being on the panel; and sample mortality, the consequence of panel members moving, dying or losing interest.

panopticism J. Bentham (1748–1832) proposed a new type of prison, a circular building constructed around a central hub that housed the prison guards, which would allow the guards to maintain complete visual surveillance of all the prisoners. He called this the 'panopticon'. The concept of panopticism was developed by FOUCAULT in *Discipline and Punish* (1975) to describe any form of rational, detailed and bureaucratic SURVEILLANCE, for example in factories and hospitals.

SEE ALSO: *total institution*.

paradigm In its sociological use, this term derives from the work of T. S. Kuhn (1970) on the nature of scientific change. For Kuhn, scientists work within paradigms, which are general ways of seeing the world and which dictate what kind of scientific work should be done and what kinds of theory are acceptable. These paradigms provide what Kuhn calls 'normal science', the kind of science routinely done day after day. Over time, however, normal science produces a series of anomalies which cannot be resolved within the paradigm. Kuhn argues that at this point there is a sudden break, and the old paradigm is replaced by a new one, leading to a new period of normal science. In sociology, the term has a still vaguer usage, denoting schools of sociological work or meta-theories, each of which is relatively self-contained, with its own methods and theories.

SEE ALSO: *meta-theory*.

Pareto, Vilfredo (1848–1923) An Italian engineer, economist and sociologist, his most significant contribution to the social sciences was as a founder of mathematical economic theory. As a sociologist, he is best known for his discussion of elites and his view that there existed a cyclical process leading to the replacement or 'circulation' of elites over time. He distinguished between elites and non-elites, and, within the ranks of the ELITE, between the governing fraction and the rest. In his view, 'circulation' occurred because some people (the 'lions') were more suited to the maintenance of the *status quo* under stable conditions, while others (the 'foxes') were adaptive and innovative and coped better during periods of change.

His major sociological work was *Trattato di sociologia generale*, published in Italy in 1916 and translated as *The Mind and Society* (1963), in which he put forward his elite theory and a general analytical scheme for sociology. He distinguished sociology from economics on the grounds that the latter discipline dealt only with one aspect of human action, namely logical action, which was the rational choice of the most appropriate means for a given end, in this case the acquisition and allocation of scarce resources. Sociology, however, dealt with the non-logical actions that made up most of social life. These were non-logical because they did not derive from methodical observation and rational deliberation, and were determined by 'sentiments' rather than scientific method. He saw non-logical beliefs – explanations of social phenomena in terms other than those of natural science – as having a major influence in society.

Within the realm of the non-logical he distinguished *residues* and *derivations*. He saw residues as universal elements that reflected basic human sentiments, and derivations as variable elements. Of six types of residue, Pareto identified two as especially important: the tendency for people to make connections even if they are unaware of any logical or observed link between the elements, which he called the 'residue of combinations'; and the propensity to preserve the things combined, which he referred to as 'residues of the persistence of aggregates'. In the circulation of elites, the 'foxes' represented the residue of combination and the 'lions' the residue of persistence. Derivations were the non-logical arguments used to justify the conclusions drawn from residues as premises, which included assertion, appeal to authority, accordance with sentiment and verbal proofs. Pareto's influence on the subsequent development of sociology has been twofold. His distinction between non-logical social action and logical economic action informed the position of the HUMAN RELATIONS school, that workers were guided by irrational sentiments whereas managerial policies were rational economic decisions. His view that societies could be analysed as systems with self-equilibriating properties, deriving from theoretical mechanics, later influenced PARSONS and other structural functionalists.

READING: Parsons (1968b)

Park, Robert E. (1864–1944) After a varied career as journalist, student of G. Simmel and political worker, Park joined the Department of Sociology at Chicago University in 1914, where he remained for twenty years. He was a major figure in the CHICAGO SCHOOL and was responsible for its focus on urban life, community and race relations, its empirical slant and the development of PARTICIPANT OBSERVATION as a research technique. With E. Burgess he wrote *Introduction to the Science of Society* in 1921. He saw social relations as being dominated by four principles: cooperation, competition, ACCOMMODATION and ASSIMILATION. He applied these to the study of social change in the city. His influence extended beyond his own writings, which were mainly essays, and he trained a whole generation of American sociologists. E. C. Hughes and J. Masuoka, with others, collected and edited Park's papers, which were published in three volumes between 1950 and 1955.

SEE ALSO: *urban ecology*.

parole See: SAUSSURE.

Parsons, Talcott (1902–79) The son of a Congregational minister, Parsons spent the whole of his adult life in academic positions in the United States, with a short period of postgraduate training in Europe. He had a powerful influence on sociology after the Second World War, particularly in America, although, being a theorist, he was not in the dominant tradition of US empirical research. As often criticized as supported, Parsons' work was at the centre of debate in sociological theory until the mid 1970s. He wrote a great deal, his principal publications being: *The Structure of Social Action* (1937); *Toward a General Theory of Action* (1951), edited with E. A. Shils; *The Social System* (1951); *Working Papers in the Theory of Action* (1953), with R. F. Bales and E. A. Shils; *Economy and Society* (1956), with N. Smelser; *Social Structure and Personality* (1964); *Societies: Evolutionary and comparative perspectives* (1966); *The System of Modern Societies* (1971).

Parsons' aim was nothing less than to provide a conceptual structure for the whole of sociology which would serve also to integrate all the social sciences. This was to be accomplished by a synthesis between the analysis of individual action and analysis of large-scale social systems. His starting point is the theory of social *action*, the essential feature of which is the relationship between actors and features of their environment, social and natural, to which they give meaning. The most important features of the environment are other people, which suggests further that social *interaction*, in which actors have to take notice of the actions, wishes and aims of others, should be the focus of inquiry. In these interactions, norms and values are critical as they regulate and make predictable the behaviour of others. SOCIALIZ-ATION ensures that individuals internalize norms and values as they grow up. Parsons treats personality and social systems as complementary, though in his analysis the latter ultimately determine the former.

Parsons notes that social interaction has a *systematic* character, hence his use of the term SOCIAL SYSTEM. The concept that bridges social action and social system is that of *pattern variables*. He defines these as the fundamental dilemmas that face actors. Social systems may be characterized by the combinations of solutions offered to these dilemmas. There are four sets of dilemmas. (1) Particularism versus universalism: actors have to decide whether to judge a person by general criteria (universalism) or criteria unique to that person (particularism). (2) Performance versus quality: actors have to decide whether to judge persons by what they do (performance) or by their personal characteristics (quality). (3) Affective neutrality versus affectivity: actors can either engage in a relationship for instrumental reasons without the involvement of feelings (affective neutrality) or for emotional reasons (affectivity). (4) Specificity versus diffuseness: actors have to choose, in any situation, between engaging with others totally across a wide range of activity (diffuseness) or only for specific, structured purposes (specificity).

These pattern variables structure any system of interaction. Such systems, however, also have certain needs of their own which have to be met, required both by the relationship between the social system and its environment and by the internal workings of the system. There are four such *functional needs* (known as AGIL): (1) adaptation: the need to relate to the environment by taking resources from it; (2) goal attainment: the setting of goals for the system; (3) integration: the maintenance of internal order; (4) latency or pattern maintenance: the generation of sufficient motivation to perform tasks. In order to meet each of these functional requirements, groups of actions or sub-systems of action develop. At the most general level, for example, the cultural sub-system discharges the function of integration. Each of these sub-systems in turn is also faced by the same four functional needs and consequently each sub-system can be divided into four sub-sub-systems. In the social system as a whole, the economy performs the function of adaptation, for example. In theory, there is no limit to the subdivision of systems and Parsons does describe in detail the structure of the economy and the relations between it and the other sub-systems of the social system.

Parsons holds that systems of social action tend to equilibrium even if they never actually reach it, and that social change is movement from one state of equilibrium to another. Change in the system is achieved by DIFFERENTIATION and in his later work Parsons used EVOLUTIONARY THEORY to describe the progressive changes in society that result from this. A number of criticisms have been levelled at Parsons: (1) his is a GRAND THEORY of little empirical use; (2) he gives too much importance to values and norms; (3) he does not pay enough attention to social conflict; (4) he is unable to reconcile action theory and system theory, and in effect sees individual action as structurally determined; (5) his functionalism involves TELEOLOGY.

SEE ALSO: *action theory; actor/social actor*.

participant observation In its strict usage, this refers to a research technique in which the sociologist observes a social collectivity of which he or she is also a member. Such participation allows the sociologist to observe covertly, without the collectivity being aware. This is easiest in large and 'open' communities. Classic examples are the two studies of an American town known as 'Middletown', conducted by R. S. and H. M. Lynd (1929; 1937). The method has occasionally been used successfully in smaller and more 'closed' collectivities in the study of organizations and occupations, when researchers have taken employment among the population being studied. A notable example is the study of restriction of output among industrial employees conducted by D. Roy (1952; 1953; 1955). In its looser usage, the term describes the form of observation in which the observer is known to be an outside investigator by those being studied. This is the case in ethnographic studies by anthropologists and in much sociological research.

The advantage of the covert approach is that the setting remains natural and the presence of the observer creates no artificial changes, which is a major risk of open observation. But it raises an ethical dilemma, whether one should observe people as objects of study without their consent. Both forms are confronted by the same problem, that the observer may gain only a restricted and partial understanding of the situation, because the observer's role may not provide access to the total population under investigation. For this reason, participant observation is sometimes supplemented by other forms of data collection.

When done well, this technique can provide data that may well have greater authenticity and validity than the more common sample survey approach. It is far more time-consuming, however, and makes greater demands on the research worker's skill and personality.

SEE ALSO: *ethnography; qualitative research*.

READING: Cicourel (1964)

pastoralism This refers to a form of SUBSISTENCE ECONOMY in which communities derive their livelihood from tending species of domesticated animals and wander in search of adequate grazing. Historically, the relationship between nomadic and settled agriculturalists was conflictual and, in the modern period, there are strong governmental pressures to settle nomads who are perceived as a threat to stable communities.

paternalism The use of a term describing the relationship between a father and a child to characterize that between superiors and subordinates captures much of the quality of paternalism. The father–child analogy provided M. Weber with his model of traditional political authority as PATRIMONIALISM, in which the authority of a master over his household (patriarchalism) was extended to the administration of whole territories. In the political case, subordinates gave their loyalty and obedience to a patriarch in return for his protection. Paternalism refers to the organization of economically productive units, agricultural and industrial, and is a way of regulating relationships between the owners of the means of production or their agents and subordinates that also draws on the patriarchal model. It has a number of features. (1) It depends on differential access to power and resources: the subordinate is unable to command sufficient resources to support himself or herself but must depend on the paternalist. (2) There is an ideological dimension that justifies subordination, emphasizing the caring role of the paternalist. (3) It is a collective form of social organization: the paternalist may be a single person, but his subordinates are treated collectively. (4) Paternalism has a tendency to become systematized and institutionalized when it occurs in modern industry, forming part of the organizational rule system. (5) Paternalism is typically a diffuse relationship which covers all aspects of subordinates' lives, which deals with the whole person rather than confining itself to specific activities.

Paternalism differs from conventional capitalist relations: (1) it assumes inequality of power, whereas the formal ideology of capitalism is that economic exchanges are contracts between equals; (2) the diffuse involvement of subordinates contrasts with the typical capitalist employment relationship based on the segmental involvement of employees and the separation of work and non-work life, where the CASH NEXUS may be the only tie binding employees and employers.

The classic cases of agricultural paternalism were found in the plantations of the Old and New Worlds. Industrial paternalism in Europe and America was mainly confined to the early years of the factory system and the transition to a modern industrialized economy. In Japan, however, among modern, large-scale corporations, it continued into the second half of the twentieth century.

SEE ALSO: *latifundia; patron–client relations*.

path analysis This is a particular application of the statistical technique of REGRESSION. In its multiple form, regression permits relations among several variables and their interactions to be studied simultaneously. In path analysis, one assumes that a particular causal model explains the relationships among variables. A causal linkage means that one variable precedes another in time and that influence is one-directional. The path coefficient (standardized regression coefficient) is computed for each assumed causal linkage. The model is then presented diagrammatically as a mapping of the variables and their causal linkages, with the relevant path coefficient attached to each linkage. The geneticist S. Wright first used this technique in the 1920s, and sociologists began to use it widely in the 1960s. The most celebrated use of path analysis in sociology was in P. M. Blau and O. D. Duncan's study (1967) of the relative importance of different factors in influencing occupational attainment in the United States.

SEE ALSO: *causal modelling; interaction of variables; multivariate analysis.*

READING: Duncan (1966; 1975)

path dependency See: INSTITUTIONAL THEORY.

patriarchy This concept is used to describe the dominance of men over women, a dominance which appears in several quite different kinds of society. It is also used to describe a type of household organization in which an older man dominates the whole household, including younger men. While male dominance is often explained biologically, usually by reference to the necessary reproductive functions of women, most sociologists argue that patriarchy refers to social, not natural relations. There is considerable debate about the sociological explanation of patriarchy. It has been suggested, for example, that compulsory heterosexuality, male violence, the way men are organized in the workplace and socialization into GENDER roles are all causal factors.

There are three recent accounts of patriarchy offered by feminist sociologists. (1) Patriarchy functions as ideology. This is a view deriving from the work of the French psychoanalyst and structuralist J. Lacan (1966), who argues that a society's culture is dominated by the symbol of the phallus. (2) Patriarchy is essentially based on the household in which men dominate women, economically, sexually and culturally. More narrowly, women exchange their unpaid domestic services for their upkeep. In this perspective, the marriage contract is a labour contract through which the husband controls the labour of his wife. (3) Marxist feminists have argued that the domination of women by men is intimately connected with capitalism, because patriarchy and capitalism are mutually supportive. Within the household, women's DOMESTIC LABOUR supports men, an expense which would otherwise fall on capital. Outside the home, the segregation of women into certain occupations has, it is argued, enabled employers to keep their wages down.

SEE ALSO: *division of labour; feminism; matriarchy; mode of production; sex roles; stereotypes; women and work.*

READING: Evans (1982)

patrilineal A system of descent in which kinship is traced through the father.

SEE ALSO: *agnatic; cognate/cognatic; descent groups; matrilineal.*

patrimonialism In M. Weber's sociology, patrimonialism is a form of traditional political domination in which a royal household exercises arbitrary power through a bureaucratic apparatus. In patrimonial systems, administration and political force are under the direct, personal control of the ruler. The support for patrimonial power is provided, not by forces recruited from a landowning aristocracy, but by slaves, conscripts and mercenaries. Weber regarded patrimonialism as (1) politically unstable because it is subject to court intrigue and palace revolts, and (2) a barrier to the development of rational capitalism. Patrimonialism was thus an aspect of

Weber's explanation of the absence of capitalist development in Oriental societies in which personal rulership was dominant.

SEE ALSO: *feudalism; Oriental despotism; paternalism; slavery.*

READING: Weber (1922)

patron–client relations Unlike PATERNALISM, patronage involves a relationship between two individuals, namely a patron and a client. The relationship is found universally, though it is institutionally recognized and sanctioned on a limited scale since patronage offends the achievement culture of many Western societies. However, it has been argued by R. Jackall (1988), that patronage is an important aspect of management in contemporary US organizations. Patron–client relations make good the inadequacies of formal institutions, and the special relationship with someone of influence or wealth protects the subordinate client from a potentially hostile environment. Developed systems of patronage are found in Latin American and Mediterranean societies.

pattern variables See: PARSONS.

peasants Peasants are a class characterized by small-scale agricultural production, economic self-sufficiency, low division of labour and relative political isolation from urban working classes. The peasantry is often differentiated into separate social strata, according to the amount of land they cultivate and the security of their rights over land. Thus it is common for sociologists to distinguish between 'rich peasants', 'middle peasantry' and 'landless peasants', although the dividing line between these strata is often arbitrary. Peasants owning only small plots of land are typically forced to rent land in return for labour, cash or a share of the harvest (known as 'sharecropping'), or to engage in petty trade, or to become migrant, urban workers. In the twentieth century, the growth of international trade and the spread of capitalist relations of production have had a profound effect on peasants, often increasing their impoverishment through rent increases and the rising price of materials, such as fertilizers. Peasants have become increasingly dependent on the production of commercial crops for export, the prices of which are subject to major fluctuations on the world market. Peasant indebtedness to rural moneylenders typically forces the peasant into the category of landless rural proletariat. Both historically and in the contemporary situation, the nature of peasant ownership of land is complex and variable. Peasants may have customary rights to cultivation either as individuals or as a village community, they may have a legal entitlement to land, or they may be landless. In FEUDALISM, peasant serfdom meant that the economic surplus was raised by landlords through rent (in kind, money or labour). The development of capitalist agriculture converts the peasant into a rural labourer by undermining customary peasant ownership (typically by land enclosures) and by destroying the self-sufficiency of the peasant producer (typically by increasing rent and reducing the size of land tenures).

In the nineteenth century, a number of writers argued that the geographical isolation and economic independence of peasant communities made the peasantry a politically conservative factor in European societies. Contemporary studies, however, have concentrated on peasant participation in revolutionary changes in the Third World. Three important changes radicalize the peasantry: (1) the DEMO-GRAPHIC TRANSITION has profoundly altered land/population ratios, leading to population pressure on agricultural resources; (2) capitalist development of agriculture, production of export commodities and land reform have disturbed traditional methods of farming and altered the range of crops produced; (3) rural society has been transformed as landowners and merchants have responded to the new market forces.

There has also been much discussion as to the nature of peasant radicalism and peasant class consciousness. In pre-capitalist societies, peasant rebellions against land-tenure conditions and rent increases were very widespread in Europe and 'social banditry' was a seasonal occupation for many peasants. In modern times, it has been argued that peasant consciousness is in fact traditional (in wanting to restore customary practices and village conditions) and that peasant rebelliousness cannot become genuinely revolutionary without an alliance with urban workers and external political leadership. Without political direction and political education, Marxist sociologists suggest that peasant rebelliousness will either remain traditional or ephemeral. It is thus claimed that MILLENARIANISM is a typical example of a traditional peasant consciousness.

SEE ALSO: *mobilization; subsistence economy.*

READING: Wolf (1971)

pedagogical practices Pedagogy is the art of teaching. Different practices are informed by different educational philosophies and their assumptions about learning, the intellectual status of the child, teaching style and curricula. Conservative or *closed* pedagogy sees learning as the absorption of specific bodies of knowledge, the child's ability as determined by hereditary and environmental factors external to the school, the appropriate teaching style as one where teachers are experts, and have authority over pupils, and direct the learning of subordinates, and the curriculum as the relevant CLASSROOM KNOWLEDGE as defined by teachers. Liberal or *open* pedagogy conceives of learning as a process and not the acquisition of specific knowledge, the child's mind as capable of development, teaching as simply guiding this development, and curricula as tailored to suit pupils' own expressed interests.

The spread of 'progressive' and 'child-centred' teaching methods since the 1960s, the open pedagogy, has been interpreted in different ways. While P. Freire (1972) argues that it has radical political implications because it emphasizes personal autonomy rather than social control, others claim that fully developed 'progressive' methods are rarely found beyond the early years of the primary school and are unlikely to have any lasting influence on attitudes, or that open pedagogy reflects the middle-class value system and is therefore unlikely to have radical implications beyond the school. Within the school, B. B. Bernstein (1977) suggests that the move towards integrated studies, an aspect of this pedagogy, may alter the power structure within the teaching staff. In principle, it also disturbs traditional authority relations between teachers and pupils, though in practice teachers resist change. The power of the HIDDEN CURRICULUM and the manner in which schools modify 'progressive' ideals in practice suggest that pedagogical practices remain fundamentally conservative.

peer group Technically a peer group is any collectivity in which the members share some common characteristic, such as age or ethnicity. It most commonly refers to age groups in general, but more specifically to adolescent groups where members are closely bound together by YOUTH CULTURE. Adolescent peer groups tend to have: (1) a high degree of social solidarity; (2) hierarchical organization; (3) a code which rejects, or contrasts with, adult values and experience. From an adult perspective, peer groups are often deviant because delinquency is supported by the rewards of group membership.

SEE ALSO: *subculture.*

penology The scientific study of the treatment and punishment of criminals, penology is conventionally regarded as a branch of CRIMINOLOGY and is associated with the movement away from retribution to correction in nineteenth-century penal reform. FOUCAULT showed that the development of penology was an aspect of an elaboration of discipline in the nineteenth century which employed new forms of knowledge to regulate individuals.

periodization Most accounts of historical change divide the sequence of events into periods. For example, the periodization adopted by Marxist theories of history is determined by changes in the dominant MODE OF PRODUCTION. Thus, one may speak of periods of history in which society is dominated by the feudal mode of production, or the monopoly stage of the capitalist mode of production. Sociologists have also argued that the development of electronic communication has brought about a revolutionary transformation of society, namely a transition to POST-INDUSTRIAL SOCIETY. Philosophers of history have claimed that we are now in a period of post history, or POSTHISTOIRE, because there is no agreement that human history has any purpose, direction or meaning.

SEE ALSO: *postmodernism; postmodernity.*

READING: Niethamma (1992)

petite bourgeoisie A term used rather loosely to designate a CLASS of persons on the fringes of both the middle class and the working class who may own productive property but whose income is fairly low and whose conditions of work are relatively poor. For example, peasants and small farmers own land, shopkeepers and small traders own their businesses, and self-employed craftsmen will be highly skilled and own tools and equipment. Sociologists, particularly Marxist sociologists, have had difficulty in fitting the petite bourgeoisie into a social-class framework based on the ownership of productive property, because its members have both middle-class and working-class characteristics. Furthermore, the class does have distinctive features. For instance, despite the fact that many members of the petite bourgeoisie live in working-class communities, their political behaviour and other attitudes are much more middle-class. Indeed, in recent history in continental Europe, the petite bourgeoisie has constituted an important base for fascist movements.

The distinctiveness, marginality and separation of the petite bourgeoisie is illustrated in empirical studies of small shopkeepers. The market share of small shops has declined but the number of shops has not declined proportionally. Shopkeepers typically work long hours, in poor conditions, for incomes little higher than those of manual workers. However, at the same time, small traders can accumulate money and tend to own houses and consumer durables to a greater extent than their working-class neighbours. Despite the apparent economic unattractiveness of shop-keeping, there is no shortage of recruits and small traders value independence and working for themselves above all else.

SEE ALSO: *bourgeoisie; fascism; Marxist sociology; stratification.*

READING: Bechhofer and Elliott (1981)

phenomenological sociology This is a type of sociology derived from phenomenological philosophy. It takes as its main aim the analysis and description of everyday life – the LIFE-WORLD and its associated states of consciousness. This study is carried out by 'bracketing off' judgements about social structure; that is, making no assumptions about the existence or causal powers of social structure. Phenomenologists argue that, although people generally take the everyday world for granted, a phenomenological analysis must show how it is made up.

Considered in this way, phenomenological sociology is part of that movement criticizing positivist methods in sociology. In particular, practitioners of the subject have objected to the notion that human beings are formed by social forces rather than creating the social world themselves, to the neglect of the meaning of human actions and to the use of causal analysis of human action. Phenomenologists have felt that these features tend to neglect the uniquely human character of social interaction.

Phenomenology has entered sociology largely through the work of SCHUTZ. However, the best-known sociological study informed by phenomenological principles is that by P. L. Berger and T. Luckmann (1967). Their starting point is a phenomenological analysis of the knowledge appropriate to everyday life. Such knowledge is almost always characterized by TYPIFICATION and is essentially oriented to solving practical problems. They then suggest that this everyday knowledge is creatively produced by individuals who are also influenced by the accumulated weight of institutionalized knowledge produced by others.

Phenomenological sociology has not greatly influenced sociology as a whole and has also been subjected to extensive criticism. It has been argued that it deals with trivial topics, is purely descriptive, has had very little empirical application and neglects the notion of social structure.

SEE ALSO: *agency and structure; ethnomethodology; Garfinkel; hermeneutics; sociology of everyday life; Verstehen.*

READING: Wolff (1978)

pilot study Prior to the main data collection phase of a research project, it is recommended that the investigator should pre-test the research design, including the techniques of data collection, in a small-scale, pilot study. This allows the final design to be modified, if need be.

plural societies These are societies fragmented into different racial, religious or linguistic groups. It originally had a more restricted meaning, describing the separate existence of ethnic communities within the division of labour, where the market provided the only context of social interaction between these ethnic groups. The degree of fragmentation will vary considerably from society to society, as will the relationship of social class to the different groups. In some societies, race and class tend to overlap, so that certain racial groups are found mainly in particular social classes, as appears to be the case in the United States, for example. In others, Brazil for instance, races may be fairly evenly distributed in the class structure.

SEE ALSO: *class; stratification; underclass.*

pluralism (1) This was a political philosophy developed by British liberals and socialists in the early twentieth century. Pluralism asserted the desirability of diffusing sovereign power widely among a variety of the associations of CIVIL SOCIETY – religious, economic, professional, educational and cultural – and fragmenting government into decentralized units. The goal was a society that would be dominated neither by the state nor by a single class. *Laissez-faire* capitalism, which ostensibly upheld individualistic values, in practice appeared to let a minority class control employment and regulate markets, and thus coerce the majority. The centralized state apparatus found in continental Europe at the time also threatened the individual. Pluralists saw small, closely knit groups as the natural form of association and the best defence of individual rights. In pluralist political philosophy, the STATE was to have a greatly reduced scope, and was to act as a fairly neutral mediator between conflicting interests. In its socialist form, pluralism became GUILD socialism.

(2) Pluralism in modern sociology was developed by US political sociologists in the 1960s and refers to social organizations, whether societies or smaller collectivities such as firms, in which power is diffused among various groups and institutions. A well-established analysis of business organizations holds that POWER is distributed between labour, management and capital (sometimes customers as well), that no party dominates the others, that all the parties therefore freely choose to cooperate with each other rather than being forced. This analysis has been challenged by the argument that capital and management do have far more power than labour and thus compel workers' cooperation. In the political context, pluralism has been thought to enhance democracy, because power is distributed among competing groups, none of which is powerful enough to dominate the others. Therefore each group can maintain its own interests. There has also been considerable debate whether pluralism is an accurate description of the political system, since the visible and apparently pluralistic exercise of power in democracies may conceal the fact that some groups or interests actually dominate. Thus pluralism may also be an IDEOLOGY that is used to describe a political system or some other imperatively coordinated social organization as pluralist when in reality it is not.

(3) The two approaches have been combined by P. Hirst (1989). He suggests that associationalism can be joined with group competition to create *associational democracy*. This would be an appropriate form of political organization for a socialist society.

SEE ALSO: *conflict theory*; *industrial conflict*; *pressure group*; *socialist societies*.

READING: Drum (1978)

policy research Sociologists may be hired to deploy the research methods and/or the substantive findings of sociological research to throw light on problems identified by clients. 'Policy research' describes this consultancy role. The aim normally is to enable clients to act on the social world in order to change it in desired ways. For example, specialists in the sociology of organizations might be hired by a company that is about to introduce a major organizational redesign, with the brief to research its ORGANIZATIONAL CULTURE and employee attitudes, and to recommend, in the light of these findings and prior sociological understanding of other organizations, how this should be achieved.

political behaviour A term largely specific to American political science, this refers to the political activity of individuals and its consequences for political institutions. The study of political behaviour covers issues such as participation and non-participation in politics and political organization, VOTING behaviour, political attitude formation and PUBLIC OPINION.

SEE ALSO: *political culture; political participation.*

political culture This concept describes the attitudes, beliefs and rules that guide a political system, which are determined jointly by the history of the system and the experiences of its members. It is used to characterize differences between national political systems and to analyse these in behavioural terms which draw on psychology and sociology. The study of political culture focuses on the content of this culture and the processes of socialization and internalization of political values. These include the various agencies of political socialization, such as family, education, mass media and political parties. It also focuses on the compatibility of political culture with the values and attitudes current in the wider national culture, elite and mass cultures. Attempts have been made to find common elements of political culture that relate to common political structures; for example, the elements of a 'civic culture' that G. A. Almond and S. Verba (1963) identified in five countries and have suggested is a vital ingredient of stable democracies. In the individual, this combines acceptance of and respect for political authority with a detachment and independence of such authority. The concept has proved too general in scope to be useful in comparative research.

SEE ALSO: *civil religion; democracy; dominant ideology thesis; ideology.*
READING: Almond and Powell (1978)

political economy This term was originally used to describe the work of certain eighteenth-century writers, such as Adam Smith, whose principal interest lay in the analysis of the production of wealth in relation to the wider constitution of society. In distinction from the way that economics developed as a highly specialized social science, nineteenth-century sociologists adhered to the eighteenth-century tradition of political economy and continued to insist that the study of economics and of society generally were inseparable. MARX, for example, argued that one could only understand the constitution of societies by analysing the MODE OF PRODUCTION, but also that it was impossible to understand the mode of production without an analysis of social arrangements, including property rights, IDEOLOGY and the class structure. In contemporary sociology, the term political economy is often applied to Marxist work in which the economy is the most important factor in social development, an apparently paradoxical change in the meaning of the term.

SEE ALSO: *economic determinism.*

political participation Taking part in the political processes that lead to the selection of political leaders and determine or influence public policy is referred to as political participation. The right to participate is a defining feature of democratic political systems, but is not fully exercised. Levels of political interest and apathy have often been taken as criteria of participation and non-participation, including party membership, expressed interest in politics and awareness of issues. Research shows that apathy is extensive and the politically concerned public is everywhere in the minority. Apart from party membership, however, these criteria do not really measure participation in the political process. The major criterion remains VOTING in elections, which is consistently somewhat higher than the other measures would suggest. There are wide national variations on all these indicators, including voting (the United States, for example, has notably lower election turn-outs than the majority of European nations). There have been attempts to correlate the different participation criteria with other variables such as occupation, age, gender, race, religion, education and social mobility. In America, where most of these studies have been conducted, there are small but consistent correlations which are not repeated for other nations. The lack of consistent relationships among the measures themselves, as well as between these measures and the other variables on an international scale, frustrates attempts to create overarching theories of political participation.

SEE ALSO: *democracy; mobilization; political parties; political process.*

READING: Dunleavy *et al.* (1997)

political parties These link the STATE to political forces in society by giving organized expression to interests and making them effective politically. The sociology of political parties covers a number of interrelated issues: the goals or political ideologies of different parties; the social bases of party support and the way support is mobilized; the distribution of power within party organizations. Parties need to mobilize the votes of non-members in elections, and this electoral necessity may constrain policies and modify goals, an aspect of the electoral process that is central to the political theory of representation though not always appreciated in studies of party organization.

Since MICHELS argued for the inevitability of OLIGARCHY in political parties, with its consequential betrayal of parties' political philosophies and the manipulation of rank-and-file by leadership, the analysis of organizational power has received considerable attention, with goals and membership frequently being studied in relation to this. Those who believe in the importance of ELITES suggest that the leaders of political parties are composed of people with common backgrounds, interests and values, mainly drawn from the higher social classes, and that the few who enter the elite from lower social backgrounds absorb this culture. Evidence from Britain, Canada and the United States confirms part of this argument, since all major parties are dominated by leaders recruited from restricted social backgrounds. Nevertheless, oligarchic tendencies do vary. Members of party elites do not all hold similar values and conflicts within elites may occur. These weaken leadership power and reduce the gap between members and leaders if different sections attempt to mobilize the rank-and-file in support of their views. Nor is the rank-and-file always willing to cede control of policy to leaders, and membership participation varies. Irrespective of the strength of oligarchic tendencies, parties have to retain members to maintain an effective electoral organization (except in single-party states where elections are predetermined), which limits how far leaders can ignore party goals and members' convictions.

Political systems are often studied in terms of the number of legitimate political parties which are constitutionally permitted to compete for the government of a society. F. von der Mehden (1969) considers political systems in terms of a continuum including societies without parties, one-party non-competitive states, one-party semi-competitive systems, two-party democratic systems and multi-party democratic systems. In developing societies, D. Apter (1965) has argued, the one-party system is crucial for the formation of national identity and rapid economic development, since a single political authority is more effective in the management of industrial development. Another contrast is between SOCIALIST SOCIETIES, where the party dominated the distribution of social rewards and the organization of the economy, and Western capitalist societies where there is a pluralistic competition between parties for electoral support.

Parties in Western political systems have tended to polarize between left- and right-wing ideologies, though the electoral system has an effect on the number of parties and the balance of political power: proportional representation tends to produce contests between a multiplicity of parties which have to combine to create governments, while non-proportional VOTING is more likely to result in contests that are in effect between two major parties (even in multi-party political systems). It is sometimes suggested that left–right party divisions reflect the class divisions in capitalist society. Against this, T. B. Bottomore (1979) argues that: (1) parties are alliances between a variety of distinctive groups with divergent interests; (2) these alliances are unstable and this results in the periodic development of splinter groups which typically occupy a centre position between left and right; (3) political parties are relatively autonomous from their class basis. In addition, there is often a gap between local class support for a party (the 'politics of support') and the capacity of any government to fulfil these aspirations at the state level (the 'politics of government'). This gap partly explains why parties often rapidly lose electoral support when in office.

While a multi-party state is often thought to be a system which is compatible with the pluralistic features of capitalist society, in historical terms capitalism has developed under a wide variety of political systems from FASCISM to liberal DEMOCRACY.

READING: Drum (1978); Dearlove and Saunders (1991); Dunleavy *et al.* (1997)

political process When people try to gain access to political power and to wield this for their own or group ends, they constitute the political process. The notion of a political process assumes that politics can be treated as an autonomous institutional sphere, not a view that finds much favour among contemporary sociologists. The study of this process focuses on the activities of POLITICAL PARTIES and interest groups, their internal organization, the nature of political decision-making, and the roles and backgrounds of politicians.

SEE ALSO: *voting*.

political sociology This is the study of politics at four levels: (1) political conflicts and struggles between states, namely the sociology of international relations; (2) the nature and role of the STATE within societies; (3) the nature and organization of political movements and parties; (4) the participation of individuals in politics, as shown, for example, in VOTING behaviour.

SEE ALSO: *authority; citizenship; civil society; democracy; dominant ideology thesis; elite; fascism; Gramsci; ideological state apparatus; incorporation; labour movement; Leninism; Lipset; Marx; Marxist sociology; Michels; Mosca; nationalism; oligarchy; Pareto; pluralism; political behaviour; political culture, political participation; political parties; political process; populism; power, psephology; relative autonomy; revolution; socialist societies; voluntary associations; Weber, working-class conservatism.*

READING: Dowse and Hughes (1986)

polity A generic term for the set of political institutions within a society.

polysemy While many writers argue that most texts (e.g. television programmes, newspaper articles, novels) contain a PREFERRED READING, they also contain several other meanings that may be less powerful: these texts are polysemic. It is almost impossible to produce a single, unified meaning for a text, and many producers or writers deliberately aim for multiple meanings – polysemy – by the use of such devices as irony.

Popper, Karl Raimund (1902–1996) Professor of logic and scientific method at the London School of Economics until his retirement in 1969, Sir Karl Popper contributed to a variety of philosophical debates in science and social philosophy. In the philosophy of science, he was famous for his principle of falsification, namely that a valid science aims to refute and not to defend its hypotheses. The ultimate criterion of science, as opposed to ideology, is its falsifiability. This position was developed in *The Logic of Scientific Discovery* (1959) and elaborated in *Conjectures and Refutations* (1963). In social theory, he was critical of determinism, which he associated with HISTORICISM and authoritarian politics in *The Open Society and Its Enemies* (1945) and *The Poverty of Historicism* (1957). Societies should be organized like philosophical arguments: they should be open to question and conjecture. He maintained that large-scale, planned social change cannot succeed and that only piecemeal social reform is possible. In his studies of physics, biology and natural sciences – *Of Clouds and Clocks* (1966), *Objective Knowledge* (1972), *Unended Quest* (1974), *The Open Universe* (1982a), *Quantum Theory and the Schism in Physics* (1982b) and *Realism and the Aim of Science* (1983) – he defended the HYPOTHETICO-DEDUCTIVE MODEL and REALISM. His views on science have been challenged as artificial, because in practice scientists attempt to defend their views by verification and not by refutation; they seek to maintain, not destroy, existing paradigms. His perspective on the limitations on planned social change has been criticized for its conservatism.

  SEE ALSO: *epistemology; falsificationism; positivism.*
  READING: Magee (1973)

popular culture Crudely, popular culture is often understood as the CULTURE of the mass of people or of subordinate classes. The contrast is with high culture, understood as the culture of an educated elite. Popular culture, according to this view, is therefore Hollywood cinema, most television, popular music and romantic fiction. High culture is French cinema, opera on television, classical music and poetry. In public debate, and sociological work up until the early 1970s, the contrast between high and popular culture was also seen as a contrast between the serious and the trivial, the educated and the uneducated, the demanding and the passive, the uncommercial and the commercialized, the authentic and the fake. The FRANKFURT SCHOOL, for instance, tended to describe the contrast in this way. More recently, there has been increased, sociological interest in forms of popular culture, often accompanied by more positive evaluations. Sociological studies of television and rock music, for example, have become branches of the discipline in their own right. Major theoretical approaches to sociology as a whole, such as feminism or POSTMODERNISM, have been very substantially involved in the study of popular culture. This explosion of sociological interest has accompanied a marked increase in the economic importance of the CULTURE INDUSTRIES in the period since the Second World War.

Theories of popular culture can be ranged along a continuum. At one extreme are those theories which propose that popular culture supports a dominant ideology, discourages critical thinking, reinforces conventional stereotypes and produces passive audiences. At the other extreme are arguments that celebrate popular culture as a creative expression of popular sentiments, appealing to an AUDIENCE that is far from passive and is capable of critical thought. While the former emphasizes the power of a constraining text, the latter argues for an active audience. While most sociological theories of popular culture fall short of celebrating all forms of popular culture, there has been a marked shift over the past twenty years towards the pole of the continuum that emphasizes the active audience.

SEE ALSO: *dominant ideology thesis; feminist social theory; mass society; subculture; youth culture.*

READING: Storey (1993)

population See: DEMOGRAPHY.

populism Social scientists use populism as a generic category to cover a variety of political phenomena. There has been considerable debate as to whether it is a movement or an ideology, or whether it exists at all. It is possible, however, to identify some common features. Populism is a distinctive form of political rhetoric that sees virtue and political legitimacy residing in 'the people', sees dominant elites as corrupt, and asserts that political goals are best achieved by means of a direct relationship between governments and the people, rather than being mediated by existing political institutions.

Following M. Canovan (1981), three forms of populism may be identified. (1) *Populism of the Little Man* describes the political orientation of small proprietors such as peasants, farmers and small businessmen who support private property and cooperation between small producers, but are distrustful of big business and government. Typically, this populism decries 'progress', whether it be urbanization, industrialization, or the growth of monopoly capitalism, which it sees as leading to moral decay, and calls for a return to the virtues of past eras. It distrusts politicians and intellectuals and may lead people to support either direct popular democracy or strong leaders who share the populist ideology. Examples include the agrarian populism of the American Populist Party in the 1890s, the European peasant parties and the Canadian Social Credit Party of the early twentieth century, and the non-agrarian populism of the post-war Scottish National Party (in its early years) and the nineteenth-century Norwegian Left. (2) *Authoritarian Populism* describes charismatic leaders who bypass the political elite to appeal directly to the people, often to their reactionary sentiments. Examples include fascists such as Hitler, and right-wing leaders such as de Gaulle. (3) *Revolutionary Populism* describes the idealization of the people and their collective traditions by intellectuals who reject elitism and 'progress'. This leads to a rejection of existing political institutions in favour of the seizure of power by the people, or in favour of charismatic leaders who claim to represent the people. Examples include the Russian Populists (Narodniks), intellectuals who during the 1860s claimed that socialism could be achieved without first going through capitalism, by building on existing peasant communes, and the later support of FASCISM among certain European intellectuals.

Populism cannot be fitted easily into the conventional frameworks of political analysis. It may be either right or left, or neither. It is often reactionary, calling for a return to traditional virtues, but some populist leaders, such as Perón in Argentina, have worked for social and economic modernization and eschewed reactionary rhetoric. Nor is it possible to identify a definite pattern of social and economic conditions under which populism occurs; particular types of populism are not systematically related to particular social classes nor to specific economic circumstances.

READING: Laclau (1977)

positional goods Those goods or services whose desirability lies in the fact that they are scarce, such as Rolls-Royce cars, hand-made furniture or antique Chinese porcelain. Their scarcity can lie in their high price or in their cult status. There is a paradox in their acquisition in that, if more people acquire them, they therefore become less desirable.

SEE ALSO: *consumer society*.

positivism An approach in the philosophy of science, positivism is characterized mainly by an insistence that science can deal only with observable entities known directly to experience and is opposed to metaphysical speculation without concrete evidence. The positivist aims to construct general laws or theories which express relationships between phenomena. Observation and experiment will then show that the phenomena are or are not related in the predicted way; explanation of phenomena consists in showing that they are instances of the general laws or regularities. In sociology, positivism is identified with a conviction that sociology can be scientific in the same way as, say, physics, a marked preference for measurement and quantification, and a tendency towards social structural explanations as distinct from those which refer to human intentions and motives.

The term was introduced into sociology by COMTE, who held that the subject should be scientific, which meant dealing only with propositions that were directly testable. DURKHEIM was also a positivist in that he believed in the importation into sociology of the methods of science, in the establishment of laws of the causal relations of social phenomena, and in the rejection, in favour of social structures, of motives and intentions as causal agents. Durkheim's *Suicide* (1897) has been taken as a textbook example of a scientific sociology and was particularly influential in the development of American sociology in the 1930s and in the immediate post-war period. Much research at the time favoured the minute OPERATIONALIZATION of classical concepts like anomie and alienation and the importance of research techniques leading to quantifiable conclusions. In this tradition, sociological notions that were not measurable were deemed meaningless.

In recent sociological debate, positivism has been the subject of three main lines of criticism. (1) REALISM rejects the insistence of positivism that only observable phenomena can be analysed and that explanation takes the form of showing that phenomena are instances of regularities. Realists argue that causal explanation proceeds by identifying the underlying mechanisms, perhaps unobservable, that connect phenomena. (2) Other sociologists argue that sociology cannot be like

science at all. Most radically, it is suggested that the aim of sociology is not explanation but understanding. Less extremely, it has been argued that sociological
accounts must pay some attention to the intentions and motives of actors. Since
these latter phenomena are unique to the social world and do not characterize the
objects of the natural world, the methods of natural science cannot be utilized in
sociology. (3) Members of the FRANKFURT SCHOOL were early critics of positivism,
particularly in American sociology. They felt that positivism tended to stop at
producing quantified facts and did not go deeper towards genuine sociological
interpretation. Opinion surveys, for example, simply recorded opinions held by
individuals without asking why they held them. More recently, HABERMAS has
argued that positivism in social science is an aspect of RATIONALIZATION and is
associated with the requirement to control societies.

Despite these criticisms, many sociologists would consider themselves to be positivists in a more limited sense, in that they oppose speculative theorizing and prefer
sociological theory to be empirically testable.

SEE ALSO: *empiricism; hermeneutics; methodological individualism; naturalism; phenomenological society; qualitative research; scientific method; sociology as science; Verstehen.*

READING: Craib (1997)

post-colonialism From as early as the sixteenth century, several European countries greatly benefited their economies by forming colonies, dependent territories
overseas, in the Americas, Australasia, Africa and Asia. Colonialism, which reached
its height in the nineteenth century, was reversed in the second part of the twentieth
century when colonies gained their independence. There is some disagreement,
however, as to whether post-colonialism is any less exploitative than colonialism.
Although there may not be as much direct intervention in the affairs of previously
colonial countries, their economies are still dominated by the activities of large
international companies based in the former colonial powers or the United States.

SEE ALSO: *globalization; imperialism.*

post-Fordism Threats to FORDISM in the late twentieth century, both as a production system and as a mode of economic governance or regulation, have prompted
people to ask what will replace it. The term post-Fordism was given currency in the
1980s by the journal *Marxism Today* and is now used as a generic description of the
changing nature of CAPITALISM and theoretical accounts of these changes. It is an
imprecise and contested concept. One account is the theory of FLEXIBLE SPECIALI-
ZATION. A second, associated with S. Lash and J. Urry (1987), sees a movement from
an 'organized' and state-regulated monopoly capitalism to a 'disorganized' form,
with more competition among firms and less state regulation of the economy.
These economic and political shifts are parallel to and associated with the cultural
fragmentation of modern societies known as POSTMODERNISM. A third approach
refers to *neo-Fordism*. In this, the likely future of Fordist production systems is
thought to be their refinement rather than their demise. Because it concentrates on
markets and production, the concept of neo-Fordism is less concerned than the two
other approaches with the linkage of the economy to modes of regulation and
governance or to culture.

Neo-Fordist production systems use programmable automation to introduce some
flexibility into dedicated machinery, which allows a number of products and variants

to be manufactured on one set of equipment. They retain the principle of moving assembly, but where appropriate this is updated to include computer-controlled, programmable carriers rather than fixed conveyors. Managerial control of the labour process and tight discipline over workers are continued, even where group working is encouraged in order to overcome imperfections in the older and often excessive fragmentation of tasks. Semi-skilled labour continues to be the norm. Product-market demands for increased variety are met by designing a range of models, and variants of each model, which have a high degree of commonality in manufacturing terms. Commonality and the greater flexibility of the machinery now used in production allow neo-Fordist producers to manufacture in sufficient volumes to meet the economic requirements of Fordism.

SEE ALSO: *automation; globalization; globalization of production; postmodernity; regulation school.*

READING: Kumar (1995)

posthistoire 'Posthistory' as a theory emerged in Germany in the 1980s and was made popular by L. Niethammer in *Posthistoire: Has history come to an end?* (1992). It refers to the 'end of meaning' in a world where, with the collapse of communism and the SECULARIZATION of Christianity, history no longer has a beginning, middle and conclusion. In Christianity, the idea of salvation meant that history had a purpose. In Marxism, history involved a class struggle for justice. For philosophers like J. F. Lyotard in *The Postmodern Condition* (1979), these 'grand narratives' of history have no authority or validity.

SEE ALSO: *postmodernism; postmodernity.*

post-industrial society This concept was first formulated in 1962 by BELL, and subsequently elaborated in *The Coming of Post-Industrial Society* (1974) to describe economic and social changes in the late twentieth century. He suggested that, in modern societies, theoretical knowledge forms the 'axial principle' of society and is the source of innovation and policy formulation. In the economy this is reflected in the decline of goods-producing and manufacturing as the main forms of economic activity, and their replacement by services. With regard to the class structure, the new axial principle fosters the supremacy of professional and technical occupations which constitute a new class. In all spheres – economic, political and social – decision-making is crucially influenced by new intellectual technologies and the new intellectual class.

Other writers have also commented on what they perceive as the growing power of technocrats in economic and political life: J. K. Galbraith (1967) asserted that power in the US economy, and therefore in American society as a whole, lies in the hands of a technical bureaucracy or the 'technostructure' of large corporations; A. Touraine (1969) suggested similar technocratic control of French economic and political life.

These approaches have been criticized for greatly exaggerating the power and importance of new professional and technical occupations: there is no evidence that these constitute a discrete social class, that they effectively control business corporations, or that they exercise significant political power. While it is true that theoretical knowledge has become steadily more significant as a force of production throughout this century, this implies no change in the locus of power in the economy nor within society. Somewhat similar arguments were once put forward about the new professional managers during the MANAGERIAL REVOLUTION, and were subsequently shown to have little foundation. Conversely, other writers have argued that the centrality of knowledge in modern economies has created a NEW WORKING CLASS of technical employees. However, given the interest in knowledge and information as an aspect of the debate about POSTMODERNISM, there is now much greater recognition of the foresight of Bell's emphasis on knowledge in post-industrialism.

SEE ALSO: *information society*.

postmodernism A movement in painting, literature, television, film and the arts generally. There is disagreement as to what its main features are but they include the following. (1) Pastiche: a putting together of elements of style from radically different contexts and historical epochs. (2) Reflexivity: the capacity to be self-aware, often accompanied by a sense of irony. (3) Relativism: the absence of objective standards of truth. (4) An opposition to certain classical artistic techniques such as narrative – telling a story in an ordered sequence closed off at the end – and representation – attempting to depict reality. (5) A disrespect for, and a wish to cross, traditional artistic boundaries such as those between popular and high culture and between different artistic forms. (6) A lessened belief in the importance of the author as the creator of the text.

Postmodernism is often opposed to MODERNISM. However, the two movements share many of the features listed above and they are probably both best seen as artistic avant-gardes which have to separate themselves off from conventional artistic practice only to become conventional themselves in time.

Sociologically, the interesting question is the relationship of postmodernism to POSTMODERNITY – whether the former is the culture of the latter. The issue for both is whether they represent genuinely new cultural and social forms or whether they are merely transitional phenomena produced by rapid social change.

READING: Connor (1989); Kumar (1995)

postmodernity A term, usually contrasted with MODERNITY, which designates a new condition which contemporary advanced industrial societies are alleged to have reached. A very large number of features are said to characterize postmodernity and they may be placed into four groups – social, cultural, economic and political.

(1) *Social.* INDUSTRIALIZATION and the economic system of CAPITALISM brought with them a system of social classes. This was one of the most important elements of social structure and of social differentiation. In postmodern societies, on the other hand, social classes are no longer so important. The social structure is more fragmented and complex, with a number of sources of differentiation, including CLASS, but also including gender, ethnicity and age.

(2) *Cultural.* Many theories of postmodernity give cultural factors the central role. These include the growing importance of the CULTURE INDUSTRIES; the AESTHETICIZATION OF EVERYDAY LIFE, in which an individual's life is increasingly seen as an aesthetic or cultural project; the construction of identity by individual choice rather than by traditional ascription; the fragmentation of personal identity, which changes over the life-course and between different social settings; different ways of experiencing space and time; POSTMODERNISM.

(3) *Economic.* Modern societies are dominated by Fordist methods of production

and marketing. In FORDISM, large companies produce goods by mass-production methods involving semi-skilled labour for mass markets. The techniques of SCIEN-TIFIC MANAGEMENT are used and national trade unions are involved in wage bargaining. In postmodern societies, by contrast, the economic system is post-Fordist: specialized batch production methods are used, involving multi-skilled workers. Markets are segmented and niche – not everyone wants the same thing. Firms are smaller and use sub-contracting a great deal more. HUMAN RELATIONS management techniques are used and trade unions are either not involved at all or only function at the plant level. One of the outcomes of post-Fordist economic organization is that competitive relations in the market are replacing bureaucratic forms of organization.

(4) *Political.* Modern societies are characterized by big government – well-established welfare states, public ownership of important utilities and service providers, and significant intervention in the economy. Postmodern states have begun to reverse these trends largely by promoting the virtues of self-reliance, competitiveness, the market and private enterprise. The result is that many aspects of the welfare state are being dismantled; benefits and services are being targeted at the most needy, the rest buying private provision. Publicly owned companies are being sold off and governments are increasingly reluctant to take responsibility for managing all aspects of the economy.

The debate on the alleged transition from modernity to postmodernity is still at an early stage and there is a remarkable absence of empirical evidence for the more abstract speculations. There is argument about: the extent to which the four features discussed above are genuinely related to one another; the extent of the spread of some of the processes, many of which may well be confined to particular sectors of society – such as POST-FORDISM and identity choice; the most appropriate theory explaining the changes, some writers attributing them to transformations in capitalism, others to fundamental cultural changes; specific features of postmodernity, such as the decline of class.

SEE ALSO: *reflexive modernization.*

READING: Lash and Urry (1987); Harvey (1989); Kumar (1995)

poststructuralism A form of analysis, primarily in literary criticism, particularly associated with the French philosopher Jacques Derrida. It is often opposed to STRUCTURALISM although Derrida sees his work as consistent with the real principles of structuralism. The fundamental idea is that we cannot apprehend reality without the intervention of language. This prioritizes the study of language – or texts. Texts can be understood only in relation to other texts, not in relation to an external reality against which they can be tested or measured. The principle of intertextuality holds that the meaning of a text is produced in reference to other texts.

Poststructuralism adopted the position of anti-humanism; that is, it criticized the residual humanism of social theory which privileged speech over writing. Radical versions of poststructuralism also argue that sociology is no longer feasible as a discipline, because it is based on outmoded notions of the social.

SEE ALSO: *postmodernism; relativism; semiotics.*

poverty Sociologists distinguish between relative and absolute poverty. *Absolute* poverty occurs when people fail to receive sufficient resources to support a minimum of physical health and efficiency, often expressed in terms of calories or nutritional levels. *Relative* poverty is defined by the general standards of living in different societies and what is culturally defined as being poor rather than some absolute level of deprivation. When poverty is defined relatively, by reference to the living standards enjoyed by the bulk of a population, poverty levels vary between societies and within societies over time.

It was popularly believed that poverty had been eradicated in Britain in the quarter-century following the Second World War. Absolute poverty was abolished by high and sustained levels of economic growth which provided full employment and high wages, and a state welfare system that cared well for those who were not part of the labour market or received low incomes from their employment. Relative poverty was much lessened by more equal DISTRIBUTION OF INCOME AND WEALTH. This belief has been challenged by sociologists and economists, however, who suggest that poverty still exists and, moreover, is rising.

In the UK, two main means of measuring relative poverty have been employed, using the level at which income support (or supplementary benefit in the 1970s) is payable and the level of average income as benchmarks. In 1979, over 4 million people were on supplementary benefit, while ten years later that figure had reached 7.5 million. Utilizing the second measure, throughout the 1960s the proportion of the population with incomes below half of the average stood at about 10 per cent. This proportion shrank in the 1970s, reaching a low of 6 per cent in 1977. In the early 1980s, however, there was a very sharp rise in poverty and by the early 1990s the proportion of the population with incomes of less than half the average had reached over 20 per cent. There have also been changes in the composition of the population in poverty. The majority are non-pensioners, the bulk of whom are represented by couples with children (at about 7 per cent of the population). Pensioners represent about 5 per cent and single parents about 3 per cent.

A good deal of recent sociological work on poverty has concentrated on the idea of social exclusion. The proposition is that since the poor are excluded by their poverty from mainstream society, they in effect lose the benefits and privileges of their CITIZENSHIP. That exclusion may not only be wrong in principle, it also means that the poor have no stake in society and one of the foundations of social order is thereby undermined.

SEE ALSO: *Booth; deprivation; poverty trap; relative deprivation; underclass; unemployment; welfare state.*

READING: Scott, J. (1993); Hills (1995)

poverty trap Many poor families in receipt of means-tested (i.e. income-related) state welfare benefits find it difficult to escape POVERTY if they increase their earnings from employment, because these may be offset by the loss of benefits and by the payment of income tax.

power There are a number of distinctive perspectives on power. For WEBER, it is the probability that a person in a social relationship will be able to carry out his or her own will in the pursuit of goals of action, regardless of resistance. He defined 'domination' in a similar manner, as the probability that a command would be obeyed by a given group of people. This definition has the following characteristics:

(1) power is exercised by individuals and therefore involves choice, agency and intention; (2) it involves the notion of agency; that is, an individual achieving or bringing about goals which are desirable; (3) power is exercised over other individuals and may involve resistance and conflict; (4) it implies that there are differences in interests between the powerful and powerless; (5) power is negative, involving restrictions and deprivations for those subjected to domination. Weber argued that, when the exercise of power was regarded by people as legitimate, it became AUTHORITY. One criticism of the Weberian approach is that, by its emphasis on agency and decision-making, it fails to recognize that non-decision-making may also be an exercise of power. For example, failure or refusal to act may be evidence of inequalities of power. Holders of power may also shape the wants or interests of subordinates. For example, advertising campaigns may involve an exercise of power through the artificial creation of needs. Weber's definition of power raises the problem of 'real' versus 'subjective' interests.

In MARXIST SOCIOLOGY, power has been regarded as a structural relationship, existing independently of the wills of individuals. The notions of agency and intentionality are not essential to the definition. The existence of power is a consequence of the class structure of societies. Thus, N. Poulantzas (1978) defined power as the capacity of one class to realize its interests in opposition to other classes. In this perspective, power has the following features: (1) power cannot be separated from economic and class relations; (2) power involves class struggle, and not simply conflicts between individuals; (3) the analysis of power cannot be undertaken without some characterization of the MODE OF PRODUCTION.

Within the Marxist tradition, the concept of HEGEMONY was developed by GRAMSCI, in order to explain why the powerless appear to accept the domination of the powerful. One aspect of this is the ability of a dominant class to impose on subordinate classes an IDEOLOGY or world view which endorses and supports the position of the dominant class. The mass media, the educational system and other agencies of civil society (e.g. churches and trade unions) disseminate ideas which subordinates internalize and which shape their views about society. This is an aspect of false CLASS CONSCIOUSNESS. It played an important role in the work of ALTHUSSER.

In American sociology, power has not been seen as necessarily involving conflict and COERCION. PARSONS defines power as a positive social capacity for achieving communal ends; power is analogous to money in the economy as a generalized capacity to secure common goals of a social system. In these terms, it is difficult to distinguish between power and influence. Indeed, R. Dahl (1970) defines 'power', 'authority' and 'influence' as 'influence-terms', where influence is the ability of one person to change the behaviour of another. Power is thus regarded as widely diffused through society rather than being concentrated in a ruling ELITE. The political system is seen to be open and pluralistic, permitting the whole community to participate to some degree in the political process. It is conventional to distinguish between pluralistic, Marxist and Weberian approaches. It is held that pluralistic theories conceptualize power as diffused through the political system, whereas Marxist sociology sees power concentrated in the RULING CLASS. Weber emphasized the importance of force and defined the STATE as an institution which had a monopoly of force. These distinctions are, however, simplistic. Dahl, for example, noted that power was concentrated in a minority which he called the 'political class', but defended liberal democracies against the Marxist charge that an economic ruling class governed society. He also accepted implicitly the Weberian view of the state as a legitimate monopoly of force.

Contemporary approaches have been greatly influenced by FOUCAULT, who examined the exercise of power through DISCOURSE and expert knowledge, and in its local and micro-manifestations. He also emphasized the productive as well as negative effects of power.

These attempts to define power serve to confirm the difficulty of reconciling AGENCY AND STRUCTURE in sociology. There is little agreement over whether power has to be intentional or whether it is structural or both. Existing definitions also fail to deal systematically with contradictory views of power as repressive and coercive, while also productive and enabling. Power is a contested concept, the use of which inevitably raises critical issues of value and perspective.

SEE ALSO: *conflict theory; leadership; pluralism; sanction.*

READING: Clegg (1989)

power elite See: ELITE; POWER.

pragmatic acceptance In contrast to accounts of working-class beliefs that explain the quiescence of subordinates in the face of social and political inequality by reference to their incorporation into dominant values, or that assert on the contrary that there is a coherent oppositional ideology that for various reasons has not been effective, M. Mann (1973) argues that subordinates accept the *status quo* on a pragmatic basis that is devoid both of normative involvement and opposition.

SEE ALSO: *class consciousness; dominant ideology thesis; dual consciousness; incorporation.*

praxis The concept, as part of the early work of MARX, has two closely related meanings. (1) It suggests action as opposed to philosophical speculation. (2) It implies that the fundamental characteristic of human society is material production to meet basic needs. Man primarily acts on the natural world – he works – and only secondarily thinks about it.

SEE ALSO: *materialism.*

READING: Lefebvre (1968)

preferred reading A term introduced by S. Hall (1980) to indicate the way in which texts (e.g. television programmes or newspapers), while they are polysemic, generally fit in with the dominant IDEOLOGY. Audience members, however, will react differently to this preferred meaning. Many will oppose it (*oppositional* reading), while others will accept some parts and not others (*negotiated* reading).

SEE ALSO: *audience; dominant ideology thesis; hegemony; incorporation; polysemy.*

prejudice This is a term usually used in the literature on race relations to denote an individual attitude of antipathy or active hostility against another social group, usually racially defined. Prejudice, often the object of psychological study, is to be contrasted with *discrimination*, which refers to the outcome of social processes which disadvantage social groups racially defined. Prejudiced individuals may participate in discriminatory activities but do not necessarily do so.

SEE ALSO: *authoritarian personality; racism.*

pressure group This is a formally constituted organization which is designed at least partly to bring pressure to bear on government, civil service and other political institutions to achieve ends that it favours. The Confederation of British Industries is a pressure group in this sense, even if it was set up with other aims in mind as well. The idea that pressure groups play a significant part in society is related to the concept of PLURALISM, since the political process is seen to result from a large number of often competing pressures.

SEE ALSO: *state; voluntary association.*

prestige The view that the STATUS or 'honour' of different groups is an important dimension of social STRATIFICATION has a long tradition in American approaches to occupational inequality, going back at least to the 1920s. L. Warner's *Social Class in America* (1949) is a celebrated early contribution. Within this tradition, it is argued that occupational prestige is determined by the system of values in a society and by the perceived functional importance of different occupations in that society. The measurement of occupational prestige is made using prestige scales. These are created by asking people to rank occupations according to their social standing or desirability, and respondents' rankings are aggregated by taking the average. The evaluation of occupations proves remarkably stable when various measurement procedures are used, and there is also considerable similarity across different societies in the evaluation of the relative prestige of occupations.

Prestige remains somewhat ambiguous. In the European sociological tradition, M. Weber conceptualized status as social honour and saw this as a dimension of social stratification that was clearly distinct from CLASS. Class inequality was based on unequal access to material rewards and different LIFE-CHANCES. Despite some awareness of Weber's work, the American tradition has conflated a number of dimensions of occupational inequality, and joins together income, power, educational level as well as social honour. The validity of prestige scales has also been questioned on the following grounds: (1) it is not always clear whether attitude surveys indicate what respondents believe is the actual or the desirable ranking of occupations; (2) different respondents have different knowledge of occupational structure; (3) there are considerable variations in attitudes, which are disguised when replies are averaged and consolidated into a single prestige scale.

SEE ALSO: *positional goods; status inconsistency; upper class.*
READING: Trieman (1977)

primary group See: GROUP.

primary labour market See: LABOUR MARKET SEGMENTATION.

primary relationship These are interpersonal relations characterized by emotional intensity, total commitment and mutual satisfaction. In a primary relationship, the total person is involved in the interaction. By contrast, secondary relationships are partial and ephemeral. For example, interactions between strangers are secondary, while mutual love is primary. This contrast is usually associated with that between primary and secondary groups.

SEE ALSO: *group.*

primitive society In evolutionary anthropology, primitive societies represented a particular stage from which more complex societies developed. The term often implied that modern man was more intelligent than his savage, irrational forebears. Without these prejudicial connotations, a primitive society is pre-industrial, small-scale, non-literate, technologically simple and traditional. In sociology, there is a preference for alternative terms such as 'pre-capitalist' or 'traditional society'. The term is commonly used in juxtaposition to modern, urban, industrial society; many of the judgemental implications of 'primitive' are still carried over into such allegedly neutral descriptions as 'traditional' society.

Prisoner's Dilemma See: GAME THEORY.

privatism A term used to describe the way in which people live their lives less in public and more in private or within the family. For example, religion is said to be now less a matter of public acts of worship and more a question of private prayer or privately held beliefs. Similarly, it is claimed that family life is more based on the home and involves parents and children only. There is less contact with neighbours, friends and wider kin and greater absorption in home-based leisure pursuits.

Some sociologists see these tendencies to privatism in spheres such as religion or the family as part of a wider process affecting all of society. They suggest that people are withdrawing more into themselves or their immediate family, even to the point of NARCISSISM. The public sphere, everything from participation in politics to involvement in public festivals, is thought to be decaying. The result is that people have less control over their society while at the same time having scant regard for other people beyond themselves or their immediate family. However, there is no general agreement as to whether this process of privatism is taking place, or what its causes might be.

SEE ALSO: *affluent worker; extended family; legitimation crisis; nuclear family; secularization; symmetrical family*.

READING: Saunders (1990a)

privatization In sociology, two rather different meanings are given to this term. First, it refers to the process whereby assets that are held by the state, such as the gas or electricity industries, are sold to private investors. This process has been initiated by governments to encourage the ENTERPRISE CULTURE, reduce government borrowing, promote greater efficiency, spread ownership of companies to a wider section of the population, and make the provision of services more responsive to consumer needs. It is by no means clear that any of these aims have been met. Secondly, privatization is used in the same sense as PRIVATISM.

READING: Saunders and Harris (1994)

problematic This assumes that sociological concepts do not exist separately from one another but are related together in a theoretical framework, known as a problematic.

profane The contrast between the profane and SACRED world is a universal cultural distinction. The sacred is set apart by ritual from the profane world which is the secular, everyday reality of work, toil and domestic duties. There are two basic attitudes to the profane world: (1) world rejection, for example the mystical flight from mundane reality; (2) mastery of the profane world, for example the ascetic control of the body by prayer, diet and self-denial. The decline of the sacred in industrial society involves a SECULARIZATION of life, which is devoid of religious significance, ritual festivity and CHARISMA.

SEE ALSO: *invisible religion; religion.*

profession G. Millerson (1964) lists these characteristics of a profession: (1) the use of skills based on theoretical knowledge; (2) education and training in these skills; (3) the competence of professionals ensured by examinations; (4) a code of conduct to ensure professional integrity; (5) performance of a service that is for the public good; (6) a professional association that organizes members. These criteria can also be used to measure the *degree* to which occupations are professionalized.

Professionals normally have high pay, high social status and autonomy in their work. Functionalists such as J. Ben-David (1963–4) explain this privileged position on the grounds that professions perform services which are socially valued. Others, for example F. Parkin (1979), suggest that strategies of occupational closure are used to restrict access to professions by means of educational requirements that may bear little relationship to the difficulty of professional work (now known as CREDEN-TIALISM), and that these account for the privileges. Professions can pursue exclusionary strategies because the state gives the right to practise certain occupations to accredited members of professions. The relationship between gender and occupational closure in the formation of professions is considered by A. Witz (1992), with particular reference to medical professionalization. She argues that men and women have unequal access to the resources (credentials and access to the law and the state) that are needed to make a successful claim to professional status, and this gender-based inequality has shaped professionalization in the medical world. Exclusionary strategies by men successfully prevented most women from becoming doctors in the nineteenth century and for part of the twentieth, and kept them in subordinate positions when they were admitted. Midwifery and nursing, which are both medical occupations dominated by women, have long tried to gain recognition of their claims to full professional status, but the dominant medical profession has prevented their achieving this equal status. T. J. Johnson (1972; 1977) and F. Parkin (1979) consider the relationship of professions to state power, the location of professions within the upper class, and their ambivalent character as part of a class that carries out CAPITAL FUNCTIONS while they also perform the functions of the COLLECTIVE LABOURER.

Another issue concerns the implications of the modern tendency for professionals to work in bureaucratic organizations, in both public and private sectors of the economy, instead of remaining independent. There may be a conflict between certain professional and organizational values: (1) between professional ethics and organizational practices; (2) between the individual's orientation to the wider professional community and the expectation that he or she should identify with the organization; (3) between professional autonomy at work and bureaucratic control and direction.

SEE ALSO: *career; labour market; labour market segmentation; middle class; proletarianization; social closure.*

READING: Macdonald (1995)

progress Most nineteenth-century sociology was based on the assumption of progress which was equated with industrialization. Technological advance was assumed to result in improvements in material welfare, reflected in enhanced standards of health and longer life-expectancy. Industrialization was also associated with a growth in rights of CITIZENSHIP, literacy and education. Progress was the social manifestation of reason, knowledge and technology. With the advent of mass warfare, fascism and totalitarian governments in the twentieth century, sociology generally took a more pessimistic turn as confidence in the progressive nature of industrial society waned. However, the assumption of progress as societies have evolved was implicit in FUNCTIONALISM, while the sociological analysis of POST-INDUSTRIAL SOCIETY has been informed by an optimistic view of twentieth-century development.

Conventional theories of progress have failed to provide adequate answers to three fundamental questions about social change. (1) Which social groups benefit from progress? (2) Who defines what is to count as progressive? (3) Who decides what personal or social costs are tolerable in relation to what degree of progress?

SEE ALSO: *evolutionary theory*.

READING: Kumar (1995)

proletarianization This is a process by which parts of the MIDDLE CLASS become effectively absorbed into the WORKING CLASS. The issue of proletarianization was widely debated in the 1970s and 1980s, particularly by Marxist sociologists. The criteria by which one judges whether or not this absorption has taken place are complex and this has led to much debate, in that proletarianization may have occurred as measured by one criterion but not by another. Proletarianization of condition must be distinguished from proletarianization of action. The former is determined by market, work and status considerations: the more closely white-collar workers' pay, holidays, chances of promotion, fringe benefits, relationships with employers, autonomy at work and status in the community approach those of manual workers, the more proletarianized they have become. Proletarianization of action has been chiefly measured by voting behaviour or the propensity to join TRADE UNIONS. But these are now thought to be poor indicators, because radical political parties no longer align with the working class and trade unionism is in decline. Hence proletarianization of condition need not lead to proletarianization of action. There is evidence from Britain that, among groups once thought to be part of the lower middle class, only personal-service workers (e.g. shop assistants) are being proletarianized, in that they are being de-skilled, have reduced autonomy at work, and have political and social attitudes closer to those of manual workers.

SEE ALSO: *class*; *de-skilling*.

READING: Marshall *et al.* (1988)

proletariat As used in sociology, proletariat is equivalent to WORKING CLASS.

SEE ALSO: *bourgeoisie*; *Marx*.

property This is usually conceived in sociology as a collection of rights over both inanimate (land, houses, etc.) and animate (animals, people) objects. These rights are socially determined and thus vary from society to society and within a particular society over time. Property rights imply social relationships between people, because they define who does and does not have authorized access to objects, because possession of property may give the possessors power over others, and because in some societies people are themselves property objects (as in slave societies and, in effect, in those feudal societies were agricultural workers were bound to the land as serfs and as such were subject to the will of the lord and could be transferred along with the land). The main concerns of sociological accounts of property are the following. (1) Acquisition, which is how individuals or collectivities gain access to property. (2) Distribution, which includes the patterns of property ownership and control, the principles that underlie these, and the institutions including law that maintain patterns of distribution. (3) The consequences of property for individuals and social structures. (4) The social values or ideologies that justify property rights.

In capitalist societies, property rarely includes rights over people. The main rights attached to property are the rights to control, benefit from and dispose of property on an exclusive basis. Historically, property was mainly private and personal and all property rights belonged to individuals (unless the disposal right was restricted by the legal device of entail), though corporate institutions such as the church or collegiate bodies did possess collective property rights. A major change since the mid nineteenth century has been the growth of corporate property, with the rise of joint-stock companies which are owned by a number of individual shareholders but at law are considered as single entities with their own corporate personalities. In advanced CAPITALISM, productive property (property that has an economic role) is increasingly corporate and impersonal as economic activity becomes concentrated in large corporations that replace individual entrepreneurs and family firms.

Recent sociological interest has concentrated on topics such as home ownership, intellectual property and inheritance. In the first case, there have been studies of the rapidly increasing home ownership in Britain on voting patterns, participation in the community and attitudes to domestic life.

SEE ALSO: *feudalism; managerial revolution; relations of production; slavery.*

READING: Reeve (1986); Saunders (1990b)

Protestant ethic Following two essays of 1904–5 by WEBER, later published as *The Protestant Ethic and the Spirit of Capitalism* (1930), it has been argued that the secular culture of capitalist society originated paradoxically in the ASCETICISM of the Protestant Reformation, and that the Protestant ethic and the spirit of capitalism have an ELECTIVE AFFINITY for each other. Protestantism emphasized the autonomy and independence of the individual rather than dependence on the church, priesthood and ritual. The religious doctrines of Calvinism held that believers could no longer depend for their salvation on the institutionalized means of grace found in the Catholic Church (confession, eucharist, baptism), on the intermediary role of priests or on good works. Individual faith in Christ as a personal saviour of sinful humanity became the key element of Protestant doctrines. Protestants were subject to a 'salvational anxiety', since, while they believed that only the elect were predestined for salvation, they did not have complete confidence in their own personal salvation. Pastoral counselling in Protestantism maintained that the answer to such anxiety could be found in a secular vocation, self-control, hard work and communal service, because these qualities might provide a sign of election. Protestantism provided much of the cultural content of early capitalism – INDIVIDUALISM, ACHIEVEMENT MOTIVATION, hostility to inherited wealth and luxury, legitimation of entrepreneurial vocations, opposition to magic and superstition, a commitment to organization and calculation in personal and public life. Protestantism provided an element in the RATIONALIZATION of Western society. However, Weber thought that, while this ethic was supremely important in the development of the rational spirit of capitalism, the Protestant ethic was not a requirement of CAPITALISM after its establishment.

Weber's thesis has been criticized on a number of grounds: (1) some historians object that the empirical evidence on which Weber's interpretation of Protestantism was based was too narrow and unrepresentative; (2) the precise relationship between capitalism and Protestantism was not adequately formulated; (3) there were aspects of traditional Catholic teaching which were equally compatible with capitalism; (4) Weber ignored crucial developments in Catholicism which occurred after the Reformation and which modernized Catholicism from within; (5) capitalism is contradictory in that it requires the consumption of commodities as well as saving for future investment; Protestant asceticism aids the latter, but the former may require hedonism. Despite these criticisms, Weber's thesis has shown a remarkable ability to survive damaging objections.

SEE ALSO: *entrepreneurship*.

READING: Marshall, G. (1982)

psephology This is the study of elections, particularly of voting behaviour, and the forecasting of election results. Psephologists use opinion-poll data on voting intentions, post-election surveys of how and why people voted and, occasionally, in-depth qualitative research.

psychologism As a term of abuse in sociology, this refers to explanations of the social structure exclusively in terms of the attributes of individual psychology. For example, adherence to religious beliefs is sometimes explained in terms of the psychological need for a way of coping with death.

SEE ALSO: *Homans*; *methodological individualism*.

public opinion The collection of people's opinions on topics of public interest, and the analysis of these by statistical techniques using a sample from the population in question, is what is normally meant by public opinion. Public-opinion polling techniques are widely used by market researchers and by psephologists interested in forecasting how people will vote in elections.

SEE ALSO: *psephology*; *questionnaire*; *sampling*; *survey*.

public relations See: COMMUNICATION MANAGEMENT.

public sphere This is an area of public life within which a debate about public issues can be developed, leading to the formation of an informed public opinion. A number of institutions are associated with the development of a public sphere – the formation of the state, newspapers and periodicals, the provision of public spaces such as parks, cafés and other public spaces – as well as a culture which favours a public life. Some theorists (e.g. HABERMAS; Sennett, 1974) have argued that the public sphere was at its most developed in eighteenth-century Europe and that, since then, there has been a withdrawal from public involvement and a growing division between public and private life under the impact of the development of CAPITALISM and the COMMODIFICATION of everyday life. This has meant a split between family, domestic and household life, on the one hand, and the world of work and politics, on the other. The division is also gendered, the private sphere being organized by women and the public dominated by men.

There has been an extensive debate (Dahlgren, 1995) about the contemporary role of the mass media, especially television, in the maintenance of a public sphere. Some argue that television trivializes issues and is biased, so that it discourages reasoned public debate. Others argue that television in effect provides the raw material which people use to discuss matters of public concern in their everyday lives.

SEE ALSO: *privatism; privatization.*

Q

qualitative research The qualitative research tradition in the social sciences and humanities is defined partly by the research methods which are employed, and partly by the EPISTEMOLOGY, or the theory of knowledge, which is propounded by many users of these methods. Qualitative research has often been contrasted with quantitative research and the epistemology of POSITIVISM. However, while many qualitative researchers are opposed to positivism, not all are, so there is no necessary incompatibility between qualitative research methods and positivism.

Commonly used qualitative research methods include: ethnography and PARTICIPANT OBSERVATION; unstructured interviews; the CASE STUDY; historical analysis based on documents, oral histories and life-histories of individuals; the textual analysis of documents; and the use of visual images such as photographs, pictures and video recordings. The aims of research may involve understanding of social phenomena in ways that do not require measurement and quantification; while the nature of the phenomena themselves may rule out quantification. For example, in a piece of ethnographic research, the aims may be to observe and understand social behaviour, and the researcher may have no interest in counting the frequency of particular behaviours; while in historical research, the artefacts the researcher has to rely on as the record of social phenomena in the past may not permit adequate quantification, even if this were his or her aim. In comparison, quantitative research assumes that a proper understanding of social phenomena requires measurement, which, in turn, opens the way to the use of statistical and mathematical techniques in the analysis of the resulting data.

The epistemological position of many adherents to qualitative research is explicitly anti-positivistic. First, they maintain that knowledge of social phenomena comes from observing these as they occur naturally in the environment and via an interpretative understanding by the researcher of the meanings of action. This position is found within a number of sociological traditions: ACTION THEORY, PHENOMENOLOGICAL SOCIOLOGY, the Weberian concept of VERSTEHEN and HERMENEUTICS. Second, they are critical of the positivistic view that there is an external social reality which can be observed, measured and understood. One claim is that social reality can never be fully understood and the best that can be achieved is some approximation of reality. A more radical claim, made in particular by poststructuralist and postmodernist qualitative researchers, is that positivism in any form constitutes only one of several ways of representing the social world and has no privileged place. Their claim is that positivism produces representations of the social world which are just different rather than more correct.

Not all qualitative researchers reject all aspects of positivism. Recently developed computer software packages for the analysis of textual material (e.g. tape-recorded interviews which have been transcribed into written text and documents of a contemporary or historical nature) have extended the range of analysis that can now be undertaken and facilitate the quantification of qualitative data. Their widespread use is evidence that some qualitative researchers do not oppose measurement and quantification.

SEE ALSO: *interview; postmodernism; poststructuralism*.

READING: Denzin and Lincoln (1994)

questionnaire Used in survey research, this is a set of questions given to respondents and designed to provide information relevant to the research area. Questionnaires may be completed by the respondents themselves or be completed by an interviewer. The questions may be *closed-ended*, in which case the respondent simply selects from predetermined answers such as yes/no in the simplest form, or from a list of predetermined answers in more complicated forms. Or the questions may be *open-ended*, in which case respondents answer as they wish. When questionnaires are completed by the respondents, for example when the research is conducted by mail, or when the level of literacy among respondents is not high, it is common to use the closed-ended format as much as possible. When questionnaires are used in interviews or given to more literate respondents, the open-ended format may be used. Strictly, a questionnaire is any standardized set of questions, but some people use the term to describe only self-completed forms and refer to the interviewer-completed instrument as an *interview schedule*.

SEE ALSO: *attitude scales; interview; public opinion; survey*.

R

race, sociology of See: SOCIOLOGY OF RACE.

racism The term may be defined as the determination of actions, attitudes or policies by beliefs about racial characteristics. Racism may be (1) overt and individual, involving individual acts of oppression against subordinate racial groups or individuals, and (2) covert and institutional, involving structural relations of subordination and oppression between social groups. While individual racism consists of intended actions, institutional racism involves the unintended consequences of a system of racial inequality. Racism may be accompanied by either implicit or explicit racist theories, which seek to explain and justify social inequality based on race.

SEE ALSO: *ethnic group; plural societies; prejudice; stereotypes.*

Radcliffe-Brown, Alfred R. (1881–1955) He was noted, with MALINOWSKI, for his contribution to the development of FUNCTIONALISM as a theoretical perspective in British anthropology. Through a comparative approach, Radcliffe-Brown stressed the important interdependence of institutions within a SOCIAL SYSTEM. Society was seen as a self-regulating organism, the needs of which were satisfied by certain basic social institutions. His major publications were *The Andaman Islanders* (1922), *Structure and Function in Primitive Society* (1952), *The Social Organization of Australian Tribes* (1931) and *Taboo* (1936).

SEE ALSO: *Lévi-Strauss; taboo.*

random sample See: SAMPLING.

rational choice theory The theory of rational choice derives from economics and informs a rapidly developing branch of sociological theory, which is more accurately labelled the rational choice approach or PARADIGM. It is one of a broader class of models of purposive action which are to be found in all the social sciences. These assume that actors are purposive; that is, they intend their actions to produce certain results. A basic postulate of rational choice, a metatheoretical assumption rather than an empirical generalization, is that people act rationally. Purposive models in general make the same assumption and the distinctive element of rational choice is its notion of *optimization*: in acting rationally, individuals optimize, by maximizing benefits or minimizing costs, when they make their choices from sets of alternatives for action. Actors choose the actions with the best outcomes according to their own preferences. Following economics, sociologists using a rational choice approach have often assumed that actors are concerned primarily with their own welfare and their preferences are self-interested. In particular, actors wish to control resources in which they have an interest (e.g. wealth and other sources of material well-being, security, leisure). Thus the approach is in the tradition of UTILITARIAN-ISM and many exponents assume that individual actors are egoistic. This is not a necessary requirement of the theory, however, which postulates that action is goal-directed and optimizing but not what the goals are. It has been suggested that some people may have other-regarding, altruistic preferences, which they pursue rationally and by means of optimization.

The primary aim of rational choice is to explain the behaviour of social systems, both large and small, rather than individual behaviour. Theorists assume that the explanation of a system should be in terms of the behaviour of the actors who make it up. This in turn requires explanations of the actions of individuals and of the transition between individual and system behaviour. As the taken-for-granted postulate is that people act rationally, individual actions are modelled fairly simply, as the outcomes of rational choice (purposive action, optimization and, for many theorists, egoism), and the complexities of individual psychology are ignored. Exponents of the approach are much more interested in the *transition* from individuals to systems and vice versa. Unlike utilitarianism, the rational choice approach does not believe that social systems can be modelled simply as aggregations of individual actors and actions. In the first place, when individual actors combine, their *interaction* often produces social outcomes that differ from the intentions of the purposive individuals who make up the social system. In the second, social systems have properties that both constrain individuals and influence their preferences. The approach therefore attempts to unite sociological explanations at the macro level (e.g. the institutional structure of a society) with those at the micro level (how actors behave within this structure) and so to resolve the dualism of AGENCY AND STRUCTURE.

These general concepts can be illustrated with reference to COLLECTIVE ACTION and social cohesion, which rational choice sees as inherently problematic. An example is the issue of trade-union membership: if a group of employees is represented by a trade union which negotiates wages on behalf of everyone in the group and union membership is voluntary, why do individuals choose to join the union and pay its membership fee? They know that the employer will pay everyone the union-negotiated wage rises, whether or not they are union members, so there appears to be no material incentive to join. The rational choice for an egoistic individual looks to be a 'free rider'; that is, not to pay to join the union but to accept the wage rises gained by the collective action of his or her workmates who are union members. However, if all individuals made this rational choice, there would be no union and no wage rises. The 'free rider' issue shows: (1) the focus on individual actions as the basic building blocks of analysis; (2) explanation of these actions by reference to the choices of self-interested actors in response to the incentive structure given by the social system; (3) that individuals acting rationally may create a collective outcome which is not rational and optimal either for the group or the individual. In fact, many people do of course join trade unions and rational choice could suggest various alternative hypotheses why this is so: individuals may be aware of the consequences of the union being weakened by low membership and believe it to be in their own long-term self-interest to join, in order to maintain union strength; individual preferences may include the wish to be liked by co-workers who are union members; individuals may have internalized group norms which value trade-union membership and these form part of their preferences.

Rational choice is a theory about how people make choices, *given* their preferences. In order to explain phenomena, therefore, one has to have additional knowledge of, or reasonable hypotheses about, the nature and origins of these preferences. There is a division of opinion here. One common account of these is egoism. Another maintains that preferences also reflect values and beliefs, which are not reducible to egoistic self-interest nor amenable to rational choice. In this view, preferences are formed by socialization, therefore the approach requires auxiliary assumptions about culture and social structure. Equally, the opportunity sets from which actors choose alternatives are socially structured and there are social constraints on choice. The evidence is that people do routinely act in ways that place the interests of others and groups before their own self-interest, and therefore egoism is neither a plausible nor a useful assumption. Advocates of egoism suggest in reply, however, that other-regarding choices, such as social norms of cooperation and trust, even of ALTRUISM, may indeed be explained within a framework of self-interest: individual actors learn by experience that cooperation, trust and promoting the good of the group are rational ways of maximizing self-interest in situations where individuals are interdependent and each controls resources that others need.

The approach recognizes that RATIONALITY is itself a problematic concept. In the first place, BOUNDED RATIONALITY means that optimization is impossible, therefore actors' choices are boundedly rather than strictly rational. Secondly, what appears to be rational to the actor may not seem so to others, and there is some discussion as to whose frame of reference should be adopted. Should the theorist take as given an actor's preferences, without inquiring whether these are themselves rational (from the theorist's perspective)? Does the theorist define an actor's choice as rational when it is apparent that there are better alternatives that the actor has failed to consider? Given that bounded rationality affects observers as well as actors, can a theorist adequately judge the rationality of actors' preferences and choices? The absence of a strict criterion of rational choice, because of bounded rationality, means that the rational choice approach can be quite indeterminate at times.

Rational choice is committed to analytical theorizing based on explicit premises, logical deduction and clear argument, and which leads to explanation rather than description. It also seeks simplicity of explanation and to reduce theory to a small number of fundamental elements. Rational choice is notable for the way it builds explicit models, often expressed in formal terms, similar to those found in economics. As a theoretical paradigm based on purposive action and METHODOLOGICAL INDIVIDUALISM, it stands within the Weberian tradition of sociological theory. Its closest sociological precursor is EXCHANGE THEORY, although that has concentrated on small groups rather than larger social systems.

SEE ALSO: *actor/social actor; game theory*.

READING: Coleman and Fararo (1992a); Marini (1992); Abell (2000)

rationalism A philosophical tradition originating in the seventeenth and eighteenth centuries, rationalism asserts that reason is the only basis of valid knowledge of reality. Rationalist philosophers thus rejected revelation as a source of genuine knowledge. More technically, only deductive or inductive reasoning could provide precise and reliable information about the world. In sociology, rationalism was associated with POSITIVISM in the nineteenth century. Rationalism, however, often led to an implicit value judgement asserting the superiority of Western civilization over other societies and over 'primitives' who were regarded as irrational. These assumptions were subsequently challenged by anthropological field work which testified to the rationality of the human species at all levels of development.

Some twentieth-century writers have altered the original meaning of the term. CRITICAL THEORY, for example, sees rationalism as being opposed to positivist sociology, which it regards as providing meaningless quantification.

SEE ALSO: *rationality; understanding alien belief systems.*

rationality It is important to make a distinction between the truth of beliefs and their rationality, which refers to the grounds on which they are held. Beliefs that are coherent, not contradictory, and compatible with experience are said to be rational. It is irrational to hold beliefs which are known to be false, incoherent and contradictory. It is often suggested that science, which involves the systematic testing of propositions by observation, experiment and logical reasoning, is the example of rationality *par excellence*.

The concept of rationality, especially in anthropology and comparative sociology, does raise considerable problems. In the nineteenth century, anthropologists typically regarded magic and religion as irrational and as the product of a pre-logical mentality. It is difficult, however, to concede that a society could exist in which irrational beliefs were widespread, since the existence of language itself implies the presence of logical norms (of negation, identity and non-contradiction). There has to be some public agreement that certain terms refer consistently to specific objects and that, for example, 'up' is the opposite of 'down'. Modern anthropology argues that: (1) beliefs which appear absurd, such as 'all twins are birds', are in fact reasonable once located in their appropriate cultural context; (2) understanding other beliefs is thus a matter of correct translation; (3) religious beliefs are expressive and symbolic, not informative and literal; religious beliefs are thus non-rational rather than irrational. Critics of this view have argued that by these three criteria no belief could ever be shown to be irrational. In contemporary sociology, the influence of POSTMODERNISM has reinforced scepticism as to the possibility of trans-social agreements about what would constitute universal criteria of rationality.

SEE ALSO: *Gellner; rational choice theory; rationalism; understanding alien belief systems.*

rationalization This term has two very separate meanings: (1) it was employed by PARETO to refer to the use of spurious explanations to justify actions; (2) it was the master concept of M. Weber's analysis of modern capitalism, referring to a variety of related processes by which every aspect of human action became subject to calculation, measurement and control.

For WEBER, rationalization involved: (1) in economic organization, the organization of the factory by bureaucratic means and the calculation of profit by systematic accounting procedures; (2) in religion, the development of theology by an intellectual stratum, the disappearance of magic and the replacement of sacraments by personal responsibility; (3) in law, the erosion of *ad hoc* law-making and arbitrary case-law by deductive legal reasoning on the basis of universal laws; (4) in politics, the decline of traditional norms of legitimacy and the replacement of charismatic leadership by the party machine; (5) in moral behaviour, a greater emphasis on discipline and training; (6) in science, the decline of the individual innovator and the development of research teams, coordinated experiment and state-directed science policies; (7) in society as a whole, the spread of BUREAUCRACY, state control and administration. The concept of rationalization was thus part of Weber's view of capitalist society as an 'iron cage' in which the individual, stripped of religious meaning and moral value, would be increasingly subject to government surveillance and bureaucratic regulation. Like K. Marx's concept of ALIENATION, rationalization implies the separation of the individual from community, family and church, and his subordination to legal, political and economic regulation in the factory, school and state.

SEE ALSO: *industrial society; metaphysical pathos; rational choice theory; secularization*.

READING: Turner, B. S. (1992a)

realism (1) In opposition to POSITIVISM, realists claim that explanation in both natural and social science consists of uncovering the (real) underlying and often unobservable mechanisms that connect phenomena causally, and not merely in showing that the phenomena are instances of some observed regularity.

Sociological writers often claim that K. Marx was a realist, in that he believed that the observable features of capitalist society were to be explained by the mechanisms of the capitalist MODE OF PRODUCTION, which could not be observed directly. Marx objected to the positivist methods of his day, which, he claimed, treated only the surface level of social life. Positivists would respond to arguing that Marxists, in postulating some unobservable structures or mechanisms that generate social phenomena, are not laying their theory open to test.

(2) In a quite different sense, the term is applied to forms of art, especially literature, painting, film and television, which attempt to depict reality.

SEE ALSO: *falsificationism; naturalism*.

READING: Keat and Urry (1975)

realist criminology Also referred to as Left Realism, this perspective was developed in British CRIMINOLOGY in the 1980s. It explained crime in terms of SOCIAL DEPRIVATION and INEQUALITY; as a result, it was particularly interested in the causal role of SUBCULTURE in DELINQUENT BEHAVIOUR. Against the POSITIVISM of mainstream criminology, it adopted CRITICAL THEORY as a response to the limitations of CRIMINAL STATISTICS. However, Left Realism also came to recognize the brutal facts relating to the victims of crime, especially women, ethnic minorities and the old, which permitted no romantic picture of the criminal as hero. Unlike CRITICAL CRIMINOLOGY, realist criminology did not neglect crimes against women or regard crimes against property as a justifiable attack on the wealth of the BOURGEOISIE. Realist criminology adopted a new agenda that involved (1) empirical studies of the victims of crime, including working-class victims; (2) recognition that policing was necessary to protect communities; and (3) development of effective policies that recognized the interactions between government, police, offenders and social circumstances. For some commentators, the reformist policies of Left Realism (such as building youth hostels and improving street lighting) were in fact little different from conventional criminology.

SEE ALSO: *feminist criminology; women and crime*.

READING: Lowman and Maclean (1992)

reciprocity (1) In functionalism and exchange theory, the reciprocal exchange of rewards is said to be a necessary basis for social interaction between individuals.

When reciprocity is not present, social actors will withdraw from interaction which has become unrewarding. The denial of reciprocity is thus an element of social control. Mutual reciprocity between social actors A and B is contrasted with univocal or directional reciprocity in which A gives to C in return for what A receives from B. The theory of reciprocal exchange suggests that social stability requires a principle of equality of rewards between social actors. Since rewards are very generally defined, the notion of reciprocity tends to be vacuous.

(2) In terms of social systems, it can be argued that the degree of reciprocity between parts of the system is variable. Where part of a social system has considerable functional autonomy (that is, satisfies its own requirements without being entirely dependent on the total system), there will be strong pressures to maintain that autonomy. Social systems may thus be seen in terms of a conflict between system interdependence and functional autonomy.

SEE ALSO: *exchange theory; functionalism; social system; systems theory.*

reductionism A sociological explanation is said to be reductionist when it attempts to account for a range of phenomena in terms of a single determining factor. It is said of some Marxist theories that they are reductionist because they explain the diversity of social behaviour by reference simply to the economy.

SEE ALSO: *base and superstructure; Marxist sociology.*

reference group In forming their attitudes and beliefs, and in performing their actions, people will compare or identify themselves with other people, or other groups of people, whose own attitudes, beliefs and actions are taken as appropriate measures. These groups are called reference groups. People do not actually have to be members of the groups to which they refer. For example, an explanation of working-class conservative voting in Britain was that the attitudes of these voters were formed by comparison or identification with the middle class. Furthermore, attitudes can be formed, not only by a positive identification with a reference group, but also by negative comparisons or rejections of it.

It is useful to distinguish normative from comparative functions of reference groups. The first refers simply to the manner in which people form attitudes in relation to a reference group, as in the working-class conservatism example. Reference groups may have a comparative function when they form a basis for evaluating one's own situation in life. For example, if middle managers compare themselves with others who have been promoted, they are more likely to feel deprived when they are not promoted than if they compared themselves with those who have not been promoted.

SEE ALSO: *relative deprivation.*

READING: Runciman (1966)

reflexive/reflexivity This term is used in three senses. (1) Theories that are reflexive are those that refer to themselves; for example, theories in the SOCIOLOGY OF KNOWLEDGE refer to themselves, since they argue that all knowledge, including sociological knowledge, can be explained socially. (2) The term is used to describe the way in which, particularly in modern societies, people constantly examine their own practices and, in the light of that examination, alter them. In his recent work, GIDDENS (1990 and 1991) has formulated an account of the reflexive project of the self in which individuals' identities are no longer based just on external factors but are constructed by a constant reflection on, and a working and reworking of, their own biographies. (3) Reflexivity is an important idea in ETHNOMETHODOLOGY. In this usage, social order is not imposed from outside but is rather created by people in their reflections on, and talk about, the social world.

SEE ALSO: *identity; reflexive modernization; risk/risk society.*

reflexive modernization U. Beck, in his *Risk Society* (1992), argued that the further development of industrial societies has a number of consequences. Technological expertise now has to be used reflexively – that is to moderate the effects of the earlier application of science and technology. More importantly, there has been increasing development of a process of individualization whereby individuals are becoming disembedded from their traditional ties of family, locality or social class. They are linked together only via market relations. One result of this is that individuals who are isolated from social ties and constraints can reflect on who they are and would like to be, and increasingly make their own choices and fashion their own identities and biographies.

SEE ALSO: *disembedding; identity; individualism; reflexive/reflexivity; risk/risk society.*

Registrar General See: SOCIO-ECONOMIC GROUPS.

regression (1) A statistical term which represents the variation in one variable as being partly determined by its dependence on another, plus an error factor. Like COR-RELATION, regression is a measure of association. It is used, however, to estimate

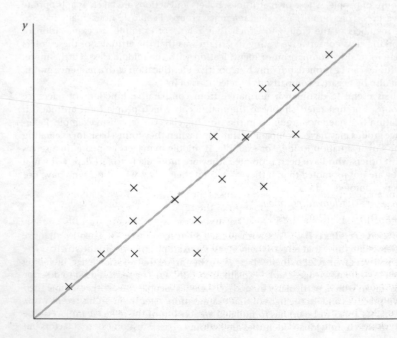

values of a dependent variable from the values of an independent variable. A simple linear regression is represented graphically opposite by means of a scatter diagram. The values of the two variables, x and y, are plotted as coordinates and the regression line of the dependent variable y on the independent variable x is a statistical construction which simply provides the line of best 'fit' to the data. Normally the regression line is expressed as an equation which provides estimates of the dependent values. Typically, regressions are used in a more complicated *multiple* form, in which a dependent variable varies with several others simultaneously (*multiple linear regression*). For example, a simple linear regression of road casualties and the number of vehicles on the road might show some association, but a complete analysis would require additional variables since accidents vary in relation not only to vehicle numbers but also with average vehicle mileage, average vehicle speed, the types of road and so on. In *multivariate regression* more than one dependent variable is analysed simultaneously.

Regression assumes interval or ratio levels of measurement. Many sociological data are not measured at these levels, but a common technique is to create dichotomous 'dummy' variables which will meet the measurement requirements of regression.

SEE ALSO: *causal modelling; dependent/independent variables; log linear analysis; measurement levels; path analysis.*

(2) A psychological term which describes how individuals under stress revert to behaviour characteristic of an earlier and more impulsive stage of development; for example, when adults respond to stress by behaving in a childlike manner.

Regulation School A group of French economists, known collectively as the French School of Economic Regulation, argues that there are no constant, ahistorical economic principles of CAPITALISM, because capitalist economic development is shaped by institutional and social factors which are specific to particular historical periods. These include social-class relations and political action. The theoretical writings of members of the school and their detailed historical accounts of capitalist development, notably M. Aglietta's (1979) analysis of the USA, have greatly influenced sociologists and political scientists concerned with crises and change in capitalism in the late twentieth century. Particular attention has been paid to the school's analysis of the apparent decline of FORDISM as the dominant mode of economic, political and social organization, and the issue of POST-FORDISM.

Regulation theory sees capitalism as developing through a series of distinct phases or *modes of development*. Each mode comprises: a *regime of accumulation*, a particular pattern of economic activity that has its own internal dynamics; and a *mode of regulation*, the institutional structures that regulate the relationships central to all capitalist economies (although the forms of these relationships vary among regimes). Modes of regulation govern: the form of the capital–labour relation; the nature of competition between firms; monetary and credit arrangements; how the national economy is inserted into the international economy; the form of state economic management. Each mode of development has its own sources of contradiction and instability, but for a while the crises that these produce are capable of regulation. However, the crises become more acute over time and regulation fails, leading to a *structural* crisis of unregulated conflicts between social classes, companies, political interest groups and governments. New modes of regulation emerge out of these struggles, but the outcomes of struggles are indeterminate and so new modes of development cannot be predicted in advance.

Three modes of development have been identified in the history of industrial capitalism in the West. These reflect different combinations of two regimes of accumulation, the *extensive* and *intensive*, and two modes of regulation, the *competitive* and the *monopoly*. Extensive regimes are based on craft production, in which economic growth is created by hiring more labour, lengthening the working day and intensifying worker effort. The potential for increased productivity and larger consumer markets are both restricted. Intensive regimes create growth by means of investment in new production technologies, which increase productivity and provide the potential for mass consumption. Regulationists are particularly interested in the capital–labour relation, notably the labour process and wage labour, and their analyses of modes of regulation mainly concentrate on this narrow aspect of the broader class of regulation. Competitive regulation is characterized by craft control of the labour process, and competition determines wages and prices. The monopoly mode is characterized by SCIENTIFIC MANAGEMENT in the labour process, prices are fixed by companies in collusion, while wages result from employers bargaining collectively with their employees' trade unions and from state intervention in the economy.

The first mode of development, in the nineteenth century, was an extensive regime with a competitive mode of regulation. Class struggle and technical change destabilized this mode in the early part of the twentieth century in the USA, and a new mode of development based on intensive accumulation and competitive regulation developed. This was short-lived, because mass production in the regime of accumulation required guaranteed and stable mass consumer markets, which the mode of regulation could not deliver. This contradiction produced a structural crisis of overinvestment and underconsumption combined with class struggle – the Great Depression of the 1930s. The third mode of development combined intensive accumulation with the monopoly mode of regulation, and solved the contradiction by laying the foundations for mass consumption. Fordism is the name given to this mode, dominant in the middle of the century in the USA and elsewhere. However, the continued refinement of the Fordist manufacturing system led to reducing rates of productivity growth, resulting in a new structural crisis in the late 1970s, which the Regulation School have conceptualized as the crisis of productivity.

Critics suggest that the primacy given to the regulation of the capital–labour relation, especially to the labour process, wage labour and class struggle, produces misleading and one-sided explanations. They also suggest that the historical account of Western capitalism in this century may be inaccurate, since Fordist manufacturing methods were only dominant in those industries producing standardized goods in high volumes for mass consumption and varieties of craft production were common elsewhere; while in some economies (e.g. Germany), Fordist methods were relatively unimportant. Moreover, US industry in the 1980s did not have declining rates of productivity growth, so the source of its economic malaise must have lain elsewhere.

SEE ALSO: *flexible specialization; labour process approach*.

READING: Boyer (1990)

reification Literally meaning a process of making 'thing-like', the concept of reification was popularized by LUKÁCS. He used it to describe a situation in which social relations seem to be beyond human control because they acquire a fixed and immutable quality, almost as if they were features of the natural, rather than social, world. In Lukács' view, reification particularly arises in capitalist societies in which goods are produced for exchange, not for immediate use. These exchanges conceal the social relations involved. For example, men come to see the exchange of wages for labour as an exchange of things, rather than a social relation between people (employers and workers) which is at heart exploitative. Reification is also often related to ALIENATION, in that men feel alienated from the social world as they feel that its thing-like quality removes it from their control.

SEE ALSO: *commodity fetishism*.

relations of production This is a concept central to Marxist social theory. The customary view is that the economy, which for Marxists is the main determinant of social phenomena, is made up of the FORCES OF PRODUCTION and the relations of production. The latter have always proved difficult to define. One influential view is that, in any MODE OF PRODUCTION, the relations of production are the relations between the owners and non-owners of the means of production. The difficulty with such a definition is that ownership appears to be a legal category and, since law is something that is supposed to be determined by the economy, including the relations of production, one should not define relations of production in legal terms. Otherwise the definition of relations of production appears to include the very thing that such relations are supposed to determine.

Attempts to solve this difficulty have pursued non-legal definitions. In essence, these attempts see relations of production in terms of control and the capacity to possess the product. Thus, in capitalist societies, the relations of production are those relations that obtain between capitalist and worker such that the former both controls the means of production and can dispose of the goods and services that are produced by the worker. Of course, the capitalist can behave like this partly because he legally owns the means of production. However, this legal power does not enter into the *definition* of relations of production which could, theoretically, function without this legal sanction.

However defined, relations of production are treated as fundamental to the constitution of societies and more fundamental than the forces of production, which they organize in different ways in different societies.

The concept does not typically refer to the relations between individual capitalists and workers but is generalized to refer to social classes. Thus it is the relations of production that determine the constitution of the two classes, of capitalists and workers. Furthermore, because the relations of production are essentially antagonistic, in that the worker has his product taken away from him, so are the relations between classes.

SEE ALSO: *base and superstructure; class; class struggle; Marx; Marxist sociology*.

relative autonomy Marxist accounts of the state in capitalist societies traditionally regarded it as simply an outpost of the bourgeois ruling class and completely controlled by ruling-class personnel. Later Marxist theorists, notably N. Poulantzas (1973), suggested that the STATE can act with some independence or relative autonomy from this class, though it is never totally independent. Such autonomy allows the state to serve the ruling class more effectively for two reasons. (1) The ruling class tends to split into fractions according to its various economic interests, and to lack the coherence to use state power for the general interests of the class as effectively as a relatively autonomous state does. (2) The state can take a broader and longer-term view of the interests of capital than do members of the ruling class, and can pursue social and political reforms which members may oppose but which contribute to their long-term welfare; for example, raising taxation to provide a welfare state that keeps the working class content with capitalism.

Criticism of the Marxist account has centred on its failure to specify how relative 'relative autonomy' is; hence its refusal to consider that the state may be far more independent of the bourgeoisie in modern industrial capitalism than Marxists are willing to concede. The Weberian analysis of the state, by contrast, has emphasized its independence as a separate bureaucracy that follows its own rules.

SEE ALSO: *capital fractions; elite.*

READING: Parkin (1979)

relative deprivation This concept, formulated by S. A. Stouffer *et al.* (1949) and developed by R. K. Merton (1957), suggests that people mainly experience feelings of deprivation when they compare their own situations unfavourably with those of other individuals or groups. Comparisons can be made both with individuals with whom people interact and with outsiders; what matters is which REFERENCE GROUP the person or group chooses as the focus of comparison. The emphasis on people's subjective frames of reference is a useful addition to the study of DEPRIVATION, but the concept itself does not determine at what point relative deprivation becomes objective and absolute deprivation.

SEE ALSO: *poverty; revolution.*

relativism A theory is said to be relativistic when it cannot provide criteria of truth which are independent and outside of itself; beliefs, theories or values are claimed to be relative to the age or society that produced them and not valid outside those circumstances. Relativism denies the existence of universal criteria of truth and falsity. For example, some theories in the SOCIOLOGY OF KNOWLEDGE are relativist in that they suggest that all knowledge is socially produced and is therefore defective since it is distorted by social interests. Since all knowledge is thus distorted, there are no independent standards of truth. This is an important difficulty, for it implies that there is also no way of validating relativistic theories themselves.

SEE ALSO: *cultural relativism; understanding alien belief systems.*

reliability The reliability of any test employed in research is the extent to which repeated measurements using it under the same conditions produce the same results. Reliability differs from *validity*, which is the success of a test in measuring correctly what it is designed to measure. For example, an attitude scale may be reliable in that it consistently produces the same results, but have little validity since it does not in fact measure the intended attitude but some other.

SEE ALSO: *attitude scales.*

religion In sociology, there are broadly two approaches to the definition of religion. The first, following E. Durkheim (1912), defines religion in terms of its social functions: religion is a system of beliefs and rituals with reference to the SACRED which binds people together into social groups. In this sense, some sociologists have extended the notion of religion to include nationalism. This recent perspective is criticized for being too inclusive, since almost any public activity – football, for example – may have integrative effects for social groups. The second approach, following M. Weber and the theologian P. Tillich, defines religion as any set of coherent answers to human existential dilemmas – birth, sickness or death – which make the world meaningful. In this sense, religion is the human response to those things which concern us ultimately. The implication of this definition is that all human beings are religious, since we are all faced by the existential problems of disease, aging and death.

SEE ALSO: *civil religion; ideology; invisible religion; secularization; sociology of religion; world religions.*

replication This involves the duplication or repetition of an experiment or piece of research. In sampling design it has a more technical meaning, when a number of sub-samples (rather than a single complete sample) are selected from a population with the aim of comparing the estimates of population characteristics arising from the different sub-samples. This comparison is sometimes used to estimate sampling error, but more often to highlight non-sampling errors such as the variation between interviewers who are assigned to different sub-samples in survey research.

repressive state apparatus See: IDEOLOGICAL STATE APPARATUS.

reproduction of labour power K. Marx argued that the reproduction of LABOUR POWER, involving the housing, feeding and health care of workers, is essential for the continuation of capitalist societies, and an understanding of the mechanisms by which this reproduction is achieved is crucial to the adequate analysis of capitalism. This idea has been used in a wide variety of Marxist analyses. The STATE is seen, for example, as having functions in the reproduction of labour power, particularly in respect of housing and health care. Similarly, the family and women's DOMESTIC LABOUR perform the same general function.

SEE ALSO: *collective consumption.*

residue See: PARETO.

restricted code BERNSTEIN introduced this concept, contrasting it with *elaborated code*. Restricted code privileges context-dependent meanings, where principles are implicit, and presupposes closely shared identifications, beliefs and practices. Such a system of meanings acts selectively on syntactic and lexical choices. Elaborated codes privilege relatively context-independent systems of specialized meanings, where principles are more likely to be more explicit. Bernstein argued that the lower working class uses restricted code and the middle class uses both codes and, since the educational system transmits class-regulated elaborated codes, the working-class child is potentially at a disadvantage. Bernstein has continued to use the concepts of restricted and elaborated codes in his later theoretical and empirical work developing relationships between meanings, linguistic realizations and social context. Furthermore, they now form part of a more general theory of the transmission of forms of consciousness which relates social-class relations to the distribution of power, and to principles of control where language codes are positioning devices.

SEE ALSO: *classroom interaction; classroom knowledge.*

READING: Bernstein (1977)

revolution In everyday usage, a revolution is any sudden, usually violent, change in the government of a society. However, social scientists regard such events as 'palace revolutions' or *coups d'état*, reserving the term 'revolution' for a total change in the social structure, of which political changes in government are only a manifestation. The explanations of revolution may be political (e.g. the failure of a government to fulfil electoral commitments or to function adequately); economic (e.g. the combination of long-term poverty and short-term failures); or sociological (e.g. the curtailment of social mobility). Some explanations combine a variety of factors, as in the 'J-curve theory of rising expectations', which suggests that revolutions are not the result of absolute but of RELATIVE DEPRIVATION, occurring when long periods of rising economic prosperity are sharply reversed.

The debate about the nature of revolutions has been dominated by Marxist theory, in which there is a clear distinction between political changes in governments and radical changes in the economic organization of society. In his analysis of India, K. Marx suggested that periodic changes in government or dynasties did not fundamentally change the static nature of the prevailing MODE OF PRODUCTION. For Marx, a revolution involved the replacement of one mode of production by another, as in the transition from feudalism to capitalism. Marxist approaches to revolution may, however, either emphasize the importance of the struggles between social classes – the history of societies is the history of class conflict – or the CONTRADICTION within the mode of production between the forces and the RELATIONS OF PRODUCTION. Marxists who treat class conflict as the essential feature of Marxist analysis are likely to see revolution as the uncertain outcome of a complex combination of forces – CLASS CONSCIOUSNESS, historical circumstance, political organization and the repression of the working class. Marxists concerned with the analysis of modes of production suggest that revolutions are an inevitable outcome of contradictions in the economic base.

Revolutions have, in addition, to be considered in a global context. While Marx and Engels assumed that the revolutionary collapse of capitalism would occur in core states (such as France and Britain), the major revolutions of the twentieth century mainly occurred in the so-called peripheral regions of Latin America and Asia. L. Althusser (1966) argued that revolution would be most likely in the weak link of the chain of capitalist society, where social contradictions were most prominent. The collapse of socialist governments in Eastern Europe and the former Soviet Union after 1989 were initially 'palace revolutions'. But the fundamental changes in political systems, as multi-party democracy was introduced, and in the economy, as capitalism replaced socialism, allow these events to be described as true revolutions. The survival of European capitalism and the collapse of socialism represent a major problem for Marxist theories of revolution, and these are now widely regarded as discredited.

SEE ALSO: *citizenship*; *conflict theory*; *Gramsci*; *institutionalization of conflict*; *Marxist sociology*; *peasants*.

READING: Kramnick (1972); Lane and Ross (1999)

Rex, John (b. 1925) Research professor in ethnic relations at the University of Aston, Birmingham (1984–90), his contribution to contemporary sociology lies in two areas. First, he has defended the classical sociological tradition in *Key Problems of Sociological Theory* (1961), *Discovering Sociology* (1973a), *Sociology and the Demystification of the Modern World* (1974) and *Social Conflict* (1981) against what he regards as the dogmatic fashions of contemporary theory. Secondly, he has contributed to the study of race relations in *Race, Community and Conflict* (1967), with R. Moore, *Race Relations in Sociological Theory* (1970), *Race, Colonialism and the City* (1973b), *Colonial Immigrants in a British City* (1979), with S. Tomlinson, and *Race and Ethnicity* (1986).

rhetoric Traditionally, rhetoric is the art of formulating arguments, or of using language, to persuade others. In classical civilizations, it was taught as a body of rules. In contemporary social science, the term has been employed to point to the importance of argument and persuasion in spoken word or written text. For example, in M. Billig's (1991) view, social science underrates the importance of rhetoric in everyday life. The formation of attitudes and opinions, even thinking itself, are intrinsically processes of argument. The idea of rhetoric has close overlaps with the concept of IDEOLOGY, in that both refer to the ways in which people are persuaded.

rights This umbrella concept covers a range of issues to do with CITIZENSHIP, EQUALITY, JUSTICE and LEGITIMACY. Rights are either passive or active, and can be defined as: (1) a claim (e.g. to have a loan repaid); (2) a power (e.g. to distribute property through a will); (3) a liberty (e.g. to express political opinions); (4) an immunity (e.g. from interference). Rights are said to be the mirror image of duties. A right to claim the repayment of a loan implies a duty to repay. Therefore, rights define the relationships between rights-bearers (who are typically individuals) and rights-upholders (which are typically states). This taxonomy of contrasting claims and obligations (privilege/duty, power/disability and immunity/liability) was first developed by the jurist W. N. Hohfeld in *Fundamental Legal Conceptions* (1919). The Hohfeldian model gave rise to a distinction between choice theory and benefit theory, which examines the issue of who or what can enjoy rights. The former, as the term suggests, asserts that rights can be exercised only by beings who are rational and capable of choice, that is by human beings. Choice theory suggests that animals cannot, properly speaking, enjoy rights. In benefit theory, which associates rights with permission, rights may be enjoyed as benefits by any creature which can be benefited. The two positions attempt to distinguish between a right as something claimed by an individual and as due to an individual or being.

There are also fundamentally different schemes or frameworks for expressing the characteristics of rights. We can distinguish the following categories.

(1) *Natural rights* are derived from NATURAL LAW. Natural law theory claims either, that rights are derived from the eternal moral order created by God, or, that rights are derived from the laws of nature, which are rational. Individuals have rights and obligations because there is a fundamental law which morally regulates the social order.

(2) With SECULARIZATION, natural law theory evolved into a theory of *human rights*; for example, in the work of H. Grotius in *On the Law of War and Peace* (1625). Contemporary human rights theory is a product of the human suffering resulting from twentieth-century GENOCIDE. The concept of a human right has been defined by M. Freeden (1991), as a legal device which assigns priority to certain attributes that are regarded as necessary for the functioning of a human being, which protects those attributes, and which promotes intervention to guarantee those attributes and conditions.

(3) Whereas natural or human rights (as outlined in the 1948 United Nations Declaration of Human Rights) are said to be held by individuals simply by virtue of

their being human, *civil rights* are claims within a specific STATE or political community which are upheld and recognized by specific legal systems. Civil rights in contemporary society have often been associated with SOCIAL MOVEMENTS and their protests for the recognition of civil liberties, such as the civil rights movement in the United States in the mid twentieth century.

(4) *Welfare rights* include claims on the provision of material assistance to individuals in need, and they may also attempt a redistribution of wealth and other resources in society. Welfare rights typically include the provision of education and health, and thus make some assumption about the importance of justice. Critics sometimes argue that no reform of society is possible through welfare rights without a radical redistribution of private property.

Rights are often associated with liberalism and INDIVIDUALISM, and thus criticized as the expression of Western conceptions of the individual. The liberal doctrine of individual rights tends to associate rights with property ownership, hence it has been criticized by FEMINIST SOCIAL THEORY for its implicit assumptions about male control of the household. COMMUNITARIANISM also denies the notion that rights should be understood within the tradition of liberal individualism.

READING: Steiner (1994)

risk/risk society The concept of risk has been fundamental to economic theory, in which choices with respect to economic ends (such as investment and profit) are always uncertain, because knowledge of the situation is imperfect. For example, J. Schumpeter (1934) defined entrepreneurship as risk-taking behaviour and, in classical economics, A. Smith's labour market theory in the *Wealth of Nations* (1776) argued that risk factors were not fully reflected in the wages of risky occupations such as seafaring.

In anthropology, DOUGLAS developed a notion of pollution and taboo, that saw social relations as inherently risky and uncertain. Religious ideas about purity and danger can be interpreted as cultural responses to risk.

Contemporary sociology has elaborated the economic notion of risk as uncertainty to argue that MODERNIZATION has produced a new type of society, which U. Beck (1992) calls a 'risk society'. In the early development of industrial societies, risks such as industrial smog were obvious, palpable and observable. But the risks of advanced societies are both less obvious and frequently also the unanticipated effects of scientific and technological advances. Risks created by environmental pollution or medical science, for example, often remain unknown to the public until their presence is exposed by a crisis. Medical catastrophes such as thalidomide babies or the victims of Creutzfeldt-Jakob disease can remain undetected until the problem is widespread. The hole in the ozone layer is for the public not a directly observable or palpable risk. This new order of risk presents problems and issues which traditional social science theories cannot readily understand or explain. For example, economics has traditionally conceptualized the economy as a mechanism for the distribution of goods, but a risk society is based on the production of 'bads'.

Beck's theory can be criticized on the grounds that it fails to produce a systematic definition of risk. For example, while he attempts to understand the risky characteristics of social relations, most of his examples refer not so much to social and political risk as to environmental hazard. The debate about a risk society has consequently focused primarily on the spread of environmental pollution. Indeed, risk theory is interpreted as a 'new ecology' by S. Lash *et al.* in *Risk, Environment and Modernity* (1996). Alternatively, a risk society is seen as a criticism of POSTMODERNISM, because of its emphasis on the idea of REFLEXIVE MODERNIZATION (Beck *et al.*, 1994). It recognizes the importance of expert knowledge and rational criticism in response to environmental pollution. A risk society represents a new view of modernity, namely one in which disputes about knowledge are paramount. The theory of risk society has produced a useful bridge between political criticisms of environmental damage in industrial capitalism and the critical analysis of instrumental reason in the Frankfurt School.

SEE ALSO: *industrialization; post-industrial society; rationalization.*

rites of passage A term first used systematically in anthropology to denote public ceremonies celebrating the transition of an individual or group to a new status, for example initiation ceremonies. Such rites, typically associated with transitions in the LIFE-CYCLE, are less prominent in industrial than in traditional societies, though they may persist in such ceremonies as marriage services.

ritual In anthropology, any formal actions following a set pattern that express through SYMBOL a public or shared meaning are rituals. They are typically the practical aspects of a religious system and they express sacred VALUES rather than seek to achieve some utilitarian end. In sociology, ritual is often used to refer to any regular pattern of interaction; thus the expression 'How do you do?' as a routine method of starting conversations could be regarded as a ritual of everyday interaction.

SEE ALSO: *Durkheim.*

role This concept assumes that, when people occupy social positions, their behaviour is determined mainly by what is expected of that position rather than by their own individual characteristics – roles are the bundles of socially defined attributes and expectations associated with social positions. For example, an individual school-teacher performs the role of 'teacher', which carries with it certain expected behaviours irrespective of his or her own personal feelings at any one time, and therefore it is possible to generalize about the professional role behaviour of teachers regardless of the individual characteristics of the people who occupy these positions. Role is sociologically important because it demonstrates how individual activity is socially influenced and thus follows regular patterns. Sociologists have used roles as the units from which social institutions are constructed. For example, the school as a social INSTITUTION may be analysed as a collection of teacher and pupil roles which are common across all schools.

There are broadly two approaches to the theory of social roles. The first systematic use of the concept was by George H. MEAD in 1934, a forerunner of SYMBOLIC INTERACTIONISM. In this usage, roles are depicted as the outcome of a process of interaction that is tentative and creative. Meadian social psychology was primarily concerned with how children learn about society and develop their own social beings (the 'self') by *role-taking*, that is imaginatively taking the roles of *others* such as fathers, mothers, doctors, teachers. In adult social behaviour, individuals were also thought to use role-taking to work out their own roles. For symbolic interactionism, every role involves interaction with other roles; for example, the role of 'teacher' cannot be conceived without the role of 'pupil' and may only be defined as expected behaviour in relation to the expected behaviour of the pupil. The interaction process means that people in roles are always testing their conceptions of other-roles, and the response of people in other-roles reinforces or questions such conceptions. This in turn leads people to maintain or change their own role behaviour. *Role-making* describes how expected behaviour is created and modified in interaction, a 'tentative process in which roles are identified and given content on shifting axes as interaction proceeds' (R. H. Turner, 1962). Symbolic interactionists attempt to avoid the extreme relativism implied by role-making, namely that roles are fluid and indeterminate and that every single interaction produces a different and unique role, and assert that role-making produces consistent patterns of behaviour which can be identified with various types of social actors. They adhere to the sociological concern with the regularities of expected behaviour.

A second approach to role theory derived from R. Linton (1936) and was subsequently incorporated into FUNCTIONALISM. This moves away from role-taking as the characteristic form of interaction with role-making as its outcome, and sees roles as essentially prescribed and static expectations of behaviour, as prescriptions inherent in particular positions. These prescriptions derive from the society's CULTURE, typically regarded in functionalist accounts as a unified cultural system, and they are expressed in the social norms that guide behaviour in roles. The cultural-prescriptions approach recognizes that roles are often defined in relation to other roles, but not that interaction creates or modifies roles. However, individuals may become aware of their culturally defined roles in the course of interaction with people in other roles. Carried to extremes, this approach assumes a rigid determination of behaviour that effectively makes 'role' synonymous with 'culture' and 'norms' and thus largely redundant.

Investigation of actual roles often demonstrates a considerable indeterminacy of expected behaviour associated with social positions, which is what symbolic interactionism postulates. Nevertheless, indeterminacy can also be explained from within the cultural-prescriptions approach: the cultural norms that guide behaviour may be vague and capable of various interpretations; individual roles may be subject to incompatible expectations from the other roles to which they relate (e.g. the role of first-line supervisor in industry is known to be subject to conflicting pressures from the occupants of worker and managerial roles which embody different conceptions of expected supervisory behaviour, even though it may be shown that both conceptions are culturally determined).

Culture and norms are rarely completely specific about concrete behaviour. Nor do they form that integrated system of mutually compatible elements which in turn are universally accepted, as functionalism postulates: the cultures of modern societies are frequently fragmented, containing diverse and inconsistent elements, and different groups (e.g. workers and managers) may adhere to different elements.

Subsequent accounts of roles produced several refinements. *Role distance*, a term coined by GOFFMAN (1959), refers to the detachment of the performer from the role he or she is performing. This makes an important distinction between the existence of expectations concerning a social role, the performance of a role and an individual's commitment to a role. In role distance, performers of a role adopt a subjective detachment from it. *Role conflict* is used in various senses: (1) when a person finds he or she is playing two or more roles at one time that make incompatible demands, as often happens, for example, with those married working women who feel that they have to satisfy simultaneously the role expectations of employee, wife and mother, which may conflict; (2) when a person defines his or her role in one way while those in related roles define it differently, as may happen, for example, when teachers adhere to their own codes of professional behaviour, which are disputed by parents or education authorities; (3) when related roles have incompatible expectations of the focal role, as is the case in the example above of supervisors receiving conflicting expectations from workers and managers. Also, the freedom of individuals to role-make is now seen to vary according to the type of position they occupy. At one extreme are the bureaucratic roles found in formal organizations and the military, where rules of behaviour are explicit and formalized and the scope for improvisation is reduced – though never eliminated, as ORGANIZATION THEORY shows. At the other are ill-defined roles such as parent or friend, where the scope is far greater.

SEE ALSO: *norm*; *sex roles*; *status*.

READING: Jackson (1972); Turner, J. H. (1991)

role, conjugal See: CONJUGAL ROLE.

role, sick See: SICK ROLE.

role conflict See: ROLE.

role distance See: ROLE.

rule One school in the philosophy of social science argues that social behaviour should be understood as following a rule and not as causally generated. The best-known exponent of this position is P. Winch (1958), who argues that human behaviour is intrinsically meaningful and that one cannot *causally* understand how it is that human beings give meaning to actions. The giving of meaning is a function of following rules which are essentially social since the appeal to others' following of rules is the only way of deciding whether an attribution of meaning is correct or incorrect. For Winch, therefore, connections between actions are conceptual, not causal, and it follows that the reasons given by an actor for his or her action cannot be seen as causes of the action.

READING: Keat and Urry (1975)

ruling class A somewhat archaic term in sociology, ruling class has come to mean a social CLASS, usually the economically dominant class, that controls a society through whatever political institutions are available. In some societies this control may be overt, as in feudal times, while in others it may be less obvious. Many Marxists, for example, argue that parliamentary democracies are really controlled by the capitalist class, the economically powerful, although this control is by no means obvious or even deliberate, being exercised by such methods as the recruitment of members of parliament with particular class backgrounds.

ELITE theorists argue that true democracy is impossible and that all societies will be dominated by a ruling class whatever their social structure.

SEE ALSO: *Mosca*; *Pareto*; *state*.

READING: Scott, J. (1991)

rural sociology In its nineteenth- and early-twentieth-century origins, rural sociology was dominated by a contrast with, and a dislike of, urban life. Attempts were made to describe a rural way of life which differed significantly from its urban counterpart. The former was variously characterized as having GEMEINSCHAFT relationships, as being based on close family ties, as exhibiting a high degree of social order and as demonstrating personal as opposed to impersonal social relations. As the rural sector shrank in size in most Western societies, it became increasingly difficult to sustain a notion of well-marked differences between rural and urban life. As a result, the rigid distinction was replaced by the idea of a RURAL–URBAN CONTINUUM.

From the 1960s onwards, rural sociology in Britain was transformed by studies of the social structure of villages and the countryside, of rural community life, of changes in farming methods, and of tourism. Rural life has been substantially affected by the decline in demand for labour in agriculture, by the development of national and international markets for agricultural produce, by the tendency for country dwellers to commute to work in nearby towns, by second-home ownership, by retirement to rural settings and by the use of the country for tourism. The result has been a greater diversification of the rural population, which is much less local in orientation, with a much smaller proportion earning their living from working the land.

READING: Newby (1979)

rural–urban continuum In much nineteenth-century sociology, it was argued that there was a definite contrast between urban and rural societies. It gradually became clear that a dichotomy of this kind was too simple; there were gradations of urban and rural. R. Redfield (1930), for example, constructed a continuum from small rural villages (or folk societies) to large cities, the more urban being more secular, more individualistic, and with a greater division of labour and consequent social and cultural disorganization. There have been many similar attempts by investigators of rural and urban communities. R. Frankenberg (1966) differentiated rural from urban by means of the concepts of ROLE and network. In urban areas there is much greater differentiation of roles and the network of social relationships is less dense. The notion of the rural–urban continuum has recently passed out of use, mainly because there no longer seem to be significant differences between urban and rural ways of life. What differences in ways of life that do exist between communities or social groups are mostly attributable to such factors as social class and not geographical location.

SEE ALSO: *community; Gemeinschaft; network/social network; Toennies; urban way of life.*

S

sacred For E. Durkheim, all religious beliefs classify phenomena as either sacred or PROFANE. The sacred includes phenomena which are regarded and experienced as extraordinary, transcendent and outside the everyday course of events. In modern societies, there has been a shrinkage of sacred reality, brought about by the RATIONALIZATION of culture.

SEE ALSO: *charisma; invisible religion; religion; secularization.*

Saint-Simon, Claude H. (1760–1825) Regarded as simultaneously the founder of French socialism and sociology, Saint-Simon led a remarkable life. Born into the French aristocracy, he was a captain in the French army which fought the British in the West Indies and North America. Changing his name to Bonhomme during the Revolution, he was imprisoned under the Terror. Under the Directory and later, he was the architect of a number of educational experiments and the centre of an influential *salon*. From 1806 onwards, Saint-Simon lived in abject poverty as an independent scholar. In 1823 he attempted suicide, losing an eye as a result. While his doctrines reflect the bizarre character of his private life, Saint-Simon was particularly influential on K. Marx and, via A. Comte and E. Durkheim, on sociology.

The principal components of his thought were: (1) the history of human society passes through three distinct stages, to which correspond distinct modes of thought – polytheism and slavery, theism and feudalism, positivism and industrialism; (2) by the application of scientific POSITIVISM, it is possible to discover the laws of social change and organization; (3) the organization and direction of modern society should be in the hands of scientists and industrialists, since bureaucrats, lawyers and clerics are essentially unproductive and parasitic; (4) the crisis of modern society could be solved by the development of a new religion based on positivism and under the control of a new priesthood, namely sociologists.

READING: Taylor, K. (1975)

sampling For practical and cost reasons, it is often impossible to collect information about the entire population of people or things in which social researchers are interested. In these cases, a sample of the total population is selected for study. The main criteria when sampling are (1) to ensure that a sample provides a faithful representation of the totality from which it is selected, and (2) to know as precisely as possible the probability that a sample is reliable in this way. Randomization meets these criteria, because (1) it protects against bias in the selection process and (2) provides a basis on which to apply statistical distribution theory, which allows an estimate to be made of the probability that conclusions drawn from the sample are correct.

The basic type of random sample is known as a *simple random sample*, one in which each person or item has an equal chance of being chosen. Often a population contains various distinct groups or strata which differ on the attribute that is being researched. *Stratified random sampling* involves sampling each stratum separately. This increases precision, or reduces time, effort and cost by allowing smaller sample sizes for a given level of precision. For example, poverty is known to be most common among the elderly, the unemployed and single-parent families, so research on the effects of poverty might well sample separately each of these three strata as part of a survey of poverty in the population as a whole, which would permit the total sample size to be reduced because the investigator would know that the groups most affected by poverty were guaranteed inclusion. *Cluster sampling* is sometimes used when the population naturally congregates into clusters. For example, managers are clustered in organizations, so a sample of managers could be obtained by taking a random sample of organizations and investigating the managers in each of these. Interviewing or observing managers on this basis would be cheaper and easier than using a simple random sample of managers scattered across all organizations in the country. This is usually less precise than a simple random sample of the same size, but in practice the reduction in cost per element more than compensates for the decrease in precision.

Sampling may be done as one process or in stages, known as *multi-stage sampling*. Multi-stage designs are common when populations are widely dispersed. Thus a survey of business managers might proceed by selecting a sample of corporations as first-stage units, perhaps choosing these corporations with a probability proportionate to their size, and then selecting a sample of managers within these corporations at the second stage. Alternatively, a sample of individual factories or office buildings within each corporation could be chosen as the second-stage units, followed by a sample of managers in each of these as a third stage. Stratification can also be used in the design, if, for example, occupational sub-groups are known to differ from each other, by selecting strata such as personnel, production and finance management and sampling within each of these.

For sampling to be representative, one needs a complete and accurate list of the first-stage units that make up the relevant population, a basic requirement that is not always easily met. This list forms the *sampling frame*. Selection from the frame is best done by numbering the items and using a table of random numbers to identify which items form the sample, though a quasi-random method of simply taking every nth item from the list is often appropriate.

The reliability of a sample taken from a population can be assessed by the spread of the sampling distribution, measured by the STANDARD DEVIATION of this distribution, called the *standard error*. As a general rule, the larger the size of the sample, the smaller the standard error.

SEE ALSO: *sampling error*; *significance test*; *survey*.

sampling error Many sociological investigations depend on a randomly selected sample drawn from a wider population. However, a single sample may not be an accurate representation of the population, so sample estimates are subject to sampling error. Repetitive sampling would in the long run average out fluctuations between individual samples and so provide a true representation. However, it is possible to estimate the degree of sampling error from a single sample, and thus to construct confidence intervals and to use statistical significance tests. Sampling errors are more likely to be large if samples are too small or the population has a high degree of variability.

SEE ALSO: *bias; non-response; sampling; significance test.*

sanction Sanctions may be either positive or negative. Positive sanctions reward behaviour that conforms to social norms, while negative sanctions restrain deviant behaviour. Sanctions are heterogeneous, ranging, for example, from financial reward or legal restraint to praise or verbal abuse. The concept has thus played an important part in the explanation of social order. Societies exist because, through the INTERN-ALIZATION of sanctions, human agents monitor their own behaviour in anticipation of reward or punishment from other social actors. In CONFLICT THEORY there is a greater emphasis on the external and coercive nature of sanctions; the enforcement of sanctions is thus seen not as evidence of agreement about values but of social control and power.

SEE ALSO: *norm.*

Saussure, Ferdinand de (1857–1913) A Swiss linguist who founded the Geneva School of Linguistic Structuralism, Saussure emphasized the collective nature of language: like culture, language is a collectively produced and shared system of meaning. He was influenced by DURKHEIM. In his *Course in General Linguistics* (1916), he distinguished between speech or language-behaviour (*parole*) and language as a system of regularities (*langue*). Language is a system of signs. The meaning of language is determined by a structure of mutually defining units, which is a self-referential and conventional system. The linguistic unit or sign has two dimensions: the signifier and the signified. The radical nature of Saussurian linguistics was to claim that the relationship between signifier and signified is arbitrary: there is no necessary, natural or intrinsic relationship between linguistic forms and their designated meanings.

SEE ALSO: *denotation; semiotics; structuralism.*
READING: Culler (1976)

scatter diagram See: REGRESSION.

Schutz, Alfred (1899–1959) Born in Austria, Schutz emigrated to the United States in 1939 where he taught and wrote part time, only taking a full-time academic post in 1952. His main publications are: *Collected Papers* (1971); *The Phenomenology of the Social World* (1972); *The Structures of the Life-World* (1974), with T. Luckmann. Schutz was a major influence in the development of PHENOMENOLOGICAL SOCIOLOGY in the English-speaking world. He was primarily interested in three problems: (1) he wanted to construct an adequate theory of social action, partly based on a critique of M. Weber; (2) he carried out a series of investigations into the constitution of the LIFE-WORLD; (3) he tried to investigate the manner in which a sociology that took human action as important could be scientific. In a dispute with PARSONS, Schutz did much to advance and clarify the problems of action theory and VERSTEHEN. His posthumous works included an analysis of the role of relevance in structuring the life-world (1970).

READING: Grathoff (1978)

scientific management At the end of the nineteenth century, workshop administration in manufacturing industry in America and Europe was still largely in the hands of foremen and skilled workers who, in addition to performing the physical tasks of production, decided how jobs were to be done, how the labour force was to be organized and supervised, and often who was to be hired. The scientific management movement of the early twentieth century, associated with the name of its main advocate, F. W. Taylor, attempted to transform the administration of the workplace so as to increase profitability.

Taylor put forward three principles of reorganization. (1) Greater DIVISION OF LABOUR: production processes were to be analysed systematically and broken down to their component parts, so that each worker's job was simplified and preferably reduced to a single, simple task. Greater specialization would lead to greater efficiency, while the DE-SKILLING that followed simplification of tasks would also allow cheaper, unskilled labour to be hired. Greater division of labour would in turn remove the planning, organizing and hiring functions from the shop floor. Greater specialization was also to be encouraged among managers. (2) Full managerial control of the workplace was to be established for the first time, and managers were to be responsible for the coordination of the production process that greater division of labour had fragmented. (3) Cost accounting based on systematic time-and-motion study was to be introduced to provide managers with the information they needed in their new roles as the controllers of the workplace.

Taylor believed that financial considerations determined employees' motivation. He assumed that if employees felt that they were sharing fairly in the increased profitability created by new workshop organization, they would willingly cooperate with management. An important aim was to design a system of payment by results that was scientific and just, to allow labour to share in the profits arising out of their efforts. In practice, companies that adopted scientific management largely ignored this aim.

Scientific management proposed two major transformations of industry simultaneously: the removal of manual skills and organizational autonomy from the work of lower-level employees; and the establishment of managing as a role distinct from ownership, with a set of technical functions to do with organization. As a movement, scientific management had some success in America prior to the First World War and later in Europe and the Soviet Union under Lenin. Its real influence, however, was more pervasive, because it provided an important legitimation of MANAGEMENT in the early days of the MANAGERIAL REVOLUTION and, in addition, established the central philosophy of work organization that dominated industry until new philosophies of work, such as FLEXIBLE SPECIALIZATION, emerged in the final quarter of the twentieth century. Scientific management was also linked with the revolution in manufacturing methods introduced by H. Ford. Between 1908 and 1914, Ford pioneered mechanized mass production, notably the moving assembly line. FORDISM is sometimes seen as separate from Taylorism, but in fact the moving line and other aspects of the mechanization of production depended on the rationalization of work outlined in the first of Taylor's principles.

SEE ALSO: *human relations*; *labour process approach*; *managerial strategies of control*.
READING: Taylor, F. W. (1964); Littler (1985)

scientific method See: SOCIOLOGY AS SCIENCE.

Scottish Enlightenment In the period 1707 to 1830, Scotland experienced considerable economic growth, which was associated with a flowering of Scottish culture, particularly moral and social philosophy and POLITICAL ECONOMY. The Scottish Enlightenment, which in many respects anticipated the development of sociology by COMTE and SPENCER in the nineteenth century, is chiefly associated with D. Hume (1711–76), A. Ferguson (1723–1816), J. Millar (1735–1801) and A. Smith (1723–90).

The Scottish Enlightenment's social philosophy had a number of common themes: (1) its sceptical EMPIRICISM emphasized the importance of observation and critical assessment of experience over religious revelation and philosophical speculation; (2) it recognized the importance of social change and social organization in the development of morals, and the difficulties of RELATIVISM; (3) while recognizing the material benefits brought about by industrialization, it did not suggest that social progress necessarily contributed to individual happiness; (4) the need for a new conceptual apparatus to understand the changes taking place in Scottish society was recognized.

The background to the Scottish Enlightenment was the economic and commercial development of Scotland, which reinforced the traditional division between Catholic, feudal Highlands and Protestant, capitalist Lowlands. The contrast between 'civil society' in the Lowlands (with its new system of social ranks, urban conflicts and moral change) and 'barbaric' society in the Highlands (with its traditional hierarchies, stable agrarian structure and static morality) provided the original focus of the theory of CIVILIZATION.

SEE ALSO: *civil society*.

READING: Schneider (1967)

secondary analysis Data that are collected and analysed for one purpose may later be analysed for other purposes, often by different researchers. Secondary analyses have always been common in economics and population studies, where the major data sets have been OFFICIAL STATISTICS. They have also become more common in sociology over the last two decades.

SEE ALSO: *survey*.

secondary labour market See: LABOUR MARKET SEGMENTATION.

sect This is a small, voluntary, exclusive religious group, demanding total commitment from its followers and emphasizing its separateness from and rejection of society. There has been considerable debate about these characteristics and a wide variety of sub-types have been identified and studied by sociologists, but the 'church–sect typology' remains a central focus of the SOCIOLOGY OF RELIGION.

It is argued that, when sects are successful in recruiting members and grow in size and complexity, they tend to approximate the denomination, which is a mid-point on the church–sect continuum. (A denomination is an inclusive religious organization with voluntary membership, doctrinal toleration and a professional ministry.) Religious commitment becomes less intense, because over time members are born into rather than converted to the sect. This is often referred to as 'the second-generation problem' and the whole process as 'denominationalization'. While this is true of so-called 'conversionist sects', denominationalization may not be characteristic of 'gnostic sects', which do not seek to change the world by large-scale conversion.

SEE ALSO: *charisma; church; cult; secularization.*

READING: Wilson, B. (1982)

secularization B. Wilson (1966) defined secularization as the process in which religious thinking, practice and institutions lose social significance. In Europe, secularization is held to be the consequence of the social changes brought about by urban, industrial society. Critics of this account argue: (1) it has to assume the existence of a 'golden age' of RELIGION, when religious institutions did have widespread social significance; (2) it exaggerates the presence of rational, secular belief in modern society, ignoring the evidence of superstition and magic; (3) it cannot account for the prevalence of cults among the young, especially those deriving from Oriental religions such as Hare Krishna, Divine Light Mission and the Meher Baba movement; (4) it underestimates the importance of organized Christianity as a political force in Europe and North America; (5) in a comparative perspective, the vitality of Zionism, militant Islam and radical Catholicism in Latin America suggests that there is no necessary connection between MODERNIZATION and secularization; (6) by adopting a narrow definition of religion, it equates secularization with de-Christianization; (7) there are processes in modern societies which ascribe a transcendental or SACRED significance to the self; these processes constitute an INVISIBLE RELIGION.

While these criticisms have not been adequately overcome, it can be argued that the diversity of religious cults and practices in modern society demonstrates that religion has become a matter of personal choice rather than a dominant feature of public life. It is further suggested that, while religion may play an important role in fundamentalist struggles against modernization, as in contemporary Afghanistan and nationalist movements in Russia, in the long term the modernization of society does bring about secularization.

The process of secularization is, however, highly variable between different industrial societies and in some European societies (such as France, Ireland, Italy and Holland), Christianity still has an important social role. Understanding secularization is thus necessary for any analysis of the culture of capitalist societies. Finally, some theorists of GLOBALIZATION suggest that religion contributes in significant ways to the emergence of global cultures.

SEE ALSO: *church; civil religion; new religious movements; profane; rationalization; sect.*

READING: Luckmann (1967); Beyer (1994)

segmented labour markets See: LABOUR MARKET SEGMENTATION.

segregated conjugal role See: CONJUGAL ROLE.

segregation Societies may be divided on ethnic or racial lines in such a way that communities may be segregated from one another. Such segregation is usually spatial and can be enforced by law as happened in South Africa. More commonly it is produced by non-formal means. The term also has other uses as in occupational segregation.

SEE ALSO: *ghetto; prejudice; sociology of race; women and work.*

selective/universal benefit See: WELFARE STATE.

self See: IDENTITY; INDIVIDUALISM; MEAD, GEORGE H.; ROLE; SYMBOLIC INTERACTIONISM.

semiology See: SEMIOTICS.

semiotics Used synonymously with semiology, the term semiotics is defined as the study of signs. It has had some influence in those areas of sociology which deal with communication in any form, for it seeks to provide a method for the analysis of messages, both verbal and non-verbal.

The starting point of semiotics is the distinction between *signifier, signified* and *sign*. The signifier can be a physical object, a word or a picture of some kind. The signified is a mental concept indicated by the signifier. The sign is the association of signifier and signified. For example, a Valentine card (signifier) can signify adoration (signified). Both card and adoration can exist separately, perhaps with other signifiers or signifieds, but their association constitutes a specific sign. The relationship between signifier and signified can be fairly direct. A photograph of a baby, for example, indicates the signified (the baby) relatively straightforwardly. In other cases, however, what signified is indicated by a signifier is largely a matter of social convention, as is the case with language, for example. Those signs relatively free of social mediation are termed *iconic*, while those more dependent on such mediation are *arbitrary*.

Signifiers may also indicate different signifieds at different levels; there may be different levels of signification or different layers of meaning of signs. A photograph of a baby, for example, may signify a baby, but it may also signify, at a second level, the innocence of childhood or the sanctity of family life. BARTHES argues that there are two ways in which signs may function at a second level of signification. (1) They may form myths, in that a sign stands for a whole range of cultural values. (2) A sign not only associates an image or object with a concept, it also engenders various feelings in us; signs not only denote, they also connote.

Signs may also be organized into codes. Again cultural conventions determine how codes are constructed for they decide which signs may meaningfully go together. Particular fashions in dress may constitute a code, for example. As the word implies, some codes may be hidden and less obvious than those of fashion and it requires detailed analysis to bring them out.

Semiotics is valuable in that it identifies a problem. That is, it goes beyond the immediate impact of a sign to ask questions about the wider meanings and social functions of sign systems. There is some doubt, however, whether it does any more than provide a set of concepts for tackling these issues. Furthermore, the problem of validating a semiotic analysis has not received any distinctive solution.

SEE ALSO: *discourse; hermeneutics; ideology; myth; polysemy; sociology of the mass media; Saussure; structuralism.*

READING: Hawkes (1977)

sentiment The concept of sentiment has two different meanings: (1) sentiments are culturally patterned EMOTIONS – the emotion of rage corresponds to the sentiment of indignation; (2) in EXCHANGE THEORY, interaction between individuals in social groups produces collective sentiments of loyalty, friendship, altruism and group commitment, which in turn reinforce common norms. Sentiments are not internal, subjective feelings but overt, observable signs of solidarity between individuals emerging from interaction. Both perspectives, however different, treat sentiments as an essential feature of social exchange.

service class The term was coined by K. Renner and adapted by R. Dahrendorf (1959) to categorize the class position of certain higher-level, non-manual groups such as business managers, professionals employed by institutions rather than self-employed, public officials, who exercise power and expertise on behalf of (i.e. they 'serve') corporate bodies or the capitalist class. This concept fell out of use until it was revived by J. Goldthorpe in the 1970s. It became part of the class categorization used in the investigation of SOCIAL MOBILITY in Britain that was carried out by the Social Mobility Group at Oxford University and is reported by J. H. Goldthorpe (1987). Goldthorpe argues that most managers, professionals and administrators have an employment relationship which is based on a contract of service rather than a labour contract to provide a certain amount of labour. In this type of relationship, employers reward employees for their service by trusting them and allowing them considerable autonomy at work, as well as by paying them well. Goldthorpe subsequently dropped the notion of trust as one defining feature of the relationship. He now claims that service-class employees have their more privileged employment contract (the service contract) because their work is very difficult to monitor and supervise, and they have general skills and specific knowledge which firms cannot easily replace if they leave.

SEE ALSO: *class*; *middle class*.

READING: Savage *et al.* (1992)

service crimes See: CRIMES WITHOUT VICTIMS.

service sector The sector of the economy which provides services rather than physical products. This sector has grown relative to manufacturing in all contemporary capitalist economies. There are a multitude of service industries, including, for example, finance, sales, distribution, education, health and personal services. They range from the financial activities of the City of London or Wall Street to caring for the elderly or infirm. The relative decline of manufacturing and rise of services has been an important focus of sociological accounts of POST-INDUSTRIAL SOCIETY.

SEE ALSO: *de-industrialization*.

sex ratio The ratio of males to females, normally expressed as the number of males per thousand females in a society, at any given age. While fewer girls than boys are born each year, males have a higher mortality rate, thus their excess numbers reduce with age and in older age groups men are outnumbered by women. In Western societies, due to improvements in health care and the decline in warfare, men now live longer. Consequently, the point at which there were fewer men than women in the British population rose from 25 to nearly 60 years of age between the opening and the closing years of the twentieth century. Changes in adult sex ratios of this magnitude have had significant effects on the rates of female employment and the number and pattern of marriages.

sex roles ROLE refers to the bundles of socially defined attributes and expectations associated with social positions. Sex roles are the attributes and expectations associated with the different genders, with being a man or a woman in a society. The *sexual division of labour* is another term that is sometimes used to describe these specialized sexual roles. Like roles in general, sex roles may be viewed as only partly fixed, because they are defined in the course of interaction; or they may be conceptualized as being firmly fixed and prescriptive, because, following the theory of FUNCTIONALISM, sex roles (like other roles) reflect enduring social NORMS and patterns of SOCIALIZATION.

In the middle of the twentieth century, socially defined sex roles in Britain and the USA distinguished sharply between the roles of men and women. Women were expected to be family- and home-centred, caring and nurturing of children and husbands, either not working outside the home at all or working part time so as to accommodate their domestic responsibilities. If women entered paid employment, they were expected to do the sort of 'women's work' which was an extension of their other sex roles (e.g. working as teachers, nurses, secretaries to male managers, or serving in shops and restaurants). At this time, functionalism was particularly influential in sociology and its view of sex roles was largely unchallenged. Since then, both the real world and sociology have changed to a certain extent. The sexual division of labour is less fixed. FEMINISM has helped to modify the views of both women and men about the content of sex roles. The pattern of women's employment shows that many women no longer follow traditional prescriptions regarding appropriate jobs and the absolute priority of domestic responsibilities. Relations between men and women have changed with the gradual development of the SYMMETRICAL FAMILY. Within sociology, roles in general are now regarded as being less fixed. At the same time, the analysis of PATRIARCHY and the SOCIOLOGY OF GENDER have questioned the nature and origin of traditional sex roles. However, sociologists' views about the social determination of sex roles are disputed by certain psychologists, who believe that biological differences between men and women mean that there are basic and unchangeable differences in their roles.

SEE ALSO: *domestic labour; feminist social theory; women and work.*

sexism Sexist attitudes or actions are those that discriminate against men or women purely on the grounds of GENDER. While these may often be explicit, they may also be implicit, being an assumed and unrecognized part of the culture. For example, sociological studies of stratification have been accused of being sexist because they do not take account of women's place in the class structure.

SEE ALSO: *class; patriarchy; sex roles; stereotypes.*

sexual division of labour See: DIVISION OF LABOUR; DOMESTIC LABOUR; SEX ROLES.

sexualities Sociology has traditionally distinguished between sex, conceived as the biological and physiological differences between men and women which are contrasted in terms of reproductive function, and GENDER, conceived as the social roles allocated to men and women in society. More recently, sociologists have also identified sexuality as the mode by which sexual interest and sexual preference are expressed. Thus masculinity is the form of sexuality which is expected of heterosexual men, and femininity of heterosexual women. Critics of these distinctions claim that mainstream sociology merely reproduces the dichotomous assumptions of society, in which PATRIARCHY determines a bi-modal distribution of sexuality, thereby ignoring lesbian women, gay men and people who have multiple sexualities. With POSTMODERNITY, it is assumed there will be an increasing differentiation of sexualities. Furthermore, sexuality will no longer be closely connected with, or determined by, either sex or gender. It is further assumed that the sexuality of an individual will vary over time with the life-cycle.

SEE ALSO: *affective individualism; embodiment; intimacy; Beauvoir; Irigaray; Kristeva; feminist social theory; sociology of gender.*

shame In anthropology, there is a distinction between guilt-cultures in which social control operates through internal sanctions and shame-cultures in which individuals are controlled by public threats to personal reputation and honour. Public shame reflects not only on the individual, but on his or her family and kin, and there are, therefore, strong familial sanctions on deviation from communal norms. Shame as a mechanism of social control can only operate in small groups where visibility and intimacy are prominent, and is thus characteristic of village rather than urban existence.

SEE ALSO: *sanction.*

sharecropping See: PEASANTS.

sick role The concept was first outlined in L. J. Henderson (1935) and then elaborated by PARSONS (1951). From a sociological perspective, illness can be regarded as a form of social deviance, in which an individual adopts a specific role. This sick role has four major characteristics: (1) the incumbent is exempted from normal social responsibilities; (2) the sick person is not blamed for being sick; (3) the person is expected to seek out competent professional help, since the illness is socially undesirable; (4) the incumbent of a sick role is expected to comply with the regimen prescribed by a competent physician. Since doctors in Western society have a professional monopoly, they are the principal legitimators of the sick role. The concept of the sick role has been criticized on a number of grounds: (1) it fails to distinguish between the patient and the sick role, since being sick does not automatically lead to the adoption of a patient status; (2) it does not recognize the possibility of conflicting interests between physician and patient; (3) the concept does not have universal application, since some 'conditions' (alcoholism, physical disability or pregnancy) do not necessarily result in a suspension of normal social responsibilities; (4) the concept is useful in the analysis of acute but not chronic illness; (5) there are problems related to so-called 'abnormal illness behaviour' (like hypochondriasis and Munchausen's syndrome) where there is a conflict of definitions of illness between doctor and patient; (6) the concept does not provide a phenomenology of the experience of being ill. For some critics, Parsons' model of the sick role is itself a legitimation of the power of doctors over patients. It did, however, lay the foundations for a sociological critique of the MEDICAL MODEL.

SEE ALSO: *sociology of health and illness.*

READING: Levine and Kozloff (1978)

sign See: SEMIOTICS.

significance test When researchers study a sample drawn from a population rather than investigating the whole population, they need to know how far they can trust the quantities calculated on the basis of the elements of the sample. Values derived from samples may be subject to SAMPLING ERROR and so be inaccurate as estimates of population values. For example, if a public opinion poll were to show that a sample was divided into one-third opposing and two-thirds supporting the reintroduction of capital punishment, the investigator would need to know the likelihood that this result was due simply to sampling error; the problem is to know whether the same statistic would have emerged if a different sample of people had been chosen.

Significance testing starts with a *null hypothesis*, which in this example states that there is no significant difference between the observed sample estimates, because they are chance results due to random variations in the population. A test statistic is calculated, and if its value falls within a specified range which has a small probability of occurring under the null hypothesis, the hypothesis will be rejected. In this example, rejection means that it is highly probable that there *is* a real difference in the proportions who support or reject capital punishment. Significance tests can be used at various *levels* of significance or confidence, most commonly in sociology at the 0.01 or 0.05 levels, which indicate, respectively, a 1 in 100 or 5 in 100 probability that the null hypothesis has been rejected when it is true. These are also referred to as the 99 per cent and 95 per cent levels of significance. Some researchers now prefer to use the 0.001 (1 in 1,000) level, in order to be sure that their results are so unlikely to be the result of chance that they can therefore be accepted as true. Various statistics exist for the testing of means, proportions, variances, correlations and goodness of fit.

Sociologists distinguish between *statistical* and *substantive* significance. Findings may have substantive significance in terms of a theory or because they reinforce other results, even though they fail to reach statistical significance at a given level of confidence. This often occurs when the total sample size or the size of individual sub-groups within the sample are small. Conversely, certain findings may have statistical but not substantive significance, when the observations are unimportant in terms of the substance of an investigation.

significant others This is a term derived from George H. MEAD, who argued that the SOCIALIZATION of the child proceeds in a number of stages. At the earliest of these, the child is unable to distinguish him- or herself from other people. Gradually, however, the child begins to establish this difference and is able to 'take the role of the other'; that is, imagine what it is like to be somebody else. Some of these others are particularly important to the rearing of the growing child – mother, father, sister or brother – and are often referred to as 'significant others'. The term is also used more loosely, simply to designate anybody important in the life of an individual, whether as an adult or a child.

signifier/signified See: SEMIOTICS.

Sikhism See: WORLD RELIGIONS.

Simmel, Georg (1858–1918) A German professor of philosophy who wrote extensively on aesthetics, EPISTEMOLOGY, the philosophy of history as well as sociology, Simmel's views were formed by opposition both to the structural sociology of writers like COMTE and to the German tradition of GEISTESWISSENSCHAFTEN, in which social and historical events were to be seen as unique and not generalizable. Simmel's solution was to picture society as a web of interactions between people. He stressed the interaction. For example, in his analysis of power, he argued that the powerful could not exercise their power without the complicity of their subordinates; power is an interaction. If there are social structures like the family, they are to be considered as mere crystallizations of interactions between individuals.

Simmel's proposed method of analysing human interactions was by FORMAL SOCIOLOGY. He suggested that one could isolate the form of interactions from their content, so that apparently very different interactions (with different contents) could be shown to have the same form. An example of this approach (although not one cited by Simmel himself) would be the form of the relationship between a writer and an aristocrat in eighteenth-century England and the relationship between a peasant and his landlord in twentieth-century Latin America, which are apparently different interactions. However, they do have the same form, in that they are both examples of patronage relationships. Examples of the forms investigated by Simmel are COMPETITION, the DIVISION OF LABOUR, and superiority and subordination. In this context, Simmel was particularly fascinated by numbers. For example, he argued that social situations involving two or three parties have the same formal similarities whether the parties are people or nation states. This similarity of form means that certain properties of the relationships are manifested in very different situations. For example, the options open to three nation states, and their consequent behaviour, are much the same as those applying to three people. Another way in which Simmel applied his formal sociology was in the analysis of social types. Thus he argued that certain social types, the stranger for example, appear in different societies at different times and the behaviour of the stranger, and the behaviour of others towards him or her, is very similar in these different social situations.

Although subsequent commentators have concentrated on his formal sociology, his analyses of social interaction and his views about the functions of social conflict and competition, Simmel was also concerned with the study of social development, as characterized by social differentiation and the emergence of a money economy. The translation into English of *The Philosophy of Money* (1900), which, among other topics, presents an alternative to the Marxist LABOUR THEORY OF VALUE, has inspired a new interest in the whole corpus of Simmel's work. The evolution of economic exchange from barter to paper money to credit represents a RATIONALIZATION of daily life. This economic quantification of social interaction was a further illustration of the separation of the form from the content of social life. Simmel's analysis of money provided a phenomenological alternative to Marxist economic categories.

Simmel's main works available in English include *The Problems of the Philosophy of History* (1892) and two collections of essays: *The Sociology of Georg Simmel*, ed. K. Wolff (1950), and *Conflict and the Web of Group Affiliations* (1955). Although some aspects of Simmel's work have been picked up by later sociologists, he has generally been neglected. This neglect may be due, in part, to the fact that he never tried to systematize his work in the manner of Marx, Weber and Durkheim.

SEE ALSO: *conflict theory; neo-Kantianism.*

READING: Frisby (1981; 1984)

single-parent families There has been a marked increase in single-parent families in the UK over the last thirty years. In 1994, 23 per cent of all families with dependent children were headed by a single parent, compared with 8 per cent in 1971. To put the matter differently, 20 per cent of dependent children in the UK in 1995 were living in single-parent families, compared with 7 per cent in 1972. More recently, there are indications that the rapid rise is slowing down or is being reversed.

The rise in the number of single-parent families is due entirely to an increase in single mothers, the proportion of lone fathers having remained almost constant over the past thirty years. Up to the mid 1980s, the main cause of the increase in lone mothers was increasing rates of DIVORCE coupled with declining rates of remarriage. Since the mid 1980s, the principle source of growth has been among never-married women, most of whom will have been in cohabiting unions. Lone parenthood is not a permanent status. Current estimates are that half of lone parents will cease to be so in less than four years.

SEE ALSO: *household*.

skewness The degree of asymmetry in a distribution.

SEE ALSO: *distribution*.

skill See: DE-SKILLING.

slavery As an institution, slavery is defined as a form of PROPERTY which gives to one person the right of ownership over another. Like any other means of production, the slave is 'a thing'. Slave labour has existed under a variety of social conditions – in the ancient world, in the colonies of the West Indies and in the plantations of the southern states of America. From the point of view of efficient production, slave labour presents a number of problems. (1) A barrack slave system does not reproduce itself and slaves have to be obtained either through purchase on a slave market or by conquest; slave systems tend, therefore, to experience acute labour shortages. (2) Slaves require considerable political surveillance, because of the threat of slave revolts. (3) It is difficult to force slaves to perform skilled labour tasks without additional incentives. These problems suggest that slavery does not provide an appropriate basis for long-term economic growth. There is some debate as to whether slavery is compatible with a capitalist economy: M. Weber (1922) has argued that CAPITALISM requires free labour markets if it is to fulfil its potential; while B. Moore (1967) believes that slavery is incompatible only with a particular form of capitalism – competitive, democratic capitalism – and not with capitalism as such.

Slavery presupposes the existence of private property and, in Marxism, is an economic rather than a political category. Support for the view that the essential feature of slavery is not political domination can be found in classical Greece and Mameluke Egypt, where slaves often performed crucial administrative and military roles. While in Marxism the slave MODE OF PRODUCTION is often regarded as a distinctive form, there are few systematic treatments of this mode of production and the nature of the transition between slavery and FEUDALISM remains obscure. For example, the dividing line between serfdom in feudalism and servitude in slavery is empirically fluid and uncertain.

It is generally acknowledged, however, that classical Greece and Rome were based on slave labour. In antiquity, the dominant class was an urban citizenry that drew its wealth from the countryside, in which slave labour was preponderant. Because slaves were acquired largely through conquest, every citizen was threatened by the prospect of servitude. While slaves provided certain obvious economic benefits – as highly movable commodities – it has been argued by P. Anderson (1974) that slavery inhibited the development of the forces of production because there was little incentive to develop labour-saving technology.

While slavery was the basis of the classical societies of Greece and Rome, it also flourished in the plantation system of the Americas. Cotton produced by slave labour in the southern states of North America played a crucial role in the development of American industrial capitalism. Marxists regard those southern states as a form of agrarian capitalism employing slave labour and not as a slave mode of production as such. As a capitalist system, the plantation economy of the southern states had distinctive characteristics: it was a rural, not urban, form and gave rise to an aristocratic rather than a bourgeois culture.

In a comparative perspective, it has also been argued that slavery in North America was far more repressive than in Latin America. There are a number of reasons for this. (1) The Protestants of North America regarded the slave as sinful and in need of sexual restraint, while Catholicism in South America was more tolerant. (2) The ethnic diversity of Latin America was extensive and therefore the division between black and white was less sharply drawn. (3) It was possible for slaves to purchase their freedom in South America, but this was uncommon in North America. Although the American Civil War put an end to slavery, the legacy of racial hatred has been a decisive influence on contemporary politics in North America.

SEE ALSO: *racism*.

READING: Davis, B. D. (1970)

snowball sample In some research settings, it is impossible to compile a complete list of the population to be studied; for example, studies of prostitutes. In the absence of such a list, it is impossible to construct a random sample. There are also research settings where the complete population can be listed but the researcher cannot generate a truly random sample, because most subjects refuse to participate in the research. This is particularly an issue in research into social elites. For example, all the directors of major British companies are listed but only a tiny minority are likely to agree to participate in research. Snowball samples begin with a group of known subjects. They grow in size as the first participants add names to the list and these in turn identify more subjects. The analogy is with a snowball rolling down a slope and picking up more snow as it goes. In the prostitution example, a group of known prostitutes, who are interviewed at the start of a project, give the researcher the names of other prostitutes to approach. They may also recommend to their contacts that they should participate in the project. In the case of a project involving the directors of major companies, a small group who have chosen to participate (perhaps because they find the topic interesting or because they know the researcher personally) may then recommend the research to their friends and acquaintances. It is important to appreciate that, because snowball SAMPLING is not random, the research results cannot be taken as representative of the wider population.

social and system integration LOCKWOOD first made this conceptual distinction in a paper of 1964. *Social* integration refers to the basis on which people relate to each other in society; that is, whether social relationships are orderly or conflictual. *System* integration refers to relationships among parts of the social system; that is, whether social institutions are compatible or incompatible. Lockwood claimed that

CONFLICT THEORY had prioritized social integration among social actors, while FUNCTIONALISM had concentrated on system integration and ignored social actors. He argued that the two forms of integration are not necessarily related to each other. Thus the institutions of society might be functionally well integrated, yet there could be major conflicts between individuals or social groups. The Marxist analysis of capitalism provides an example, with its suggestion that, while the major social institutions (e.g. economy, polity, family, education) are functionally very well integrated, social integration is low because of class conflict between capitalists and workers. Conversely, there may be societies that are highly integrated socially but where system integration is weaker.

Lockwood also intended that his distinction should contribute to a resolution of what later became known as the AGENCY AND STRUCTURE dualism. Social integration deals with issues of human agency and system integration with structure, and Lockwood criticized theories which emphasized one at the cost of the other. The concepts were later adapted by GIDDENS in his discussion of agency and structure.

READING: Mouzelis (1997)

social change The problem of explaining social change was central to nineteenth-century sociology. This preoccupation arose from (1) an awareness of the radical social effects of industrialization on European societies, and (2) an appreciation of the fundamental gap between European industrial societies and so-called 'primitive societies'. Theories of social change thus centred on the nature of capitalist or industrial development and the apparent absence of social development in those societies which had become part of the colonial empires of Europe. These theories of social change were concerned with long-term and large-scale or macro-development.

Sociological theories of change, especially nineteenth-century ones, may be divided into theories of social evolution and theories of REVOLUTION. In the first, social change was thought to involve basic stages of development such as 'military society' and 'industrial society', by which society progressed from simple, rural, agrarian forms to more complex, differentiated, industrial–urban ones. This type of EVOLUTIONARY THEORY was developed by COMTE, SPENCER and E. Durkheim. The analysis of social change in FUNCTIONALISM continues to depend, to some extent, on evolutionary theory by regarding change as the adaptation of a social system to its environment by the process of mental differentiation and increasing structural complexity. Theories of revolutionary social change, particularly deriving from MARX, emphasized the importance of class conflict, political struggle and imperialism as the principal mechanisms of fundamental structural changes.

This distinction between evolutionary and revolutionary theories is a fundamental analytical division, but theories of social change can be further classified in terms of: (1) the level of analysis (whether macro or micro); (2) whether change derives from factors internal or external to the society, institution or social group; (3) the cause of social change (variously demographic pressure, class conflict, changes in the MODE OF PRODUCTION, technological innovation or the development of new systems of belief); (4) the agents of change (innovative elites of intellectuals, social deviants, the working class); (5) the nature of change (whether a gradual diffusion of new values and institutions, or a radical disruption of the social system).

Although the issue of long-term structural change is still alive in contemporary social science, it is thought that a general theory of change is necessarily too vague to be of much use in the explanation of historical change. In the main, the trend in twentieth-century sociology was towards MIDDLE-RANGE THEORY, which accounts for the development of particular institutions, social groups, items of culture, or particular beliefs rather than for the transformation of societies as a whole. However, towards the end of the century, theories of macro-level and societal change became more popular, with various accounts of POST-FORDISM and POSTMODERNITY, which attempted to account for what were perceived as fundamental and systemic social changes.

SEE ALSO: *differentiation; historical materialism; progress; underdevelopment.*

READING: Smith, A. D. (1973); Kumar (1995)

social closure Used by M. Weber to describe the action of social groups who maximize their own advantage by restricting access to rewards (usually economic opportunities) to their members, thus closing access to outsiders, this term was re-introduced into the modern analysis of social CLASS by F. Parkin (1974; 1979), who treats closure as an aspect of the distribution of power between classes. Parkin identifies strategies of *exclusion*, by which collectivities with privileged access to rewards attempt to exclude outsiders and pass on privileges to their own kind, a classic example being how members of a PROFESSION restrict access. *Usurpation* refers to the process by which outsiders, often organized collectively, try to win a greater share of resources. Trade unionism is an example of this latter process.

SEE ALSO: *caste; labour market segmentation; trade unions.*

social constructionism This is a term with both a more general and a more specific meaning. Generally, it is used to designate an approach to the study of the social world which insists on social explanation instead of explanations in terms of individual characteristics or genetic or biological aspects of human life. In this sense, the term is more or less synonymous with sociology itself. For example, sociologists of science insist that science has to be studied as a social construction, not simply as the product of scientists following the dictates of their individual scientific interest. More specifically, the term refers to the process whereby people actively construct their social world rather than have it imposed upon them, and it thereby owes a great deal to phenomenological approaches to sociology.

SEE ALSO: *action theory; agency and structure; biologism/biological reductionism; phenomenological sociology; symbolic interactionism.*

social contract Contract theory seeks to explain the origins and binding force of mutual obligations and rights in society. T. Hobbes, in *Leviathan* (1651), argued that in the pre-social 'state of nature' people enjoy absolute personal freedom, but this very freedom means that they are exposed to the threat of physical violence and exploitation. In order to remove this threat, people enter into a social contract with each other whereby they surrender their absolute individual freedom to a third party (the state), which then acts to guarantee SOCIAL ORDER and stability. Social contract theory simultaneously legitimates state power and provides a right of revolution if the state fails to guarantee the minimum conditions of civilized life.

It should be recognized that social contract theory does not literally assume that at a given period in history people decided to band together to form society. To form a contract presupposes that people possess a language in which the terms of a contract could be formulated. The existence of human language in turn presupposes the existence of social relations. Contract theory suggests that we examine the relationship between state and society 'as if' people were bound by mutual obligations and privileges. In other words, it is an early theoretical attempt to analyse the basis of CONSENSUS and COERCION. In social theory, the idea of a contract has played an important analytical role in justifying power relations and for limiting the boundaries of the state in relation to individual rights. The theory of social contract was a crucial ingredient of J. Locke's analysis of property rights, which provided a legitimation of the constitutional settlement in Britain in 1688. It was also central to J.-J. Rousseau's account of the 'general will' as the basis of government, which provided a model for democratic rights. In sociology, contract theory has been less important. T. Parsons (1937) attempted to show that the fundamental basis of society is not social contract and the coercive apparatus of the state, but the existence of a consensus over values and norms. The classical theory of the social contract has thus been replaced in sociology by theories of consensus, RECIPROCITY and exchange.

SEE ALSO: *exchange theory.*

READING: Dunn (1990)

social control The majority of sociologists argue that social control is achieved through a combination of compliance, COERCION and commitment to social values. For example, PARSONS (1951) defined it as the process by which, through the imposition of sanctions, DEVIANT BEHAVIOUR is counteracted and social stability maintained. The concept has primarily been encountered in the analysis of deviant behaviour, as an aspect of LABELLING THEORY. It is argued that, paradoxically, the attempt to increase forms of coercive social control by, for example, increasing police surveillance of particular crimes or social groups tends to amplify deviance rather than diminish it. The implication is that social control depends more on the stability of social groups, community relations and shared values than it does on mere coercion. Social control was also important for FOUCAULT, who studied how individuals were disciplined and regulated by means of surveillance, the power of expert knowledge and other regulatory structures. The concept is somewhat vague, however, and embraces a number of other, more precise, sociological categories.

SEE ALSO: *deviance amplification; managerial strategies of control; sanction; social order.*

Social Darwinism Late nineteenth-century sociology was dominated by various theories of social evolution, one of which was Social Darwinism – nothing to do with C. Darwin himself. This doctrine, most prominent in the United States, took various forms but most versions had two central assumptions. (1) There are underlying, and largely irresistible, forces acting in societies which are like the natural forces that operate in animal and plant communities. One can therefore formulate social laws similar to natural ones. (2) These social forces are of such a kind as to produce evolutionary progress through the natural conflicts between social groups. The best-adapted and most successful social groups survive these conflicts, raising the evolutionary level of society generally ('the survival of the fittest').

Such a theory, like that of SPENCER, has been interpreted as well suited to *laissez-faire* conceptions of society. It also, in some authors, especially L. Glumpowicz and, to a lesser extent, W. Sumner, had racial overtones, with the belief that some races, being innately superior, were bound to triumph over inferior ones. In other authors the doctrine took a weaker form. A. Small, for example, based his sociology on the notion that social groups necessarily had interests which conflicted.

SEE ALSO: *biologism/biological reductionism; competition; eugenics; evolutionary theory; organic analogy; sociobiology; urban ecology.*

READING: Timasheff (1967)

social distance This term refers to the perceived feelings of separation or distance between social groups. It is most commonly used to indicate the degree of separation or closeness between members of different ethnic groups, as revealed in answers to questions such as 'Would you buy a house next door to a white or black person?' A social distance scale (the Bogardus scale) attempts to measure degrees of tolerance or prejudice between social groups. This scale is assumed to be cumulative. For example, a white respondent who is prepared to contemplate marriage between blacks and whites is likely also to be prepared to live in the same street as blacks.

social division of labour See: DIVISION OF LABOUR.

social fact DURKHEIM (1895) insisted that social phenomena could not be reduced to individual states, either biological or psychological, but depended instead on social factors. Thus he argued that the rate of SUICIDE in a social group could not be explained by, for example, the proneness to depression of individuals within that social group; rather, it was explained by the degree of cohesiveness of the social group, as expressed, for example, by the prevalence and type of religious belief. Durkheim formulated this principle in the doctrine of social facts, which, he argued, are external, coercive and objective. As social forces they are external to and outside of the individual; they are coercive, in that individuals are compelled to act by them; and they are objectively measurable. The *rate* of suicide in any society is a social fact of this kind. It exists independently of the properties of individuals, represents a determining external force and can be measured.

SEE ALSO: *agency and structure; social constructionism.*

social mobility A concept used in the sociological investigation of inequality, social mobility refers to the movement of individuals between different levels of the social hierarchy, usually defined in terms of broad occupational or social-class categories. The amount of social mobility is often used as an indicator of the degree of openness and fluidity of a society. The study of mobility looks at mobility rates, mobility patterns (both short-range between adjacent hierarchical levels and long-range between widely separated levels), who is recruited to various positions and the determinants of this selection. *Intergenerational* mobility compares the present position of individuals with those of their parents. *Intragenerational* mobility compares the positions attained by the same individual at different moments in the course of his or her work-life.

Sociological interest in mobility has been informed by several issues. S. M. Lipset and R. Bendix (1959) believed that mobility was essential for the stability of modern industrial society, since open access to elite positions would allow able and ambitious people to rise from lower social levels, acting as a safety valve that reduced the likelihood of revolutionary collective action by lower classes. Others have been more concerned with issues of efficiency and social justice: P. M. Blau and O. D. Duncan (1967) argued that the efficiency of modern societies required mobility if the most able people were to perform the most important jobs, and D. V. Glass (1954) believed that justice in a democratic society depended on an egalitarian opportunity structure.

Various theories of INDUSTRIAL SOCIETY have also given social mobility an important place. The CONVERGENCE THESIS, that all industrial societies converge on a single model as they develop economically, has specified the following characteristics of mobility in mature industrial societies: high rates of mobility; more mobility upwards than downwards as the structure of employment is continuously upgraded; more equal opportunities for mobility for individuals of different social backgrounds as societies become more egalitarian; increasing rates of mobility and equality of opportunity. Differences between nations reflect different levels of economic development and will reduce with time. Conversely, the LABOUR PROCESS APPROACH maintained that the development of capitalist industrialism would create DE-SKILLING and PROLETARIANIZATION, and so lead to large-scale downward mobility, particularly for women. Theories of cross-national variation suggest that national differences in mobility will persist despite industrialism. Others claim that there are enduring similarities across industrialized nations, which are quite unrelated either to the extent of industrialism or the level of economic development.

Three of the findings of the Social Mobility Group at Oxford University, reported in J. H. Goldthorpe (1987), have challenged older beliefs about the lack of social mobility in Britain: (1) absolute mobility rates over the last half century are higher than previously believed; (2) there is considerable long-range mobility from the WORKING CLASS into the upper class (labelled the 'service' class in this study) as well as short-range mobility; (3) membership of the upper ('service') and intermediate classes is more fluid than expected. What others have called the *occupational transition*, that the growth of professional, technical, managerial and lower-level white-collar occupations and the contraction of manual jobs, which all advanced industrial societies have experienced, is the main explanation of why absolute rates of social mobility are high and the CLASS hierarchy appears fluid and open at the top. Goldthorpe (1987) adjusts the Nuffield data to 'allow' for structural changes in the occupational system, and he suggests that the class structure would have been stable without much openness but for these changes. One limitation of this research is that it deals mainly with the mobility of men.

Modern studies of social mobility make a major distinction between *absolute* and *relative* rates of mobility. Absolute rates refer to the percentage of individuals in some base category who are mobile (or immobile). Relative mobility rates express the relative chances of access to different class destinations for individuals of differing class origins. Technically, relative mobility rates are known as *odds ratios* and they measure the statistical independence of categories of origins and destinations: a ratio of 1 equals complete statistical independence, which, if it were ever to occur, would translate as 'perfect mobility' or 'complete openness'. This would mean that the chances of individuals ending up in a certain occupation or class are completely unaffected by their parents' occupation or class level (in the case of intergenerational mobility). The Oxford research defined perfect mobility or complete openness in this statistical fashion and measured the extent to which relative mobility rates fell short of the theoretical model. The results showed that increased rates of absolute mobility due to the changing occupational structure coexisted with fairly constant rates of relative mobility.

The comparison of mobility rates and patterns among industrial societies is difficult, given differences between occupational structures. However, the use of relative rates allows the effects of such structural differences and other specific features of national economic, demographic and political histories to be disentangled. In their comparison of mobility rates in twelve industrial countries at different stages of economic development, including two state socialist countries, R. Erikson and GOLDTHORPE (1992) report that relative rates show a broadly similar degree of openness and similar patterns of social fluidity, irrespective of the level of economic development or type of economic system. Britain is in the middle of this group of nations. The study concludes that relative mobility rates in industrial societies are similar and static; that is, not only are these nations similar now, but there is no indication that mobility rates are changing over time.

SEE ALSO: *career; educational attainment; middle class; service class; sponsored mobility; stratification.*

social movements The term covers a great variety of forms of collective action aimed at social reorganization. The aims of social movements can be broad, as in the overthrow of an existing government, or narrow, as in the installation of traffic-calming measures in a suburban street. Forms of organization are also diverse. Some social movements are highly organized with a well-developed bureaucracy and leadership, others are fluid and informal. Examples of social movements include MILLENARIANISM, campaigns for gay rights and movements against tobacco advertising.

It has been argued that a distinctive form of social movement has arisen since the Second World War, first coming to prominence with the radical student movements of the 1960s. These new social movements (NSMs) are distinguished from interest groups, which represent a small group pursuing a narrow interest, and political movements, such as political parties, which aim at social transformation through the political process. Examples of NSMs are ecological, feminist and black movements.

NSMs have been identified in terms of four features.

(1) *Aims.* These tend to be to do with the alteration of social and cultural values, especially those concerning individual autonomy, rather than the transformation of social structures as a whole.

(2) *Social base.* Traditional political movements are based in social CLASS; NSMs are based in other groupings, such as women.

(3) *Means of action.* NSMs do not use the traditional political means of influencing the state but rely on mass mobilization to change values and attitudes, as in the deployment of 'green' social action.

(4) *Organization.* NSMs repudiate formal and bureaucratic modes of organization, preferring loose, flexible modes that actively involve ordinary members.

The distinctive nature of NSMs may be exaggerated. They do use traditional political processes, they are often middle class and their mode of organization is becoming more formal.

SEE ALSO: *collective behaviour; new religious movements; political participation; political parties; revolution; urban social movements; voluntary associations.*

READING: Scott, A. (1990)

social order Sociologists have long been fascinated by the question 'How is society possible?' That is, although in everyday life we may take social order for granted, for sociologists it is something that requires explanation. For example, why, when there is such manifest injustice, oppression and poverty in the world, are there not more revolutions? What is it that stops people routinely breaking windows? How is it that everyday social life is generally ordered and predictable and people do not generally break the unspoken rules of how to behave towards one another?

Four types of answer to these sorts of questions about social order have been provided.

(1) The utilitarian approach suggests that it is in the self-interest of all individuals to maintain social order, particularly in complex societies where the DIVISION OF LABOUR is high and the people are interdependent. UTILITARIANISM has had less influence on social than on economic theory, except in EXCHANGE THEORY, and enlightened self-interest does not figure prominently in sociological accounts of order.

(2) The cultural approach emphasizes the role of shared norms and VALUES. The proposition is that the members of society have certain beliefs in common; for example, the sanctity of life, the legitimacy of properly constituted AUTHORITY, the importance of marriage. It is this CONSENSUS about the right way to behave that provides stability and order. Arguments along these lines frequently point to the importance of religion in many societies, in uniting a population around a common set of values. DURKHEIM and PARSONS are influential sociological exponents of this cultural approach. There are also Marxist varieties of the argument. These suggest that, although there may be a sharing of values, this is really imposed on others by the powerful. The shared culture that provides for order is therefore essentially an IDEOLOGY which favours the interests of the powerful in a society.

(3) Another approach emphasizes power and domination – that is, compulsion. Order is ensured by the use of the military, the police, the courts, by the internal discipline of organizations such as schools, bureaucracies, places of work, hospitals and prisons, or by the sheer weight of economic POWER. Among sociological theorists, MARX and WEBER are notable exponents of the role of compulsion in social order, although it is also notable that both believed that culture and values also play an important part. Theorists who stress the role of COERCION implicitly or explicitly raise an important issue. Order is not a neutral idea, for one always has to ask in whose interests a particular social order is constructed.

(4) The interactionist approach essentially concentrates on how social order is brought about and owes much to the work of GOFFMAN and ethnomethodologists. These writers focus, unlike those mentioned above, on how order is constructed at the small-scale level of everyday social interaction. They demonstrate that there are a multitude of rules governing social interaction of which we are largely unaware. Indeed participants only become aware when the rules are accidentally or experimentally broken.

SEE ALSO: *conflict; dominant ideology thesis; ethnomethodology; Gramsci; hegemony; ideological state apparatus; social contract; social control.*

social pathology This nineteenth-century notion is based on an analogy between organic disease, or pathology, and social deviance. In E. Durkheim's discussion of crime and SUICIDE, social pathology was based on a distinction between normal and abnormal social conditions rather than individual deviance. Furthermore, he argued that the distinction was objective rather than a moral judgement and that social pathology could be scientifically measured. Unfortunately, Durkheim's use of the concept is confused and treated social pathology as merely the obverse of social normality.

SEE ALSO: *Durkheim; organic analogy.*

social problems The definition of a social problem is fraught with difficulty for a variety of reasons. (1) Cultural relativism means that what is a social problem for one group may be nothing of the sort for another. (2) Historically, the nature of social problems has changed over time with changes in law and MORES. (3) There is a political dimension, that the identification of a 'problem' may involve one group in the exercise of social control over another. Sociologists reject taken-for-granted views that social problems have an objective status like some organic pathology, and search for the socially created definitions of what constitutes a 'problem'.

Symbolic interactionists, for example, suggest that social problems are not social facts, and that some problems result simply from processes of social change that create conflicts between groups, when one group succeeds in winning public acceptance of its claim that the other's behaviour should be labelled as problematic. Mass media, official agencies and 'experts' typically exaggerate the extent of social problems and over-react to social pressures. The concept of MORAL PANICS illustrates how the media of communication help define social problems and create public anxiety.

Other sociologists criticize the assumption implicit in many official definitions of social problems, particularly in the area of social welfare policy, that such problems derive from the personal characteristics of individuals rather than from structural features of the social system over which individuals have little influence. For example, emphasis on the 'problem' that many people are unemployed because they are 'work-shy' diverts attention from the actual causes of mass UNEMPLOYMENT, some of which may be the actions of government.

SEE ALSO: *addiction; alcoholism; criminology; deviance amplification; deviant behaviour; divorce; labelling theory; poverty; social fact; symbolic interactionism.*

social reproduction Just as people reproduce physically over the generations, so they also tend to reproduce their social organization, and social reproduction is the name given to this phenomenon.

SEE ALSO: *cultural reproduction.*

social structure This is a concept often used in sociology but rarely discussed at any length. It is possible to identify two broad approaches. The first envisages social structure as observable patterns in social practices. An example of this approach is FUNCTIONALISM. The second finds structure in the underlying principle of social arrangements, which may not be observable. REALISM would be an example of this. Social structure has been defined simply as any recurring pattern of social behaviour. However, for most sociologists such a definition might tend to include trivial behaviours as well as the significant ones. A more generally preferred approach is to say that social structure refers to the enduring, orderly and patterned relationships between elements of a society, a definition that prompted some nineteenth-century sociologists to compare societies with machines or organisms. There is some disagreement as to what would count as an 'element'. RADCLIFFE-BROWN, for example, thought of social structures as relationships of a general and regular kind between people. S. F. Nadel, on the other hand, suggested roles as the elements. Even more generally, social institutions, as organized patterns of social behaviour, are proposed as the elements of social structure by a wide range of sociologists, particularly functionalists, who then define societies in terms of functional relations between social institutions. Furthermore, for them, certain elements of social structure – social institutions – are necessary because they are functional prerequisites.

Sociologists typically wish to use concepts of social structure to explain something, and this usually means that the explanation is a causal one. Such a view can present difficulties in that social structures are not directly observable entities but are rather abstract formulations. This and other difficulties have led to criticism of the use of social structure. Thus it has been seen as a reified concept, as unobservable and therefore unverifiable, and as denying human creativity and freedom by suggesting that human action is determined by structures. One solution to these criticisms is to demonstrate, as P. L. Berger and T. Luckmann (1967) do, the way in which social structures are themselves the creation of active human beings.

SEE ALSO: *agency and structure; functional imperative; hermeneutics; methodological individualism; organic analogy; phenomenological sociology; poststructuralism; role; realism; social institution; social system; Spencer; structuralism; structuration.*

READING: Smelser (1988)

social system The notion of 'system' is not peculiar to sociology, but is a conceptual tool with widespread currency in the natural and social sciences. A system is any collection of interrelated parts, objects, things or organisms. It is often seen to be purposeful or functional; that is, it exists to satisfy some purpose or goal. In the work of PARSONS (1951), a *social* system is defined in terms of two or more social actors engaged in more or less stable interaction within a bounded environment. The concept is not, however, limited to interpersonal interaction, and refers also to the analysis of groups, institutions, societies and inter-social entities. It may, for example, be employed in the analysis of the university or the state as social systems which have structures of interrelated parts. There are two further features typically associated with the concept: (1) social systems tend over time towards equilibrium or 'homoeostasis', because they are 'boundary-maintaining systems'; (2) social systems can be regarded, from a cybernetic point of view, as information systems or input–output systems. In FUNCTIONALISM in the 1950s, it was common to draw an analogy between living organisms and social systems as homoeostatic systems. For example, exercise in human beings increases the blood sugar level, heart rate and temperature. We perspire, which has the effect of controlling our body temperature. The body depends on a variety of such feedback mechanisms in order to maintain an equilibrium. Similarly, the parts of a social system are linked together by media of exchange, which include a variety of information-carrying symbols such as language, money, influence or commitments. Equilibrium may thus be defined as a balance between inputs and outputs. This view of social systems has been criticized by GIDDENS, who argues that social systems are rarely like biological systems and, in any case, cannot be regarded as entities with properties over and above those possessed by individual actors.

The concept of social system has been used most explicitly and self-consciously in modern functionalism, but it was implicit in much nineteenth-century social thought. Any social theory which treats social relations, groups or societies as a set of interrelated parts that functions to maintain some boundary or unity of the parts is based implicitly or explicitly on the concept of 'social system'. For some theorists, therefore, the concept is inescapable as the basis of a scientific approach to social data.

SEE ALSO: *boundary maintenance*; *functional imperative*; *holism*; *Pareto*; *reciprocity*; *social structure*; *society*; *systems theory*.

READING: Luhmann (1995)

socialist societies While there were historically various strands of socialist thought (such as utopian and scientific), most socialists have identified the following as the important characteristics of socialist societies: (1) there was common ownership of the means of production and distribution; (2) economic activities were planned by the state and the market played little or no role in the allocation of resources; (3) with the disappearance of private property, economic classes also disappeared and hence the state had an administrative rather than repressive function; (4) there were important changes in criminal and property law, since the legal system was now primarily concerned with administration; (5) these structural changes also brought about the disappearance of ideology, especially religion; (6) human ALIENA-TION was abolished with the disappearance of private property.

Three claims were typically made about the superiority of socialist over capitalist societies: (1) socialist societies were more efficient economically, because in a command economy they did not experience the waste (unemployment, overproduction, idle machinery, inflation and stagnation) associated with capitalist market economies; (2) socialist societies did not have colonial markets, because they did not require an outlet for capital or commodities; (3) socialist societies were more democratic than capitalist societies, because decisions about the satisfaction of human needs were taken collectively and publicly. Socialist economic development was thus regarded as the only successful alternative to capitalism in the Third World, because it offered the possibility of growth without dependency.

Critics of socialist societies argued that, in practice, the societies that emerged in Russia, Eastern Europe, Asia and Africa that claimed to be socialist did not exhibit these characteristics. The following arguments were typically raised: (1) socialist societies did not prove more economically efficient and dynamic than capitalist societies, since they became dependent on the West for imports of food, technology and skill, without which they would not have been able to satisfy the needs of their populations; (2) socialist societies were not democratic, because major decisions were taken by the Party, which controlled all appointments to important political and social positions in society; (3) they were imperialist because, to satisfy the requirements of rapid industrialization and economic accumulation, they were forced to exploit their indigenous workers or the peasants of underdeveloped nations; (4) while economic classes may have become less important with the abolition of private ownership, social stratification persisted in the form of income inequality, differences in prestige, and inequalities of power; (5) inequality was determined not by the market but by the Party and its bureaucratic apparatus, which enjoyed a monopoly of power; (6) in practice, it was difficult to remove entirely the operation of economic markets within a planned economy and the black market served to reinforce social inequalities associated with political monopoly;

(7) ideology was important in legitimating Party power, although it did not prove particularly effective (for example, the persistence of Catholicism in Poland or Orthodox opposition in Russia).

In defence of socialist societies, it was often claimed that: (1) these empirical departures from socialism were defects of the transition to advanced socialist society rather than inevitable and inherent failures; (2) socialist societies could not fully develop in a global situation that remained dominated by capitalist societies, since capitalism was able to impose certain restraints on independent socialist development; (3) more radically, societies like the former Soviet Union were not socialist but 'state capitalist', since the state merely replaced private owners in the exercise of capitalist functions. Critics of socialist societies claim that the fall of organized socialism in the old Soviet Union and across Eastern Europe after 1989 demonstrated that socialist societies could not successfully solve the fundamental problems of a planned economy, nor establish the popular LEGITIMACY of their political institutions.

SEE ALSO: *convergence thesis; industrial society.*

READING: Szelenyi and Kostello (1998); Lane and Ross (1999)

socialization Sociologists use this term to describe the process whereby people learn to conform to social norms, a process that makes possible an enduring society and the transmission of its culture between generations. The process has been conceptualized in two ways. (1) Socialization may be conceived as the internalization of social norms: social rules become internal to the individual, in the sense that they are self-imposed rather than imposed by means of external regulation and are thus part of the individual's own personality. The individual therefore feels a need to conform. (2) It may be conceived as an essential element of social interaction, on the assumption that people wish to enhance their own self-image by gaining acceptance and status in the eyes of others; in this case, individuals become socialized as they guide their own actions to accord with the expectations of others. The two conceptualizations may be combined, as in the work of PARSONS.

Socialization may be divided into three stages: the primary stage involves the socialization of the young child in the family; the secondary stage involves the school; and the third stage is adult socialization, when actors enter roles for which primary and secondary socialization may not have prepared them fully (such as becoming an employee, a husband or wife, a parent).

In the mid twentieth century, particularly in Parsonian FUNCTIONALISM, sociologists displayed what D. H. Wrong (1961) called the OVERSOCIALIZED CONCEPTION OF MAN; that is, they saw socialization as all-powerful and effective rather than as a more tentative process that influences but may not determine actors' behaviours and beliefs. Symbolic interactionists have also criticized the conventional usage, emphasizing socialization as a process of transaction between individual and society, in which both are mutually influential. It is now accepted that individuals are rarely totally moulded by the culture of their society.

SEE ALSO: *agency and structure; anticipatory socialization; identity; internalization; Mead, George H.; norm; role; significant others.*

READING: Danziger (1971)

societal This term refers to the characteristics of a society as a whole.

societal reaction See: FOLK DEVILS.

society The concept is a commonsense category in which 'society' is equivalent to the boundaries of nation states. While sociologists in practice often operate with this everyday terminology, it is not adequate because societies do not always correspond to political boundaries (as in 'Palestinian society'). GLOBALIZATION, in particular, has exposed the limitations of traditional theories which equated society with the nation state. Some Marxists, in order to avoid this difficulty, substituted 'social formation' for 'society', but in practice these two terms are equivalent. It is more useful to argue that SOCIOLOGY is the analysis of the social, which can be treated at any level (e.g. dyadic interaction, social groups, large organizations or whole societies).

society of the spectacle A term invented by G. Debord (1994) to describe the way in which, in contemporary society, the social and natural worlds are presented as images or spectacles. As Debord says, what was once directly lived, has now become a representation. He explains this transformation by suggesting that CAPITALISM has colonized everyday life and has made everything into a commodity.

SEE ALSO: *commodification*.

sociobiology This applies modern evolutionary ideas developed within the biological sciences to the analysis of human behaviour. The theory of natural selection, which was pioneered by C. Darwin in the nineteenth century, holds that, within any living species, some individual organisms will do better than others in the struggle for existence and will have more surviving offspring. As a consequence, the inherited characteristics of these more successful individuals will become dominant in future generations of the species. Evolutionary theory holds that organisms seek to maximize their reproductive success, that is the number of their surviving offspring at some point in the future. The development of genetics in the twentieth century led to the identification of genes as the basic units of inheritance and it is assumed that genes act to maximize their reproductive success. Genes that enable some individuals to leave more surviving offspring will become more numerous over time as the result of natural selection. However, in any population at any moment, there will still be some range of genetic variation, because genes combine and recombine via cross-breeding over the generations and may also mutate (fail to replicate accurately). Finally, natural selection occurs within an environment. Thus genes that maximize reproductive success do so within certain environmental conditions and, should conditions change significantly, may be less well adapted.

Sociobiologists assume that human behaviour is conditioned by biological evolution, because traits that have been favoured by selection in the past will condition our behaviour today. One fundamental principle of social evolution is *inclusive fitness*. Fitness is another way of describing reproductive success, and behaviours that enhance inclusive fitness have been winnowed by natural selection. The principle of inclusive fitness states that individuals have evolved in ways which maximize the likelihood of transmitting as much of their genetic endowment as possible to succeeding generations. Transmission occurs via individuals' own direct descendants and also via those of their relatives (siblings, half-siblings, cousins, etc.). This general principle has been used to inform the analysis of social relations of cooperation and altruism among kin (and their progressive weakening as ties of kinship become more distant), clan and ethnic solidarity, and the differential investment of mothers and fathers in their children. However, under certain conditions, natural selection will also be expected to favour cooperation where relatedness is too distant for kin selection to be a factor. The argument is that, where the trait of reciprocal altruism produces benefits, in the form of the exchange of many altruistic acts with others, which outweigh the costs, then selection will favour altruists over those who decline to cooperate. That is, reciprocal altruists will have greater reproductive success. Moreover, some sociobiologists have hypothesized that reciprocal altruism will create a sense of justice in participants and that this might be a trait which increases evolutionary fitness.

There is a distinction between species-wide features of evolution, which affect all humans, and those which are sex-specialized. Sociologists have addressed various sexually differentiated behaviours of men and women, which include unequal access to material and political resources, the application of different standards of sexual behaviour, different involvements in child rearing and different strategies for attracting and selecting mates. The conventional sociological approach is that culture and socialization explain how sex differences are manifest and perpetuated. Sociobiologists accept culture and socialization as important variables, but maintain that the fundamental roots of sex-differentiated behaviours are to be found in the evolved aspects of human nature. They argue that biological differences and how these have affected human evolution are additional to, and complement, conventional sociology.

A basic tenet is that individuals and the genes that they embody are self-benefiting; this has been described, one-sidedly, as the 'selfish gene' (Dawkins, 1989). The analytical task is to explain how different forms of social behaviour may be explained by the principle of natural selection acting on the self-benefiting imperative to maximize reproductive success. Sociobiologists therefore share a common orientation with RATIONAL CHOICE THEORY, that social life needs to be explained as an outcome of the activities of self-interested individuals. Indeed, many also use the Prisoner's Dilemma, tit-for-tat strategies and other aspects of GAME THEORY in their analyses. However, for sociobiologists, cooperative and altruistic behaviours have been favoured over time by natural selection and thus are innate to human nature under certain conditions.

The concept of evolved behaviour looks to the past to explain how people behave in the present: individuals today are genetically predisposed to certain behaviours because these maximized the fitness of their ancestors over many previous generations. Many human behavioural traits have been explained in terms of their evolutionary fitness to the hunter-gatherer and simple agrarian societies which have prevailed during much the greater part of human existence. Under conditions of major environmental change, of the sort experienced in many places in the world over the last few hundred years, evolved behaviour may prove less adapted. An example is the taste for fatty foods: this increased fitness in societies where fat was scarce and often had to be hunted, but may reduce fitness now that fat is abundant, if excessive consumption shortens the life-span of individuals and thus their chances of reproductive success. But the only way to determine whether or not certain evolved behaviours now reduce fitness is to wait for the future, when reproductive success will resolve the issue.

Sociobiology has been treated with great scepticism by the majority of sociologists. There have been a variety of criticisms.

(1) *Biological determinism.* It is claimed that sociobiologists believe that human

behaviour is determined by biology in the form of genetic inheritance. Sociobiologists reply that evolved traits which are encoded genetically are not so much determining as predisposing. Thus people may choose to behave differently, although it is assumed that, on average, the majority will not. For example, women may choose to take advantage of historically new opportunities, provided by the invention of effective contraception which women control and a labour market which allows them material independence, to make new choices about how they will live their lives. These even include the possibility of minimizing rather than maximizing their direct reproductive success by remaining childless. The issue for sociobiologists would be whether evolved traits, which have been favoured by natural selection and predispose women to certain forms of behaviour, ensure that most women do not make radically different choices.

(2) *Cultural diversity.* The diversity of human societies and behaviour throws into doubt the usefulness of explanations based on universal human traits, because, even if such traits exist, they do not explain very much. The response to this criticism has three parts. (i) Certain common features of behaviour and social life can be found underlying apparent diversity. (ii) In any population there will always be a range of variation in its genetic endowment which will underpin a range of behavioural variations. (iii) Natural selection is the product of the genetic endowments of organisms in interaction with pressures from the environment. But for humans, environmental pressures are *both* physically given (e.g. the relative abundance or, more typically, scarcity of resources such as food, shelter and sexual partners) and socially/culturally constructed (i.e. by other people). In principle, therefore, cultural diversity can be incorporated into evolutionary accounts, although it is not clear that it has been to date.

(3) *Justification of inequalities.* The Darwinian 'survival of the fittest' metaphor is said to justify the existing distribution of wealth, power and sexual and racial advantage as being inevitable and unchangeable, because naturally selected. Sociobiologists reply, in general with justification, that this implication of their work is something which others have chosen to find and is not part of their own endeavour.

SEE ALSO: *competition; ethology; nature/nurture debate; organic analogy; Social Darwinism.*

READING: Trivers (1985); Lopreato and Crippen (1999)

sociodrama A term used to describe events, usually games or rituals, that have come to have a particular symbolic significance for certain social groups or society at large; it is as if these events were dramas, watched, perhaps via the mass media, by a society. For example, it has been suggested that the coronation of Queen Elizabeth II unified British society. Similarly, cricket or football matches may dramatize social conflicts that might otherwise be really acted out.

socio-economic classification (SEC) The Office for National Statistics (ONS) has devised a single classificatory scheme, which replaces socio-economic groups (SEGs) and social class based on occupation (SC), for use in the 2001 census and in other official statistics. This is an occupationally based classification, taken from employment relations and conditions, which derives from the social-class schema developed by the Oxford University Social Mobility Group.

SEE ALSO: *class; Goldthorpe; social mobility.*

socio-economic groups (SEGs) A now outmoded official classification of occupations in Britain, originally devised by the Registrar General for the 1951 census and used by government until the end of the 1990s. SEGs contained people whose lifestyles were similar with respect to social, cultural and leisure behaviour, and people were allocated to the various SEGs on the basis of their occupation and employment status. There were originally thirteen SEGs, which increased to seventeen in 1961. The Office for National Statistics (ONS) has replaced SEGs with a new SOCIO-ECONOMIC CLASSIFICATION (SEC) for use in the 2001 census.

SEE ALSO: *class*; *lifestyle*.

sociogram Relationships among members of a group may be presented diagrammatically in a sociogram which plots, for example, who interacts with whom and who are the effective leaders. Sociograms were developed in the 1940s and are a forerunner of modern social network analysis.

SEE ALSO: *network/social network*; *sociometry*.

sociology The term has two stems – the Latin *socius* (companion) and the Greek *logos* (study of) – and literally means the study of the processes of companionship. In these terms, sociology may be defined as the study of the bases of social membership. More technically, sociology is the analysis of the structure of social relationships as constituted by social interaction, but no definition is entirely satisfactory because of the diversity of perspectives which is characteristic of the modern discipline.

The study of society can, of course, be traced back to Plato and Aristotle in Greek philosophy, Ibn Khaldun in Islamic jurisprudence and to the European and SCOTTISH ENLIGHTENMENT, but the term 'sociology' dates from the correspondence of COMTE in 1824 and became more publicly used through his *Positive Philosophy* (1838). The sociological approach of SAINT-SIMON, Comte and SPENCER was based on the optimistic belief that POSITIVISM would provide a scientific basis for the study of society. Sociology would discover general laws of social change similar to those found in Newtonian physics or Darwinian biology, but these aims proved overly ambitious. By the end of the nineteenth century, sociologists adopted far more limited goals for the new discipline.

For WEBER, sociology would have to concern itself with the meaning of social action and the uniqueness of historical events rather than with the fruitless search for general laws. By contrast, DURKHEIM exhibited a far more confident view of the achievements of sociology, claiming that it had shown how certain moral and legal institutions and religious beliefs were the same in a wide variety of societies, and that this uniformity was the best proof that the social realm was subject to universal laws.

While Durkheim's research attempted to show that sociology was an autonomous and distinctive science of social phenomena, there is considerable disagreement with respect to sociology's place in the social sciences. Against Durkheim, it can be argued that: (1) sociology is not a separate discipline, but one that integrates the findings of economics, politics and psychology, since the social is not an autonomous datum but is constituted by the intersection of economics, politics, geography, history and psychology; (2) sociology is a perspective or a form of imagination which seeks to ground individuals and events in a broad social context, and this imagination is not peculiar to the discipline of sociology but is shared by historians, geographers, economists, journalists, etc.; (3) for some Marxists, sociology does not have a scientific status, because it has no definite object of analysis, no distinctive methodology and no scientific frame of analysis, and should be seen as an IDEOLOGY appropriate to a particular stage of capitalist development.

Sociology is sometimes seen as the intellectual and often conservative response to the specific social problems which were produced by the French Revolution and the transition from a traditional to an industrial society. It attempted to measure and analyse urban poverty, political instability, mortality rates, disease, crime, divorce, suicide, etc.

However, the subject was also deeply influenced by Saint-Simon, MARX and ENGELS in its analysis of SOCIAL STRUCTURE, CLASS and SOCIAL CHANGE. The philosophical and political inheritance of sociology is complex and no single tradition can be regarded as entirely dominant.

While there is disagreement about the nature of sociology, there is some agreement about its importance. A defence of the discipline could rightly claim: (1) it has contributed in detail, through numerous empirical studies, to knowledge and understanding of modern societies; (2) it raises important questions about the nature of individual responsibility in law and morality by studying the social context of action; (3) it has contributed significantly to developments in other disciplines, especially history, philosophy and economics; (4) it can be regarded as a new form of consciousness, particularly sensitive to the dilemmas of a secular, industrial civilization.

SEE ALSO: *sociology as science*.

READING: Nisbet (1967); Willis (1996)

sociology as science A long-standing controversy in sociology is to what extent or in what ways sociology is a science. Sciences are commonly understood as having certain objectives and using particular methods to reach those objectives. Most fundamentally, they aim at CAUSAL EXPLANATION (by means of theories) of regularities in the natural world. They attempt to provide theories which in turn generate testable hypotheses. Theories, generalizations or even laws may survive this process of testing and become more and more firmly accepted, only being rejected if they are shown to be logically incoherent or if evidence piles up against them. One of the most important ways in which evidence is brought to bear on theory is by experiments, which can be repeated and which will often involve an attempt to quantify variables, provide techniques of measurement and apply mathematical and statistical methods to the results.

Many sociologists (often called positivists) believe that their subject has many of these features of sciences. They are interested in causal explanations of phenomena in the social world by confronting theories with empirical evidence which is often quantified. It is even said that certain types of CAUSAL MODELLING may be equivalent to the experimental method. It should be noted here that much practice in the natural sciences does not in fact conform precisely to this scheme. For example, it is often difficult to repeat experiments in the same form, while some branches of science, such as astronomy or the theory of evolution in biology, do not use experiments in the strict sense. Even positivist sociologists, however, will concede that sociology cannot conform to the scientific method precisely. It is certainly very difficult to experiment with social behaviour in such a way that variables can be controlled precisely and experiments can be repeated.

There are, however, more fundamental objections to the view that sociology is, with some relatively minor exceptions, like the natural sciences. These objections are of two kinds. First, it has been argued that human beings cannot be treated in the same way as objects in the natural world because, among other things, they have the capacity to reason and to make active sense of their world. Sociologists, on this view, cannot aim to produce theories which give causal explanations of social behaviour but only ones which provide understanding, perhaps by the operation of VERSTEHEN. One extreme version of this position is provided by P. Winch (1958), who argues that social behaviour cannot be seen as causally regular behaviour but must be seen as rule-following behaviour. Sociologists do not causally explain, they detect rules. The second objection to the positivist view of sociology is that, unlike natural science, sociology cannot be separated from value judgements about social behaviour. Because sociologists are themselves members of the society that they study, they simply cannot make objective studies of society; they can see social reality only as it is filtered through a set of value judgements.

SEE ALSO: *empathy; empiricism; ethnomethodology; experimental method; falsificationism; grounded theory; hermeneutics; hypothesis; hypothetico-deductive model; induction; Methodenstreit; naturalism; neo-Kantianism; objectivity; operationalization; phenomenological sociology; positivism; qualitative research; realism; replication; understanding alien belief systems; value freedom; value neutrality; value relevance.*

sociology of development This involves the analysis of the social and political effects of INDUSTRIALIZATION on Third World societies. In the 1960s, the sociology of development was dominated by perspectives and assumptions drawn from FUNCTIONALISM and regarded industrial change as largely beneficial. In the 1970s, MARXIST SOCIOLOGY emphasized the negative effects of capitalist industrialization by arguing that development programmes, which were financed by Western societies, did not necessarily result in economic growth or social improvement. The experience of rapid economic growth in many previously underdeveloped societies in the 1980s and their inclusion into a globalized economy, the decline of Marxism as a significant intellectual strand in sociology in the 1990s, and the realization that the nation state may no longer be so important as a unit of analysis, given GLOBALIZATION, have greatly reduced sociological interest in development as a subject for investigation.

SEE ALSO: *capitalism; centre/periphery; convergence thesis; dependency theory; differentiation; dual economy; imperialism; internal colonialism; migration; mobilization; modernization; nationalism; new international division of labour; peasants; secularization; social change; underdevelopment; uneven development; urbanization.*

READING: Roxborough (1979); Mouzelis (1988)

sociology of economic life See: ECONOMIC SOCIOLOGY.

sociology of education The main focus of British educational sociology in the 1950s and 1960s was on the contribution of education to SOCIAL MOBILITY and LIFE-CHANCES, social-class differences in EDUCATIONAL ATTAINMENT and the explanation of these. Since then the subject has developed in several ways. (1) School ethnographies provided descriptions of the social systems of schools, and drew attention to the significance of pupil–teacher interactions for educational attainment. (2) Reflecting the interest within mainstream sociology in accounts of ideologies, educational sociologists have looked at schools as agencies of CULTURAL REPRODUCTION and purveyors of a HIDDEN CURRICULUM. (3) Feminist sociologists investigate the role of the school in reinforcing gender STEREOTYPES among children. (4) Empirical research into teaching methods attempts to identify the effectiveness of different teaching styles.

SEE ALSO: *Bernstein; class; classroom interaction; classroom knowledge; cultural capital; cultural deprivation; intelligence; nature/nurture debate; pedagogical practices; restricted code; sponsored mobility.*

sociology of everyday life Although much of sociology is preoccupied with the analysis of large-scale structures, such as the family, work institutions or the state, an important branch of the discipline has been concerned with the small-scale analysis of the practices, reciprocities and cultural arrangements of everyday life. For some approaches, for example ETHNOMETHODOLOGY, everyday life represents the only valid level of sociological analysis.

There are various sociological approaches to the study of the everyday world. SCHUTZ attempted to analyse the taken-for-granted assumptions of commonsense thought in everyday interaction. In the work of HABERMAS there is an important contrast between LIFE-WORLD (everyday life) and social system, in which the process of MODERNIZATION and RATIONALIZATION brings about a colonization of the life-world. The life-world is regarded as authentic, while the institutions of the rationalized social system are false and manufactured. In Marxism, H. Lefebvre (1947) argued that we must understand how capitalism brings about an ALIENATION of daily life through the separation of work, household and leisure. The CONSUMER SOCIETY resulted in the COMMODIFICATION of daily life. Postmodern studies of culture have claimed that there has been an AESTHETICIZATION OF EVERYDAY LIFE in which mundane objects in the everyday world are increasingly influenced by style and fashion. Ordinary objects are not developed merely for their utility but are influenced by fashion: they are now designed. GOFFMAN was very interested in the way in which everyday life is a PERFORMANCE.

BOURDIEU has developed the notion of 'habitus' to describe the everyday world as a system of practices which embody our fundamental preferences or taste for objects, values and people. The habitus determines our response to reality by organizing these preferences into a system of distinctions which structure social reality. The habitus is a cultural organization of everyday practices, which includes taste and the emotions.

SEE ALSO: *Marxist sociology; micro-sociology; symbolic interactionism.*

sociology of the family This is the study of how human sexual reproduction is institutionalized and of how children, who are the product of sexual unions, are assigned places within a kinship system. Two issues have dominated contemporary sociological approaches to the family. (1) The relationship between types of family structure and industrialization has been debated. (2) Critics of modern family life suggest that a woman's place in the home compounds female inequality in society at large and that the modern family based on intimacy and emotional attachment in fact masks a system of exploitation of wives by husbands and children by parents.

SEE ALSO: *conjugal role; demography; descent groups; divorce; domestic labour; extended family; marriage; maternal deprivation; matriarchy; nuclear family; patriarchy; sex roles; symmetrical family.*

READING: Allan (1985); Jamieson (1998)

sociology of gender The sociology of gender considers the ways in which the physical differences between men and women are mediated by culture and social structure. These differences are culturally and socially elaborated so that (1) women are ascribed specific feminine personalities and a 'gender identity' through socialization; (2) women are often secluded from public activities in industrial societies by their relegation to the private domain of the home; (3) women are allocated to inferior and typically degrading productive activities; (4) women are subjected to stereotypical ideologies which define women as weak and emotionally dependent on men.

There have been two major debates within the sociology of gender. The first has addressed the issue of whether GENDER is a separate and independent dimension of social STRATIFICATION and of the social DIVISION OF LABOUR. The second debate concerns the appropriateness of general theoretical perspectives for the analysis of gender differences and divisions in society. For example, one aspect of the debate is whether feminism is compatible with Marxism.

SEE ALSO: *class; domestic labour; educational attainment; feminism; feminist social theory; labour market segmentation; maternal deprivation; Mead, Margaret; patriarchy; sex roles; sociology of the family; stereotypes; women and work.*

READING: Abbott and Wallace (1990); Robinson and Richardson (1997)

sociology of health and illness This term is often preferred to the SOCIOLOGY OF MEDICINE, because it reflects the theoretical interests of sociology rather than the professional interests of medicine. The sociological study of health and illness has the following features: (1) it is critical of the MEDICAL MODEL and treats the concepts of health and illness as highly problematic and political; (2) it is concerned with the phenomenology of health and illness and gives special attention to how patients experience and express their distress; (3) it has been significantly influenced by the concept of the SICK ROLE but is also critical of this legacy; (4) it argues that modern societies have a residual conception of health, because the medical PROFESSION has been primarily concerned with illness; (5) it has been critical of the MEDICALIZATION of social problems. In practice, there is considerable overlap between the sociology of medicine and the sociology of health and illness.

SEE ALSO: *clinical sociology.*

READING: Samson (1999)

sociology of industry See: SOCIOLOGY OF WORK AND EMPLOYMENT.

sociology of knowledge This is a branch of sociology often mentioned but only slightly developed. In its earlier stages it was dominated by the debate with the ideas of MARX, and MANNHEIM, an early practitioner, spent much effort showing that forms of belief or knowledge could not all be explained by the economy or the class structure. Since Mannheim the subject has become defined very generally as the relation between knowledge and a social base. In much sociology of knowledge this relation is understood causally; social base produces particular kinds of knowledge. This point has been attacked by HERMENEUTICS.

Not a great deal of empirical work has been done in the sociology of knowledge itself, but there has been considerable activity in some of its branches, particularly in the sociologies of literature and science. The former typically asks how social institutions influence particular literary forms or novelists. In the latter, these macro-sociological questions are left aside in favour, for example, of investigations of how scientists decide what is to count as knowledge.

SEE ALSO: *base and superstructure; critical sociology; discourse; Frankfurt School; ideology; Marxist sociology; semiotics; world view.*

READING: Abercrombie (1980)

sociology of law This field of sociology involves the study of how social conditions influence the making and enforcement of law. One controversy within the subject is between Marxist and Weberian sociologists concerning the relationship of law to the economy. For Marxists, the law ultimately serves the interests of the dominant class by, for example, protecting property rights, whereas WEBER argued that a stable system of abstract, general law was a requirement of capitalism. Symbolic interactionists have also argued that sociologists should not study why people break laws but why the laws are made in the first place.

One legacy of Weber's sociology of law was a relativistic criticism of the normative basis of law. As a result, sociologists were sceptical of the universalistic claims of NATURAL LAW. In recent debates, however, sociologists have attempted to defend the notion of rights as a universalistic discourse.

SEE ALSO: *criminal statistics; criminology; deviant behaviour; Durkheim; ideological state apparatus; labelling; legitimacy; property; state; symbolic interactionism.*

READING: Baumgarten (1998)

sociology of the mass media Three main issues currently preoccupy practitioners in this subject. (1) The study of media messages is a major concern and various approaches have been suggested. However, there are still no widely agreed procedures as to the proper methods of analysing the content of, say, television programmes. (2) One way of understanding how particular messages are produced is to study media institutions and personnel. There have been many investigations of the ownership and control of newspapers and television companies and of the background, education and basic assumptions of journalists in these media. (3) Studies of audiences have not been so common in recent years, although most investigations of the mass media do speculate as to the effects of the media on the AUDIENCE. In work done after the Second World War, audiences were thought to be passive while the media were all-powerful. This view was replaced by an account of audiences as active, selecting and often rejecting media opinions. More recent work suggests some compromise between these two.

SEE ALSO: *content analysis; culture industries; discourse; dominant ideology thesis; ideological state apparatus; ideology; mass society; semiotics.*

READING: McQuail (1987)

sociology of medicine Although medical sociology emerged rather late in the 1950s as a specialized area of sociology, it has subsequently developed rapidly, partly because the medical profession has recognized the importance of sociology in the education of medical students. There are now a number of important journals dealing with the subject – *Journal of Health and Social Behavior; Millbank Memorial Fund Quarterly; Social Science and Medicine; Sociology of Health and Illness.*

Medical sociology covers a variety of topics: (1) the sociology of the healing professions; (2) the sociology of illness, illness behaviour and 'help-seeking' behaviour; (3) medical institutions and health service organizations; (4) social factors in the aetiology of illness and disease; (5) social factors in fertility and mortality; (6) social factors influencing the demand for and use of medical facilities; (7) the sociology of doctor–patient interaction; (8) the social effects of different medical systems, such as between private and public provision of health care; (9) international patterns of illness and health services.

It is important to recognize a distinction between sociology *in* medicine and sociology *of* medicine as perspectives in research. The former involves the use of sociology to clarify medically defined problems and objectives, such as the nature of patient compliance to medical regimens. J. Roth (1962) claims that sociology in medicine exhibits a 'management bias', because research is guided by the dominant values of professional medicine. Controversial issues, such as medical malpractice, tend to be ignored. By contrast, the sociology of medicine has been more concerned with issues of power between doctors and patients, and between medicine and the state. For example, writers like I. Illich (1977) have drawn attention to the issue of iatrogenesis – that is, the risks to human health brought about by medical intervention itself. MEDICALIZATION has produced dependency on antibiotics, amphetamines and barbiturates, which can be harmful to health. In the USA in 1979, for example, there were 65 million prescriptions for tranquillizers written by physicians. There has been a corresponding shift in paradigms from SYMBOLIC INTERACTIONISM and FUNCTIONALISM, which neglected the politics of medicine, to various Marxist paradigms which adopt a far more critical perspective on health-service organizations and healing professions. Another radical perspective on medicine has come from FEMINISM, which regards inequalities in health provision and differences in illness behaviour as the products of PATRIARCHY and GENDER. Feminist critics have argued: (1) that modern medicine converts women into 'natural' patients by regarding women as emotional and complaining; (2) modern surgery often inflicts unnecessary procedures on women as patients (such as mastectomy and hysterectomy) where the benefit of these operations is uncertain; (3) modern obstetrics prevents women from exercising some control over the birth of their children; (4) medicine in general prevents women from having control over their bodies (especially with respect to reproduction). These critical perspectives in contemporary medical sociology argue that the health of human populations is not a consequence of medical intervention but of the socio-political environment.

SEE ALSO: *clinical sociology; demography; epidemiology; gerontology; rick role; sociology of health and illness.*

READING: Mumford (1983); Turner, B. S. (1995)

sociology of race Sociologists do not regard 'race' as a useful scientific category and there is widespread agreement that the biological notion of race cannot provide a causal explanation of human behaviour. Thus the sociology of race is the study of a form of social STRATIFICATION in which race relations between ethnic groups are constructed around an IDEOLOGY of imputed racial differences. The sociology of race involves the following issues: (1) the study of RACISM and racial ideologies which claim that cultural differences between groups can be explained wholly by reference to genetic differences, and that social inequalities between ethnic groups are genetic in origin; (2) the study of the social structures which produce and maintain racism and racial hatred; (3) the study of the interaction between social class and ethnicity in social stratification, giving rise to both vertical and horizontal segments in the social structure of societies; (4) the analysis of racism and racial inequality in the history of colonialism and anti-colonialism, and the continuity of such racial systems of SEGREGATION under GLOBALIZATION; (5) the study of the function of ethnic groups within the domestic labour market and the role of race relations in global patterns of MIGRATION; (6) the historical inquiry into the role of ethnicity and racism in the shaping of NATIONALISM, national identity and the formation of the modern STATE; (7) the sociological analysis of how these issues have contributed to the specific features of social stratification in contemporary societies. Despite the importance of these empirical studies, it is argued that, in order to conceptualize racism, sociologists must set aside the notion of race as an analytical category (M. Wieviorka, 1991).

SEE ALSO: *accommodation; assimilation; caste; citizenship; eugenics; ghetto; heredity; imperialism; internal colonialism; Orientalism; plural societies; prejudice; slavery; social closure; sociobiology; stereotypes; stigma; underclass.*

READING: Miles (1989)

sociology of religion In classical sociology, the study of RELIGION was primarily concerned with two broad issues: (1) how did religion contribute to the maintenance of social order? (2) what was the relationship between religion and capitalist society? These two issues were typically combined in the argument that industrial capitalism would undermine traditional religious commitment and thereby threaten the cohesion of society. More recently, the subject has been narrowly defined as the study of religious institutions.

SEE ALSO: *church; civil religion; cult; Durkheim; Freud; Halévy thesis; invisible religion; millenarianism; myth; new religious movements; profane; Protestant ethic; rationalization; ritual; sacred; sect; secularization; taboo; theodicy; Weber; witchcraft; world religions.*

READING: Turner, B. S. (1991); Hamilton (1995)

sociology of work and employment This is the successor to what was once known as *industrial sociology*. Sociologists working in the area have traditionally been concerned mainly with two issues: (1) to investigate the nature of the social relations involved in the production of goods and services, broadly to determine whether these are cooperative and harmonious, or conflictual; (2) to determine whether the tasks that people perform at work provide for the satisfaction of human needs.

Early work was heavily influenced by a Durkheimian perspective, that conflict was pathological rather than inherent, and a belief that the low morale of employees, interpreted as the result of uninteresting jobs and work that provided little opportunity to participate in a social community in the firm, was a major cause of conflict. Although associated with the old HUMAN RELATIONS movement, these views have retained some influence with the continuing concern to 'humanize' jobs and to increase employees' sense of belonging to their companies. Sociologists broke with Human Relations in the 1960s to argue that employees did not have fixed or universal expectations of work, and that boring jobs and lack of community did not necessarily lead to low morale. The older approach was also accused of technological determinism, believing that technology was responsible for the nature of social relations at work and individual job satisfaction. A further shift of perspective occurred during the 1970s, with the revival of the Marxist view that capitalism contained an inherent conflict of interest between capital and labour and the parallel interest in M. Weber's belief that all modern organizations, whether in capitalist or socialist economies, dominated the individual. By the 1980s, the focus was on the history of the social relationships involved in production, the labour process, managerial control systems and employee resistance, and the effects of technological change. Alternative forms of organizing the enterprise, such as industrial democracy, self-management and cooperatives, were also studied. The idea of human needs reappeared with the notion of alienation. The position of women and ethnic groups in employment was also a growing area of research.

During the later 1980s and through the 1990s, the concern with conflict, domination and alternatives waned to some extent. More sociologists became interested in understanding the transformations of work that resulted from POST-FORDISM, the continued decline of manufacturing jobs and the rise of services, the increasing participation of women in the labour force, the organizational restructuring of large companies which shed many employees and created insecure jobs for the remainder, and the growing GLOBALIZATION of the capitalist economy. New theoretical interpretations of the subject matter have included the cultural 'turn' associated with the importation of Foucaultian ideas about discourse and power, and a concern to engage with the ideas of economics.

In the course of this evolution, the scope of the sociology of industry and work has widened, from the focus on a restricted selection of factors internal to the enterprise that largely ignored labour markets, TRADE UNIONS and MANAGEMENT, to a more complete analysis of work and employment which also includes their social, economic and political environments. At its margins, the subject merges with mainstream sociology.

SEE ALSO: *affluent worker; alienation; automation; bureaucracy; capitalism; class imagery; collective bargaining; cooperative; corporatism; economic sociology; flexible specialization; Fordism; human capital; industrial conflict; industrial democracy; institutional theory; institutionalization of conflict; labour market; labour market segmentation; labour movement; labour process approach; managerial revolution; managerial strategies of control; organizational culture; organization theory; orientation to work; paternalism; pluralism; privatization; scientific management; socio-technical systems; strikes; technology; unemployment; unionateness; women and work.*

sociometry This was an early attempt to study small-group social relations using sociograms and was associated with work in the 1940s by the social psychologist J. L. Moreno. It did not prove influential in sociology at the time and should be seen as a precursor of network analysis.

SEE ALSO: *network/social network; sociogram.*

socio-technical systems This term was coined by members of the Tavistock Institute of Human Relations to describe their view that industry would operate efficiently only if both the social–psychological needs of employees – for satisfying tasks and group working, and the technical requirements of production – were met simultaneously. Their research suggested that production technology could often be redesigned so as to meet human needs without any loss of technical efficiency. There is usually a range of viable technological arrangements, which are equally efficient in terms of production but have different effects on the job satisfaction of employees. Industrial engineers need to choose arrangements which jointly optimize social and technical factors.

SEE ALSO: *alienation; human relations; labour process approach; technology.*

Sorokin, Pitirim A. (1880–1968) Born and educated in Russia, Sorokin was exiled in 1922 and eventually came to the United States. He became the first professor of sociology at Harvard University in 1930. His main interests included: social mobility in *Social Mobility* (1927); assessments of sociological theory in *Contemporary Sociological Theories* (1928), *The Social Philosophies of an Age of Crisis* (1950), *Fads and Foibles in Modern Sociology* (1956) and *Sociological Theories of Today* (1966); and analysis of social change in *Social and Cultural Dynamics* (1937–41) and *Sociocultural Causality, Space, Time* (1943).

Spencer, Herbert (1820–95) The principal feature of Spencer's sociology was its attempt to combine utilitarian individualism with an organic model of the evolution of social systems. Influenced by the biological theories of natural selection, Spencer used two separate versions of social evolution. (1) He argued that social systems, like organisms, adapt to their environments by a process of internal differentiation and integration. (2) The evolutionary progress of societies was from simple homogeneity in 'militant' society to complex heterogeneity in industrial society. The political doctrine that Spencer derived from his sociology was that social planning, social welfare and state intervention interfered with the natural process of social evolution and progress, which guaranteed personal freedom in industrial society. Spencerian sociology is often associated with the principle of 'the survival of the fittest' (the phrase coined by Spencer) and SOCIAL DARWINISM, but Spencer thought that competitive struggle was dominant only in early militant societies. An advanced industrial society would rely on cooperation, persuasion and altruism rather than aggression and conflict. Spencer contributed to the emergence of FUNCTIONALISM, but little of his work has survived in contemporary sociology.

SEE ALSO: *differentiation; evolutionary theory; organic analogy; social system.*
READING: Turner, J. H. (1985)

spiralist This term describes the typical ORGANIZATION MAN, whose upward career movement is a spiralling progression of new posts that involve frequent relocation around the country and abroad. C. Bell (1968) contrasts *burghers*, locally based middle-class people who stay in one place and run family businesses or professional practices.

sponsored mobility R. H. Turner (1960) contrasted the British and American educational systems with respect to upward SOCIAL MOBILITY in terms of 'sponsored' and 'contest' mobility. Until the introduction of comprehensive schools, sponsorship in Britain involved the early identification of able children, by means of an examination in the final year of primary education (the 11+ examination), who were chosen to progress through selective secondary education and to attain high-level occupations. The American system delayed selection as long as possible, at least to the tertiary stage of education, and was seen as more egalitarian, because social mobility depended on a contest open to all. The notion has become dated with the abolition of selection in British state schools and the realization that mobility patterns in America and Britain do not greatly differ.

SPSS These initials refer to the *Statistical Package for the Social Sciences*, the most widely used standard computer program for the analysis of sociological research data.

standard deviation To measure the variability of any set of data, the standard deviation and its square, the VARIANCE, are the most commonly used statistics. The standard deviation measures the spread of the DISTRIBUTION about the mean value of the data. It is calculated by measuring the deviation (x) of each datum from the mean, taking the squared value of each deviation (x^2), summing these squared deviations (Σx^2), dividing the sum of the squared deviations by the total number (N) of elements in the set to establish the average squared deviation, and extracting the square root to convert squared back into linear units. Thus the basic formula for the standard deviation (σ) is:

$$\sigma = \sqrt{\frac{\Sigma x^2}{N}}$$

In the analysis of survey data, it is important that the likely accuracy of a single sample estimate can be assessed, for which a measure of the variability or the fluctuations of the various sample estimates is needed. This measure is provided by the *standard error of the mean* (or the *proportion*, if the relevant estimates are proportions rather than means), which is partly determined by the standard deviation of the population. In practice, of course, population values are usually unknown and the actual standard deviation cannot be used. However, from any one randomly selected sample it is possible to estimate the likely average magnitude of SAMPLING fluctuations (i.e. the variability) using the variability in the sample which is measured by the standard deviation of the sample. For large numbers, the sampling distribution of the sample mean is approximately Normal, and statistical theory provides procedures for assessing the sample results.

SEE ALSO: *sampling error; significance test.*

stakeholder society A term used in recent political discussion, and particularly influential with New Labour in Britain, to describe a society that suffers neither from the evils of the totally free market economy nor from those of bureaucratic socialism. The former produces inequality, while the latter stifles freedom. The solution is a society that recognizes the interests, rights and responsibilities of the whole population and of each group that has a *stake* in that society. While continuing to operate in a free market economy, major institutions have to be persuaded to moderate the costs on individuals of that free market.

SEE ALSO: *state.*

READING: Hutton (1997)

state This is a set of institutions governing a particular territory, with a capacity to make laws regulating the conduct of the people within that territory, and supported by revenue deriving from taxation. The capacity to make and enforce law is dependent on the state's enjoyment of a monopoly of legitimate force. Defined in this way, there are difficulties in establishing the boundaries of the state in modern society. These difficulties are of two kinds – territorial and institutional. Although the state governs particular territory, the increasing GLOBALIZATION of the modern world means that governments have decreasing control over activities within the territory. For example, commercial enterprises operate on an international scale and can move resources from state to state at will. The activities of global financial markets can totally destabilize governments, which have to a large extent lost control over their own economies. Institutionally, the boundary between state and non-state organizations has been made unclear by recent privatizations of state enterprises, on the one hand, and the creation of regulatory organizations responsible to the state on the other. For many theorists, there is a distinction between the state and a CIVIL SOCIETY which includes the institutions of the family and voluntary organizations, for example. Other writers point out that the institutions of civil society are so intimately bound up with the state that separation between the two is difficult.

Theories of the state may be divided into three main groups – pluralist, elitist and Marxist. In the pluralist model, power is dispersed and fragmented. Large numbers of interest groups try to influence policy but no one ever retains dominance. Political life is thus a competition between rival interests and elections are one manifestation of that competition. The state is not captured by any one interest but is in some sense neutral to them all. There are different ways of being neutral and different theories emphasize different ones. For example, a neutral state can be passive, simply responding to the interest group that is temporarily the strongest; it may be a referee, making sure that the conditions for political conflict are fair; it may be interventionist to protect the weak who are less able to compete: or it may mediate between the various political pressures but have interests of its own which state functionaries pursue.

Although pluralist theories of the state are, on the whole, optimistic, some recent accounts in the tradition have worried that the modern pluralist state is overloaded or ungovernable (e.g. BELL). Demands for better health care have increased hugely, for example. At the same time, the state is unable to meet those demands and so respect for its AUTHORITY diminishes.

The ELITE view of the state challenges the pluralist account. It argues that the political process actually ensures the dominance of particular political groups. There is an inequality of influence between interest groups and some social groups do not have their interests represented at all. There is no serious competition between political groups and elections are therefore not especially meaningful. In support of claims of this kind, elite theorists cite studies of the ruling institutions of Britain – Parliament, civil service, judiciary, church, armed forces, business, press – which show that the leaders of these bodies have very similar backgrounds and form a network of influence. They form, in short, an elite whose interests are not seriously challenged by the political process. Elite theory has both right-wing and left-wing versions. Proponents of the former – for example, MICHELS and PARETO – take Marxist theory as their target. For proponents of the latter – for example, MILLS – pluralist theory is the object of attack.

For Marxist sociologists, the determining feature of capitalist society is the contradiction between capital and labour. The culture, law, social arrangements and politics of such societies reflect the interests of capitalists. Marxists therefore agree with elite theorists in arguing that the conduct of modern politics, especially elections, is largely without meaning; it is ideological. There are varieties of Marxist theories of the state. Some writers – for example, Miliband (1983) – see the state as an instrument of the capitalist class actually promoting its interests, and helped in doing so by the common social origin of state functionaries and members of the capitalist class. Other authors, such as ALTHUSSER, adopt a functionalist view, in which the state functions to support the capitalist mode of production. In such a view, the characteristics and behaviour of state functionaries are deemed irrelevant. In a third variant, some Marxists, such as Poulantzas (1973), come closer to a pluralist version, arguing that state agencies are *relatively* autonomous of CAPITALISM, though in the last instance, the requirements of capital will prevail.

SEE ALSO: *citizenship; feudalism; functionalism; ideological state apparatus; ideology; legitimation; Marxist sociology; pluralism; power; pressure group; socialist societies; Weber.*

READING: Dunleavy and O'Leary (1987); Pierson (1996)

state capitalism See: CAPITALISM; SOCIALIST SOCIETIES.

statistical control This is a commonly used practice in the statistical analysis of data, in order to exclude ('control for') the influence of a particular variable. For example, there is some evidence that girls do better academically in single- than mixed-sex schools, but it is also known that more middle-class parents send their daughters to single-sex schools and that middle-class children on average do better at school than other children. When analysing whether single-sex education accounts for superior attainments among girls, it would be highly advisable to partition the data by social class (e.g. into middle- and working-class categories). This would indicate whether single-sex education was associated with better performance for girls in all social classes, or whether social-class background was the more important factor.

statistical interaction See: INTERACTION OF VARIABLES.

statistical significance See: SIGNIFICANCE TEST.

status This has three sociological uses. (1) R. Linton (1936) defined status simply as a position in a social system, such as 'child' or 'parent'. Status refers to what a person is, whereas the closely linked notion of ROLE refers to the behaviour expected of people in a status. (2) Status is also used as a synonym for honour or PRESTIGE, when social status denotes the relative position of a person on a publicly recognized scale or hierarchy of social worth. WEBER employed *status group* as an element of social STRATIFICATION distinct from CLASS to describe certain collectivities distinguished from other social groups in a society by socially defined criteria of status, such as CASTE or ethnicity. (3) It is increasingly associated with LIFESTYLE and distinctive patterns of consumption in recent sociology. BOURDIEU, for example, approaches status hierarchy from the perspective of culture.

SEE ALSO: *status inconsistency.*

status crystallization See: STATUS INCONSISTENCY.

status group See: STATUS.

status inconsistency In multi-dimensional systems of STRATIFICATION, individuals may occupy inconsistent statuses. For example, individuals with a high level of educational attainment, which provides a high social STATUS along one stratification dimension, may be employed in occupations that are poorly paid and carry low PRESTIGE, indicating low status along other dimensions. G. Lenski (1954) coined this term along with *status crystallization*, which denotes consistency between an individual's various statuses. He cites four important statuses: income, occupational prestige, education and ethnicity. Inconsistency is believed to promote resentment among individuals, who may therefore favour either radical social change designed to alter the system of stratification or attempt to crystallize their own statuses by changing their own personal situations (in the above example, by raising their occupational level).

SEE ALSO: *class.*

stereotypes A stereotype is a one-sided, exaggerated and normally prejudicial view of a group, tribe or class of people, and is usually associated with RACISM and SEXISM. Stereotypes are often resistant to change or correction from countervailing evidence, because they create a sense of social solidarity.

Sociologists have long used the notion in the analysis of DEVIANT BEHAVIOUR, notably to explain DEVIANCE AMPLIFICATION, and of race relations. Recently it has been used in accounts of gender stereotyping and SEX ROLES in education and at work. Schools, it is claimed, reinforce gender stereotyping by socializing children into traditional male and female roles: school books depict girls helping mothers with domestic chores and boys helping fathers repair cars, for example, while teachers believe that boys are more suited to technical and scientific subjects and girls to domestic subjects, the humanities or biology, and instil these ideas in their pupils. At work, employers stereotype all women as being more likely than men to be absent from work or to interrupt their careers because of their family commitments, regardless of whether an individual woman employee in fact fits the stereotype, and also have fixed ideas about what is appropriate 'women's work'. Thus they deny women equal opportunities with men on the basis of the ascriptive criterion of gender.

SEE ALSO: *ascription; authoritarian personality; labour market segmentation; management; prejudice; socialization; stigma; women and work.*

stigma A stigma is a social attribute which is discrediting for an individual or group. There are stigmas of the body (e.g. blemishes and deformities), of character (e.g. homosexuality) and of social collectivities (e.g. race or tribe). Stigma theories explain or justify the exclusion of stigmatized persons from normal social interaction.

SEE ALSO: *Goffman; symbolic interactionism.*

strata See: SAMPLING; STRATIFICATION.

stratification Social differences become social stratification when people are ranked hierarchically along some dimension of inequality. Members of the various layers or strata tend to have common LIFE-CHANCES or lifestyles and may display an awareness of common identity, and these characteristics further distinguish them from other strata. It is safe to say that all large complex societies are stratified, although there is some disagreement as to whether the same can be said of all simple or tribal societies. There are theories of stratification – for example, the FUNCTIONAL THEORY OF STRATIFICATION – which argue that stratification is universal, because societies need the best-qualified people to undertake crucial tasks and have to reward them accordingly, or because social order and integration require a measure of stratification.

Stratification systems can be founded on a variety of social characteristics; for example, social CLASS, race, gender, birth or age. These can be ranged from those that are essentially to do with PRESTIGE and STATUS, for example, to those that are more to do with economic characteristics, such as social class. Modern societies are likely to emphasize economic characteristics, while traditional, ancient or feudal societies will be founded rather more on status characteristics. However, all societies will be mixtures of the two. So, while feudal European societies may have been founded on the principles of aristocratic birth, those social strata were only clearly defined by the position of unequal wealth and income. In modern societies, stratification systems may be particularly complex, with the various social bases interacting with each other. For example, although class is the fundamental basis of stratification, it clearly interacts with ethnicity and gender. In the United States, for instance, black people are heavily over-represented in the poorest stratum; thus a status characteristic – ethnicity – is heavily bound up with an economic one – social class.

Stratification systems can be more or less rigid. There is, for example, a fair degree of social mobility between social classes in contemporary society. In other societies, those based on CASTE, for example, the boundaries between strata are rigid and impermeable and there are well-developed mechanisms whereby higher strata can exclude lower.

SEE ALSO: *estate; functionalism; lifestyle; social mobility; status inconsistency; teleology.*

Strauss, Anselm L. (1916–96) Formerly professor emeritus at the University of California, San Francisco, he made major contributions to qualitative sociology in a variety of substantive fields, including the SOCIOLOGY OF HEALTH AND ILLNESS, the study of PROFESSIONS and the sociology of organizations. His first major study was *Social Psychology* (1949). With B. G. Glaser, he developed GROUNDED THEORY and was a founder of SYMBOLIC INTERACTIONISM. A classic study of medical professionalization was published in *Boys in White* (H. S. Becker *et al.*, 1961). He employed these perspectives to study identity in *Mirrors and Masks* (1959) and the meaning of urban life in *The American City* (1968). He also made a fundamental contribution, with B. G. Glaser, to the sociological study of death, in *Awareness of Dying* (1965) and *Time for Dying* (1968b). He made contributions to the study of work in *Social Organization of Medical Work* (1985). His general theoretical perspective was summarized in *Continual Permutations of Action* (1993).

SEE ALSO: *Chicago School; dramaturgical; Goffman; symbol.*

strikes Industrial sociologists have regarded strike action, the refusal of employees collectively to continue working, as an instance of INDUSTRIAL CONFLICT and are mainly concerned with this broader phenomenon rather than strikes as such. Researchers concerned with strikes as such have approached these in three ways. (1) Case studies, for example A. Gouldner (1955), T. Lane and K. Roberts (1971), and

E. Batstone *et al.* (1978), have provided detailed ethnographic accounts of individual strikes. (2) Official statistics on strike activity are analysed to find trends over time and between different industries, often on a comparative basis among different countries. (3) Strike activity is taken as an indicator of something else, worker militancy and sometimes even class consciousness.

The second and third approaches face methodological and substantive problems. The methodological problem is that official strike statistics are known to be inaccurate. They depend on employers, often voluntarily, reporting stoppages and their causes, which leads to under-recording and misclassification. Unofficial strikes (those not sanctioned by a union) are notably prone to under-recording, particularly when the stoppages are of short duration or in countries where such activity is illegal. Different societies have different criteria of what counts as a strike: some exclude all small stoppages; others disregard 'political' strikes. Employers' perceptions of the causes of strikes are often highly contentious. Comparative analysis compounds inaccuracies because different national statistics are biased in different ways. The substantive problem is that strikes are not necessarily good indicators of workers' attitudes: strike activity also depends on contextual factors such as the efficacy of COLLECTIVE BARGAINING, managerial attitudes and behaviour, the organizational strength of unions, labour market conditions and the legal framework of industrial relations. Workplace militancy may not even show up in strike data if labour is powerful and managements give way without strikes.

SEE ALSO: *official statistics; trade unions.*

structural differentiation See: DIFFERENTIATION.

structuralism This term is frequently used to refer to a particular style of sociological work, although it is not at all distinctive. At its most general level, it simply refers to a sociological perspective based on the concept of SOCIAL STRUCTURE and the view that society is prior to individuals. However, the label has also been used in a more specific sense for those theorists who hold that there is a set of social structures that are unobservable but which generate observable social phenomena. The best-known exponent of this position is the anthropologist LÉVI-STRAUSS, who was a member of an intellectual movement, particularly in France, that embraced anthropology, sociology, linguistics and literary criticism. He held that cultural forms, especially myths, typically take the form of the combination of opposite qualities, called binary oppositions, such as sweet and sour or red and green. Analysis of myths, and by extension of literary texts, takes the form of showing what binary oppositions are manifested. For Lévi-Strauss, explanation of the form of myths was to be found in unvarying qualities (structures) of the human mind. Certain Marxists, particularly ALTHUSSER, adopted a structuralist framework in seeking to explain social phenomena by reference to the underlying structures of the MODE OF PRODUCTION. These structuralist positions have been heavily criticized as ahistorical, unverifiable and neglectful of human creative activity.

SEE ALSO: *agency and structure; Barthes; Foucault; myth; poststructuralism; realism; Saussure.*

READING: Keat and Urry (1975); Bottomore and Nisbet (1978a)

structuration This concept is fundamental to the sociology of GIDDENS and has been a feature of his criticism of EVOLUTIONARY THEORY and FUNCTIONALISM.

Structuration identifies the importance of social practices over both actions and structures. It refers to the ways in which SOCIAL STRUCTURE is produced, reproduced and transformed in and through practice. The notion of structuration is therefore associated with Giddens' concept of the 'duality of structure', in which structures are both produced by human action and are the medium of social action. Structuration theory can be regarded as a summary of the basic concerns of Giddens' sociology, which include the knowledgeability of actors, the temporal and spatial dimensions of action, the openness and contingency of action in everyday life, and the false separation of AGENCY AND STRUCTURE in sociology.

Giddens' attempt to transcend the limitations of functionalism and his concern to transform the agency and structure dichotomy have been well received in contemporary sociology. However, the failure of structuration theory to produce a distinctive programme of empirical research in terms of testable hypotheses has been an issue of critical debate.

SEE ALSO: *action theory; actor-network theory; embodiment; time–space distanciation.*
READING: Craib (1992); Giddens (1984)

subculture This is a system of values, attitudes, modes of behaviour and lifestyles of a social group within a larger whole, whether that is a whole society or an organization. Potentially the term can be used for any social group, but is applied most commonly to deviant or youth cultures that possess a culture opposed to the dominant CULTURE of the larger whole. For example, BECKER described groups of marijuana users who formed a subculture, with developed rituals, slang and ways of behaving which emphasized the differences between them and the wider society. Similarly, studies of exponents of youth cultures, such as punks or skinheads, show how the group is united by dress, attitudes and tastes in opposition to the dominant culture. It has been argued, for example by S. Hall and T. Jefferson (1976), that deviant or youth cultures provide a solution to the problems faced by their members, disadvantaged by youth, criminality or social position. Membership of such subcultures gives a sense of identity and some compensation for 'failure' in conventional society. One of the difficulties of the notion is that it implies the existence of an identifiable dominant culture, but the fragmentation of contemporary society makes the identification of such a common or dominant culture problematic. Indeed, it is arguable that postmodern society is simply composed of large numbers of subcultures that are differentiated from each other by their lifestyles.

SEE ALSO: *deviant behaviour; gang; lifestyle; organizational culture; popular culture; postmodernity; youth culture.*

subject/subjectivity The concept of 'the subject' in contemporary STRUCTURALISM has a paradoxical and contradictory significance. The subject implies agency, action and authorship, but also subjection. While the term is often used synonymously with 'the person' or 'the actor', it has the merit of bringing out the complexity of the debate over DETERMINISM, since 'the subject' suggests both agency and subjection. In structuralist theories of literature, the text is analysed as a product which is independent of the author (subject). In contemporary Marxism, the function of IDEOLOGY is to constitute subjects as the occupants of roles and bearers of social structures. Both perspectives thus deny the creative agency of human subjects.

'Subjectivity' is the self-conscious awareness of subjects, but it is also suggested in structuralism that subjectivity is a mode of awareness which is historically specific to modern Western culture. Recent developments in psychoanalysis, Marxism and structuralism have brought into question most traditional assumptions about subjective agency and the primacy of subjectivity. Subjectivity and self-consciousness are, in these approaches, no longer seen as innate, a part of human nature, but as socially constructed in different forms in different societies. In this sense, subjectivity clearly overlaps with IDENTITY.

SEE ALSO: *action theory*; *agency and structure*; *Freud*; *Lacan*; *methodological individualism*; *objectivity*; *semiotics*.

READING: Benoist (1975)

subsistence economy Also referred to as a 'self-sufficient economy' or 'natural economy', economic subsistence is characterized by the following: (1) the unit of production, such as the peasant family, produces for its own immediate consumption; (2) the unit does not depend on the market for consumption; (3) there is little specialization or division of labour. The subsistence economy is regarded as typical of pre-capitalism or peripheral regions where capitalism has not penetrated. It is thus defined by the absence of economic exchange within a market. The concept has been criticized, since so-called 'self-sufficient' economies do in fact buy and sell on the market. Subsistence economies are thus in reality dependent on external market forces, which in the modern world force them into DEPENDENCY.

SEE ALSO: *peasants*; *underdevelopment*.

substantive significance See: SIGNIFICANCE TEST.

sub-system See: PARSONS; SOCIAL SYSTEM.

suburban way of life It has been argued that those who live in suburbs have a distinctive way of life. In some versions, this is described as 'privatized', families being inward-looking, separated from wider family and neighbours and manifesting a more equal domestic division of labour. In other accounts, while it is admitted that suburban life may be privatized in this sense, there may also be close, almost family-like, relationships with neighbours and friends.

SEE ALSO: *domestic labour*; *metropolitan fringe*; *privatization*; *urban way of life*.

suicide A major sociological tradition derives from E. Durkheim's theory that suicide rates and different types of social context are related, in particular that suicide is related to the level of social integration so that increased disintegration leads to increased numbers of suicides. Three other characteristics of Durkheim's works have also been adopted: (1) a concern with aggregate rates of suicide rather than individual acts and motives; (2) a positivistic approach that relates suicide rates to 'objective', external variables; (3) the use of government statistics as the data source. M. Halbwachs (1930) concluded that Durkheim's analysis could be simplified to a direct relationship between social complexity and suicide rates, demonstrated by the fact that suicides were lower in rural areas, where lifestyles were simpler than in towns. Modern theories usually assume that rapid changes of socio-economic status are the cause of suicide, though unlike Durkheim they include various psychological factors to explain why only certain individuals commit suicide in these circumstances. Outside the Durkheimian tradition, 'ecological' accounts such as R. Cavan's (1928) also focus on social disorganization, which is conceptualized in terms of population variables such as high rates of social mobility and social complexity that weaken the influence of social values on individuals.

The devastating criticisms of sociological theories made by J. B. Douglas (1967) indicate that existing accounts lack foundation and are misguided. He shows that OFFICIAL STATISTICS are highly inaccurate and systematically biased in ways that support disintegration theories: suicides are more accurately reported in towns than rural areas, highly integrated groups are more likely than poorly integrated ones to conceal suicides by ensuring that other causes of death are recorded; the medical competence of those who categorize deaths for official purposes varies and may be assumed to be greater as societies modernize (and grow more complex). Thus Durkheimian and ecological theories simply and uncritically reproduce the distortions inherent in official statistics. Existing theories are also misguided, because they impute social meanings to suicide such as 'egoistic' and 'anomic' acts that are based merely on untested commonsense judgements and ignore the actual meanings for those involved. In Douglas' view, particular social acts like suicides cannot be explained by abstract social meanings such as values favouring suicide.

SEE ALSO: *Durkheim; social pathology.*

READING: Atkinson, J. M. (1978)

superstructure See: BASE AND SUPERSTRUCTURE.

surplus value In Marxist analysis, this is the value remaining when the worker's daily costs of subsistence have been subtracted from the value that he produces. Let us say the worker has a working day of ten hours. In a portion of this, say eight hours, the worker will produce goods of a value equal to his costs of subsistence. In the two hours remaining, the worker will be creating surplus value, which is appropriated by the capitalist. For MARX, this theory provided an account of exploitation in capitalist societies, but it has been criticized: (1) there is no absolute definition of necessary labour time, because the costs of subsistence vary from society to society; (2) the LABOUR THEORY OF VALUE is deficient.

SEE ALSO: *labour power; Marxist sociology.*

surveillance Literally meaning 'keeping a watch over' 'guarding' or 'supervising', surveillance has acquired a rather more technical meaning in sociology, referring to the relationship between information and power. Exercises of POWER, whether at the level of the state, the organization or between individuals, involve surveillance. Those in power need to gather information on subordinates, issue commands and then ensure that the commands have been carried out.

While pre-industrial states do not have particularly efficient means of surveillance, and depend more on direct physical coercion, modern states rely more on surveillance, involving very good information systems, which are often located in bureaucracies. As FOUCAULT points out, in contemporary societies power is exercised by administration: populations are counted, registered, docketed and filed. This surveillance system provides a precise kind of supervision which effectively prevents infractions of rules.

The growth of surveillance systems has prompted some writers, G. Orwell in *Nineteen Eighty-Four* (1949), for example, to speculate on the totalitarian possibilities of modern states, which will come to know so much about their citizens that effectively they will be watched over continuously. Such extremes are improbable, since complete surveillance of that kind demands very great resources.

SEE ALSO: *authority; bureaucracy; panopticism.*

READING: Dandekar (1990)

survey Survey research is the systematic gathering of information about individuals and collectivities, using INTERVIEW or mail QUESTIONNAIRE methods to elicit information directly and interpreting the resulting data by means of statistical analysis. It provides an alternative to the EXPERIMENTAL METHOD or PARTICI-PANT OBSERVATION and is widely used in sociology. Surveys may use SAMPLING, in order that inferences may be made from the sample to a wider population with a known degree of accuracy, as in government surveys and the investigation of PUBLIC OPINION. When the populations are small, sociological surveys may cover whole groups rather than samples. Even when taking a sample from a wider population, sociologists may treat the sample as a self-contained whole and may not attempt to generalize to the wider population from the sample. Surveys may be used in CASE STUDY research.

The purpose of surveying may be description or causal analysis. Large-scale descriptive surveys have a long history in social research, including two notable surveys of poverty in Britain in the 1890s, C. Booth's *Life and Labour of the People in London* (1889–91) and B. S. Rowntree's *Poverty: A study of town life* (1902) based on York, and the national sample surveys carried out by government such as the *New Earnings Survey* and *Family Expenditure Survey* in Britain.

Sociologists are often less interested in description as such than in charting relationships among variables and the analysis of causation. This interest influences the design of surveys, but its main effect is on the data analysis; whereas descriptive surveys mainly analyse their findings as percentage frequency counts that are presented in a tabular form, sociologists are more likely to use various statistical techniques of MULTIVARIATE ANALYSIS or engage in CAUSAL MODELLING in order to test theoretical hypotheses. A recent trend has been the re-analysis of existing surveys – rather than designing and administering their own surveys, a number of sociologists have used modern statistical techniques for the causal analysis of survey material collected by others. This secondary analysis may pose problems when, as is often the case, the aims of the original survey differ from those of the re-analyst.

SEE ALSO: *Booth; mass observation.*

READING: Marsh (1982)

survival of the fittest See: COMPETITION; EVOLUTIONARY THEORY; ORGANIC ANALOGY; SOCIAL DARWINISM; SPENCER; URBAN ECOLOGY.

symbol Any gesture, artefact, sign or concept which stands for, signifies or expresses something else is a symbol. The study of symbols is important because they are public and convey shared emotions, information or feeling, and may therefore function for social cohesion and commitment. However, they may also have social dysfunctions representing social conflicts and, like RITUAL, 'symbol' is often defined so broadly that it includes all human culture.

SEE ALSO: *Durkheim; semiotics; symbolic interactionism.*

symbolic interactionism This theoretical tradition has its intellectual roots in the concept of the self as developed by George H. MEAD, who argued that reflexivity was crucial to the self as a social phenomenon. Social life depends on our ability to imagine ourselves in other social roles, and this taking the role of the other depends on our capacity for an internal conversation with ourselves. Society was conceived by Mead as an exchange of gestures which involves the use of symbols. Symbolic interactionism is thus the study of the self–society relationship as a process of symbolic communications between social actors. The perspective has made important contributions to the analysis of ROLE, SOCIALIZATION, communication and action. It has been particularly influential in the sociology of deviance for the concept of CAREER in the study of DEVIANT BEHAVIOUR. The interactionist perspective provided the theoretical basis for LABELLING THEORY, STEREOTYPES and STIGMA. It has been valuable in medical sociology for the study of doctor–patient interaction and the SICK ROLE. While Mead emphasized his social objectivism (society has an objective existence and is not merely the subjective awareness of actors), modern symbolic interactionism tends to see society as emerging from the infinite transactions of social actors, and it has been criticized for failing to give sufficient weight to the objective restraints on social action.

Although symbolic interactionism was criticized in the 1970s for its lack of attention to macro-structures, historical change and power, it also became successfully institutionalized in American sociology after a symposium in 1974, which gave rise to the Society for the Study of Symbolic Interaction (SSSI). As symbolic interactionism has matured, it has become possible to identify distinct areas of research interest and theoretical development. (1) There is a specific concern for the sociology of everyday life, with particular attention to the sociology of the emotions, conversational analysis and CULTURAL STUDIES. (2) The emphasis on empirical research and the attempt to overcome any division between abstract theory and empirical investigation continue to inform the work of symbolic interactionism. (3) In the work of N. K. Denzin (1991; 1992) symbolic interactionism has attempted to engage with new developments in sociology, such as POSTMODERNISM and cultural studies. These empirical research topics have indicated five major developments in symbolic interactionism in the 1990s. These are: (1) a concern to move beyond the conventional distinction between micro- and macro-sociology; (2) the adoption of developments in literary theory to study metaphors in social life and to understand the textual characteristics of interaction; (3) an interest in SEMIOTICS that has resulted in a more sophisticated grasp of the basic concept of the symbol; (4) an awareness that symbolic interaction needs to develop a more formal, general and coherent theory of interaction; and finally (5) a realization that symbolic interactionists can and should engage more fully and consciously with political issues, for example issues associated with gay and lesbian SOCIAL MOVEMENTS. These developments suggest that the criticisms raised against earlier forms of symbolic interactionism have produced a more robust and diverse tradition of sociological analysis of social interaction.

SEE ALSO: *actor/social actor; action theory; Chicago School; ethnomethodology; dramaturgical; Goffman; symbol.*

READING: Fine (1990); Plummer (1996)

symmetrical family A term employed by M. Young and P. Willmott (1973) to describe the family form which they believe is emerging in modern Britain. There are three characteristics of the symmetrical family. (1) Husband and wife, especially when children are young, are centred on the home. (2) The EXTENDED FAMILY counts for less and the NUCLEAR FAMILY for more. (3) There is less division of labour between husband and wife in domestic work. Men are taking more responsibility for housekeeping and child care, and married women are working outside the home rather more.

The symmetrical family represents a third stage in the development of the family. In the first stage, the family was the unit of production, with all family members working together in home and field. Stage two, corresponding to industrialization, saw a disruption of the family unit, with men working outside the home, women confined to the home as domestic workers and children in compulsory schooling. The symmetrical family represents a reuniting of the family, but around consumption not production. There does indeed seem to be evidence of increased home-centredness, at least among nuclear-family households. However, it is not clear that the extended family counts for less. As for DOMESTIC LABOUR, although there are still substantial gender inequalities, the evidence is that these are declining.

SEE ALSO: *conjugal role; privatization; sociology of the family.*

synchronic See: DIACHRONIC.

system integration See: SOCIAL AND SYSTEM INTEGRATION.

systems theory This was the dominant PARADIGM in sociology in the 1950s and 1960s, being associated in particular with a group of social theorists centred around PARSONS at Harvard University. Much of the early inspiration for systems theory came from an attempt to establish parallels between physiological systems in medical science and social systems in the social sciences. In Parsons (1951), a voluntaristic theory of action is combined with a systemic approach to two-person interactions. In later work, Parsons provided a general theory of social systems as problem-solving entities, which sought to integrate sociological theory with developments in biology, psychology, economics and political theory. Every social system has four sub-systems corresponding to four FUNCTIONAL IMPERATIVES, namely adaptation (A), goal-attainment (G), integration (I) and pattern-maintenance or latency (L). These four sub-systems can be conceptualized at various levels so that, for example, the basic AGIL pattern also corresponds to the economy, polity, societal community and institutions of socialization. In adapting to their internal and external environments, social systems have to solve these four problems in order to continue in existence, and they evolve by greater differentiation of their structures and by achieving higher levels of integration of their parts. Parsons attempted to show the validity of the systems approach through a diversity of studies – of the university, politics, religion and professions.

Although widely influential in the study of political processes, industrialization, development, religion, modernization, complex organizations, international systems and sociological theory, the theory has been extensively criticized. The arguments against social systems theory are: (1) it cannot deal adequately with the presence of conflict and change in social life; (2) its assumptions about equilibrium and social order are based on a conservative ideology; (3) it is couched at such a level of abstraction that its empirical referents are often difficult to detect and hence the approach is of little value in actual sociological research; (4) its assumptions about value consensus in society are not empirically well grounded; (5) it is difficult to reconcile notions about structural processes and functional requirements with the theory of action, which emphasizes the centrality of purposeful choice by individual actors; (6) the teleological assumptions of systems theory cannot explain why certain societies experience underdevelopment or de-industrialization; (7) many of the propositions of the theory are tautological and vacuous. For example, in the last analysis the existence of a social system is the only real evidence of its adaptation to its environment. In short, modern systems theory appears to reproduce all the essential weaknesses of nineteenth-century EVOLUTIONARY THEORY.

In the late 1950s and early 1960s, critics of FUNCTIONALISM and systems theory argued in favour of CONFLICT THEORY as an alternative perspective. In the 1970s, Marxist theory, with its focus on change, conflict and contradiction, came to be seen as the major alternative to systems theory. However, there is now a recognition that: (1) Marxist theory itself is based on a concept of the SOCIAL SYSTEM; (2) systems theory is not inevitably tied to assumptions about static equilibria or to a conservative ideology; (3) there are models of systems other than those developed in the biological sciences, which do not depend on an ORGANIC ANALOGY. For example, cybernetic models of social systems provide an alternative to crude analogies between social and biological systems by examining the importance of information in exchanges between sub-systems. Further possibilities for the development of systems theory were opened up by HABERMAS in the analysis of the *legitimation crisis* (1973) of contemporary capitalism. Systems theory does not in principle preclude notions of contradiction, conflict and change in the analysis of social systems. The consequence of these developments is that the concept of social system is not uniquely tied to any particular branch of sociology, but is a concept which is basic to all sociological paradigms. After the death of Parsons in 1979, there was a revival of interest in Parsonian sociology, especially in Germany. In turn, this development produced a re-evaluation of systems theory in the work of LUHMANN.

READING: Wallace (1969); Alexander (1982; 1984)

T

taboo (tabu) The term, which came into the English language from Captain Cook's travels in Polynesia, refers to anything (food, place, activity) which is prohibited and forbidden. For E. Durkheim, observation of a taboo has the social consequence of binding a social group together behind common rituals and sentiments. The taboo is the SYMBOL of group membership. Contemporary analysis of TOTEMISM has been revolutionized by LÉVI-STRAUSS, for whom the taboo is a message, a symbolic system, which gives expression to the interchange between nature and culture, animality and society. The concept of taboo has been central to the work of DOUGLAS, who has enlarged the anthropological notion to develop a theory of knowledge based on the idea of pollution.

tautology A tautology is a statement that is true by virtue of its logical form. In sociology, the term is applied to explanations which are circular and therefore unfalsifiable. The classic example is the common criticism of FUNCTIONALISM that it explains the origins of social institutions in terms of their effects on society.

Tawney, R. H. (1880–1962) Professor of economic history at London University (1931–49), he made a major contribution to the theory of social DEMOCRACY in *The Acquisitive Society* (1921) and *Equality* (1931). He was a critic of INDIVIDUALISM in *Religion and the Rise of Capitalism* (1926).

SEE ALSO: *equality*; *Protestant ethic*; *Weber*.

taxonomy This is a classification of phenomena as opposed to their explanations. For example, T. Parsons' notion of pattern variables is intended to offer a taxonomy of human action.

SEE ALSO: *Parsons*.

Taylorism See: SCIENTIFIC MANAGEMENT.

technical division of labour See: DIVISION OF LABOUR.

technical rationality See: HABERMAS; RATIONALITY.

techniques of neutralization See: ACCOUNTS; DELINQUENT DRIFT; NEUTRALIZATION.

technological determinism This is the notion that social change is produced by changes in productive technique, such as the invention of the steam engine. The industrial revolution, in this light, is then simply a bundle of such techniques. Most sociologists regard such an account as misleading, since it neglects the social changes that are necessary for technical inventions to be made and applied. The idea has also been applied to the analysis of work. It was once common for industrial sociologists to argue that production technology determined other phenomena (e.g. job satisfaction, the social organization of the workplace, industrial militancy), but the notion is now discredited.

SEE ALSO: *industrial society; Marx; socio-technical systems.*

technology In sociological usage, technology embraces all forms of productive technique, including hand-working, and is not synonymous with machinery as in some popular accounts. In the SOCIOLOGY OF WORK AND EMPLOYMENT, the term also includes the physical organization of production; that is, the way in which production hardware is arranged in the place of work, and thus embraces the DIVISION OF LABOUR and organization of work that is built into or required for efficient operation by the production technique. Productive techniques and the organization of production are social products, the consequences of human decision-making, and so technology can be analysed as the outcome of social processes.

Sociologists in the HUMAN RELATIONS tradition focused on the relationships between technology and employee morale and alienation, specifically on the direct worker–machine interaction and on the influence of technology on work groups, both of which were shown to have some limited effects on morale. Later, attention turned to technology as an aspect of social CLASS and class relations. The Marxist LABOUR PROCESS APPROACH treated technology as a manifestation of the relations between social classes, arguing that new productive techniques that dominate and control employees are developed in order to alleviate the consequences of an inherent conflict of interests between employees (labour) and management (capital) in capitalist economies. Several Weberian theories of class see 'work situation' as a criterion of class position and technology as a major determinant of work situation.

SEE ALSO: *alienation; automation; de-skilling; flexible specialization; Fordism; labour process; post-Fordism; scientific management; socio-technical systems.*

teleology Sociological explanations are teleological when they try to explain social processes, particularly processes of social change, by reference to an end-state to which they are alleged to be working, or to an ultimate function which they are said to serve. For example, COMTE argued that human societies necessarily evolved to higher and higher states of civilization. PARSONS and other functionalists are often said to be offering teleological accounts when they explain, say, systems of STRATIFICATION by reference to the 'need' which societies have for the efficient discharge of tasks. Thus the cause of a social phenomenon is said to be its effects on some other phenomenon, a circular or tautological explanation.

SEE ALSO: *functionalism; systems theory.*
READING: Ryan (1970)

theodicy A theodicy in RELIGION justifies divine justice, despite the existence of evil. The concept was used by M. Weber to explore how religious beliefs may legitimate social privilege or compensate the suffering of the disprivileged. The most frequently quoted illustration of a theodicy is:

> The rich man in his castle,
> The poor man at his gate –
> God made them high and lowly,
> And ordered their estate.

Like CHARISMA, the term illustrates how sociology often takes its vocabulary from other disciplines.

theories of the middle range See: MIDDLE-RANGE THEORY.

theory-laden A proposition or empirical finding is theory-laden if it is necessarily produced by, or only makes sense in the context of, a particular theory; it is not *theory-neutral*. Such propositions are already influenced by the theory that they are intended to support. Some sociologists argue that all sociological findings are necessarily theory-laden.

SEE ALSO: *objectivity*.
READING: Keat and Urry (1975)

thick description A term proposed by the anthropologist C. Geertz (1973) to indicate what kind of enterprise ETHNOGRAPHY is. Any description of human conduct is 'thick' in the sense that it depends on the multiple layers of meaning given by human beings to their actions. Every description given in an ethnographic account is actually based on descriptions provided by participants, which in turn are dependent on other descriptions. All these descriptions are embedded in different, and sometimes incompatible, systems of meaning.

third way politics A term used at the end of the 1990s to describe attempts to revive and update the political philosophy of social democracy. The term itself is particularly associated with the British Labour government elected in 1997, although the renewal of social democracy was a much wider movement that embraced newly elected centre-left governments throughout Europe at the end of the century. The idea of a 'third way' had previously been used in the 1950s to describe social democracy itself, as an alternative to SOCIALIST SOCIETIES of the Soviet type and the free-market liberalism of the USA, and in the 1970s to describe 'market socialism'.

GIDDENS (1998) has analysed third way politics from a sociological perspective. In his analysis, old-style social democracy (the 'old left') in Britain and the rest of Europe had a number of features. (1) There was considerable state involvement in social and economic life. This was manifest in the domination of CIVIL SOCIETY by the state. Government intervention in the economy put restrictions on entrepreneurs and companies, placed many economic activities into public ownership and, via the management of economic demand, attempted to regulate the overall level of activity in the economy. Full employment was a major policy goal. (2) CORPORATISM was a characteristic feature of decision-making in the political and economic realms, and egalitarianism and collectivism were important social values which constrained INDIVIDUALISM. (3) There was a strong commitment to extending CITIZENSHIP via a comprehensive and well-funded WELFARE-STATE. (4) Whilst professing internationalism, the social democratic view of the world was bi-polar and reflected the division between the USA and the former Soviet Union which dominated thinking during the era of the Cold War (1945–89).

With the political ascendancy of the neo-liberal NEW RIGHT in Britain and the

USA between the early 1980s and late 1990s and the influence of New Right ideas elsewhere, old-style social democratic political parties became less influential. In contrast to social democracy, neo-liberalism stood for minimal government, autonomous civil society, a free economy and free markets, individualism, inequality, moral authoritarianism and a minimal welfare state. In the same period, there were major changes in the world economic system associated with GLOBALIZATION, which reduced the capacity of national governments to regulate their economies. There was also an important cultural shift, which was marked by the greater strength of individualism, the decline of tradition and greater personal autonomy. This shift in social values initially favoured the political agenda of the New Right.

The object of third way politics has been to develop social democracy to be compatible with a globalized economy and changing values among voters. The argument is that social democratic goals of promoting social justice, reducing economic inequalities and democratizing institutions, thereby giving people more control over their lives, remain valid. But they need to be adapted to a changed world and new policies developed. There is a reasonable consensus on the analysis of the challenge facing social democratic politics, but there is far less agreement on how policies should be changed. Different political thinkers emphasize different elements, in particular how far to accommodate the ideas of the New Right and how much influence nation states, acting alone or in concert in the European Union, retain within a globalized economy. Nor do all societies start from the same point: traditional social democratic institutions and values remain stronger in some societies (e.g. Germany) than in others (e.g. the UK), thus different policies may be appropriate.

SEE ALSO: *voting*.

time While sociologists have made a significant contribution to the analysis of space through urban sociology, regionalism and the sociology of the city, the analysis of time in sociology has been relatively neglected. Time was seen as a collective representation in E. Durkheim's analysis of classification in his sociology of religion (1912). In Durkheim's approach, time was not an a priori but a social category. Similar studies in the anthropology of time were undertaken by M. Mauss (1906) and by E. E. Evans-Pritchard on the Nuer (1940) in an analysis of Eskimo society. Anthropologists have studied the cross-cultural variations in the methods by which societies measure sequence and duration. In traditional societies, time was measured by the repetition of religious events or festivals within a sacred calendar; in modern societies, time is measured by a flow of units within a linear conception. Precision in the measurement of differentiated units of time or a conception of long periods of time are uncommon in traditional societies. Chinese and Arabic civilizations developed both water-clocks and sundials. Chinese water-clocks were used to regulate irrigation and water supplies. Arabic sundials were used to regulate daily patterns of prayer in Islam. Exact notions of time are essential to the functioning of an urban civilization. For example, M. Weber's study of the Protestant sects (1930) demonstrated that the precise calculation of time was a fundamental feature of the organization of labour in capitalism. By the middle of the nineteenth century, the development of cheap watches for a mass market made the precise regulation of individual lifestyles a general aspect of industrial society.

The neglect of the temporal dimension of social relations is an important issue because, as A. Giddens (1984) has pointed out in the concept of TIME–SPACE

DISTANTIATION, social action is stretched over time and space dimensions. A shared conception of time is essential for social organization, if individuals are to regulate their lives in order to meet collective goals. Being punctual (for work, for example) is a necessary requirement for the operation of modern social institutions. The organization of time requires a commonly agreed unit of measurement, based either on natural cycles (such as the cycles of the Moon) or human measures (such as the week). In his *Time, an Essay*, N. Elias (1984) argued that this collective sharing of time is a feature of the CIVILIZING PROCESS in which individuals learn to monitor and direct their lives according to a personal notion of constraint.

Empirical research has been undertaken in time–space analysis on the constraints on individual and collective behaviour in time–space budgets for given periods of time (the day, the week or the year). A TIME BUDGET is a diary of the sequence of activities undertaken by an individual in a given time period, typically a day. Time–space analysis has been employed to study the diffusion of innovations, technology, institutions and epidemics. Time budgets are useful for understanding the allocation of duties and responsibilities within the household.

time budget This technique of social inquiry requires people to record in detail how they have spent their time in a day or several days. Most commonly, this takes the form of recording activities on a chart subdivided into short periods of time, say half an hour, immediately after the activity. The technique permits precise quantification and it avoids the biases and inadequacies that are necessarily involved in a respondent trying to remember what she or he has done, and for how long, some time after the event. Time budgets have been used in a variety of sociological areas, most of which are concerned with everyday life. One study of DOMESTIC LABOUR, for example, used time budgets to estimate how much domestic work men and women do.

time series Data that are ordered in time, typically at regular intervals, constitute a time series. In sociological research, the most commonly used time-series data are derived from censuses or panel studies.

SEE ALSO: *census; panel study.*

time–space distantiation It is argued that social theory has yet to take into account the revolution which has occurred in the physical and biological sciences, where the notion of relativity has transformed twentieth-century science. In sociology, TIME in nature is still understood in terms of Cartesian and Newtonian science, where there is a concept of absolute, unchanging time. Contemporary natural science, on the other hand, has concentrated on the rhythmic, changeable and variable nature of time.

GIDDENS in *The Constitution of Society* (1984) defines it as the 'stretching' of social systems over time–space on the basis of various mechanisms of social and system integration. His STRUCTURATION theory argues that the organization of social time–space should be considered as an aspect of the authoritative organization of society, namely as a feature of POWER. With technological innovation, neither individuals nor groups are fixed in a single point in time–space; social interaction can be stretched across time. Because people can move through time and space at much greater speeds, this shrinking of distance is described by Giddens as a *time–space convergence*. Social interaction often occurs between people who are absent in real time–space; for example, by long-distance telephone calls. With the advent of information technology, individuals and societies are dispersed in VIRTUAL REALITY. Finally, he argues that there is a DISEMBEDDING of time and space from social activities, whereby social relations are taken out of their local environments. Giddens has employed these arguments to criticize evolutionary theories which assume a unitary rather than varied notion of time.

Giddens' notion of distantiation has been criticized on the grounds that (1) it does not consider important differences in the organization of time–space in modern societies; (2) he fails to conceptualize time and space as resources; (3) it does not analyse travel (such as tourism) as temporal play.

SEE ALSO: *information superhighway*.

READING: Urry (1996)

Tocqueville, Alexis de (1805–59) A French aristocrat who wrote on comparative political systems. He visited the United States in 1831–2 to examine the prison system. His views on the negative psychological effects of solitary confinement and the problems of comparative CRIMINOLOGY were reported (with Gustave de Beaumont) in *On the Penitentiary System in the United States* (1833). His major contribution to POLITICAL SOCIOLOGY was *Democracy in America*, which was published in two sections in 1835 and 1840. Tocqueville made a comparison between the highly centralized and powerful apparatus of the STATE in France and the decentralized democratic system of government in the United States. His primary focus in the first part was the principle of EQUALITY, which eroded traditional distinctions of STATUS and was the fundamental principle of modern societies. Although he admired the American system, he argued that the universal franchise would produce a tyranny of the majority, which would obliterate hierarchy, local differences and regionalism. He thought that in a democracy voluntary associations would be crucial as a counterweight to the tyranny of the majority. In the second part, he considered the consequences of political democracy on religion, philosophy, art and science. While the egalitarian principle was dominant at the political level, he argued that American culture was thoroughly penetrated by INDIVIDUALISM.

In *The Old Regime* (1856), he reflected on the causes of the French Revolution, arguing that REVOLUTION occurs when there is a sudden improvement in social conditions or when there is a deterioration after a period of social improvement. He argued that the French Revolution was caused by the contradiction between the new principles of individualism emerging with the growth of trade, markets, and a money economy, and the traditional principles of hierarchy and status characteristic of French FEUDALISM and aristocracy. *The Old Regime* can also be regarded as an exercise in the COMPARATIVE METHOD. The absence of a violent revolution in England was a consequence of the fact that the English class system was relatively open and fluid, without a rigid system of privilege. Reflecting on the Revolution of 1848 in France, Tocqueville came, in the posthumously published *Recollections* (1893), to a set of conclusions rather similar to MARX, namely that the Revolution of 1848 was a continuation of the social processes underlying the Revolution of 1789, primarily the struggle by the WORKING CLASS for a new set of principles associated with democracy and equality. The development of a comparative political sociology can be regarded as an elaboration of the sociological studies of MONTESQUIEU.

READING: Aron (1965c); Poggi (1972)

Toennies, Ferdinand (1855–1936) A German sociologist and a founder of the German Sociological Association, he is best known for his distinction between 'community' and 'association', which he elaborated in *Gemeinschaft und Gesellschaft* (1887), translated as *Community and Association*. Toennies identified three separate branches of sociology: pure or theoretical, applied and empirical. The distinction between 'community' (*Gemeinschaft*) and 'association' (*Gesellschaft*) constituted the core of his theoretical sociology. These 'fundamental concepts' were to guide empirical and applied sociology in the study of the transformation of society from communal to associational relationships. Although they are ideal types, Toennies wanted to use his pair of concepts to describe the historical transformation of Germany from a rural to an industrial society. He was influenced by the philosophy of A. Schopenhauer (1788–1860) and F. Nietzsche (1844–1900), from whom he adopted the notion of 'the will to life'. Toennies argued that social relations are the products of human will; he identified two types of will. Natural will (*Wesenwille*) is the expression of instinctual needs, habit, conviction or inclination. Rational will (*Kurwille*) involves instrumental rationality in the selection of means for ends. Whereas natural will is organic and real, rational will is conceptual and artificial. These forms of will correspond to the distinction between community and association, since communal life is the expression of natural will and associational life is a consequence of rational will.

SEE ALSO: *ideal type; teleology; rural–urban continuum; urban way of life.*

READING: Atoji (1984)

total institution GOFFMAN (1961b) defined this as 'a place of residence and work where a large number of like-situated individuals, cut off from the wider society for an appreciable period of time, together lead an enclosed, formally administered round of life' (p. 11). Examples include prisons, mental hospitals, monastic settlements, boarding schools and work camps. Goffman's primary interest is in the inmate culture of such institutions, by which inmates adapt to and modify the formal system of SURVEILLANCE.

totemism A totem is a plant, animal or object which is the SYMBOL of a social group, particularly a clan or tribe. The totem is TABOO. A totem animal or plant may be eaten on ritual occasions (the totemic feast), but otherwise it is carefully avoided as SACRED. In the 1950s, RADCLIFFE-BROWN argued that totemism is essentially a system of classification with respect to the relationship between man and nature. This view provided the basis of structuralist interpretations in which totemism as a mode of classification provides an analysis of the structure of human thought.

SEE ALSO: *Lévi-Strauss.*

trade-union consciousness See: LENINISM.

trade unions These are organizations of employees who have joined together to improve pay and conditions at work. Sociological interest in trade unions has had a variety of foci. (1) The contribution that unions make to the INSTITUTIONALIZATION OF CONFLICT in society and industry. In this context, attention is paid to COLLECTIVE BARGAINING, the extent to which union officials represent their members when they negotiate, and the likelihood that members will honour bargains. It is generally agreed that unions have been fairly effective in institutionalization, and Marxist sociologists criticize them for promoting among workers a commitment to reformism and piecemeal improvement that inhibits the development of a revolutionary CLASS CONSCIOUSNESS. (2) Trade-union democracy has been of concern since MICHELS claimed that union administrations inevitably developed into oligarchies that no longer represented members' interests. Oligarchic tendencies clearly exist, but modern research suggests that representativeness is maintained under certain conditions, notably when there are strong workplace rank-and-file organizations based on shop stewards. (3) The amount of power unions have to pursue members' interests is sometimes raised, with research suggesting that unions are normally weaker than employers, particularly large corporations, the precise power imbalance varying with economic conditions. (4) The relationship between unions and politics was debated in the 1970s, when the notion of CORPORA-TISM was used to describe a certain political strategy regarding trade unions. (5) Marxists have been exercised by the effects of unions on the unity of labour, since occupationally based unionism, which once dominated Britain and America and still has some force, divides labour into segments that inhibit united action or consciousness. (6) Union membership has occasionally been used as an indicator of PROLETARIANIZATION. Union membership as such bears no relation to class consciousness or proletarian social imagery, since the reasons people join unions range from ideological commitment to the labour movement, through a calculative assessment of the benefits unions bring, to coercion as, for example, when closed-shop arrangements (now illegal in Britain) used to force people into unions against their will. However, some sociologists argued that the unionization of white-collar employees in Britain during the 1960s and 1970s reflected their proletarianization.

Trade-union membership has declined throughout the advanced economies over the last twenty years and the influence of trade unions on employers and politicians has also declined. These trends have been particularly marked in Britain and the USA. Sociologists now pay far less attention to trade unionism.

SEE ALSO: *citizenship; class imagery; industrial conflict; labour market; labour market segmentation; labour movement; Leninism; middle class; oligarchy; strikes; unionateness; working class.*

READING: Crouch (1982)

tradition In its literal sense, tradition refers to any human practice, belief, institution or artefact which is handed down from one generation to the next. While the content of traditions is highly variable, it typically refers to some elements of culture regarded as part of the common inheritance of a social group. Tradition is often regarded as a source of social stability and LEGITIMACY, but appeals to tradition may also provide the basis for changing the present. The concept is important in sociology in making a contrast with modern society and in debates on the nature of AUTHORITY.

In contemporary sociology, the concept of risk society has stimulated interest in REFLEXIVE MODERNIZATION, which claims that the critical theory of society has been replaced by a theory of societal self-critique. Reflexive criticism of society has become democratized, which marks a major break between tradition and a modernity in which traditional authority is continually challenged.

SEE ALSO: *risk/risk society.*

READING: Shils (1981); Beck *et al.* (1994)

traditional society See: PRIMITIVE SOCIETY.

transmitted deprivation See: DEPRIVATION.

triangulation A method used by land surveyors and map-makers to locate a spot, by taking bearings from three known points and plotting their intersection. N. Denzin has recommended the use of multiple methods to explain phenomena in sociology and borrowed 'triangulation' to describe this approach. It is a widely adopted practice, particularly among qualitative researchers. Indeed, sociologists who employ multiple methods often use more than three, thus triangulation may not be the most accurate descriptor. Denzin identified four forms of triangulation: (1) *data triangulation* – use of a number of types of data in a project; (2) *investigator triangulation* – use of several different researchers; (3) *theory triangulation* – application of multiple perspectives to interpret the data; (4) *methodological triangulation* – use of multiple methods to study a single issue.

READING: Denzin (1989)

trust See: DOUGLAS; REFLEXIVE MODERNIZATION.

typification The great bulk of knowledge of the LIFE-WORLD is typified. That is, it refers, not to the individual or unique qualities of things or persons, but to their typical features. Typification refers to the process by which people typify the world around them.

SEE ALSO: *phenomenological sociology*.

unanticipated/unintended consequences Clearly, people will undertake actions deliberately with a firm set of intentions. But their actions may have consequences which they did not intend. These unintended consequences become interesting sociologically when they have social effects. For example, when the Hopi indians engage in rain dancing, they intend the dancing to produce rain. This ceremony, like other ceremonies, may, however, have the unintended consequence of unifying the tribe in a common ritual. Unintended consequence is sometimes used with the same meaning as LATENT FUNCTION.

underclass A somewhat inexact notion, indicating a CLASS of people who are in some sense at the bottom of society, or separated from the bulk of society. The class has been defined in various ways. Most commonly, members of the underclass are seen as those in long-term unemployment, in receipt of welfare benefits and, perhaps, involved in the black economy or crime. As such, various groups will be over-represented in the underclass, particularly the old, disabled or long-term sick, unemployed, especially the young unemployed, single-parent families and those of ethnic origin. In debates in the United States, the last has been of particular importance: the American underclass is chiefly black. In both American and British discussions, attention has focused on the alleged destruction of secure family life in the underclass environment. Single parenthood, particularly, is said to produce children who themselves, through lack of qualification and welfare dependency, are unable to rise out of the underclass. The position is thus inherited and passed on.

The idea has been at the centre of political debate in both Britain and the United States, because it relates directly to questions of welfare reform. In particular, it lies behind proposals to reduce the welfare budget by encouraging (and forcefully persuading) welfare recipients into paid work.

SEE ALSO: *poverty*; *status*; *welfare state*; *women and work*; *working class*.
READING: Scott, J. (1993)

underdevelopment Against the classical view that trade produces mutual advantages to societies involved in exchange, underdevelopment theory claims that capitalist development retards independent economic change in peripheral regions, because the conditions of exchange are unequal. The penetration of capitalism does not necessarily transform traditional society, but may create backward socioeconomic conditions. Underdevelopment involves dependence on the export of raw materials, and on manufactured imports. Because commodities are subject to external price fluctuations, underdeveloped economies are exposed to inflationary pressures. Underdeveloped societies have characteristics of ECONOMIC DUALISM, combining small industrial sectors with large backward sectors. Local markets are blocked by imports, low wages and low productivity. Underdevelopment theory has been critical of modernization theory and Marxist development theory, both of which assumed the inevitability of capitalist development.

SEE ALSO: *centre/periphery; dependency theory; development; dual economy; imperialism; internal colonialism; new international division of labour; modernization; uneven development; world-system theory.*

READING: Roxborough (1979)

understanding See: EMPATHY; HERMENEUTICS; QUALITATIVE RESEARCH; RULE; UNDERSTANDING ALIEN BELIEF SYSTEMS; VERSTEHEN.

understanding alien belief systems Insofar as sociology attempts to arrive at propositions which have general validity, comparative study of cultures is a necessary feature of sociological research. While some sociologists have adopted a thorough RELATIVISM, most sociologists argue that valid knowledge of other cultures is in principle possible, despite the difficult methodological problems which such knowledge involves. The problems of comparative understanding can be illustrated by two issues. (1) How can we know that what counts as X (honour, religion, madness, etc.) in our culture also counts as X in some other culture? (2) How can we know that a sociological explanation of X in our culture will be valid for another culture? Cross-cultural comparisons involve difficulties of identification and explanation.

Followers of philosophers like L. Wittgenstein and P. Winch have argued that understanding X in terms of the actor's own DEFINITION OF THE SITUATION is the best way of avoiding misidentification, since we no longer impose our categories on their behaviour. However, this procedure can be criticized on two grounds: (1) it involves 'contextual charity' to such an extent that no behaviour or belief in another culture could ever be regarded as irrational once it is located in its appropriate cultural context; (2) sociologists and anthropologists often, regardless of their intentions, inherit frameworks (or discourses) which organize culture in such a way as to rule out any genuine understanding of the subjective experience of actors in other cultures. Good intentions not to impose alien categories are never in themselves sufficient to rule out bias.

SEE ALSO: *comparative method; cultural relativism; rationality; rule.*

READING: Peel (1969b)

unemployment A person is unemployed if he or she is eligible for work but does not have a job. He or she may be voluntarily unemployed (i.e. have chosen not to work), or involuntarily unemployed (i.e. be willing to work but unable to find a job). Involuntary unemployment is what most people have in mind when they refer to unemployment.

After three decades of relatively full employment following the Second World War, unemployment in advanced capitalist economies grew substantially after the mid 1970s. The exception was Japan up until the early 1990s, when unemployment increased. Rates of unemployment fluctuate according to the state of the world economy, but the average level since 1976 has been far higher than before and substantial rates of unemployment are now normal. In the European Union, the average has been over 6 per cent since 1980 and in the 1990s was often higher. The causes of unemployment are low economic growth-rates, structural economic changes, such as higher productivity for each person employed and the decline of the older, labour-intensive industries, and an increase in the size of the potential labour force as the result of population growth and more women seeking employment. In the second half of the 1990s, the USA managed to reduce unemployment significantly, creating large numbers of new jobs on the basis of rapid and sustained economic growth, but it is not clear whether this will be a long-term trend or will spread to other societies.

Unemployment statistics reflect the assumptions of those who collect the information as well as the actual number of people who may be regarded as out of work. Thus rates will also vary according to how unemployment is defined and how the size of the workforce is calculated (e.g. whether or not the self-employed are included). In Britain, for example, the government made changes in the way the unemployment rate was calculated on approximately twenty occasions between 1981 and 1991. The cumulative effect was to reduce both the numbers of people defined as being unemployed and unemployment as a proportion of the workforce, compared to the internationally recognized method of calculating unemployment adopted by the International Labour Organization (ILO). The figures traditionally quoted by the British government were based on the receipt of unemployment benefit. The ILO basis for calculating unemployment is the number of people without a job who are available to start work within two weeks, and have either looked for a job in the last four weeks, or are waiting to start a job already obtained. The British government has published statistics on both the traditional and the ILO basis since 1996.

Official statistics in Britain are likely to underestimate the numbers seeking work, or underemployed, for several reasons. (1) A number of workers, especially women, do not claim or are not eligible for benefit when unemployed. (2) Temporary employment and training schemes take large numbers out of the 'normal' LABOUR MARKET for a while. (3) Workers may be underemployed by being on short-time working. (4) Many otherwise unemployed people choose early retirement and a pension on losing their jobs, while some are classified as disabled by doctors and receive a disability benefit rather than the lower allowance for unemployment.

It was once possible to conceive of unemployment as a 'flow': people flow out of work into unemployment, and then back into work after a short interval. This model still holds good for part of the unemployed population, but in the 1980s and 1990s between one-third and a half of those without work failed to find a job within one year: for them, the 'flow' petered out. Some groups are more affected by unemployment than others. The young, the old, the disabled, the low-paid, ethnic minorities, the unskilled and inhabitants of depressed regions are all disproportionately unemployed. In Britain, the continued growth of jobs for women, particularly in part-time work, has kept female unemployment reasonably low.

The social consequences of unemployment for those out of work include higher incidences of POVERTY, ill-health and death, demoralization and strained family relationships. For society as a whole, they include the failure to realize the social investment in HUMAN CAPITAL made through the educational system, and a loss of tax revenue combined with increased outgoings in unemployment benefits that threaten the financing of other parts of the welfare state.

SEE ALSO: *automation; de-industrialization; official statistics; underclass; women and work.*

READING: Worswick (1991)

unequal exchange See: WORLD-SYSTEM THEORY.

uneven development The notion of 'combined and unequal development' was first employed by L. Trotsky and V. Lenin to analyse the uneven features of Russian capitalist development prior to the Revolution. They argued that capitalist development is not a smooth, upward trajectory from traditional to modern society by noting that pre-capitalist social structures are often conserved and reinforced by capitalist economic growth, and development is a contradictory and complex process.

SEE ALSO: *underdevelopment*.

unionateness This concept was proposed by British sociologists in the 1960s as a measure of the commitment of employees' collective organizations to the principles and ideology of trade unionism. It defined the relevant characteristics of 'unionate' organizations in Britain as COLLECTIVE BARGAINING, willingness to take industrial action against employers (especially to strike), and affiliation to the Trades Union Congress and to the Labour Party. The concept was used especially to compare manual TRADE UNIONS with those of non-manual workers.

READING: Blackburn and Prandy (1965)

universal benefits See: WELFARE STATE.

unobtrusive measures These research techniques are 'non-reactive' since they involve no interaction between the investigator and the population being studied, unlike research that involves interviewing, observation or even self-completed questionnaires. For example, the effect of changing the social conditions within a workplace might be assessed by company records of absenteeism, sickness and output rather than by direct investigation of the employees concerned. Unobtrusive measures can be used imaginatively in sociological research and are a useful addition to more conventional methods, but they do not entirely remove reactive error or subjective judgement.

upper class The upper class can be distinguished from the MIDDLE CLASS and the WORKING CLASS by its wealth, its coherence and its POWER.

Wealth is unevenly distributed in the UK. The top 1 per cent of wealth-holders own about one-third of the nation's wealth. This proportion has fallen considerably from an estimated two-thirds before the First World War, but from the late 1970s onwards the proportion has, if anything, actually increased. The upper class should be seen very much in terms of families. Wealth is distributed among close family members, both by means of inheritance and by gifts designed to avoid taxes on death. Similarly, family background continues to be important in gaining certain upper-class occupations. Family and kinship give a certain coherence to the class, which is reinforced by similar educational experiences, intermarriage and continuing friendship and business contacts. These same people are likely also to have contacts in business, at least partly by means of interlocking directorships – the practice of companies having directors on each other's boards. The result is that a relatively small group of people, who hold several directorships in the largest companies, can form an inner circle of wealthy people.

The way in which ELITE positions are interconnected by a variety of factors may also give the upper class real power. Those who hold senior jobs in business, politics, the civil service, the church and the army, tend to have a similar education, giving a similarity of outlook as well as frequency of contact. Those without these common experiences are likely to be socialized into the outlook of the class. It should be pointed out, however, that common origins and education do not, of themselves, *necessarily* mean common interests or common action, and little in fact is known about how holders of upper-class positions *actually* interact.

SEE ALSO: *class; distribution of income and wealth; management; prestige; ruling class; stratification.*

READING: Scott, J. (1991)

urban ecology The CHICAGO SCHOOL introduced ecological theory into urban studies. It derives from the ORGANIC ANALOGY, specifically from the attempted application of C. Darwin's theory of natural selection to social life. The city is defined as an environment like those found in nature. All parts of the environment are interdependent and are moved by natural forces. The most important of these forces is competition. Competition between social groups for scarce urban resources, especially land, means that the best-adapted, the fittest, groups become dominant. Competition also forces societies to a greater division of labour which, by promoting more efficient social organization, provides greater adaptive capacity. The competitive struggle also tends to create numbers of sub-environments or natural areas within the city. Each of these areas is occupied by a distinctive social group which has adapted to it in much the same way as a plant or animal species adapts to a specialized natural environment. The city tends to EQUILIBRIUM and any disturbance is met by forces which restore equilibrium. One illustration of this is the process of succession. If a social group (defined largely by racial or national characteristics) leaves a NATURAL AREA, its place will be taken by another group, which will be subject to the same ecological forces, eventually even having, for example, the same rate of delinquency. Urban ecologists used their theory in a large number of empirical studies. The concepts of competition, natural area and succession are best illustrated in the CONCENTRIC ZONE THEORY.

The crucial assumption of urban ecology is that the social structure of the city is formed by underlying natural and impersonal forces. It suggests, therefore, that social structure is not greatly influenced by individual interventions such as planning. Culture also takes on a secondary role; ecologists argued that culture only had significance when ecological forces had already established an equilibrium. The neglect of culture, and the conviction that cities operated like environments in nature, formed the basis of a critique of urban ecology and ultimately its collapse. Although there have been attempts to revive ecological thinking, it has degenerated into the minute statistical examination of urban areas.

READING: Saunders (1981)

urban managerialism As codified by R. Pahl (1975), this approach in urban sociology concentrates on the role of various managers, for example council housing officials or building society managers, in the distribution of urban resources. Studies have been done on such managers, often concentrating on the values and ideologies which guide their decisions. The approach has been criticized because it tends to assume that urban managers are relatively independent and have freedom of action.

More recent studies have stressed the way that managers are constrained by economic factors or by bureaucratic rules, and have limited independence.

SEE ALSO: *housing class; rural–urban continuum*.

READING: Saunders (1981)

urban social movements A term derived from Marxist urban sociology and popularized by M. Castells (1977; 1978), urban social movements arise out of the politicization of access to various publicly provided and generally urban goods and services; for example, housing, education or transport. The argument is that the provision of these services necessarily becomes increasingly restricted – there is a crisis in COLLECTIVE CONSUMPTION – which, after a period of active political organization, generates urban social movements in protest. Since a restricted access to collective consumption tends to affect all classes, urban social movements will be an alliance of classes. Class struggles promoted by urban social movements will not, however, engender fundamental change, if they have any effect at all, since that can only come from change in the ownership and control of the FORCES OF PRODUCTION. The concept has been heavily criticized as not being empirically productive. It is not clear how specific urban social movements are related to crises in collective consumption, most movements are not class alliances, and the term has been over-generalized to include any urban protest movement, whatever its origins or effects.

SEE ALSO: *social movements; state*.

urban way of life In an article said to be the most widely cited in sociology, L. Wirth (1938) attempted to describe and explain a way of life peculiar to cities. For Wirth, cities have a whole range of features including the loss of primary relationships, weaker social control, a great DIVISION OF LABOUR, greater importance of the mass media and the tendency for urbanites to treat each other instrumentally. These features are caused by three basic factors – the numbers, density and heterogeneity of the population. In this theory Wirth was faithful to the principles of URBAN ECOLOGY in holding that fundamental features of the urban environment produce the entire range of urban social behaviour. He has been criticized, firstly because empirical research showed that there was not one urban way of life but several, and, secondly, because it does not seem possible to derive all aspects of urban life from the three basic factors.

Other sociologists, SIMMEL, for example, regard anonymity as the principal characteristic of urban life.

SEE ALSO: *Chicago School; primary relationship; rural–urban continuum; suburban way of life; zone of transition*.

READING: Savage and Warde (1993)

urbanization Urbanization refers properly to a growth in the *proportion* of a country's population living in urban centres of a particular size. Although cities have always been socially, politically and economically important, the urbanization of industrial Western societies in the nineteenth century was very rapid: for example, in the United Kingdom in 1800 some 24 per cent of the population was urban, while by 1900 it was 77 per cent. For almost all these societies, urbanization has followed an S-shaped curve, building up very slowly, expanding very quickly, and then slowing down, or even reversing slightly, with greater suburban development. The proportional increase in urban populations in the nineteenth century was largely by migration from the countryside. However, in contemporary underdeveloped societies, which are urbanizing even more rapidly, the increase comes rather more from simple growth in the urban population, as public health and medical facilities have improved, and tends to be concentrated in a single city.

In general, periods of urbanization appear to be associated with INDUSTRIALIZ-ATION. There is, however, some controversy about the nature of the association and about the role that capitalism plays in the process. Urbanization has contradictory consequences for economic growth, since it cheapens the cost of providing services such as health and education while increasing the cost of labour that can no longer supplement its wages by small-scale agricultural production.

SEE ALSO: *demographic transition; industrial society; modernization; rural–urban continuum.*

READING: Friedmann and Wulff (1975)

use value See: LABOUR THEORY OF VALUE.

uses and gratifications See: AUDIENCE; SOCIOLOGY OF THE MASS MEDIA.

utilitarianism This social philosophy, associated with J. Bentham and J. S. Mill (though precursors such as T. Hobbes, J. Locke and D. Hume are sometimes called utilitarians as well) placed the satisfaction of the individual's wants (utility) at its core. Consequently, the greatest good was defined simply as the greatest happiness of the greatest number of people. Its main impact on the social sciences has been via its model of social action in which individuals rationally pursue their own self-interests, and its conception of society as the aggregation of atomized individuals united by self-interest. Behavioural psychology and economics have been influenced by these conceptions, as have EXCHANGE THEORY and RATIONAL CHOICE THEORY in sociology. Sociology, however, has been more influenced by the French collectivist tradition that gave society greater weight than the individual and saw SOCIAL ORDER as the outcome of cultural traditions that were not reducible to individuals' interests, mainly via the work of E. Durkheim.

SEE ALSO: *atomism; social contract.*

READING: Parsons (1968c)

Utopia MANNHEIM used this term to describe the beliefs of subordinate classes, especially beliefs which emphasized those aspects of a society which pointed to the future collapse of the established order. By contrast, the ideology of the dominant class emphasized the enduring stability of existing social arrangements. While Mannheim suggested that utopian thought would not be characteristic of the twentieth century, some sociologists claim that modern pessimism over, for example, nuclear warfare represents *dystopian* thought – a collapse of civilization without a subsequent social reconstruction.

SEE ALSO: *millenarianism.*

V

validity See: RELIABILITY.

value freedom In sociology, this has a variety of meanings: (1) sociology can successfully exclude ideological or non-scientific assumptions from research; (2) sociologists should not make evaluative judgements about empirical evidence; (3) value judgements should be restricted to the sociologist's area of technical competence; (4) sociologists are indifferent to the moral implications of their research; (5) sociologists should make their own values open and clear; (6) sociologists should refrain from advocating particular values.

SEE ALSO: *objectivity; value neutrality; value relevance; Weber.*

READING: Albrow (1990)

value neutrality While research topics, approaches and perspectives are selected according to the criterion of VALUE RELEVANCE, social science is not in a privileged position to pronounce on social values, because there is a logical gap between empirical evidence and moral actions. Empirical discoveries about the nature of poverty, inequality or suicide do not tell us what we *ought* to do. It is consequently argued that sociologists have to strive for value neutrality with respect to research and policy formation. Value neutrality operates at two levels: (1) at a personal level, sociologists should make clear their own values; (2) at an institutional level, sociologists should not use their professional status as teachers to dictate values to students.

There are three objections to this conventional account. (1) Despite personal declarations of neutrality, values may unwittingly obtrude in research. (2) It is not clear that neutrality, even in principle, is possible. (3) It is not always evident that value neutrality is desirable; on some questions nobody should be neutral.

SEE ALSO: *value freedom; Weber.*

READING: Gouldner (1975)

value relevance In M. Weber's discussion of the philosophy of social science, there is a definite but complex distinction between value judgement and value interpretation. As social scientists, sociologists have to avoid making *ad hoc*, personal value judgements on social phenomena and, in particular, they are not in a position to recommend courses of action by suggesting that their recommendations are necessary and inevitable deductions from objective facts. However, given that Weber thought sociology involved the interpretative understanding of social action, interpretation depends on value interpretation. The values of a social scientist determine which questions will be asked in any inquiry, which topics will be selected for investigation and which methods will be employed for gathering data. For WEBER, value relevance operates at three levels. (1) There is philological interpretation which establishes the meaning of texts and documents. (2) There is ethical interpretation in assigning a value to an object of inquiry. (3) There is rational interpretation in which the sociologist seeks the meaningful relationship between phenomena in terms of causal analysis. The point of value interpretation is to establish the values towards which an activity is directed; it is not to judge such activities as either good or bad.

SEE ALSO: *objectivity; value freedom; value neutrality.*

READING: Albrow (1990)

values There is a conventional distinction between values, which are seen to be permanent and important to society, and attitudes, which are fleeting and unstable. While people's attitudes may often change, society depends on more or less stable values.

In Parsonian sociology, social order depends on the existence of general, shared values which are regarded as legitimate and binding, and act as a standard by means of which the ends of action are selected. The linkage between social and personality systems is achieved by the INTERNALIZATION of values through the process of SOCIALIZATION. Values cannot be reduced to or explained by interests, biological need or class. Three criticisms of this interpretation of values are pertinent: (1) societies exist despite considerable disagreement over values; (2) values may be accepted pragmatically rather than normatively; (3) it disregards the constraining force of social structures.

In Marxism, value has an entirely different meaning in the LABOUR THEORY OF VALUE, where the exchange value of a commodity is determined by the labour time it contains.

SEE ALSO: *attitude; coercion; consensus; norm; Parsons; pragmatic acceptance; social order.*

variable Any quantity which varies in value. For example, variables that we commonly use to distinguish individuals, such as height, weight and colour of eyes, are quantities that vary in value. Sociological variables are normally social constructs (e.g. social class, ethnicity, childhood) rather than physical characteristics. However, they are constructed in such a way that they can be measured and used in numerical analysis.

variance This is a statistical measure of variability or dispersion closely related to the STANDARD DEVIATION. The *analysis of variance* is a commonly used technique for the evaluation of differences among several groups.

Veblen, Thorstein (1857–1929) An American social critic who held university posts at Chicago, Stanford and Missouri but remained an outsider in the academic community. He developed an economic sociology of capitalism that criticized the acquisitiveness and predatory competition of American society and the power of the corporation. His best-known publication was *The Theory of the Leisure Class* (1899). In this he argued that the dominant class in American capitalism, which he labelled as the 'leisure class', pursued a lifestyle of conspicuous consumption, ostentatious waste and idleness. In *The Higher Learning in America* (1918a), he claimed that the universities were dominated by considerations of profitability, economic patronage, and self-interest, and had no commitment to true academic values.

In *The Instinct of Workmanship* (1914), *The Place of Science in Modern Civilization* (1918b) and *The Engineers and the Price System* (1921), Veblen optimistically suggested that engineers, who embodied the spirit of science and technology, would replace the parasitic leisure class. In *The Theory of the Business Enterprise* (1904) and *Absentee Ownership and Business Enterprise* (1923), he considered the distinctive features of U S capitalism, namely the separation of ownership and control and the oligopolistic power of the giant corporation.

During the First World War, he published *Imperial Germany and the Industrial Revolution* (1915). He regarded warfare as a threat to economic productivity, which he defined as the production of useful commodities and services. Contrasting the authoritarian politics of Germany with the British democratic tradition, he noted that in Germany industrialization had not produced a progressive political culture. He contributed to the analysis of American diplomatic strategy in *An Inquiry into the Nature of Peace and the Terms of its Perpetuation* (1917).

READING: Diggins (1978)

verification See: FALSIFICATIONISM; SIGNIFICANCE TEST.

Verstehen Usually translated as 'understanding', this concept has formed part of a critique of positivist or naturalist sociology. It is argued that sociology should not analyse human action from 'the outside' by copying the methods of natural science. Instead, sociology should recognize the meanings that people give to their actions. *Verstehen* is the procedure by which sociologists can have access to these meanings. The concept has come into sociology largely via the work of WEBER, who defined sociology as being concerned with meaningful action. *Verstehen* consists of placing oneself in the position of other people to see what meaning they give to their actions, what their purposes are, or what ends they believe are served by their actions. For example, if sociologists wish to analyse the social circumstances of waving, they must have some basis for deciding which cases of flapping one's arm up and down are waving and which mean something else. Not to be able to investigate the meaning of the actions may be seriously misleading, in that actions might all be put together in one category when they actually belong in different ones. To some extent, the inspection of meaning involved here is simply an extension of everyday attempts to understand action.

However, Weber wishes to go further, by reconciling interpretation of action by *Verstehen* with causal explanation. It is not entirely clear what is meant here and interpreters of Weber have variously suggested that *Verstehen* merely generates causal hypotheses or that meanings can function as causes.

The use of *Verstehen* has been criticized from two points of view. On the one hand, sociologists have argued that there is no way of validating *Verstehen* interpretations, while, on the other, it has been suggested that the attempt to reconcile causal and *Verstehen* analysis actually ends up by denying the actor's point of view.

SEE ALSO: *agency and structure; empathy; ethnomethodology; Geisteswissenschaften; hermeneutics; meaningful action; naturalism; phenomenological sociology; positivism; rule; social structure; understanding alien belief systems.*

READING: Albrow (1990)

victimology Until the 1980s, the study of crime and deviance focused on the criminal or deviant, or on the social processes that labelled particular actions as criminal or deviant. From the 1980s onwards, there has been an interest in the study of the victims – who they are, the interactions between criminal and victim, and the effect of crime or other deviance on the victim. For example, there has been much criticism of the original focus of CRIMINOLOGY from feminists, who argue that women are often the victims of male crime, whether directly victims, as in rape, or indirectly as a member of a criminal's family. Again, much sociological interest was generated by the findings of successive crime surveys in Britain and America, which showed the existence of a substantial number of crimes not reported to the police. These showed that a concentration on the criminal, or the criminal justice system, would ignore a large number of victims of crime who, for some reason, had not reported the crime.

The more recent emphasis on victimology – the study of the victims of crime – has been related to a greater public interest in the welfare of victims rather than criminals.

SEE ALSO: *criminal statistics; deviance amplification; deviant behaviour.*

virtual reality Mistakenly equated with CYBERSPACE, this refers to the technological management of the senses to create alternative realities. M. Featherstone and R. Burrows in *Cyberspace, Cyberbodies, Cyberpunk* (1995) define it as both a tactile and audible multi-media experience, whereby 'bioapparatuses' – headphones, eyephones (head-mounted stereo television goggles) and datagloves – surround the body with an artificial 'sensorium' of sound, sight and touch. Social critics of communication technologies claim that the natural and social worlds have been replaced by a virtual world, in which electronic signs and images simulate reality.

SEE ALSO: *hyperreality; information superhighway; time–space distantiation.*

vocabulary of motives See: ACCOUNTS.

voluntarism This term is applied to those sociological theories based on the intentions or motives of actors who are thus assumed to act 'voluntarily' and not as 'determined' by the social structure. Sociologists often dislike voluntaristic explanations, because in neglecting the role of social structure they appear to be anti-sociological.

SEE ALSO: *action theory; agency and structure; methodological individualism; Parsons; psychologism.*

voluntary associations Participation in voluntary associations such as political parties, churches, trade-union and professional bodies has been regarded as integrating marginal groups such as immigrants and ethnic minorities into society. In America, voluntary associations are regarded as important elements in participatory democracy. As secondary groups, they bridge the gulf between the individual or family and the wider society.

With the decline in state support for welfare services, voluntary associations (sometimes known as the third sector) play an increasing role in the provision of social services. However, these associations differ from charitable organizations of earlier periods, because they are governed by more commercial and professional performance criteria. Indeed, in some cases, for example housing associations in the UK, they are in receipt of state funding for which they are accountable to government.

SEE ALSO: *group; pressure group.*

READING: Kendall and Knapp (1996)

voting Sociological analysis of electoral behaviour, how and why people vote, has traditionally been based on a structural approach which seeks to identify the social structural determinants of voting. The *party identification* model is the main example of the approach. This assumes that voting patterns are associated primarily with the particular socio-economic factors that form the basis of enduring party loyalty via long-term political socialization. In contrast, political scientists have often given purely political factors more weight, including party programmes and election campaigns, political issues of the day and the public standing of political leaders. The fact that most voters have little interest in politics or political issues, may even dislike some of the policies of the party for which they vote, yet continue to vote for the same party time and time again, provides some support for the party identification model. It must be borne in mind, however, that a minority of voters *do* change their party allegiance or abstain at each election and these people largely decide the outcome (when the voting of others remains stable). Furthermore, the size of this minority has grown.

For the first thirty years after the Second World War, the main influence on voting in Britain, as in many Western nations, appears to have been the family: political socialization in the home meant that people tended to vote like their parents. Social class was also closely associated with voting: typically in the post-war period about two-thirds of the manual working class voted Labour and four-fifths of the non-manual, middle class voted Conservative. Parental and class influences are difficult to disentangle, however, since parental occupation is also a major determinant of the class position of offspring. The other important influence was community: middle-class voters living in predominantly working-class communities were more likely to vote Labour than if they lived in a middle-class area; conversely, working-class voters in middle-class areas showed some tendency to vote Conservative.

Voting began to change during the late 1960s. Increasing numbers of people began to vote against their supposedly 'natural' class alignment, a process known as *class dealignment*. Even among core supporters of the Labour and Conservative parties, the strength of their commitment to party policies weakened, which is called *partisan dealignment*. There was also growing support for a third party, the Liberal Democrat Party (formerly the Liberal–SDP Alliance), during the 1980s and 1990s. The Labour Party won four out of five elections between 1964 and 1974. The Conservative Party won majorities in four consecutive general elections between 1979 and 1992, and Labour seemed permanently set to be in second place. However, the 1997 election witnessed the largest swing in voting for over fifty years, in which the Labour Party gained its greatest ever number of seats, the Liberal Democrats doubled their representation and Conservative seats were halved. With 31.4 per cent of the votes, this was the weakest Conservative performance since 1832. Labour votes in 1997 came from all social classes and ethnic groups, and across most of the age range. Nevertheless, Labour's share of the vote in 1997 (43.2 per cent) was below its 1966 peak (48 per cent) and virtually the same as when it lost in 1970 (43.1 per cent). These developments show that the party identification model and the traditional structural determinants have weakened. Over the last twenty years, considerable effort has been devoted to understanding changes in voting behaviour. Understanding has been complicated by the way that voting has continued to change from election to election, thus researchers have been chasing a moving target. Another complication is that developments in statistical techniques over the last decade have greatly extended how voting data can be analysed, notably in the modelling of complex interactions among many variables; thus earlier attempts to understand voting behaviour are probably oversimplified.

The overall linear trend since the end of the 1960s has been a decline in class voting – that is, class dealignment. In 1997, class voting dipped to its lowest level. But there have also been large fluctuations at each election, which have disguised this underlying decline, so that the trend has not been steady and smooth. Equally, social class is not unimportant: class origins and attitudes still remain a major influence on how people vote, despite their lower salience in comparison with the past. A number of factors have contributed to this change.

Structural change in British society is one. There has been a fragmentation of the old class structure, following the expansion of middle-class jobs and a decline of the working class. This has been accompanied by an increase in social mobility from working-class into middle-class positions and in households containing members from different social classes. B. Sarlvik and I. Crewe (1983) suggested that fragmentation would weaken collective influences on voting and encourage people to make more individual choices, based on their assessment of their own self-interest. P. Dunleavy and C. T. Husbands (1985) thought that a modified structural approach might be more appropriate, as a consequence of what they regarded as new constellations of interests that cut across older political ties. These included: whether people depended on public services for their housing, transport, health and social security, or whether they made private provision; whether or not they were trade unionists; whether they were employed in the public or private sectors of the economy. Manual workers who were not trade-union members, worked in the private sector, and owned their own homes would have a low probability of voting Labour despite their class position. This was related to a wider sociological argument at the time, that differences in patterns of consumption created CONSUMPTION CLEAVAGES which were replacing class as a basic division in society. Subsequent empirical work has shown that all these factors have some influence on voting, but their effects are weak and do not support a new structural model.

Both the above accounts represent an alternative theoretical approach to voting behaviour which uses *rational* models. These models derive from RATIONAL CHOICE THEORY and indicate that individuals make rational choices which maximize their own interests and preferences. Rational models may either replace the party identification model or complement it. Voters search for the best fit between their own preferences and what parties have to offer at each election, and make a rational choice about how to vote on the basis of this assessment. Their preferences may include, of course, a desire to vote for the party with which they have voted in the past, which is why rational choice is not incompatible with identification.

A second factor is that POLITICAL PARTIES have realigned their ideological base, in order to compete for votes. The activities of political parties in mobilizing support can have real effects and political factors should not be downplayed in favour of changes in social structure. The two go together when structural change erodes the basis of party identification and reduces the relevance of older ideologies for many voters, while enabling the creation of political programmes with a wider appeal to a new alignment of social groups. In the last three decades of the twentieth century, the political ideologies of major British parties were remodelled. During the 1970s and 1980s, the rise of a NEW RIGHT agenda within the Conservative Party was an ideological shift that appealed to a substantial proportion of those voting at elections, including parts of the manual working class which had previously voted Labour. During the 1990s, the Labour Party moved into the ideological central ground, leaving the Conservatives to its right and, for the first time, the Liberal Democrats to its left. Analysis of its 1997 election programme has shown that Labour endorsed the free market economy, economic individualism and restraints on public spending, and had shifted from its traditionally more radical position on what was, historically, the major left–right ideological cleavage in British politics. It also adopted a conservative position on the emerging political agenda of social values relating to the family and law and order.

Institutional changes are a third factor. These include: the effects of lowering of the voting age from 21 to 18 years in 1968, because younger people tend to have a weaker identification (partisan alignment) with any one party; the increase in the numbers of Liberal Democrat candidates, which has allowed tactical voting in a larger number of constituencies (i.e. voting for the candidate you feel has most chance of keeping out the candidate you least want, rather than voting for your first choice); and the continuing revision of the boundaries of electoral constituencies, which have favoured different parties at different times.

Comparative analyses of other European political parties – for example, by Giddens (1998) – also point to the changing basis of support elsewhere in Europe. By the end of the century, the European working class had been fragmented in various ways which undermined support for left-wing social democratic parties: the numerical and proportional decline of the manual working class and the rise of non-manual wage labour; wider differentiation within the manual working class following a growing divergence of market conditions and life-chances; age as a new source of stratification among wage-earners; the feminization of the work force; growing ethnic diversity and its attendant racism that erodes cultural solidarity. There is a further claim, that the rise of a more global capitalist economy has restricted the range of policies which political parties can now pursue in their search for votes, notably their capacity to determine national economic policies.

However, there have also been important cultural changes in many European societies, and these have a significant influence on voting, independently of structural changes. Cultural change is a fourth factor that contributes to the changing nature of party identification. It dissolves old loyalties but also provides the opportunity for ideological realignment, in which parties can remodel their political ideologies in order to reposition themselves in stronger segments of the 'market' for votes. It may even allow new partisan alignments to be created. There is now a politically significant ethical division, between libertarian and progressive values, which guide personal and social morality, and an authoritarian and traditional morality. The libertarian position is individualistic, anti-authoritarian and against state involvement on issues such as law and order, dutifulness and discipline, civil rights, personal and sexual morality. Authoritarians expect the state to take a strong line in all areas, including morality and economic life, and to preserve traditional values. This division now cuts across social classes. It is additional to the traditional split between left and right political ideologies over the distribution of material rewards and the role of the state in this. There is now a more complex set of demands that can be mobilized politically. Playing the progressive hand, while backpedalling on economic redistribution, has allowed the social democratic parties of continental Europe to create new electoral coalitions without forfeiting the votes of the declining working class.

SEE ALSO: *third way politics; working-class conservatism.*

READING: Dearlove and Saunders (1991); Dunleavy *et al.* (1997); Norris and Evans (1999)

W

wealth See: DISTRIBUTION OF INCOME AND WEALTH.

Weber, Max (1864–1920) Weber is often regarded as the founder of modern sociology, because: (1) he provided a systematic statement of the conceptual framework of the sociological perspective; (2) he developed a coherent philosophy of social science, which recognized the essential problems of explanation of social action; (3) in a variety of substantive fields, he grasped the basic characteristics of a modern, industrial civilization; (4) through these empirical studies of modern society, he identified a number of key issues which have become the foci of the principal debates within the discipline; (5) his own life in many respects provides a forceful example of sociology as a vocation.

The details of Weber's life have been fully and sympathetically examined in an extensive biography by his wife, Marianne Weber (1975). Born in Erfurt, Weber grew up in a family context characterized by merchant wealth, liberal politics and Protestant pietism. He attended the universities of Heidelberg, Göttingen and Berlin, and completed his academic training by research on the history of commercial societies in the Middle Ages and on Roman agrarian history. While Weber held professorial posts at Freiburg, Heidelberg and Munich, his teaching and research were interrupted by illness, following a mental breakdown in 1897. Despite this, his academic productivity was formidable. Weber has suffered in English translation from a highly selective and discontinuous publication of his work, much of which originally took the form of essays, papers, lectures and even speeches. However, the major German text *Wirtschaft und Gesellschaft* (1922), published posthumously, has been translated in its entirety as *Economy and Society* (1968). The complexity and controversy of Weber's sociology has been repeatedly illustrated by the contradictory interpretations of his work. Both the nature of his work and the diversity of exegesis can be examined by summarizing Weber's contribution to modern social science under the following topics: (1) philosophy of social science (1949; 1975); (2) RATIONALIZATION (1922; 1930); (3) the PROTESTANT ETHIC thesis (1930); (4) Weber's relationship to MARX and Marxism (1922); (5) his analysis of power politics in relation to German society (1946; 1978).

(1) Weber's analysis of the methodological and philosophical problems of sociology is conventionally regarded as a form of NEO-KANTIANISM. In his early commentaries on the methodology appropriate to sociology, Weber denied that sociology could: (i) discover universal laws of human behaviour comparable with those of natural science; (ii) confirm any evolutionary progress in human societies; (iii) provide any evaluation of, or moral justification for, any existing or future state

of affairs; (iv) develop any collective concepts (like 'the state' or 'the family') unless they could be stated in terms of individual action. Sociology had to aim at the understanding of the meaning of actions, on the basis of which sociology could work towards formal models or ideal types of action on a comparative basis. Concepts in sociology like BUREAUCRACY would have the same analytical status as those in economics such as 'perfect competition'. Sociology was not simply a subjective interpretation of action, because sociologists were guided by certain public norms (such as VALUE NEUTRALITY) and their findings were open to academic scrutiny and criticism. Weber regarded statistics and social surveys as an essential aid to sociological research, but statistical data still had to be interpreted and evaluated. While Weber rejected as unwarranted the claims of POSITIVISM and Marxism, it is not clear from his actual studies of society that he fully adhered to his own methodological principles.

(2) Having denied the possibility of developmental laws in sociology, Weber implicitly presented rationalization as the master trend of Western capitalist society. Rationalization is the process whereby every area of human relationships is subject to calculation and administration. While Marxists have noted the prominence of rational calculation in factory discipline and the labour process, Weber detected rationalization in all social spheres – politics, religion, economic organization, university administration, the laboratory and even musical notation. Weber's sociology as a whole is characterized by a METAPHYSICAL PATHOS, whereby the process of rationalization eventually converted capitalist society into a meaningless 'iron cage'.

(3) One source of rationalization in Western societies lay in the cultural changes brought about by the Protestant Ethic, Protestantism was not a direct cause of CAPITALISM, but it did provide a culture which emphasized individualism, hard work, rational conduct and self-reliance. This ethic had an 'affinity' with early capitalism, but Weber thought that advanced capitalist societies would no longer require any religious legitimation.

(4) It is conventional to regard Weber as one of the major critics of Marx and Marxism. The reasons for this position are: (i) that Weber's emphasis on the role of culture, especially religion, in shaping human action appears to be a refutation of economic DETERMINISM; (ii) the importance of subjective orientation of individuals in Weber's analysis of social relations is said to be in contrast to the analysis of objective structural effects in Marxism; (iii) Weber's account of status groups and markets appears to run counter to Marx's emphasis on economic CLASS and relations of production; (iv) Weber was explicitly critical of Marxist analysis of the imminent collapse of capitalism, since he argued that the planned economy in socialist society would enhance rationalization, not terminate it. An alternative view is that: (i) Weber regarded Marx, along with Nietzsche, as one of the most important thinkers of the nineteenth century; (ii) Weber's criticisms were directed at institutionalized Marxism (in the form of the German Democratic Party) rather than at Marx; (iii) the Protestant Ethic thesis was not intended to be a refutation of Marx; (iv) Weber often wrote in a manner that suggests a strong element of determinism; (v) Weber's description of the nature of capitalism as an 'iron cage' was often very close to Marx's analysis and, in particular, there is a close relationship between the concepts of ALIENATION and rationalization; (vi) Weber came to regard capitalist society as having a logic which operated independently of the subjective attitudes of social actors.

(5) Weber's sociology and his attitude towards Marxism have to be seen in the

context of German society between 1870 and 1918. For Weber, Germany lacked an independent, politically educated middle class, while the working class was underdeveloped, partly because of the late development of industrialization. The political and economic development of Germany had been brought about by a strong state under Bismarck, and political power rested in the hands of the feudal land-owning class of Junkers. With the death of Bismarck, the German bureaucracy and state lacked leadership, which neither the middle nor working class could provide. This political vacuum partly explains the importance of power and power conflicts in Weber's writing on AUTHORITY and CHARISMA. There are basically two responses to Weber's political sociology: (i) Marxists tend to regard Weber's analysis of German politics as a precursor of fascism; (ii) Liberals suggest that Weber's sociology is in fact grounded in an anxiety that rationalization will destroy individual freedom and creativity. There is evidence for both views, since Weber thought Germany would require strong state leadership to beat off the economic threat posed by the United States and Great Britain, but he also sought to encourage a situation in which the importance of the individual could be maximized. The debate about the political implication of Weber's sociology has continued to be important in modern Germany, while controversy about his contribution to contemporary sociology continues unabated.

Weber also contributed to the sociology of comparative religions (1951; 1952; 1958a), urban sociology (1958b), the sociology of music (1958c), economic history (1950), the sociology of law (1922; 1977) and the analysis of ancient civilization (1976).

Recent interpretations of Weber have emphasized his contribution to cultural sociology and his critical attitude towards capitalist modernization. These reinterpretations suggest that we should see Weber's cultural critique as part of the legacy of Nietzsche; they also show that Weber's analysis of religious orientations to the world is fundamental for an understanding of his analysis of modern society.

SEE ALSO: *action theory; ideal type; legal–rational authority; Marxist sociology; meaningful action; methodological individualism; rational choice theory; rationality; social closure; status; value freedom; value relevance; Verstehen.*

READING: Bendix (1960); Käsler (1988); Löwith (1993); Swedberg (1998); Turner, B. S. (1996b)

welfare rights See: RIGHTS.

welfare state The basic premise of a welfare state is that government has the responsibility for the well-being of its citizens and that this cannot be entrusted to the individual, private corporation or local community. Welfare states typically protect people against poverty by means of unemployment benefits, family allowances, income supplements for the poorly paid, and old-age pensions; they provide comprehensive medical care, free education and public housing. These services are financed by state insurance schemes and taxation.

The earliest state welfare programme was the national social insurance system that Bismarck introduced to Germany in the 1880s, and which Lloyd George imitated in Britain in 1911 with national insurance for health and UNEMPLOYMENT. BEVERIDGE, whose vision was of state care 'from the cradle to the grave', had a key influence over the British measures and the subsequent introduction of the first comprehensive welfare state by the Labour government of 1945–50, which included the National Health Service. Labour intended both to promote welfare and at the same time to use welfare spending, financed out of taxation that bore more heavily on the rich, as a means to reduce social inequality by redistributing resources. The British welfare state has had real success in caring for its citizens, though the nation's relatively poor economic performance over many decades, and the disinclination of governments since 1979 to increase public spending, means that most programmes are now underfunded, and the family and VOLUNTARY ORGANIZATIONS still perform welfare roles. However, it has not achieved as much as was once expected in redistributing resources and, indeed, it has been shown that the middle classes actually receive disproportionately large amounts of certain sorts of welfare, education in particular. Most Western European and Scandinavian societies have comprehensive welfare states, as do Australia and New Zealand, leaving America and Japan with the most poorly developed welfare provision among advanced industrial societies.

Particularly since the start of the 1980s, governments in Britain and other countries have been intent on rolling back the welfare state, placing more responsibility on individuals, perhaps via private insurance schemes, for the provision of their own health, education, old-age pension and housing. Such a policy has been initiated partly out of conviction, whether this has been Thatcherism or New Labour, and partly out of a belief that the level of public spending, especially on unemployment and disability benefits, state pensions and other support for the poor, is far too high. The intention is that private sources should provide as much welfare as possible (with the exception, perhaps, of health and education) while leaving the STATE to provide a safety net for those unable to fund their own welfare.

A major debate in the sociology of the welfare state has been between those who argue that welfare genuinely serves the needs of the relatively disadvantaged and those, chiefly Marxists, who argue that it functions as an instrument of repression by mitigating the worst excesses of capitalism and providing a form of state supervision of the disadvantaged. Another debate focuses on selectivity versus universality in welfare provision. Should welfare be for all or only for disadvantaged groups? The proponents of the first argue that universality of welfare emphasizes the nation as a community, enhances social order and reinforces the notion of CITIZENSHIP. Advocates of the latter, on the other hand, argue that selective welfare provision focuses benefit on those genuinely in need, is cheaper and is potentially redistributive.

SEE ALSO: *deprivation; distribution of income and wealth; poverty; rights.*

READING: Pierson (1991); Taylor-Gooby (1991)

Weltanschauung See: WORLD VIEW.

white-collar crime As originally used by E. Sutherland (1945), this referred to crimes committed by members of the business community and large corporations, including false advertising, infringement of copyright, unfair competition, tax evasion, fraud and unfair labour practices. This is usually called CORPORATE CRIME. The concept has since been broadened to include the large volume of hidden crime committed by white-collar employees at work (e.g. pilfering and fiddling expenses). While such activities are technically illegal, white-collar crime is often not regarded by public opinion as crime, because it does not necessarily carry a criminal STIGMA, and because they are often crimes against institutions rather than people. White-collar crimes are not obvious or violent, unlike rape or assault; their consequences are usually diffuse rather than directly affecting single individuals. The legal response to such crimes tends, therefore, to be lenient.

SEE ALSO: *criminal statistics*.

white-collar worker A term sometimes used to describe all non-manual employees, but increasingly confined to the lower levels of this occupational hierarchy.

Williams, Raymond (1921–88) Formerly professor of drama at Cambridge University, he made a major contribution to the emergence of CULTURAL STUDIES, where he developed the concept of 'the structure of feeling' to describe the emergence of everyday beliefs and perceptions outside an official IDEOLOGY. He published a number of influential volumes on the cultural and social history of Britain in *Culture and Society 1780–1950* (1958), *The Long Revolution* (1961) and *The Country and the City* (1973). He also fostered the growth of media studies in *Television* (1974) and the acceptance of a language of cultural analysis in *Keywords* (1976).

SEE ALSO: *culture; Hall; Hoggart*.

READING: Inglis (1995)

Willmott, Peter (b. 1923) A British sociological researcher and currently a senior fellow at the Policy Studies Institute, Willmott has been chiefly active in studies of family, community and youth, especially in association with Michael Young and the Institute of Community Studies. His best-known works are: *Family and Kinship in East London* (1957) and *Family and Class in a London Suburb* (1960) (both with M. Young), which are studies of the relationship of family with community and the relevance of the extended family to modern life in different parts of the city; *The Evolution of a Community* (1963) and *Adolescent Boys of East London* (1966), both investigations of East London; and *The Symmetrical Family* (1973), also with M. Young, which is a study of changing family forms.

SEE ALSO: *symmetrical family*.

Wilson, Bryan R. (b. 1926) Former reader in sociology at Oxford and fellow of All Souls, he has made a major contribution to the contemporary sociological study of religion, with special reference to the religious SECT. In *Patterns of Sectarianism* (1967) and *Religious Sects* (1970a), he has formulated an ideal type of sectarian groups which has resolved many of the traditional problems in the classical legacy of M. Weber. Wilson has also defended a strong version of the theory of SECULARIZATION, and argues that religious institutions have been robbed of their social significance, in *Religion in a Secular Society* (1966) and *Religion in Sociological Perspective* (1982). He has evaluated his analyses of sects and secularization on a world scale in *Magic and the Millennium* (1973) and *Contemporary Transformations of Religion* (1976). Wilson has also taken a critical stand in relation to contemporary educational issues, YOUTH CULTURE and modern values, in *Youth Culture and the Universities* (1970b). The general theme of his sociology is that the powerful and transformative values which characterized both primitive Christianity and Protestantism have declined, leaving the modern world exposed to social processes which have trivialized contemporary culture and intellectual activity.

witchcraft In anthropology, this is defined as the belief that members of a community employ supernatural means to harm others in ways which are socially disapproved. Witchcraft is occasionally distinguished from sorcery, which is the use of RITUAL to control supernatural forces in ways that do not evoke strong social disapproval. Various explanations have been offered for the presence of witchcraft beliefs: (1) they provide an account for the misfortunes of everyday life; (2) they are a vehicle for interpersonal conflict in small communities; (3) witchcraft accusations serve to re-affirm more general social values, such as cooperation or neighbourliness; (4) since most suspects were women, witchcraft accusations were an expression of male control; (5) accusations and trials of witches were a form of social control over deviants. The decline of witchcraft is seen as a consequence of changes in communal life with urbanization and in changes in intellectual life with SECULARIZATION.

READING: Douglas, M. (1970a)

Wittgenstein, Ludwig (1889–1951) A philosopher who was born in Austria and spent much of his professional life in Britain, Wittgenstein has had a considerable influence on some branches of sociology, especially ETHNOMETHODOLOGY. This influence has been mostly exercised via his later work (partly published as *Philosophical Investigations*, 1958). In this work, Wittgenstein rejected the view that words name some feature of the external world and that their meaning is given in relation to the external world. Instead, he argued that meaning is given by the use that people make of utterances. Such uses are rule-bound, and in learning language people learn these rules. Sociologists have therefore taken Wittgenstein's work as a warrant for a sociological approach to language and meaning; meaning is not a fixed invariant quality but is given by the use of words in the social context, which may vary from society to society.

women and crime The influence of FEMINISM and FEMINIST SOCIAL THEORY means that CRIMINOLOGY now pays greater attention to women as victims and perpetrators of crime. Women commit fewer serious crimes than men and are over-represented in shoplifting and minor sex offences. Various criminological explanations have been suggested: (1) sex-role socialization; (2) sex differences in opportunities to commit crimes; (3) differences in police and court responses; (4) variations in societal reaction. It is assumed that women are more likely to be victims rather than offenders, but changes in the sexual division of labour and the increase of women in the labour force suggests that the differential rate of crime between men and women will decline.

SEE ALSO: *criminal statistics; feminist criminology; sex roles; sociology of gender.*

women and work There was a major shift in the employment patterns of Western industrialized economies over the last four decades of the twentieth century, as women increasingly sought paid employment in the labour market. For example, in the USA in 1963, approximately 38 per cent of working-age women were employed, and by 1995 this proportion had risen to 65 per cent. In the UK, 37 per cent were employed in 1961, rising to 63 per cent by 1995. In America in the mid 1990s, a quarter of all women employees worked part-time, while in Britain the proportion was 44 per cent. Most of the growth in employment since the 1950s can be accounted for by the increasing proportions of married women who return to work after bearing children and choose to spend less time out of the labour market for domestic reasons.

Nearly all the growth has been in part-time jobs rather than full-time jobs. The proportion of women of working age who work full time remained stable, at around 30 per cent from the early 1950s until the late 1970s, then rose steadily to a peak of 38 per cent in 1990, followed by a decline to around 36 per cent in the mid 1990s. A similar growth of women working part time rather than full time can be found in many other European societies. But in the USA, most of the expansion has been among women working full time. Women now account for about 50 per cent of the total labour force in the USA and 45 per cent in the UK.

In Britain, women's employment profiles (often referred to as 'career patterns') fall into two categories, which are labelled by C. Hakim (1996) as *working woman* and *homemaker*. Women in the first category work full time for at least twenty years after entering the labour market, either in continuous employment or with some breaks. It appears that women in this group expect a long-term career in paid employment and plan on this basis. Planning includes regulating their fertility, with some choosing to be childless while others plan the number and timing of their children to minimize disruption of their careers. Women in the second category work full time until early in adult life (until marriage or, more commonly, the birth of a child), then either leave the labour force for good or return to part-time employment after breaks in employment. Those who return to employment seek jobs that fit their domestic role (e.g. close to home, with convenient hours and part-time). Increasingly over the last few decades, women in this group have also tended to work more intermittently, with numerous breaks over the remainder of their working lives. However, employment discontinuity is growing among both groups, because all women now take more breaks from paid work than in the past, so the boundary between two models is not rigid. About two-fifths of women in Britain fit the working-woman model and about three-fifths the homemaker. It is difficult to make comparisons with careers in other countries, but evidence of rising full-time employment in the USA indicates that the working woman category could be more significant there.

The reasons for the shifting pattern of employment may be divided into demand and supply. Among the factors leading to a greater demand for women employees are: the growth of routine non-manual work and personal services where women have traditionally been employed; interest among employers in hiring part-time employees to match fluctuations in work flow; the fact that part-timers are often less well protected by employment legislation and are, therefore, cheaper to hire and easier to dismiss; labour shortages in the 1960s and early 1970s when the supply of male labour was inadequate. Among the factors increasing the supply of female labour are: limitations on family size, giving women more opportunity to work and for longer periods; changing social conceptions of women's roles; the increasing qualification of women via the educational system; the desire to increase personal and household income.

Historically, women and men have tended to do different jobs. The term *occupational segregation* describes this division of occupations into some which are dominated by women and others by men. Women have always been heavily concentrated and heavily over-represented (in proportion to the number of women in the labour force) in low-skill, routine, non-manual occupations, including work as clerks, cashiers, typists, secretaries and receptionists, and in unskilled manual jobs in retailing, clothing, catering and personal services. This pattern still holds. The small numbers of women who entered higher-level jobs traditionally worked in certain professional and related jobs in education, welfare and health. There is also an issue of *vertical segregation*, when men dominate higher-paid and higher-status occupations or, within an occupation, earn more because they are promoted to higher levels than women. In Britain, occupational segregation declined sharply in the 1970s but more slowly subsequently. The overall decline conceals different trends, however, because segregation has declined for full-time employees while it is stable (or even may have widened slightly) for part-timers. About a fifth of men and women (mainly in full-time employment) now work in occupations that are integrated rather than segregated; that is, they have a mix of men and women that is reasonably proportionate to the balance in the labour force. These include a considerable number of the senior professional and management occupations which constitute the SERVICE CLASS. These are highly paid and high-status jobs; thus women's share of more senior positions has risen (although there are still high-level occupations where women are seriously under-represented, e.g. professional engineers, architects, senior military and police officers). In this case, less occupational segregation also means less vertical segregation. But women are still not fully represented across all service-class occupations and so this component of vertical segregation remains significant. Nor do women fill the most senior positions within occupations in proportion to their numbers. Indeed, even in feminized occupations, the top jobs are disproportionately filled by men (e.g. most teachers are women but most directors of education are men).

On average, men earn more than women in all Western economies, although the gap has somewhat closed in most countries over the last fifteen years. Part of this difference is due to the fact that, on average, men put in a longer working week than women; nevertheless, average hourly rates are still lower for women than men. In Britain, the gap began to close more rapidly after the mid 1980s, perhaps reflecting the somewhat greater number of women working full time and in service-class jobs.

There is no agreed explanation of occupational and vertical segregation, or of differential remuneration. HUMAN CAPITAL explanations point to the significance of the greater education and training, and the continuous work experience of men. Some sociologists believe that these explanations have considerable relevance to the majority who choose the homemaker model. Others point to discrimination as the reason women enter only certain jobs, fail to reach senior positions and tend to be poorly paid. Discrimination within the family leads to different patterns of childhood socialization, so that boys and girls have different aspirations, and later assigns women domestic roles that prevent them participating fully in work. Discrimination may also occur in the labour market when employers fail to treat men and women on equal terms, and in the workplace when male employees expect women to be treated unequally. Trade unions or professional associations dominated by men may also reinforce women's disadvantage. It is estimated that about three-quarters of the difference in earnings can be explained by vertical segregation within occupations and about a quarter by horizontal occupational segregation.

Legislation may redress discrimination. In Britain, the Equal Pay Act and the Sexual Discrimination Act (both of which became fully operational in 1975) together accounted for some closing of the earnings differential between men and women and an initially sharp reduction in occupational segregation. The maternity provisions of the 1975 Employment Protection Act provided for maternity pay and the right to return to a job for women who met the qualifying conditions. Elsewhere in Europe, improvements in women's relative pay seem to have owed less to legislation.

The lifetime employment patterns of most women workers clearly reflect a sexual DIVISION OF LABOUR that gives men and women different roles in relation to the family and domestic organization. These patterns in turn are part of any explanation of the inequalities of condition that occur. Equally, women's attitudes to work are influenced by their family roles, since many women appear to have distinctive WORK ATTITUDES that relate to their life-cycles.

It is often said that women are part of the secondary market in a system of LABOUR MARKET SEGMENTATION. Occupational segregation means that women in the main sell their labour in a separate market from men and this indicates segmentation. However, the view that the market for female labour is 'secondary', in the sense that it provides low pay, unstable jobs, little chance to acquire skills, and little career progression, is not true for all women. Women employees are not homogeneous and have polarized into at least two different groups which occupy different sorts of market: professional and managerial occupations have 'primary' labour-market characteristics, while many other jobs done by women do have 'secondary' characteristics.

SEE ALSO: *class; domestic labour; emotional labour; feminism; gender; management; middle class; patriarchy; profession; sex roles; sociology of gender; stereotypes.*

READING: Milkman and Townsley (1994); Hakim (1996)

women's studies See: SOCIOLOGY OF GENDER.

work and employment, sociology of See: SOCIOLOGY OF WORK AND EMPLOYMENT.

work attitudes The sociological analysis of work attitudes historically covered a number of issues: orientations to work, motivation, satisfaction and other job-related attitudes. Sociologists have continued to investigate work orientations (also referred to as expectations), but it is psychologists rather than sociologists who, over the last twenty years or so, have systematically investigated motivation and satisfaction.

A traditional assumption, shared by sociologists and psychologists, was that people's needs of work were universal and stable. The most widely accepted account was the NEEDS HIERARCHY of A. Maslow. Given universal needs, it was possible to argue that contextual factors, such as the type of technology or the size of a workplace, would have fairly consistent consequences for everyone. However, this assumption was challenged by J. H. Goldthorpe *et al.* (1968a) in the AFFLUENT WORKER study. They argued that orientations were a mediating variable between the nature of work and employees' attitudes and behaviour. They further claimed that orientations were shaped by the social experiences of employees outside work. *Solidarism* applied to people who expected social community and job satisfaction at work. The need to identify with a workplace social community was often associated with conflictual employment relations, because solidarism was defined in relation to co-workers and in opposition to employers. The external social setting that gave rise to solidarism was the traditional working-class community. INSTRUMENTALISM described workers who sought only high pay and security, were indifferent to job content and were concerned primarily with their own interests. They lived in newer communities which lacked the dense social networks of traditional working-class areas. However, subsequent research could not identify these orientations among other manual workers. *Bureaucratic* orientation described people who committed themselves to the service of an organization, in return for employment security, promotion prospects and guaranteed movement up an incremental salary scale, and where employment relations were ones of trust. This applied primarily to white-collar, middle-class employees. Goldthorpe's later development of the concept of SERVICE CLASS had affinities with the bureaucratic orientation.

Analysis of a national survey of work attitudes among full-time employees in the USA has identified six features of work that are more or less important to different people (A. L. Kalleberg, 1978). The *intrinsic* dimension refers to whether work tasks are interesting and use a person's skills. *Convenience* refers to working hours, ease of travel to work and the pleasantness of the workplace. The *financial* dimension deals with pay and security. *Relations with co-workers* covers the possibilities of sociability. *Career* refers to promotion. *Resource adequacy* covers the provision by the employer of sufficient resources for the employee to do the job properly.

There are differences in work orientations or expectations between women and men, and also among different groups of women. Investigation of attitudes towards the sexual DIVISION OF LABOUR and SEX ROLES in Britain indicates that about two-thirds of women give primacy to their domestic roles, whereas men mainly see themselves as 'breadwinners'. Women who work part time, or who do not work at all, are more domestically oriented than the minority who are in full-time work (who are more work- and career-oriented). The orientations of women who are in work are multi-stranded, with financial considerations dominating, followed by the intrinsic dimension and the company of other people. The priorities of women working part time generally differ from those of full-timers, and notably in the importance given to convenience.

Psychologists have remained interested in motivation. There are several theories of motivation which regard behaviour as being caused by innate psychological needs, the needs hierarchy being the best-known. Another if F. Herzberg's thesis of two separate factors: motivators and hygiene factors. Hygiene factors cause dissatisfaction. They are part of the extrinsic context of work, including salary, co-workers, company policies, managerial styles. When these are improved, people stop being dissatisfied but they will still not be positively motivated. Positive motivators are intrinsic to the job content: the work itself, achievement, recognition, responsibility, advancement and personal growth. But other theorists deny innate needs. They regard behaviour as determined by cognition, because individuals make deliberate and rational choices. Expectancy theory, developed for the work context by V. H. Vroom (1964), maintains that effort is determined by two factors: the values that individuals place on particular work-related rewards (e.g. pay, career, sociability, intrinsic satisfaction) and the calculations that they make as to whether their efforts will deliver what they value.

Job satisfaction is now seen primarily as a set of cognitions (beliefs). It is not necessarily related to the affective responses (i.e. feelings of happiness/unhappiness) that work stimulates. Typically, satisfaction and dissatisfaction are judgements that people make about fairness, because they have expectations of work which function as rules of justice. Individuals feel a sense of injustice (become dissatisfied) when their expectations are not met. Furthermore, the tendency to be satisfied or dissatisfied with work is, in part, a personal predisposition which is not related to the features of any specific work situation.

There has been much interest in the linkage between attitudes and work performance, because of the common assumption that happy employees work better. The relationship is controversial, both for motivation and satisfaction. The research evidence that either motivation or satisfaction are associated with performance is inconclusive. There is disagreement about what attitudes are and how they might be measured. There is no agreed definition of work performance, or whether this is better studied at the level of the individual or the work team. Even the causal sequence is questioned: do good attitudes produce good performance or is the relationship reversed? If there is a linkage, might this be due to an unspecified third factor?

SEE ALSO: *alienation; achievement motivation; attitude; human relations.*

READING: Hakim (1996); Steers *et al.* (1996)

work situation See: CLASS; TECHNOLOGY.

working class The working class in Britain, following the traditional but now disputed definition of this as manual workers, is declining, from 75 per cent of the employed population in 1911 to 42 per cent in 1991. Changes in the occupational structure have led to a steady increase in the number of non-manual jobs along with the contraction of manual work. The distinctiveness of the working class has not, however, been eroded: on average it has lower incomes, less job security and more UNEMPLOYMENT, a greater likelihood of poverty, more boring jobs and worse conditions of employment, fewer chances of a structured CAREER, higher rates of morbidity and an earlier age of mortality, and less chance of success within the educational system than the intermediate and upper classes. Sociological interest has focused on two issues: (1) why the working class appears to have tolerated such inequalities of condition and not organized more effectively to reduce the depth of CLASS divisions; (2) how far the working class is unified and internally homogeneous.

(1) Investigations of working-class consciousness have typically revealed dualism: people simultaneously reject and accept the social, economic and political structures that create such inequalities, and their views are incoherent. Evidence indicates that proletarian CLASS IMAGERY is quite widespread but does not develop into a radical CLASS CONSCIOUSNESS. Sociologists have advanced various reasons for this, though none is universally accepted: (i) the EMBOURGEOISEMENT of manual workers; (ii) the ideological HEGEMONY of those who benefit from and dominate the existing structures; (iii) the PRAGMATIC ACCEPTANCE by the working class of its lot. The failure to organize effectively is seen to derive partly from the lack of a coherent and single-minded commitment to change, and also from the failure of working-class organizations such as trade unions and the old Labour Party to press for change. This in turn has been interpreted as a consequence of oligarchical tendencies in these organizations and processes of INCORPORATION, and as a result of the growth of rights of CITIZENSHIP, the INSTITUTIONALIZATION OF CONFLICT, and social welfare which, by allowing for some amelioration of living and working conditions, give the appearance of change without effecting major transformations.

(2) Homogeneity relates partly to the above issue, in that the less homogeneous

the working class the less likely its members are to share a common consciousness or act in concert. Historically, in Britain, the LABOUR ARISTOCRACY marked a major division within the class. Skill divisions have become less significant as the result of DE-SKILLING and declining differentials in the areas of pay and working conditions. Since the 1950s other divisions have been postulated, including the typology in the AFFLUENT WORKER research of affluent, traditional-proletarian, and traditional-deferential workers, and the notion of a NEW WORKING CLASS. Neither has withstood scrutiny. Another division may be the development of an UNDERCLASS. Given that social mobility takes people out of the working class but does not replace them with outsiders from other classes because the class is shrinking, and that the shift from agriculture to industry has long been complete and with it the influx of peasants and agricultural workers into the industrial working class, the working class is fairly homogeneous. Elsewhere, in Western Europe and America, the movement of population from agriculture to industry and fairly recent waves of immigration make homogeneity less. In America, a dual labour market creates a privileged stratum that also divides the working class.

SEE ALSO: *deferential worker; distribution of income and wealth; dominant ideology thesis; dual consciousness; labour market segmentation; labour process approach; Leninism; Michels; middle class; migration; proletarianization; social mobility; upper class; welfare state; working-class conservatism.*

READING: Goldthorpe (1987)

working-class conservatism A substantial minority of the British manual working class, varying between about one-third and two-fifths, used to vote Conservative from the late 1940s until the late 1960s. Since this behaviour deviated from the class norm at the time and, for some sociologists and political commentators, appeared to be against workers' class interests, working-class conservatism was of considerable sociological interest for many years. Explanations included EMBOURGEOISEMENT, the DEFERENTIAL WORKER and the prevalence of a false CLASS CONSCIOUSNESS as the result of the ideological HEGEMONY of the ruling class. VOTING behaviour after the 1960s showed a relative weakening of class-based decisions for *all* classes, as more middle-class individuals voted Labour as well as with workers voting Conservative and with the rise of third parties, and sociologists lost interest in the conservative-voting manual worker.

SEE ALSO: *affluent worker; class imagery; class interest; dominant ideology thesis.*

world religions The idea that only certain religions are 'world religions' is problematic, since most religious movements claim universality. Classifications traditionally included the Abrahamic faiths (Judaism, Christianity and Islam) and the great Asian religions (Hinduism, Buddhism and Confucianism). These classifications also contain the problematic assumptions that each religion is homogeneous and that they are static. Alternative terminologies such as the 'religions of humanity' or the 'living religions' present their own difficulties. Classificatory schemes often refer also to 'religions in primal societies', which include the pre-literate religious systems of traditional societies and the new religious movements of the Third World, and the modern 'alternative religions' of Western society, especially the United States. A more neutral terminology classifies the major religions of the world into the following.

(1) *Abrahamic faiths*. (i) Judaism; (ii) Christianity; (iii) Islam.
(2) *Asian religions*. (i) Hinduism; (ii) Buddhism; (iii) Sikhism; (iv) Jainism.
(3) *Other Asian religions*. (i) Chinese religions; (ii) Japanese religions.

From a comparative perspective, the principal characteristics of the world religions can be analysed within the framework of the SOCIOLOGY OF RELIGION. We can classify religions from a sociological point of view in terms of prophetic leadership, emphasis on salvation and methods of recruitment, nature of formal AUTHORITY, conception of divinity, ritualistic practices and worship, and social organization (priesthood and CHURCH) and relation to the STATE.

(1.i) *Judaism*. This is a monotheistic belief system which is documented in the Bible and the Law (Torah). Its monotheistic doctrine was guarded by the prophets, who were the vehicles of religious CHARISMA. Judaism has no priesthood as such and its rabbinate is a stratum of learned interpreters of law and scripture. It has no church, but the synagogue is a house of assembly for study and prayer. Judaism does not seek to convert people, and a child is regarded as a Jew if it is born of a Jewish mother. Circumcision is the rite of passage by which boys enter into a covenant with God. Jewish theology came to be organized around the theme of God–Torah–community–land. Religious disobedience was in Jewish mythology punished by exile, leading to expectations of a Messiah who will return the people to their ancient homeland.

According to M. Weber in *Ancient Judaism* (1952), the quest for personal salvation was eventually codified into a formal RITUAL of dietary practices. Much controversy surrounds Weber's argument that Judaism did not contribute significantly to the rise of CAPITALISM.

Jews have been the target of much persecution, leading in the Middle Ages to the mysticism of the Kabbalah and in eighteenth-century Eastern Europe to the ecstatic piety of Hasidism. The European Jewish community suffered a GENOCIDE in the 1930s and 1940s, resulting in mass migration to the United States and Palestine. Jews who do not live in the Holy Land occupy the Diaspora, and the aspiration of many secular and religious Jews is to return to contemporary Israel. SECULARIZATION and political conflict have produced a wide variety of reform movements in contemporary Judaism, namely Orthodox, Reformist, Conservative and Reconstructionist.

SEE ALSO: *rites of passage*.

(1.ii) *Christianity*. A faith grounded in the teaching of Jesus, a prophet from the first-century Palestine, it was originally a social movement within Judaism. The term 'Christian' was first used in Antioch between 35 and 40 CE (Christian Era) to designate people who were attached to 'Christos', the Greek translation of the Hebrew word for Messiah. Christianity, unlike Islam, quickly formed a church or body of believers, of which Jesus was the head. The charisma of Jesus was thought to be stored in the church and distributed by the apostolic AUTHORITY of its bishops. The prophetic teaching of Jesus was eventually collected into the gospels of the New Testament. Christianity spread through the ancient world as an evangelical, literate, and monotheistic religion, although the trinitarian doctrine of the Father, Son and Holy Spirit has been interpreted by critics as a diminution of monotheism. Christianity also acquired the philosophical legacy of Greece and the juridical legacy of Rome. This combination produced an enduring tension of legitimation, namely reason versus revelation.

Christianity was originally characterized by MILLENARIANISM and recruited among the marginal and lower-class sectors of the ancient world. As a result, there has been an important radical component to Christian social teaching about JUSTICE. However, when in 313 Constantine established Christianity as the official religion of the Roman Empire, it became hierarchical and conservative. With the institutionalization of charisma, E. Troeltsch argued in *The Social Teaching of the Christian Churches* (1912) that Christianity oscillated between two dominant forms of organization, namely church and SECT. In the West, from the sixteenth century onwards, the Catholic Church claimed a continuity with early Christian practice, while the Protestant Church followed the teaching of John Calvin (1509–64) and Martin Luther (1483–1546), and the Anabaptists attempted to break the connection between church and state. Calvinism developed as a religious movement with a strong emphasis on INDIVIDUALISM, asceticism and discipline, which led WEBER in *The Protestant Ethic and the Spirit of Capitalism* (1930) to detect a meaningful connection between capitalism and the Protestant sects. In the nineteenth century, various pietist movements such as Wesleyan Methodism spread among the urban working class, leading MARX to argue that religion was the 'opium of the people'. The HALÉVY THESIS suggested that Methodism encouraged social EMBOURGEOISEMENT. In the twentieth century, evangelical sects in North America have been popular among black communities and ethnic minorities, thereby alleviating social ALIENATION. With secularization, the social authority of the Christian churches has declined in the West, but both the Catholic Church and the Christian sects continue to enjoy considerable growth through missionary work in Africa and South America. In Russia, following the collapse of organized communism after 1989, there has also been a significant revival of the Russian Orthodox Church, which is closely associated with Russian NATIONALISM. In North America, television evangelism has allowed Protestantism to exercise considerable influence over the Republican Party and right-wing politics.

SEE ALSO: *social movements.*

(1.iii) *Islam.* Often falsely referred to as Muhammadanism, Islam means 'submission to God'. The faith requires an absolute commitment to the idea of the unity of God. Muslims hence criticize Christianity for its trinitarian doctrine. Muhammad the Prophet of God received the Word of God (the Qur'an), but He was not a Messiah as such. Unlike Christianity, Islam has no church, no priesthood and no sacraments (baptism, confession or absolution). The three principal sources of authority for the Muslim community (*umma*) are the Qur'an, customs (*hadith*) and the Law (*Shariah*). As a religious system, Islam is defined by the Five Pillars: profession of faith (*Shahada*); worship (*Salat*); alms-giving (*Zakat*); fasting (*saum*); and pilgrimage (*Hajj*). Western observers of Islam have often argued that, while the Christian Church struggled to be ideologically orthodox, Islam sought conformity to practice.

Muhammad was born at about 570 (CE) and from around 610 he began to receive revelations which he proclaimed to the people of Mecca. His criticisms of idolatry were rejected and in 622 he made the *hijra* (migration) to Medina. Within ten years, Muhammad and his disciples had secured military control of central and western Arabia. Weber in *The Sociology of Religion* (1966) argued that Islam was a warrior religion which spread by military force. This view underestimates the importance of trade in the diffusion of Islam. Weber also claimed, in *The City* (1958b), that Muslim cities were merely military camps which did not support the growth of an urban

BOURGEOISIE. He claimed, too, in *Economy and Society* (1922), that Islamic law was arbitrary, because there was always a gap between Holy Law which remained fixed and social circumstances which changed. The inevitable gaps were filled by arbitrary law-finding procedures. These circumstances – military ethic, authoritarian urban structures, the absent bourgeoisie and irrational law – inhibited the development of capitalism. Weber's sociology of Islam has been criticized by B. S. Turner (1978) for its Orientalism.

When Muhammad died in 632, Islam was ruled by a series of caliphs who were descendants of the Prophet. The Umayyad dynasty ruled from Damascus (661–750), and the Abbasid dynasty from Baghdad (750–1258).

After the death of the fourth caliph, Ali (d. 661), the Muslim community split into the majority, who are referred to as Sunnis, and the Shi'ites, who over time became dominant in Persia (modern-day Iran). The Shi'ites were radical, because they came to believe that the true ruler of Islam was hidden but would return to restore justice. Shi'ism, with its belief in the Occultation of the Hidden Imam, rejected the secular authority of the caliphate. In the twentieth century, this radical rejection of secular authority provided a religious criticism of the rule of Pahlavi Shahs. The Ayatollah Khomeini (1902–89) subsequently led a political revolution against the Shah's regime.

Anthropologists like GELLNER have argued that Islam is divided between an urban tradition based on puritanical values, hierarchy and the Qur'an and a rural or nomadic tradition of Sufism which is based on saints, mysticism and folk traditions. Because the folk religion has a stronger social solidarity, nomadic elites periodically replace urban regimes. In North Africa, there has been a circulation of tribal elites. In the twentieth century, puritanical reformers have been able to capture the towns and impose their values, resulting in a decline of the authority of Sufi saints. Islamic fundamentalism – for example, the Muslim Brotherhood in Egypt, the Jamaat-i-Islami in Pakistan, Shi'ite radicalism in Iran, or the Islamique du Salut in Algeria – has spread through the Muslim world (in North Africa, the Middle East and in South-east Asia). As a movement, it has been anti-colonial and anti-Western, and has claimed that militant, reformist Islam can provide a radical social ideology as an alternative to both liberalism and communism. Western critics tend to see Islam, after the demise of communism, as the only global threat to Western political and economic dominance.

(2.i) *Hinduism.* Unlike the Abrahamic religions, Hinduism has no founder, no historical origin, no formal creed and no ecclesiastical organization. Hindu self-consciousness has evolved originally through its confrontation with Buddhism and Jainism, and more recently with Christianity and Islam. The term 'Hinduism' was first employed in English in 1829 to designate the religion of the Hindus. Evidence of religious life in India dates from around 4000 BCE in the Indus valley civilization. The Vedic religion flourished until 500 BCE, culminating in the literature of the Upanishads, which describe the doctrine of endless birth and rebirth (*samsara*) until the soul achieves liberation in *brahman*. The conditions of rebirth are determined by various acts (*karma*) performed in previous lives. During the classical period of Hinduism between 500 BCE to 500 CE, these doctrines were formulated as sacred texts in Sanskrit under the guardianship of the Brahmans, a religious ELITE. The Brahmans developed a series of religious texts which embraced the principal doctrine of *varnashrama dharma*, specifying the rights and duties of the four main social classes of society. The four varnas are Brahmans (priests and teachers), Kshatriya (rulers and warriors), Vaishyas (merchants and cultivators), and Shudras (manual labourers). Those marginal tribes and social groups that could not fulfil the Vedic prescriptions were regarded as outside Hindu culture and were 'untouchables'. These religious prescriptions formed the ideological basis of social STRATIFICATION by CASTE.

Hinduism is characterized by a diversity of religious beliefs and practices, but its central concept is *dharma*, which broadly describes the laws which govern nature and society. This law also describes the cycle of birth and rebirth, and the determinant consequences of all human actions. The *dharma–karma–samsara* doctrinal system specifies the core elements of Hindu belief. In *The Religion of India* (1958a), Weber argued that the soteriology (theory of human salvation) in Hinduism promoted withdrawal from the world in various forms of mysticism, with the result that no radical version of this-worldly asceticism and rational ethic could emerge. As a result, Hinduism did not contribute to the rise of capitalism.

(2.ii) *Buddhism*. This describes the teachings and practices of Siddhartha Guatama (563–483 BCE), who became the Buddha. The word 'Buddha' is not a proper name, but denotes 'The Enlightened One'. The Guatama Buddha was born into a wealthy Kshatriya clan in the foothills of the Himalayas. His teaching was a version of the *dharma–karma–samsara* doctrine of Hinduism, but Buddhism rejects the view that God or soul have any ultimate reality. The goal of Buddhist existence (Nirvana) is nothingness. Buddhist practices are demanding and only monks who adopt poverty and dedication can fulfil the obligations of Buddha's teaching. In *The Religion of India* (1958a), Weber described ancient Buddhism by contrast with Islam as an apolitical religious technology of meditation that was developed by wandering monks.

After the death of the Buddha, various branches of the religion developed separate and distinctive schools. Theravada (the Southern School or 'Lesser Vehicle') is a strict version which is prevalent in Sri Lanka, Burma, Thailand, Cambodia and Laos. Mahayana (the Northern School) has a broader base and is called the 'Greater Vehicle'; it is prevalent in Nepal, Tibet, China, Korea, Mongolia and Japan. Other forms include Zen Buddhism, which teaches inner awareness of spiritual truth through meditation, and Pure Land Buddhism, which developed millenarianism. In the twentieth century, Buddhism spread in Europe and North America, where intellectuals welcomed its philosophy of non-violence and its vegetarian diet. Buddhist meditation techniques have also been integrated into the psychoanalytic framework of FREUD.

(2.iii) *Sikhism*. A Punjabi religious movement whose formative period was 1469 to 1708, the religious doctrines of Sikhism were produced by a line of ten gurus, the most important of whom was Guru Nanak (1469–1539). Following a religious conversion, Guru Nanak became a religious teacher travelling widely throughout India and establishing a community. The Punjab term for disciple is *sikh*. The tenth leader, Gobind Singh, who was the community leader from 1675–1708, founded the Khalsa brotherhood, created a distinctive initiation ceremony and established a specific mode of dress including the turban, sword, short trousers and steel wristlet. The Khalsa community rejected their Hindu caste position by raising their status in the caste hierarchy to that of a warrior (Kshatriya caste). To prevent disputes over his succession, the tenth Guru invested his charismatic powers in the community itself (the Khalsa Panth).

Sikhism acquired a distinctive egalitarian ethos, partly through the incorporation of an agrarian militant group from northern India (the Jats) in the sixteenth century, who were opposed to the hierarchical Hindu traditions of Brahmanism. The other feature of Sikhism is that it was shaped by a profound military and cultural struggle against Islam of the Mughal or Timuri Empire in the eighteenth century. The Sikhs established their own crafts and industry, building their own city of Amritsar. In 1799, Maharaja Ranjit Singh established a Sikh kingdom after the capture of Lahore. The Sikh kingdom lasted until 1849 when, after the second Punjab war, it came under British control. Religious teaching and practice were revived under British rule by the Singh Sabha movement.

The Sikh community participated in the Independence struggle but found their homeland divided between India and Pakistan in 1947; in 1966, the movement for a separate Sikh state (Punjabi Suba) was partly successful in achieving some autonomy. There was an important migration of male Jat Sikhs out of the Punjab as a result of their recruitment into the British army when many were stationed in Hong Kong and Singapore. In the post-war period, there has been further Sikh migration (of approximately 10 per cent of the population) to Britain and the United States.

From a sociological perspective, Sikhism can be regarded as a reform movement that opposed the traditional caste structure of Hinduism, placed an emphasis on communal equality, and rejected both mysticism and asceticism as necessary for salvation.

(2.iv) *Jainism.* This religious tradition of India is derived from the teachings of the ancient *jinas* or 'those who overcame'. Twenty-four *jinas* are recognized by Jainism but Vardhamana Mahavira (540–468 BCE), a contemporary of Buddha, was its founding teacher. Born in north-east India, he practised detachment and poverty. The basic teaching of Jainism is the ability of human beings to conquer the limitations of physical existence through ascetic discipline. The goal of monastic asceticism is to release the soul from the infinite wheel of birth and rebirth. Lay asceticism developed between 500 and 1500 CE, involving the creation of manuals guiding lay religiosity through pilgrimages, temple worship and observation of holy days. Jainism rejects the idea of monotheism and has embraced the worship of images in Jain temples. In its social teaching, Jainism encourages an egalitarian ethic and participation in charitable works. Mohandas K. Gandhi, the Hindu nationalist leader of India, was influenced by the social teaching of Jain laymen like R. Mehta. Jains in modern India have not been less confined by hierarchical views of caste and SOCIAL MOBILITY has not been significantly constrained by their religious beliefs.

(3.i) *Chinese religions.* These were primarily concerned with the celebration of major events in the LIFE-CYCLE, where religious rituals played a significant part in the recognition of birth and death as rites of passage. In this traditional system, three forms of religious teaching were recognized: Confucian ethics in relation to public life, Taoist teachings about nature, and Buddhist ideas about salvation. In *The Religion of China* (1951), Weber, recognizing that there was no special word for 'religion' in the Chinese language, argued that religious rituals had a traditional function in regulating secular activities – getting married, having children and supporting the family.

Confucius (551–479 BCE) was a famous Chinese philosopher who, in his early years, wandered from state to state advising rulers about social and administrative reform. His main achievements were to provide a code of humanistic ethics for the conduct of everyday life. The key components of his teaching were the notions of respect and restraint. Government had to be responsible for its actions and could not depend on force alone. Weber (1951) regarded Confucianism as 'the gentleman ideal' which provided an ethical code for the educated bureaucratic stratum of the Chinese patrimonial administration. As a code of this-worldly conduct, it was not concerned with questions of religious grace and salvation.

Although the 'cultural revolution' in 1966 under the leadership of Chairman Mao Zedong (1893–1976) during the communist period had a radical impact on traditional society, these traditional patterns of religious life survived among the peasantry and in the countryside. With the subsequent growth of capitalist enterprises in mainland China and the rise of so-called 'tiger' economies, there has been much discussion about the compatibility of Confucianism with both capitalism and democracy. One argument is that Confucianism is a basis for human rights because it is less individualistic than liberalism.

(3.ii) *Japanese religions.* The religious traditions of Japan can be divided into the formal religions of Buddhism, Confucianism and Christianity, and the local religious tradition of Shinto. The term Shinto means 'way of the gods' and was introduced in the eighth century to distinguish Buddhism from Shintoism. Shinto tradition was derived from ancient agricultural ceremonies and as such it had no theology or formal system of belief. The emperor was the chief priest of Shinto belief and practice, and hence the unity of society depended on this close relationship between the emperor, the state system and Shinto. In the nineteenth century, Shinto became the official state religion. This religious system, which lasted from 701 until the fall of Japan in the Second World War in 1945, ensured that loyalty to the state was a religious duty. Shinto also guaranteed, through devotions to shrines, the continuity of family and clan as sources of authority. The Shinto calendar has been associated with celebrations and festivals at places of significant geographical importance; for example, the powers of nature are specifically associated with sacred mountains. Its main focus has been on the issue of avoiding pollution and employing rites of purification. Its principal ethical teachings have been concerned with the proper conduct of the community in terms of the avoidance of pollution.

Christian and Buddhist missions were reluctantly tolerated only where they too embraced loyalty to the emperor. The post-war period brought in a constitution which formally promoted religious freedom and the separation of state and religious institutions. There has been much inconclusive debate as to whether Shintoism (as the religion of emperor-worship) did or did not delay the MODERNIZATION of Japanese culture.

READING: De Bary (1998)

world-system theory A perspective on the origins and development of capitalism as a global economic system, this theory was originally outlined by I. Wallerstein (1974). The theory argues: (1) the economic organization of modern CAPITALISM is on a global, not national, basis; (2) this system is composed of core regions, which are economically and politically dominant, and peripheries which are economically dependent on the core; (3) core regions are developed as industrial systems of production, whereas the peripheries provide raw materials, being thereby dependent on prices set in the core regions; (4) there are also semi-peripheries which have a mixture of social and economic characteristics from both core and periphery; (5) this world economic order began to develop in Europe in the fifteenth century with the slow evolution of capitalist agriculture. Wallerstein makes the important point that pre-modern empires had a common political–bureaucratic structure but diverse economic systems, whereas the modern world has diverse political systems but a common interlocking economic organization. The principal implication of this approach is that we cannot understand the nation state in isolation, because the 'internal' economic processes of any society will be completely shaped by its location in the world system.

World-system theory has been criticized on the following issues: (1) it is not entirely evident that peripheral societies are underdeveloped by core regions, because most trade and investment takes place between societies which are already developed and industrialized; (2) it is not clear how socialist societies fit into the world system; (3) it is not clear that external forces of the world economy are more significant for social change than internal processes (such as class struggle); (4) by emphasizing economic processes, world-system theory has neglected cultural change, and some theorists, such as R. Robertson and F. Lechner (1985), have argued that there is a world system of global culture which is entirely autonomous from the economic processes of capitalism. During the 1990s, the concept of GLOBALIZATION largely replaced world-system theory.

SEE ALSO: *centre/periphery; dependency theory; feudalism; imperialism; industrialization; new international division of labour; Marxist sociology; peasants.*

READING: Corbridge (1986)

world view A term used synonymously with world vision and the German *Weltanschauung*, world view refers to the set of beliefs constituting an outlook on the world characteristic of a particular social group, be it a social class, generation or religious sect. For example, the world view of the nineteenth-century entrepreneur is said to comprise individualism, thrift, a sense of family propriety, moral order and moderate religious devotion. Sociologists of knowledge will want to explain why a particular group holds a particular world view. However, the analytical problem consists in what justification the sociologist has for putting particular elements into a world view, for it will never be the case that all members of a group believe all elements of the world view that is ascribed to them.

SEE ALSO: *hermeneutics.*

Wrong, Dennis Hume (b. 1923) Formerly editor of *Social Research* (1962–4) and *Contemporary Sociology* (1972–4), and professor of sociology at New York University, his early work was concerned with demography (1966), but he is best known for his criticisms of FUNCTIONALISM, theories of SOCIALIZATION and functionalist theories of social STRATIFICATION. His criticisms emphasized the continuing importance of conflict, opposition and resistance to cultural integration, against the sociology of PARSONS. In his evaluation of socialization theory, Wrong drew upon the work of FREUD, to reassert the significance of the conflict between sexual needs and social order within the Freudian tradition. Many of these influential articles have been reprinted in *Sceptical Sociology* (1977). In his research on the perennial problems of POWER, Wrong (1979) has identified various forms of power, such as force, manipulation, persuasion and AUTHORITY, and located the bases of power in various individual and collective resources. While Wrong has made a significant contribution to modern sociological theory, his influence spreads far beyond the formal academy, especially through his contributions to the journals *Commentary* and *Dissent*. His essays and commentaries on intellectuals and politics were published as *The Modern Condition* (1998).

Y

youth culture Within the last sixty years or so, 'youth' has become a more sharply defined category in most Western countries. Young people have developed their own culture and a distinctive social identity which is more clearly differentiated from that of their parents. Three general features distinguish youth culture. (1) It is a culture of leisure rather than work. (2) Social relations are organized round the peer group rather than families or individual friends. (3) Youth groups are particularly interested in 'style', by which is meant an interest in external markers such as the use of distinctive language forms, taste in music or clothes, the adoption of particular leisure pursuits or a concern with personal appearance. There are a number of reasons for the appearance of youth culture, the most important of which are the rise in the disposable income available to young people and a lengthening of the period of childhood into adulthood, caused partly by a greater involvement in part-time or full-time education up to the age of 21.

It may be misleading to talk of one single youth culture. Rather there is a multiplicity of youth cultures, differentiated, for example, by social class, gender and ethnicity. Clearly, young people from different social classes or ethnic groups have very different attitudes, tastes, ways of behaving and styles, as do young men and women. Some youth cultures are also more spectacular, dressing or behaving in a very flamboyant way which draws the attention and censure of parents, teachers or the police and courts. Examples of these spectacular cultures are mods, rockers, skinheads, punks and crusties. Public attention has concentrated on these groups because they seem to be defiant and oppositional. Until fairly recently, sociologists also focused on these groups and on why working-class youth cultures seem to be more spectacular than middle-class ones. Answers to the questions were heavily influenced by S. Hall and T. Jefferson (1976), who argued that there are certain problems faced by working-class youth because of their class position which are intensified by their age. The adoption of a particular culture provides an IDENTITY, rewards of status and approval and some sense of being in control. The adoption of a youth culture of this kind is therefore a *symbolic* resistance to the definition of working-class life promulgated by the wider society.

A large number of criticisms have been levelled at the Hall and Jefferson approach – the difficulty of interpreting symbolic resistance, the lack of empirical evidence, the presence of spectacular middle-class cultures and the obvious fact that most young people do not belong to spectacular cultures. As far as this last point is concerned, there is evidence that most young people are very like their parents in their attitudes and are, in general, conforming and conventional. This does not of course mean the more conforming young people do not have distinctive cultures based on leisure, peer group and style. Recent arguments suggest that the commercialization of youth style has eliminated the spectacular youth cultures of the 1960s, 1970s and early 1980s. An interest in style no longer signifies resistance of any kind but only conveys a loose sense of identity as part of CONSUMER SOCIETY.

SEE ALSO: *adolescence; aging; consumption; generation; subculture.*

Z

zero sum See: GAME THEORY.

Zola, Irving Kenneth (1935–94) Mortimer Gryzmish Professor of Human Relations at Brandeis University, he was founder-editor of *Disability Studies Quarterly* and contributed to the study of MEDICALIZATION. His *Missing Pieces* (1982) shaped the SOCIOLOGY OF HEALTH AND ILLNESS and the study of EMBODIMENT.

SEE ALSO: *stigma*.

zone of transition E. Burgess (1925) invented the term 'zone in transition' in his CONCENTRIC ZONE THEORY, although the common usage is now 'zone of transition', to describe the area of the city immediately adjacent to the city centre. As economic activity in the centre expands, land in the zone of transition is developed for offices, big shops or large hotels, for example. As a result, the zone of transition is typically a run-down area, landlords being reluctant to improve property since they are waiting for land values to rise so that they can sell profitably. In Burgess' view, the outcome is that the zone of transition (or *inner city*, in contemporary idiom) is an area of marginal light manufacturing or service industry, houses in multi-occupation, a shifting population without any sense of community and a high crime rate. Many studies have confirmed this view of the inner city but others have suggested that there may be more community life in slums than there appears.

SEE ALSO: *Chicago School; urban ecology; urban way of life*.

Bibliography

Where a book was originally published in a foreign language, or some time ago, we have given the original date of publication in the text and in the bibliography, followed by bibliographical details of an accessible English edition. In many cases, as with the work of M. Weber or J. Habermas, for example, the work available in English is extracted or selected from the original foreign-language source. For these references we have given the date of the first English edition, not of the often rather different original.

Abbott, P., and Wallace, C. (1990), *An Introduction to Sociology: Feminist perspectives*, London, Routledge

Abel-Smith, B., and Townsend, P. (1965), *The Poor and the Poorest*, London, Bell

Abell, P. (2000), 'Sociological theory and rational choice theory', in B. S. Turner (ed.), *The Blackwell Companion to Social Theory*, 2nd edn, Oxford, Blackwell, pp. 223–44

Abercrombie, N. (1980), *Class, Structure and Knowledge*, Oxford, Blackwell

Abercrombie, N., Hill, S., and Turner, B. S. (1980), *The Dominant Ideology Thesis*, London, Allen & Unwin

Abercrombie, N., Hill, S., and Turner, B. S. (1986), *Sovereign Individuals of Capitalism*, London, Allen & Unwin

Abercrombie, N., and Longhurst, B. (1998), *Audiences*, London, Sage

Abercrombie, N., and Urry, J. (1983), *Capital, Labour and the Middle Classes*, London, Allen & Unwin

Abercrombie, N., and Warde, A. (1992), *Social Change in Contemporary Britain*, Cambridge, Polity Press

Abercrombie, N., Warde, A., Soothill, K., Walby, S., and Urry, J. (1994), *Contemporary British Society*, 2nd edn, Cambridge, Polity Press

Abrams, P. (1982), *Historical Sociology*, Shepton Mallet, Open Books

Adam, B. (1990), *Time and Social Theory*, Cambridge, Polity Press

Adorno, T. W. (1967), *Prisms: Cultural criticism and society*, London, Spearman

Adorno, T. W. (1974), *Minima Moralia: Reflections from a damaged life*, London, New Left Books

Adorno, T. W., Frankel-Brunswik, E., Levinson, D. J., and Sanford, R. N. (1950), *The Authoritarian Personality*, New York, Harper

Adorno, T. W., and Horkheimer, M. (1973), *Dialectic of Enlightenment*, London, Allen Lane The Penguin Press

Aglietta, M. (1979), *A Theory of Capitalist Regulation: The US experience*, London, New Left Books

Albrow, M. (1990), *Max Weber's Construction of Social Theory*, Basingstoke, Macmillan

Albrow, M. (1996), *The Global Age: State and society beyond modernity*, Cambridge, Polity Press

Albrow, M. C. (1970), *Bureaucracy*, London, Macmillan

Ald, R. (1970), *The Youth Communes*, New York, Tower

Alexander, J. C. (1982), *Theoretical Logic in Sociology*, vol. 1, London, Routledge & Kegan Paul

Alexander, J. C. (1984), 'The Parsons revival in German sociology', in R. Collins (ed.), *Sociological Theory 1984*, San Francisco, Jossey-Bass, pp. 394–412

Allan, G. (1979), *Friendship and Kinship*, London, Allen & Unwin

Allan, G. (1985), *Family Life*, Oxford, Blackwell

Allan, G. (1989), *Friendship*, London, Harvester Wheatsheaf

Almond, G. A., and Powell, G. B. (1978), *Comparative Politics*, 2nd edn, Boston, Little-Brown

Almond, G. A., and Verba, S. (1963), *The Civic Culture: Political attitudes and democracy in five nations*, Princeton, Princeton University Press

Althusser, L. (1966), *For Marx*, London, Allen Lane The Penguin Press, 1969

Althusser, L. (1971), *Lenin and Philosophy and Other Essays*, London, New Left Books

Althusser, L., and Balibar, E. (1968), *Reading Capital*, London, New Left Books, 1970

Alvesson, M. (1993), *Cultural Perspectives on Organizations*, Cambridge, Cambridge University Press

Amin, S. (1976), *Unequal Development: An essay on the social formations of peripheral capitalism*, Hassocks, Harvester Press

Amsden, A. H. (ed.) (1980), *The Economics of Women and Work*, Harmondsworth, Penguin Books

Anderson, M. (1975), *Sociology of the Family*, Harmondsworth, Penguin Books

Anderson, P. (1974), *Passages from Antiquity to Feudalism*, London, New Left Books

Anderson, P. (1976a), 'The Antimonies of Antonio Gramsci', *New Left Review*, no. 100, pp. 5–80

Anderson, P. (1976b), *Considerations on Western Marxism*, London, New Left Books

Andorka, R. (1978), *Determinants of Fertility in Advanced Societies*, New York, Free Press

Anthony, P. O. (1977), *The Ideology of Work*, London, Tavistock

Appadurai, A. (1986), 'Introduction: commodities and the politics of value', in A. Appadurai (ed.), *The Social Life of Things*, Cambridge, Cambridge University Press

Apter, D. W. (1965), *The Politics of Modernization*, Chicago, Chicago University Press

Aries, P. (1960), *Centuries of Childhood*, Harmondsworth, Penguin Books

Aron, R. (1935), *German Sociology*, London, Heinemann, 1957

Aron, R. (1938), *Introduction to the Philosophy of History: An essay on the limits of historical objectivity*, Boston, Beacon Press, 1961

Aron, R. (1951), *The Century of Total War*, New York, Doubleday, 1954

Aron, R. (1955), *The Opium of the Intellectuals*, London, Secker & Warburg, 1957

Aron, R. (1961), *Peace and War: A theory of international relations*, New York, Doubleday, 1966

Aron, R. (1963a), *The Great Debate: Theories of nuclear strategy*, New York, Doubleday, 1965

Aron, R. (1963b), *Eighteen Lectures on Industrial Society*, London, Weidenfeld & Nicolson, 1967

Aron, R. (1965a), *Democracy and Totalitarianism*, New York, Praeger, 1969

Aron, R. (1965b), *An Essay on Freedom*, New York, World, 1970

Aron, R. (1965c), *Main Currents in Sociological Thought*, 2 vols, New York, Basic Books, 1965, 1967

Aron, R. (1966), *The Industrial Society: Three essays on ideology and development*, New York, Simon & Schuster

Aron, R. (1968a), *De Gaulle, Israel and the Jews*, New York, Praeger, 1969

Aron, R. (1968b), *The Elusive Revolution: Anatomy of a student revolt*, New York, Praeger, 1969

Aron, R. (1969), *Progress and Disillusion: The dialectics of modern society*, New York, Praeger

Aron, R. (1973a), *History and the Dialectic of Violence: An analysis of Sartre's* Critique de la raison dialectique, Oxford, Blackwell, 1975

Aron, R. (1973b), *The Imperial Republic: The United States and the world 1945–1973*, Englewood Cliffs, NJ, Prentice Hall, 1974

Aron, R. (1976), *Clausewitz*, London, Routledge & Kegan Paul, 1983

Aron, R. (1978), 'Introduction' to M. B. Conant (ed.), *Politics and History: Selected essays by Raymond Aron*, New York, Free Press, pp. xvii–xxx

Atkinson, A. B. (ed.) (1980), *Wealth, Income and Inequality*, 2nd edn, Oxford, Oxford University Press

Atkinson, J. M. (1978), *Discovering Suicide*, London, Macmillan

Atkinson, P. (1985), *Language, Structure and Reproduction: An introduction to the sociology of Basil Bernstein*, London, Methuen

Atoji, Y. (1984), *Sociology at the Turn of the Century: On G. Simmel in comparison with F. Toennies, M. Weber and E. Durkheim*, Tokyo, Dobunkan

Austin, J. L. (1962), *How to Do Things with Words*, Oxford, Clarendon Press

Averitt, R. T. (1968), *The Dual Economy: The dynamics of American industry structure*, New York, Norton

Axelrod, R. M. (1984), *The Evolution of Cooperation*, New York, Basic Books

Babbage, C. (1832), *On the Economy of Machinery and Manufactures*, London, Knight

Bakhtin, M. (1981), *The Dialogic Imagination*, Austin, University of Texas Press

Bailey, A., and Llobera, J. R. (eds) (1981), *The Asiatic Mode of Production: Science and politics*, London, Routledge & Kegan Paul

Baker, W. (1984), 'The social structure of a national securities market', *American Journal of Sociology*, vol. 89, pp. 775–811

Banks, O. (1976), *The Sociology of Education*, 3rd edn, London, Batsford

Baran, P. (1957), *The Political Economy of Growth*, New York, Monthly Review Press

Barbalet, J. M. (1998), *Emotion, Social Theory and Social Structure: A macrosociological approach*, Cambridge, Cambridge University Press

Barker, E. (1984), *The Making of a Moonie*, Oxford, Blackwell

Barnard, A., and Spencer, J. (eds) (1996), *Encyclopaedia of Social and Cultural Anthropology*, London, Routledge

Barratt Brown, M. (1974), *The Economics of Imperialism*, Harmondsworth, Penguin Books

Barratt, M. (1991), *The Politics of Truth*, Cambridge, Polity Press

Barratt, M., and McIntosh, M. (1982), *The Anti-Social Family*, London, Verso

Barthes, R. (1953), *Writing Degree Zero*, London, Cape, 1967

Barthes, R. (1957), *Mythologies*, London, Cape, 1972

Barthes, R. (1970), *S/Z*, London, Cape, 1975

Barthes, R. (1971), *Sade, Fourier, Loyola*, London, Cape, 1977

Barthes, R. (1975), *The Pleasure of the Text*, London, Cape, 1976

Barton, R. (1959), *Institutional Neurosis*, Bristol, Wright

Bataille, G. (1955), *Prehistoric Painting: Lascaux or the birth of art*, London, Macmillan

Bataille, G. (1962), *Eroticism*, London, Boyers, 1987

Bataille, G. (1976), *The Accursed Share*, 3 vols, New York Zone Books, 1988

Bataille, G. (1988), *Theory of Religion*, New York Zone Books

Batstone, E., Boraston, I., and Frenkel, S. (1978), *The Social Organization of Strikes*, Oxford, Blackwell

Baudrillard, J. (1972), *For a Critique of the Political Economy of the Sign*, St Louis, Telos Press, 1981

Baudrillard, J. (1973), *The Mirror of Production*, St Louis, Telos Press

Baudrillard, J. (1976), *L'Echange symbolique et la mort*, Paris, Gallimard

Baudrillard, J. (1978), *In the Shadow of the Silent Majorities*, New York, Semiotexte, 1983

Baudrillard, J. (1979), *Seduction*, London, Macmillan, 1990

Baudrillard, J. (1981), *Simulations*, New York, Semiotexte, 1983

Baudrillard, J. (1983), *Fatal Strategies*, London, Pluto Press

Baudrillard, J. (1986), *America*, London, Verso, 1988

Bauman, Z. (1973), *Culture as Praxis*, London, Routledge

Bauman, Z. (1976), *Socialism: The active utopia*, London, George Allen & Unwin

Bauman, Z. (1978), *Hermeneutics and Social Science*, New York, Columbia University Press

Bauman, Z. (1982), *Memories of Class: The pre-history and after-life of class*, London, Routledge & Kegan Paul

Bauman, Z. (1987), *Legislators and Interpreters: On modernity, postmodernity and intellectuals*, Cambridge, Polity Press

Bauman, Z. (1989), *Modernity and the Holocaust*, Cambridge, Polity Press

Bauman, Z. (1991), *Modernity and Ambivalence*, Cambridge, Polity Press

Bauman, Z. (1992), *Intimations of Postmodernity*, London, Routledge

Bauman, Z. (1993), *Postmodern Ethics*, Oxford, Blackwell

Bauman, Z. (1995), *Life in Fragments: Essays in postmodern morality*, Oxford, Blackwell

Baumgarten, M. P. (1998), *The Social Organization of Law*, Orlando, Fla., Academic Press

Beauvoir, S. de (1949), *The Second Sex*, Harmondsworth, Penguin Press, 1972

Beauvoir, S. de (1970), *Old Age*, London, Weidenfeld & Nicolson, 1972

Bechhofer, F., and Elliott, B. (eds) (1981), *The Petite Bourgeoisie: Comparative studies of the Uneasy Stratum*, London, Macmillan

Beck, U. (1992), *Risk Society: Towards a new modernity*, London, Sage

Beck, U., Giddens, A., and Lash, S. (1994), *Reflexive Modernization: Politics, tradition and aesthetics in the modern social order*, Cambridge, Polity Press

Becker, H. (1932), *Systematic Sociology*, New York, Wiley

Becker, H. S. (1963), *Outsiders: Studies in the sociology of deviance*, Glencoe, Free Press

Becker, H. S. (1970a), *Campus Power Struggle*, Chicago, Aldine

Becker, H. S. (1970b), *Sociological Work, Method and Substance*, Chicago, Chicago University Press

Becker, H. S., *et al.* (1961), *Boys in White: Student culture in the medical world*, Chicago, Chicago University Press

Becker, H. S., *et al.* (1968), *Making the Grade: The academic side of college life*, New York, Wiley

Bell, C. (1968), *Middle-Class Families*, London, Routledge & Kegan Paul

Bell, C., and Newby, H. (1971), *Community Studies*, London, Allen & Unwin

Bell, D. (1960), *The End of Ideology*, New York, Collier

Bell, D. (1974), *The Coming of Post-Industrial Society*, New York, Basic Books

Bell, D. (1976), *The Cultural Contradictions of Capitalism*, New York, Basic Books

Bellah, R. N. (1967), 'Civil religion in America', *Daedalus*, vol. 96, pp. 1–21

Bellah, R. N. (1970), *Beyond Belief*, New York, Harper & Row

Bellah, R. N. (1974), 'American civil religion in the 1970s', in R. Richey and D. Jones (eds), *American Civil Religion*, New York, Harper & Row, pp. 255–72

Bellah, R. N. (1975), *The Broken Covenant*, New York, Seabury

Bellah, R. N., and Hammond, P. E. (1980), *Varieties of Civil Religion*, New York, Harper & Row

Belsey, C. (1980), *Critical Practice*, London, Methuen

Ben-David, J. (1963–4), 'Professions in the class system of present day societies: a trend report and bibliography', *Current Sociology*, vol. 12

Bendix, R. (1956), *Work and Authority in Industry: Ideologies of management in the course of industrialization*, New York, Wiley; 2nd edn, New York, Harper, 1963

Bendix, R. (1960), *Max Weber: An intellectual portrait*, New York, Doubleday

Bendix, R. (1964), *Nation-Building and Citizenship: Studies of our changing social order*, New York, Wiley

Benjamin, W. (1973a), *Illuminations*, London, Fontana

Benjamin, W. (1973b), *Understanding Brecht*, London, New Left Books

Benjamin, W. (1979), *One Way Street*, London, New Left Books

Benoist, J.-M. (1975), *The Structural Revolution*, London, Weidenfeld & Nicolson, 1978

Benton, T. (1977), *Philosophical Foundations of the Three Sociologies*, London, Routledge & Kegan Paul

Benton, T. (1984), *The Rise and Fall of Marxism*, London, Macmillan

Berg, I. (ed.) (1981), *Sociological Perspectives on Labor Markets*, New York, Academic Press

Berger, B., and Berger, P. L. (1983), *The War Over the Family*, New York, Doubleday

Berger, P. L. (1963), *Invitation to Sociology*, New York, Doubleday

Berger, P. L. (1967), *The Sacred Canopy*, New York, Doubleday

Berger, P. L. (1977), *Facing up to Modernity*, New York, Basic Books

Berger, P. L. (1986), *The Capitalist Revolution*, New York, Basic Books

Berger, P. L. (1997), *Redeeming Laughter: The comic dimension of human experience*, Berlin, Walter de Gruyter

Berger, P. L., and Berger, B. (1976), *Sociology: A biographical approach*, Harmondsworth, Penguin Books

Berger, P. L., Berger, B. and Kellner, P. (1973), *The Homeless Mind*, New York, Random House

Berger, P. L., and Luckmann, T. (1963), 'Sociology of religion and sociology of knowledge', *Sociology and Social Research*, vol. 74, pp. 417–27

Berger, P. L., and Luckmann, T. (1967), *The Social Construction of Reality*, New York, Doubleday

Berle, A. A., and Means, G. C. (1932), *The Modern Corporation and Private Property*, New York, Macmillan

Bernstein, B. B. (1961), 'Social class and linguistic development: a theory of social learning', in A. Halsey, J. Floud and C. A. Anderson (eds), *Education, Economy and Society*, New York, Free Press, pp. 288–314

Bernstein, B. B. (1971, 1973, 1975), *Class, Codes and Control*, vols 1–3, London, Routledge & Kegan Paul

Bernstein, B. B. (1977), *Class, Codes and Control*, vol. 3, 2nd edn, London, Routledge & Kegan Paul

Bernstein, H. (1973), *Underdevelopment and Development*, Harmondsworth, Penguin Books

Bernstein, R. J. (1976), *The Restructuring of Social and Political Theory*, Oxford, Blackwell

Beyer, P. (1994), *Religion and Globalization*, London, Sage

Biddle, B. J., and Thomas, E. J. (eds) (1966), *Role Theory: Concepts and research*, New York, Wiley

Billig, M. (1991), *Ideology and Opinions*, London, Sage

Bilton, T., Bonnett, K., Jones, P., Sheard, K., Stanworth, M., and Webster, A. (1996), *Introductory Sociology*, 3rd edn, Basingstoke, Macmillan

Blackburn, R. M., and Mann, M. (1979), *The Working Class in the Labour Market*, London, Macmillan

Blackburn, R. M., and Prandy, K. (1965), 'White-collar unionization: a conceptual framework', *British Journal of Sociology*, vol. 16, pp. 111–22

Blalock, H. M., and Blalock, A. B. (eds) (1968), *Methodology in Social Research*, New York, McGraw-Hill

Blane, D. (1985), 'An assessment of the Black Report's "explanations of health inequalities"', *Sociology of Health & Illness*, vol. 7 (3), pp. 423–45

Blau, F. D., and Ferber, M. A. (1985), 'Women in the labor market: the last twenty years', in L. Larwood, A. H. Stromberg and B. A. Guteck (eds), *Women and Work: An annual review*, Beverly Hills, Sage, pp. 19–49

Blau, P. M. (1955), *The Dynamics of Bureaucracy: A study of interpersonal relations in two government agencies*, Chicago, Chicago University Press

Blau, P. M. (1964), *Exchange and Power in Social Life*, New York, Wiley

Blau, P. M., and Duncan, O. D. (1967), *The American Occupational Structure*, New York, Wiley

Blau, P. M., and Schoenherr, R. A. (1971), *The Structure of Organizations*, New York, Basic Books

Blau, P. M., and Scott, W. R. (1962), *Formal Organizations: A comparative approach*, San Francisco, Chandler

Blauner, R. (1964), *Alienation and Freedom*, Chicago, Chicago University Press

Bocock, R. (1983), *Sigmund Freud*, London, Tavistock

Bonar, J. (1942), *Malthus and his Work*, London, Cass

Bonte, P. (1981), 'Marxist theory and anthropological analysis: the study of nomadic pastoralist societies', in J. S. Kahn and J. R. Llobera (eds), *The Anthropology of Pre-capitalist Societies*, London, Macmillan, pp. 22–56

Booth, C. (1889–91), *Life and Labour of the People in London*, London, Macmillan

Bott, E. (1957), *Family and Social Network*, London, Tavistock

Bottomley, K., and Pease, K. (1986), *Crime and Punishment: Interpreting the data*, Milton Keynes, Open University Press

Bottomore, T. B. (1962), *Sociology*, London, Allen & Unwin

Bottomore, T. B. (1965), *Classes in Modern Society*, London, Allen & Unwin

Bottomore, T. B. (1966), *Elites and Society*, Harmondsworth, Penguin Books

Bottomore, T. B. (1975), *Marxist Sociology*, London, Macmillan

Bottomore, T. B. (1978), 'Marxism and sociology', in T. B. Bottomore and R. Nisbet (eds), *A History of Sociological Analysis*, New York, Basic Books, 1978, pp. 118–48

Bottomore, T. B. (1979), *Political Sociology*, London, Hutchinson

Bottomore, T. B. (ed.) (1983), *A Dictionary of Marxist Thought*, Oxford, Blackwell

Bottomore, T. B. (1984), *Sociology and Socialism*, Brighton, Wheatsheaf

Bottomore, T. B. (1985), *Theories of Modern Capitalism*, London, Allen & Unwin

Bottomore, T. B., and Goode, P. (eds) (1978), *Austro-Marxism*, Oxford, Oxford University Press

Bottomore, T. B., and Nisbet, R. (1978a), 'Structuralism', in T. B. Bottomore and R. Nisbet (eds), *A History of Sociological Analysis*, New York, Basic Books, 1978, pp. 557–98

Bottomore, T. B., and Nisbet, R. A. (eds) (1978b), *A History of Sociological Analysis*, New York, Basic Books

Bottomore, T. B., and Rubel, M. (eds) (1961), *Karl Marx: Selected writings in sociology and social philosophy*, Harmondsworth, Penguin Books

Bourdieu, P. (1972), *Outline of a Theory of Practice*, Cambridge, Cambridge University Press, 1977

Bourdieu, P. (1973), 'Cultural reproduction and social reproduction', in R. Brown (ed.), *Knowledge, Education and Cultural Change*, London, Tavistock, pp. 71–112

Bourdieu, P. (1979), *Distinction: A social critique of the judgement of taste*, London, Routledge & Kegan Paul, 1984

Bourdieu, P. (1980), *The Logic of Practice*, Cambridge, Polity Press, 1990

Bourdieu, P. (1984a), *Homo Academicus*, Stanford, Stanford University Press, 1988

Bourdieu, P. (1984b), *Sociology in Question*, London, Sage, 1993

Bourdieu, P. (1987), *In Other Words: Essays towards a reflexive sociology*, Cambridge, Polity Press, 1990

Bourdieu, P. (1988), *The Political Ontology of Martin Heidegger*, Cambridge, Polity Press, 1991

Bourdieu, P. (1992), *The Rules of Art*, Cambridge, Polity Press, 1996

Bourdieu, P. (1993), *The Field of Cultural Production*, Cambridge, Polity Press

Bourdieu, P. (1990), Boltanski, L., Castel, R., Camberedon, J.-C., and Schnapper, D., *Photography: A middlebrow art*, Cambridge, Polity Press

Bourdieu, P., and Passeron, J.-C. (1970), *Reproduction in Education, Society and Culture*, London, Sage, 1990

Bourdieu, P., and Wacquant, L. J. D. (1992), *An Invitation to Reflexive Sociology*, Cambridge, Polity Press

Bourricaud, F. (1981), *The Sociology of Talcott Parsons*, Chicago, Chicago University Press

Bowlby, J. (1953), *Child Care and the Growth of Love*, Harmondsworth, Penguin Books

Bowles, S., and Gintis, H. (1976), *Schooling in Capitalist America*, London, Routledge & Kegan Paul

Box, S. (1971), *Deviance, Reality and Society*, London, Holt, Rinehart & Winston

Box, S. (1983), *Power, Crime, and Mystification*, London and New York, Tavistock

Boyer, R. (1990), *The Regulation School: A critical introduction*, New York, Columbia University Press

Boyers, R., and Orrill, R. (1972), *Laing and Anti-Psychiatry*, Harmondsworth, Penguin Books

Bradley, K., and Gelb, A. (1983), *Cooperation at Work*, London, Heinemann Educational Books

Braudel, F. (1966), *The Mediterranean and the Mediterranean World of Philip II*, Glasgow, Collins, 1972–3

Braudel, F. (1969), *On History*, Chicago, Chicago University Press, 1980

Braudel, F. (1979), *Civilization and Capitalism*, Glasgow, Collins, 1981–2

Braverman, H. (1974), *Labor and Monopoly Capitalism: The degradation of work in the twentieth century*, New York, Monthly Review Press

Bredemeier, H. C. (1979), 'Exchange theory', in T. Bottomore and R. Nisbet (eds), *A History of Sociological Analysis*, London, Heinemann Educational Books, pp. 418–56

Brenner, R., and Glick, S. (1991), 'The regulation approach: theory and history', *New Left Review*, no. 188, July/August, pp. 45–119

Bronner, S. E., and Kellner, D. M. (eds) (1989), *Critical Theory and Society: A reader*, London, Routledge

Brown, M., and Madge, N. (1982), *Despite the Welfare State*, London, Heinemann Educational Books

Brown, R. (1976), 'Women as employees: some comments on research in industrial sociology', in D. L. Barker and S. Allen (eds), *Dependence and Exploitation in Work and Marriage*, London, Longman, pp. 1–46

Brown, R. (1992), *Understanding Industrial Organisation*, London, Routledge

Buckley, W. (1967), *Sociology and Modern Systems Theory*, Englewood Cliffs, NJ, Prentice Hall

Burawoy, M. (1979), *Manufacturing Consent: Changes in the labor process under monopoly capitalism*, Chicago, Chicago University Press

Burgess, E. W. (1925), 'The Growth of the City' in R. E. Park *et al.*, *The City*, Chicago, University of Chicago Press

Burke, P. (1980), *Sociology and History*, London, Allen & Unwin

Burnham, J. (1941), *The Managerial Revolution: What is happening in the world*, New York, Day

Burns, T. (1992), *Erving Goffman*, London, Routledge

Burns, T., and Stalker, G. M. (1961), *The Management of Innovation*, London, Tavistock

Burridge, K. O. L. (1960), *Mambu – a Melanesian Millennium*, London, Methuen

Burrow, J. W. (1966), *Evolution and Society: A study of Victorian social theory*, Cambridge, Cambridge University Press

Burt, R. S. (1992), *Structural Holes: The social structure of competition*, Cambridge, Mass., Harvard University Press

Butler, D. E., and Stokes, D. (1974), *Political Change in Britain*, 2nd edn, London, Macmillan

Callinicos, A. (1976), *Althusser's Marxism*, London, Pluto Press

Canguilhem, G. (1996), *The Normal and the Pathological*, New York, Zone Books, 1989

Canovan, M. (1981), *Populism*, New York, Harcourt Brace

Cant, S., and Sharma, U. (eds) (1996), *Complementary and Alternative Medicine: Knowledge in practice*, London, Free Association Books

Carpenter, E., and McLuhan, M. (1960), *Explorations in Communication*, Boston, Beacon Press

Castells, M. (1977), *The Urban Question*, London, Edward Arnold

Castells, M. (1978), *Class, City and Power*, London, Macmillan

Castells, M. (1996), *The Rise of the Network Society*, Cambridge, Mass., Blackwell

Castles, S., and Kosack, G. (1973), *Immigrant Workers and Class Structure in Western Europe*, London, Oxford University Press

Cavan, R. (1928), *Suicide*, Chicago, Chicago University Press

Centre for Contemporary Cultural Studies (1982), *The Empire Strikes Back*, London, Hutchinson

Chandler, A. D., and Daems, H. (1980), *Managerial Hierarchies: Comparative perspectives on the rise of the modern industrial enterprise*, Cambridge, Mass., Harvard University Press

Child, J. (1969), *The Business Enterprise in Modern Industrial Society*, London, Collier-Macmillan

Child, J. (1972), 'Organisational structure, environment and performance: the role of strategic choice', *Sociology*, vol. 6, pp. 1–22

Chodorow, N. (1989), *Feminism and Psychoanalytic Theory*, New Haven, Yale University Press

Cicourel, A. (1964), *Method and Measurement in Sociology*, New York, Free Press

Cixous, H. (1975), 'The laugh of Medusa', *Signs*, vol. 1, pp. 875–99

Cixous, H. (1976), 'Castration or decapitation', *Signs*, vol. 7, pp. 41–55, 1981

Clegg, S. (1989), *Frameworks of Power*, London, Sage

Clinard, M. B. (1965), 'Criminological research', in Robert K. Merton *et al.*, *Sociology Today*, New York, Harper, vol. 2, pp. 509–36

Cloward, R. A., and Ohlin, L. E. (1960), *Delinquency and Opportunity*, New York, Free Press

Cloward, R. A., and Piven, F. F. (1979), 'Female protest, the channeling of female innovative resistance', *Signs*, vol. 4, pp. 661–9

Cohen, A. K. (1955), *Delinquent Boys: The culture of the gang*, New York, Free Press

Cohen, G. A. (1978), *Karl Marx's Theory of History*, Oxford, Oxford University Press

Cohen, I. J. (1996), 'Theories of Action and Praxis', in B. S. Turner (ed.), *The Blackwell Companion to Social Theory*, Oxford, Blackwell, pp. 111–42

Cohen, J. L., and Arato, A. (1995), *Civil Society and Political Theory*, Cambridge, Mass., MIT Press

Cohen, J. L., and Rogers, J. (1995), *Associations and Democracy*, London, Verso

Cohen, P. S. (1968), *Modern Social Theory*, London, Heinemann Educational Books

Cohen, S. (ed.) (1971), *Images of Deviance*, Harmondsworth, Penguin Books

Cohen, S. (1991), *Folk Devils and Moral Panics*, 2nd edn, Oxford, Martin Robertson

Coleman, D., and Salt, J. (1992), *The British Population*, Oxford, Oxford University Press

Coleman, J. S. (1957), *Community Conflict*, New York, Free Press

Coleman, J. S. (1961), *Adolescent Society*, New York, Free Press

Coleman, J. S. (1964), *Introduction to Mathematical Sociology*, New York, Free Press

Coleman, J. S. (1973), *Power and the Structure of Society*, New York, Norton

Coleman, J. S. (1986), *Individual Interests and Collective Action: Selected essays*, Cambridge, Cambridge University Press

Coleman, J. S. (1990a), *Equality and Achievement in Education*, Boulder, Westview Press

Coleman, J. S. (1990b), *Foundations of Social Theory*, Cambridge, Mass., The Belknap Press

Coleman, J. S., and Fararo, T. J. (1992a), 'Introduction', in J. S. Coleman and T. J. Fararo (eds), *Rational Choice Theory*, Newbury Park, Calif., Sage, pp. ix–xxi

Coleman, J. S., and Fararo, T. J. (1992b), *Rational Choice Theory: Advocacy and critique*, Newbury Park, Calif., Sage

Coleman, J. S., Hoffer, T., Kilgore, S. and Peng, S. S. (1982), *Public and Private Schools*, Washington, DC, National Centre for Education Statistics

Coleman, J. S., and Schneider, B. L. (1993), *Parents, their Children and the School*, Boulder, Westview Press

Coleman, J. S., *et al.* (1966), *Equality of Educational Opportunity*, Washington DC, Government Printing Office

Comte, A. (1838), *The Positive Philosophy of Auguste Comte*, London, Bell, 1896

Connerton, P. (ed.) (1976), *Critical Sociology*, Harmondsworth, Penguin Books

Connor, S. (1989), *Postmodernist Culture*, Oxford, Blackwell

Connor, W. D. (1979), *Socialism, Politics and Equality: Hierarchy and change in Eastern Europe and the USSR*, New York, Columbia University Press

Cook, K. (1987), *Social Exchange Theory*, London, Sage

Cooley, C. H. (1902), *Human Nature and the Social Order*, New York, Scribner's

Cooley, C. H. (1909), *Social Organization*, New York, Scribner's

Coombs, R. (1985), 'Automation, management strategies and labour-process change', in D. Knights, H. Willmott and D. Collinson (eds), *Job Redesign: Critical perspectives on the labour process*, Aldershot, Gower, pp. 142–70

Corbridge, S. (1986), *Capitalist World Development: A critique of radical development geography*, London, Macmillan

Cornforth, C., Thomas, A., Lewis, J., and Spear, R. (1988), *Developing Successful Worker Cooperatives*, London, Sage

Coser, L. A. (1956), *The Functions of Social Conflict*, New York, Free Press

Coser, L. A. (1968), 'Conflict: social aspects', in D. L. Sills (ed.), *International Encyclopedia of the Social Sciences*, vol. 3, New York, Macmillan and Free Press, pp. 232–6

Coser, L. A. (1971), *Masters of Sociological Thought: Ideas in historical and social context*, New York, Harcourt Brace

Cousins, M., and Hussain, A. (1984), *Michel Foucault*, New York, St Martin's Press

Craib, I. (1992), *Anthony Giddens*, London, Routledge

Craib, I. (1997), *Classical Social Theory*, Oxford, Oxford University Press

Cressey, D. R. (1955), 'Changing criminals: The application of the theory of differential association', *American Journal of Sociology*, vol. 61, pp. 112–18

Crompton, R. (1976), 'Approaches to the study of white-collar unionism', *Sociology*, vol. 10, no. 3, pp. 407–26

Crompton, R. (1993), *Class and Stratification: an introduction to current debates*, Cambridge, Polity Press

Crompton, R., and Jones, G. (1984), *White-Collar Proletariat*, London, Macmillan

Crompton, R., and Mann, M. (eds) (1986), *Gender and Stratification*, Oxford, Polity Press

Crouch, C. (1982), *Trade Unions: The logic of collective action*, Glasgow, Fontana

Crouch, C. (1992), *Industrial Relations and European State Traditions*, Oxford, Clarendon Press

Crow, G., and Allan, G. (1994), *Community Life*, London, Harvester Wheatsheaf

Crozier, M. (1964), *The Bureaucratic Phenomenon*, London, Tavistock

Cuff, E. C., and Payne, G. C. F. (eds) (1979), *Perspectives in Sociology*, London, Allen & Unwin

Culler, J. (1976), *Saussure*, London, Fontana

Culler, J. (1983), *Barthes*, Glasgow, Fontana

Cutler, A., Hindess, B., Hirst, P., and Hussain, A. (1977), *Marx's 'Capital' and Capitalism Today*, London, Routledge & Kegan Paul

Dahl, R. A. (1970), *Modern Political Analysis*, 2nd edn, Englewood Cliffs, NJ, Prentice Hall

Dahl, R. A. (1989), *Democracy and its Critics*, New Haven, Yale University Press

Dahlgren, P. (1995), *Television and the Public Sphere: Citizenship, democracy, and the media*, London, Sage

Dahrendorf, R. (1959), *Class and Class Conflict in an Industrial Society*, London, Routledge & Kegan Paul

Dahrendorf, R. (1967a), 'Conflict after Class', Noel Buxton Memorial Lecture, Longmans for the University of Essex

Dahrendorf, R. (1967b), *Society and Democracy in Germany*, New York, Doubleday

Dahrendorf, R. (1975), *The New Liberty*, London, Routledge & Kegan Paul

Dahrendorf, R. (1979), *Life Chances*, London, Weidenfeld & Nicolson

Dandekar, C. (1990), *Surveillance, Power and Modernity*, Cambridge, Polity Press

Daniel, W. W. (1981), *The Unemployed Flow*, London, Policy Studies Institute

Danziger, K. (1971), *Socialization*, Harmondsworth, Penguin Books

Darwin, C. (1872), *The Expression of Emotion in Man and Animals*, Chicago, Chicago University Press, 1965

Davies, J. C. (1962), 'Toward a theory of revolution', *American Sociological Review*, vol. 27, pp. 5–19

Davis, B. D. (1970), *The Problem of Slavery in Western Culture*, Harmondsworth, Penguin Books

Davis, H. B. (1978), *Toward a Marxist Theory of Nationalism*, New York and London, Monthly Review Press

Davis, K., and Moore, W. E. (1945), 'Some principles of stratification', *American Sociological Review*, vol. 10, pp. 242–9; reprinted in R. Bendix and S. M. Lipset (eds) (1966), *Class, Status and Power*, 2nd edn, New York, Free Press

Dawe, A. (1978), 'Theories of social action', in T. B. Bottomore and R. Nisbet (eds), *A History of Sociological Analysis*, New York, Basic Books, pp. 362–417

Dawkins, R. (1989), *The Selfish Gene*, 2nd edn, Oxford, Oxford University Press

De Bary, W. T. (1998), *Asian Values and Human Rights: A Confucian communitarian perspective*, Cambridge, Mass., Harvard University Press

Dearlove, J., and Saunders, P. (1991), *Introduction to British Politics*, 2nd edn, Cambridge, Polity Press

Debord, G. (1994), *The Society of the Spectacle*, New York, Zone Books

Deetz, S. (1992), 'Disciplinary power in the modern corporation', in M. Alvesson and H. Willmott (eds), *Critical Management Studies*, London, Sage

Denzin, N. K. (1989), *The Research Act*, 3rd edn, Englewood Cliffs, NJ, Prentice Hall

Denzin, N. K. (1991), *Images of Postmodern Society*, London, Sage

Denzin, N. K. (1992), *Symbolic Interactionism and Cultural Studies*, Oxford, Blackwell

Denzin, N. K., and Lincoln, Y. S. (1994), 'Introduction: entering the field of qualitative research', in N. K. Denzin and Y. S. Lincoln (eds), *Handbook of Qualitative Research*, Thousand Oaks, Calif., Sage Publications, pp. 1–17

Derrida, J. (1982), *Margins of Philosophy*, Chicago, Chicago University Press

Dex, S. (1988), 'Gender and the labour market,' in D. Gallie (ed.), *Employment in Britain*, Oxford, Blackwell, pp. 281–309

DHSS (Black Report) (1980), *Inequalities in Health: Report of a Research Working Group*, London, Department of Health and Social Security

Diggins, J. P. (1978), *The Bard of Savagery: Veblen and modern social theory*, Hassocks, Harvester Press

Ditton, J. (1979), *Contrology: Beyond the new criminology*, London, Macmillan

Doeringer, P. B. and Piore, M. J. (1971), *Internal Labor Markets and Manpower Analysis*, Lexington, Heath

Donzelot, J. (1977), *The Policing of Families*, New York, Pantheon, 1979

Dore, R. P. (1958), *City Life in Japan*, London, Routledge & Kegan Paul

Dore, R. P. (1959), *Land Reform in Japan*, Oxford, Oxford University Press

Dore, R. P. (1965), *Education in Tokugawa Japan*, London, Routledge & Kegan Paul

Dore, R. P. (1973), *British Factory, Japanese Factory: The origins of national diversity in industrial relations*, London, Allen & Unwin

Dore, R. P. (1976), *The Diploma Disease*, London, Allen & Unwin

Dore, R. P. (1978), *Shinohata: A portrait of a Japanese village*, London, Allen Lane The Penguin Press

Dore, R. P. (1986), *Flexible Rigidities: Industrial policy and structural adjustment in the Japanese economy*, London, Athlone

Douglas, J. B. (1967), *The Social Meanings of Suicide*, Princeton, Princeton University Press

Douglas, J. D. (ed.) (1973), *Introduction to Sociology*, New York, Free Press

Douglas, M. (1963), *The Lele of the Kasai*, Oxford, Oxford University Press

Douglas, M. (1966), *Purity and Danger: An analysis of concepts of pollution and taboo*, London, Routledge & Kegan Paul

Douglas, M. (ed.) (1970a), *Witchcraft, Confessions and Accusations*, London, Tavistock

Douglas, M. (1970b), *Natural Symbols: Explorations in cosmology*, London, Barrie & Rockcliff

Douglas, M. (ed.) (1973), *Rules and Meaning: The anthropology of everyday life*, Harmondsworth, Penguin Books

Douglas, M. (1975), *Implicit Meanings: Essays in anthropology*, London, Routledge & Kegan Paul

Douglas, M. (1978), *Cultural Bias*, London, Royal Anthropological Institute

Douglas, M. (1980), *Evans-Pritchard*, London, Fontana

Douglas, M. (1982a), *In the Active Voice*, London, Routledge & Kegan Paul

Douglas, M. (ed.) (1982b), *Essays in the Sociology of Perception*, London, Routledge & Kegan Paul

Douglas, M. (1986), *How Institutions Think*, Syracuse, Syracuse University Press

Douglas, M., and Isherwood, B. (1978), *The World of Goods: Towards an anthropology of consumption*, London, Allen Lane The Penguin Press

Douglas, M. (1992), *Risk and Blame: Essays in cultural theory*, London, Routledge

Douglas, M., and Wildavsky, A. (1982), *Risk and Culture: An essay on the selection of technical and environmental dangers*, Berkeley, University of California Press

Downes, D., and Rock, P. (1995), *Understanding Deviance*, 3rd edn, Oxford, Oxford University Press

Dowse, R. E., and Hughes, J. (1986), *Political Sociology*, 2nd edn, New York, Wiley

Doyal, L. (1979), *The Political Economy of Health*, London, Pluto Press

Dreyfus, H. L. (1991), *Being-in-the-World*, Cambridge, Mass., MIT Press

Drum, A. M. (1978), *Introduction to Political Sociology*, Englewood Cliffs, NJ, Prentice Hall

Dumm, T. L. (1996), *Michel Foucault and the Politics of Freedom*, London, Sage

Dumont, L. (1970), *Homo Hierarchicus*, Chicago, Chicago University Press

Duncan, O. D. (1966), 'Path analysis: sociological examples', *American Journal of Sociology*, vol. 72, pp. 1–16

Duncan, O. D. (1975), *Introduction to Structural Equation Models*, New York, Academic Press

Dunleavy, P., Gamble, A., Holliday, I., and Peele, G. (eds) (1997), *Developments in British Politics 5*, New York, St Martin's Press

Dunleavy, P., and Husbands, C. T. (1985), *British Democracy at the Crossroads: Voting and party competition in the 1980s*, London, Allen & Unwin

Dunleavy, P., and O'Leary, B. (1987), *Theories of the State*, Basingstoke, Macmillan

Dunn, J. (1990), *Interpreting Political Responsibility*, Cambridge, Polity Press

Durkheim, E. (1893), *The Division of Labor in Society*, Glencoe, Free Press, 1960

Durkheim, E. (1895), *The Rules of Sociological Method*, Glencoe, Free Press, 1958

Durkheim, E. (1897), *Suicide: A study in sociology*, Glencoe, Free Press, 1951

Durkheim, E. (1912), *The Elementary Forms of the Religious Life*, London, Allen & Unwin, 1954

Durkheim, E. (1950), *Professional Ethics and Civic Morals*, London, Routledge, 1992

Durkheim, E. (1978), *On Institutional Analysis*, Chicago, Chicago University Press

Durkheim, E., and Mauss, M. (1903), *Primitive Classification*, Chicago, Chicago University Press, 1963

Duster, T. S. (1970), *The Legislation of Morality: Law, drugs and moral legislation*, New York, Free Press

Duverger, M. (1964), *Political Parties*, London, Methuen

Dworkin, R. (1991), *Law's Empire*, London, Fontana

Dyer, G. (1982), *Advertising as Communication*, London, Methuen

Eckstein, H. (1965), 'On the etiology of internal wars', *History and Theory*, vol. 4, pp. 133–63

Edwards, R. (1979), *Contested Terrain*, London, Heinemann Educational Books

Ehrenreich, B., and Ehrenreich, J. (1970), *The American Health Empire: Power, profits and politics*, New York, Random House

Eisenstadt, S. N. (1956), *From Generation to Generation*, Glencoe, Free Press

Eisenstadt, S. N. (1968a), 'Evolution: social evolution', in D. L. Sills (ed.), *International Encyclopedia of the Social Sciences*, vol. 5, New York, Macmillan and Free Press, pp. 228–34

Eisenstadt, S. N. (1968b), 'Social institutions: the concept', in D. L. Sills (ed.), *International Encyclopedia of the Social Sciences*, vol. 14, New York, Macmillan and Free Press, pp. 409–21

Eisenstadt, S. N. (1968c), 'Social institutions: comparative study', in D. L. Sills (ed.), *International Encyclopedia of the Social Sciences*, vol. 14, New York, Macmillan and Free Press, pp. 421–9

Ekeh, P. (1974), *Social Exchange Theory: The two traditions*, London, Heinemann Educational Books

Elias, N. (1939a), *The Civilizing Process: The history of manners*, vol. 1, Oxford, Blackwell, 1978a

Elias, N. (1939b), *The Civilizing Process: State formation and civilization*, vol. 2, Oxford, Blackwell, 1982

Elias, N. (1969), *The Court Society*, Oxford, Blackwell, 1983

Elias, N. (1970), *What is Sociology?*, London, Hutchinson, 1978b

Elias, N. (1982), *The Loneliness of the Dying*, Oxford, Blackwell, 1985

Elias, N. (1984), *Time, an Essay*, Oxford, Blackwell, 1992

Elias, N. (1986), *Involvement and Detachment*, Oxford, Blackwell

Elias, N., and Scotson, J. L. (1965), *The Established and the Outsiders*, London, Cass

Elliott, G. (ed.) (1994), *Althusser: A critical reader*, Oxford, Blackwell

Emmanuel, A. (1972), *Unequal Exchange*, London, New Left Books

Emmanuel, A. (1974), 'Current myths of development', *New Left Review*, no. 85, pp. 61–82

Engels, F. (1845), *The Condition of the Working Class in England*, Oxford, Blackwell, 1958

Engels, F. (1877–8), *Anti-Dühring: Herr Eugen Dühring's revolution in science*, Moscow, Foreign Languages Publishing House, 1959

Engels, F. (1884), *The Origin of the Family, Private Property and the State*, New York, International Publishers, 1942

Engels, F. (1952), *Dialectics of Nature*, New York, International Publishers, 1960

Erikson, R., and Goldthorpe, J. H. (1992), *The Constant Flux: A study of class mobility in industrial societies*, Oxford, Clarendon Press

Etzioni, A. (1968), 'Mobilization as a macrosociological conception', *British Journal of Sociology*, vol. 19, pp. 243–53

Etzioni, A. (1993), *The Spirit of Community: The reinvention of American society*, New York, Touchstone

Evans, M. (ed.) (1982), *The Woman Question*, London, Fontana Books

Evans-Pritchard, E. E. (1937), *Witchcraft, Oracles and Magic among the Azande*, Oxford, Clarendon Press

Evans-Pritchard, E. E. (1940), *The Nuer: A description of the modes of livelihood and political institutions of a Nilotic people*, Oxford, Clarendon Press

Everitt, B. S. (1980), *Cluster Analysis*, 2nd edn, London, Heinemann Educational Books

Eyerman, R., and Turner, B. S. (1998), 'Outline of a theory of generations', *European Journal of Social Theory*, vol. 1 (1), pp. 91–106

Featherstone, M. (1991), *Consumer Culture and Postmodernism*, London, Sage

Featherstone, M., and Burrows, R. (eds) (1995), *Cyberspace, Cyberbodies, Cyberpunk*, London, Sage

Fenton, S. (1984), *Durkheim and Modern Sociology*, Cambridge, Cambridge University Press

Ferguson, A. (1767), *An Essay on the History of Civil Society*, Edinburgh, Edinburgh University Press, 1966

Festinger, L. (1957), *A Theory of Cognitive Dissonance*, Evanston, Row

Feuerbach, L. (1841), *The Essence of Christianity*, New York, Harper, 1957

Field, F. (1982), *Poverty and Politics*, London, Heinemann Educational Books

Finch, J. (1989), *Family Obligations and Social Change*, Cambridge, Polity Press

Finch, J., and Mason, J. (1993), *Negotiating Family Responsibility*, London, Routledge

Fine, B. (1975), *Marx's 'Capital'*, London, Macmillan

Fine, G. A. (1990), 'Symbolic interactionism in the post-Blumerian age', in G. Ritzer (ed.), *Frontiers of Social Theory: The new synthesis*, New York, Columbia University Press, pp. 117–57

Firestone, S. (1970), *The Dialectics of Sex: The case for feminist revolution*, New York, Morrow

Fiske, J. (1990), *Introduction to Communication Studies*, London, Routledge

Fletcher, R. (1971), *The Making of Sociology: Beginnings and foundations*, vol. 1, London, Nelson

Foucault, M. (1961), *Madness and Civilization*, London, Tavistock, 1971

Foucault, M. (1963), *The Birth of the Clinic*, London, Tavistock, 1973

Foucault, M. (1966), *The Order of Things: An archaeology of the human sciences*, London, Tavistock, 1974

Foucault, M. (1969), *The Archaeology of Knowledge*, London, Tavistock, 1974

Foucault, M. (1973), *I Pierre Rivière, Having Slaughtered My Mother, My Sister and My Brother . . .*, London, Tavistock, 1978

Foucault, M. (1975), *Discipline and Punish: The birth of the prison*, London, Tavistock, 1977

Foucault, M. (1976), *History of Sexuality*, London, Tavistock, 1979

Foucault, M. (1984a), *The Care of the Self: The history of sexuality*, vol. 3, Harmondsworth, Penguin Books, 1990

Foucault, M. (1984b), *The Use of Pleasure: The history of sexuality*, vol. 2, Harmondsworth, Penguin Books, 1987

Foucault, M. (1991), 'Governmentality', in G. Burchell, C. Gordon, and P. Miller (eds), *The Foucault Effect: Studies in governmentality*, London, Harvester Wheatsheaf, pp. 87–104

Foucault, M. (1993), 'About the beginning of the hermeneutics of the self: two lectures at Dartmouth', *Political Theory*, vol. 21 (2), pp. 198–227

Fowler, B. (1997), *Pierre Bourdieu and Cultural Theory*, London, Sage

Fox, A. (1974), *Beyond Contract: Work, power and trust relations*, London, Faber & Faber

Frank, A. G. (1969), *Capitalism and Underdevelopment in Latin America*, New York, Monthly Review Press

Frankenburg, R. (1966), *Communities in Britain*, Harmondsworth, Penguin Books

Freeden, M. (1991), *Rights*, Minneapolis, University of Minnesota Press

Freeman, D. (1983), *Margaret Mead and Samoa: The making and unmaking of an anthropological myth*, Canberra, Australian National University Press

Freire, P. (1972), *Pedagogy of the Oppressed*, Harmondsworth, Penguin Books

Freud, S. (1900), *The Interpretation of Dreams*, London, Hogarth, 1958

Freud, S. (1901), *The Psychopathology of Everyday Life*, London, Hogarth, 1960

Freud, S. (1905a), *Jokes and their Relation to the Unconscious*, Harmondsworth, Penguin Books, 1976

Freud, S. (1905b), *Three Essays on the Theory of Sexuality*, London, Hogarth, 1953

Freud, S. (1910a), *Five Lectures on Psycho-Analysis*, Harmondsworth, Penguin Books, 1962

Freud, S. (1910b), *Leonardo da Vinci: A memory of his childhood*, London, ARK edn, 1984

Freud, S. (1910 and 1926), *Two Short Accounts of Psycho-Analysis*, Harmondsworth, Penguin Books, 1962

Freud, S. (1914), *On the History of the Psycho-Analytical Movement*, New York, Norton, 1966

Freud, S. (1923), *The Ego and the Id*, London, Hogarth, 1961

Freud, S. (1925), *An Autobiographical Study*, London, Hogarth, 1959

Freud, S. (1927), *The Future of an Illusion*, London, Hogarth Press

Freud, S. (1930), *Civilization and its Discontents*, London, Hogarth Press

Freud, S. (1934–8), *Moses and Monotheism: Three essays*, London, Hogarth Press

Freud, S., and Breuer, J. (1895), *Studies on Hysteria*, Harmondsworth, Penguin Books, 1974

Freund, J. (1966), *The Sociology of Max Weber*, London, Allen Lane The Penguin Press, 1968

Friedman, A. L. (1977), *Industry and Labour*, London, Macmillan

Friedman, J. (1994), *Cultural Identity and Global Process*, London, Sage

Friedmann, J., and Wulff, R. (1975), *The Urban Transition*, London, Arnold

Frisby, D. (1981), *Sociological Impressionism: A reassessment of Georg Simmel's social theory*, London, Heinemann Educational Books

Frisby, D. (1984), *Georg Simmel*, London, Tavistock

Frith, S. (1984), *The Sociology of Youth*, Ormskirk, Causeway Press

Frobel, F., Heinrichs, J., and Kreye, O. (1980), *The New International Division of Labour*, Cambridge, Cambridge University Press

Fromm, E. (1993), 'Infantilization and Despair, Masquerading as Radicalism', *Theory, Culture and Society*, vol. 10 (2), pp. 197–206

Galbraith, J. K. (1967), *The New Industrial State*, London, Hamish Hamilton

Gallie, D. (1978), *In Search of the New Working Class: Automation and social integration within the capitalist enterprise*, Cambridge, Cambridge University Press

Gallie, D. (1988), 'Introduction', in D. Gallie (ed.), *Employment in Britain*, Oxford, Blackwell, pp. 1–30

Gallie, D., White, M., Cheng, Y., and Tomlinson, M. (1998), *Restructuring the Employment Relationship*, Oxford, Clarendon Press

Gans, H. J. (1968), 'Urbanism and suburbanism as ways of life', in R. E. Pahl, *Readings in Urban Sociology*, Oxford, Pergamon Press, pp. 95–118

Garfinkel, H. (1967), *Studies in Ethnomethodology*, Englewood Cliffs, NJ, Prentice Hall

Gay, P. (1966–9), *The Enlightenment: An interpretation*, New York, Vintage

Geertz, C. (1973), *The Interpretation of Cultures*, New York, Basic Books

Gellner, E. (1959), *Words and Things*, London, Routledge & Kegan Paul

Gellner, E. (1964), *Thought and Change*, London, Weidenfeld & Nicolson

Gellner, E. (1969), *Saints of the Atlas*, London, Weidenfeld & Nicolson

Gellner, E. (1974), *Legitimation of Belief*, Cambridge, Cambridge University Press

Gellner, E. (1982), *Muslim Society*, Cambridge, Cambridge University Press

Gellner, E. (1983), *Nations and Nationalism*, Oxford, Blackwell

Gellner, E. (1985), *The Psychoanalytic Movement or The Coming of Unreason*, London, Paladin Books

Gellner, E. (1992), *Postmodernism, Reason and Religion*, London, Routledge

Gellner, E. (1995), *Revolutions in the Sacred Grove*, Oxford, Blackwell

Geoghegan, V. (1981), *Reason and Eros: The social theory of Herbert Marcuse*, London, Pluto Press

Geras, N. (1971), 'Fetishism in Marx's *Capital*', *New Left Review*, no. 65, pp. 69–85

Gershuny, J. (1992), 'Change in the Domestic Division of Labour in the UK, 1975–1987; Dependent Labour versus Adaptive Partnership', in N. Abercrombie and A. Warde, *Social Change in Contemporary Britain*, Cambridge, Polity Press

Gerth, H. H., and Mills, C. W. (eds) (1946), *From Max Weber: Essays in sociology*, New York, Oxford University Press

Giddens, A. (1971), *Capitalism and Modern Social Theory*, Cambridge, Cambridge University Press

Giddens, A. (1972), *Politics and Sociology in the Thought of Max Weber*, London, Macmillan

Giddens, A. (1973), *The Class Structure of the Advanced Societies*, London, Hutchinson

Giddens, A. (ed.) (1974), *Positivism and Sociology*, London, Heinemann Educational Books

Giddens, A. (1976), *New Rules of Sociological Method*, London, Hutchinson

Giddens, A. (1977), *Studies in Social and Political Theory*, London, Hutchinson

Giddens, A. (1978), *Emile Durkheim*, London, Fontana

Giddens, A. (1979), *Central Problems in Social Theory*, London, Macmillan

Giddens, A. (1981), *A Contemporary Critique of Historical Materialism*, London, Macmillan

Giddens, A. (1982), *Sociology: A brief but critical introduction*, London, Macmillan

Giddens, A. (1983), *Profiles and Critiques in Social Theory*, London, Macmillan

Giddens, A. (1984), *The Constitution of Society: Outline of the theory of structuration*, Cambridge, Polity Press

Giddens, A. (1985), *The Nation-State and Violence: Volume two of a contemporary critique of historical materialism*, Cambridge, Polity Press

Giddens, A. (1990), *The Consequences of Modernity*, Cambridge, Polity Press

Giddens, A. (1991), *Modernity and Self-Identity: Self and society in the late modern age*, Cambridge, Polity Press

Giddens, A. (1992), *The Transformation of Intimacy: Sexuality, love and eroticism*, Cambridge, Polity Press

Giddens, A. (1994), *Beyond Left and Right: The future of radical politics*, Cambridge, Polity Press

Giddens, A. (1997), *Sociology*, 3rd edn, Cambridge, Polity Press

Giddens, A. (1998), *The Third Way*, Cambridge, Polity Press

Giddens, A. (1999), *Runaway World: How globalisation is shaping our lives*, London, Profile Books

Giddens, A. (2000), *The Third Way and its Critics*, Cambridge, Polity Press

Gilbert, G. N. (1981), *Modelling Society*, London, Allen & Unwin

Gilbert, M. (1986), *Inflation and Social Conflict: A sociology of economic life in advanced societies*, Brighton, Wheatsheaf

Gilligan, C. (1982), *In a Different Voice*, Cambridge, Mass., Harvard University Press

Giner, S. (1976), *Mass Society*, London, Martin Robertson

Glaser, B. G., and Strauss, A. L. (1965), *Awareness of Dying*, Chicago, Aldine

Glaser, B. G., and Strauss, A. L. (1968a), *The Discovery of Grounded Theory: Strategies for qualitative research*, Chicago, Aldine & Atherton

Glaser, B. G., and Strauss, A. L. (1968b), *Time for Dying*, Chicago, Aldine

Glaser, D. (1956), 'Criminality theories and behavioral images', *The American Journal of Sociology*, vol. 61, pp. 433–45

Glasgow University Media Group (1993), *Getting the Message*, London, Routledge

Glass, D. V. (ed.) (1954), *Social Mobility in Britain*, London, Routledge & Kegan Paul

Glass, D. V., and Eversley, D. E. C. (eds) (1965), *Population in History*, London, Arnold

Glass, D. V., and Revelle, R. (1972), *Population and Social Change*, London, Arnold

Glassner, B., and Freedman, J. A. (1979), *Clinical Sociology*, New York and London, Longman

Goffman, E. (1959), *The Presentation of Self in Everyday Life*, Garden City, New York, Doubleday Anchor

Goffman, E. (1961a), *Encounters: Two studies in the sociology of interaction*, Indianapolis, Bobbs-Merrill

Goffman, E. (1961b), *Asylums*, Harmondsworth, Penguin Books

Goffman, E. (1963), *Behavior in Public Places: Notes on the social organization of gatherings*, New York, Free Press

Goffman, E. (1964), *Stigma: Notes on the management of spoiled identity*, Englewood Cliffs, New Jersey, Prentice-Hall

Goffman, E. (1967), *Interaction Ritual: Essays in face-to-face behavior*, Chicago, Aldine

Goffman, E. (1969), *Strategic Interaction*, Philadelphia, University of Philadelphia Press

Goffman, E. (1971), *Relations in Public: Microstudies of the public order*, New York, Basic Books

Goffman, E. (1974), *Frame Analysis: An essay on the organization of experience*, Cambridge, Mass., Harvard University Press

Goffman, E. (1979), *Gender Advertisements*, London, Macmillan

Goldthorpe, J. H. (1980), *Social Mobility and Class Structure in Britain*, Oxford, Clarendon Press

Goldthorpe, J. H. (ed.) (1984), *Order and Conflict in Contemporary Capitalism*, Oxford, Oxford University Press

Goldthorpe, J. H. (1987), *Social Mobility and Class Structure in Modern Britain*, 2nd edn, Oxford, Clarendon Press

Goldthorpe, J. H., and Hope, K. (1974), *The Social Grading of Occupations: A new approach and scale*, Oxford, Clarendon Press

Goldthorpe, J. H., Lockwood, D., Bechhofer, F., and Platt, J. (1968a), *The Affluent Worker: Industrial attitudes and behaviour*, Cambridge, Cambridge University Press

Goldthorpe, J. H., Lockwood, D., Bechhofer, F., and Platt, J. (1968b), *The Affluent Worker: Political attitudes and behaviour*, Cambridge, Cambridge University Press

Goldthorpe, J. H., Lockwood, D., Bechhofer, F., and Platt, J. (1969), *The Affluent Worker in the Class Structure*, Cambridge, Cambridge University Press

Goode, E., and Ben-Yehuda, N. (1994), *Moral Panics*, Oxford, Blackwell

Goode, W. J. (1964), *The Family*, Englewood Cliffs, NJ, Prentice Hall

Gordon, D. M., Edwards, R., and Reich, M. (1982), *Segmented Work, Divided Workers*, Cambridge, Cambridge University Press

Gorz, A. (1964), *Strategy for Labour*, Boston, Beacon Press, 1967

Gouldner, A. W. (1954), *Patterns of Industrial Bureaucracy*, New York, Free Press

Gouldner, A. W. (1955), *Wildcat Strike*, London, Routledge & Kegan Paul

Gouldner, A. W. (1965), *Enter Plato: Classical Greece and the origins of social theory*, New York, Basic Books

Gouldner, A. W. (1970), *The Coming Crisis of Western Sociology*, New York, Basic Books

Gouldner, A. W. (1975), *For Sociology: Renewal and critique in sociology today*, Harmondsworth, Penguin Books

Gouldner, A. W. (1976), *The Dialectic of Ideology and Technology*, New York, Seabury Press

Gouldner, A. W. (1979), *The Future of Intellectuals and the Rise of the New Class*, New York, Seabury Press

Gouldner, A. W. (1980), *The Two Marxisms: Contradictions and anomalies in the development of theory*, New York, Seabury Press

Gouldner, A. W. (1985), *Against Fragmentation: The origins of Marxism and the sociology of intellectuals*, Oxford, Oxford University Press

Gouldner, A. W., and Peterson, R. A. (1962), *Notes on Technology and the Moral Order*, New York, Bobbs-Merrill

Gove, W. R. (1975), *The Labeling of Deviance: Evaluating a perspective*, Beverly Hills, Sage

Gramsci, A. (1971), *Selections from the Prison Notebooks*, London, New Left Books

Granovetter, M. (1974), *Getting a Job*, Cambridge, Mass., Harvard University Press

Grathoff, R. (ed.) (1978), *The Theory of Social Action: The correspondence of Alfred Schutz and Talcott Parsons*, Bloomington and London, Indiana University Press

Gray, R. (1981), *The Aristocracy of Labour in Nineteenth-Century Britain c. 1850–1914*, London, Macmillan

Greer, G. (1970), *The Female Eunuch*, London, Verso

Grint, K. (1993), *The Sociology of Work: An introduction*, Oxford, Blackwell

Grint, K. (1995), *Management: A sociological introduction*, Cambridge, Polity Press

Grotius, H. (1625), *On the Law of War and Peace*, New York, Wiley and Sons, 1964

Grunig, J. E., and Hunt, T. (1984), *Managing Public Relations*, Fort Worth, Holt, Rinehart & Winston

Gurevitch, M., Bennett, T., Curran, J., and Woollacott, J. (eds) (1982), *Culture, Society and the Media*, London, Methuen

Habakkuk, H. J. (1963), 'Population problems and European economic development in the late eighteenth and nineteenth century', *American Economic Review*, vol. 53, pp. 607–18

Haber, J., and Schneider, B. E. (eds) (1992), *The Social Context of AIDS*, Newbury Park, Sage

Habermas, J. (1962), *The Structural Transformation of the Public Sphere*, Cambridge, Polity Press

Habermas, J. (1963), *Theory and Practice*, London, Heinemann Educational Books, 1973

Habermas, J. (1968), *Knowledge and Human Interests*, London, Heinemann Educational Books, 1971

Habermas, J. (1970a), 'On systematically distorted communication', *Inquiry*, vol. 13, pp. 205–18

Habermas, J. (1970b), 'Towards a theory of communicative competence', *Inquiry*, vol. 13, pp. 360–75

Habermas, J. (1970c), *Towards a Rational Society*, London, Heinemann Educational Books, 1971

Habermas, J. (1973), *Legitimation Crisis*, London, Heinemann Educational Books, 1976

Habermas, J. (1979), *Communication and the Evolution of Society*, London, Heinemann Educational Books

Habermas, J. (1981), *The Theory of Communicative Action*, Boston, Beacon Press, 2 vols, 1984

Habermas, J. (1988), *The Philosophical Discourse of Modernity: Twelve Lectures*, Cambridge, Mass., MIT Press

Habermas, J. (1997), *Between Facts and Norms: Contributions to a discourse theory of law and democracy*, Cambridge, Polity Press

Habermas, J., and Luhmann, N. (1971), *Theorie der Gesellschaft oder Sozialtechnologie?*, Frankfurt, Suhrkamp Verlag

Hakim, C. (1979), *Occupational Segregation*, Department of Employment Research Paper No. 9, London, Her Majesty's Stationery Office

Hakim, C. (1996), *Key Issues in Women's Work*, London, Athlone

Halbwachs, M. (1930), *Les Causes du suicide*, Paris, Alcan

Halévy, E. (1961), *A History of the English People in the Nineteenth Century*, 2nd edn, vols 1 and 2, London, Benn

Hall, J. A. (1981), *Diagnoses of Our Time: Six views of our social condition*, London, Heinemann Educational Books

Hall, J. A. (1985), *Powers and Liberties: The causes and consequences of the rise of the West*, Oxford, Blackwell

Hall, R. (1969), *Occupations and the Social Structure*, Englewood Cliffs, NJ, Prentice Hall

Hall, S. (1978), *Policing the State: Mugging, the state, and law and order*, London, Macmillan

Hall, S. (1980), 'Encoding/Decoding', in S. Hall *et al.*, *Culture, Media, Language*, London, Hutchinson

Hall, S. (1988), *The Hard Road to Renewal: Thatcherism and the crisis of the left*, London, Verso

Hall, S., and du Gay, P. (1996), *Questions of Cultural Identity*, London, Sage

Hall, S., and Gieben, B. (1992), *Formations of Modernity*, Cambridge, Polity Press

Hall, S., and Jacques, M. (1983), *The Politics of Thatcherism*, London, Lawrence & Wishart

Hall, S., and Jefferson, T. (eds) (1976), *Resistance through Rituals*, London, Hutchinson

Hall, S., and Whannel, P. (1964), *The Popular Arts*, London, Hutchinson

Halsey, A. H. (1957), *Social Class and Educational Opportunity*, London, Heinemann

Halsey, A. H. (1961), *Education, Economy and Society*, New York, Free Press

Halsey, A. H. (1965), *Power in Co-operatives*, Oxford, Blackwell

Halsey, A. H. (1968), *Social Survey of the Civil Service*, London, Her Majesty's Stationery Office

Halsey, A. H. (1971), *The British Academics*, London, Faber & Faber

Halsey, A. H. (1977), *Heredity and Environment*, London, Methuen

Halsey, A. H. (1978), *Change in British Society*, Oxford, Oxford University Press

Halsey, A. H. (1988), *Trends in British Society since 1900*, 2nd edn, London, Macmillan

Halsey, A. H. (1992), *Decline of Donnish Dominion*, Oxford, Oxford University Press

Halsey, A. H. (1995), *Change in British Society*, 4th edn, Oxford, Oxford University Press

Halsey, A. H., Heath, A. F., and Ridge, J. M. (1980), *Origins and Destinations: Family, class, and education in modern Britain*, Oxford, Clarendon Press

Halsey, A. H., and Karabel, J. (1977), *Power and Ideology in Education*, Oxford, Oxford University Press

Ham, C. (ed.) (1997), *Health Care Reform: Learning from the international experience*, Buckingham, Open University Press

Hamilton, M. B. (1995), *The Sociology of Religion: Theoretical and comparative perspectives*, London, Routledge

Hamilton, P. (1983), *Talcott Parsons*, London, Tavistock

Haralambos, M. (1980), *Sociology: Themes and perspectives*, Slough, University Tutorial Press

Hargreaves Heap, S. P., and Varoufakis, Y. (1995), *Game Theory: A critical introduction*, London, Routledge, 1995

Harman, H. H. (1967), *Modern Factor Analysis*, 2nd edn, Chicago, Chicago University Press

Harris, C. C., (1969), *The Family*, London, Allen & Unwin

Harris, D. K. (1990), *Sociology of Aging*, New York, Harper & Row

Hart, N. (1976), *When Marriage Ends: A study in status passage*, London, Tavistock

Harvey, D. (1989), *The Condition of Postmodernity*, Oxford, Blackwell

Hawkes, T. (1977), *Structuralism and Semiotics*, London, Methuen

Hawkins, K. (1979), *Unemployment*, Harmondsworth, Penguin Books

Hawthorne, G., and Busfield, J. (1968), 'A sociological approach to British fertility', in J. Gould (ed.), *Penguin Social Science Survey*, Harmondsworth, Penguin Books, pp. 168–210

Heath, A. (1981), *Social Mobility*, Glasgow, Fontana

Heath, A., and Evans, G. (1988), 'Working-class conservatives and middle-class socialists', in R. Jowell, S. Witherspoon, and L. Brook (eds), *British Social Attitudes: The 5th report*, Aldershot, Gower, 1988, pp. 53–69

Heath, A., and Topf, R. (1987), 'Political Culture', in R. Jowell, S. Witherspoon, and L. Brook (eds), *British Social Attitudes: The 1987 report*, Aldershot, Gower, pp. 51–67

Hechter, M. (1975), *Internal Colonialism: The Celtic fringe in British national development, 1536–1966*, London, Routledge & Kegan Paul

Heelas, P. (1996), *The New Age Movement*, Oxford, Blackwell

Hegel, G. W. F. (1837), *The Philosophy of History*, New York, Dover, 1956

Heidegger, M. (1927), *Being and Time*, Oxford, Blackwell, 1962

Heidegger, M. (1954), *The Question Concerning Technology and Other Essays*, New York, Harper & Row, 1977

Held, D. (1980), *Introduction to Critical Theory*, London, Hutchinson

Held, D. (1995), *Democracy and the Global Order: From the modern state to cosmopolitan governance*, Cambridge, Polity Press

Heller, A. (1974), *The Theory of Need in Marx*, London, Allison & Busby

Henderson, L. J. (1935), 'Physician and patient as a social system', *New England Journal of Medicine*, vol. 212, pp. 819–23

Herberg, W. (1955), *Protestant, Catholic, Jew*, New York, Doubleday

Heritage, J. (1987), 'Ethnomethodology', in A. Giddens and J. Turner (eds), *Social Theory Today*, Cambridge, Polity Press, pp. 224–272

Hill, M. (1973), *A Sociology of Religion*, London, Heinemann Educational Books

Hill, S. (1976), *The Dockers: Class and tradition in London*, London, Heinemann Educational Books

Hill, S. (1981), *Competition and Control at Work*, London, Heinemann Educational Books

Hills, J. (1995), *Joseph Rowntree Foundation Inquiry into Income and Wealth*, vol. 2, York, Joseph Rowntree Foundation

Hinde, R. A. (1982), *Ethology*, Glasgow, Fontana

Hindess, B. (1973), *The Use of Official Statistics in Sociology*, London, Macmillan

Hindess, B. (1977), 'The concept of class in Marxist theory and Marxist politics', in J. Bloomfield (ed.), *Class, Hegemony and Party*, London, Lawrence & Wishart, pp. 95–108

Hindess, B., and Hirst, P. Q. (1975), *Pre-Capitalist Modes of Production*, London, Routledge & Kegan Paul

Hirsch, F., and Goldthorpe, J. H. (eds) (1978), *The Political Economy of Inflation*, London, Martin Robertson

Hirst, P. (ed.) (1989), *The Pluralist Theory of the State: Selected writings of G. D. H. Cole, J. N. Figgis and H. J. Laski*, London, Routledge

Hirst, P. (1990), *Representative Democracy and its Limits*, Cambridge, Polity Press

Hirst, P., and Zeitlin, J. (1991), 'Flexible specialization and post-Fordism: theory, evidence and policy implications', *Economy and Society*, vol. 20, pp. 1–56

Hobbes, T. (1651), *Leviathan*, Glasgow, Fontana, 1962

Hochschild, A. R. (1983), *The Managed Heart*, Berkeley, University of California Press

Hofstadter, R. (1955), *Social Darwinism in American Thought*, Boston, Beacon Press

Hoggart, R. (1957), *The Uses of Literacy*, Harmondsworth, Penguin Press

Hoggart, R. (1970), *Speaking to Each Other*, 2 vols, London, Chatto & Windus

Hoggart, R. (1982a), *An English Temper: Essays on education, culture and communication*, London, Chatto & Windus

Hoggart, R. (1982b), *The Future of Broadcasting*, London, Macmillan

Hohfeld, W. N. (1919), *Fundamental Legal Conceptions*, London and New Haven, Greenwood Press, 1964

Hollowell, P. (ed.) (1982), *Property and Social Relations*, London, Heinemann Educational Books

Holsti, O. R. (1969), *Content Analysis for the Social Sciences and Humanities*, Reading, Mass., Addison-Wesley

Holton, R. J. (1985), *The Transition from Feudalism to Capitalism*, London, Macmillan

Holton, R. J., and Turner, B. S. (1986), *Talcott Parsons on Economy and Society*, London, Routledge

Homans, G. C. (1950), *The Human Group*, New York, Harcourt Brace

Homans, G. C. (1961), *Social Behavior: Its elementary forms*, New York, Harcourt Brace

Homans, G. C. (1962), *Sentiments and Activities*, New York, Free Press

Homans, G. C. (1964), 'Bringing men back in', *American Sociological Review*, vol. 29, pp. 809–18

Homans, G. C. (1967), *The Nature of Social Science*, New York, Harcourt Brace

Hoogvelt, A. M. (1976), *The Sociology of Developing Societies*, London, Macmillan

Hooks, B. (1984), *Feminist Theory: From margin to center*, Boston, Mass., South End Press

Hough, M., and Mayhew, P. (1985), *Taking Account of Crime: Key findings from the second British Crime Survey*, Home Office Research Paper No. 85, London, Her Majesty's Stationery Office

Hoy, D. C. (ed.) (1986), *Foucault: A critical reader*, Oxford, Blackwell

Hughes, E. C., and Masuoka, J. (eds) (1950–55), *Collected Papers of Robert Ezra Park*, 3 vols, New York, Free Press

Hunt, A. (1978), *The Sociological Movement in law*, London, Macmillan

Hutton, W. (1997), *The State to Come*, London, Vantage Books

Hyman, R. (1977), *Strikes*, 2nd edn, Glasgow, Fontana

Illich, I. (1977), *Limits to Medicine*, Harmondsworth, Penguin Books

Inglis, F. (1995), *Raymond Williams*, London, Routledge

Irigaray, L. (1974), *Speculum of the Other Woman*, Ithaca, NY, Cornell University Press, 1985

Irigaray, L. (1977), *This Sex Which is Not One*, Ithaca, NY, Cornell University Press, 1985

Jackall, R. (1988), *Moral Mazes: The world of corporate managers*, Oxford, Oxford University Press

Jackson, J. A. (ed.) (1970), *Professions and Professionalisation*, Cambridge, Cambridge University Press

Jackson, J. A. (ed.) (1972), *Role*, Cambridge, Cambridge University Press

James, W. (1884), 'What is an emotion?', *Mind*

James, W. (1890), *The Principles of Psychology*, 2 vols, New York, Smith, 1962

James, W. (1902), *The Varieties of Religious Experience: A study of human nature*, ed. J. Ratner, New Hyde Park, NY, University Books, 1963

James, W. (1907), *Pragmatism: A new name for some old ways of thinking*, New York, Longman, 1949

Jameson, F. (1991), *Postmodernism*, London, Verso

Jamieson, L. (1998), *Intimacy*, Cambridge, Polity Press

Jay, M. (1973), *The Dialectical Imagination: A history of the Frankfurt School and the Institute of Social Research 1923–50*, Boston, Little, Brown

Jay, M. (1984), *Adorno*, London, Fontana

Jenkins, R. (1996), *Social Identity*, London, Routledge

Jenks, C. (1993), *Culture*, London, Routledge

Jenks, C. (1996), *Childhood*, London, Routledge

Jerrome, D. (ed.) (1983), *Ageing in Modern Society: Contemporary approaches*, London, Croom Helm

Johnson, T. J. (1972), *Professions and Power*, London, Macmillan

Johnson, T. J. (1977), 'The professions in the class structure', in R. Scase (ed.), *Industrial Society: Class, cleavage and control*, London, Allen & Unwin

Kalleberg, A. L. (1978), 'Work values and job rewards: a theory of job satisfaction', *American Sociological Review*, vol. 42, pp. 124–43

Käsler, D. (1988), *Max Weber: An introduction to his life and work*, Cambridge, Polity Press

Katz, S. (1996), *Disciplining Old Age: The formation of gerontological knowledge*, Charlottesville, University Press of Virginia

Kay, J. (1993), *Foundations of Corporate Success*, Oxford, Oxford University Press

Keat, R., and Abercrombie, N. (eds) (1991), *Enterprise Culture*, London, Routledge

Keat, R., and Urry, J. (1975), *Social Theory as Science*, London, Routledge & Kegan Paul

Keddie, N. (1971), 'Classroom knowledge', in M. F. D. Young (ed.), *Knowledge and Control*, London, Collier-Macmillan, pp. 133–61

Keesing, R. M. (1975), *Kin Groups and Social Structure*, New York, Holt, Rinehart & Winston

Kemper, T. D. (ed.) (1990), *Research Agendas in the Sociology of Emotions*, New York, State University of New York Press

Kendall, J., and Knapp, M. (1996), *The Voluntary Sector in the United Kingdom*, Manchester, Manchester University Press

Kerr, C., *et al.* (1962), *Industrialism and Industrial Man*, London, Heinemann Educational Books

Keynes, J. M. (1936), *The General Theory of Employment, Interest and Money*, London, Macmillan

Kilminster, R. and Varcoe, I. (eds) (1996), *Culture, Modernity and Revolution: Essays in honour of Zygmunt Bauman*, London, Routledge

Kitchen, M. (1976), *Fascism*, London, Macmillan

Kolakowski, L. (1978a), *Main Currents of Marxism*, vol. 1, Oxford, Oxford University Press

Kolakowski, L. (1978b), *Main Currents of Marxism*, vol. 2, Oxford, Oxford University Press

Kramnick, I. (1972), 'Reflections on revolution: definition and explanation in recent scholarship', *History and Theory*, vol. 2, pp. 26–63

Kristeva, J. (1974), *Revolution in Poetic Language*, New York, Columbia University Press, 1984

Kristeva, J. (1980), *Powers of Horror*, New York, Columbia University Press, 1982

Kristeva, J. (1983), *Tales of Love*, New York, Columbia University Press

Kruskal, J. B., and Wish, M. (1978), *Multidimensional Scaling*, London, Sage

Kuhn, A., and Wolpe, A. (eds) (1978), *Feminism and Materialism: Women and modes of production*, London, Routledge & Kegan Paul

Kuhn, T. S. (1970), *The Structure of Scientific Revolutions*, 2nd edn, Chicago, Chicago University Press

Kumar, K. (1978), *Prophecy and Progress: The sociology of industrial and post-industrial society*, Harmondsworth, Penguin Books

Kumar, K. (1995), *From Post-Industrial to Post-Modern Society: New theories of the contemporary world*, Oxford, Blackwell

Lacan, J. (1966), *Ecrits: A selection*, London, Tavistock, 1977

Laclau, E. (1977), *Politics and Ideology in Marxist Theory: Capitalism, fascism, populism*, London, New Left Books

Ladurie, E. Le Roy (1975), *Montaillou*, Harmondsworth, Penguin Books, 1978

Laing, R. D. (1959), *The Divided Self*, London, Tavistock

Lane, D. (1971), *The End of Inequality?*, Harmondsworth, Penguin Books

Lane, D. (1985), *Soviet Economy and Society*, Oxford, Blackwell

Lane, D., and Ross, C. (1999), *The Transition from Communism to Capitalism: Ruling elites from Gorbachev to Yeltsin*, New York, St Martin's Press

Lane, R. E. (1991), *The Market Experience*, Cambridge, Cambridge University Press

Lane, T., and Roberts, K. (1971), *Strike at Pilkingtons*, London, Fontana

Lanternari, V. (1963), *The Religions of the Oppressed: A study of modern messianic cults*, London, MacGibbon & Kee

Larrain, J. (1979), *The Concept of Ideology*, London, Hutchinson

Lash, S., Szerszynski, B., and Wynne, B. (eds) (1996), *Risk, Environment and Modernity: Towards a new ecology*, London, Sage

Lash, S., and Urry, J. (1987), *The End of Organized Capitalism*, Cambridge, Polity Press

Laslett, P. (ed.) (1972), *Household and Family in Past Time*, Cambridge, Cambridge University Press

Law, J., and Hassard, J. (eds) (1999), *Actor Network Theory and After*, Oxford, Blackwell

Lazarsfeld, P. F. (1954), *Mathematical Thinking in the Social Sciences*, New York, Russell & Russell

Lazarsfeld, P. F. (1971), *Qualitative Analysis: Historical and critical essays*, Boston, Allyn & Bacon

Lazarsfeld, P. F., and Henny, N. W. (1968), *Latent Structure Analysis*, New York, Houghton Mifflin

Lazarsfeld, P. F., and Katz, E. (1955), *Personal Influence: The part played by people in the flow of mass communications*, New York, Free Press

Lazarsfeld, P. F., *et al.* (1969), *The People's Choice: How the voter makes up his mind in a presidential campaign*, 3rd edn, New York, Columbia University Press

Leach, E. R. (1967), *The Structural Study of Myth and Totemism*, London, Tavistock

Leach, E. R. (1970), *Lévi-Strauss*, London, Fontana

Le Bon, G. (1895), *The Crowd*, New York, Macmillan, 1947

Lefebvre, H. (1947), *Critique of Everyday Life*, London, Verso, 1991

Lefebvre, H. (1968), *The Sociology of Marx*, London, Allen Lane The Penguin Press

Lee, D. J., and Turner, B. S. (eds) (1996), *Conflicts about Class: Debating inequality in late industrialism*, London, Longman

Lemaire, A. (1977), *Lacan*, London, Routledge & Kegan Paul

Lemert, E. M. (1951), *Social Pathology: A systematic approach to the study of sociopathic behavior*, New York, McGraw-Hill

Lemert, E. M. (1967), *Human Deviance, Social Problems and Social Control*, Englewood Cliffs, NJ, Prentice Hall

Lenin, V. I. (1902), 'What is to be done?', *Collected Works*, vol. 5, Moscow, Foreign Languages Publishing House, 1961

Lenin, V. I. (1915), *Imperialism, as the Highest Stage of Capitalism*, Moscow, Progress Publishers

Lenski, G. E. (1954), 'Status crystallization: a non-vertical dimension of social status', *American Sociological Review*, vol. 19, pp. 405–14

Lerner, D. (1958), *The Passing of Traditional Society*, Glencoe, Free Press

Lessnoff, M. (1974), *The Structure of Social Science*, London, Allen & Unwin

L'Etang, J., and Pieczka, M. (1996), *Critical Perspectives in Public Relations*, London, International Thomson Business Press

Lévi-Strauss, C. (1949), *The Elementary Structures of Kinship*, London, Eyre & Spottiswoode, 1969

Lévi-Strauss, C. (1955), *Tristes Tropiques*, New York, Atheneum, 1968

Lévi-Strauss, C. (1958), *Structural Anthropology*, London, Allen Lane The Penguin Press, 1968

Lévi-Strauss, C. (1962a), *Totemism*, Harmondsworth, Penguin Books, 1969

Lévi-Strauss, C. (1962b), *The Savage Mind*, Chicago, Chicago University Press, 1966

Lévi-Strauss, C. (1964), *Introduction to a Science of Mythology*, 4 vols, London, Cape, 1970–81

Levine, S., and Kozloff, M. A. (1978), 'The sick role: assessment and overview', *Annual Review of Sociology*, vol. 4, pp. 317–43

Lewis, O. (1961), *The Children of Sanchez*, New York, Random House

Lindesmith, A. R. (1968), *Addiction and Opiates*, Chicago, Aldine

Lindholm, C. (1993), *Charisma*, Oxford, Blackwell

Linton, R. (1936), *The Study of Man: An introduction*, New York, Appleton

Lipset, S. M. (1950), *Agrarian Socialism, The Co-operative Commonwealth Federation in Saskatchewan: A study of political sociology*, Berkeley, University of California Press

Lipset, S. M. (1960), *Political Man: The social bases of politics*, Garden City, NY, Doubleday

Lipset, S. M. (1963), *The First New Nation: The United States in historical and comparative perspective*, New York, Basic Books

Lipset, S. M. (1969), *Revolution and Counter-Revolution*, London, Heinemann Educational Books

Lipset, S. M., and Bendix, R. (1959), *Social Mobility in Industrial Society*, Berkeley, University of California Press

Lipset, S. M., and Raab, E. (1971), *The Politics of Unreason*, London, Heinemann Educational Books

Lipset, S. M., Trow, M. A., and Coleman, J. S. (1956), *Union Democracy: The internal politics of the International Typographical Union*, Glencoe, Free Press

Littler, C. R. (1982), *The Development of the Labour Process in Capitalist Societies*, London, Heinemann Educational Books

Littler, C. R. (1985), 'Taylorism, Fordism and job design', in D. Knights, H. Willmott and D. Collinson (eds), *Job Redesign: Critical perspectives on the labour process*, Aldershot, Gower, pp. 30–51

Littler, C. (1990), 'The Labour Process Debate: a theoretical review 1974–1988', in D. Knights and H. Willmott (eds), *Labour Process Theory*, Basingstoke, Macmillan, pp. 46–94

Loader, C. (1985), *The Intellectual Development of Karl Mannheim*, Cambridge, Cambridge University Press

Lockwood, D. (1956), 'Some remarks on "The Social System"', *British Journal of Sociology*, vol. 7, pp. 134–46

Lockwood, D. (1958), *The Blackcoated Worker*, London, Allen & Unwin

Lockwood, D. (1964), 'Social integration and system integration', in G. K. Zollschan and W. Hirsch (eds), *Explorations in Social Change*, London, Routledge & Kegan Paul, pp. 244–57

Lockwood, D. (1966), 'Sources of variation in working-class images of society', *Sociological Review*, vol. 14, pp. 249–67

Lockwood, D. (1992), *Solidarity and Schism: 'The problem of order' in Durkheimian and Marxist sociology*, Oxford, Clarendon Press

Lopreato, J., and Crippen, T. (1999), *Crisis in Sociology: The need for Darwin*, New Brunswick, NJ, Transaction Publishers

Löwith, K. (1993), *Max Weber and Karl Marx*, London, Routledge

Lowman, J., and Maclean, B. (eds) (1992), *Realist Criminology: Crime control and policing in the 1990s*, Toronto, University of Toronto Press

Luckmann, T. (1967), *The Invisible Religion: The problem of religion in modern society*, New York, Macmillan

Luhmann, N. (1982), *The Differentiation of Society*, New York, Columbia University Press

Luhmann, N. (1984), *Religious Dogmatics and the Evolution of Society*, Lewiston, NY, Edwin Mellen

Luhmann, N. (1986), *Love as Passion: The codification of intimacy*, Cambridge, Polity Press

Luhmann, N. (1989), *Ecological Communication*, Cambridge, Polity Press

Luhmann, N. (1993), *Risk: A sociological theory*, New York, De Gruyter

Luhmann, N. (1995), *Social Systems*, Stanford, Stanford University Press

Lukács, G. (1923), *History and Class Consciousness*, London, Merlin Press, 1971

Lukács, G. (1954), *The Destruction of Reason*, London, Merlin Press

Lukács, G. (1955), *The Historical Novel*, London, Merlin Press, 1962

Lukács, G. (1964), *Essays on Thomas Mann*, London, Merlin Press

Lukács, G. (1968), *Goethe and his Age*, London, Merlin Press

Lukács, G. (1972), *Studies in European Realism*, London, Merlin Press

Lukács, G. (1978), *The Ontology of Social Being*, London, Merlin Press

Lukes, S. (1967), 'Alienation and anomie', in P. Laslett and W. G. Runciman (eds), *Philosophy, Politics and Society*, 3rd series, Oxford, Blackwell, pp. 134–56

Lukes, S. (1972), *Emile Durkheim, his Life and Work: A historical and critical study*, London, Allen & Unwin

Lukes, S. (1974), *Power: A radical view*, London, Macmillan

Lury, C. (1996), *Consumer Culture*, Cambridge, Polity Press

Lynd, R. S., and Lynd, H. M. (1929), *Middletown: A study in contemporary American culture*, New York, Harcourt Brace

Lynd, R. S., and Lynd, H. M. (1937), *Middletown in Transition: A study in cultural conflicts*, New York, Harcourt Brace

Lyotard, J. F. (1979), *The Postmodern Condition: A report on knowledge*, Manchester, Manchester University Press, 1984

Macdonald, K. M. (1995), *The Sociology of the Professions*, London, Sage

Macedo, S. (1990), *Liberal Virtues: Citizenship, virtue and community in liberal constitutionalism*, Oxford, Clarendon Press

MacIntyre, A. (1981), *After Virtue: A study in moral theory*, London, Duckworth

Magee, B. (1973), *Popper*, London, Fontana

Malinowski, B. (1922), *Argonauts of the Western Pacific*, London, Routledge & Kegan Paul

Malinowski, B. (1927), *Sex and Repression in Savage Society*, London, Routledge & Kegan Paul

Malinowski, B. (1935), *Coral Gardens and their Magic*, London, Allen & Unwin

Malinowski, B. (1944), *A Scientific Theory of Culture*, Oxford, Oxford University Press

Malinowski, B. (1948), *Magic, Science and Religion and Other Essays*, Glencoe, Free Press

Mallet, S. (1963), *The New Working Class*, Nottingham, Spokesman, 1975

Malthus, T. R. (1803), *An essay on the principle of population and a summary view of the principle of population*, edited with an introduction by Antony Flew, Harmondsworth, Penguin, 1970

Man, P. de (1983), *Blindness and Insight: Essays in the Rhetoric of Contemporary Criticism*, 2nd edn, London, Methuen

Mandel, E. (1975), *Late Capitalism*, London, New Left Books

Mangen, S. P. (1982), *Sociology and Mental Health*, Edinburgh, Churchill Livingstone

Mann, M. (1973), *Consciousness and Action in the Western Working Class*, London, Macmillan

Mannheim, H. (1965), *Comparative Criminology*, London and Boston, Routledge & Kegan Paul

Mannheim, K. (1936), *Ideology and Utopia*, London, Routledge & Kegan Paul

Mannheim, K. (1940), *Man and Society in an Age of Reconstruction*, London, Routledge & Kegan Paul

Mannheim, K. (1943), *Diagnosis of Our Time*, London, Kegan Paul/Trench, Trubner

Mannheim, K. (1951), *Freedom, Power and Democratic Planning*, London, Routledge & Kegan Paul

Mannheim, K. (1952a), 'The problem of generations', in *Essays on the Sociology of Culture*, London, Routledge & Kegan Paul, pp. 276–320

Mannheim, K. (1952b), *Essays on the Sociology of Knowledge*, London, Routledge & Kegan Paul

Mannheim, K. (1953), *Essays on Sociology and Social Psychology*, London, Routledge & Kegan Paul

Mannheim, K. (1956), *Essays on the Sociology of Culture*, London, Routledge & Kegan Paul

March, J. G., and Simon, H. A. (1958), *Organizations*, New York, Wiley

Marcuse, H. (1954), *Reason and Revolution: Hegel and the rise of social theory*, New York, Humanities Press

Marcuse, H. (1955), *Eros and Civilization: A philosophical inquiry into Freud*, Boston, Beacon Press

Marcuse, H. (1961), *Soviet Marxism: A critical analysis*, New York, Columbia University Press

Marcuse, H. (1964), *One-Dimensional Man: Studies in the ideology of advanced industrial society*, London, Routledge & Kegan Paul

Marcuse, H. (1968), *Negations: Essays in critical theory*, London, Allen & Unwin

Marcuse, H. (1969), *An Essay on Liberation*, London, Allen Lane The Penguin Press

Marini, M. M. (1992), 'The role of models of purposive action in sociology', in J. S. Coleman and T. J. Fararo (eds), *Rational Choice Theory*, Newbury Park, California, Sage, pp. 21–48

Marsh, C. (1982), *The Survey Method: The contribution of surveys to sociological explanation*, London, George Allen & Unwin

Marshall, G. (1982), *In Search of the Spirit of Capitalism*, London, Hutchinson

Marshall, G., Rose, D., Newby, H., and Vogler, C. (1988), *Social Class in Modern Britain*, London, Unwin Hyman

Marshall, T. H. (1963), *Sociology at the Crossroads*, London, Heinemann Educational Books

Marshall, T. H. (1965), *Social Policy in the Twentieth Century*, 5th edn, edited by A. M. Rees, London, Hutchinson, 1985

Marshall, T. H. (1981), *The Right to Welfare and Other Essays*, London, Heinemann Educational Books

Martin, D. (1965), *Pacifism: A sociological and historical study*, London, Routledge & Kegan Paul

Martin, D. (1967), *A Sociology of English Religion*, London SCM Press

Martin, D. (1969a), *The Religious and the Secular*, London, Routledge & Kegan Paul

Martin, D. (1969b), *Anarchy and Culture*, London, Routledge & Kegan Paul

Martin, D. (1973), *Tracts against the Times*, London, Lutterworth Press

Martin, D. (1978a), *A General Theory of Secularization*, Oxford, Blackwell

Martin, D. (1978b), *The Dilemmas of Contemporary Religion*, Oxford, Blackwell

Martin, D. (1980), *The Breaking of the Image*, Oxford, Blackwell

Martin, J., and Roberts, C. (1984), *Women and Employment: A lifetime perspective*, London, Her Majesty's Stationery Office

Marx, K. (1845), *Theses on Feuerbach*, reprinted in K. Marx and F. Engels, *Selected Works*, London, Lawrence & Wishart, 1970

Marx, K. (1847), *The Poverty of Philosophy*, Moscow, Progress Publishers, 1956

Marx, K. (1852), *The Eighteenth Brumaire of Louis Bonaparte*, Moscow, Progress Publishers, 1934

Marx, K. (1867, 1885, 1894), *Capital*, London, Lawrence & Wishart, 1970

Marx, K. (1964), *The Economic and Philosophical Manuscripts of 1844*, New York, International Publishers

Marx, K. (1973), *Grundrisse*, Harmondsworth, Penguin Books

Marx, K., and Engels, F. (1845a), *The Holy Family*, Moscow, Progress Publishers, 1956

Marx, K., and Engels, F. (1845b), *The German Ideology*, London, Lawrence & Wishart, 1965

Marx, K., and Engels, F. (1848), *Manifesto of the Communist Party*, in K. Marx and F. Engels, *Selected Works*, London, Lawrence & Wishart, 1968

Maslow, A. H. (1954), *Motivation and Personality*, New York, Harper & Row

Matza, D. (1964), *Delinquency and Drift*, New York, Wiley

Matza, D. (1969), *Becoming Deviant*, Englewood Cliffs, NJ, Prentice Hall

Mauss, M. (1906), 'Essai sur les variations saisonnières des sociétés eskimos: étude de morphologie sociale', in *Sociologie et Anthropologie*, Paris, Presses Universitaires de France, pp. 389–477

Mauss, M. (1925), *The Gift*, New York, Free Press, 1954

McCarthy, T. (1978), *The Critical Theory of Jürgen Habermas*, London, Hutchinson

McClelland, D. C. (1961), *The Achieving Society*, Princeton, Princeton University Press

McClelland, D. C. (1971), *Assessing Human Motivation*, New York, General Learning Press

McLellan, D. (1973), *Karl Marx*, London, Macmillan

McLellan, D. (1977), *Engels*, Glasgow, Fontana

McLuhan, M. (1962), *The Gutenberg Galaxy: The making of typographic man*, London, Routledge & Kegan Paul

McLuhan, M. (1987), *Understanding Media: The extensions of man*, London, ARK, 1987

McQuail, D. (1987), *Mass Communication Theory*, London, Sage

Mead, G. H. (1934), *Mind, Self and Society*, Chicago, Chicago University Press

Mead, G. H. (1938), *The Philosophy of the Act*, Chicago, Chicago University Press

Mead, G. H. (1959), *The Philosophy of the Present*, Seattle, Open Court Publishing

Mead, M. (1928), *Coming of Age in Samoa*, Harmondsworth, Penguin Books, 1961

Mead, M. (1930), *Growing Up in New Guinea*, Harmondsworth, Penguin Books, 1967

Mead, M. (1935), *Sex and Temperament in Three Primitive Societies*, New York, Morrow, 1963

Mead, M. (1949), *Male and Female: A study of the sexes in a changing society*, New York, Morrow, 1963

Mead, M. (1956), *New Lives for Old*, New York, Morrow

Mead, M. (1970a), *Culture and Commitment: A study of the generation gap*, London, Bodley Head

Mead, M. (ed.) (1970b), *Science and the Concept of Race*, New York, Columbia University Press

Mead, M. (1972), *Twentieth Century Faith: Hope and survival*, New York, Harper

Mechanic, D. (1968), *Medical Sociology*, New York, Macmillan

Mennell, S. (1985), *All Manners of Food: Eating and taste in England and France from the Middle Ages to the present*, Oxford, Blackwell

Mennell, S. (1989), *Norbert Elias: Civilisation and the human self-image*, Oxford, Blackwell

Merleau-Ponty, M. (1962), *Phenomenology of Perception*, London, Routledge & Kegan Paul

Merquior, J. G. (1980), *Rousseau and Weber: Two studies in the theory of legitimacy*, London, Routledge & Kegan Paul

Merton, R. K. (1957), *Social Theory and Social Structure*, New York, Free Press

Merton, R. K., and Nisbet, R. (eds) (1961), *Contemporary Social Problems*, New York, Harcourt Brace

Michels, R. (1911), *Political Parties: A sociological study of the oligarchical tendencies of modern democracy*, New York, Free Press, 1962

Miles, R. (1989), *Racism*, London, Routledge

Miliband, R. (1969), *The State in Capitalist Society*, London, Weidenfeld & Nicolson

Miliband, R. (1970), 'The capitalist state: reply to Nicol Poulantzas', *New Left Review*, no. 59, pp. 53–60

Miliband, R. (1983), *Class Power and State Power*, London, Verso

Milkman, R. and Townsley, E. (1994), 'Gender and the economy', in N. J. Smelser and R. Swedberg (eds), *The Handbook of Economic Sociology*, Princeton, NJ, Princeton University Press, pp. 600–619

Millerson, G. L. (1964), *The Qualifying Association*, London, Routledge & Kegan Paul

Millett, K. (1969), *Sexual Politics*, London, Virago

Mills, C. W. (1940), 'Situated actions and vocabularies of motive', *American Sociological Review*, vol. 5, pp. 904–93

Mills, C. W. (1951), *White Collar: The American middle classes*, New York, Oxford University Press

Mills, C. W. (1956), *The Power Elite*, New York, Simon & Schuster

Mills, C. W. (1959), *The Sociological Imagination*, New York, Oxford University Press

Mirrless-Black, C., Budd, T., Partridge, S., and Mayhew, P. (1998), *The 1998 British Crime Survey, England and Wales*, London, Her Majesty's Stationery Office

Mitchell, J. (1974), *Women: The longest revolution*, Harmondsworth, Penguin, 1984

Moi, T. (ed.) (1986), *The Kristeva Reader*, Oxford, Blackwell

Mommsen, W. J. (1980), *Theories of Imperialism*, London, Weidenfeld & Nicolson

Montesquieu, C.-L. (1721), *Persian Letters*, Harmondsworth, Penguin Books, 1973

Montesquieu, C.-L. (1734), *Considérations sur les causes de la grandeur des Romains et de leur décadence*, in *Oeuvres complètes de Montesquieu*, NRF, Bibliothèque de la Pléiade, vol. 2, 1951

Montesquieu, C.-L. (1748), *The Spirit of the Law*, New York, Hafner, 1962

Moore, B. (1950), *Soviet Politics – The Dilemma of Power: The role of ideas in social change*, Cambridge, Mass., Harvard University Press

Moore, B. (1954), *Terror and Progress USSR: Some sources of change and stability in the Soviet dictatorship*, Cambridge, Mass., Harvard University Press

Moore, B. (1958), *Political Power and Social Theory*, Cambridge, Mass., Harvard University Press

Moore, B. (1967), *Social Origins of Dictatorship and Democracy: Lord and peasant in the making of the modern world*, London, Allen Lane The Penguin Press

Moore, B. (1972), *Reflections on the Causes of Human Misery and upon Certain Proposals to Eliminate Them*, Boston, Beacon Press

Moore, B. (1978), *Injustice: The social bases of obedience and revolt*, White Plains, New York, M. E. Sharpe

Moore, B. (1984), *Privacy: Studies in social and cultural history*, New York, Pantheon Books

Moore, B., and Wolff, K. H. (eds) (1967), *The Critical Spirit: Essays in honor of Herbert Marcuse*, Boston, Beacon Press

Moores, S. (1993), *Interpreting Audiences*, London, Sage

Moorhouse, H. F. (1976), 'Attitudes to class and class relationships in Britain', *Sociology*, vol. 10, pp. 469–96

Moorhouse, H. F. (1978), 'The Marxist theory of the labour aristocracy', *Social History*, vol. 3, pp. 61–82

Morgan, D. H. J. (1985), *The Family, Politics and Social Theory*, London, Routledge

Morley, D., and Chen, K.-H. (eds) (1996), *Stuart Hall: Critical dialogues in cultural studies*, London, Routledge

Morris, L. (1990), *The Workings of the Household*, Cambridge, Polity Press

Morris, R. (1968), *Urban Sociology*, London, Allen & Unwin

Morriss, J. A., and Feldman, D. C. (1996), 'The dimensions, antecedents, and consequences of emotional labor', *Academy of Management Review*, vol. 21, pp. 986–1010

Mosca, G. (1896), *The Ruling Class*, New York, McGraw-Hill, 1939

Moser, C. A., and Kalton, G. (1979), *Survey Methods in Social Investigation*, 2nd edn, London, Heinemann Educational Books

Mosteller, F. (1968), 'Errors: nonsampling errors', in D. L. Sills (ed.), *International Encyclopedia of the Social Sciences*, vol. 5, pp. 113–32, New York, Macmillan and Free Press

Mouffe, C. (ed.) (1979), *Gramsci and Marxist Theory*, London, Routledge & Kegan Paul

Mouzelis, N. P. (1967), *Organisations and Bureaucracy*, London, Routledge & Kegan Paul

Mouzelis, N. P. (1988), 'Sociology of development: reflections on the present crisis', *Sociology*, vol. 22, pp. 23–44

Mouzelis, N. P. (1997), 'Social and system integration: Lockwood, Habermas, Giddens', *Sociology*, vol. 31, pp. 111–19

Mumford, E. (1983), *Medical Sociology: Patients, providers and policies*, New York, Random House

Nandan, Y. (1977), *The Durkheimian School*, Westport, Conn., Greenwood

Navarro, V. (1977), *Medicine under Capitalism*, London, Croom Helm

Nelson, D. (1975), *Managers and Workers*, Madison, University of Wisconsin Press

Neuwirth, G. (1969), 'A Weberian outline of a theory of community: its application to the "Dark Ghetto" ', *British Journal of Sociology*, vol. 20, pp. 148–63

Newby, H. (1977), *The Deferential Worker*, London, Allen Lane The Penguin Press

Newby, H. (1979), *Green and Pleasant Land?* London, Hutchinson

Nicholson, L. J. (ed.), (1990), *Feminism and Postmodernism*, New York and London, Routledge

Niethammer, L. (1992), *Posthistoire: Has history come to an end?*, London, Verso

Nisbet, R. A. (1953), *The Quest for Community: A study in the ethics of order and freedom*, New York, Oxford University Press

Nisbet, R. A. (ed.) (1965), *Emile Durkheim*, Englewood Cliffs, NJ, Prentice Hall

Nisbet, R. A. (1967), *The Sociological Tradition*, London, Heinemann Educational Books

Nisbet, R. A. (1968), *Tradition and Revolt: Historical and sociological essays*, New York, Random House

Nisbet, R. A. (1969), *Social Change and History*, New York, Oxford University Press

Nisbet, R. A. (1970), *The Social Bond: An introduction to the study of society*, New York, Knopf

Nisbet, R. A. (1974a), *The Social Philosophers: Community and conflict in Western thought*, London, Heinemann Educational Books

Nisbet, R. A. (1974b), *The Sociology of Emile Durkheim*, London, Heinemann Educational Books

Nisbet, R. A. (1976), *Sociology as an Art Form*, London, Heinemann Educational Books

Nisbet, R. A. (1980), *History of the Idea of Progress*, New York, Basic Books

Nisbet, R. A. (1982), *Prejudices: A philosophical dictionary*, Cambridge, Mass., Harvard University Press

Nisbet, R. A. (1986), *Conservatism*, Milton Keynes, Open University Press

Norman, P. (1975), 'Managerialism: Review of recent work', in M. Harloe (ed.), *Proceedings of the Conference on Urban Change and Conflict (1975)*, London, Centre for Environmental Studies, pp. 62–86

Norris, C. (1988), *Paul de Man: Deconstruction and the critique of aesthetic ideology*, New York and London, Routledge

Norris, P., and Evans, G. (1999), 'Introduction: understanding electoral change', in P. Norris and G. Evans (eds), *Critical Elections: British parties and voters in long-term perspective*, London, Sage, pp. xix–xl

North, N., and Bradshaw, Y. (eds) (1997), *Perspectives in Health Care*, Basingstoke, Macmillan

Nozick, R. (1974), *Anarchy, State and Utopia*, New York, Basic Books

Oakeshott, R. (1978), *The Case for Workers' Co-ops*, London, Routledge & Kegan Paul

Oakley, A. (1972), *Sex, Gender and Society*, Melbourne, Sun Books

Oakley, A. (1974), *The Sociology of Housework*, London, Martin Robertson

Oakley, A. (1981), *Subject Women*, Oxford, Martin Robertson

O'Connor, J. (1973), *The Fiscal Crisis of the State*, New York, St Martin's Press

Ogburn, W. F. (1950), *On Culture and Social Change*, Chicago, Chicago University Press

Ollman, B. (1971), *Alienation: Marx's critique of man in capitalist society*, Cambridge, Cambridge University Press

Olson, M. (1965), *The Logic of Collective Action: Public goods and the theory of groups*, Cambridge, Mass., Harvard University Press

Oppenheim, C. (1990), *Poverty: The facts*, London, Child Poverty Action Group

Orwell, G. (1949), *Nineteen Eighty-Four*, London, Secker & Warburg, 1992

Ossowski, S. (1963), *Class and Class Structure in the Social Consciousness*, London, Routledge & Kegan Paul

Outhwaite, W. (1975), *Understanding Social Life*, London, Allen & Unwin

Oyen, E. (ed.) (1990), *Comparative Methodology: Theory and practice in international social research*, London, Sage

Pahl, R. E. (ed.) (1968), *Readings in Urban Sociology*, Oxford, Pergamon Press

Pahl, R. E. (1975), *Whose City?*, Harmondsworth, Penguin Books

Pakulski, J., and Waters, M. (1996), *The Death of Class*, London, Sage

Pareto, V. (1963), *The Mind and Society: A treatise on general sociology*, New York, Dover

Park, R. E. (1950), *Collected Papers of Robert Ezra Park*, New York, Free Press

Park, R. E., and Burgess, E. (1921), *Introduction to the Science of Society*, Chicago, Chicago University Press, 2nd edn, 1929

Parkin, F. (1971), *Class, Inequality and Political Order*, London, MacGibbon & Kee

Parkin, F. (1974), 'Strategies of social closure in class formation', in F. Parkin (ed.), *The Social Analysis of the Class Structure*, London, Tavistock, pp. 1–18

Parkin, F. (1978), 'Social stratification', in T. Bottomore and R. Nisbet (eds), *A History of Sociological Analysis*, New York, Basic Books, pp. 599–632

Parkin, F. (1979), *Marxism and Class Theory: A bourgeois critique*, London, Tavistock

Parkin, F. (1982), *Max Weber*, London, Tavistock

Parkin, F. (1992), *Durkheim*, Oxford, Oxford University Press

Parsons, T. (1937), *The Structure of Social Action*, New York, McGraw-Hill

Parsons, T. (1951), *The Social System*, New York, Free Press

Parsons, T. (1953), 'A revised analytical approach to the theory of social stratification', in R. Bendix and S. M. Lipset (eds), *Class, Status and Power: A reader in social stratification*, Glencoe, Free Press

Parsons, T. (1954), *Essays in Sociological Theory*, rev. edn, New York, Free Press

Parsons, T. (1963), 'On the concept of political power', *Proceedings of the American Philosophical Society*, vol. 107, pp. 232–62

Parsons, T. (1964), *Social Structure and Personality*, New York, Free Press

Parsons, T. (1966), *Societies: Evolutionary and comparative perspectives*, Englewood Cliffs, NJ, Prentice Hall

Parsons, T. (1967), *Sociological Theory and Modern Society*, New York, Free Press

Parsons, T. (1968a), 'Durkheim, Emile', in D. L. Sills (ed.), *International Encyclopedia of the Social Sciences*, vol. 4, pp. 311–20, New York, Macmillan and Free Press

Parsons, T. (1968b), 'Pareto, Vilfredo: contributions to sociology', in D. L. Sills (ed.), *International Encyclopedia of the Social Sciences*, vol. 11, New York, Macmillan and Free Press, pp. 411–15

Parsons, T. (1968c), 'Utilitarianism: sociological thought', in D. L. Sills (ed.), *International Encyclopedia of the Social Sciences*, vol. 16, New York, Macmillan and Free Press, pp. 229–36

Parsons, T. (1971), *The System of Modern Societies*, Englewood Cliffs, NJ, Prentice Hall

Parsons, T. (1977), *Social Systems and the Evolution of Action Theory*, New York, Free Press

Parsons, T., Bales, R. F., Olds, J., Zelditch, M., and Slater, P. E. (1955), *Family, Socialization and Interaction Process*, New York, Free Press

Parsons, T., Bales, R. F., and Shils, E. A. (1953), *Working Papers in the Theory of Action*, New York, Free Press

Parsons, T., and Shils, E. A. (eds) (1951), *Toward a General Theory of Action*, Cambridge, Mass., Harvard University Press

Parsons, T., and Smelser, N. (1956), *Economy and Society*, New York, Free Press

Peel, J. D. Y. (1969a), 'Spencer and the Neo-Evolutionists', *Sociology*, vol. 3, pp. 173–92

Peel, J. D. Y. (1969b), 'Understanding alien belief systems', *British Journal of Sociology*, vol. 20, pp. 69–84

Peel, J. D. Y. (1971), *Herbert Spencer: The evolution of a sociologist*, London, Heinemann Educational Books

Perrow, C. (1986), *Complex Organizations: A critical essay*, 3rd edn, New York, McGraw-Hill

Petersen, W. (1979), *Malthus*, London, Heinemann Educational Books

Phillipson, C. (1998), *Reconstructing Old Age: New agendas in social theory and practice*, London, Sage

Pierson, C. (1991), *Beyond the Welfare State?*, Oxford, Polity Press

Pierson, C. (1996), *The Modern State*, London, Routledge

Pilcher, J. (1995), *Age and Generation in Modern Britain*, Oxford, Oxford University Press

Piore, M., and Sabel, C. F. (1984), *The Second Industrial Divide*, New York, Basic Books

Plant, S. (1992), *The Most Radical Gesture: The situationist international in a postmodern age*, London, Routledge

Plummer, K. (1996), 'Symbolic Interactionism in the twentieth century: the rise of empirical social theory', in B. S. Turner (ed.), *The Blackwell Companion to Social Theory*, Oxford, Blackwell, pp. 223–51

Poggi, G. (1972), *Images of Society: Essays on the sociological theories of Tocqueville, Marx and Durkheim*, Stanford, Stanford University Press

Poggi, G. (1978), *The Development of the Modern State: A sociological introduction*, Stanford, Stanford University Press

Pollert, A. (ed.) (1991), *Farewell to Flexibility?*, Oxford, Blackwell

Poole, M. (1986), *Towards a New Industrial Democracy*, London, Routledge & Kegan Paul

Popham, R. E. (ed.) (1970), *Alcohol and Alcoholism*, Toronto, University of Toronto Press

Popper, K. R. (1945), *The Open Society and Its Enemies*, 2 vols, London, Routledge & Kegan Paul

Popper, K. R. (1957), *The Poverty of Historicism*, London, Routledge & Kegan Paul

Popper, K. R. (1959), *The Logic of Scientific Discovery*, London, Hutchinson

Popper, K. R. (1963), *Conjectures and Refutations: The growth of scientific knowledge*, London, Routledge & Kegan Paul

Popper, K. R. (1966), *Of Clouds and Clocks*, St Louis, Washington University Press

Popper, K. R. (1972), *Objective Knowledge: An evolutionary approach*, Oxford, Clarendon Press

Popper, K. R. (1974), *Unended Quest*, Glasgow, Fontana

Popper, K. R. (1982a), *The Open Universe*, London, Hutchinson

Popper, K. R. (1982b), *Quantum Theory and the Schism in Physics*, London, Hutchinson

Popper, K. R. (1983), *Realism and the Aim of Science*, Totowa, NJ, Rowman & Littlefield

Portes, A. (ed.) (1995), *The Economic Sociology of Immigration: Essays on networks, ethnicity and entrepreneurship*, New York, Russell Sage Foundation Press

Poulantzas, N. (1969), 'The problems of the capitalist state', *New Left Review*, no. 58, pp. 67–78

Poulantzas, N. (1973), *Political Power and Social Classes*, London, New Left Books

Poulantzas, N. (1974), *Fascism and Dictatorship*, London, New Left Books

Poulantzas, N. (1978), *State, Power, Socialism*, London, New Left Books

Prawer, J., and Eisenstadt, S. N. (1968), 'Feudalism', in D. L. Sills (ed.), *International Encyclopedia of the Social Sciences*, vol. 5, New York, Macmillan and Free Press, pp. 393–403

Pullinger, J., and Summerfield, C. (eds) (1997), *Social Focus on the Family*, London, Her Majesty's Stationery Office

Punnett, R. M. (1980), *British Government and Politics*, 4th edn, London, Heinemann Educational Books

Purcell, K. (1988), 'Gender and the experience of employment', in D. Gallie (ed.), *Employment in Britain*, Oxford, Blackwell, pp. 157–86

Pye, L. W., and Verba, S. (eds) (1965), *Political Culture and Political Development*, Princeton, Princeton University Press

Radcliffe-Brown, A. R. (1922), *The Andaman Islanders*, New York, Free Press

Radcliffe-Brown, A. R. (1931), *The Social Organization of Australian Tribes*, Glencoe, Free Press

Radcliffe-Brown, A. R. (1936), *Taboo*, Cambridge, Cambridge University Press

Radcliffe-Brown, A. R. (1952), *Structure and Function in Primitive Society*, London, Cohen & West

Ragin, C. C. (1987), *The Comparative Method: Moving beyond qualitative and quantitative strategies*, Berkeley, University of California Press

Rapoport, R. N., and Rapoport, R. (1971), *Dual Career Families*, Harmondsworth, Penguin Press

Rapoport, R. N., and Rapoport, R. (1976), *Dual Career Families Re-examined*, Oxford, Martin Robertson

Rasmussen, D. M. (1990), *Reading Habermas*, Oxford, Blackwell

Rawls, J. (1971), *A Theory of Justice*, Oxford, Oxford University Press, 1973

Reasons, C. E., and Rich, R. M. (eds) (1978), *The Sociology of Law*, London, Butterworth

Redfield, R. (1930), *Tepoztlan, a Mexican Village: A study of folk life*, Chicago, Chicago University Press

Reed, M. I. (1992), *The Sociology of Organizations*, London, Harvester Wheatsheaf

Reeve, A. (1986), *Property*, London, Macmillan

Regini, M. (ed.) (1992), *The Future of Labour Movements*, London, Sage

Reich, M., Gordon, D. M., and Edwards, R. C. (1973), 'A theory of labour market segmentation', *American Economic Review*, vol. 63, pp. 359–65

Reich, W. (1933), *The Mass Psychology of Fascism*, Harmondsworth, Penguin Books, 1975

Reinharz, S. (1992), *Feminist Methods in Social Research*, Oxford, Oxford University Press

Rex, J. (1961), *Key Problems of Sociological Theory*, London, Routledge & Kegan Paul

Rex, J. (1970), *Race Relations in Sociological Theory*, London, Weidenfeld & Nicolson

Rex, J. (1973a), *Discovering Sociology: Studies in sociological theory and method*, London, Routledge & Kegan Paul

Rex, J. (1973b), *Race, Colonialism and the City*, London, Routledge & Kegan Paul

Rex, J. (1974), *Sociology and the Demystification of the Modern World*, London, Routledge & Kegan Paul

Rex, J. (1981), *Social Conflict: A conceptual and theoretical analysis*, London, Longman

Rex, J. (1986), *Race and Ethnicity*, Milton Keynes, Open University Press

Rex, J., and Moore, R. (1967), *Race, Community and Conflict: A study of Sparkbrook*, London, Oxford University Press

Rex, J., and Tomlinson, S. (1979), *Colonial Immigrants in a British City*, London, Routledge & Kegan Paul

Richardson, M. (1994), *Georges Bataille*, London, Routledge

Rigby, A. (1974), *Alternative Realities*, London, Routledge & Kegan Paul

Riley, D. (1988), *Am I That Name?*, London, Macmillan

Ritzer, G. (1993), *The McDonaldization of Society*, Thousand Oakes, Pine Forge Press

Robbins, T. (1988), *Cults, Converts, and Charisma*, London, Sage

Roberts, J. (1982), *Walter Benjamin*, London, Macmillan

Roberts, K. (1978), *The Working Class*, London, Longman

Roberts, K., Cook, F. G., Clark, S. C., and Semeonoff, E. (1977), *The Fragmentary Class Structure*, London, Heinemann Educational Books

Robertson, R. (1974), 'Towards the identification of the major axes of sociological analysis', in J. Rex (ed.), *Approaches to Sociology: An introduction to major trends in British sociology*, London, Routledge & Kegan Paul, pp. 107–24

Robertson, R. (1992), *Globalization: Social theory and global culture*, London, Sage

Robertson, R. (1995), 'Globalization: time–space and homogeneity–heterogeneity', in M. Featherstone, S. Lash and R. Robertson (eds), *Global Modernities*, London, Sage, pp. 25–44

Robertson, R., and Lechner, F. (1985), 'Modernization, globalization and world-systems theory', *Theory, Culture and Society*, vol. 2 (3), pp. 103–17

Robinson, V., and Richardson, D. (eds) (1997), *Introducing Women's Studies*, London, Macmillan

Roche, M. (1992), *Rethinking Citizenship: Welfare, ideology and change in a modern society*, Cambridge, Polity Press

Rocher, G. (1974), *Talcott Parsons and American Sociology*, London, Nelson

Rock, P. (1979), *The Making of Symbolic Interactionism*, London, Macmillan

Rojek, C. and Turner, B. S. (eds) (1993), *Forget Baudrillard?*, London, Routledge

Rose, G. (1975), *The Problem of Party Government*, London, Macmillan

Rose, M. (1979), *Servants of Post-Industrial Power?*, London, Macmillan

Rose, M. (1988), *Industrial Behaviour*, London, Allen Lane

Rose, N. (1989), *Governing the Soul: The shaping of the private self*, London, Routledge

Ross, J. C. (1972), 'Towards a reconstruction of voluntary association theory', *British Journal of Sociology*, vol. 23, pp. 20–32

Roth, J. (1962), 'Management bias in social science research', *Human Organization*, vol. 21, pp. 47–50

Rousseau, J.-J. (1762), *The Social Contract*, London, J. M. Dent & Sons (Everyman Edition), 1913

Rowntree, B. S. (1902), *Poverty: A study of town life*, London, Longman

Roxborough, I. (1979), *Theories of Underdevelopment*, London, Macmillan

Roy, D. (1952), 'Quota restriction and goldbricking in a machine shop', *American Journal of Sociology*, vol. 57, pp. 427–42

Roy, D. (1953), 'Work satisfaction and social reward in quota achievement: an analysis of piecework incentive', *American Sociological Review*, vol. 18, pp. 507–14

Roy, D. (1955), 'Efficiency and "the fix": informal intergroup relations in a piecework machine shop', *American Journal of Sociology*, vol. 60, pp. 255–66

Royal Commission on the Distribution of Income and Wealth (1980), *An A to Z of Income and Wealth*, London, Her Majesty's Stationery Office

Rubinson, R., and Browne, I. (1994), 'Education and the Economy', in N. J. Smelser and R. Swedberg (eds), *The Handbook of Economic Sociology*, Princeton, NJ, Princeton University Press, pp. 581–99

Runciman, W. G. (1966), *Relative Deprivation and Social Justice*, London, Routledge & Kegan Paul

Runciman, W. G. (1972), *A Critique of Max Weber's Philosophy of Social Science*, Cambridge, Cambridge University Press

Rutter, M. (1972), *Maternal Deprivation Reassessed*, Harmondsworth, Penguin Books

Rutter, M., Maugham, B., Mortimore, P., and Ouston, J. (1979), *Fifteen Thousand Hours: Secondary schools and their effects on children*, London, Open Books

Ryan, A. (1970), *The Philosophy of the Social Sciences*, London, Macmillan

Sahlins, M. (1977), *The Use and Abuse of Biology: An anthropological critique of sociobiology*, London, Tavistock

Said, E. (1978), *Orientalism*, New York, Pantheon

Salaman, G. (1979), *Work Organizations*, London, Longman

Salmon, J. W. (ed.) (1984), *Alternative Medicines: Popular and policy perspectives*, London, Tavistock

Samson, C. (ed.) (1999), *Health Studies: A critical and cross-cultural reader*, Oxford, Blackwell

Sandel, M. (1982), *Liberalism and the Limits of Justice*, Cambridge, Cambridge University Press

Santos, T. Dos (1970), 'The structure of dependence', *American Economic Review*, vol. 60, pp. 231–6

Sarlvik, B., and Crewe, I. (1983), *Decade of Dealignment: The Conservative victory of 1979 and electoral trends in the 1970s*, Cambridge, Cambridge University Press

Sartori, G. (1976), *Parties and Party Systems: A framework for analysis*, Cambridge, Cambridge University Press

Saunders, P. (1980), *Urban Politics*, Harmondsworth, Penguin Books

Saunders, P. (1981), *Social Theory and the Urban Question*, London, Hutchinson

Saunders, P. (1990a), *A Nation of Home Owners*, London, Unwin Hyman

Saunders, P. (1990b), *Social Class and Stratification*, London, Routledge

Saunders, P., and Harris, C. (1994), *Privatization and Popular Capitalism*, Buckingham, Open University Press

Saussure, F. de (1916), *Course in General Linguistics*, London, Fontana, 1974

Savage, M., Barlow, J., Dickens, P., and Fielding, T. (1992), *Property, Bureaucracy and Culture: Middle class formation in contemporary Britain*, London, Routledge

Savage, M., and Warde, A. (1993), *Urban Sociology, Capitalised modernity*, London, Macmillan

Scheff, T. J. (1966), *Being Mentally Ill: A sociological theory*, London, Weidenfeld & Nicolson

Schein, E. H. (1985), *Organizational Culture and Leadership*, San Francisco, Jossey-Bass

Scherer, K. R. (1984), 'On the nature and functions of the emotions', in K. R. Scherer and P. Ekman (ed.), *Approaches to Emotion*, New Jersey, Lawrence Erlbaum, pp. 293–317

Schneider, L. (ed.) (1967), *The Scottish Moralists, on Human Nature and Society*, Chicago, Chicago University Press

Schudson, M. (1984), *Advertising: The uneasy persuasion*, New York, Basic Books

Schumpeter, J. A. (1934), *The Theory of Economic Development*, Cambridge, Mass., Harvard University Press

Schumpeter, J. A. (1950), *Capitalism, Socialism and Democracy*, 3rd edn, London, Allen & Unwin

Schumpeter, J. A. (1951), *Imperialism and Social Classes*, New York, Kelley

Schur, E. M. (1965), *Crimes without Victims*, Englewood Cliffs, NJ, Prentice Hall

Schutz, A. (1970), *Reflections on the Problem of Relevance*, ed. R. M. Zaner, New Haven, Conn., Yale University Press

Schutz, A. (1971), *Collected Papers*, vols 1 and 2, The Hague, Nijhoff

Schutz, A. (1972), *The Phenomenology of the Social World*, London, Heinemann Educational Books

Schutz, A., and Luckmann, T. (1974), *The Structures of the Life-World*, London, Heinemann Educational Books

Scott, A. (1990), *Ideology and the New Social Movements*, London, Unwin Hyman

Scott, J. (1979), *Corporations, Classes and Capitalism*, London, Hutchinson

Scott, J. (1982), *The Upper Class: Property and privilege in Britain*, London, Macmillan

Scott, J. (1988), 'Ownership and employer control', in D. Gallie (ed.), *Employment in Britain*, Blackwell, pp. 437–64

Scott, J. (ed.) (1990), *The Sociology of Elites*, 3 vols, Aldershot, Edward Elgar

Scott, J. (1991), *Who Rules Britain?*, Cambridge, Polity Press

Scott, J. (1992), *Social Network Analysis*, London, Sage

Scott, J. (1993), *Poverty and Wealth*, London, Longman

Scott, J. (1997), *Corporate Business and Capitalist Classes*, Oxford, Oxford University Press

Scott, W. R. (1995), *Institutions and Organizations*, London, Sage

Scull, A. (1977), *Decarceration – Community Treatment and the Deviant: A radical view*, Englewood Cliffs, NJ, Prentice Hall

Seeman, M. (1959), 'On the Meaning of Alienation', *American Sociological Review*, vol. 24, pp. 783–91

Seidler, V. (1989), *Rediscovering Masculinity: Reason, language and sexuality*, London, Routledge

Sennett, R. (1974), *The Fall of Public Man*, Cambridge, Cambridge University Press

Senter, R. J. (1969), *Analysis of Data: Introductory statistics for the behavioral sciences*, Glenview, Illinois, Scott, Foresman

Sharpe, S. (1979), *Just Like a Girl: How girls learn to be women*, Harmondsworth, Penguin Books

Sharrock, W., and Anderson, B. (1986), *The Ethnomethodologists*, London, Tavistock

Sheridan, A. (1980), *Michel Foucault: The will to truth*, London, Tavistock

Shils, E. (1962), 'The theory of mass society', *Diogenes*, vol. 39, pp. 45–66

Shils, E. (1975), *Center and Periphery: Essays in macrosociology*, Chicago, Chicago University Press

Shils, E. (1981), *Tradition*, London, Routledge & Kegan Paul

Shonfield, A. (1965), *Modern Capitalism*, London, Oxford University Press

Shorter, E. (1977), *The Making of the Modern Family*, Glasgow, Fontana

Siegel, S. (1956), *Nonparametric Statistics for the Behavioral Sciences*, New York, McGraw-Hill

Silverman, D. (1970), *The Theory of Organisations*, London, Heinemann Educational Books

Simey, T. S., and Simey, M. B. (1960), *Charles Booth, Social Scientist*, Oxford, Oxford University Press

Simmel, G. (1892), *The Problems of the Philosophy of History*, New York, Free Press, 1977

Simmel, G. (1900), *The Philosophy of Money*, London, Routledge & Kegan Paul, 1978

Simmel, G. (1955), *Conflict and the Web of Group Affiliations*, New York, Free Press

Simons, J. (1995), *Foucault and the Political*, London, Routledge

Sklair, L. (1970), *The Sociology of Progress*, London, Routledge & Kegan Paul

Sklair, L. (1991), *Sociology of the Global System*, Hemel Hempstead, Harvester Wheatsheaf

Smart, B. (1985), *Michel Foucault*, Chichester, Ellis Horwood, and London, Tavistock

Smart, C. (1977), *Women, Crime and Criminology: A feminist critique*, London, Routledge & Kegan Paul

Smelser, N. J. (1959), *Social Change in the Industrial Revolution*, London, Routledge & Kegan Paul

Smelser, N. J. (1962), *Theory of Collective Behavior*, New York, Free Press

Smelser, N. J. (1988), 'Social Structure', in N. J. Smelser (ed.), *The Handbook of Sociology*, London, Sage, pp. 103–29

Smelser, N. J., and Swedberg, R. (1994a), 'The Sociological Perspective on the Economy', in N. J. Smelser and R. Swedberg (eds), *The Handbook of Economic Sociology*, Princeton, NJ, Princeton University Press, pp. 3–26

Smelser, N. J. and Swedberg, R. (eds) (1994b), *The Handbook of Economic Sociology*, Princeton, NJ, Princeton University Press

Smith, A. (1776), *An Inquiry into the Nature and Causes of the Wealth of Nations*, ed. E. Cannan, London, Methuen, 1950

Smith, A. D. (1973), *The Concept of Social Change*, London, Routledge & Kegan Paul

Smith, A. D. (1991), *National Identity*, Harmondsworth, Penguin Books

Smith, D. (1983), *Barrington Moore Jr: A critical appraisal*, Armonk, New York, M. E. Sharpe

Social Trends 16 (1986), London, Her Majesty's Stationery Office

Social Trends (1997), London, Her Majesty's Stationery Office

Sociology (1978), special issue on *Language and practical reasoning*, vol. 12, no. 1

Sohn-Rethel, A. (1978), *Intellectual and Manual Labour: A critique of epistemology*, London, Macmillan

Sombart, W. (1930), 'Capitalism', in A. Johnson and E. R. A. Seligman (eds), *Encyclopaedia of the Social Sciences*, vol. 3, pp. 195–208, New York, Macmillan

Sorensen, A. B., and Spilerman, S. (eds) (1993), *Social Theory and Social Policy: Essays in honor of James S. Coleman*, Westport, Connecticut, Praeger

Sorokin, P. A. (1927), *Social Mobility*, New York, Harper

Sorokin, P. A. (1928), *Contemporary Sociological Theories*, New York, Harper

Sorokin, P. A. (1937–41), *Social and Cultural Dynamics*, New York, American Book Company

Sorokin, P. A. (1943), *Sociocultural Causality, Space, Time*, Durham, Duke University Press

Sorokin, P. A. (1950), *The Social Philosophies of an Age of Crisis*, republished as *Modern Historical and Social Philosophies*, New York, Dover, 1963

Sorokin, P. A. (1956), *Fads and Foibles in Modern Sociology*, Chicago, Regnery

Sorokin, P. A. (1966), *Sociological Theories of Today*, New York, Harper

Spencer, B., and Gillen, F. J. (1904), *The Northern Tribes of Central Australia*, London, Routledge/Thoemmes Press, 1997

Spencer, H. (1876–96), *Principles of Sociology*, New York, Appleton

Spencer, H. (1884), *The Data of Ethics*, London, Williams & Norgate

Stanworth, M. (1983), *Gender and Schooling: A study of sexual divisions in the classroom*, London, Hutchinson

Stark, T. (1990), *Incomes and Wealth in the 1980s*, 2nd edn, London, The Fabian Society

Steers, R. M., Porter, L. W., and Bigley, G. A. (1996), 'Motivation and leadership: an introduction', in R. M. Steers, L. W. Porter and G. A. Bigley (eds), *Motivation and Leadership at Work*, 6th edn, New York, McGraw-Hill, pp. 2–33

Steiner, H. (1994), *An Essay on Rights*, Oxford, Blackwell

Stockman, F., Ziegler, R., and Scott, J. (1985), *Networks of Corporate Power: A comparative analysis of ten countries*, Cambridge, Polity Press

Stoett, P. L. (1995), 'This age of genocide: conceptual and institutional implications', *International Journal*, vol. 1, pp. 594–618

Stone, L. (1965), 'Theories of revolution', *World Politics*, vol. 18, pp. 159–76

Storey, J. (1993), *An Introductory Guide to Cultural Theory and Popular Culture*, London, Harvester Wheatsheaf

Stouffer, S. A., *et al.* (1949), *The American Soldier*, vol. 1, Princeton, Princeton University Press

Strauss, A. L. (1949), *Social Psychology*, New York, Dryden

Strauss, A. L. (1959), *Mirrors and Masks: The search for identity*, New Brunswick, NJ, Transaction Publishers, 1997

Strauss, A. L. (1964), *George Herbert Mead on Social Psychology*, Chicago, Chicago University Press

Strauss, A. L. (1968), *The American City: A source book of urban imagery*, Chicago, Aldine

Strauss, A. L. (1978), *Negotiations, Varieties, Contexts, Processes and Social Order*, San Francisco, Jossey-Bass

Strauss, A. L. (1993), *Continual Permutations of Action*, New York, Aldine De Gruyter

Strauss, A. L., Fagerhaugh, S., Suczek, B., and Wiener, C. (1985), *Social Organization of Medical Work*, Chicago, Chicago University Press

Sturmthal, A., and Scoville, J. G. (1973), *The International Labor Movement in Transition*, Urbana, University of Illinois Press

Sumner, W. G. (1906), *Folkways*, New York, Dover

Sutherland, E. H. (1934), *Principles of Criminology*, Chicago, Lippincott

Sutherland, E. H. (1939), *Principles of Criminology*, Philadelphia, Lippincott, rev. edn, 1955

Sutherland, E. H. (1945), 'Is "white-collar crime" crime?', *American Sociological Review*, vol. 10, pp. 132–9

Sutherland, E. H., and Cressey, D. R. (1955), *Principles of Criminology*, Chicago, Lippincott

Swedberg, R. (1994), 'Markets as social structures', in N. J. Smelser and R. Swedberg (eds), *The Handbook of Economic Sociology*, Princeton, NJ, Princeton University Press, pp. 255–83

Swedberg, R. (1998), *Max Weber and the Idea of Economic Sociology*, Princeton, NJ, Princeton University Press

Swedberg, R., and Granovetter, M. (1992), 'Introduction', in M. Granovetter and R. Swedberg (eds), *The Sociology of Economic Life*, Boulder, Col., Westview Press, pp. 1–28

Swingewood, A. (1977), *The Myth of Mass Culture*, London, Macmillan

Sykes, G., and Matza, D. (1957), 'Techniques of neutralization, a theory of delinquency', *American Sociological Review*, vol. 22, pp. 664–70

Szasz, T. (1971), *The Manufacture of Madness*, London, Paladin

Szelenyi, I., and Kostello, E. (1998), 'Outline of an institutional theory of inequality: the case of socialist and postcommunist eastern Europe', in M. C. Brinton and V. Nee (eds) (1998), *The New Institutionalism in Sociology*, New York, Russell Sage Foundation, pp. 305–26

Tawney, R. H. (1921), *The Acquisitive Society*, London, Bell

Tawney, R. H. (1926), *Religion and the Rise of Capitalism: A historical study*, London, Murray, 1960

Tawney, R. H. (1931), *Equality*, New York, Barnes & Noble

Taylor, F. W. (1964), *Scientific Management*, New York, Harper

Taylor, I., Walton, P., and Young, J. (1973), *The New Criminology: For a social theory of deviance*, London, Routledge & Kegan Paul

Taylor, K. (1975), *Henri Saint-Simon 1760–1825: Selected writings on science, industry and social organisation*, London, Croom Helm

Taylor-Gooby, P. (1991), *Social Change, Social Welfare and Social Science*, London, Harvester Wheatsheaf

Therborn, G. (1980), *The Ideology of Power and the Power of Ideology*, London, New Left Books

Thomas, W. I. (1927), 'The behavior pattern and the situation', *Publications of the American Sociological Society*, papers and proceedings, 22nd Annual Meeting, vol. 22, pp. 1–13

Thomas, W. I. (1928), *The Child in America, Behavior Problems and Programs*, New York, Knopf

Thomas, W. I. (1966), *On Social Organization and Social Personality*, Chicago, Chicago University Press

Thompson, E. P. (1978), *The Poverty of Theory*, London, Merlin Press

Thompson, P. (1983), *The Nature of Work: An introduction to debates on the labour process*, London, Macmillan

Thornley, J. (1981), *Workers' Co-operatives: Jobs and dreams*, London, Heinemann Educational Books

Thrasher, F. M. (1927), *The Gang: A study of 1,313 gangs in Chicago*, Chicago, Chicago University Press

Tilly, C., and Tilly, C. (1994), 'Capitalist work and labour markets', in N. J. Smelser and R. Swedberg (eds), *The Handbook of Economic Sociology*, Princeton, NJ, Princeton University Press, pp. 283–312

Timasheff, N. S. (1967), *Sociological Theory*, New York, Random House

Titmuss, R. (1970), *The Gift Relationship*, London, George Allen & Unwin

Tocqueville, A. de (1835–1840), *Democracy in America*, Glasgow, Collins, 1968

Tocqueville, A. de (1856), *The Old Regime and the French Revolution*, New York, Doubleday, 1955

Tocqueville, A. de (1893), *Recollections*, New York, Doubleday, 1970

Tocqueville, A. de, and Beaumont, G. de (1833), *On the Penitentiary System in the United States and its Application to France*, Carbondale and Edwardsville, Southern Illinois University Press, 1964

Toennies, F. (1887), *Community and Association*, Michigan, Michigan State University Press, 1957

Touraine, A. (1969), *The Post-Industrial Society*, New York, Random House, 1971

Treiman, D. J. (1977), *Occupational Prestige in Comparative Perspective*, New York, Academic Press

Trivers, R. L. (1985), *Social Evolution*, Menlo Park, Calif., Benjamin/Cummings

Troeltsch, E. (1912), *The Social Teaching of the Christian Churches*, New York, Macmillan, 1931

Turner, B. S. (1978), *Marx and the End of Orientalism*, London, George Allen & Unwin

Turner, B. S. (1981), *For Weber: Essays on the sociology of fate*, London, Routledge & Kegan Paul

Turner, B. S. (1983), *Religion and Social Theory: A materialist perspective*, London, Heinemann Educational Books

Turner, B. S. (1986a), *Citizenship and Capitalism: The debate over reformism*, London, Allen & Unwin

Turner, B. S. (1986b), *Equality*, London, Tavistock

Turner, B. S. (ed.) (1990), *Theories of Modernity and Postmodernity*, London, Sage

Turner, B. S. (1991), *Religion and Social Theory*, 2nd edn, London, Sage

Turner, B. S. (1992a), *Max Weber: From history to modernity*, London, Routledge

Turner, B. S. (1992b), *Regulating Bodies: Essays in medical sociology*, London, Routledge

Turner, B. S. (ed.) (1993), *Citizenship and Social Theory*, London, Sage

Turner, B. S. (1995), *Medical Power and Social Knowledge*, London, Sage

Turner, B. S. (1996a), *The Body and Society*, 2nd edn, London, Sage

Turner, B. S. (1996b), *For Weber: Essays on the sociology of fate*, 2nd edn, London, Sage

Turner, J. H. (1985), *Herbert Spencer: A renewed appreciation*, London, Sage

Turner, J. H. (1991), *The Structure of Sociological Theory*, 5th edn, Belmont, Calif., Wadsworth

Turner, R. (ed.) (1974), *Ethnomethodology*, Harmondsworth, Penguin Books

Turner, R. H. (1960), 'Sponsored and contest mobility and the school system', *American Sociological Review*, vol. 25, pp. 855–67

Turner, R. H. (1962), 'Role taking: process versus conformity', in A. M. Rose (ed.), *Human Behavior and Social Processes*, Boston, Houghton Mifflin, pp. 20–40

Urry, J. (1980), *The Anatomy of Capitalist Society – the Economy, Civil Society and the State*, London, Macmillan

Urry, J. (1996), 'Sociology of time and space', in B. S. Turner (ed.) *The Blackwell Companion to Social Theory*, Oxford, Blackwell, pp. 369–95

Urry, J., and Wakeford, J. (eds) (1973), *Power in Britain: Sociological readings*, London, Heinemann Educational Books

Vallier, I. (ed.) (1971), *Comparative Methods in Sociology*, Berkeley, University of California Press

Vattimo, G. (1988), *The End of Modernity: Nihilism and hermeneutics in post-modern culture*, Cambridge, Polity Press

Veatch, R. M. (1981), 'The medical model, its nature and problems', in A. L. Caplan, H. T. Englehardt and J. J. McCartney (eds), *Concepts of Health and Disease: Interdisciplinary perspectives*, London, Addison, pp. 523–54

Veblen, T. (1899), *The Theory of the Leisure Class*, New York, Mentor, 1953

Veblen, T. (1904), *The Theory of the Business Enterprise*, New York, Kelley, 1965

Veblen, T. (1914), *The Instinct of Workmanship and the State of the Industrial Arts*, New York, Norton, 1964

Veblen, T. (1915), *Imperial Germany and the Industrial Revolution*, New York, Kelley, 1964

Veblen, T. (1917), *An Inquiry into the Nature of Peace and the Terms of its Perpetuation*, New York, Kelley, 1964

Veblen, T. (1918a), *The Higher Learning in America*, Gloucester, Mass., Peter Smith

Veblen, T. (1918b), *The Place of Science in Modern Civilization and Other Essays*, New York, Russell & Russell, 1961

Veblen, T. (1921), *The Engineers and the Price System*, New York, Harcourt, 1963

Veblen, T. (1923), *Absentee Ownership and Business Enterprise in Recent Times*, Boston, Beacon Press, 1967

Venturi, F. (1963), 'Oriental despotism', *Journal for the History of Ideas*, vol. 24, pp. 133–42 von der Mehden, F. R. (1969), *Politics of the Developing Nations*, Englewood Cliffs, NJ, Prentice Hall

Vroom, V. H. (1964), *Work and Motivation*, New York, Wiley

Walker, M. (ed.) (1995), *Interpreting Crime Statistics*, Oxford, Oxford University Press

Wallace, W. L. (1969), *Sociological Theory: An introduction*, London, Heinemann Educational Books

Wallerstein, I. (1974), *The Modern World-System: Capitalist agriculture and the origins of the European world-economy in the sixteenth century*, New York, Academic Press

Wallis, R. (1984), *The Elementary Forms of the New Religious Life*, London, Routledge & Kegan Paul

Warner, L. (1949), *Social Class in America: A manual of procedure for the measurement of social status*, New York, Harper, 1960

Watson, L. (1996), *Victims of Violent Crime Recorded by the Police, England and Wales 1990–1994*, Home Office Statistical Findings, Issue 1/96, London, Home Office

Waxman, C. I. (ed.) (1968), *The End of Ideology Debate*, New York, Funk & Wagnalls

Webb, E. J., *et al.* (1966), *Unobtrusive Measures: Nonreactive research in the social sciences*, Chicago, Rand McNally

Weber, Marianne (1975), *Max Weber: A biography*, New York, Wiley

Weber, M. (1922), *Economy and Society: An outline of interpretive sociology*, New York, Bedminster Press, 1968; 2 vols, Berkeley, University of California Press

Weber, M. (1930), *The Protestant Ethic and the Spirit of Capitalism*, London, Allen & Unwin

Weber, M. (1946), *From Max Weber: Essays in sociology*, London, Routledge & Kegan Paul, edited by H. H. Gerth and C. W. Mills

Weber, M. (1949), *The Methodology of the Social Sciences*, Glencoe, Free Press, edited by E. Shils and H. Finch

Weber, M. (1950), *General Economic History*, New York, Collier

Weber, M. (1951), *The Religion of China*, New York, Macmillan

Weber, M. (1952), *Ancient Judaism*, Glencoe, Free Press

Weber, M. (1958a), *The Religion of India*, Glencoe, Free Press

Weber, M. (1958b), *The City*, Glencoe, Free Press

Weber, M. (1958c), *The Rational Foundations of Music*, Carbondale, Southern Illinois University Press

Weber, M. (1966), *The Sociology of Religion*, London, Methuen

Weber, M. (1975), *Roscher and Knies: The logical problems of historical economics*, New York, Free Press

Weber, M. (1976), *The Agrarian Sociology of Ancient Civilizations*, London, New Left Books

Weber, M. (1977), *Critique of Stammler*, New York, Free Press

Weber, M. (1978), *Selections in Translation*, Cambridge, Cambridge University Press, edited by W. G. Runciman

Weedon, C. (1987), *Feminist Practice and Post-structuralist Theory*, Oxford, Blackwell

Weitz, S. (1977), *Sex Roles: Biological, psychological and social foundations*, New York, Oxford University Press

West, J. (ed.) (1982), *Work, Women and the Labour Market*, London, Routledge & Kegan Paul

Wieviorka, M. (1991), *The Arena of Racism*, London, Sage, 1995

Whyte, W. F. (1956), *The Organization Man*, New York, Simon & Schuster

Whyte, W. F. (1961), *Street Corner Society: The social structure of an Italian slum*, 2nd ed, Chicago, Chicago University Press

Whyte, W. F., and Whyte, K. K. (1988), *Making Mondragon*, Ithaca, NY, ILR Press

Wilkins, L. (1965), 'Some sociological factors in drug addiction control', in D. Wilner and G. Kassebaum (eds), *Narcotics*, New York, McGraw-Hill

Wilkins, L. T. (1964), *Social Deviance: Social policy, action and research*, London, Tavistock

Williams, K., Cutler, T., Williams, J., and Haslam, C. (1987), 'The end of mass production?', *Economy and Society*, vol. 16, pp. 404–38

Williams, R. (1958), *Culture and Society 1780–1950*, London, Chatto & Windus

Williams R. (1961), *The Long Revolution*, London, Chatto & Windus

Williams, R. (1973), *The Country and the City*, London, Chatto & Windus

Williams, R. (1974), *Television: Technology and cultural form*, London, Collins

Williams, R. (1976), *Keywords: A vocabulary of culture and society*, London, Fontana

Willis, E. (1996), *The Sociological Quest: An introduction to the study of social life*, 3rd edn, New Brunswick, NJ, Rutgers University Press

Willmott, P. (1963), *The Evolution of a Community*, London, Routledge & Kegan Paul

Willmott, P. (1966), *Adolescent Boys of East London*, London, Routledge & Kegan Paul

Willmott, P., and Young, M. (1960), *Family and Class in a London Suburb*, London, Routledge & Kegan Paul

Wilson, B. (1966), *Religion in a Secular Society*, London, Watts

Wilson, B. (1967), *Patterns of Sectarianism: Organization and ideology in social and religious movements*, London, Heinemann Educational Books

Wilson, B. (1970a), *Religious Sects: A sociological study*, London, Weidenfeld & Nicolson

Wilson, B. (1970b), *Youth Culture and the Universities*, London, Faber & Faber

Wilson, B. (1973), *Magic and the Millennium: A sociological study of religious movements of protest among tribal and third-world peoples*, London, Heinemann Educational Books

Wilson, B. (1976), *Contemporary Transformations of Religion*, London, Oxford University Press

Wilson, B. (1982), *Religion in Sociological Perspective*, Oxford, Oxford University Press

Wilson, E. O. (1975), *Sociobiology*, Cambridge, Mass., Harvard University Press

Winch, P. (1958), *The Idea of a Social Science*, London, Routledge & Kegan Paul

Wirth, L. (1931), 'Clinical sociology', *American Journal of Sociology*, vol. 37, pp. 49–66

Wirth, L. (1938), 'Urbanism as a way of life', *American Journal of Sociology*, vol. 44, pp. 1–24

Wittfogel, K. A. (1957), *Oriental Despotism: A comparative study of total power*, New Haven, Yale University Press

Wittgenstein, L. (1958), *Philosophical Investigations*, London, George Allen & Unwin

Wittig, M. (1973), *The Lesbian Body*, New York, Avon

Witz, A. (1992), *Professions and Patriarchy*, London, Routledge

Wolf, E. (1971), *Peasant Wars of the Twentieth Century*, London, Faber & Faber

Wolff, K. H. (ed.) (1950), *The Sociology of Georg Simmel*, New York, Free Press

Wolff, K. H. (1978), 'Phenomenology and Sociology', in T. B. Bottomore and R. Nisbet (eds), *A History of Sociological Analysis*, New York, Basic Books, pp. 499–556

Wolfgang, M. (1957), 'Victim-precipitated criminal homicide', *Journal of Criminal Law, Criminology and Police Science*, vol. 48, pp. 1–11

Wolfgang, M., Savitz, L., and Johnston, N. (eds) (1970), *The Sociology of Crime and Delinquency*, New York, Wiley

Wollstonecraft, M. (1792), *A Vindication of the Rights of Woman: With strictures on political and moral subjects*, Harmondsworth, Penguin Books, 1975

Wolpe, H. (ed.) (1980), *The Articulation of Production*, London, Routledge & Kegan Paul

Wood, S. (ed.) (1982), *The Degradation of Work?*, London, Hutchinson

Worswick, D. (1991), *Unemployment: a problem of policy*, London, National Institute for Economic and Social Research

Wright, E. O. (1976), 'Class boundaries in advanced capitalist societies', *New Left Review*, no. 98, pp. 3–41

Wright, E. O. (1985), *Classes*, London, Verso

Wrigley, E. A. (ed.) (1966), *An Introduction to English Historical Demography from the Sixteenth to the Nineteenth Century*, London, Weidenfeld & Nicolson

Wrigley, E. A. (1969), *Population and History*, London, Weidenfeld & Nicolson

Wrigley, E. A., and Schofield, R. (1982), *The Population History of England 1541–1871: A reconstruction*, London, Arnold

Wrong, D. H. (1961), 'The oversocialized conception of man in modern sociology', *American Sociological Review*, vol. 26, pp. 183–93

Wrong, D. H. (1966), *Population and Society*, New York, Random House

Wrong, D. H. (1977), *Sceptical Sociology*, London, Heinemann Educational Books

Wrong, D. H. (1979), *Power: Its forms, bases and uses*, Oxford, Blackwell

Wrong, D. H. (1998), *The Modern Condition: Essays at the century's end*, Stanford, California, Stanford University Press

Yin, R. K. (1989), *Case Study Methods*, 2nd edn, London, Sage

Young, A. (1990), *Femininity in Dissent*, London, Routledge

Young, J. (1971), *The Drugtakers: the social meaning of drug use*, London, Paladin

Young, M. (1958), *The Rise of the Meritocracy*, London, Thames & Hudson

Young, M., and Willmott, P. (1957), *Family and Kinship in East London*, London, Routledge & Kegan Paul

Young, M., and Willmott, P. (1973), *The Symmetrical Family*, Harmondsworth, Penguin Books

Zeldin, T. (1994), *An Intimate History of Humanity*, New York, Harper Collins

Zimbalist, A. (ed.) (1979), *Case Studies on the Labor Process*, New York, Monthly Review Press

Zola, I. K. (1972), 'Medicine as an institution of social control: the medicalizing of society', *Sociological Review*, vol. 20, pp. 487–504

Zola, I. K. (1982), *Missing Pieces: A chronicle of living with a disability*, Philadelphia, Temple University Press

Zollschan, G. K., and Hirsch, W. (eds) (1964), *Explorations in Social Change*, London, Routledge & Kegan Paul